D1754793

Wissenschaftliche Untersuchungen
zum Neuen Testament

Herausgeber / Editor
Jörg Frey (München)

Mitherausgeber / Associate Editors
Friedrich Avemarie (Marburg)
Judith Gundry-Volf (New Haven, CT)
Hans-Josef Klauck (Chicago, IL)

222

The Resurrection of Jesus
in the Gospel of John

Edited by
Craig R. Koester and Reimund Bieringer

Mohr Siebeck

CRAIG R. KOESTER is Professor of New Testament at Luther Seminary in St. Paul, Minnesota, USA.

REIMUND BIERINGER is Professor of New Testament Exegesis at the Faculty of Theology of the Catholic University of Leuven, Belgium.

ISBN 978-3-16-149588-5
ISSN 0512-1604 (Wissenschaftliche Untersuchungen zum Neuen Testament)

Die Deutsche Nationalbibliothek lists this publication in the Deutsche Nationalbibliographie; detailed bibliographic data is available in the Internet at *http://dnb.d-nb.de*.

© 2008 by Mohr Siebeck, Tübingen, Germany.

This book may not be reproduced, in whole or in part, in any form (beyond that permitted by copyright law) without the publisher's written permission. This applies particularly to reproductions, translations, microfilms and storage and processing in electronic systems.

The book was printed by Gulde-Druck in Tübingen on non-aging paper and bound by Großbuchbinderei Spinner in Ottersweier.

Printed in Germany.

Preface

The resurrection of Jesus plays a central and yet disputed role in the narrative and theology of Johns gospel. At the time of his death Jesus says, "It is finished" (19:30), yet readers find that as a narrative the gospel is not finished but continues with accounts of the empty tomb and Jesus' appearances to his disciples. During his ministry Jesus calls himself "the resurrection and the life" (11:25–26) and says that those who believe in him have true life now (5:24), yet he also speaks about the resurrection of believers on the last day (5:25–29; 6:39–40). In the Farewell Discourses Jesus says that he will see his disciples again, but it is not always clear whether this promise is fulfilled by the resurrection appearances or whether the gospel speaks of another encounter that is yet to come (14:18–19; 16:16–24). The importance of Jesus' resurrection seems clear, but how it fits into the overall perspective of the gospel continues to generate debate.

The essays in this collection take up key questions concerning the significance of Jesus' resurrection and its implications. Included are studies of the relationship of Jesus resurrection to his ministry of signs, his crucifixion, and the faith of later generations. The embodied quality of the resurrection and its importance for understanding Johannine eschatology and life within the Christian community is given special attention. Literary studies explore the interplay between the Farewell Discourses and the resurrection narratives, the problematic role of John 21 within the gospel as a whole, and the way the theme of recognition informs the interpretation of the gospels message. Careful attention is also given to the theme of Jesus' ascension and the commission to forgive and retain sins. Together, these essays give a rich sense of the many facets of Jesus resurrection and its importance for the study of Johns gospel. We hope that this volume will make a substantial contribution to the ongoing discussion of this central theme in Christian theology.

The idea for this series of studies originated in the "Johannine Writings Seminar" of the Society for New Testament Studies (SNTS). Some of essays were originally presented during the annual meetings of the society in Halle (2005), Aberdeen (2006), and Sibiu (2007), while others were written later specifically for this collection. The contribution of Sandra M. Schneiders was previously published in *Proceedings of the Catholic*

Theological Society of America (2006), 13–35. We are grateful for the permission of the Catholic Theological Society of America to reprint this text.

As editors we thank Tom Vollmer and Ilse Bacqué for their editorial assistance support and Victoria Smith for her careful preparation of the camera-ready copy. The indices were prepared with the assistance of Cosmin Murariu and Gabrielle Christenhusz. Special thanks goes to Jörg Frey (München), the editor of the series Wissenschaftliche Untersuchungen zum Neuen Testament, for offering us the opportunity to publish this volume. We also thank Henning Ziebritzki, Jana Trispel, and the staff at Mohr Siebeck for all they have done to bring this project to completion.

Easter 2008

Craig R. Koester, St. Paul
Reimund Bieringer, Leuven

Table of Contents

Preface V

Table of Contents VII

1. *Harold W. Attridge*
"From Discord Rises Meaning. Resurrection Motifs in the
Fourth Gospel" 1

2. *John Painter*
"'The Light Shines in the Darkness. . .' Creation, Incarnation,
and Resurrection in John" 21

3. *Craig R. Koester*
"Jesus' Resurrection, the Signs, and the Dynamics of Faith in
the Gospel of John" 47

4. *Ruben Zimmermann*
"The Narrative Hermeneutics in John 11. Learning with
Lazarus How to Understand Death, Life, and Resurrection" 75

5. *Jean Zumstein*
"Jesus' Resurrection in the Farewell Discourses" 103

6. *Udo Schnelle*
"Cross and Resurrection in the Gospel of John" 127

7. *Sandra M. Schneiders*
"Touching the Risen Jesus. Mary Magdalene and Thomas the
Twin in John 20" 153

8. *Jesper Tang Nielsen*
"Resurrection, Recognition, Reassuring. The Function of
Jesus' Resurrection in the Fourth Gospel" 177

9. *Reimund Bieringer*
"I am ascending to my Father and your Father, to my God and your God" (John 20:17). Resurrection and Ascension in the Gospel of John 209

10. *Johannes Beutler*
"Resurrection and the Remission of Sins. John 20:23 Against Its Traditional Background" 237

11. *R. Alan Culpepper*
"Realized Eschatology in the Experience of the Johannine Community" 253

12. *Hans-Ulrich Weidemann*
"Eschatology as Liturgy. Jesus' Resurrection and Johannine Eschatology" 277

13. *Martin Hasitschka*
"The Significance of the Resurrection Appearance in John 21" 311

Index of References 329

Index of Modern Authors 353

Chapter 1

From Discord Rises Meaning
Resurrection Motifs in the Fourth Gospel

Harold W. Attridge

1. The Tensive Elements in John's Gospel

On the subject of the resurrection, the Fourth Gospel is, as in so many other areas, full of tensive elements. Most obviously, resurrection is, in a fashion traditional within Judaism,[1] an event of the end times, when the dead shall arise to either positive or negative judgment (5:28), but that end time is already palpable (5:24). The resurrection is yet to come (11:24), but is also present in and through Jesus here and now (11:25).

Ambiguity in what the gospel teaches about resurrection thus parallels a significant element of tension in the treatment of the resurrection of Jesus and, more specifically, the relationship between the cross, empty tomb, and paschal appearances.[2] Much of the gospel focuses on the event of the

---

[1] As argued strongly by N. T. Wright, *The Resurrection of the Son of God* (Christian Origins and the Question of God 3; London: SPCK, 2003). Among the many reactions see especially Markus Bockmuehl, "Compleat History of the Resurrection: A Dialogue with N.T. Wright," *JSNT* 26 (2004): 489–504, and Robert H. Smith, "Wright Thinking on the Resurrection?" *Dialog: A Journal of Theology* 43 (2004): 244–51. Wright downplays the diversity in pre-Christian Jewish beliefs about the resurrection. For a similar approach to the Jewish evidence, see Richard Bauckham, "Life, Death, and the Afterlife in Second Temple Judaism," in *Life in the Face of Death: The Resurrection Message of the New Testament* (ed. Richard N. Longenecker; MacMaster New Testament Studies; Grand Rapids: Eerdmans, 1998), 80–95. For an alternative perspective, see George W. E. Nickelsburg, *Resurrection, Immortality, and Eternal Life in Intertestamental Judaism* (HTS 26; Cambridge, MA: Harvard University Press; London: Oxford University Press, 1972), and with more data from the Scrolls, John J. Collins, *Seers, Sibyls and Sages in Hellenistic-Roman Judaism* (JSJSup 54; Leiden: Brill, 1997). A critical point for assessing the possibilities available to the Fourth Gospel is how to construe the Wisdom of Solomon.

[2] For an insightful essay dealing with the whole issue see Andrew T. Lincoln, "'I am the Resurrection and the Life': The Resurrection Message of the Fourth Gospel," in Longenecker, ed., *Life in the Face of Death,* 122–44.

cross, which is the point where Jesus is "lifted up/exalted," where the work he has come to do is completed (19:30), where an effective sign is given that epitomizes and encapsulates the previous "signs." Like the serpent in the desert (3:14), the body of Jesus on the cross will heal when seen with the eyes of faith. Like the Son of Man coming in glory, Jesus lifted up on the cross will draw all people to himself (12:32). From the side of Jesus, who is suspended on the cross, comes the water and the blood that will nourish and cleanse (2:1–11; 4:10; 6:51–58; 7:37–39).[3] The cross is certainly a focal point of the text, both in its symbolism and in its underlying theology.[4] So why does the text continue with resurrection appearance accounts?[5] Are they merely afterthoughts, unavoidable elements of the resurrection tradition, simple illustrations of pious themes? Or do they serve an essential function in John's story of Jesus? The problem is exacerbated by the presence of chapter 21, which may have been added later,[6] but it is there already in chapter 20.

Two major strategies have marked the attempts to deal with these various tensive elements. First, there are the redactional hypotheses, which have loomed large in the world of twentieth-century Johannine scholarship.[7] Second, many readers of John have attempted to find an

---

[3] On the motifs involved see especially John P. Heil, *Blood and Water: The Death and Resurrection of Jesus in John 18–21* (CBQMS 27; Washington, D.C.: Catholic Biblical Association, 1995).

[4] See Harold W. Attridge, "The Cubist Principle in Johannine Imagery: John and the Reading of Images in Contemporary Platonism," in *Imagery in the Gospel of John. Terms, Forms, Themes and Theology of Figurative Language* (ed. Jörg Frey, Jan G. van der Watt, Ruben Zimmermann, with Gabi Kern; WUNT 200; Tübingen: Mohr Siebeck, 2006), 47–60.

[5] Wright, *Resurrection*, 441, n. 122, cites C. F. Evans, *Resurrection and the New Testament* (London: SCM, 1970), 116. Strictly speaking, there is no place in the Fourth Gospel for resurrection stories, since the ascent or exaltation has already taken place." He also cites M.J.J. Menken, "Interpretation of the Old Testament and the Resurrection of Jesus in John's Gospel," in *Resurrection in the New Testament: FS J. Lambrecht* (ed. R. Bieringer, V. Koperski, and B. Lataire; Leuven: Peeters, 2002), 189–205.

[6] Most commentators still judge chapter 21 to be an appendix or "epilogue" (so D. Moody Smith, *John* [ANTC; Nashville: Abingdon, 1999] 389), but there have been recent vigorous defenses of its integral relationship with the rest of the Gospel. See Hartwig Thyen, *Das Johannesevangelium* (HNT 6; Tübingen: Mohr Siebeck, 2005), 772–74.

[7] For a review of literature on John 5:28–29, which treats those verses as redactional, see Hans Christian Kammler, *Christologie und Eschatologie: Joh 5,17–30 als Schlüsseltext johanneischer Theologie* (WUNT 126; Tübingen: Mohr Siebeck, 2000), 188–90. For a review of the redactional hypotheses about John 11, see Josef Wagner, *Auferstehung und Leben: Joh 11,1–12,19 als Spiegel johanneischer Redaktions-und Theologiegeschichte* (BU 19; Regensburg: Pustet, 1988), 29–94. Wagner defends a

integral eschatological framework within which realized and future understandings of resurrection cohere.[8] We will consider each of these approaches in turn.

From a redactional or diachronic perspective the characteristic core position of the Johannine tradition would be an interpretation of "resurrection" as a category relevant to the life of the believer in the here and now. This interpretation would mark a radical rethinking of the apocalyptic heritage of the early followers of Jesus. Such a radical departure could not stand in a religious movement that found a prominent place for eschatological hope. The radical impulse was blurred in the final stages of the Gospel which insisted on the reality of the physical resurrection of Jesus and on the futurity of resurrection hope for his followers. One interesting version of this position is represented by those who see Johannine theology engaging in critical dialogue with another identifiable branch of early Christianity, which was associated with the name of the apostle Thomas and attested by texts such as the *Gospel of Thomas* and *Acts of Thomas*.[9] For "Thomasine" Christians, resurrection would have been understood as an allegorical cipher for the spiritual transformation of individuals rather than a future reality. This is a position that many scholars have deemed to be characteristic of one stage of the development of the Gospel. For the Gospel in its final form, the reality of the physical resurrection is vital. This analysis recognizes the importance of the final chapters of the Gospel, although its reading of the physical character of the resurrected body may need correction. This position does not, however, do justice to the strain of "realized" eschatology in the gospel, except as an otiose remnant of a rejected alternative view.

Among those who would find a coherent eschatological framework integrating the tensive elements of resurrection language, some insist that the "realized" pole dominates and serves as the interpretive framework within which the "future" elements must be understood.[10] One prominent example of the latter is N. T. Wright's sometimes provocative treatment of resurrection in the NT, which offers a comprehensive reading of the Fourth

---

redactional approach, based on that of Georg Richter, to the tensions in the resurrection passages.

[8] Kammler (*Christologie*, 191–94) usefully catalogs those who find John 5:28–29 integral to Johannine eschatology, a position that he himself espouses. In general, of course, see Jörg Frey, *Die johanneische Eschatologie*, Vol. 3: *Die eschatologische Verkündigung in den johanneischen Texten* (WUNT 117; Tübingen: Mohr Siebeck, 2000).

[9] See especially Gregory Riley, *Resurrection Reconsidered: Thomas and John in Controversy* (Minneapolis: Fortress, 1995).

[10] E.g., Kammler, *Christologie*, 195–230.

Gospel.¹¹ Wright's overall project is not focused primarily on the Gospel of John, but on the issue of the historicity of the resurrection and its role as the cornerstone of the early Christian movement. He vigorously argues that there was a uniformity and coherence among early Christian proclamations of the resurrection. Not surprisingly, then, the Fourth Gospel fits the general pattern and the tensive elements find a home within that picture. The lynchpin of Wright's approach is provided by the hints that the Fourth Gospel portrays the resurrection as the beginning of a new creation.¹² Through the outpouring of the Spirit on Easter, a new way of living is made possible in the present, and it will have its consummation in a final resurrection. A "realized" eschatology is there, to be sure, but it does not exhaust the gospel's eschatological hope.

Wright's synthesis, whatever else it may do for understanding resurrection in early Christianity, is instructive, but may be in need of some refinement. I suggest that it does not do justice to the fact that there are tensions within the text. In what follows I would like to explore those tensions with a view to seeing how they might function in leading a reader (implied or otherwise) into an understanding of the meaning of resurrection generally.¹³

2. The Principal Resurrection Texts in John

It is important to follow the sequence of resurrection texts in John and to note the structure of what the gospel says about resurrection. Here we will consider the principal passages in which resurrection is mentioned, later asking how the tensions reflected here are – or are not – resolved in the conclusion of the gospel.

---

[11] See note 1 above.

[12] This reading plays on the faint allusions to Genesis often found in the Resurrection stories, the tomb in the *garden* (20:15), on the *first day* (20:19) of a new week, with the new inbreathing of the Spirit (20:22). Thyen, *Johannesevangelium*, 767, also highlights these allusions in the Johannine account.

[13] My debt to the many Johannine scholars of recent years who have offered various reader-response and other literary readings of John should be obvious. For a brief presentation of my basic understanding of the way in which this Gospel works, see "Genre Bending in the Fourth Gospel," *JBL* 121 (2002): 3–21, and "The Restless Quest for the Beloved Disciple," in *Early Christian Voices: In Texts, Traditions, and Symbols: Essays in Honor of François Bovon* (ed. David H. Warren, Ann Graham Brock, and David W. Pao; Biblical Interpretation Series 66; Leiden: Brill, 2003), 71–80.

Resurrection and the Son's Equality with the Father[14]

The first passage appears in the forensic debate of John 5, where Jesus refutes the charge of blasphemy for having made himself equal to God. There is an element of irony in the apologia, since all the defenses that Jesus offers finally are based on his in fact being equal to God.[15] The references to resurrection are woven into that defense. Jesus, the Son, has been taught to do all that the Father does. As instructed Son he is therefore not "equal to God." But what has the Father instructed him to do? The first type of act is raising the dead (5:21), but the description of the act has about it a studied ambiguity: "For as the Father raises the dead and gives them life, so also the Son gives life to those whom he will." The present tense could have a generalizing force without any consideration of time. The point at which the Son "gives life" could be the eschatological future, where a literal resurrection takes place, or the present, when resurrection is a matter of spiritual rebirth.

Before the ambiguity reaches any resolution, the discourse turns to the theme of judgment, a notion hardly unexpected in a context where resurrection is in view. Resurrection and judgment usually hang together like Siamese twins.[16] The Gospel's treatment of the theme simply continues the tension. Jesus first (5:22) denies that the Father judges at all. Instead, he has given over the right to judge to the Son, with the explicit result that the Son will be honored as the Father is honored (5:24). The text thus makes a Christological point. Jesus, as the divine emissary, is functionally indistinguishable from God, but when he does his judging remains unclear. The reader who has in mind the text's earlier affirmation about judgment taking place when the light comes into the world (3:19)

---

[14] See Frey, *Die johanneische Eschatologie*, 3.322–402, and Kammer, *Christologie*.

[15] See my "Argumentation in John 5," in *Rhetorical Argumentation in Biblical Texts* (ed. Anders Eriksson, Thomas H. Olbricht, and Walter Übelacker; Emory Studies in Early Christianity 8; Harrisburg, Pa.: Trinity Press International, 2002), 188–99. Whatever we might say about the perspectives on resurrection in these verses, the discussion of the subject is formally subordinated to the basic theme of the discourse of chapter 5. That discourse focuses on the issue of the relationship between Jesus and the Father. Has Jesus (or the community that reveres him) made himself "equal to God" (5:18)? The response (5:19–47) consists of a playfully ironic forensic defense, which apparently begins by denying the charge. The defense insists that Jesus simply does what he sees the Father do. Yet every instance of that "imitation" of God by Jesus suggests that he has a very special status indeed, that he sees things from the perspective of heaven and that he "imitates" things that only God can do, particularly to raise people from the dead. Frey, *Die johanneische Eschatologie*, 2.398, rightly insists on the predominance of Christology over eschatology in the dynamics of the discourse.

[16] See Dan 12:1–3; Matt 25:1–46; Rev 20:11–15; etc.

might be forgiven for suspecting that judgment is not an event of the distant future but is a present reality.

What immediately follows, in the two solemn, "Amen, Amen" sayings, tends to confirm those suspicions. The first saying combines the themes of resurrection, expressed in terms of eternal life and judgment (5:24). The hint from 5:21 that the Son gives life in the here and now is made explicit: "The one who hears my word and believes in the one who sent me has eternal life, and does not come to judgment but has passed over from death to life." In the words of Hymenaeus and Philetus, the resurrection has already occurred (2 Tim 2:17–18)! Resurrection as metaphor triumphs. The point is reinforced in the second "Amen, Amen" saying (5:25). The "hour is coming and *now is* when the dead hear the voice of the Son of God and those who have heard will come to life." Readers have yet to hear of a story of resurrection or even resuscitation, though when they later come to the story of Lazarus, who hears the voice of Jesus and comes from his tomb, this solemn proclamation may echo in their ears. The Son gives life as the agent of the Father, but the ante is upped even further in the next verse (John 5:26): The Father has given the Son to have life "in himself." His equality with God is not simply a matter of imitation. As plenipotentiary, he has all the powers that the Father has. Jesus provides life, and that claim shapes the understanding of "resurrection." Whenever one encounters the one whom the Father has sent, one has the possibility and the reality of life. Such a "realized" view of resurrection in the presence of such a Son has already been anticipated by those Johannine passages that have applied eschatological categories to the moment of encounter with Jesus (e.g., 3:36).

What follows in 5:28–29 introduces a discordant note. The "hour" in which those in the tomb will hear the voice of Jesus is "coming" (ἔρχεται). The hearer should not be amazed. The dead will arise, as they do in Daniel, Matthew, and Paul, to face judgment: those who have done what is good will experience the "resurrection of life," while those who have done ill will experience a "resurrection of judgment" (5:29).[17] In these verses a literal, future resurrection triumphs,[18] although the gospel does not explain how the relationship between the two resurrections works.

---

[17] The judgment is in the hands of a "son of man" (v. 27). Whether this is an allusion to an eschatological "Son of Man" or simply to the status of Jesus as a human being is an intriguing question, but it does not affect the construal of resurrection in these verses. For the construal of the anarthrous *huios anthropou* as "human being" see Delbert Burkett, *The Son of Man in the Gospel of John* (JSNTSup 56; Sheffield: Sheffield Academic Press, 1991), 42, followed now by Thyen, *Johannesevangelium,* 315–18.

[18] Wright (*Resurrection,* 442) appeals to the verses with a decidedly futurist eschatology (chapters 5 and 6) as important data connecting John and the general Pharisaic and early Christian belief in the futurity of the "transphysical" resurrection.

In fact, by insisting that the future resurrection will lead to a judgment based on deeds, rather than on the will of the Son (5:21), these verses only exacerbate the tension.[19]

The intricate interplay between the "realized" and "future" aspects of resurrection, within which Jesus can so fully imitate the Father, may possibly be the result of redactional activity; but if so, what has the redactor achieved?[20] The references to a "realized" eschatology stand and have not been eliminated by the affirmation of a future resurrection. Would a reader notice the tension and be surprised by it? Would she be confirmed in a dominant theology that works, as does Paul, with a tension between the already and not yet? Or might she simply be confused, "wondering" (5:28) how the eschatological hope works?

Resurrection and the Bread of Life

The next large block of conversation about the resurrection appears in chapter 6, in the heart of the "bread of life" discourse, where "resurrection on the last day" is mentioned four times. The first reference appears in the initial midrashic interpretation of the "bread" of Psalm 78, paraphrased in John 6:31.[21] Jesus identifies himself as the "bread" of the scriptural text, and says that partaking of him provides "eternal life" plus "resurrection on the last day." The promise is repeated like a refrain through the chapter

---

[19] Some commentators attempt to reconcile the two divergent perspectives on resurrection by importing a distinction between the resurrection that believers experience in the present and the general resurrection that all will experience before final judgment. In that final judgment Jesus as judge "will decide between people who have died *before his advent* on the basis of their deeds." So Smith, *John,* 138. Such a limitation on who is affected by the final judgment seems quite arbitrary.

[20] A position resisted by Nils A. Dahl, "'Do Not Wonder!' John 5:28–29 and Johannine Eschatology Once More," in *The Conversation Continues: Studies in Paul and John in honor of J. Louis Martyn* (ed. Robert T. Fortna, Beverly R. Gaventa; Nashville: Abingdon, 1990), 322–36, cited by Frey, *Die johanneische Eschatologie,* 2.400. Both correctly point to the continuous interweaving of realized and future eschatological affirmations in the Gospel as a warrant for rejecting redactional hypotheses here. But have they done justice to the problem, at this stage of the gospel, of integrating the two perspectives? The command by Jesus not to wonder (v. 28) may constitute a recognition that the reader is doing just that.

[21] The fundamental analysis of the chapter remains that of Peder Borgen, *Bread from Heaven: An Exegetical Study of the Concept of Manna in the Gospel of John and the Writings of Philo* (NovTSup 10; Leiden: Brill, 1965). See also idem, "John 6: Tradition, Interpretation and Composition," in *Critical Readings of John 6* (ed. R. Alan Culpepper; Biblical Interpretation Series 22; Leiden/New York/ Cologne: Brill, 1997), 95–114, repr. in Peder Borgen, *Early Christianity and Hellenistic Judaism* (Edinburgh: Clark, 1996), 205–29. Among recent treatments see Paul N. Anderson, *The Christology of the Fourth Gospel: Its Unity and Disunity in the Light of John 6* (WUNT 2.77; Tübingen: Mohr Siebeck, 1995).

with cloying frequency. In 6:39, who or whatever the Father gives to the Son will not perish, but Jesus will raise that one on the last day. In 6:40, whoever contemplates (θεωρῶν) the Son and believes in him will have eternal life, and Jesus will raise that contemplating believer on the last day. In 6:44, echoing 6:39 at a new stage of the midrash, whomever the Father draws to Jesus, Jesus will raise on the last day. In 6:54, whoever munches (τρώγων) on the flesh and drinks the blood of Jesus will have eternal life and Jesus will raise that one on the last day.

Whatever the redactional history of this text – and I suspect it is less complex than many theories have proposed – references to "resurrection on the last day" run through the discourse. They are, at several points, balanced with a-temporal promises of the "eternal life" that follows from "belief." Two of these appear in tandem with a resurrection promise (6: 40, 54). The second is an affirmation (6:47) at a climactic moment in the discourse, after the introduction of Isa 54:13, "They will be taught of God" (John 6:45). This set of affirmations concludes with a reference to the mutual abiding of eater and eaten, and the life that the eater will have through the true bread (6:56–58). Important textual variants could increase the number of references to a "realized eschatology." At the very least they show that scribes were somewhat confused by Johannine eschatology.[22]

It is, of course, possible to read this complex web of statements concerning resurrection/eternal life as the result of redactional interference, which has perhaps been made more complicated by the possible addition of 6:52–58. But if so, the balanced, tensive result is remarkable. In other words, if a redactor inserted the realistic sacramental and eschatological materials, he produced a final product that does not leave a clear and simple theological picture, but one that keeps odd elements bumping against one another. The creative tension, moreover, is a feature of both major portions of the discourse. The first, more "sapiential" portion, resembles depictions of wisdom as the true bread, and the actions involved are "seeing/believing" (θεωρῶν, πιστεύων, 6:40) and "hearing/learning" (ἀκούσας, μαθών, 6:45).[23] This part favors a metaphorical understanding of what consuming the true bread is all about. Whatever may happen "on the last day" is directly connected to the life that the believer has here and now (5:47–48).

---

[22] See especially the tenses of the verb ζάω in v. 51.
[23] On the motif involved here see Craig R. Koester, "Hearing, Seeing and Believing in the Gospel of John," *Bib* 70 (1989): 327–48.

The second, more "sacramental" portion of the discourse (5:52–58),[24] although it lacks specific resurrection language, also holds out hope for a future life with the repeated promises that the one who eats "will live" (5:57, 58). One might be tempted to expect a simple correlation between an eschatology that insists on the physical character of end-time events and an interpretation of the ritual actions that focuses on the tangible dimensions of those actions, but the discourse is not so simple. What appears to be the concrete actions of eating flesh and drinking blood moves into the language of relationship between Jesus and the one who eats and drinks (5:56), a relationship that in turn extends the relationship between the Father and Jesus (5:57). It is that relationship that grounds the hope of future life (ζήσει/ζήσεται, 5:57).

The "bread of life" discourse thus reinforces the dioptic view of resurrection encountered in chapter 5. The gospel expresses hope for some future resurrection while insisting that some form of "eternal life" is available in the life of the believer in the present, and it maintains that the two are intimately connected. The insistence on the "realized" pole of the eschatological horizon and its relationship with the "realistic" understanding of the sacramental act might well be a corrective to an overly mechanistic understanding of the way in which the φάρμακον ἀθανασίας, to use Ignatius's phrase, works.[25] The final stage of the development of the resurrection and life themes in the discourse as we have it suggests that true life, both present and future, is a function of a relationship[26] with the Father that is mediated by the Son (6:56–58). The suggestion here comes close to the implicit resolution of the tensions in resurrection language that the Gospel will later offer.[27]

The entire chapter, whose canonical form there is no good reason to ignore, provides the context for the references to resurrection. The text construes the meaning of Christian ritual dining as a constitutive part of the relationship with the Father and with his Son, who gives himself in flesh and blood. Similarly, the references to a future corporeal resurrection

---

[24] As always in John, more is going on in any given pericope than the surface themes indicate. In the case of this passage, the Christological significance of the "body and blood" certainly remains part of the picture, although an allusion to some ritual practice is hard to deny. See Maarten J.J. Menken, "John 6:51c–58: Eucharist or Christology?" in Culpepper, *Critical Readings*, 183–204.

[25] Eph 20.2. For a useful discussion of that text and the nuanced sense of the "medicine of immortality" in Ignatius, see Anderson, *Christology*, 119–27.

[26] The pregnant Johannine term "abide" (μένω)" appears here (v. 56) with its full connotations for the first time.

[27] For a suggestion about the centrality of these verses, see Joseph Grassi, "Eating Jesus' Flesh and Drinking His Blood: The Centrality and Meaning of John 6:51–58," *BTB* 17 (1987): 24–30.

reaffirm a widespread early Christian belief. The discourse, however, frames that hope in terms of understanding (*seeing, hearing, learning from*) the one who is himself the true bread. The understanding and the relationship, which stand in parallel as the interpretive frame of the traditional elements, are surely related, but our attentive reader may again wonder how to interpret the connection. Is it the case that the relationship is simply a matter of knowing the truth of who Jesus is?

Raising a Friend from the Dead

The tensive perspectives on resurrection continue into the story of the resurrection of Lazarus. The well-known story, in fact, epitomizes the "realized" pole of the Johannine resurrection, although it also has elements, whether redactional or compositional,[28] that resist that "realized" reading.

The key points arise in the exchanges between Jesus and Martha. The dramatic irony in the dialogue is patent. Martha reproaches Jesus, since he could have prevented the death of Lazarus (11:21). Jesus offers the reassurance that Lazarus will rise. Martha takes the reassurance to be an expression of the conventional hope in eschatological resurrection, "on the last day." Jesus responds with the solemn declaration that he is resurrection and life (11:25). For the believer, life is a reality even in the face of death. Indeed, the life that comes with belief in Jesus eternally negates death (11:26). Martha confesses belief in what Jesus has said, although that confession displays a wooden, formulaic quality that suggests lack of conviction.

The reproachful encounter with a conventionally pious Martha is repeated in the first stage of the encounter with a worshipful Mary (11:32). An emotional Jesus, perhaps frustrated that his friends do not seem to understand, does not bother to repeat that he is the resurrection and life for the believer. Instead, he raises his dead friend from the tomb.[29] Jesus is, quite dramatically, the resurrection and the life for Lazarus.

---

[28] For a general review of earlier source and redactional theories, see Wagner, *Auferstehung*, 29–94, and Frey, *Die johanneische Eschatologie*, 3.403–62. See also Delbert Burkett, "Two Accounts of Lazarus' Resurrection in John 11," *NovT* 36 (1994): 209–32, positing two contrasting sources. Hartwig Thyen has argued forcefully for derivation from the Synoptics. See Hartwig Thyen, "Die Erzählung von den bethanischen Geschwistern (Joh 11,1–12,19) als 'Palimpsest' über synoptischen Texten,'" in *The Four Gospels, 1992: Festschrift Frans Neirynck* (ed. F. Van Segbroeck, Christopher M. Tuckett, Gilbert Van Belle, J. Verheyden; BETL 100; 3 vols.; Leuven: Leuven University Press/Peeters, 1992), 2021–50, and his *Johannesevangelium*, 510–11.

[29] For a good review of the usual readings of the narrative flow, and a sensitive approach to the differences between Martha and Mary, see Francis J. Moloney, "Can Everyone be Wrong? A Reading of John 11.1–12.8," *NTS* 45 (2003): 505–27, as well as

Now with the raising of Lazarus, the declaration that those in the tombs would hear the voice of Jesus and come forth (5:28–29) is dramatically realized.[30] At one level the "realized" pole of the resurrection sayings of the previous chapters is now transparent. It all refers to the acts that the historical Jesus performed. But the meaning of the "realized" resurrection sayings transcends their function in the narrative. The general, universalizing language of 11:24–26 invites an application of the significance of the "sign" of Lazarus' resurrection to the world of the Gospel's audience.[31] It is precisely that transference that sidelines questions about the duration of Lazarus's resurrected life. Once he has been raised from the dead and the act has been interpreted, narrative interest in Lazarus largely disappears. He makes a brief cameo dinner appearance at Bethany (12:2), which gives the narrator an opportunity to tell us that the high priests were seeking to kill him (12:20). His resuscitation thus seems to be qualitatively different from that of Jesus, since he remains liable to death. The Gospel has offered a significant story, a "sign" that, whatever its historical value, has immediate symbolic significance for people wanting to become followers of Jesus. The event of Lazarus' resurrection symbolically affirms that any who come to Christ will enjoy life full and complete in the present as well as renewed "on the last day."[32]

The tension between present and future eternal life remains formally unresolved at this stage of the narrative.[33] In fact, the Lazarus story

---

his earlier piece, "The Faith of Martha and Mary: A Narrative Approach to John 11,17–40," *Bib* 75 (1994): 471–93.

[30] The intimate connection between John 5 and 11 is often recognized. See Frey, *Eschatologie* 2.401.

[31] For one reading that realizes that universalizing potential of the text, see Sandra Schneiders, "Death in the Community of Eternal Life: History, Theology, and Spirituality in John 11," *Int* 41 (1987): 44–56.

[32] For various narrative-critical approaches to the text that offer similar readings, see Wilhelm Wuellner, "Rhetorical Criticism and its Theory in Culture-Critical Perspective: The Narrative Rhetoric of John 11," in *Text and Interpretation: New Approaches in the Criticism of the New Testament* (ed. P. J. Hartin and J. H. Petzer; NTTS 15; Leiden: Brill, 1991), 171–85; idem, "Putting Life Back into the Lazarus Story and Its Reading: The Narrative Rhetoric of John 11 as the Narration of Faith," *Semeia* 53 (1991): 113–132; Mark W. G. Stibbe, "A Tomb with a View: John 11.1–44 in Narrative-Critical Perspective," *NTS* 40 (1994): 38–54; Ingrid Rosa Kitzberger, "Mary of Bethany and Mary of Magdala – Two Female Characters in the Johannine Passion Narrative: A Feminist, Narrative-Critical Reader Response," *NTS* 41 (1995): 564–86, here 570–78.

[33] Some readings move too quickly to resolve the tension, e.g., Paul S. Minear, "The Promise of Life in the Gospel of John," *ThTo* 49 (1993): 485–99, who interprets the death from which believers are delivered here and now as the metaphorical death of sin. The interpretation, which has merit, only comes from a survey of the whole gospel. The tensive character of the affirmations at this point are obscured.

continues and intensifies the tensions that have been present in earlier chapters. Jesus is the resurrection and the life for the believer in the here and now. That is physically true for Lazarus, who hears the voice of the Son of Man and comes out of his tomb. Is the promise of a present realization of eschatological hope reduced to a miraculous event in the past? Or does that event signify something in the present reality of the believer? The obvious choice is the second option, but it is not at all clear what the present reality of resurrected life really means. The evangelist, as usual, teases as the thematic structure of the gospel weaves ahead.

The first half of the gospel has left the reader with a riddle. Resurrection in the future, on the "last day," which is a standard hope of pious Pharisee and follower of Jesus alike, is assumed. Alongside that postulate is a set of strong claims, even more insistent than their parallels in chapters 5 and 6, that resurrection and participation in "eternal life" are a reality experienced in the encounter with Jesus. How the two are combined remains something of a mystery, particularly because the realized pole remains largely an assertion. What it means to have eternal life here and now remains opaque.

The development of the theme of resurrection parallels the theme of revelation. As Bultmann famously described it, Jesus reveals only that he is the revealer. This is certainly the case, but only for the first half of the gospel. In the farewell discourses and in the event of cross and resurrection that they interpret, revelation achieves a content, which is to love one another. This is expressed in example (13:15), command (13:31), parable (15:1–7), and proverb (15:13).[34]

What is true for the content of revelation is also true for the specification of the contemporary reality of resurrection, and the two are intimately connected. By the end of the Lazarus story a present resurrection remains a cipher, an unfulfilled, tantalizing lure. A reader schooled in Christian tradition may have had some suspicions about what the story might mean, particularly on the basis of the relational language of 5:56–57. The suspicion might have been reinforced by one prominent feature of the Lazarus story, which is that the resurrected one was a friend whom Jesus loved (11:3; 5, 11, 36). A relationship of intimacy was critical to this signal "resurrection" and may be an important part of how this "sign" signifies.

---

[34] Example: 13:15; command: 13:31; parable (and proverb) 15:13. On the latter see K. Scholtissek, "'Eine grossere Liebe als diese hat niemand, als wenn einer sein Leben hingibt für seine Freunde' (Joh 15,13): Die hellenistische Freundschaftsethik und das Johannesevangelium," in *Kontexte des Johannesevangeliums: Das vierte Evangelium in religions- und traditionsfeschichtlicher Perspektive* (ed. Jörg Frey and Udo Schnelle; Tübingen: Mohr Siebeck, 2004), 413–41.

Anointing for Resurrection

With the anointing scene of John 12:1–8 attention shifts from the present and/or future promises of resurrection to the resurrection of Jesus. The details of the account have intrigued commentators. The fact that Mary wipes the precious nard from Jesus' feet with her hair may perhaps hint at the notion that Jesus body will not need embalming unguents.[35] The aroma of the ointment filling the house evokes other olfactory images.[36] Judas's stingy comment (12:6) sets the stage for his possession by Satan in the next chapter (13:27).[37] Whatever connotations the details may suggest, Jesus' explanation of Mary's action (12:7) orients the reader's attention to the future, to his burial, a destiny that awaits him, in part at least, because of his raising of Lazarus (12:9–11). But if the entombment of the dead Jesus is a result of his resurrection of Lazarus, what will his resurrection accomplish?

Resolution anticipated: The Farewell Discourses?[38]

One of the often noted features of the last supper discourses is their collapse of temporal horizons.[39] Jesus seems to speak as one already glorified, while he promises future support and consolation for his persecuted flock through the person of the Paraclete. The topic of resurrection does not explicitly surface in these discourses, but the eschatological horizon does, and it does so in a way that reinforces the "realized" pole of the resurrection antinomies of the earlier chapters. The two related images through which this occurs are the motif of "abiding" and the promise of the Paraclete.

The conceptual structure of the first image replicates that of the image of resurrection and the structural homology is significant. The way in which the image works is familiar to any reader of John. The departure of Jesus, solemnly announced at the beginning of chapter 14, has as its goal the preparation of the dwellings (μοναί: condos? flats?) for the disciples

---

[35] Charles H. Giblin, "Mary's Anointing for Jesus' Burial-Resurrection (John 12,1–8)," *Bib* 73 (1992): 560–64.

[36] See 2 Cor 2:14. The passage may be one intertext in the complex trope on sacred aroma by second-century homilist who gave us the *Gospel of Truth* NHC 1,4: 33.33–34.33.

[37] The relationship between the two passages recalls the comments at 2:20–21 about those who do base deeds not being the elect.

[38] Literature on the final discourses is vast. Among recent work, see especially Udo Schnelle, "Die Abschiedsreden im Johannesevangelium," *ZNW* 80 (1989): 64–79.

[39] On temporal categories in John see especially Frey, *Die johanneische Escahtologie*, 2.208–83.

(14:2).⁴⁰ Jesus will, he says, return and gather up (παραλήμψομαι) the disciples with him – perhaps a Johannine acknowledgment of notions of the "rapture" (1 Thess 4:17).⁴¹ The result will be a blissful cohabitation (John 14:3). All of this future-oriented language finds a new twist in the subsequent plays on "abiding" (μένω). Later in chapter 14, the mutual abiding of God, Christ, and the believers is made possible by the "abiding" (μένει) presence of the Paraclete, the Spirit of Truth (14:17). It is presumably because of that Spirit that Jesus will not leave his disciples as orphans but will come to them (14:18). Here is certainly one stage of the return promised in 14:2. When that happens, Jesus and the disciples will "live" (14:19). The Father will abide in Christ and in them, and vice versa.

Whether by the same or a different hand,⁴² the same troping on future promises that are made present in contemporary abiding continues in chapter 15.⁴³ The branches "abide" in Jesus their vine through obedience to his command to love (15:5–7, 10). That abiding saves them from the threat of being cut off and burned (15:6), an image with none too subtle hints of eschatological judgment.⁴⁴ The Paraclete/Spirit that has made the abiding possible will also empower people for witness (15:26–27) and exercise judgment over the world (16:8–10).

As the voice of Jesus in the final discourses sounds from a virtually exalted state, combining history and eschatology, so do the promises that he offers. Life with Jesus in God's house will be, from the point of view of the narrative, a future reality; but from the point of view of the reader/hearer it is a present fact. That life is made possible by the presence of the Spirit of Truth, the abiding divine presence that instructs and empowers the disciples while it judges "the world." Whatever the long-range possibilities for the created order, those who believe already experience eschatological reality, but the key to that reality is the presence of the Spirit; and before the Spirit comes it is necessary that Jesus depart

---

⁴⁰ For the interpretation of this complex text see especially Frey, *Die johanneische Eschatologie*, 3.119–78.

⁴¹ See Thyen, *Johannesevanglium*, 620–21.

⁴² See Wayne Brouwer, *The Literary Development of John 13–17: A Chiastic Reading* (SBLDS 182; Atlanta: SBL, 2000); George Parsenios, *Departure and Consolation: the Johannine farewell Discourses in light of Greco-Roman Literature* (NovTSup 117; Leiden: Brill, 2005), both of which wrestle with the issue of the unity of the composition. Parsenios, drawing on ancient dramatic conventions, in particular provides an ingenious literary framework within which to understand some of the *aporias* of the discourses.

⁴³ In general see Klaus Scholtissek, *In ihm sein und bleiben: Die Sprache der Immanenz in den johanneischen Schriften* (HBS 21; Freiburg im Breisgau/New York: Herder, 2000).

⁴⁴ Cf. Matt 15:30; Heb 6:8; Rev 20:14.

(16:7). Here is where the resurrection of Jesus begins to emerge as a pivotal point.

The Resurrection Accounts

As Wright notes, the two chapters on the resurrection in John constitute remarkable pieces of literature.[45] They are richly textured, with dramatic encounters between the resurrected Jesus and his disciples, with implications for the Johannine understanding of faith, of community, of what it might mean to be raised from the dead, of love, longing, and fulfillment. How then, do they resolve the tensions that have built through the gospel?

The very existence of the chapters is, as we initially noted, something of an anomaly.[46] The description of the crucifixion is a nodal point where several important themes and images of the gospel come together. Much of the gospel leading up to chapter 19 has pointed to the cross as the moment of glorification and to the "seeing" that provides healing. Jesus himself declares on the cross that his work is complete just before he breathes his last and becomes the font of bloody, but therefore life-giving, water.

The gospel's insistence on the real death of the truly human Jesus on that cross is indeed central to its construal of who Jesus is and what he, as revealer, in fact reveals.[47] But it is also clear from various hints in the text that the cross is only one facet of a complex moment of "glorification." The final discourses, despite their anticipation of hearing the voice of the glorified one, tell of the coming of the Paraclete, the Spirit of Truth. As of chapter 19, the Spirit has been given up, but not given out. Another moment is needed, another side of "glorification" must be seen, and so comes John 20, and on its heels, John 21. Of all the things that these chapters do, they above all celebrate the reality of resurrection in a way that resolves, but at the same time extends the tensions of the previous

---

[45] Wright, *Resurrection*, 662: "among the most glorious pieces of writing on the resurrection" . . . a "deceptively simple account of the Easter events, warm with deep and human characterization, pregnant with new possibilities."

[46] Lincoln ("'I am the Resurrection,'" 124) usefully cites Bultmann, "If Jesus' death on the cross is already his exaltation and glorification, his resurrection cannot be an event of special significance. No resurrection is needed to destroy the triumph which death might be supposed to have gained in the crucifixion. For the cross itself was already triumphant over the world and its ruler" (*Theology of the New Testament* [2 vols.; New York: Scribners, 1955] 2.56).

[47] As pointed out by the many critics of Käsemann. See, e.g., Udo Schnelle, *Antidocetic Christology in the Gospel of John* (trans. Linda M. Maloney; Minneapolis: Fortress, 1992); trans. of *Antidoketische Christologie im Johannesevangelium* (FRLANT 144; Göttingen: Vandenhoeck & Ruprecht, 1987).

accounts into the life of the reader. Reflecting on how that is so will consume the remainder of this essay.

3. The Tension Resolved?

The reader of the rest of the gospel may ask how the future of resurrected life is a present reality. If attentive to the hints of chapters 6 and 14, she will know that it has to do with relationship, with abiding in the Son who abides in the Father. And she may know, from the command that Jesus gave (13:31; 15:11) and parable he told that abiding has to do with love (15:13), an extravagant love that is willing to sacrifice all for the sake of the "friend." Abiding in such all-consuming, radical love, is to abide in God, as the Johannine epistolographer will remind his addressees (1 John 4:16). But is that not, as critics will aver, a romantic, or sectarian notion?[48] Our hypothetical attentive reader will also have heard something about the coming of the Paraclete, who will teach and intercede for believers. She may suspect that in the presence of the Paraclete the reality of new, resurrected life is grounded. Such hopes and suspicions are confirmed, perhaps even rewarded, in the account of the appearance of Jesus to the disciples on Easter night. Jesus now fulfills the promise to provide the Spirit to his disciples in what many have dubbed the Johannine Pentecost.[49]

---

[48] For stern modern critiques of the Johannine perspective, see Maurice Casey, *Is John's Gospel True?* (London/New York: Routledge, 1996) and, with more restraint, Wayne Meeks, "The Ethics of the Fourth Evangelist," in *Exploring the Gospel of John: In honor of D. Moody Smith* (ed. R. Alan Culpepper and C. Clifton Black; Louisville: Westminster/John Knox, 1996), 317–26.

[49] For another view of the significance of the verse, focusing on the Christological implications of the relationship of Christ and Spirit, see Gavin D' Costa, "Resurrection, the Holy Spirit and World Religions," in idem, ed., *Resurrection Reconsidered* (Oxford: OneWorld, 1996), 163; Pamela Kinlaw, *The Christ is Jesus: Metamorphosis, Possession, and Johannine Christology* (Academia Biblica; Leiden and Boston: Brill , 2005), 161. The Christological point here is surely misplaced: The resurrection is hardly the confirmation of the Paraclete's permanent indwelling in Jesus. The account has something to say about what the presence of the Spirit means to the followers of Jesus. For a carefully nuanced reading of the Paraclete passages and their theological and Christological significance, see Hans-Christian Kammler, "Jesus Christus und der Geistparklet: Eine Studie zur johanneischen Verhältnisbestimmung von Pneumatologie und Christologie," in *Johannesstudien: Untersuchungen zur Theologie des vierten Evangeliums* (ed. Otfried Hofius and Hans-Christian Kammler; WUNT 88; Tübingen: Mohr-Siebeck, 1996), 88–190. For an alternative, setting the notions of the Spirit and the resurrection of Jesus into a Stoic framework, see Gitte Buch-Hansen," It is the Spirit that

The importance of the verse in tying Johannine threads together has often been noted. Yet the variety of interpretations of John 20:22 illustrates the principle that there is nothing like solutions to cause problems.[50] Comparison with the Synoptics and with Acts raises numerous questions about the evangelist's timetable for Jesus on earth. Was the ascension yet to come or had it taken place after Jesus left Mary in the garden (more likely). Was this a proleptic bestowal of the Spirit in order to enable mission, with more to come at Pentecost, or was this the real and final thing?[51] Such questions, which arise in a canonical context, are beside the point in the narrative world of the Gospel. Now the reader will have some sense that the way to follow the love displayed on the cross is to abide in the community where forgiveness is practiced. What the Spirit/Paraclete teaches is how to provide that forgiveness. In that act resides eternal life.

Spirit-powered forgiveness is, in the structure of resurrection chapters, surrounded by relationships with Jesus, which are built on new encounters with his mysterious transformed presence.[52] In those encounters, those relationships, faith happens – on the basis of physical signs (20:8),[53] on the basis of a personal address of shepherd to his own sheep (20:16),[54] in the

---

Makes Alive (6:63): A Stoic Understanding of Pneuma in John" (Ph.D. Diss. Copenhagen, 2007).

[50] James Swetnam, S.J., "Bestowal of the Spirit in the Fourth Gospel," *Bib* 74 (1993): 556–76, although the story extends beyond a claim about the bestowal of apostolic authority on the disciples; T. R. Hatina, "John 20,22 in Its Eschatological Context: Promise or Fulfillment?" *Bib* 74 (1993): 196–219.

[51] See the discussion by Cornelis Bennema, "The Giving of the Spirit in John's Gospel – A New Proposal?" *Evangelical Quarterly* 74 (2002): 195–213. See also his *The Power of Saving Wisdom: An Investigation of Spirit and Wisdom in Relation to the Soteriology of the Fourth Gospel* (WUNT 2.148; Tübingen: Mohr Siebeck, 2002).

[52] As noted among others by P. Benoit, "Marie-Madeleine et les Disciples au Tombeau selon Joh 20,1–18," in *Judentum–Urchristentum–Kirche: FS Joachim Jeremias* (ed. Walther Eltester; BZNW 26; Berlin: Töpelmann, 1960), 141–52; Raymond Brown, "The Resurrection in John 20–A Series of Diverse Reactions," *Worship* 64 (1990): 194–206; Dorothy A. Lee, "Partnership in Easter Faith: The Role of Mary Magdalene and Thomas in John 20," *JSNT* 58 (1995): 37–49.

[53] But what does the Beloved Disciple really believe? The answer is ambiguous, but even if, in the narrative world, he only believes Mary's report that the tomb is empty, the reader is invited to come to a deeper belief. For the reading of the belief in simple narrative terms, see James H. Charlesworth, *The Beloved Disciple: Whose Witness Validates the Gospel of John?* (Valley Forge, Pa.: Trinity Press International, 1995), 177.

[54] Much has been made, in the decade of Dan Brown, of the relationship between Jesus and Mary, and its evocation of John 10:4. See Teresa Okure, "The Significance Today of Jesus' Commission of Mary Magdalene," *IRM* 81 (1992): 177–88; I. R. Kitzberger, "Mary of Bethany and Mary of Magdala – Two Female Characters in the Johannine Passion Narrative: A Feminist, Narrative-Critical Reader Response," *NTS* 41 (1995): 564–86; Dorothy A. Lee, "Partnership in Easter Faith: The Role of Mary

challenge to believe without seeing (20:29),⁵⁵ and in the sharing of a meal with a stranger (21:12). The encounters of John 20 and 21 might be taken as a typology of kinds of faith-producing moments, which may or may not have some hierarchical value.

The encounters with the resurrected one also serve one other important function in the economy of this Gospel's theology, which is so much concerned with the foundations of belief. Sarah Coakley suggests that the ensemble serves to illustrate a fundamental hermeneutical principle that sounds familiar to modern ears, that belief and knowledge come not in the abstract, but precisely from an experience of lived engagement.⁵⁶ Another way of framing her insight is to consider the way in which the resurrection appearance stories at the end of the gospel offer a subtle critique of their own role in the life of faith. For the Fourth Gospel the resurrection of Christ is the *conditio sine qua non* for the life of faith, but it is not a warrant for that faith. It is the ultimate *semeion* in the text, an event that has meaning only as a pointer to a reality beyond itself. The gospel's critique of a naïve belief on the basis of signs hangs as a background warning to the reader who would take the resurrection as an event that suffices to compel belief in the Resurrected One.⁵⁷ The Gospel knows him to be elusive, now inaccessible to the sight of potential disciples, not easily

---

Magdalene and Thomas in John 20," *JSNT* 58 (1995): 37–49; Sandra Schneiders, "John 20:11–18: The Encounter of the Easter Jesus with Mary Magdalene – A Transformative Feminist Reading," in *"What is John?" Readers and Readings of the Fourth Gospel* (ed. Fernando F. Segovia; SBLSS 3; Atlanta: Scholars, 1996), 155–68; Adeline Fehribach, *The Women in the Life of the Bridegroom: A Feminist Historical-Literary Analysis of the Female Characters in the Fourth Gospel* (Collegeville: Liturgical Press, 1998), 143–67.

⁵⁵ For the suggestion that the "signs" referred to in John 20,30–31 refer not to the miraculous deeds of Jesus, but to the grounds of resurrection belief, see Paul Minear, "The Original Function of John 21," *JBL* 102 (1983): 85–98, and Hans-Christian Kammler, "Die 'Zeichen' des Auferstandenen: Überlegungen zur Exegese von Joh 20,30–31," in *Johannesstudien: Untersuchungen zur Theologie des vierten Evangeliums* (ed. Otfried Hofius and Hans-Christian Kammler; WUNT 88; Tübingen: Mohr-Siebeck, 1996), 191–211. Contra, Thyen, *Johannesevangelium*, 774.

⁵⁶ Sarah Coakley, "The Resurrection: The Grammar of 'Raised'," in *Biblical Concepts and Our World* (ed. D. Z. Phillips and Mario von der Ruhr; Claremont Studies in the Philosophy of Religion; New York and Houndmills, UK: Palgrave Macmillan, 2004), 169–89.

⁵⁷ See especially 2:18; 4:48; 6:26. Among more recent literature on the topic see Marinus De Jonge, "Signs and Works in the Fourth Gospel," in *Miscellanea Neotestamentica* (ed. Tjitze Baarda, A. F. J. Klijn and Willem C. van Unnik; NovTSup 48; Leiden: Brill, 1978), 107–25; Marianne Meye Thompson, "Signs and Faith in the Fourth Gospel," *BBR* 1 (1991): 89–108; Loren L. Johns and Douglas R. Miller, "The Signs as Witnesses in the Fourth Gospel: Reexamining the Evidence," *CBQ* 56 (1994): 519–35; Andreas J. Köstenberger, "The Seventh Johannine Sign: A Study in John's Christology," *BBR* 5 (1995): 87–103.

recognizable even when he was with his own. Tokens of his resurrection (i.e., the accounts of the empty tomb in resurrection narratives) and visions (i.e., the list of authoritative witnesses that Paul provided[58]) could cause some to believe in the reality of his abiding presence. But it is only the experience of that presence that provides any ground for belief, and that presence is encountered in the community where the Spirit resides.

The overall thrust of the resurrection stories, therefore, seems to reinforce the "realized" dimension of the Johannine resurrection theme. And yet, all the stories are grounded in the presence of one who came back from the dead, in however mysterious a form.[59] The dialectic that pervades the narrative also informs the ending, although in a reverse or chiastic order. Previously the hopes for a future literal resurrection, while affirmed, were constantly refracted onto the life of the believer, but in a way that remained formal and tantalizing. In the conclusion, the reality of resurrected life in the present is given definition as a life of Spirit-filled love that issues in forgiveness. But that realized experience of the way in which a believer abides with Father and Son in a mysteriously glorious present is rooted in the physical (or to take up Wright's term, "transphysical") reality of the resurrected Christ. The evangelist seems most interested in the ways in which resurrected life have meaning in the present,[60] but he insists that they are intimately tied to the resurrected reality of Christ, and with this reality abides a hope for the continued relationship that the presence of the Spirit portends.

---

[58] 1 Cor 15:1–8.

[59] For another approach to the issue of bodily resurrection in the text, see Sandra M. Schneiders, "The Resurrection (of the Body) in the Fourth Gospel," in *Life in Abundance: Studies of John's Gospel in Tribute to Raymond E. Brown* (ed. John R. Donahue; Collegeville: Liturgical Press, 2005), 168–99.

[60] For a comparable reading of the reality of the resurrection, see Rowan Williams, "Between the Cherubim: The Empty Tomb and the Empty Throne," in *Resurrection Reconsidered* (ed. Gavin D'Costa; Oxford: OneWorld, 1996), 87–101. Taking his cue from the two angels of John 20:12, understood as an allusion to the Cherubim over the ark of the covenant, Williams insists on the messy indeterminacy of the resurrection stories.that point in complex ways to the reality of Jesus, bestower of the Spirit, active in the corporate life of the Church (p. 93). Although his point is more general, the archbishop relies heavily on the treatment of resurrection in the Fourth Gospel.

Chapter 2

"The Light Shines in the Darkness..."
Creation, Incarnation, and Resurrection in John

John Painter

"The Light shines in the darkness" is a title that reveals the narrative unity of creation, incarnation and resurrection in John. This motif is announced early (John 1:5) and re-echoes throughout the gospel (1:4–5, 9–10; 3:19–21 [cf. 9:39]; 8:12; 9:4–5; 12:35–36, 46). The images of night and day function as metaphors of darkness and light in 3:2 and 13:30. In the former, Nicodemus comes out of the night into the presence of the light of the world. In the latter, Judas leaves the light of Jesus' presence and goes out into the night and his fate is sealed. Elsewhere Jesus says that work must be done while it is day and that as long as he is in the world he is the light of the world (9:4–5). This implies the darkness of the world without the presence of Jesus as well as that Jesus' withdrawal through death marks the coming of the night. Yet the resurrection of Jesus is marked by the dawning of a new day (20:1), where again the light shines in the darkness.

The relevance of the light shining in darkness (1:5) for our understanding of creation and incarnation seems obvious from the placement of this statement. It stands between the Prologue's statements that all things were made through the Word (1:3) and that the Word became flesh (1:14), as well as between the reference to creation and the light entering the world (1:3, 9). But there is no *specific* mention of the resurrection in the Prologue or of creation and incarnation in the resurrection narrative (John 20–21). Accordingly, we will argue here that the Johannine understanding of creation implies the incarnation and resurrection, and that resurrection presupposes creation and incarnation.[1] The incompleteness of the creation, implied by the struggle with the darkness (1:5), presupposes the incarnation in which God became united with the creation to bring it to completion. The incarnation presupposes the resurrection because the Logos made flesh was on his way to dusty death and corruption. In the resurrection the

---

[1] This is the view of Brooke Foss Westcott. See especially chapter 1 of his *The Gospel of the Resurrection* (8th ed.; London: Macmillan 1898).

creative power of the divine life was reasserted and became communicable in a new way. God's purpose in creation was affirmed by the incarnation and the resurrection.

My approach utilizes the hermeneutical circle in which the proper approach to this topic is, through the formal analysis of John, to reveal its structure and style. Such an analysis presupposes understanding the individual elements from the perspective of the whole and the whole on the basis of the individual elements. Logically this involves beginning with individual words and building the whole bit by bit. The possible meaning of a word is found from the use of language (the whole) in the period of the text, which is narrowed by the use of an author in particular texts and more precisely by the context in which it is used (the part). In this process, the understanding of the parts and the whole is continually renegotiated, each in the light of the other.[2] Only when a sophisticated grasp of the whole informs the reading of the parts can there be a significant comprehension of such a text as the Gospel of John.

My analysis of the gospel reveals the following structure: Prologue (1:1–18); The Quest for the Messiah (1:19–4:54); The Rejection of the Messiah (5:1–12:50); The Farewell of the Messiah (13:1–17:26); The Death of the Messiah (18:1–19:42); The Resurrection of the Messiah [and conclusion] (20:1–29 [30–31]); Epilogue: resurrection appearance and unfinished business (21:1–25). This analysis is consistent with that of many other contemporary Johannine scholars, despite some differences. Although I treat the gospel as a unity, my analysis of the text has led me to see it as the consequence of a lengthy process of composition in which, for example, John 5 has been relocated or inserted, separating John 4 from John 6. John 5 marks the beginning of hostilities between Jesus and the Jews and the rejection of Jesus (5:16–18). The sign of John 5, like that of John 9, is surprisingly identified as a Sabbath breach only at its conclusion (5:9–10; 9:13–14, 16, 22, 34). The former leads to the beginning of action against Jesus, while the latter marks the excommunication of believers in Jesus. It seems to be the latter that led to the reorganization of the order of John 5 and 6, the reinterpretation of some traditions, and expansion of the gospel. The final addition was probably John 21, which falls outside what looks like the original conclusion, but was part of the published gospel from the beginning. Other small explanatory notes may also have been

---

[2] See Rudolf Bultmann, "Das Problem der Hermeneutik," *ZTK* 47 (1950): 47–69, reprinted in *Glauben und Verstehen II* (Tübingen: Mohr Siebeck, 1955), 211–35; ET: "The Problem of Hermeneutics," in *Essays Philosophical and Theological* (trans. J. C. G. Greig; London: SCM, 1955), 234–61. See esp. p. 236. Bultmann drew on the work of Aristotle and Wilhelm Dilthey. See also his Gifford lectures, *History and Eschatology* (Edinburgh: Edinburgh University Press, 1955).

made at this time, preparing the gospel for a wider audience.³ John 21 deals with the death of the substantial author and other "loose ends," such as Peter's threefold denial of Jesus, the relation of Peter to the Beloved Disciple, and the tradition of Galilean as well as Jerusalem appearances. The final verses (21:24–25) attest the veracity of the witness of the Beloved Disciple as the gospel was prepared for a wider readership beyond the circle where the Beloved Disciple was well known.

John is a misleadingly simple text, having a relatively small vocabulary that is used repetitively. Yet it is not a text suited to first time readers because it perplexingly presupposes the recognition of resonances forwards and backwards.⁴ Indeed, the echoes are not only intratextual (within the text of John), though these abound and are significant. They are also intertextual (connected to texts outside the gospel), and a number of these resound from the beginning of the Prologue. The gospel opens, "In the beginning," an expression that involves just two words in Greek (LXX and John) and one in Hebrew (בראשית), and which by that time might have been used to identify Genesis. Thus there is no serious doubt that the opening words of John echo the opening of Genesis.⁵ That echo is confirmed because the expression "In the beginning" is an unusual beginning for a book, and the creation theme is common to both texts. Genesis deals immediately with creation, but John turns first to the status and relation of the Logos to God. Elaboration of this relationship using Wisdom tradition signals that John has a new understanding of God, which goes beyond Genesis. This relationship is fundamental for John's story of creation, laying the foundation for the account of the incarnation and resurrection, which is

---

³ The 2007 San Diego SBL paper given by R. Alan Culpepper ("John 21:24–25: The Johannine Sphragis") adopts a similar position.

⁴ See 11:2, which refers forward to the event of 12:3 as if it had already happened! See also 1:15 in relation to 1:27 and 30. The use of the imperfect ἦν in 1:15 and the present ἐστιν in 1:30 is a puzzle.

⁵ Though John refers to the Logos, the echoes in the Prologue are predominantly with divine Wisdom and are found in the Wisdom literature where Wisdom is often found in parallel with Logos and as a metaphor of Torah. Recognition of this was established by J. Rendel Harris's *The Origin of the Prologue to St John's Gospel* (Cambridge: Cambridge University Press, 1917). His position was adopted by J. H. Bernard, A Critical and Exegetical Commentary on the Gospel according to St. John (ICC; Edinburgh: T. & T. Clark, 1928) and by C. H. Dodd, *The Interpretation of the Fourth Gospel* (Cambridge: Cambridge University Press, 1953), esp. 274–75. Since then the Wisdom background of Johannine thought and language has been a common assumption. Though drawing conclusions different from Harris, Rudolf Bultmann also appealed to the Wisdom background of the Johannine Prologue in his "Der Religionsgeschichtliche Hintergrund des Prologs zum Johannes-Evangelium," in ΕΥΧΑΡΙΣΤΗΡΙΟΝ. *Studien zur Religion und Literatur des Alten und Neuen Testaments : Hermann Gunkel zum 60. Geburtstage* (ed. Hans Schmidt; 2 vols. Göttingen: Vandenhoeck & Ruprecht, 1923), 2.3–26.

fundamental for his story of Jesus. John's intertextual reference to Genesis is designed to elaborate the understanding of God who is named there. The understanding of creation is also elaborated in an unexpected way.

What used to be attributed to the role of the evangelist is these days generally referred to as the role of the narrator, who overtly inserts comments into the narrative as well as providing the narrative framework of the story. In the "new" literary criticism or narrative criticism the narrator is understood as the overt expression of the role of the implied author. The narrator, like the implied author, may or may not express the views of the actual author. In John, the intrusions of the narrator's commentary are prominent and correspond closely to the point of view of Jesus – so closely that at times it is unclear where the words of Jesus end and the words of the narrator begin (3:10–21). Whoever is speaking in these passages, it is clear that by the end they are no longer addressed to characters within the story but directly to the reader. It is this that makes attribution to the narrator appropriate. The same is true in the relationship between the words of John [the Baptist] and the words of the narrator (1:15–18; 3:27–36). It is likely that 1:16–18 and 3:31–36 should be attributed to the narrator. The crucial role of the narrator in John is nowhere more apparent than in the critical placement of the Prologue. Given its content and its position at the beginning, it provides the reader with privileged insight into the way to read the gospel.

My argument is that both creation and the incarnation flow from the relationship between the Logos and God and between the Father and Son, and that the incarnation is the source of the resurrection of Jesus, which both foreshadows and is instrumental in fulfilling the purposes of God in creation. In order to support this thesis, my approach works with the intricate interdependence of the Prologue and the body of the gospel, as is intimated by the introduction of the major motifs of the gospel in the language of the Prologue.[6]

---

[6] See C. K. Barrett, *The Gospel according to St John* (2d ed. London: SPCK, 1978), 150, 151. There he argues that "the whole passage [the Prologue] shows, on careful exegesis, a marked internal unity, and also a distinct unity of theme and subject-matter with the remainder of the gospel." "Many of the central ideas in the Prologue are central also in the body of the gospel; see, e.g., the notes on ζωή, φῶς (v. 4), μαρτυρία (v. 7), ἀληθινός (v. 9), κόσμος (v. 10), δόξα, ἀλήθεια (v.14). If the Prologue was intended to express in eighteen verses the theological content of twenty chapters a good deal of condensation was necessary; and much of John's Christology is condensed in the word λόγος."

> The Prologue is necessary to the gospel, just as the gospel is necessary to the Prologue. The history explicates the theology, and the theology interprets the history.[7]

I would say that the Prologue and the body of the gospel are each a combination of history and interpretation (theology). Though the balance of history is greater in the body of the gospel, the Johannine story is a profound theological interpretation.[8] The interdependence one on the other is to be seen in that the Prologue provides the key insights for a full reading of the gospel and the body of the gospel fills out in some detail what is found only *in nuce* in the Prologue.

The argument follows an analysis of the Prologue (read in the light of the gospel) in the following stages:

1. The relation of the Logos to God as the ground of creation (1:1–3).
2. 'The Light shines in the Darkness': Intimations of an incomplete creation (1:4–5).
3. Intimations of the incarnation (1:6–13).
4. The Incarnation and its consequences (1:14–18).
   The relationship of 1:14, 18 to 1:1–3 and to the body of the gospel.
   The Incarnation as God's life-giving gift.
   Understanding 1:18
   Incarnation, Resurrection and Creation.

1. The Relationship of the Logos to God as the Ground of Creation (1:1–3)

The Prologue initially describes the being and role of the Logos and then refers to God, whereas the body of the gospel follows the reverse order, typically referring to the Father and then the Son. In the Prologue the Logos is given priority because the Logos explicates or exegetes the unseen God. In the body of the gospel the Father commissions and sends the Son into the world. It hardly needs to be argued that the one explicates the other. John 1:14–18, which forms an *inclusio* with 1:1–2, is a bridge between these two conceptual formulations.

In the Prologue, the narrator provides the readers with a perspective not shared by characters in the story. We begin with the Prologue to see how it crystallizes what is found in the body of the gospel and how the body of the gospel fills out the Prologue. Whereas Genesis follows the opening word(s), "In the beginning" with a reference to God and God's action in

---

[7] C. K. Barrett, "The Prologue of St John's Gospel," in *New Testament Essays* (London: SPCK, 1972), 27–48, esp. 48.

[8] See John Painter, *John Witness and Theologian* (London: SPCK, 1975), 7–9.

creation, the Prologue makes the Logos the subject. John 1:1–2 first establishes that "In the beginning" the Logos already "was," before dealing with the status and relationship of the Logos to God as a basis for the creation of all things by the Logos in 1:3. John here signals a development in the understanding of God. This prepares for what is to follow in 1:14. The creation of all things is linked to the incarnation of the Logos (1:14) by the use of ἐγένετο in a creative sense in 1:3 and 14.[9] The Logos, through whom all things were created, became part of the creation.

The Prologue portrays the Logos in a hypostatized relation to God already "in the beginning." Nowhere in the Prologue is this relationship *explicitly* expressed in terms of the Father and Son. In 1:18 the UBS GNT gives the reading μονογενὴς θεός a B rating. It is more strongly supported than μονογενὴς υἱός with or without the definite article (cf. 3:16). Had the latter been original it is unlikely any variations would have been made while the former accounts for variants. In the light of 3:16, the language of 1:14 and 18 moves from the conception of the Logos as θεός in 1:2 in the direction of 3:16 in 1:14, 18, but without the body of the gospel the expressions in 1:14 and 18 are enigmatic.[10] Before addressing the relationship and differences between 1:1–2 and 14–18, some comments on 1:1–13 may be helpful.

First, in 1:1–2 the Logos is both identified as θεός and distinguished from θεός. The presence of the Logos with God in the beginning has a precedent in the role of Wisdom in the Wisdom literature, but John's tension between relationship and identity in 1:1–2 extends the personification of the attributes of God to another level. This becomes especially clear when the Logos made flesh is identified with Jesus who claims, with reference to God, "My Father is working until now and I am working" and "I and my Father are one" (5:17; 10:30).

In 1:1 the Prologue tells us that the Logos was πρὸς τὸν θεόν and the Logos shared divine being (θεός). Further, *this* divine status or being (οὗτος) was not acquired but was in the beginning with God (1:2).[11] Thus, the repeated use of πρὸς τὸν θεόν in 1:1–2 progressively clarifies and provides the initial description of the relationship of the divine Logos as "turned towards God." In the light of 1:14–18 and the body of the gospel, we can render this as "the Son turned towards the Father."[12]

---

[9] See Brooke Foss Westcott, *The Gospel According to St. John: The Greek Text with Introduction and Notes* (2 vols.; London: John Murray, 1908), 1.21.

[10] On the Father Son relationship and the Son as the emissary of the Father in the body of the Gospel see John Painter, *The Quest for the Messiah* (2d ed.; Edinburgh: T & T Clark and Nashville: Abingdon, 1993), 242–43, 245–49.

[11] Barrett, *The Gospel according to St John*, 155–56.

[12] See Francis J. Moloney, "John 1:18: 'In the bosom of' or 'turned towards' the Father?" *ABR* 31 (1983): 63–71. Moloney argues that this is the meaning in 1:18, and takes

The Prologue speaks of God from the perspective of the Logos. Being turned towards God means to be centered there, to be turned there in love. While "love" is not used in the Prologue, the noun and the two verbs are together used 56 times in the gospel, predominantly in chapters 13–21.[13] To use this term here is to read the relationship of the Logos to God (πρὸς τὸν θεόν) in the Prologue in the light of the body of the gospel.[14]

John 1:1–3 make clear that the creation of all things by the Logos arises from the relationship of the Logos to God. That is the point of the emphatic double use of πρὸς τὸν θεόν in 1:1–2, which underlies the statement that all things without exception were created by the Logos. With this in mind, we note that the creative role of the Logos is described in terms of agency.[15] The Logos is the agent of God in creation because the Logos is turned towards God. In the body of the gospel, the Son is the agent of the Father. This change in conceptual terms is foreshadowed by the transitional terminology of 1:14–18. Our discussion will show that the language used there and in the body of the gospel should not be restricted to the scope of the relationship of Jesus to God in his historical mission.

2. "The Light shines in the Darkness": Intimations of an Incomplete Creation (1:4–5)

John 1:4 seems to be the beginning of a new sentence.[16] Reference to the life-giving power (ζωή) in the Logos as the light of human beings (1:4) resonates with Jesus' claim to be (as the incarnate Logos) the light of the world, the light of life (φῶς τῆς ζωῆς) in 8:12 (see also 1:9; 3:19).[17] This

---

this as a reference to the relationship of the incarnate Word (Jesus) to the Father in his work on earth making the Father known. While I disagree with this conclusion I found much that was stimulating and helpful in the article and have taken his caption as one that captures the relationship of 1:1–2.

[13] See Painter, *John Witness and Theologian*, 92.

[14] Thus also Moloney ("John 1:18: 'In the bosom of' or 'turned towards' the Father").

[15] Agency is expressed by δι' αὐτοῦ. On the importance of divine agency in John and first century Judaism see Peder Borgen, *Bread from Heaven: An Exegetical Study of the Concept of Manna in the Gospel of John and the Writings of Philo*, NovTSup 10; Leiden: Brill, 1965), 158–64; idem, "God's Agent in the Fourth Gospel," in *LOGOS was the True Light and Other Essays on the Gospel of John* (Trondheim: Tapir Academic Publishers, 1983); also in *The Interpretation of John* (ed. John Ashton, Philadelphia: Fortress, 1986), 67–78; idem, "The Gospel of John and Hellenism: Some Observations," in *Exploring the Gospel of John: In honor of D. Moody Smith* (ed. R. Alan Culpepper and C. Clifton Black; Louisville: Westminster John Knox, 1996), 98–123 esp. 101–2, 110.

[16] For the evidence and argument in support of this position see Barrett, *The Gospel according to St John*, 156–57.

[17] See Painter, *John Witness and Theologian*, 43–46, especially 44–45.

light springs from the one who, as the life (11:25; 14:6), is life-giving light (1:4). In 5:26 Jesus says, "just as the Father has life in himself (ἔχει ζωὴν ἐν ἑαυτῷ), in the same way also he has given to the Son to have life in himself (ἔδωκεν ζωὴν ἔχειν ἐν ἑαυτῷ)." The Son (Logos) shares this life-giving power of the Father. In the Prologue the Logos already mediates the life-giving power of God (ἐν αὐτῷ ζωὴ ἦν), and in 5:21–29 the Son is the agent of the Father's power to judge and to make alive (ζῳοποιεῖ). The words, "For just as the Father raises the dead and makes alive, so also the Son makes alive whomsoever he wills" (5:21), should be read with 11:25–26 in mind, and especially Jesus' words, "I am the resurrection and the life." The use of ζωή in relation to the Logos, the Father and the Son, is primarily a reference to creative life-giving power. In John 5 that life-giving power issues in eternal life (ζωὴ αἰώνιος) and the resurrection of life for those who believe and do good (5:24–25, 28–29). The source of that life is in the Father, and the Son mediates the life giving power because the Father "has given to the Son to have life in himself." The Logos, in whom there is ζωή, is the agent of God (the Father).

Andrew Lincoln associates the temporal human life of Jesus (his ψυχή) with his flesh (σάρξ) as distinct from his divine life (ζωή), which he could not give up because it is imperishable.[18] Contrary to this view it seems to me that in John 10:11 ψυχὴν αὐτοῦ has the sense of *himself*.[19] It is anachronistic to suggest that John thinks of Jesus having both a human life and a divine life. Such a view belongs in the debates leading up to the Council of Chalcedon (451 CE). Rather I think that John perceives the paradox in that the divine Logos became flesh and that the giver of life dies. Does Charles Wesley capture the Johannine paradox with the words, "Tis mystery all, the immortal dies"? The sense of ψυχή in John corresponds to the LXX rendering of Gen 2:7, καὶ ἔπλασεν ὁ θεὸς τὸν ἄνθρωπον χοῦν ἀπὸ τῆς γῆς καὶ ἐνεφύσησεν εἰς τὸ πρόσωπον αὐτοῦ πνοὴν ζωῆς, καὶ ἐγένετο ὁ ἄνθρωπος εἰς ψύχην ζῶσαν. Here εἰς ψύχην ζῶσαν in the LXX corresponds to לנפש חיה in the Hebrew text. Without the breath of life there is only a dead body, but the breath of life brings a living person into being. See Ezekiel 37 for the distinction between dead bodies and living persons.[20] This makes it unlikely that any contrast between human life (ψυχή) and divine life (ζωή) is to be found in the use of this language in relation

---

[18] See the insightful essay by Andrew Lincoln, "'I Am the Resurrection and the Life': The Resurrection Message in the Fourth Gospel," in *Life in the Face of Death: The Resurrection Message in the New Testament* (ed. Richard N. Longenecker; Grand Rapids: Eerdmans, 1998), 122–44, esp. 129.

[19] See Painter, *John Witness and Theologian*, 45.

[20] See Ezek 37:9 in context and Wis 15:11 for confirmation of this conclusion.

to Jesus in John. Nevertheless, death does not destroy the life of the incarnate Logos.

The light of the Logos *shines* in creation as the light of people. The use of the present tense marks no beginning or interruption of that shining. But the light shines *in the darkness* (1:5). The gospel as a whole (1:4–5, 9–10; 3:19–21 [cf. 9:39]; 8:12; 9:4–5; 12:35–36, 46 [cf. 3:2; 13:30]), and the context of 1:4–5 confirm the aggressive reaction of the darkness to the light (κατέλαβεν). Barrett rightly notes that the verb may mean to seize, overcome or, especially in the middle, "to grasp with the mind."[21] He thinks that John is probably playing on the two meanings. Given 1:10–12, this is possible, but I think that the dominant meaning is aggressive rejection and suppression. This compound verb is found only sixteen times in the NT, and five of these are associated with the text of John (1:5; 6:17; 8:3, 4; 12:35). None of these (if 1:5 does not) means "to grasp with the mind." Of these, the use of κατέλαβεν in 6:17 is found only in an unlikely textual variant, and 8:3 and 4 are part of a passage that almost certainly does not belong in John. This leaves 12:35 as our best guide to John's meaning. Jesus exhorts the crowd (12:29, 34), "For a little while the light is with you. Walk as (while?) you have light, that the darkness may not overtake/overwhelm you." Compare the variant on 6:17 for a similar use. The negative (οὐ κατέλαβεν) affirms the failure of the darkness to overwhelm the light, which implies the attack of the darkness on the light. In this metaphorical use, the darkness is not the absence of light, but an aggressive force that resists, opposes, and seeks to overpower the light. Nevertheless, the light of the life-giving power of God is not overwhelmed by the darkness. The present tense, "the light *shines* in the darkness," affirms the failure of the darkness to quench the light. As in Genesis, the darkness is there without explanation. But unlike Genesis, where the darkness is ordered into the harmony of day and night, in John the darkness has a violent, negative role from the beginning (1:5). This implies the incompleteness of the creation.

3. Intimations of the Incarnation (1:6–13)

If 1:6–8 provides a summary statement of the witness of John [the Baptist] to the coming of the true light into the world, then 1:9–13 provides an ini-

---

[21] Barrett, *The Gospel according to St John*, 158. The aggressive attempt to overwhelm the light might then be seen as a consequence of the failure to grasp the nature of the light. This perspective should not mask the malevolent nature of the darkness. See 3:19–21; 12:35–36, 46.

tial cryptic account of that coming (1:9) and its consequences both negative (1:10–11) and positive (1:12–13). Andrew Lincoln says,

> When the mission of the Logos is summarized in 1:10–13, it is depicted in terms of his coming into a world that has in some sense become separated from the divine life that created everything that exists. . . . Yet at the same time the Logos is able to mediate life to those who believe in him – that is, to put created life back into relationship with its source.[22]

First, the theme of the conflict of the light of the life of the Logos with the darkness is announced in 1:5, well before 1:10–13. I take 1:5 to relate to the period prior to the work of the Logos made flesh in the world, announced by reference to the witness of John [the Baptist] in 1:6–8 and schematically narrated in 1:9–13.[23] Thus, "from the beginning" of the creation "the light *shines* in the darkness."

Second, the present tense – "the light *shines* in the darkness" – states a principle concerning the nature of the light. It shines creatively in the darkness as the force of life-giving power in the midst of the darkness of death. Neither in the Prologue nor in the body of the gospel is there any suggestion that the world has become separated from the divine life. This view reflects the influence of an Augustinian interpretation of Paul in which Genesis 3 is interpreted as "the Fall," which alienates humanity from God with dire consequences for all creation. There is no sign of this view in John, nor did it dominate the Judaism of the time in the way it has come to dominate Christian theology since Augustine. Rather the Prologue narrates God's progressive movement to unite the Creator and the creation, which progresses in the quantum leap of the incarnation of the Logos and culminates in its consequences. To this the narrator now turns.

The introduction of the witness of John in 1:6–8 alerts the informed reader to the reference to the coming of Jesus, but in a way that is strikingly similar to the presence of Wisdom in the world. Although the *coming* of the light of the Logos into the world is announced in 1:9, everything from 1:9–13 could be understood in terms of the presence of Wisdom in the world. C. H. Dodd wrote, "The concept of חכמה, σοφία, in the Wisdom literature represents the hypostatized thought of God, immanent in the world. As such, it replaces the Word of the Lord as medium of creation

---

[22] Lincoln, "I Am the Resurrection and the Life," 125.

[23] Peder Borgen is a long-time defender of the analysis of the Prologue into two parts, the first of which (1:1–5) deals "with protological and preincarnational 'time'" and the second (1:6–18) deals "with the appearance of Jesus Christ." To the latter I would add that it includes the consequences of his appearing. See Borgen, "The Scriptures and the Words and Works of Jesus," in *What We Have Heard from the Beginning: The Past, Present, and Future in Johannine Studies* (Waco, Tex.: Baylor University Press, 2007), 45. He also provides references to his earlier works on the subject.

and revelation."²⁴ Dodd supported this statement by noting parallels between the statements concerning the Logos in the Prologue and those concerning Wisdom, and the parallels are so pervasive that Rendel Harris suggested that the Prologue was based on a hymn in praise of Wisdom.²⁵ Dodd argued that the Logos of John shares a common background and development with the Logos of Philo.²⁶ Both ancient authors link the creative role of the Logos with the Genesis creation narrative and the Wisdom tradition, but John lacks the overt philosophical tendencies of Philo, who was consciously working with the Greek philosophical tradition in relation to the Jewish Wisdom tradition.

4. The Incarnation and Its Consequences (1:14–18)

The opening words of 1:14–18 mark a dramatic shift in the narrative. John 1:14 introduces the startling language of incarnation (ὁ λόγος σὰρξ ἐγένετο).²⁷ Nothing in 1:1–13 has prepared the reader for this. Clearly this means that the Logos enters human life as a man subject to the conditions of human life including death. All of this is implicit in becoming flesh. Barrett rightly notes that the Word remains the Word in the incarnation (σὰρξ ἐγένετο) and affirms the paradox in the statement ὁ λόγος σὰρξ ἐγένετο. It would be a mistake to press on down the paths of fourth and fifth century christological formulations in the interpretation of John, even if this gospel helped to provoke the speculation that led to such formulations. Clearly the incarnate Logos is subject to death even if the life-giving power of the Logos underlies his resurrection.²⁸ The Johannine understanding of flesh is grounded in the Hebraic OT use, where to speak of humans as flesh is to accentuate weakness, finitude, and life on the way to death.

> All people (flesh) are grass, their constancy is like the flower of the field. The grass withers, the flower fades, when the breath of the Lord blows upon it; surely the people are grass. The grass withers, the flower fades; but the word of our God will stand forever. (Isa 40:6–8)

---

[24] Dodd, *Interpretaton of the Fourth Gospel*, 274.
[25] Dodd, *Interpretaton of the Fourth Gospel*, 274–75; Rendel Harris, *The Origin of the Prologue*, 6.
[26] Dodd, *Interpretaton of the Fourth Gospel*, 276–81.
[27] Westcott notes the use of ἐγένετο in both 1:3 and 1:14. With regard to the use of ἐγένετο in 1:14 he wrote, "This term forms a link between this verse and verse 3. As 'all things *became* through the Word,' so He Himself '*became flesh.*' The first creation and the second creation alike centre in Him" (*Gospel According to St. John*, 1.21).
[28] See Barrett, *The Gospel according to St John*, 164–65.

Here the flesh is set in stark contrast with the word of God, which abides forever. Yet in John the narrator confesses that the divine Word became flesh! The eternal enters the realm of death and in so doing takes on the process of dying. Apart from this implied reference in the incarnation, the dying of Jesus is not mentioned in the Prologue. Thus the dying of Jesus is seen in the context of his life. It is not the death of Jesus or the dead Jesus that is significant, but the living Jesus who gives his life. The incarnation is the giving of the life of the Word for the world.[29]

In the body of the gospel the motivation for this action is expressed in terms of God's love for the world. "God loved the world like this (οὕτως ἠγάπησεν), he gave (ἔδωκεν) his only Son (τὸν υἱὸν μονογενῆ)" (3:16). What follows describes the act of giving in terms of mission (3:17): "God sent (ἀπέστειλεν) his Son into the world . . . that the world may be saved through him (δι' αὐτοῦ)." The unique reference (in the gospel) to God's gift of his Son is immediately expressed in the more common Johannine terms of God sending (ἀπέστειλεν) his Son to save the world. Each of these parallel descriptions uses verbs in the aorist tense: God loved, God gave, God sent. In this way God's love is defined as giving, and giving is understood as mission/sending. The use of the aorist ἐγένετο in 1:14 expresses the gift/mission in terms of the incarnation. From the perspective of the narrative (Prologue and the body of the gospel), the event lies in the past. In the Prologue no explicit motivation/reason is given for the creation or the incarnation. In 3:16 the narrator (or less likely, Jesus) asserts that God loved the world in such a way that the consequence was that God gave (ὥστε ἔδωκεν) his only Son to bring eternal life to those who believe in him. This act of love (ἠγάπησεν) is expressed in the act of giving (ἔδωκεν). The mission of the Son in the incarnation to save the world is an expression of God's love for the world (3:16–17). Though the motivation for the incarnation is not expressed in the Prologue, the consequence is: "We beheld his glory, glory as of the only begotten of the Father, full of grace and truth (חסד ואמת)." The revelation of the glory that comes from the Father in the incarnate Word is here expressed in terms of the loving kindness of God, thus overlapping the ἠγάπησεν of 3:16. According to 1:1–2, the agency of the Logos in the creation of all things (1:3. cf. the world, 1:10) arises from the relationship of the Logos to God, that is, the Logos inclined to God, turned towards God. In both creation and incarnation the Logos acted as the agent of God, the Son was the agent of the Father in his loving purpose of creation and bringing creation

---

[29] See Gail O'Day, "The Love of God Incarnate: The Life of Jesus in the Gospel of John," in *Life in Abundance: Studies of John's Gospel in Tribute to Raymond E. Brown, S.S.* (ed. John R. Donahue; Collegeville: Liturgical Press, 2005), 158–67, esp. 158–61, 166–67.

to completion. The language of the agency of the Son (δι' αὐτοῦ) in bringing life to the world (3:17) echoes the agency of the Logos in the creation of all things (1:3). This shared language implies a continuity of purpose in bringing the creation to completion.

In the Prologue, verses 1:3 and 1:10 use δι' αὐτοῦ ἐγένετο, the first for the creation of all things (πάντα) and the second for the creation of the world by the Logos. Κόσμος is a frequently used term in John, where it is found 78 times. In the NT this concentration is matched only in 1 John, where it is found 23 times, but only 15 times in the Synoptics. Used here (John 1:10) it is a synonym for all things that have been created by the Logos. As distinct from the use of πάντα in 1:3, the use of κόσμος in 1:10 is colored by the negative sense, which characterizes many of the uses in John and 1 John. The paradox is that "he was in the world and the world was made by him, but the world did not know him." That is, the world did not recognize or receive him (1:10–13). Consequently κόσμος can have a positive, neutral, or negative sense in John. The negative sense is common and, if not explicit, is often lurking in the background.

If the incarnation can be described as a past event captured by the aorist tense (ἐσκήνωσεν), the verb also has a durative sense. Barrett notes the connection of ἐσκήνωσεν with the Hebrew verb שכן often used with the durative sense of the dwelling of God with Israel (Exod 25:8; 29:46), or of the dwelling of the visible manifestation of God's presence that settled on the tabernacle (Exod 24:16; 40:35), and Wisdom's tabernacling with Israel, κατέπαυσεν τὴν σκηνήν μου . . . 'Εν 'Ιακὼβ κατασκήνωσον . . . ἐν σκηνῇ ἁγίᾳ (Eccl 24:8, 10; cf. *1 En.* 42:2; *Odes of Solomon* 12:12).[30] Though ἐσκήνωσεν is also aorist, because the narrator writes from the perspective of the completed life of Jesus, it indicates a dwelling even if a temporary dwelling of Jesus' life and ministry. The incarnate Logos dwelt for a time "among us." This means, first of all, as a man among other human beings. The focus narrows to the perspective of those who saw him and saw in him the glory of God. Again the verb is an aorist, ἐθεασάμεθα τὴν δόξαν αὐτοῦ. Consistent with the three aorist tenses in 1:14, this places the vision of the glory of God in the incarnate Logos in the past.

In 1:14 the narrator, who has been an impersonal voice until now, explicitly becomes part of the corporate witness of believers ("we"). It has long been disputed whether or not this believing witness implies eyewitness testimony. The classical argument of narrowing concentric circles of evidence set out by B. F. Westcott in his commentaries on John is used to argue that it does. Westcott has been followed by many scholars. C. H.

---

[30] On ἐσκήνωσεν see Barrett, *The Gospel according to St John,* 165–66.

Dodd held a nuanced alternative to this position. Writing of the meaning expressed in the words, ἐθεασάμεθα τὴν δόξαν αὐτοῦ (1:14), he said:

> The meaning is that those who, whether in actual physical presence, or in retrospect through the witness of the Church, contemplate the historic life of Jesus, and recognize the divine quality in it – His 'glory' – have attained a knowledge of Him which is the real 'vision of God.'[31]

It is implicit in Dodd's argument that "in retrospect through the witness of the Church" the confession, "we beheld his glory," is grounded in the believing eyewitness testimony, even if the narrator is not the voice of an eyewitness author in solidarity with other eyewitnesses. I am inclined to accept that the narrator, at this point, implies the voice of an eyewitness. Those who confess their faith in company with the narrator assert "we beheld" the glory of the Logos made flesh.[32] The aorist tense implies that the glory was seen in the flesh of Jesus in the past. In the community of faith that vision remains rooted in the past. Thus the narrator's "we" is to be identified with the witnesses, not with the believers at large. John 20:29 confirms the gospel's distinction between belief based on seeing and belief based on testimony, "not having seen."

Does the juxtaposition of divine glory with flesh place the reality of the humanity in question? The debate between Bultmann and Käsemann over this crux is well known.[33] The glory of the incarnate Logos was seen, recognized and confessed by those who came to believe in him. It was recognized as δόξαν ὡς μονογενοῦς παρὰ πατρός.[34] In the light of 1:18; 3:16, 18; and 1 John 4:9 these words are recognized as characteristic and theologically important Johannine terms which should be understood as "the only begotten Son from the Father." Because the Son comes as the emissary or agent from the Father, the glory of the Logos made flesh is the glory of God. The comparative ὡς probably implies "like father like son." Here the case for a naïve docetism seems to be ready-made. The divine glory was seen in the Logos made flesh. The glory was recognized as originating with God, the Father's glory revealed in the flesh of the Father's only Son. But the nature of that glory is defined as "full of grace and

---

[31] Dodd, *Interpretation of the Fourth Gospel*, 167.

[32] See Rudolf Bultmann, *The Gospel of John* (Oxford: Blackwell, 1971; German orig. 1941), 63. He argued that the glory was seen in the human Jesus, the Logos made flesh: "We beheld *his* glory." On the whole this makes sense in John, especially the association of glorification with the death of Jesus.

[33] See Ernst Käsemann, *The Testament of Jesus. A Study of the Gospel of John in the Light of Chapter 17* (London: SCM Press, 1968; German orig. 1966), ch. 2.

[34] Barrett rightly notes that the association of μονογενοῦς with πατρός means that it must be understood as only begotten Son (*Gospel according to St John*, 166).

truth."³⁵ If the glory of God was seen in Jesus' life and acts of חסד ואמת then the perception of that glory in the Logos made flesh makes sense, especially of the giving of his life for his own, and for the world. The revelation of the glory reveals God's love for the world as the underlying motivation of the incarnation (and the creation of all things?).

Sandra Schneiders appeals to Mary Coloe's "Like Father, Like Son: The Role of Abraham in Tabernacles – John 8:31–59" to support her view that "flesh" and Tabernacle relate to Jesus' career as a mortal while body and Temple denote his glorified life. ³⁶ This seems to me to be a mistaken conclusion drawn from the use of the verb tabernacled with flesh in 1:14 and temple/body in 2:19, 21. It should be noted that the verb "tabernacled" does not have an equivalent "templed." I suspect that the Johannine meaning of these texts is that the glory of God is to be seen in the human life of Jesus but that this reality was grasped only after his death and resurrection (2:22). Schneiders also fails to note that Jesus (2:19. 21) explicitly uses temple to refer to his mortal body that was put to death, "You destroy this temple (ναός) and in three days I will raise it." In John the dominant use of σῶμα is to refer to a dead body, 19:31, 38 (twice), 40; 20:12, making the use in 2:21 the only exception. Even there, the ναός/body that the Jews destroy is his mortal body, which Jesus does not distinguish from the body he will raise up. Body no more refers specifically to Jesus' glorified life than does σάρξ. John 6:51 confirms the complex use of σάρξ in John, which is already clear in 1:14 where the σάρξ of Jesus is the theatre of the revelation of the glory of God Similarly, in 6:51 σάρξ is identified with the bread from heaven and is used in a comparable context to the Pauline and Synoptic use of σῶμα in the last supper narrative. Nothing in John's use suggests that σῶμα as distinct from σάρξ denotes the person "as self-symbolizing," as "a subject who can interact with other subjects."³⁷

---

³⁵ See Dodd (*Interpretation of the Fourth Gospel*, 175) and Barrett (*Gospel according to St John*, 167) for the identification of grace and truth with חסד ואמת and Painter, *John Witness and Theologian,* 58 for a short note on the way to read 1:14c.

³⁶ See her n. 22 in "Touching the Risen Jesus: Mary Magdalene and Thomas the Twin in John 20" below in this volume, where she refers to Mary Coloe's article in *Pacifica* 12 (1999): 1–11.

³⁷ Contrary to Schneiders, "The Resurrection (of the Body) in the Fourth Gospel: A Key to Johannine Spirituality," in *Life in Abundance: Studies in John's Gospel in Tribute to Raymond E. Brown, S.S.* (ed. John R. Donahue; Collegeville: Liturgical Press, 2005), 168–98. This is a reference to p.172. That it makes sense to treat the particularity of bodily form as a means of recognizing persons does not mean that John made use of language in this way. John's use of flesh and body does not support this hypothesis. Nor does the narrative in which Mary failed to recognize the risen Jesus and the disciples recognized him only after seeing his wounded hands and side.

If the Logos became flesh, the Father sent/gave (ἀπέστειλεν / ἔδωκεν) him. Jesus defines his being (the incarnate Logos) as the Good Shepherd, "I am the Good Shepherd." He explains, "the Good Shepherd *gives* his life (τὴν ψυχὴν αὐτοῦ τίθησιν) for the sheep" (10:11, 15, 17). The present tense signifies the characteristic behavior of the Shepherd. While it may be true that you can only die once, it is the nature of the Good Shepherd to "put his life on the line" for the sake of the sheep. Daily he risks his life to keep them safe. In the incarnation the Son, who was sent/given by the Father, daily gives his life for the world and for his own. In due course the daily self-giving comes to an end in the death of Jesus.[38]

The narrator makes the same point in direct language in 13:1. He notes that "Jesus, knowing that his hour had come to depart from this world to the Father, having loved his own in the world, he loved them to the end." The final act is of a piece with his life as a whole. The whole of Jesus' life as depicted by John is his self-giving for the life of his own, for the life of the world. Because in the incarnation the Logos/Son entered the realm of death, his actual death makes clear what was true in principle in the incarnation. The incarnation was complete self-giving, to the end, to death. The washing of the disciples' feet by Jesus is narrated as a parabolic action (ὑπόδειγμα), which reveals the character of Jesus' life and love (13:12–16).[39] It becomes the basis upon which the Johannine Jesus issues his distinctive commandment, "A new commandment I give to you, Love one another as (καθώς) I have loved you. . . . In this way all people will know that you are my disciples, if you have love for one another" 13:34–35. Just as the life-giving power of God is the power of God's love (see 3:16–17), so the eternal life that God gives is known by its loving action (see also 1 John 2:9–11; 3:14–18).

John 1:15 is a resumption of 1:6–8, with a difference. The generic statement of witness in 1:6–8 is now linked to the actual witness of John described in 1:19–34, especially 1:27, 30.[40] Almost certainly the witness of John ends with 1:15 and 1:16–18 resume the narrator's words addressed directly to the reader in 1:14. In response to the incarnation of the Logos

---

[38] See Gail R. O'Day, "The Love of God Incarnate,"158–59. O'Day rightly emphasizes that John's shaping of the theological perspective of the Gospel is not about the death but about the meaning of the life of Jesus. "Jesus *lived* to make God's love known."

[39] This emphasis is one of the major points of my 2005 Leuven English Seminar paper, "The Death of Jesus in John: A Discussion of the Tradition, History, and Theology of John," in *The Death of Jesus in the Fourth Gospel* (ed. Gilbert Van Belle; BETL 200; Leuven: Leuven University Press and Peeters, 2007), 327–61.

[40] Although there are differences between the two statements concerning the priority of Jesus in 1:30 and 1:27, the saying in 1:30 might refer back to 1:27. But in what way can 1:15 be said to refer *back* to 1:30 or 1:27?

the witnesses (narrator) confess, "we beheld his glory . . . full of grace and truth." In John the common Pauline term grace (χάρις) is used only four times, and only in 1:14, 16, 17. The two uses of 1:16 are enclosed between the two uses of "grace and truth" of 1:14, 17, reflecting the influence of the Hebrew חסד ואמת. If "grace" is not used in the body of the gospel, "love" is not used in the Prologue. The Johannine use implies a significant overlap of meaning in the Prologue's use of "grace and truth" and the use of "love" in the gospel. The revelation of grace and truth in the incarnate Logos was not only seen, it was experienced, and received in abundance, grace piled upon grace. This seems to be the best way to read χάριν ἀντὶ χάριτος.[41] Although the idiom of grace and truth in 1:14 and 17 does not suggest a Pauline reading, the polarity of Law and grace in 1:17 may indicate some Pauline influence. The evidence of the underlying influence of חסד ואמת suggests that any Pauline influence has been Johannised by the influence of the Johannine love motif.

The polarity of the Law given by (ἐδόθη + διά with the genitive) Moses (God's agent) is contrasted with grace and truth that came by (ἐγένετο διά with the genitive) Jesus Christ (God's agent).[42] There is no reason to see a denigration of Moses here (see 5:39, 45–47), though there is reason to think that the Jesus of John seeks to put Moses in his place (6:31–32). God is the giver of the manna and the Law even if the giving was via the agency of Moses. In the growing conflict with synagogue Judaism the polarity of Moses against Jesus grows, as in John 9:16, 24–34. The superior agency of Jesus as incarnate Logos is evident in the Prologue, which sets out the agency of the Logos in creation (1:1–3) and of the incarnate Logos in making the transcendent Father known. His superiority is affirmed in his superior relationship to the Father (1:18) and in his role in creation and revelation (ἐγένετο). Creation and the realization of grace and truth in the incarnate Logos (Jesus Christ) are linked by ἐγένετο in 1:3 and 14.

4.1. The Relationship of 1:18 to 1:1–3 and to the Body of the Gospel

The opening words of the Prologue deal with the beginning and creation (1:1–5). What follows (1:6–18) narrates the impact of the life of the Logos made flesh, including the end of Jesus' earthly ministry and return to the Father, as the foundation of believing witness.[43]

---

[41] Thus Barrett, *The Gospel according to St John*, 168.
[42] Note the use of ἐγένετο in relation to the *Logos* in 1:3, 10, 14. 17.
[43] Thus also Peder Borgen, "The Scriptures and the Words and Works of Jesus" in *What We Have Heard from the Beginning: The Past, Present, and Future in Johannine Studies* (Waco, Tex.: Baylor University Press, 2007), 45.

In the Prologue (1:1–18) the creation of all things (1:3) forms the beginning of a narrative that is consummated by the incarnation and return to glory of the Logos. At the beginning of the Prologue the Logos was with God. The ending forms an *inclusio* with the reference to μονογενὴς θεός in the bosom of the Father. In between, the creation of πάντα puts in motion the events of the gospel story. Underlying the account of creation is an understanding of the undergirding being of God expressed in the *inclusio* of 1:1–2, 18. Creation arises out of God's complex relationality as the source of creativity and life. The relational complexity of God is expressed in and explicated by the parallelism of 1:1–2 and 1:18. Although the Logos is not mentioned in 1:18, in 1:14 the glory of the incarnate Logos is identified as δόξα ὡς μονογενοῦς παρὰ πατρός, confirming the identification of the Logos with μονογενὴς θεός in 1:18. Although the Son is not mentioned in the Prologue, and the Father is not mentioned in 1:1–2, 1:14 speaks of the incarnate Logos ὡς μονογενοῦς παρὰ πατρός, and 1:18 describes μονογενὴς θεὸς ὁ ὢν εἰς τὸν κόλπον τοῦ πατρός.[44] The Son, who came from the Father, has returned to the Father. The use of μονογενὴς θεός in 1:18 stands half way between θεὸς ἦν ὁ λόγος of 1:1 and τὸν υἱὸν τὸν μονογενῆ in 3:16. In 1:18 μονογενὴς θεός is described as being εἰς τὸν κόλπον τοῦ πατρός, affirming the Father – Son relationship, which resumed the intimacy affected by the incarnation and was restored by the ascent/return to the Father (20:17; cf. 17:5).

1:1–2	1:18
ὁ λόγος	Implied ὁ υἱός
πρὸς τὸν θεόν	ὁ ὢν εἰς τὸν κόλπον τοῦ πατρός
θεός	μονογενὴς θεός

The Prologue implies that the Logos is to be identified with the Son in the body of the gospel. Thus the relation of the Logos to God and the Father Son relationship are mutually illuminating. This is confirmed by the *inclusio* of 1:1–2 with 1:18 where the relationship of the Logos to God and the relationship of μονογενὴς θεός to the Father, the unseen God, are mutually illuminating.[45] The relationship is described using a variety of preposi-

---

[44] Thus Barrett, *The Gospel according to St John*, 166 and Dodd, *Interpretation of the Fourth Gospel*, 305. Barrett rightly notes that (in 1:14) the glory is of the Son who proceeds from the Father (παρὰ πατρός).

[45] For attempts to analyze the Prologue as a chiastic construction see especially R. Alan Culpepper, "The Pivot of St John's prologue" *NTS* 27 (1980): 1–31. He surveys a number of chiastic approaches before setting out his own which, he argues, makes 1:12c the center and climax of the Prologue. I note that 1:1–2 match 1:18 in these chiastic analyses. Though Peder Borgen uses the criterion of the use and reuse of Genesis for his analysis, he also suggests something like a chiastic structure in his recent, "The Scriptures and the Words and Works of Jesus," 45. But his analysis is based on the specific

tions (πρὸς and εἰς τὸν κόλπον (1:1–2, 18).[46] Compared with 1:1–2, the imagery of 1:18 is more personal in an anthropomorphic way, because the Father – Son relationship is in view. That the Logos was directed towards God is emphasized by the repetition of the prepositional relationship in 1:1–2.

That directedness is critical for 1:3, which asserts the creation of all things (πάντα) without exception, by the Logos (δι' αὐτοῦ). The point of δι' αὐτοῦ is that the Logos is God's agent in the creation of all things. What the Logos does creatively arises out of the directedness of the Logos towards God (the Father). John 1:14 grounds the incarnation in the relation of the Logos to the Father, describing the incarnate Logos as the only begotten from the Father (μονογενοῦς παρὰ πατρός). In the Prologue creation and incarnation are united in the loving purpose of God and arise from the relationship between Father and Son, a theme strongly developed in the body of the gospel. There Jesus teaches that the Son was sent by the Father and does only whatever he sees and hears from the Father. Because the Father loves the (φιλεῖ) Son he shows him all things (πάντα) that he does (5:19–20, 30; 8:28). If the Father loves the Son and enables his activity, the Son loves the Father and does his will (4:34; 14:31). Earlier John [the Baptist], or more likely the narrator, has said,

> For the one whom God sent speaks the words of God, for he does not give the Spirit by measure. For the Father loves (ἀγαπᾷ) the Son and has given (δέδωκεν) all things (πάντα) by (or in) his hand" (3:34–35).

While 5:19–20 and 3:34–35 may seem to have a primary reference to the relationship of the incarnate Logos to the Father, both Jesus (17:5, 24) and the narrator (1:1–18) speak of the pre-incarnate relation of the Logos/Son to the Father. Consequently it is likely that when the narrator and Jesus say, "the Father loves the Son," this includes the pre-incarnate and pre-temporal relationship, which is explicit in 17:5, 24. In 17:5 Jesus says, "Now you glorify me, Father, with/by yourself with the glory which I had with you before the world came to be (πρὸ τοῦ τὸν κόσμον εἶναι)." More importantly, in 17:24 Jesus speaks of his relation to the Father as the Son. Where the Prologue says the Logos was with God in the beginning, in 17:24 Jesus speaking as the Son says, "you loved (ἠγάπησας) me before the foundation of the world (πρὸ καταβολῆς κόσμου)." Only here is the love of the Father for the Son expressed in any tense other than the present. Here the aorist tense is used, not to limit that love to an act in the

---

content of the Prologue so that the two parts are rather unbalanced though they follow the abc, cba of chiastic constructions.

[46] The latter should be compared with the use of ἐν τῷ κόλπῳ (13:23) and ἐπὶ τὸ στῆθος (13:25). These variations do not seem to involve different meanings.

past, but to assert that the Father already loved the Son before the foundation of the world. Thus that love is temporally delimited and underlies the creation of the world by the Logos/Son. While 3:16 provides a basis for concluding that for John the Father's love for the world was the source of the Son's mission to save the world, there is no specific statement about creation grounded in the love of God. I take that to be implied by the relation of the Son as directed towards the Father and doing his works, 1:1–3. This interpretation is confirmed by Jesus' assertion of the Father's love for the Son before the foundation of the world. In the light of this clear statement of that love prior to creation, the present tense assertions that the Father loves the Son (ἀγαπᾷ, 3:35) and (φιλεῖ, 5:20) should be understood to apply from before the creation of the world. This formulation states no temporal beginning of that love and 17:24 asserts its reality prior to the creation of the world.

In the Prologue, the creation of all things (πάντα) by the Logos arises from the relationship of the Logos to God (1:1–2), interpreted as the relationship of μονογενὴς θεός to the Father in 1:18. In the body of the gospel, two passages that deal with the Father Son relationship in terms of the Father's love for the Son also deal with all things (πάντα) in a way that includes the creation of all things.[47] First, in 3:35 the narrator (or John the Baptist) speaks with the voice of Jesus: "The Father loves (ἀγαπᾷ) the Son and has given (δέδωκεν) all things by (or in) his hand." The love relationship between Father and Son is expressed in the continuous present. The Father *loves* the Son. That is the reason all things have been given by his hand. This instrumental use of ἐν τῇ χειρὶ αὐτοῦ is comparable to the agency of δι' αὐτοῦ in 1:3. Agency is appropriate to personal action while instrumentality is for reference to the hand. The Father's love for the Son is expressed in the agency of the Son in doing all that God does. Love is linked to God initiating creation through the Logos and his continuing creation in Jesus, who says, "Amen, amen, I say to you, the Son is not able to do one thing from himself except what he sees the Father doing; for whatever he (the Father) does, these things also the Son does likewise (in the same way). For the Father loves (φιλεῖ) the Son and shows (δείκνυσιν) him all things (πάντα) that he does" (5:19–20). Here πάντα includes not only the originating creation as in 1:3, but also the consummating acts of making the creation whole. "My Father is working *until now* and I am working" (5:17) presupposes the Father working through the agency of the Son. In 3:35 and 5:20 the present tenses should not be restricted to any particular situation but state the principle of the Father working through

---

[47] In the third reference (17:24) Jesus, addressing the Father, says, "you loved me before the foundation of the world." Here the Father's love for the Son is clearly related to the creation of the world.

the Son in relation to the world. The Father loves the Son and shows him all that he does and the Son does all the Father shows him. This is true also of the perfect tense (δέδωκεν) in 3:35. No temporal situation can be identified because the ground of the giving is the present tense ἀγαπᾷ.

In John 5, Jesus changes the idiom from the narrator's description (5:3, 5, 13) dealing with sickness and healing (ἀσθενέω, ἀσθένεια, ἰαθείς) to wholeness (ὑγιής; 5:6; cf. 5:9, 11, 14, 15; 7:23).[48] In a context where failure to keep the Sabbath is not denied, the statement, "My Father is working until now (ἕως ἄρτι) and I am working" (5:17), implies that creation is not complete. The offence of this assertion cannot be overcome by distinguishing God's providential working from the initiating creative work because neither Jesus nor the narrator makes any attempt to do so. Instead Jesus increases the offence. He asserts God's continuous creative work "until now," that is, on the Sabbath. John 5:18 makes clear that the Jews understood that Jesus' appeal to "my Father" was a reference to God. If this was not enough, he adds, "and I am working (on the Sabbath)." This exacerbates the problem because Jesus claims that God is at work in all that he does (5:19–20). The narrator informs us, "Because of this the Jews sought all the more to kill him because, not only did he break the Sabbath, but he also claimed God as his own Father, making himself equal with God" (5:18). That the creation lacks wholeness is signaled by Jesus' offer to make the man whole, asserting God's continuing work on the Sabbath. By setting aside the Sabbath commandment and asserting that just as the Father works, he also works on the Sabbath, not to restore, but to make whole, he implied that creation is incomplete. His response to intensified persecution was to elaborate the Father – Son relationship in 5:19–20. Here he asserts that he does only what he sees the Father doing and because the Father loves the Son he shows him all that he does. Thus the Father does all things through the Son (see 1:3; 3:35). God's action through the Son "until now" has been with a view to making the creation whole. From the beginning of the creation the light of the Logos has been shining in the darkness and until now God's work through his Son has been to turn the night into day.

The same perspective is present in the second Sabbath sign in John 9 (see 9:14; cf. 5:9). Here also Jesus asserts the identity of his work with the work of God, the one who sent him (9:4; cf. 5:17). Here also creative work on the Sabbath implies the incomplete creation, as is confirmed by the giv-

---

[48] John's six uses of ὑγιής are all concentrated on one incident in which Jesus' choice of ὑγιής describes his action as making a man whole on the Sabbath. Linked with 5:17, this sign signifies Jesus' work of making creation whole. Elsewhere in the NT this word is rarely used, only twice in Matt 12:13; 15:31; once in Mark 5:34; once in Acts 4:10; and once in Titus 2:8.

ing of sight to a man *born* blind. His sight was not restored. Rather, eyes that had always been sightless were given sight. What is more, the description of the act of healing echoes the creation of the human in Gen 2:7, where God created the human from the dust of the earth. Here Jesus spits on the ground and makes clay from the mixture of his spittle with the dust of the earth. With this he anoints the man's eyes. The Diatessaron recognizes the echo with Gen 2:7, translating the last half of 9:6 as "he [Jesus] made eyes from his clay."[49] The newness of this act is signaled by the addition (to the dust of the earth of Gen 2:7) of Jesus' spittle and the water in the pool of Siloam. The sending of the Man to wash in the pool of Siloam is reminiscent of the Elisha episode with Naaman (2 Kings 5). Though the healing of the man in John 9 was at the initiative of Jesus, like that of John 5, completing creation, the blind man was called on to respond actively by going to wash in the pool of Siloam. This he did and came away seeing, and in so doing he became the major player in 9:13–34. In this section he becomes increasingly the active and effective witness to the absent Jesus. Having received his physical sight in 9:7, the subsequent scene in 9:13–34 depicts the growing spiritual perception of the once blind man as the Jewish authorities retreat into darkness and blindness. John 9:39–41 reveal that there is yet more creative work to be done to make creation whole.

4.2 The Incarnation as God's life-giving gift

Creation is the overflow of the love of the Father for the Son (1:3; 5:19–20; 3:35; cf. 17:24). Though the Father's love for the Son antedates and underlies the creation of the world (17:24), the first specific reference to God's love in the gospel concerns the Father's love for the world. God's love for the world is the source of the giving/incarnation of the Son (3:16) to save the world, to bring eternal life to those who believe. It includes the life of the Logos in the flesh. This gift of God's love is definitive for the Johannine understanding of God and God's love (see especially 1 John 4:9–12, 16, 19). Jesus' life of self-giving love is consistent with it (13:1). His act of washing the disciples' feet was a symbolic demonstration of the reality of his love in self-giving service, which was both an empowerment and example to be followed (13:15). The act of love has the power to initiate response and to provide an example of how to respond. It leads into the new commandment and the consequences that flow from the fulfillment of it (13:34–35).

The life giving of the Son begins with the incarnation. He came to bring life to the world through the giving of his life, not by his death but by the

---

[49] See Kurt Aland et al., *The Greek New Testament* (3d corrected ed.; New York: American Bible Society, 1983), 364 on John 9:6.

giving of his life.⁵⁰ With the incarnation a new phase in God's relationship with the world was initiated. That phase reached its climax in the resurrection of Jesus. The model of his life became life empowering through his resurrection.

4.3. Understanding 1:18

The Prologue makes no specific reference to the resurrection of Jesus. It is presupposed in the confession of 1:14–18. The fullness of that confession reflects the transformation of understanding brought about by the resurrection (2:22; 12:16). The witness presupposes that the sojourn of the Word made flesh is now a past event, and that the Word made flesh has returned to the Father (1:18). The aorist tense (ἐθεασάμεθα) places the vision of the glory in the past (1:14). The aorist tense of ἐξηγήσατο also places that action as completed in the past and in the present μονογενὴς θεός is in the bosom of the Father. The language is strongly suggestive of the Father – Son relationship so prominent in the body of the gospel. It expresses a return to the relationship expressed in 1:1–2, though in much more personal terms. The temporal relationship of the completed revelation of the transcendent and unseen Father by the incarnate Son to the Son's return to be the one who *is in the bosom of the Father* (ὁ ὢν εἰς τὸν κόλπον τοῦ πατρός) presupposes Jesus' ascent to the Father (1:18). In John, resurrection and ascent are often indistinct and can even be combined with the crucifixion of Jesus. By John 20 it has become clear that Jesus' death, resurrection, and ascent to the Father are three stages of the Son's return to the Father (see 20:17).

4.4. Incarnation, Resurrection, and Creation

In the resurrection the life that comes from God in Jesus (the Logos incarnate) proved to be indestructible and communicable. In John, Jesus, who gives up his life that his disciples may go free (10:11, 15, 17–18; 18:8), raises himself from the dead (2:18–22; 10:17–18; cf. 5:19–20, 21). As the Son, through whom the Father does all his works, Jesus raises the dead and raises himself (5:17, 19–21). The one in whom was life (1:4), who is the resurrection and the life (11:25); the way, the truth and the life (14:6) is not only alive but is the Lord and giver of life (5:21, 26). I have already noted that the resurrection of Jesus is marked by the dawning of a new day where the shining of the true light dispels the darkness (20:1). Following the scene of the coming of Mary Magdalene to the tomb, John describes

---

⁵⁰ See John Painter, "Sacrifice and Atonement in John," in *Israel und seine Heilstraditionen im Johannesevangelium* (ed. Michael Labahn, Klaus Scholtissek, and Angelika Strotmann; Paderborn: Ferdinand Schöningh, 2004), 287–313; and "The Death of Jesus in John."

Mary's report to Peter and John and their frantic race to find the "empty" tomb (20:5–8) and the extraordinary manner in which the grave clothes, once on the body of Jesus, were left behind. The manner suggests that someone has come out from within rather than the removal of the clothes from the outside. In this way the Johannine narrative portrays Jesus as the one in whom the life giving power of God was present and that life-giving power was indestructible even by death.

The scene between Mary and Jesus in the garden near the tomb is reminiscent of Gen 3:8. Mary reports to the disciples that she has seen the Lord and what he said to her. This includes the message concerning Jesus' ascent to the Father. Thus they heard first-hand witness to the risen Lord from a person they knew well and have every reason to trust. Mary Magdalene has been described as the apostle to the apostles. The treatment of the women present at the crucifixion and attending the empty tomb in the narrative of the Gospels raises questions about the credibility of the testimony of women. Although the Gospels make use of this testimony and, in John, Mary is the first witness, the disciples do not believe through her witness. Although they heard the testimony of Mary, they were totally unprepared for the appearance of Jesus to them in 20:19–29. Jesus enters a locked room and greets the disciples, "Peace be with you." This traditional Jewish greeting appears in some specific way to be the trademark of Jesus (see 14:27). From a Johannine perspective, peace is at the heart of earth made whole. Between these words and their repetition, Jesus showed the disciples his hands and his side. Only then were they glad, when they saw and recognized the Lord.[51] For them, no less than Thomas, belief was based on seeing the risen Lord. The only difference between them and Thomas is that he was missing from the first meeting with the risen Lord. Another meeting was necessary to overcome his skepticism.

The double greeting of peace precedes the commission of the disciples, "As the Father has sent me, I am sending you" (20:21; cf. 17:18). Surprisingly, in 17:18, Jesus reflects on the commission of 20:21 as a past event. This makes sense if John 17 is understood as the prayer of the exalted Lord. It should not be seen as John's equivalent of Jesus' Gethsemane prayer for which 12:27–28 is the closest parallel. It is a prayer that assumes the completion of Jesus' work and concentrates on the precarious position of the disciples in the world after his departure. The mission from the Father through the Son to the disciples continues the possibility of the transformation of the world from darkness to light, to earth made whole.

---

[51] The risen body of Jesus is not the basis for his recognition either by Mary or the disciples. Mary mistakes Jesus for the gardener. Only when he speaks her name does she recognize him. Similarly, it is not the risen body that brings recognition to the disciples but the evidence of his wounded hands and side.

The light shines in the darkness. The mission presupposes the continuing presence of the risen life of Jesus in the world through the presence of the Paraclete and in the witness of the disciples (15:26–27). Their commission is rooted in Jesus' mission, which it continues. Because of this Jesus breathes on them (the disciples, 20:19), symbolically bestowing the Holy Spirit on them with the words, "Receive (the) Holy Spirit, 20:22. Like the resonance of John 1:1 with Gen 1:1, these words resonate with the creation motif of Gen 2:7.

That an echo of creation should return in the resurrection narrative is not surprising. Again, the linguistic overlap is quite slender. John 20:22 shares with Gen 2:7 the verb ἐνεφύσησεν.[52] The verb (ἐμφυσᾶν) occurs only in John 20:22 in the NT and is rare in the LXX where it occurs only 11 times, of which only 7 fall in the books of Hebrew origin. Of these 11 uses only Gen 2:7 has the verb in the same form (ἐνεφύσησεν) as John 20:22. Of the rest, Wis 15:11 clearly appeals to Gen 2:7 and the life-giving breath of God. Ezek 37:9 is also important. In the valley of dry bones there is no life, even when the bones are gathered together and formed into bodies knit by sinews and covered with flesh, until the life giving breath of the Lord is breathed into them.

Given this evidence, there is scarcely room to doubt that John 20:22 is an echo of Gen 2:7. Here, as we have been led to expect in John, Jesus acts as the emissary or agent of God. Yet in bestowing the life-giving Holy Spirit, something new is announced. The echo does not indicate the restoration of physical life to dead bodies. Rather, it announces a new development in which human life is elevated to a new level. In Gen 2:7 God breathed the breath of life into the human fashioned from the dust of the earth with the result that the human became a living person (ψυχὴν ζῶσαν). In this way the human became like other living creatures ὃ ἔχει ἐν ἑαυτῷ ψυχὴν ζωῆς (Gen 1:30). But what Jesus breathes into his disciples is an infusion of the Holy Spirit, confirmed by his words, 'Receive the Holy Spirit.' The significance of this bestowal is illuminated by the promise of Jesus in the context of the Farewell Discourses (John 14:16–17, 26–27; 15:26–27; 16:7–15). The intertextual resonance between Gen 2:7 and John 20:22 unveils a progressive theme, from old to new creation or, better still, from incomplete creation towards the fulfillment of creation. From this perspective, the bestowal of the Spirit is the means by which the presence, teaching, and mission of the Father through the Son is

---

[52] See also Philo, *Opif.* 134, who uses ἐνεφύσησεν in his discussion of Gen 2:7. He uses this text to confirm his view that the material body is bad but the immaterial spirit/soul is good.

continued in the mission of the disciples.[53] So the mission initiated by the Father in the Son (3:16–17) continues in and through the Son to believers. In this fragile human community of faith and love, hope for the transformation of the world resides and the light continues to shine in the darkness (17:18–26).

The love command, the fulfillment of which is crucial for the success of that mission, is rooted in the Father's love for the Son, which finds expression in God's love for the world and initiates the mission of the Son to transform the world. The mission of the Son continues in the mission of the disciples and those who believe through their witness. That witness and their love for one another open the possibility for the transformation of the world (13:34–35; 17:18–26, and see especially 17:21, 23). In creation, and in the incarnate life of Jesus, including the resurrection of Jesus, the light shines in the darkness. The power of his risen life is communicated in the bestowal of the Holy Spirit to those who believe.

---

[53] For the relevance of this material to John 20:22 and the discussion of the resurrection and creation see Barrett, *The Gospel according to St John*, 570: "That John intended to depict an event of significance parallel to that of the first creation of man cannot be doubted; this was the beginning of the new creation." See also Painter, *John Witness and Theologian*, 70: "Thus the character of life for the believer is the creation of the Spirit. [John] 20:22 interprets the coming of the Spirit as a new creation in terms of Genesis 2:7. The emphasis is on the new quality of life brought by the Spirit, to be understood in terms of love. The coming of the Spirit is also the assurance that the mission, spoken of in 20:21, will be effective."

Chapter 3

Jesus' Resurrection, the Signs, and the Dynamics of Faith in the Gospel of John

Craig R. Koester

John's gospel introduces the story of Jesus by saying, "In the beginning was the Word, and the Word was with God, and the Word was God" (John 1:1). The Word is God's way of communicating. Through the Word, God creates and addresses the world. The evangelist also says that "the Word became flesh and dwelt among us" (1:14). In Jesus of Nazareth, God's Word encounters people in an embodied human life. This makes God's Word uniquely accessible to human beings, since flesh is what all people share (17:2). The Word meets human beings in human terms. He makes God known by the words he speaks, the actions he performs, and the death that he dies. The purpose of sending the Word in the flesh is that people might believe and have life (1:12). Yet the incarnation also produces a crisis, since the incarnate ministry of the Word spans a limited period of time. Jesus' farewell discourses prepare his disciples for the time when they will no longer see him as an embodied human being (16:17).

Jesus' resurrection is part of this problem. His ministry culminates in death by crucifixion, an action that he undergoes willingly in obedience to his Father's will (10:17–18). One might anticipate that death is what brings an end to seeing the embodied Jesus. But according to John, Jesus does not go away simply by dying. Instead, Jesus dies in a visible embodied way and then rises in a visible embodied way before returning to his Father (20:17). In the Fourth Gospel, the ministry that begins with Jesus' incarnation culminates in bodily resurrection. On Easter, Jesus' body is no longer in the tomb, his disciples are shown his scars, and Thomas is invited to touch him and believe (20:5–12). To be sure, the risen body of Jesus is transformed, so that it is not limited by the constraints of space and time: closed doors do not prevent him from coming to his disciples (20:19, 26). Yet the risen Jesus still meets people as an embodied person.[1] The

---

[1] See Sandra M. Schneiders, "The Resurrection (of the Body) in the Fourth Gospel: A Key to Johannine Spirituality," in *Life in Abundance. Studies of John's Gospel in Tribute to Raymond E. Brown* (ed. John R. Donahue; Collegeville: Liturgical Press, 2005), 168–

disciples who see Jesus during his ministry also see him after his resurrection – for a while. The problem is that they do not continue to see him indefinitely. And people of subsequent generations do see the incarnate or resurrected Jesus in the way that the earliest disciples do.[2]

Seeing is, of course, not the principal issue. Faith is the issue that runs throughout the Fourth Gospel. John wrote in order that people might believe.[3] The question is how they can believe in a Jesus whom they have never seen. Faith is a relationship with a living being. The gospel assumes that there is content to faith, since people are to believe *that* Jesus is the Christ, the Son of God (20:31). Yet this alone is not faith, according to John. To believe is to trust, and such trust can only be placed in one who is alive; it cannot be lodged in someone who is dead. Therefore, Jesus' resurrection is essential for John's theology, since faith cannot be faith unless Jesus is alive. The conviction that the Jesus who was crucified is now living and that people can now relate to him undergirds the whole of John's message.

Faith is important because it is the way people receive life, both now and in the future.[4] Life, according to John, is a relational matter. There is a physical dimension to life, which involves the wellbeing of the body, but life is not limited to what is physical. People have life in its truest sense when they are in relationship to the God who made them, and the proper shape of this relationship is faith. The gospel recognizes that people may be alive in a physical sense and yet dying in the relational sense through

---

98; idem, "Touching the Risen Jesus: Mary Magdalene and Thomas the Twin," in the present volume, 153–76. Andrew T. Lincoln, "'I Am the Resurrection and the Life': The Resurrection Message of the Fourth Gospel," in *Life in the Face of Death. The Resurrection Message of the New Testament* (ed. Richard N. Longenecker; Grand Rapids and Cambridge: Eerdmans, 1998), 122–44, esp. 128–31.

[2] Andreas Dettwiler, *Die Gegenwart des Erhöhten: Eine exegetische Studie zu den johanneischen Abschiedsreden (Joh 13,31–16,33) unter besonderer Berücksichtigung ihres Relecture-Charakters* (FRLANT 169; Göttingen: Vandenhoeck & Ruprecht, 1995), 11, 299–300.

[3] On John's vocabulary of faith see Raymond E. Brown, *The Gospel according to John* (2 vols.; AB 29–29A; Garden City, N.J.: Doubleday, 1966, 1970), 1.512–14; Rudolf Schnackenburg, *The Gospel according to St John* (3 vols.; New York: Herder/Seabury/Crossroad, 1968, 1980, 1982), 1.558–75; John Painter, *The Quest for the Messiah. The History, Literature and Theology of the Johannine Community* (Edinburgh: T. & T. Clark, 1991), 327–33; Ferdinand Hahn, *Das Glaubensverständnis im Johannesevangelium*, in *Glaube und Eschatologie. Festschrift für Werner Georg Kümmel zum 80. Geburtstag* (ed. Erich Grässer and Otto Merk; Tübingen: Mohr Siebeck, 1985), 50–69.

[4] On the theme of "life" see Marianne Meye Thompson, "Eternal Life in the Gospel of John," *Ex Auditu* 5 (1989): 35–55. C. F. D. Moule, *The Meaning of "Life" in the Gospels and Epistles of St John. A Study in the Story of Lazarus, John 11:1–44, Theology* 78 (1975): 114–125.

their alienation from God. Therefore, God calls people to faith and life through his Word, made flesh in Jesus of Nazareth. To believe in Jesus is to believe in the God who sent him, and this brings life eternal (12:44, 50). In John's gospel eternal life begins in the present, since faith binds people to the God who is the source of all life (5:24, 26). Eternal life also continues in the future, beyond death, through the promise of resurrection (5:28–29; 6:39–40). The gospel recognizes that people of faith do die – the death and entombment of Lazarus is a vivid example (11:14, 17; cf. 21:23). Yet the gospel also extends the promise that the relationship with God that begins in faith does not "die" but continues and holds within it the promise of future resurrection (11:25–26).[5]

Readers of the gospel are called to believe and have life during the time of "not seeing." In the past, people saw the incarnate and risen Jesus, but that kind of seeing is no longer available. Readers are also given the promise of resurrection, and with it the prospect of seeing the glory of the risen and exalted Jesus for themselves (17:24).[6] But that kind of seeing remains future. Readers live in the time after Jesus' resurrection and before their own. Therefore, the evangelist faces the formidable task of calling people to believe in a Jesus who is *no longer seen*, but who has risen from the dead and remains alive in the present time of the readers. He must also call people to believe in a Jesus whom they do *not yet see*, but whom they can hope to see, since his resurrection presages the future resurrection of all believers from the dead. The gospel does not dismiss the importance of

---

[5] In John 11:25 Jesus first speaks of death in the ordinary sense: even those who believe die. Then he affirms the promise of future resurrection: the believer "will live." In 11:26 the expressions for life and death are used in a modified sense. Since Jesus has already said that believers do "die," the statement that believers do not die (οὐ μὴ ἀποθάνῃ) cannot mean that they escape death in the ordinary sense. Rather, it means that death does not terminate the relationship that begins with faith. Many interpreters emphasize the strong element of continuity between the present and future life. See, e.g., Jaime Clark-Soles, "I Will Raise [Whom?] Up on the Last Day"? Anthropology as a Feature of Johannine Eschatology," in *New Currents through John. A Global Perspective* (ed. Francisco Lozada Jr. and Tom Thatcher; Atlanta: Society of Biblical Literature, 2006), 29–53. What is significant about resurrection in Johannine theology is that believers do die and that the threat of death is finally and fully overcome when death is no longer a factor.

[6] On 17:24 see Jörg Frey, "Eschatology in the Johannine Circle," in *Theology and Christology in the Fourth Gospel* (ed. G. Van Belle, J. G. van der Watt, and P. Maritz; BETL 184; Leuven: Leuven University and Peeters, 2005), 47–82, esp. 80; idem, *Die johanneische Eschatologie III* (WUNT 117; Tübingen: Mohr Siebeck, 2000), 223–31; C. K. Barrett, *The Gospel according to St. John* (2d ed.; Philadelphia: Westminster, 1978), 514.

either the past or the future.[7] Instead, the evangelist seeks to show that faith and life are possible now, in this time of not seeing.

There are two important dimensions to the Johannine approach to this question of faith in the present time: First, the evangelist presents Jesus to the readers through the words of his gospel. People living after the incarnation may not have seen Jesus' signs, yet they have the signs in written form. Similarly, they may not have seen the risen Jesus, but they hear of his resurrection through the witness of the gospel, and this makes faith possible (20:29–31).[8] When telling the story of Jesus' life, death, and resurrection, the gospel writer keeps the needs of the post-resurrection readers in view. The narrative describes the ways in which people come to faith during Jesus' ministry, but as it does so, it anticipates the ways in which people continue coming to faith after Jesus' ministry has ended. Similarly, when recounting how the earliest followers of Jesus come to believe in his resurrection, the evangelist anticipates how later generations come to resurrection faith. The readers of the gospel see something of themselves in the people described in the narrative.

John's post-resurrection perspective on the ministry of Jesus has often been noted.[9] Sometimes the gospel writer specifically notes that he includes later insights in his narrative. For example, he explains that only after the resurrection do the disciples understand that Jesus' saying about the destroying and raising up of the temple foreshadows the death and resurrection of his body (2:22), and that his approach to Jerusalem on the donkey before the passion fulfills the Scriptures (12:16). Elsewhere, the gospel seems to suspend the ordinary boundaries of time and space, so that readers have the sense that the crucified and risen Jesus already speaks in

---

[7] On the future dimension in Johannine thought see Frey, "Eschatology" idem, *Die johanneische Eschatologie III*; Craig R. Koester, *The Theology of John's Gospel* (Grand Rapids: Eerdmans, 2008), ch. 7. Cf. Dettwiler, *Die Gegenwart des Erhöhten*, 156–57. On John's emphasis on the present availability of life and salvation see R. Alan Culpepper, "Realized Eschatology in the Johannine Community," in the present volume, pp. 253-77. On tensions within John's eschatology see Harold W. Attridge, "From Discord Rises Meaning: Resurrection Motifs in the Fourth Gospel," on pp. 1–19 above.

[8] Thomas Söding, "Die Schrift als Medium des Glaubens. Zur hermeneutischen Bedeutung von Joh 20,30f," in *Schrift und Tradition. Festschrift für Josef Ernst zum 70. Geburtstag* (ed. Knut Backhaus and Franz G. Untergassmair; Paderborn: Fredinand Schöningh, 1996), 343–71. In the present volume see the comments by Jesper Tang Nielsen, "Resurrection, Recognition, Reassuring: The Function of Jesus' Resurrection in the Fourth Gospel," 177-208; and Hans-Ulrich Weidemann, "Eschatology as Liturgy: Jesus' Resurrection and Johannine Eschatology," 279–312.

[9] See, e.g., R. Alan Culpepper, *Anatomy of the Fourth Gospel. A Study in Literary Design* (Philadelphia: Fortress, 1983), 27–32; Jean Zumstein, *Kreative Erinnerung. Relecture und Auslegung im Johannesevangelium* (2d ed.; AThANT 84; Zürich: Theologischer Verlag, 2004), 47–63.

the pre-Easter narrative. For example, when addressing Nicodemus, Jesus speaks as if he has already ascended to heaven again (3:13). In the encounter with the Samaritan woman, Jesus offers her the Spirit's living water, even though the Spirit is not given until after Easter (4:10; 7:37–39). And when praying before the passion, Jesus speaks as if he has already departed from the world and is on his way to the Father (17:11).

The corollary is that the people who meet the incarnate and resurrected Jesus are portrayed in ways that foreshadow people of later generations. Many have noted that on one level the story of the man born blind and his conflict with the Pharisees takes place during the ministry of Jesus. But on another level, John tells it in a way that anticipates later disputes between the followers of Jesus and non-Christian Jews.[10] This foreshadowing of post-resurrection life is not confined to scenes of conflict. The episodes in which people come to believe in Jesus through his public ministry and resurrection appearances also address the situation of readers living in later times. John explores the dynamics of belief and unbelief through his telling of the encounters that take place during Jesus' life, death, and resurrection. And he does so to help readers discern the analogies between the situations of those who have seen Jesus and those who have not (20:29–31).

The second dimension to John's approach to the question of faith in the time of "not seeing" is the recognition that words alone do not evoke faith in the readers. The words about the risen Jesus must be made effective by the risen Jesus. The Spirit that is given to the disciples after Easter, is the means by which Jesus does this. It is the Spirit who brings about the new birth into faith (1:12–13; 3:5–8, 16–18), and the Spirit carries out its work through the witness that began with the earliest disciples (15:26–27). The words Jesus speaks during his earthly ministry become effective through the Spirit (14:26), and it is through the Spirit that the risen Jesus continues to address people (16:13–15). The witness of the gospel grounds the Spirit's work in the tradition about the incarnate, crucified, and risen Jesus. Conversely, the evangelist's witness to Jesus evokes faith when it is made effective through the Spirit given by the risen Christ.[11]

---

[10] J. Louis Martyn, *History and Theology in the Fourth Gospel* (3d ed.; Louisville: Westminster John Knox, 2003); Raymond E. Brown, *The Community of the Beloved Disciple* (New York: Paulist Press, 1979).

[11] On the importance of the Spirit's role in the shaping of the gospel see Martyn, *History and Theology*, 136–43; Zumstein, *Kreative Erinnerung*, 57–58. On the Spirit's continuing role in the community of faith see Sandra M. Schneiders, *The Revelatory Text. Interpreting the New Testament as Sacred Scripture* (2d ed.; Collegeville: Liturgical Press, 1999), 72–73; Michel Gourges, "Le paraclet, l'esprit de vérité: Deux désignations, deux fonctions," in *Theology and Christology in the Fourth Gospel* (ed. G. Van Belle, J.

We will explore the dynamics outlined here in several steps: First, we will consider the similarities between the signs and resurrection appearances, and the complex way they relate to faith. Second, we will trace the functions of the spoken word and "seeing" the signs performed during Jesus' public ministry. We recognize that each sign has its own distinctive elements and that no two are exactly alike. We also recognize that signs have multiple dimensions of meaning.[12] Our focus, however, will be on certain patterns that occur repeatedly in the accounts of signs as they relate to belief. Third, we will consider how the patterns developed in connection with the signs continue in the account of Jesus' resurrection. This will enable us to reflect on the continuing activity of the risen Jesus through the verbal witness of his disciples and the work of his Spirit.

1. Signs, Resurrection, and the Question of Faith

Jesus' public ministry involves both speech and actions, and many of these actions can be considered "signs." A sign (σημεῖον) is an action that brings the power of God into the realm of the senses. Both the signs and the resurrection appearances are forms of action that are extraordinary and yet visible to the eye. The gospel narrative also shows that the signs Jesus does during his public ministry anticipate the culmination of the story in his death and resurrection. The sign that inaugurates Jesus' ministry is turning water into wine at Cana, an action that reveals his glory in a way that anticipates the glory that will be manifested in the "hour" of his crucifixion and completed through his resurrection (2:3, 11).[13] The sign that concludes his public ministry is raising Lazarus from the dead, an act that prepares for Jesus' own death and resurrection, as well as anticipating the future resurrection of believers (11:4, 25–26).

Comments made during Jesus' ministry suggest that the resurrection appearances have a role like that of the signs. When Jesus drives the merchants out of the temple, bystanders demand that he give them a "sign" to show his authority for doing this (2:18). Rather than performing a miracle, however, Jesus gives them the promise of a sign. He speaks of the resurrection of the temple of his body (2:19–22). Later, at the end of the gospel, John recounts Jesus' resurrection appearances to his disciples and

---

G. van der Watt, and P. Maritz; BETL 184; Leuven: Leuven University Press and Peeters, 2005), 83–108.

[12] On these dimensions of meaning see Craig R. Koester, *Symbolism in the Fourth Gospel. Meaning, Mystery, Community* (2d ed.; Minneapolis: Fortress, 2003), 79–138.

[13] On the thematic interconnections of crucifixion and resurrection see Udo Schnelle, "Cross and Resurrection in the Gospel of John," in this volume, 127–52.

then says, "Now Jesus did many other signs in the presence of his disciples, which are not written in this book. But these are written that you may believe that Jesus is the Christ, the Son of God, and that by believing you may have life in his name" (20:30–31). The way the gospel writer refers to the signs at this point in the narrative suggests that the resurrection appearances function in a manner similar to the signs narrated earlier.[14]

One might think that the relationship of the signs and resurrection appearances to faith should be straightforward. Those who see the miracles or the risen Jesus should believe. There are, after all, positive connections between seeing and believing at some points in the narrative. The disciples believe when Jesus turns the water into wine, some of the people believe when he raises Lazarus from the dead, and Thomas confesses his faith when he sees the risen Jesus (2:11; 11:45; 20:26–28). But there are also many points at which the need to see something extraordinary is problematic, and the signs foster unreliable faith or unbelief. Jesus does not trust those whose faith depends on the signs (2:23–25), and his public ministry concludes on a sharply negative note: "Although he had performed so many signs in their presence, they did not believe in him" (12:37). Later, Thomas makes seeing a resurrection appearance a precondition for believing, which echoes the problematic demands for signs earlier in the gospel (2:18; 6:30; 20:25) (2:18; 6:30; 20:25). But when the risen Jesus appears to Thomas, he says "Blessed are those who have not seen and yet believe" (20:29).

Interpreters have understood the complex relationship of signs and resurrection appearances to faith in different ways. Some conclude that the gospel disparages belief based on signs.[15] Others take the opposite view,

---

[14] Udo Schnelle, *Antidocetic Christology in the Gospel of John. An Investigation of the Place of the Fourth Gospel in the Johannine School* (Minneapolis: Fortress, 1992), 139; Gilbert Van Belle, *The Signs Source in the Fourth Gospel. Historical Survey and Critical Evaluation of the Semeia Hypothesis* (BETL 116; Leuven: Leuven University Press and Peeters, 1994), 401; idem, "The Meaning of σημεῖα in Jn 20,30–31," *ETL* 74 (1998): 300–25; idem, "Christology and Soteriology in the Fourth Gospel: The Conclusion of John Revisited," in *Theology and Christology in the Fourth Gospel* (ed. G. Van Belle, J. G. van der Watt, and P. Maritz; BETL 184; Leuven: Leuven University Press and Peeters, 2005), 435–61; Willis Hedley Salier, *The Rhetorical Impact of the Sēmeia in the Gospel of John* (WUNT II/186; Tübingen: Mohr Siebeck, 2004), 148–50.

[15] Jürgen Becker, "Wunder und Christologie: Zum literarkritischen und christologischen Problem der Wunder im Johannesevangelium," *NTS* 16 (1969–70): 130–48; Luise Schottroff, *Der glaubende und die feindliche Welt. Beobachtungen zum gnostischen Dualismus und seiner Bedeutung für Paulus und das Johannesevangelium* (WMANT 37; Neukirchen-Vluyn: Neukirchener 1970), 251–58; cf. Rudolf Bultmann, *The Gospel of John: A Commentary* (Philadelphia: Westminster, 1971; German orig. 1941) 696; Wilhelm Wilkens, *Zeichen und Werke. Ein Beitrag zur Theologie des 4.*

emphasizing that signs are supposed to evoke faith, even if this does not always occur.[16] Still others propose that signs bring people to an initial immature faith, which can later grow into a mature faith that no longer needs signs.[17] We can clarify the issue by noting that signs in themselves are not the problem. People do not merely see signs, they interpret them. Their responses are not governed by seeing alone. The question is what they see *in* the sign; that is, what they think the sign means.

Everyone sees the signs from some point of view. So we must ask what shapes that point of view. For example, the Pharisees portrayed in the gospel have a worldview that is shaped by a certain approach to Jewish law. According to their tradition, no work is to be done on the Sabbath. Therefore, if Jesus heals on the Sabbath, they see this as a sign of his sinfulness, since he is breaking God's law (5:16; 9:16). Others see issues in political terms. Therefore, if Jesus feeds the crowd, this is a sign that he is aspiring to political office and they want to make him king (6:14–15). Similarly, if he raises the dead, this sign means that he is trying to attract followers in order to mount a revolt against Rome (11:47). If people are able to see the signs in a more positive way, it shows that their perspective has been shaped by something else. We will find that something similar is true in John's account of Jesus' resurrection, where those who see the open tomb and the risen Jesus readily interpret what they see in ways that do not lead to resurrection faith.

Characters in the gospel respond to the signs with genuine faith if their perspective has already been positively shaped by what they have heard from or about Jesus. The path of discipleship begins when people are called to follow or when they hear something that prompts them to trust Jesus. This trust, which is evoked by what they hear, creates a perspective from which people can see the signs in a manner helpful for faith. For them, the sign is not the beginning of a relationship with Jesus but something that occurs within an existing relationship. They begin

---

Evangeliums in Erzählungs- und Redestoff (ATANT 55; Zürich: Zwingli, 1969) 44, 141–42; Ernst Haenchen, *John* (2 vols.; Hermeneia; Philadelphia: Fortress, 1984), 1.237, 2.212

[16] Marianne Meye Thompson, *The Humanity of Jesus in the Fourth Gospel* (Philadelphia: Fortress, 1988), 63–64; Schnelle, *Antidocetic Christology*, 173–75; cf. Raymond F. Collins, *These Things Have Been Written. Studies on the Fourth Gospel* (Louvain: Peeters and Grand Rapids: Eerdmans, 1990), 183–95; Michael Labahn, "Between Tradition and Literary Art: The Miracle Tradition in the Fourth Gospel," *Bib* 80 (1999):178–203, esp. 189.

[17] Bultmann, *Gospel of John*, 131, 207–9; W. Nicol, *The Sēmeia in the Fourth Gospel. Tradition and Redaction* (NovTSup 32; Leiden: Brill, 1972) 99–106; Robert Kysar, *John. The Maverick Gospel* (2d ed.; Louisville: Westminster John Knox,1993), 80–86.

following because of something they hear, and this in turn shapes what they see. The gospel also shows that Jesus' signs bear out the truth of his words. He not only says that he is the bread of life but feeds the five thousand with barley loaves (6:11, 35). He calls himself the light of the world, then brings light to the eyes of a man who was born blind (8:12; 9:4–7). When he says that he is the resurrection and the life, he calls Lazarus out of the tomb (11:25–26, 44) – and his claim to be the resurrection is finally borne out by his own resurrection from the dead.

In John's gospel the words people hear from or about Jesus enable them truly to see who Jesus is. Without verbal testimony people interpret what they see within other frames of reference, and regularly come to misguided faith or unbelief. For readers living after Jesus' resurrection, this means that they have what is essential: they have received the words from and about Jesus, and these are what make faith possible, even if they have not had visible access to the resurrected Jesus. Those who come to believe through the words of the gospel have the promise of one day seeing of Jesus' glory in an immediate way, through their own resurrection (17:24). But such a seeing remains future. In the present, they are called to believe the verbal testimony of the gospel, which brings people to the faith that is life in relationship with the risen Christ and the God who sent him.

2. Words, Signs, and Faith in the Ministry of Jesus (John 1–12)

John's account of the first disciples establishes a pattern in which people come to faith through an initial experience of hearing, without having seen a sign. This is like the situation of the readers, who are also called to believe on the basis of what they hear about Jesus. In John's account of the first disciples, readers can see patterns that continue in their own time.[18] As the narrative begins, John the Baptist declares that Jesus is "the Lamb of God," and two people who hear this follow Jesus (1:35–37). The Baptist's words evoke a curiosity, a willingness to follow. When Jesus turns and asks them what they are looking for, they respond with a question, "Rabbi . . . where are you staying?" (1:38). Jesus could have given them an answer by telling them the name of the person's house where he was staying and giving them directions to it, but he does not do

---

[18] John 1:35–51 has sometimes been read as a glimpse into the formation of the early Johannine Community. See J. Louis Martyn, *The Gospel of John in Christian History. Essays for Interpreters* (New Yori: Paulist, 1978), 93–98; Brown, *The Community of the Beloved Disciple*, 27. My suggestion here is that the dynamics go beyond the foundations of one community to reflect broader patterns of evangelism within the Christian community. Many elements in 1:35–51 typify an ongoing experience.

so. Instead, he offers an invitation: "Come and you will see" (1:39). This statement creates a new situation for the seekers. Their question will not be answered in advance. They will only learn more by following Jesus. When they do, they "see" where he is staying, and through the encounter they come to recognize that he is the Messiah (1:39–41).

The pattern is repeated when one of these disciples tells his brother Peter, "We have found the Messiah," and he brings Peter to Jesus (1:41–42). Then Jesus calls Philip, who goes to his friend Nathanael with the astonishing claim, "We have found him about whom Moses in the law and also the prophets wrote, Jesus son of Joseph from Nazareth" (1:45). Thoroughly unimpressed, Nathanael replies, "Can anything good come out of Nazareth?" At this point Philip might have tried to marshal a collection of Scripture passages to answer Nathanael's objection, but he does not do so. Instead, he repeats the invitation, "Come and see" (1:46). This puts Nathanael in a new situation. He could demand that his question about Jesus be answered at the outset, or he could go to Jesus on the basis of what he has heard, even with his question unanswered – which is what he does.

In the encounter, Jesus tells Nathanael, "Before Philip called you, while you were under the fig tree, I saw you," and Nathanael acclaims Jesus as the Son of God and King of Israel (1:47–49). What Jesus says about the fig tree is not a miraculous sign but a playful allusion to Scripture.[19] Philip has already directed Nathanael's attention to the law and the prophets, and Jesus now points out that Nathanael was called while he was under a fig tree. This alludes to Zech 3:8, which said, "In that day, says the Lord of hosts, *a man will call his neighbor* under a vine and *under a fig tree*." In that context, being called under a fig tree marked the arrival of the messianic "Branch" (Zech 3:8), who was understood to be the Davidic Messiah foretold in the law (Gen 49:10) and the prophets (Jer 23:6; 33:16; Zech 3:8; 6:12–13), just as Philip had said. According, to the flow of the text, Nathanael catches the allusion in Jesus' words. After being reminded that he was called by his neighbor Philip, while under a fig, he connects his experience with the scriptural promise of the Messiah, and gives Jesus the messianic titles "Son of God" and "King of Israel." He believes because of what Jesus "said" to him (John 1:50). He has not seen any miracles. He believes because of what he has heard. Then Jesus says that having come to faith, Nathanael and others like him "will see" greater things. They "will see" the glory of God revealed in the Son of Man (1:51).

---

[19] The fig tree comment is sometimes taken as a sign of supernatural knowledge (e.g., Barrett, *Gospel according to St. John*, 185). It can better be taken as an allusion to Scripture. See the detailed argumentation in Craig R. Koester, "Messianic Exegesis and the Call of Nathanael (John 1.45–51)," *JSNT* 39 (1990): 23–34.

The sign Jesus performs in the next scene bears out the truth of his words. The disciples, who already believe, accompany him to a wedding at Cana. There he turns the water in six stone jars into wine. The evangelist says that by doing this he "revealed his glory" and "his disciples believed in him" (2:11). The disciples who see the glory in the sign have *already* come to believe based on what they have heard. They have already identified Jesus as the Messiah foretold in the law and the prophets, and have called him Son of God and King of Israel. Others at the wedding know that Jesus transformed the water into wine, and the steward finds it odd to serve the best wine after people have drunk so much. But only the disciples are said to see the glory or believe. Their faith does not originate with the sign. Rather, what they see confirms what they have already heard. And now, by recounting this sign, the gospel writer conveys Jesus' glory to the readers in verbal form.

The second sign involves a royal official, who has a son dying of a fever. This illness creates a crisis in which the man must act. He sets out from Capernaum and travels halfway across Galilee to find Jesus at Cana – not because he has seen Jesus do any miracles, but because he has *heard* about Jesus (4:47). The man goes with a clear sense of expectation about the proper course of action. He wants Jesus to accompany him back to his home in order to heal the dying boy. But Jesus' response runs counter to what the man anticipates. Jesus says, "Unless you see signs and wonders, you will not believe" (4:48). Undeterred, the man persists in asking that Jesus come with him before the child dies. Then Jesus says, "Go; your son will live" (4:50).

Jesus' statement poses a different kind of crisis. The man has expected Jesus to come to his home to heal the boy, but Jesus has only given him the promise that the boy will live. At this point the man must either continue asking Jesus to work on his terms, or else he must trust the word Jesus has spoken – and he will not know for some time whether Jesus' word is true. This is the moment where faith is specifically mentioned. The man "believed the word that Jesus spoke" (4:50a). He jettisons his expectation that Jesus will come along with him and sets out for home (4:50b). This belief or trust sets the man on a course of action. To believe is to return home without visible proof that the boy is alive. This, for John, is the character of faith.[20]

At the end of the story the man is still on his way, when his servants meet him along the road and tell him that his son is living. Even here the official has not actually seen the sign for himself. What he has is the report

---

[20] Klaus Wengst, *Das Johannesevangelium* (2 vols.; Theologischer Kommentar zum Neuen Testament 4; Stuttgart: Kohlhammer, 2000, 2001), 1.178; Gail R. O'Day, *The Gospel of John* (NIB 9; Nashville: Abingdon, 1995), 575.

of the servants, yet this seems to be sufficient. Jesus said the boy would live and the servants now say the same. Their words bear out the truth of Jesus' words. This sign is not the basis of the man's faith. Instead, it confirms the faith that began with what he heard from Jesus (4:51–53). John's readers are like the royal official in that they too receive a promise of life from Jesus – the gospel itself communicates Jesus' word to them. They are also like the official in that they will not know ahead of time whether the promise is true. The only way to find out is to trust it, which is what the official did. The question is whether the readers will do the same.

The third sign shows the opposite relationship of signs to faith. In the story of the invalid at Bethzatha, readers find that seeing does not necessarily lead to believing (5:1–16). Here a man is given a sign "up front," without faith, and yet this sign does not bring about belief. The story begins by a pool in Jerusalem, where many people with physical ailments come in the hope of a cure. Among the invalids is a man who cannot walk and has been lying beside the pool for a long time. Initially, nothing is said about his belief or unbelief, but the text does disclose something about the man's perspective. Jesus approaches the man and asks whether he wants to be healed. But instead of giving Jesus an affirmative answer, the man complains that he has no one to put him into the pool when the water is mysteriously troubled, and that while he is making his way into the pool someone else steps in ahead of him (5:7).

The man's perspective is shaped by the conviction that whoever enters the water at the right moment will be healed and that latecomers will not be helped. His perspective seems to have little connection with the God of Israel, who does not limit his favor to those who have the best sense of timing. The man's worldview borders on the magical. In traditional magic, a person tries to manage supernatural powers in ways that virtually guarantee results.[21] The man at the pool does not try to produce a troubling of the water, of course, but he seems to assume that a well-timed entry to the pool will make healing almost automatic. The scribes who later copied the gospel improved the man's image by ascribing the movement of the water to an angel of the Lord, which brings some vestige of God into the picture (5:4). But the verse about the angel is not included in the best ancient manuscripts and it has rightly been deleted from most modern translations. As the text stands, there is no mention of God in the healing process connected with the pool.[22]

---

[21] David E. Aune, "Magic in Early Christianity," *ANRW* II/23.2 (1980) 1507–57, esp. 1515.

[22] John 5:4 is missing from 𝔓⁶⁶ 𝔓⁷⁵ ℵ B C* D other manuscripts. On the text-critical problem see Bruce M. Metzger, *A Textual Commentary on the Greek New Testament* (2d ed.; Stuttgart: Deutsche Bibelgesellschaft and United Bible Societies, 1994), 179.

Despite the man's unresponsiveness, Jesus tells him, "Rise (ἔγειρε), take up your mat and walk" (5:8). The result is that "immediately the man was made well" (5:9a). This is significant. The immediate result of Jesus' word is that the man is healed, and only after the miraculous healing occurs does the man take up his mat and walk (5:9b). In contrast to the previous episodes, where people show faith before experiencing a sign, this man receives the sign first and then gets up to walk. Significantly, there is still no mention of faith, and the man's encounters with the Jewish authorities will reveal that the sign has not produced faith.[23] The authorities reprimand the man for carrying his mat on the Sabbath (5:10). In response, the man tries to evade responsibility by saying that he is only doing what he had been told, since his healer had directed him to carry the mat. Unfortunately, the man had not bothered to learn his healer's name (5:11–13).

Jesus identifies the issue when he says, "Do not persist in sin so that nothing worse happens to you" (5:14). In the gospel of John, sin is regularly identified with unbelief, and the use of the verbal form indicates that the man exhibits unbelief in action. By warning him not to persist in sin, Jesus tells him not to continue in the way of unbelief (μηκέτι ἁμάρτανε).[24] This makes clear to readers that persistent unresponsiveness to Jesus, which has characterized the man up to this point, manifests unbelief. Jesus also warns that continuing in unbelief will bring something "worse" than a reprimand from the Jewish authorities for a Sabbath violation. To persist in sin places one under the judgment of God.[25] Despite the warning, however, the pattern of unbelief continues,

---

[23] Some suggest that the man has some faith at this point, while acknowledging that this incipient faith disappears. See, e.g., Francis J. Moloney, *Signs and Shadows. Reading John 5 – 12* (Minneapolis: Fortress, 1996), 5–6. But since the gospel says that the man was already healed, it did not require faith for him to stand up. In a similar story, the Synoptics say that a paralytic rose in response to Jesus' command (Matt 9:6; Mark 2:11; Luke 5:24), but in John the man was *healed* in response to the command and only rose afterward.

[24] Rainer Metzner, *Das Verständnis der Sünde im Johannesevangelium* (WUNT 122; Tübingen: Mohr Siebeck, 2000), 52–57.

[25] Some have argued that Jesus warns the man that something worse than his illness will happen to him if he persists in sin. See D. A. Carson, *The Gospel according to John* (Leichester: Inter-Varsity and Grand Rapids: Eerdmans, 1991), 245–46; John Christopher Thomas, "'Stop Sinning Lest Something Worse Come upon You': The Man at the Pool in John 5," *JSNT* 59 (1995), 3–20; Metzner, *Das Verständnis der Sünde*, 48–51. Given the refusal to identify a physical ailment as the direct result of sin in John 9:1–5, it seems improbable that this is the case in John 5. Moreover, the invalid seems to respond to prospect of negative judgment by the Jewish authorities, and he therefore reports Jesus to them. But the gospel wants to show that the judgment that is worth heeding is the one that comes from God and not from human authorities.

and the man reports his healer to the authorities, who begin persecuting Jesus (5:15–16).

The sign shows Jesus' ability to give life by empowering an invalid to "rise" to his feet (ἔγειρε, 5:8). The discourse that follows indicates that the sign also manifests the power to make the dead "rise" (ἐγείρει, 5:21).[26] When the sign is interpreted in light of the discourse, readers can see that one who raises the man by the pool by a word is the same one who will raise the dead by a word in the future, in the time that "is coming" (5:28). Jesus affirms that those who believe do not come under judgment but have already passed from death to life (5:24). The man at the pool, however, has received a sign by being raised to his feet, yet he does not show faith and therefore remains in sin and under judgment (5:14). This unbelief has an ominous future, for in the coming hour the Son of Man will raise all people from their tombs, and those who have done evil – i.e., those whose actions are driven by their unbelief – are given the resurrection of judgment (5:28–29). For readers, the episode shows that seeing in no way guarantees believing. It also underscores the importance of faith, since faith means life now and in the future, just as unfaith means separation from God now and in the future.

The fourth sign is the feeding of the five thousand (6:1–15), which again shows that seeing does not lead to faith. Jesus' actions are simple but suggestive. He makes the crowd recline on the grass, then he takes five loaves and two fish, gives thanks, and distributes the food to the people until they have had all they want. Then he has the disciples gather up the leftover pieces, and they fill twelve baskets full. The discourse that follows interprets the meaning of the sign. By giving bread to the people, so that they might eat and live, Jesus communicates how God gives his Son to the world in order that people might believe and have life (6:32–35). By gathering up the fragments, "so that nothing may be lost (ἀπόληται)," Jesus conveys the promise that he will not "lose" (ἀπολέσω) anything that the Father has given him, but raise people up on the last day (6:12, 39–40).

The crowd sees the sign, but they construe it in their own way, and this eventually manifests itself as unbelief. When they see the sign they initially declare that Jesus is the prophet who is coming into the world, which is to some extent correct (6:14). At this point their frame of reference is shaped by the Passover tradition, in which the people of Israel ate unleavened bread each year to commemorate their deliverance from slavery in Egypt under the leadership of Moses (Exod 12:14–20). On their journey through the wilderness, they were given manna or bread from

---

[26] The pattern is that the two healing signs in 4:46–5:16 is followed by a discourse in 5:17–47, just as the two signs in 6:1–21 are followed by a transitional scene and discourse in 6:22–59.

heaven to eat as they made their way toward the promised land (Exod 16:4). According to the Scriptures, God also promised to raise up another prophet like Moses for the people (Deut 18:15–18). When Jesus miraculously fed the people with bread near the time of Passover, the people concluded that he must be the prophet they were expecting. And this interpretation is valid up to a point. The Fourth Evangelist assumes that Jesus does fulfill the biblical promise concerning the prophet like Moses.[27]

But the crowd's interpretation of the sign does not end there. The people want to seize Jesus and "make" (ποιήσωσιν) him king, so that Jesus flees from them (John 6:15). Now their action shows a problem in the way they perceive who Jesus is and how they understand their own role. As John portrays them, they assume that by feeding the masses with bread, Jesus shows that he has aspirations for political office. In the Roman world, rulers often placated the populace with distributions of bread or grain. Cicero recalled that the practice was agreeable to the masses, since it provided food without work (*Sest.* 48 §103). Juvenal lampooned citizens who accompanied the consul because of the free meal tickets in their wallets, and he mocked the crowds who were willing to proclaim any lucky "carcass an equal successor to Augustus," but were devoted only to the "bread and circuses" with which their leaders mollified them (*Sat.* 10.44–46, 73–80).[28]

Perceiving the sign in light of such practices, they are happy to receive the bread and want to elevate Jesus to the status of king. Yet from John's point of view, this reverses the proper flow of power. They assume that they have the ability to "make" Jesus king. But in the Fourth Gospel, Jesus' kingship is not based on his ability to curry favor with the masses "below." Rather, his power is from God "above" (John 18:36). The crowd's attempt to "make" Jesus king on their own terms runs counter to what God is doing. What they see not only fails to bring faith but places them in opposition to the purposes of God and Jesus. By the end of the chapter, those who have been given a visible sign turn against the one who

---

[27] Martyn, *History and Theology*, 101–23; Richard Bauckham, "Messianism according to the Gospel of John," *Challenging Perspectives on the Gospel of John* (ed. John Lierman; WUNT II/219; Tübingen: Mohr Siebeck, 2006), 34–68, esp. 40–53; in that same volume see John Lierman, "The Mosaic Pattern of John's Christology," 210–34.

[28] Cf. Dio Chrysostom, *Or.* 32.31; Fronto, *Correspondance* 2.17. See Edward Courtney, *A Commentary on the Satires of Juvenal* (London: Athlone, 1980), 104–5, 372, 472; Bill Salier, "Jesus, the Emperor, and the Gospel According to John," in *Challenging Perspectives on John* (ed. John Lierman; WUNT II/219; Tübingen: Mohr Siebeck, 2006), 284–301, esp. 294–95.

gives it (6:41, 52, 66).²⁹ For those living in the post-resurrection period, this passage shows that there is no reason to think that seeing might guarantee believing.

The fifth sign is Jesus walking on the sea, which immediately follows the feeding of the five thousand (6:16–21). Attention now turns to the disciples, who present a striking contrast to the crowd. The disciples have been following Jesus since the first chapter of the gospel, where they came to faith before seeing any signs. After Jesus flees from the crowd that tried to make him king, the disciples embark in a boat on the Sea of Galilee and are caught in wind, rough waves, and darkness. After rowing for three or four miles, they see Jesus walking on the sea and coming near the boat (6:19). This seeing does not alter the situation, however. The disciples respond to what they see with fear, not faith (6:19c).

The turning point in the story comes when Jesus speaks. He tells the disciples, "I Am; do not be afraid" (6:20). Only when he speaks is the disciples' fear transformed into a desire to receive him (6:21). Although the "I Am" (ἐγώ εἰμι) is a traditional element in the story (cf. Matt 14:27; Mark 6:50), John places this expression at the center of his account.³⁰ The "I Am" appears in several different forms in John's Gospel, all of which can have divine significance. The divine overtones in the "I Am" are scarcely audible when Jesus speaks to the Samaritan woman (John 4:26), but they crescendo in his words to the disciples on the sea (6:20) and in statements like "I Am the Bread of Life" (6:35, 48). In the remainder of the gospel, it will be clear that in saying, "I Am," Jesus identifies himself as the one in whom God is present and active.³¹

The disciples' response to Jesus' words is the opposite of that of the crowd. On the basis of their perception of the sign, the crowd wants to "make" (ποιήσωσιν) him king on their terms (6:15). By way of contrast, when Jesus speaks, the disciples want to "receive" (λαβεῖν) Jesus as the one who comes in the name of God (6:21). To "receive" (λαμβάνω) Jesus is an expression of faith in John's gospel (1:12; 5:43). It expresses a willingness to welcome the one who comes on God's terms, instead of

---

²⁹ The crowd's inability to believe in spite of Jesus signs is reflected in their complaining (γογγύζω) against him (John 6:41, 43). The language recalls that of the wilderness generation, who complained (γογγύζω) against God and Moses despite the signs performed on their behalf (Num 14:11, 27).

³⁰ Brown, *Gospel according to John*, 1.254–55; Schnackenburg, *Gospel according to St John*, 2.27; Gail R. O'Day, "John 6:15–21: Jesus Walking on the Water as Narrative Embodiment of Johannine Christology," in *Critical Readings of John 6* (ed. R. Alan Culpepper; Biblical Interpretation Series 22; Leiden: Brill, 1997), 149–59.

³¹ Brown, *Gospel according to John*, 1.533–38; David Mark Ball, *"I Am" in John's Gospel. Literary Function, Background and Theological Implications* (JSNTSup 124; Sheffield: Sheffield Academic Press, 1996).

contriving to make Jesus fit a role that suits the people's terms. The contrast continues to the end of the chapter, when those seeking signs fall away and Peter affirms the disciples' loyalty to Jesus by saying, "You have the words of eternal life" (6:68). The implication for the readers of later generations is that those who receive Jesus' words have what is necessary for the faith that is eternal life.

The sixth sign is the healing of the man born blind, which continues the patterns we have seen thus far (9:1–41) At the beginning of the episode the blind beggar sits in silence as Jesus' disciples ponder theoretical questions about the cause of his blindness. But Jesus alters the situation when he puts mud on the man's eyes and says, "Go, wash in the pool of Siloam" (9:7). The pool is located elsewhere in Jerusalem. The man cannot see. All he has is the directive to go and wash – and Jesus does not even explain *why* he should grope his way across town to the pool instead of wiping the mud off his eyes at the place where he is sitting. Yet Jesus' words evoke a willingness to trust. The man goes as Jesus tells him to do, even though he has not yet experienced healing.

After washing, the man discovers that he can see. His initial trust in Jesus seems well-placed. The man sees – *but he does not see Jesus*. His healing takes place at a time and place that Jesus is not visibly present. Throughout the central part of the chapter, the man is questioned about a Jesus whom he has never seen. After placing mud on the man's eyes at the beginning of the story, Jesus is nowhere to be seen until the end, when the man finally sees him face to face. In between, the man does not even know where Jesus is (9:12), but he tenaciously testifies that Jesus is a healer, prophet, and emissary of God (9:11, 17, 33). Instead of seeing Jesus, what the man sees is conflict, which starts with divided opinions among the neighbors and the authorities, but finally escalates until the man is put out of the synagogue (9:9, 16, 28, 34).

The beggar sees Jesus for the first time only at the end of the story. After he has been put out of the synagogue, Jesus finds him and asks whether he believes in the Son of Man (9:35). The beggar must ask who the Son of Man is because he has never before laid eyes on his healer (9:36). This is finally the point where Jesus can say, "You have seen him," and the beggar replies, "I believe" (9:37–38). The readers of the gospel are like the man born blind in that they must respond to words from and about Jesus, even though they have not seen him.[32] For them, as for the beggar, faith will mean believing in a Jesus whom they have not seen in the face of conflicts that they do see. Yet the story of the beggar also extends the hope that those who have responded to Jesus' words will one day see him for themselves, when visible conflict with the world gives way to visible glory

---

[32] Martyn, *History and Theology*, 36, 40.

in the presence of God (17:24). That seeing, however, remains future for the readers. At present, they are like the man in the middle of the story, coming to terms with a Jesus whom they have not seen.

The seventh sign in Jesus' public ministry is the raising of Lazarus (11:1–44). In this climactic episode it is not a question of believing without seeing. It is believing in spite of what one sees. The story opens when Lazarus's sisters send word of his illness to Jesus, who is east of the Jordan River, a day's journey away (10:40–11:1). Jesus receives the message, "Lord, he whom you love is ill," but he inexplicably delays in coming, so that death occurs in Jesus' absence. With poignant simplicity the evangelist tells about two women sending a plea to Jesus only to receive silence in return, and about a friend of Jesus who dies when Christ is not visibly present. John's account invites readers to find analogies between this story and their own situations, as they experience sickness and death in a time when Christ is not visibly present, and as they turn to a seemingly absent Christ and receive no timely answer.[33]

Jesus finally ends his delay and comes to the village, where Lazarus's sister Martha meets him and says, "Lord, if you had been here, my brother would not have died" (11:21). It is difficult to know whether this is mainly a lament over Lazarus's death or a reproach for Jesus' failure to come sooner. Regardless of the tone, Martha shows continuing trust in Jesus and is convinced that God will give him whatever he asks (11:22).[34] One might assume that Martha harbors the hope that Jesus might still do a miracle and bring her brother back to life. That would compensate for his inexplicable delay. But this is not the character of Martha's response. There is no suggestion that she thinks Jesus will do a miracle. When Jesus promises that Lazarus will rise again, she assumes it will occur in the future, on the last day, not later that same afternoon (11:23–24). She is not looking for a surprising post-mortem healing.

Then Jesus says, "I Am the resurrection and the life. Those who believe in me, even though they die, will live, and everyone who lives and believes in me will never die. Do you believe this?" (11:25–26). She replies, "Yes, Lord, I believe that you are the Messiah, the Son of God, the one coming into the world" (11:27). Martha not only believes without seeing; she believes in spite of what she sees. Lazarus is visibly dead, and Martha assumes that he will remain dead for the foreseeable future. She does not even want the stone removed from the tomb's entrance (11:39). Martha's faith will be confirmed by the sign, but it is not based on the sign. She confesses her faith in spite of Jesus' delay and her brother's death. Jesus

---

[33] Philip F. Esler and Ronald Piper, *Lazarus, Mary and Martha. Social-Scientific Approaches to the Gospel of John* (Minneapolis: Fortress, 2006), 108–11.

[34] Schnackenburg, *Gospel according to St John*, 2.329.

says that faith will enable Martha to see God's glory in the sign (11:40). The idea is not that she will initially come to faith in God by seeing her brother brought back to life. Instead, faith creates the perspective from which she will later see God's power at work in the sign. To make sure that readers get the point, the next chapter will show that those who see the raising of Lazarus from other perspectives regard Jesus as a political threat or a viable candidate for the throne (11:45–53; 12:12–18).

Martha's confession of faith in Jesus as Messiah and Son of God is the same confession the evangelist wants the readers to make (20:31).[35] Like Martha, people of later generations are called to believe in Jesus without having seen a resurrection. In this episode Martha is called to believe *before* her brother is raised from the dead, and readers are called to do something similar. They stand where Martha stands in the middle of the story, with the words of Jesus and the invitation to believe, but not with visible proof that what Jesus says is true (11:25–26). Jesus' claim to be the resurrection and the life is borne out when he calls Lazarus to come forth from the tomb (11:43–44). It is also confirmed by Jesus' own resurrection from the dead at the end of the gospel. Yet death continues to confront John's readers. They are called to believe in a Jesus who raised Lazarus and rose himself in the past, but whose presence they do not now see. They are also called to trust that Jesus will give them life, despite the continuing threat of death and the recognition that the promise of resurrection will only be fully validated in the future (6:39–40). But the gospel also affirms that in faith people do have life in relation to God and Jesus now, and that this relationship has a future.[36]

The mixed public reaction to the raising of Lazarus shows again that seeing does not guarantee believing. The Jewish authorities interpret the sign in political categories, assuming that Jesus is gathering a large following among the people in order to foment a revolt against Rome. To prevent this from happening, they determine to put the doer of the sign to death, since they assume that death will end his popularity (11:46–50). The crowds also seem to interpret the sign in political terms, but assume that the result will be more favorable. Because of the sign they receive Jesus

---

[35] Since Martha's confession does not correspond directly to Jesus' announcement that he is the resurrection and the life, some propose that it is less than adequate. See Moloney, *Signs and Shadows*, 162; Brown, *Gospel according to John*, 1.434–35. Most, however, consider it to be a genuine and developed statement of faith. See Schnackenburg, *Gospel according to St John*, 2.332–33; Wengst, *Das Johannesevangelium*, 2.28; Sandra M. Schneiders, "Death in the Community of Eternal Life: History, Theology and Spirituality in John 11," *Int* 41 (1987), 44–56, esp. 53; Colleen M. Conway, *Men and Women in the Fourth Gospel. Gender and Johannine Characterization* (SBLDS 167; Atlanta: Society of Biblical Literature, 1999), 141–43.

[36] Lincoln, "I Am the Resurrection," 140–43.

with palms, as they might do for a conquering hero, and acclaim him King of Israel (12:12–18). Yet given the signs, they assume that Jesus will reign without dying. So when Jesus speaks of being "lifted up," in anticipation of his coming crucifixion, the crowd is incredulous (12:32–34).

3. Words, Resurrection Appearances, and Faith (John 20)

Patterns that have developed in the narrative of Jesus' ministry continue in the account of his passion and resurrection. The most significant presupposition in these chapters is that Jesus truly died by crucifixion. The reality of Jesus' death is unquestioned. The Fourth Evangelist seeks to show that Jesus' death was a purposeful action and not a meaningless tragedy, and he shapes the passion narrative so that readers can see the will of God being carried out through it.[37] But everyone in the gospel – Jesus' followers as well as his foes – understands that crucifixion results in a death that is genuine and complete. In the late afternoon, the soldiers who came to break the legs of the victims on the crosses "saw" that Jesus "was already dead," and for once in John's narrative, seeing is believing (19:32). Jesus' death is real. Those who place him in the tomb may honor him by putting a hundred pounds of spices on the corpse, but this only underscores death's reality. Spices are placed on a body that is expected to decay, not on a person who is expected to return to life (19:38–42).

The genuineness of Jesus' death is a given for the Fourth Evangelist. Therefore, the question is how anyone can believe that Jesus' death is anything other than the end of the story. The evangelist understands that resurrection on the first day of the week is not the easy answer to the problem of crucifixion. The narrative itself suggests other more plausible ways of coming to terms with a tragic death. For example, Martha voiced the hope that there would be a resurrection at the end of the age (11:24). Accordingly, one might assume that Jesus' followers could have taken comfort in the hope that he would return to life on the last day, when the blessed age to come would dawn. Alternatively, one could think of death

---

[37] Some argue that Jesus' sufferings are so diminished that John's gospel does not really have a passion narrative, since "passion" means suffering. See John Ashton, *Understanding the Fourth Gospel* (Oxford: Clarendon Press, 1991), 489. By way of contrast, I understand that the suffering and reality of Jesus' death is presupposed throughout the gospel. The evangelist takes the reality of suffering and death as a given and seeks to disclose its meaning. See Craig R. Koester, "Why Was the Messiah Crucified? A Study of God, Jesus, Satan, and Human Agency in Johannine Theology," in *The Death of Jesus in the Fourth Gospel* (ed. Gilbert Van Belle; BETL 200; Leuven: Leuven University and Peeters, 2007) 163–80; idem, *Symbolism in the Fourth Gospel*, 207–46.

as a transition point, when the person's body dies and the soul is freed to ascend to life in heaven. After all, Jesus spoke about leaving the world and returning to his Father (16:28). One might assume that death brought an end to Jesus' bodily suffering and allowed his soul to depart to heavenly rest. It would be difficult to object to this point of view. Yet the gospel moves in another direction, by saying that Jesus rose, bodily, from the dead. The gospel does not divide Jesus into a body that perishes and a soul that does not. Jesus lays down his body in death and takes it up in resurrection (σῶμα, 2:21), and he does the same with his soul (ψυχή, 10:17). He dies and rises as an embodied person.[38]

The reality of Jesus' death is underscored by the opening lines of John's resurrection account. Mary Magdalene goes to the tomb and sees that the stone has been removed from the entrance (20:1). What Mary sees requires interpretation, and her conclusion is that the open tomb means that Jesus is still dead and that someone has taken the body: "They have taken the Lord out of the tomb and we do not know where they have laid him" (20:2). The evangelist makes clear that Mary has accepted the fact that Jesus has died, and that she is not clinging to the hope that somehow he might still be alive. The gospel does not explain why Mary thinks of grave robbery, but assumes that her conclusion will be plausible to the readers. For example, thieves sometimes disturbed tombs when searching for any valuables that had been placed there with the body. Again, violating a tomb could be a malicious action designed to intimidate the family and friends of the deceased.[39] Whatever the case, Mary is convinced that Jesus is dead and that the open tomb can readily be explained by the practice of grave robbery. Theologically, this is important for the evangelist. It makes clear that resurrection is not the obvious answer to an open tomb. Therefore, any belief that Jesus has risen and is alive must overcome this alternative explanation of what Mary sees.

In the next scene, Peter and the Beloved Disciple run to the burial place of Jesus (20:3–10). At each point in the passage these disciples "see" something, and this builds intensity into the narrative. Readers are told that the Beloved Disciple arrives first, looks into the tomb, and sees the grave cloths lying there (20:5). Next, Peter goes into the tomb and sees not only the grave cloths but the head cloth rolled up in a place by itself (20:6). Then the Beloved Disciple enters the tomb, and readers are told that he "saw and believed," which brings the story to its climax (20:8). Or at least it seems to do so. What is puzzling is that after speaking of the Beloved

---

[38] Emphasized by Schneiders, "Touching the Risen Jesus."

[39] A Galilean inscription from the mid-first century records an imperial ordinance that prohibits maliciously disturbing tombs. For a translation see C. K. Barrett, *The New Testament Background* (New York: Harper & Row, 1956), p. 15.

Disciple's faith, the narrator explains that these disciples do not yet understand the scriptural necessity for Jesus to rise from the dead. Then they simply return home, apparently without saying anything (20:9–10).

So what does the Beloved Disciple believe? One possibility is that he believes that Mary is right and that Jesus' body had been stolen. After all, he saw that the body was not there and did not understand the scriptural necessity of the resurrection. This would explain why the Beloved Disciple and Peter simply leave without saying anything even to Mary, who remains weeping outside the tomb.[40] Yet a second interpretation is more plausible, which is that the Beloved Disciple believes that Jesus has been released from death.[41] Elsewhere in the gospel, the Beloved Disciple is consistently insightful. He learns the identity of the betrayer at the last supper and is the only male disciple at the cross, where he is entrusted with the care of Jesus' mother (13:23–25; 19:26–27). He is probably the disciple who enters the high priest's house without denying Jesus (18:15–16), and he will be the first to recognize the risen Jesus in Galilee (21:7). If anyone could discern the meaning of the empty tomb, we would expect it to be him. Moreover, the presence of the grave cloths, and the fact that the head cloth is neatly rolled up, rules out body snatching. No one disturbing the grave would take the body while leaving the cloths, and a thief would not bother to roll up the head cloth in such a tidy fashion. In contrast to Lazarus, who comes out of the tomb still bound in the grave cloths, the grave cloths are left behind in Jesus' tomb (11:44). Accordingly, the word "believed" seems to indicate genuine faith (cf. 4:53).

What is surprising is that the narrator notes that this faith does not yet include understanding of the Scriptures or prompt the Beloved Disciple to say anything.[42] This does not mean that his faith is not genuine, since the gospel assumes that understanding comes through faith, not prior to faith. The gospel points out that after the resurrection the disciples will be able to discern connections between Jesus and the Scriptures that were not evident during his ministry (2:17, 22; 12:15–16). But the subdued

---

[40] Augustine *Tract. ev. Jo.* 120.9; cf. Godfrey C. Nicholson, *Death as Departure. The Johannine Descent-ascent Schema* (SBLDS 63; Chico, Calif.: Scholars Press, 1983), 69–71.

[41] This is the most commonly accepted view. See, e.g., Francis J. Moloney, *Glory Not Dishonor. Reading John 13 – 21* (Minneapolis: Fortress, 1998), 162; Schnackenburg, *Gospel according to St John*, 3.312; Wengst, *Das Johannesevangelium*, 2.279; Lincoln, "I Am the Resurrection," 130.

[42] Ignace de la Potterie, "Genèse de la foi pascale de'après Jn 20," *NTS* 30 (1984): 26–49, esp. 32–33; O'Day, *The Gospel of John*, 841. Brendan Byrne points out that the Beloved Disciple saw the tomb and grave cloths, but he did not see the risen Jesus himself. See "The Faith of the Beloved Disciple and the Community in John 20," *JSNT* 23 (1985): 83–97.

conclusion to this scene works against the idea that seeing the empty tomb is a sure way to believe and comprehend the resurrection. The Beloved Disciple may have seen and believed, but it was not a faith that entailed much comprehension or resulted in the announcement of resurrection. And nothing is said about Peter believing. If there is to be faith that leads to proclamation, it will have to come from something more than the empty tomb. It will require action on the part of the risen Jesus himself.

This becomes clear as the scene shifts back to Mary Magdalene, who remains unwavering in her conviction that the body has been stolen, even when she looks into the tomb and sees two angels in white, sitting where the body of Jesus had been (20:12). Readers might expect Mary to be startled when she sees these supernatural beings (cf. Matt 28:2–4; Mark 16:5; Luke 24:4–5), but seeing the angels has no affect on Mary in John's account. When the angels ask why she is weeping, she speaks to them as she spoke to the disciples. She voices her conviction that the body has been taken, then turns away without giving the angels a chance to say anything that might make her change her mind (John 20:13).

The pattern continues even when Mary sees the risen Jesus himself. Readers might expect that seeing Jesus will lead to resurrection faith, but it does not. Mary does not recognize the risen Jesus. Instead, she interprets what she sees in light of common experience. She naturally assumes that the man standing in the garden must be the gardener. So she speaks to him as she spoke to the disciples and the angels, expressing her conviction that the body was stolen: "Sir, if you have carried him away, tell me where you have laid him and I will take him away" (20:15). Readers may wonder why Mary is unable to recognize the risen Jesus, but speculating about this detracts from the flow of the narrative. The gospel does not explain why Mary cannot recognize the risen Jesus. Rather, each successive scene builds suspense and makes one wonder what it will take for her to realize that he is not dead but alive.

Mary recognizes Jesus when he calls her by name. "Jesus said to her, 'Mary!' She turned and said to him in Hebrew, 'Rabbouni!' (which means Teacher)" (20:16). This is the pivotal moment. Being called by name is what moves Mary from the conviction that Jesus is dead to the realization that he is alive. Again, her understanding is not fully developed, since she seems to assume that her relationship with Jesus the rabbi will be much as it was before. Jesus marks the shift in their relationship by directing her back to the community of disciples, which is where her future lies. That will be where subsequent encounters with the risen Christ will take place (20:17–18).

Mary's encounter with Jesus is unique in many respects, yet her experience anticipates the way people of future generations will come to faith. The gospel speaks to those who have not seen the risen Jesus (20:29), and Mary's story shows that seeing the tomb, seeing the angels, and even seeing Jesus himself does not guarantee faith. Like Mary, others will be called to faith by the risen Jesus. This is reflected in Jesus' comments about the good shepherd, who "calls his own sheep by name" and leads them out, and they recognize his voice (10:3–4, 16, 27).[43] Jesus calls Mary by name outside the empty tomb, but he will also call others to recognize him, sending them as he sent Mary to tell others what has happened. Just *how* the risen Jesus will continue calling people remains to be seen.

Mary's spoken testimony about the resurrection and her report about what Jesus has said helps to shape the context in which Jesus will meet the rest of his disciples. Before encountering the risen Christ, they have already heard the message of his resurrection from Mary. Moreover, according to the gospel narrative, they have also heard things from Jesus during the Farewell Discourses, which shape John's depiction of the resurrection appearance. Jesus said that he would "come" to the disciples and that they would see him again, which is what happens here (14:18–19; 20:19). He promised them "peace," and he meets them with the repeated expression of "peace" (14:27; 16:33; 20:19, 21). He promised to give them the Spirit, and now he breathes the Spirit into them (14:16–17, 26; 15:26; 16:7; 20:22). And he promised that they would rejoice, which is what they do (16:22; 20:20).[44] The words spoken earlier form the context in which the risen Christ works. This will also be true in time to come, as the disciples bear witness concerning the risen Christ, and their words form the context in which Jesus will work to evoke faith in those who were not present on the day of resurrection.

The call to resurrection faith occurs, for people of later generations, when the message *about* the risen Jesus is made effective *by* the risen Jesus. This is the dimension of Johannine theology that informs the story of Thomas. When Jesus appears to his disciples as a group, Thomas is not with them, but the disciples tell him, "We have seen the Lord" (20:25a). To this Thomas replies, "Unless I see the mark of the nails in his hands, and put my finger in the mark of the nails and my hand in his side, I will not believe" (20:25b). Thomas is often said to doubt, but his words actually state his refusal to believe until certain conditions are met: If he

---

[43] Dorothy Lee, *Flesh and Glory: Symbolism, Gender and Theology in the Gospel of John* (New York: Crossroad, 2002), pp. 223–26; Wengst, *Das Johannesevangelium*, 2.284.

[44] On these themes see, in the present volume, Jean Zumstein, "Jesus' Resurrection in the Farewell Discourses," 103–26; Weidemann, "Eschatology as Liturgy."

sees and touches, then he will believe.[45] In the wider context his insistence on seeing seems ironic, since seeing certainly did not lead Mary Magdalene to believe in the resurrection. Moreover, Thomas himself has apparently seen a resurrection before – he was involved in the episode where Jesus raises Lazarus from the dead. Note that the evangelist first mentions Thomas when Jesus announces that he is going to awaken Lazarus, even though his opponents are seeking to kill him. At this point Thomas declares, "Let us also go, that we may die with him" (11:16). Thomas may be mistaken in thinking that death will have the final word, but the implication is that Thomas goes along with Jesus for the raising of Lazarus. And if this is the case, then seeing Lazarus emerge from the tomb does not create in Thomas any readiness to think that Jesus will rise from the dead.

The gospel also shows that Thomas is later told two things, which create the context in which the risen Jesus will work. The first saying comes at the Last Supper, when Jesus speaks of going away and Thomas objects that he does not know where Jesus is going. After identifying himself as the way, Jesus says, "If you know me, you will know my Father also. From now on you do know him *and have seen him*" (14:7). The point is significant. Thomas is told that truly seeing Jesus means seeing God. The second saying comes after the resurrection, when the other disciples tell Thomas, "We have seen the Lord," and he responds with a refusal to believe (20:25). So before the risen Jesus comes, Thomas has already heard of those who have seen the Lord and he has heard that those who truly see Jesus *see God* his Father.

These sayings create the context in which the risen Jesus will work. When Jesus meets Thomas after the resurrection, Thomas says, "My Lord and my God" (20:28). By calling Jesus "my Lord," Thomas makes the disciples' words his own words. They have spoken about having seen "the Lord," and Thomas echoes what they have said by calling the risen Jesus "my Lord." Then, by calling Jesus "my God," Thomas makes his own what he heard from Jesus. At the Last Supper Thomas heard that to see Jesus is to see God, and Thomas makes this part of his confession by saying to Jesus, "my God."[46]

Readers of John's gospel are like Thomas in that they are not among those who initially saw the risen Christ. They are also like Thomas in that

---

[45] Moloney, *Glory Not Dishonor*, 175.

[46] On the implications of Thomas's confession see Marianne Meye Thompson, *The God of the Gospel of John* (Grand Rapids: Eerdmans, 2001), 232–35. On the importance of divine agency in bringing Thomas to faith see William Bonney, *Caused to Believe. The Doubting Thomas Story as the Climax of John's Christological Narrative* (Biblical Interpretation Series 62; Leiden: Brill, 2002), 131–73.

they have received testimony about Jesus – the gospel itself conveys such witness. John's account of the resurrection shows that seeing does not guarantee believing – one can see the empty tomb, the grave cloths, the angels, and even the risen Jesus without coming to faith. So when Jesus says, "Blessed are those who have not seen and yet believe" (20:29), the readers can be assured that those who have not seen Jesus are not disadvantaged, but are as blessed as the first group of disciples. Thomas eventually saw the risen Jesus, which will not be the case for the readers, at least until "the last day" (6:39; 17:24). Yet the gospel assumes that resurrection faith continues to be generated because the risen Christ continues to be active, encountering people through the witness of his disciples and the work of the Holy Spirit.

4. The Risen Jesus, the Gospel, and the Spirit

Faith is possible for those who have "not seen" because Jesus is alive – this conviction is basic to John's theological perspective. The Jesus who visibly encountered people in the past, through his ministry and resurrection appearances, is understood to be alive and active in the time of the gospel's readers. There are, to be sure, statements within the gospel that seem to run counter to the idea that Jesus remains present with his followers. In the Farewell Discourses Jesus speaks repeatedly about leaving the world and returning to his Father (14:28; 16:5, 28; 17:11). Accordingly, one might assume that during the time of the readers Jesus is absent, and that he will remain absent until he comes again in the future, when he takes believers to himself and to their "dwelling" in the presence of God (μονή, 14:2–3). But other passages point to Jesus' continued presence among his followers.[47]

Jesus said, "If anyone loves me he will keep my word, and my Father will love him, and we will come to him and make our dwelling (μονή) with him" (14:23). For the writer of the gospel, the dwelling of the risen Jesus and his Father with believers is understood to be a present reality. The faithful are not left waiting to enter the "dwelling" of God in the distant future; God already makes his "dwelling" among the faithful. This dwelling of the risen Jesus and his Father is not visible to the eye but is disclosed through the Spirit that abides or dwells (μένει) within the circle of believers (14:17). It is not that the risen Jesus is present "in Spirit," as if the Spirit has taken Jesus' place. The Spirit and Jesus retain their distinct

---

[47] Martyn, *History and Theology*, 39; Gary M. Burge, *The Anointed Community: The Holy Spirit in the Johannine Tradition* (Grand Rapids: Eerdmans, 1987), 147; O'Day, *John*, 774–77.

identities in John's gospel. What the Spirit does is disclose the presence of the risen and unseen Christ to believers.[48] This, in turn, makes it possible for the believers to abide or dwell (μείνατε) with Christ in the present (15:4, 9).

The continued presence of the risen Jesus means that patterns established during his ministry continue in the context of the readers in modified form.[49] We have seen that the words spoken by and about Jesus were the principal means of evoking faith during John's account of his ministry. The disciples and other exemplars of faith were called to follow Jesus before seeing any miracles. Conversely, those whose initial encounters with Jesus were based on the miraculous regularly interpreted what they saw in ways that led them away from genuine faith. Later, Mary Magdalene saw the risen Jesus and failed to recognize him until he spoke, and Thomas's climactic confession of resurrection faith meant acknowledging the truth of the words he had already heard from Jesus and the other disciples.

Words from and about Jesus continue coming to the readers in the period after the resurrection through the text of the gospel and witness of the community. Since words have been essential in fostering faith in the people depicted in the gospel, the readers have what is needed. The words of the text convey Jesus to the readers in ways that are designed to evoke and sustain faith.[50] The evangelist also recognizes that words in themselves do not generate belief. Rather, the words of the gospel are the means by which the risen Christ evokes faith through the Spirit that he sends. The witness of the early disciples becomes effective when the Spirit bears witness in and with their witness (15:26–27). Jesus both spoke and acted during the time of his incarnation and resurrection appearances. Afterward, the unseen Jesus continues to speak and act – now through the witness of his followers and the activity of the Spirit. During his ministry, Jesus performed signs that revealed his glory. Now the signs and resurrection

---

[48] Thompson, *The God of the Gospel of John*, 181–82.

[49] Schneiders, "The Resurrection (of the Body)," 187.

[50] The verb tense in 20:31 varies in the manuscripts. Some have the aorist tense πιστεύσητε ($\mathfrak{P}^{66vid}$ ℵ² A C D L W Ψ $f^{1.13}$ 33), which suggests coming to believe (NRSV), while others have the present tense πιστεύητε (ℵ* B Θ 0250 892), which suggests continuing to believe. See Gordon D. Fee, *On the Text and Meaning of John 20,30–31*, in *The Four Gospels 1992. Festschrift Frans Neirynck* (ed. F. Van Segbroeck et al.; 3 vols.; BETL, 100), Leuven: University Press and Peeters, 1992), 3.2193–205. The gospel would initially have been read within the early Christian community, where its function would have been to sustain faith rather than bringing people to an initial conversion experience. But the gospel also shaped the witness of the community, and such gospel-shaped witness was the means by which outsiders were brought into the community of faith. Cf. Salier, *Rhetorical Impact*, 152–53.

appearances of the past are presented to the readers through the words of John's text. In this way they remain accessible during this time of "not seeing."

The signs and resurrection appearances also anticipate a future seeing, which will come about through the believer's own resurrection. The readers are like the disciples, who believed on the basis of words and hoped to see greater things in the future (1:50–51; 2:11); they are like the official, who traveled home on the basis of Jesus' word, hoping to see his son delivered from death at the end of his journey (4:50–53). They are like the blind man, who responds to Jesus' word and only later comes to see Jesus face to face (9:7, 37); and they are like Martha, who must believe before seeing the glory of God revealed (11:27, 40). Finally, they are like Thomas, who has already heard words from and about Jesus, but who only later sees the risen Jesus for himself. The word of the gospel and the activity of the Spirit are what make such faith in the risen Christ possible during this time of "not seeing," a time that extends from the resurrection of Jesus until the resurrection of those who follow him.

Chapter 4

The Narrative Hermeneutics of John 11
Learning with Lazarus How to Understand Death, Life, and Resurrection

Ruben Zimmermann

1. Resurrection in John 11: Where Is the Problem?

Compared to the reports of the resurrection appearances of Jesus, John 11 does not appear, at first glance, to pose great challenges to the exegete. What we are dealing with here is resurrection in the traditional eschatological sense as "resurrection on the last day" (ἡ ἀνάστασις ἐν τῇ ἐσχάτῃ ἡμέρᾳ, John 11:24) – a concept that is controversial but nevertheless well-known in contemporary Judaism. Furthermore, the story of the actual revivification of a dead man named Lazarus is told and, although this may pose problems for a modern reader who is familiar with the irreversibility of brain death, it was no problem for a reader in ancient times. The story can be grouped into a series of well-known prophetic (1 Kgs 17:17–24; 2 Kgs 4:18.37) or magical and miraculous plots: here the problem is described and leads to a plea for healing. The miracle worker arrives and is able to save the sick or dead person, provoking, in many cases, an ambivalent reaction in the audience.[1] As a resurrection miracle, however, the story is in no way isolated in the New Testament, for resuscitations of the dead by Jesus and the apostles are also reported in other places, be it the daughter of Jairus (Mark 5:21–43 par.), the son of the widow of Nain (Luke 7:11–17) or Tabitha and Eutychus (Act 9:36–42; 20:7–12). The resurrection problem of the narrative in John 11 could thus be dealt with in a traditional way through form criticism or comparison with other religious or historical texts.

At the same time, one might ask whether a study of John 11 actually belongs in a volume on "The Resurrection of *Jesus* in the Gospel of John," since the chapter primarily deals with the resurrection of Lazarus. Never-

---

[1] On the form of miracle narrative see the study of Gerd Theißen, *The Miracle Stories of the Early Christian Tradition* (trans. F. McDonagh; Edinburgh: T. & T. Clark, 1983).

theless, Lazarus's resurrection is brought directly into connection with Jesus through the use of metaphor, because in an ἐγώ εἰμι saying Jesus describes himself as the "resurrection and life" (John 11:25–26). The value and importance or even the reference of such a statement may perhaps be up for discussion, but on the narrative level it remains the statement of a person in flesh and blood. When someone speaks like this, we may feel the mysterious element in the statement, or perhaps the meaning of the statement even remains completely hidden. However, we do not feel the need to question our worldview, as is the case in the other reports of the resurrection of Jesus.

Such an evaluation of John 11, however, demonstrates the restrictiveness of the resurrection discourse and how it often emerges in present day New Testament and theological scholarship.[2] On the one hand, a sometimes stormy debate about the historicity and human corporality of Jesus' resurrection continues,[3] and it resonates far beyond the borders of the exegetical and academic discussion.[4] On the other hand, the exegetes are con-

---

[2] See the articles in volume 19 of the *Zeitschrift für Neues Testament* (= *ZNT*), 10 (2007), especially the surveys on the subject by Eckart Reinmuth, "Ostern – Ereignis und Erzählung. Die jüngste Diskussion und das Matthäusevangelium," *ZNT* 10 (2007): 3–15; Richard B. Hays and J. R. Daniel Kirk, Auferstehung in der neueren amerikanischen Bibelwissenschaft," *ZNT* 10 (2007): 24–34; in the same volume see also the controversial debate on "Auferstehung der Toten – eine individuelle Hoffnung?" between Robert C. Neville and Hans H. Kessler, pp. 44–56. See also the different volumes *Die Wirklichkeit der Auferstehung* (ed. Hans-Joachim Eckstein and Michael Welker; Neukirchen-Vluyn: Neukirchener, 2002); *Resurrection: Theological and Scientific Assessments* (ed. Ted Peters, Robert John Russell, and Michael Welker; Grand Rapids: Eerdmans, 2002); *Resurrection in the New Testament* (ed. R. Bieringer et al.; BETL 165; Leuven: Leuven University Press and Peeters, 2002).

[3] In Germany, see especially the debate surrounding the theses of Gerd Lüdemann in his work, *Die Auferstehung Jesu. Historie, Erfahrung, Theologie* (Göttingen: Vandenhoeck & Ruprecht, 1994); Gerd Lüdemann, *The Resurrection of Christ. A Historical Inquiry*, Amherst NY: Prometheus Books, 2004; see Martin Rese, "Exegetische Anmerkungen zu G. Lüdemanns Deutung der Auferstehung Jesu," in: Bieringer, ed., *Resurrection in the New Testament*, 55–71; Jacob Neusner, ed., *Faith, Truth, and Freedom. The Expulsion of Professor Gerd Lüdemann from Theology Faculty at Göttingen University. Symposion and Documents* (Binghamton, N.Y.: Global, 2002); Carsten P. Thiede, *Auferstehung Jesu – Fiktion oder Wirklichkeit? Ein Streitgespräch* (Basel and Giessen: Brunnen, 2001). In the U.S.A. note particularly the debate surrounding the book of N. T. Wright, *The Resurrection of the Son of God* (Christian Origins and the Question of God 3; London: SPCK, 2003); for example Markus Bockmuehl, "Compleat History of the Resurrection: A Dialogue with N. T. Wright," *JSNT* 26 (2004): 489–504; Robert H. Smith, "Wright Thinking on the Resurrection?" *Dialog* 43 (2004): 244–51; *The Resurrection of Jesus. John Dominic Crossan and N. T. Wright in Dialogue* (ed. R. B. Stewart; Minneapolis: Fortress, 2006).

[4] On the paradigm of "historical facticity" see Heinzpeter Hempelmann, *Die Auferstehung Jesu Christi – eine historische Tatsache? Argumente für den Osterglauben* (3d

centrating on the evaluation of traditional-historical and form-critical contexts – whether and in what way concepts of resurrection were already present in early Judaism.[5] For both of these discussions, John 11 may at first seem to be only minimally productive. At second glance, however, the reader finds a series of insights in John 11 that not only call for a closer investigation within the scope of the resurrection of Jesus but also could break through the limits of this debate in a decisive way.

The long "warm-up" to the miraculous action at the end of John 11 (which occupies only 7 verses) leads the reader to suspect that this is more than just a miracle story. The dialogues with the disciples or with Mary and Martha seem strangely to obstruct the progress of the narrative while, at the same time, the attraction and the uniqueness of this story clearly lies in this broken narrative style.[6] The dialogues are about the basics – dealing with death, life, and faith. Even if John 11 does not directly refer to the Passion and Easter, the Lazarus story deals from beginning to end with the death and resurrection of Jesus. This is evident in the way the chapter creates a bridge between Jesus' ministry to the world and the narrative of the Passion. Furthermore, in the gospel narrative Jesus not only sets out on his last trip to Jerusalem (11:7), we also find that John 11 provides the sign (σημεῖον) – the last and greatest of the seven miracles in John – that ultimately becomes the direct cause of Jesus' death. This death perspective is formulated explicitly in 11:8 and 16 (danger of stoning) and even becomes the focus at the end of the chapter in 11:45–57 (Caiaphas prophecy, death

---

ed.; Wuppertal: Brockhaus, 2003); Walter Simonis, *Auferstehung und ewiges Leben? Die wirkliche Entstehung des Osterglaubens* (Düsseldorf: Patmos, 2002); R. O. Muncaster, *Prüfe die Beweise. Ist Jesus wirklich auferstanden?* (Hamburg: Fliss, 2004).

[5] See for example Richard Bauckham, "Life, Death, and the Afterlife in Second Temple Judaism," in *Life in the Face of Death. The Resurrection Message of the New Testament* (ed. Richard N. Longenecker; MacMaster New Testament Studies; Grand Rapids: Eerdmans, 1998), 80–95; *Auferstehung – Resurrection* (ed. Friedrich Avemarie and Hermann Lichtenberger; WUNT 135, Tübingen: Mohr Siebeck, 2001); James H. Charlesworth, "Resurrection: The Dead Sea Scrolls and the New Testament," in *Resurrection. The Origin and Future of a Biblical Doctrine* (ed. James H. Charlesworth; New York: T. & T. Clark, 2006), esp. 145–53 (with respect to 4Q521 and 4Q385); see also the articles by D. Zeller, "Erscheinungen Verstorbener im griechisch-römischen Bereich" and D. J. Harrington, "Afterlife Expectations in Pseudo-Philo, 4 Ezra, and 2 Baruch, and Their Implications for the New Testament," both in Bieringer et al., *Resurrection in the New Testament*, 1–19; 21–34. See also the older work by George W. E. Nickelsburg, *Resurrection, Immortality, and Eternal Life in Intertestamental Judaism* (HTS 26; Cambridge, Mass.: Harvard University Press and London: Oxford University Press, 1972); H. C. Cavallin, "Leben nach dem Tod im Spätjudentum und frühen Christentum," in *ANRW* 19.1 (1979), 240–345.

[6] Thus with justification Jörg Frey, *Die johanneische Eschatologie III* (WUNT 117; Tübingen: Mohr Siebeck, 2000), 407: "In dieser 'gebrochenen' Erzählweise liegt die Eigenart dieser Erzählung."

plot) as well as in 12:7–10 (preparation for burial). In addition, we find many smaller allusions and ambiguous formulations that make the reference to Jesus' fate obvious – at least for the initiated reader – such as the allusion to the motif of the "hour" (11:9–10), signal words like ὑπάγειν (11:8) or πορεύεσθαι (11:11), which are otherwise used for Jesus' path to death (7:33, 35; 8:21–22; see also the cohortative ἄγωμεν in 11:7, 15, 16; 14:31), the talk of "dying with him" (11:16), the location "near Jerusalem" (11:18) that would otherwise be superfluous from the point of view of the narrative, or the talk of the "glorification" (11:4, 40), which is connected to Jesus' death in 12:28–36. Finally, the description of the grave, down to details such as bandages and face cloth (11:44), is identical with details in the Passion and Easter narratives (see 19:40; 20:7). Thus, the subject of John 11 is Jesus' own death and resurrection.

Within that christological perspective, however, there are further questions and problems to be discussed. What relationship do the death of Jesus and that of Lazarus have to each other? And what relationship do their resurrections have? Are there two categories of resurrection because Lazarus, of course, returns to his earthly life and then must die again? What actually happens to Lazarus after his resurrection? Is he again subjected to the finitude of human life or does he become the prototype of a new life that has conquered death? Is the resurrection of Lazarus thus not only a model for the resurrection of Jesus but also ultimately a role model for the participation of the faithful in this new life?

How should the central part of the chapter, John 11:25–26, be evaluated? Is the "I Am" saying of Jesus a linguistic device, using the ambivalence of a metaphorical statement to avoid the decisive questions surrounding the historicity of the resurrection? Or do we find, in the statement of 11:25–26, the "theological climax" of the chapter, the "central statement of Johannine eschatology"[7] with which the present reality of the resurrection in the person of Jesus is expressed. However, how does this "realized resurrection" relate to the anticipation of the future resurrection of the dead on the last day, a tradition that is evident not only in John 5:28–29 (and John 6), but also in 11:24? Furthermore, there are questions about other people who, in addition to Lazarus and Jesus, play a central role in John 11. How do they react to the death of Lazarus and to his resurrection? Do they recognize – as Martha does – the close connection of this event to Jesus' own fate? What does their respectively different behavior say about their faith in Jesus, his death and his resurrection?

Question upon question draws us into the process of understanding that this narrative is designed to evoke. Let us try to enter into the process of

---

[7] Frey, *Eschatologie III*, 403: "Kernsatz der johanneischen Eschatologie"; "theologischer Höhepunkt."

the narrative search for and struggle with answers. Let us allow ourselves to be called into the narrative hermeneutic of John 11.

2. Narrative Structure of John 11

In contrast to earlier redactional hypotheses regarding the chapter,[8] it can scarcely be doubted that the entire section belongs together as one narrative entity.[9] The narrative design of John 11 has been described many times,[10] so that I can limit myself here to a few brief remarks. John 11 is an artistically composed text that is shaped down to the last detail,[11] allowing

---

[8] For a survey of scholarly discussion on of earlier sources and the redactional hypotheses in John 11, see Jacob Kremer, *Lazarus: die Geschichte einer Auferstehung: Text, Wirkungsgeschichte u. Botschaft von Joh 11,1–46* (Stuttgart: Katholisches Bibelwerk, 1985), 82–109; Josef Wagner, *Auferstehung und Leben: Joh 11,1–12,19 als Spiegel johanneischer Redaktions- und Theologiegeschichte* (BU 19; Regensburg: Pustet, 1988), 29–94, Brendan J. Byrne, *Lazarus. A Contemporary Reading of John 11.1–46* (Collegeville: Liturgical Press, 1991), 69–83; Michael Labahn, *Jesus als Lebensspender. Untersuchungen zu einer Geschichte der johanneischen Tradition anhand ihrer Wundergeschichten* (BZNW 98; Berlin: de Gruyter, 1999), 378–465; Frey, *Eschatologie III*, 403–62.

[9] See nearly all recently published commentaries. Exceptions are Wagner, *Auferstehung*, 29–94 (Wagner defends a redactional approach, based on that of Georg Richter, with respect to the tensions in the resurrection passages); Delbert Burkett, "Two Accounts of Lazarus' Resurrection in John 11," *NovT* 36 (1994): 209–32; Hartwig Thyen, "Die Erzählung von den bethanischen Geschwistern (Joh 11,1–12,19) als 'Palimpsest' über synoptischen Texten," in *The Four Gospels, 1992: Festschrift Frans Neirynck* (ed. F. van Segbroeck, Christopher M. Tuckett, Gilbert van Belle, and J. Verheyden; BETL 100; 3 vols.; Leuven: Leuven University Press and Peeters, 1992), 2021–50; idem, *Das Johannesevangelium* (HNT 6; Tübingen: Mohr Siebeck, 2005), 510–11. (Thyen argued that the account is derived from the Synoptics.)

[10] See, e.g., Gail O'Day, *The Word Disclosed, John's Story and Narrative Preaching* (St. Louis: CBP, 1987), 76–99; Wilhelm Wuellner, "Rhetorical Criticism and its Theory in Culture-Critical Perspective: The Narrative Rhetoric of John 11," in *Text and Interpretation: New Approaches in the Criticism of the New Testament* (ed. P. J. Hartin and J. H. Petzer; NTTS 15; Leiden: Brill, 1991), 171–85; idem, "Putting Life Back into the Lazarus Story and Its Reading: The Narrative Rhetoric of John 11 as the Narration of Faith," *Semeia* 53 (1991): 113–132; Mark W. G. Stibbe, "A Tomb with a View: John 11.1–44 in Narrative-Critical Perspective," *NTS* 40 (1994): 38–54; Ingrid Rosa Kitzberger, "Mary of Bethany and Mary of Magdala – Two Female Characters in the Johannine Passion Narrative: A Feminist, Narrative-Critical Reader Response," *NTS* 41 (1995): 564–86; Eckart Reinmuth, "Lazarus und seine Schwestern – was wollte Johannes erzählen?" *TLZ* 124 (1999): 127–37; Frey, *Eschatologie III*, 408–22; Francis J. Moloney, "Can Everyone be Wrong? A Reading of John 11.1–12.8," *NTS* 45 (2003): 505–27.

[11] See the effusive opinion of Stibbe, *A Tomb with a View*, 38: "In many ways, John's story of the raising of Lazarus represents the pinnacle of the New Testament literature. It

us to assume that even details that may seem unimportant were chosen with great care.

The section of the narrative that begins with 11:1 is defined very unambiguously through the introduction of new people and the naming of the location, even though John 10:40–42 clearly fulfils a bridging function.[12] It is more difficult to define the end of the passage. Although the resurrection of Lazarus comes to a kind of conclusion with the presentation of the resurrected person in 11:44, the element, typical within the genre of miracle stories, of the witnesses' reaction to the miracle is missing – this does not appear until 11:45. The subsequent section involving the death plot against Jesus remains closely connected to the former, which is why many exegetes assume a unity of John 11:1–53/54 or 11:1–57.[13] If one, however, recognizes an expansion beyond v. 44, one must also note the connection between 11:45 and 12:11, which speaks in almost literal repetition about the faith of the Jews.[14] As so often, the Johannine narrative style disallows, in my opinion, a dogmatic definition of the limits of the passage, for it is characteristic of John that he is a master of interconnectedness and overlapping. Without needing to challenge a certain independence of the sections in 11:45–57 and 12:1–11, the close relationship between 11:1–44 and the subsequent sections should be moved here into the central focus. Thus, not only the character constellation (Lazarus, Mary, Martha) of John 11 is adopted in 12:–11, but also, by way of the introduction of Mary in 11:2 as the "Mary . . . who anointed the Lord with ointment," an explicit bracketing is carried out that becomes understandable for the reader only with the narrative of the anointing. Without this conclusion, the anachronistic remark would remain a mystery. If one, following Stibbe, recognizes that throughout the entire narrative the two protagonists, who are at first far apart, are moving toward each other, this does not even reach its objective

---

is a tale artfully structured, with colourful characters, timeless appeal, a sense of progression and suspense, subtle use of focus and no little sense of drama." Further elements of narrative style or rhetorical techniques are, according to Wuellner, "internal monologue," "Katachresis" (11:4), "irony," "repetitions," and "deictic and modal features;" see Wuellner, *Putting Life back*, 120–24 with textual examples.

[12] On the contextual placement of John 10 (and 10:40–42) see Ruben Zimmermann, *Christologie der Bilder im Johannesevangelium. Die Christpoetik des vierten Evangeliums unter besonderer Berücksichtigung von Joh 10* (WUNT 171; Tübingen: Mohr Siebeck, 2004), 241–50.

[13] See, for example, Ludger Schenke, *Johannes. Kommentar* (Düsseldorf: Patmos 1998), 207–31; J. Gnilka, *Johannesevangelium* (3d ed.; NEB 4; Würzburg: Echter, 1989), 87. Frey demonstrated the attractive framing of John 10:40, 42 and John 11:45–54 through the parallel structured sections. See Frey, *Eschatology III*, 409–11.

[14] John 11:45: Πολλοὶ οὖν ἐκ τῶν Ἰουδαίων (. . .) ἐπίστευσαν εἰς αὐτόν.
John 12:11: πολλοὶ (. . .) τῶν Ἰουδαίων καὶ ἐπίστευον εἰς τὸν Ἰησοῦν.

in the resurrection.[15] After Lazarus is called out of the tomb, he is simply let go. A complete communion is not realized until John 12:1–11, where Lazarus and Jesus are reclining at the table, sharing supper (12:1–2). The sections in 11:45–57 and 12:1–11 demonstrate further, with the backdrop of threats and the death plot as well as the shared supper and faith, two absolutely contrasting reactions to the resurrection of Lazarus. The entire thought and narrative movement thus comes to an end only in 12:1–11.

The primary characters of the narrative already mentioned (Jesus, Lazarus, Martha, Mary, the Jews) need only be supplemented by the disciples who play a role especially in the first narrative section (11:6–16) and again at the conclusion (12:1–11). In each case, a disciple is singled out by name from the group of disciples (Thomas in 11:16; Judas in 12:4–6), so that through this detail an *inclusio* is once again created. In the central focus of the narrative, however, are the three different meetings of Jesus with the three siblings from Bethany. Thus Martha first meets Jesus on the outskirts of the city of Bethany in order to speak to him about the resurrection, and this ends with Martha's confession of faith (11:17–27). She then calls Mary, whose meeting with Jesus is characterized less by theological discourse than by emotions (11:28–37). Together with the Jews following her, everyone then goes to the grave, where the meeting with Lazarus takes place (11:38–44). After Jesus' prayer to the Father, he calls the dead man out of the tomb. The act of resurrection leads to a divided reaction in the accompanying crowd. Some Jews go to the Pharisees with hostile intentions which leads to a convening of the council. Out of fear that, because of such signs, "all will believe in him" (11:48: πάντες πιστεύσουσιν εἰς αὐτόν), the high priests and Pharisees decide to kill Jesus.

A great number of Jews (πολλοί in John 12:9.11), however, begin to believe and they come to witness the supper of Jesus and the three siblings from Bethany (12:1–11). As a whole, we can describe in this way a seven-element structure of this narrative unity, in whose center are the meetings with the three siblings:[16]

---

[15] Stibbe, *A Tomb with a View*, 42–43.

[16] Various sequences of scenes have been differentiated in literature, which particularly corresponds to the delimitation of the conclusion of the passage: Frey and many others see five scenes in John 11:1–44 (Frey, *Die johanneische Eschatologie III*, 416–18); Wuellner (*Putting Life back*, 118–20) places vv. 45–53 and vv. 54–57 in the sixth and seventh scenes; Stibbe works out a concentric structure, in which he separates the Martha dialogue on its own: A (vv. 1–16); B (v. 17–22); C (vv. 23–27); B' (vv. 28–32); A' (vv. 33–44); see Stibbe, *A Tomb with a View*, 43–44; Schenke sees the Martha dialogue (vv. 17–27) as a unity, differentiates based on the spatial information between v. 28–32 und v. 33–45 (at the tomb) and sees in vv. 46–53 the fifth scene, see Schenke, *Johannes*, 212–18; for Moloney, who also counts John 12:1–8 in the narration, "eight stages" can be outlined; see Moloney, "Can everyone be Wrong," 508–9.

The Narrative Structure of John 11:1–12:11

1) Exposition (11:1–5): Naming of the active characters and the topic.
2) Disciples' dialogue (11:6–16): Discussion of sickness and death; parable of walking

3) Meeting with Martha (11:17–27): Resurrection on the last day, confession of faith.
4) Meeting with Mary (11:28–37): Mary's mourning and proskynesis
5) Meeting with Lazarus (11:38–44): Prayer and act of resurrection.

6) Reaction of the hostile Jews (11:45–57): Death plot.
7) Reaction of the faithful Jews (12:1–11): Anointing and Supper.

3. The Narrative Hermeneutics in John 11

The narrative is not characterized by a stringent narrative progression or a linear increase in tension. Instead, retarding elements, puzzling elements, and misunderstandings are inserted that lead to a "broken narrative style."

Despite the urgent pleas of the sisters, Jesus lingers – incomprehensively for the disciples and the readers – where he is before he starts out on the journey (11:6). Then, on his arrival in Bethany, Jesus does not go directly to the tomb, but rather is delayed by the meetings with the sisters outside the village (11:17–37). Comments to the reader (11:2, 5, 13, 30) or "theological excurses" (11:9–10, 12–16, 19, 31, 35–37, 40, 41b–42) are repeatedly interspersed, and these do not promote the progress of the narrative. Even the scene at the tomb is again unbearably extended by the intervention of Martha and the prayer of Jesus. The reader is dying to ask, when are we getting to the point? When is Jesus going to get down to business? But what is the "business" of this narrative? In recognizing a conscious narrative strategy in this *tactic of procrastination*, the reader must have realized by the time he or she finally gets to the act of resurrection that this is not a "simple" miracle story.

However, finding the center or the object of this narrative is not made easy for the reader. Contributing to this are the many *gaps* and *riddles* that are built into the narrative. In this way, the remark about Mary, that she anointed the Lord (v. 2), is confusing, for there had been no mention of this up to this point. Jesus' statement that this sickness does not lead to death but rather to the glorification of God (v. 4) is also strangely shrouded. Or even Jesus' expression of joy at the death of a beloved friend (v. 15). A strange tension arises also between the disciples' fearful warning to Jesus of the deadly risk (v. 8) and Thomas's brave declaration of his desire to die with Jesus (v. 16), without a recognizable discussion between these two things. The brief parable in vv. 10–11 about walking by day and night seems to be in the wrong place in any case.[17] And how should Jesus' mysterious statement about life and non-death despite death (vv 25–26) be understood? The reader also wonders why Martha "secretly" calls her sister, and the questions could go on.

The individual meetings of the various characters with Jesus proceed inauspiciously and are characterized by *misunderstandings*: The disciples misunderstand Jesus' statement about Lazarus's sleep (11:11–13). Martha interprets Jesus' statement that her brother will rise wrongly as the resurrection on the last day (11:23–24). The Jews who have come to console Mary believe that she is going to the tomb when she instead is going to meet Jesus (11:31–32). Further, they misunderstand the weeping of Jesus as an expression of his mourning of Lazarus, which would, however, be in contrast to the joy mentioned before. Instead, it is Jesus' insight into the sadness of Mary and the Jews that provokes his emotions (11:33). Caiaphas does not understand his own statement about Jesus' death (11:51–52), and, finally Judas demonstrates a colossal misunderstanding in the interpretation of the act of anointing, which he interprets not in a thanatological but rather a socio-critical context (12:4–8).

However, the reader should not be confused by these elements. The fact that the narrative techniques of disguise and disclosure, or the misunderstandings and corrections, represent "calculated provocations" that correspond to those in other σημεῖον-narratives.[18] The narratological devices make it necessary for the reader to submerge himself or herself ever deeper in the process of understanding. It is especially the open, unexplained elements that urge the recipient to search for a deeper meaning. The narrative resists an instantaneous, simple solution and thus succeeds in pushing onwards to higher levels of understanding.

However, what actually should be understood? Are we dealing with a correct understanding of the miracle of the resurrection, as the earlier exegetes emphasized? The modern question of historicity would definitely not play a role in this. The facticity of miracles and also of resurrections was not contested in the ancient world. Is the goal instead a correct understanding of such a miracle? Does the evangelist want to counteract a faith that is mistakenly based on signs?

---

[17] See now R. Craig Koester, "Es ist Zeit, dem Licht zu folgen (Wandel bei Tag und Nacht) – Joh 11,9f." in *Kompendium der Gleichnisse Jesu* (ed. R. Zimmermann et al., Gütersloh: Gütersloher Verlagshaus, 2007), 793–803.

[18] So C. Welck, *Erzählte Zeichen. Die Wundergeschichten des Johannesevangeliums literarisch untersucht* (WUNT II/69; Tübingen: Mohr Siebeck, 1994), 249–54.

The central topic of the passage is contained in the two poles in Jesus' programmatic statement at the beginning of the narrative (11:4): On the one hand the subject is sickness and death; and on the other hand it is the glorification of God, concretely the glorification of the Son of God. Understanding this polarity and this tension is the task of this chapter. Terminologically heightened, the subject of John 11 is the correct understanding of death in contrast to life and resurrection. In the close connection of these elements to the person of Jesus, the narrative ultimately reaches for a correct understanding of Jesus himself and especially his death and resurrection. This understanding is, however, not explained in the form of dogmatic knowledge, but rather is conveyed through a narrative that shows the correct relationship with the protagonists of Jesus. The term used for this is "faith," which functions like a guideline throughout the whole story (11:14, 25, 26, 27, 40, 42, 45, 48; 12:11). Jesus acts in many cases "in order that you might believe" (ἵνα πιστεύσητε, 11:15; cf. 11:42) or explicitly asks Martha "Do you believe this?" (πιστεύεις τοῦτο;). The statements addressed to the characters are thus transferred to the readers. They – and we too – are challenged in their or our faith. Thus, the key hermeneutical question for John 11 is: How can one, in the Johannine sense, correctly believe in Christ? How do death and resurrection reveal themselves in faith in Jesus?

4. How to Understand Some Key Theological Terms in John 11

4.1. Death

One of the central topics, if not *the* central topic, of John 11 is death and the various human reactions to the end of life. The verb "to die" (ἀποθνῄσκω) occurs nine times in John 11, which means that about one third of all the occurrences in the Gospel of John are found in this chapter[19]; furthermore, two of the eight Johannine occurrences of "death" (θάνατος) appear in 11:4.13. This statistical evidence makes it obvious that the topic of dying and death plays an important role for John within the Lazarus passage. This is corroborated by the systematic placement and discussion of the subject in which all possible denotations and connotations of death are played out.

If we follow the path of the narrative, we find the first mention of death at the point where the connection between sickness and death is brought out. Jesus hears of the sickness and classifies it as a "non-deadly sickness"

---

[19] See John 11:14, 16, 21, 25, 26, 32, 37, 50, 51; furthermore 4:47, 49; 6:49, 50, 58; 8:21, 24, 52, 53; 12:24, 33; 18:14, 32; 19:17; 21:23.

(11:4: αὕτη ἡ ἀσθένεια οὐκ ἔστιν πρὸς θάνατον; "This sickness is not unto death"). We get the impression here that this basic differentiation between "deadly" and "non-deadly" is common in this social setting. Sickness leads to death and thus creates sensitivity to *human mortality*. This natural dimension of death is presented in the example of the illness of a concrete person – the person is mortal, finite, and corruptible, as is shown in 11:39, even with the senses!

However, the threat to humans does not only exist in our fleshly condition, that is, from the inside out. The threat arises frequently from external danger – other people take life and kill. This perspective of a *violent death* is explicitly mentioned in Jesus' case in verse 8: the Jews in Judea have tried to stone Jesus. The brief subsequent parable about walking by day and by night (11:9–10) also follows this path. It reveals, through the well-known tradition of the metaphors ("Bildfeldtradition") of light and darkness (see Ps 88:13; Sir 22:11; as well as Homer, *Il.* 4.461; Euripides, *Alc.* 266), behind the prosaic action of walking, the tension between life and death. Accordingly, in the Gospel of John "those who walk at night have started down a path that ultimately leads to death."[20] For Jesus himself, the coming of "night" brings with it betrayal and crucifixion (John 12:23–27; 13:1, 30; 17:1), but because the "hour" of his death is determined by God, there is no danger for the time being. This subject is not re-opened until after the actual miracle. The council plans to kill Jesus: "So from that day on they planned together to kill him." (11:53) This is then extended to Lazarus – they plan to kill him, just as they would do to Jesus (12:10).

In addition to natural and violent death, another dimension comes into view in 11:16 – the *representative death* for another person. Talk of "dying with someone" (ἀποθνήσκω μετά) or more generally "risking one's life for others" is not only found in the Gospel of John (10:11, 15, 17–18; 15:13[21]), but is especially well-known in the Hellenistic environment as a part of the ethics of friendship. Thus it is primarily the discussion of the high priests (11:47–53) that takes up the subject again. We are no longer dealing here with a threat to life that will lead to death, but rather very explicitly with death "for others" or "dying *for* the people" (ἀποθνῄσκειν ὑπὲρ τοῦ ἔθνους). For many exegetes, the preposition ὑπέρ, used as a signal in early Christianity, is an unambiguous allusion to the representative death of Je-

---

[20] Koester, "Es ist Zeit," 797.

[21] In this case, however, especially in the formulation "to risk his life for . . ." (τιθέναι τὴν ψυχήν), see Jens Schröter, "Sterben für die Freunde. Überlegungen zur Deutung des Todes Jesu im Johannesevangelium," in *Religionsgeschichte des Neuen Testaments. Festschrift für Klaus Berger zum 60. Geburtstag* (ed. Axel von Dobbeler et al.; Tübingen and Basel: Francke, 2000), 263–87 as well as my comments in Zimmermann, *Christologie der Bilder*, 389–96.

sus.²² In any case, it can not be doubted that in John 11:49–52 the death of Jesus is being assigned a representative function.²³ While Caiaphas unwittingly prophesies with his statement that "one man should die for the people" (11:50), the subsequent comment to the reader confirms more than clearly "that Jesus was going to die for the nation, and not for the nation only, but that he might also gather together into one the children of God who are scattered abroad"(11:51–52). Jesus' death should be for the good of all people and it is thus given a universal meaning.

A final area that describes the way of dealing with death in John 11 could be entitled *Mourning* or *Rituals of Death*. We learn not only of the sadness and the weeping of the dead man's sisters (11:31, 33) but also of their anger and resentment in the face of death (11:33). We see people who sympathize and come into the house of the family in order to comfort them (11:31.45). Furthermore, we read about the smallest details of the treatment of the dead man, such as the bandaging of his hands and feet with grave cloths (11:44).

4.2. Life and Resurrection

However, this small "thanatology" is not a compendium-like discourse for its own purposes. The narrative portrayal of the death motif in John 11 leads to the recognition that it deals, in and with the narrative progression, precisely with a discussion about death, with a treatment of the various perceptions. Thus, the remarks on death enter very often into a tense interaction with the question of life. It is especially Jesus who repeatedly counteracts death with the perspectives of life and resurrection. Long before the term "resurrection" explicitly appears, such counteractions, relativizations, and reinterpretations of death occur. I would like to mention some of these in a more systematic portrayal. In v. 4, when the topic of death is first touched upon, a fundamental tension is formulated – death is counteracted by the glory of Jesus.

Jesus uses the popular reaction of euphemizing death in order to allude to the resurrection. By speaking of Lazarus falling asleep (11:11: Λάζαρος ὁ φίλος ἡμῶν κεκοίμηται; "Our friend Lazarus has fallen asleep"), Jesus ironically adopts the death-sleep metaphor in order to remove the sharpness from death and simultaneously to allude to the original background of

---

[22] See, with many examples, Jörg Frey, "Die Deutung des Todes Jesu als Stellvertretung. Neutestamentliche Perspektiven," in *Stellvertretung I. Ein interdisziplinäres Symposium* (ed. C. Janowski et al., Neukirchen-Vluyn: Neukirchener, 2006), 87–121.

[23] Jörg Frey, "Edler Tod – wirksamer Tod – stellvertretender Tod – heilschaffender Tod. Zur narrativen und theologischen Deutung des Todes Jesu im Johannesevangelium," in *The Death of Jesus in the Fourth Gospel* (ed. G. van Belle; BETL 200; Leuven: Leuven University Press and Peeters, 2007), 65–94.

the resurrection metaphor in the sense of a "waking-up" (ἐξυπνίζω) or "getting up" (from sleep at night) (ἀνίστημι). Such a re-metaphorization is a way of speaking that John uses in other contexts (e.g., in Christological titles) in order to make theological terms more understandable.[24] Of course, the disciples do not understand this ironic trick. But sometimes – especially in the context of making a taboo of death – it can have a healing effect to speak plainly and to call the facts by name, which Jesus does when he says candidly, "Lazarus is dead" (Λάζαρος ἀπέθανεν, 11:14).

Although Jesus shares the emotional dismay at death and weeps (11:35), his "joy" in the face of death is also reported (11:15). This is a remark that must at first seem disturbing and paradoxical to the reader. Nevertheless, one can also see this change in emotions in the rapid change in mood in the parable of birth (16:21–22), which in the same way can be interpreted with the fate of Jesus.[25] It is, however, more a paradoxical refraction of the usual valuations, as we see them also in the formulation "lifting up" on the cross (12:32–33).[26]

The verb used for Jesus' calling or shouting at the tomb of Lazarus (κραυγάζω, 11:43) is taken up again in the passion story (18:40; 19:8, 12, 15), where the people shout Jesus into death. From the opposite perspective, when Jesus shouts at death here, it is not only the death of Lazarus or the death of people in general that he is shouting at, but also his own death on the cross.

Further contrasts need to be mentioned only briefly. The horribleness of the stench of decomposition is contrasted with the aesthetics of anointing. Jesus meets the silencing effect of death with a great voice that calls the name of the dead man. Violent death by others is counteracted with representative death for others.

However, in the center of these contrasting refractions of death we find the statement of the resurrection in 11:25–26, which I would like to look at more closely. It is prepared for by the dialogue with Martha, who receives Jesus with the statement that his presence could have prevented the death of her brother (11:21). Jesus then promises her brother's resurrection: ἀναστήσεται ὁ ἀδελφός σου (11:23).

According to traditional perceptions, but also corresponding to the discussion of the resurrection up to this point in the Gospel of John (6:39, 40, 44, 54), Martha understands the future tense of this promise as the resurrection on the last day. Yes, she knows that her brother, like all the dead,

---

[24] See on this with respect to such titles as "Son (of God)," "Lord" etc. Zimmermann, *Christologie der Bilder*, 167–96.

[25] See Judith Hartenstein, "Aus Schmerz wird Freude (Die gebärende Frau) – Joh 16,21f.," in Zimmermann, *Kompendium der Gleichnisse Jesu*, 840–47, esp. 845–46.

[26] See Zimmermann, *Christologie der Bilder*, 228–31.

will rise again at the end of time (11:24). But Jesus means something else, which he expresses in the subsequent, striking "I Am" saying (11:25–26):

Ἐγώ εἰμι ἡ ἀνάστασις καὶ ἡ ζωή·	I am the resurrection and the life;
ὁ πιστεύων εἰς ἐμὲ	he who believes in me
κἂν ἀποθάνῃ ζήσεται,	even if he dies, shall he live
καὶ πᾶς ὁ ζῶν	and everyone who lives
καὶ πιστεύων εἰς ἐμὲ	and believes in me
οὐ μὴ ἀποθάνῃ εἰς τὸν αἰῶνα.	shall never die.

Just as the terms "resurrection/rise" have been accumulating in the section under discussion, the fundamental poles of life and death are now connected to each other very closely. This "I Am" saying, in view of its formal arrangement, can be classified with the other "I Am" sayings in the gospel:[27] The introductory ἐγώ εἰμι is followed by a predicative classification that is somewhat unusual because, instead of one predicate nominative, two nouns are mentioned (resurrection; life) and they are abstract nouns, unlike most images such as "door," "bread," and "vine," which are taken from the concrete world around them. Even if the differentiation, common since Schulz, between "self-predication" and "soteriological apodosis" is problematical,[28] it maintains its correctness to the extent that "I Am" sayings are always followed by an explanatory sentence (see 11:25–26) that leads to the recognition of a parallel construction with four elements. A participial construction is respectively classified in synthetic *parallelismus membrorum* to a futuristic statement of healing.

The construction, however, becomes problematic in regards to semantics and logic. In both, the stichometries of "dying" and "life" are put into relation to one another. The first sentence promises life to the faithful, even if he or she dies; the second promises non-death to those who live in faith. The promise of non-death thus falls into formal-logical opposition to the concession of the first sentence, "if he dies" (κἂν ἀποθάνῃ). Are the faithful now indeed able to die or not?

---

[27] See details of the arrangement in Hartwig Thyen, "Ich-bin-Worte," *RAC* 17 (1996), 147–213, esp. 177–79, Frey, *Eschatologie III*, 448–52; Chrisitan Cebulj, *Ich bin es. Studien zur Identitätsbildung im Johannesevangelium* (SBB 44; Stuttgart: Katholisches Bibelwerk, 2000), 209–12. On the "I Am" sayings in general see also Zimmermann, *Christologie der Bilder*, 121–34.

[28] See Siegried Schulz, *Komposition und Herkunft der johanneischen Reden* (BWANT V, Stuttgart: Kohlhammer, 1960), 86–87, and my criticism in Zimmermann, *Christologie der Bilder*, 130–31.

This consciously produced tension can only be resolved by playing consciously with the nuances of meaning. Thus the main clause in v. 26 begins with the "bodily death" that is counteracted with "real, eternal life." The second sentence takes up this life given in faith and indicates that this new life is indestructible. With empathetic negation ("will certainly not die"), any threat to life is rejected.

Through the "I Am" saying, death in all its dimensions – bodily death or even eternal death[29] – is refracted and, at the same time, an explanation for the resurrection is given. It is striking that the actual terminology of resurrection has only been used for concepts of future resurrection on the last day. Only in the "I Am" saying in 11:25 is ἀνάστασις taken up and immediately supplemented with ζωή, which then remains a leading term in the subsequent text. Not only is the directly present resurrection in the person of Jesus held up against the apparent finality of death, but the resurrection, which up to this point has been experienced as a future event, is interpreted here as life experienced in the present. The future tense of ζῆν must, in line with other places in the gospel (5:25; 6:51a, 57–58; 14:19), be related to the gift of eternal life promised in present faith and may not be misunderstood in the sense of future eschatology. The resurrection is taking place now; it is the life given now and present in Jesus.

Apart from its otherwise central importance within the theology of the gospel,[30] the notion of life plays a large role in the "I Am" sayings in their entirety. Apart from the direct identification of Jesus with life in 11:25 and 14:6, "life" is mentioned in five other "I Am" sayings – in John 6:25, 48, and 51 "life" appears directly in the syntagma (e.g., "bread of life"), in John 8:12 and 10:7 and 9 it is mentioned in closer context. Jan van der Watt has worked out that the figurative domain of life can be regarded as one of the highest-level metaphorical networks of the Gospel of John, in which the "I Am" sayings fulfill the function of classification[31]: Jesus is the giver and receiver of life (6:35, 48: bread; cf. 4:10), he leads through life to the light (8:12) and promises a life in full (10:9–10); he protects life even at the risk of his own life (10:11, 14) and ultimately can himself be identified with life (11:25; 14:6). Finally, it is the close relationship to Christ, or figuratively stated, the listening to the voice of the shepherd

---

[29] Cf. the expression "the second death" in Rev 2:11; 20:6, 14; 21:8.

[30] See Labahn, *Jesus als Lebensspender*; Mira Stare, *Durch ihn leben: die Lebensthematik in Joh 6* (NTAbh 49; Münster: Aschendorff, 2004), and further the good overview in Christian Dietzfelbinger, *Das Evangelium nach Johannes* (ZBK 4/1; Zürich: Theologischer Verlag, 2001), esp. 348–50: "Exkurs: Leben im Johannesevangelium."

[31] Cf. Jan G. van der Watt, *Family of the King. Dynamics of Metaphor in the Gospel According to John* (BIS 47; Leiden et al., 2000), 201–45; with reference to the "I Am" sayings; see also 416–17; see also Stare, *Durch ihn leben*, 269–72: "Ich-bin-Worte und Lebensthematik."

(10:11), the eating of the bread of life that leads the faithful to eternal life (6:50, 58). Both of these aspects play a central role in the resurrection narrative in John 11. Lazarus hears the voice of Jesus (11:43–44), in the end he has supper with him (12:2) and thus receives the life that conquers death. However, in the Jewish tradition, God is the only giver of life[32] so that the unity proclaimed by Jesus in prayer between himself and his Father (11:41–42) corresponds to the self-identification of Jesus with life.

Let us state this once again clearly. In John 11, death is not simply negated or relativized. On the contrary, death in all its dimensions is taken seriously, but it does not receive any (super)power. What is important is the "in spite of" in the face of death. The overlapping construction of 11:25–26 expresses this particularly well. The transformation of death into life does not occur simply or clearly; rather it is paradoxically overcome through the full recognition of the depth and threat of death. This present refraction of death by the presence of Jesus takes place as an act of (re-)interpretation and finally of faith. The text itself alludes to this clearly through the clustering in 11:25–26 of the term πιστεύειν (four times). The discussion on death and life (resurrection), which up to now has been summed up rather abstractly, remains embedded in the text in a narrative framework. It is individual people who are portrayed in their own respective attempts at faith. Although I could also bring in here secondary characters such as the disciples or the Jews,[33] in what follows I would like concentrate on the three siblings as models of faith.

5. The Characters in the Narrative – Models of Misunderstanding?

At the center of the entire narrative progression we find three meetings in which models of the handling of death and resurrection, as well as of faith, are presented as ideal types.

5.1. Martha – Model of the Confessing Faithful?

Martha, the sister of the dead man, comes to the forefront (11:17–27) first. She goes to meet Jesus. She receives him with the words: "Lord, if you had been here, my brother would not have died" (11:21). We are at first not certain whether this is meant to be an expression of reproach, of resignation, or of trust.[34] However, the following clause unmistakably expresses

---

[32] See Gen 2:7; Deut 4:4; Ps 16:11; 21:5; 36:10 et al.
[33] On this see, for example Schenke, *Johannes*, 214, 216–17; Moloney, "Can Everyone be Wrong," 515–16.
[34] Thus Dietzfelbinger, *Johannes*, 344–45.

trust and hope. Even now, after death has occurred, Martha believes that Jesus will receive everything that he asks of the Father. The attentive reader thus recognizes a foreshadowing of that which will occur later. Jesus will ask his Father for the power of resurrection. Martha, however, who on the narrative level does not know how the story will end, is instead surprised when Jesus immediately promises her the resurrection of her brother: "Your brother will rise again!" She misunderstands this statement as a reference to the eschatological resurrection on the last day.

Once again, in her answer, she proves herself to be a true believer. She is familiar with the resurrection as an eschatological event. Jesus, however, answers her with an "I Am" saying and thus corrects the postponing of the resurrection into the future. The "now" is important – in resurrection as in faith. Thus the question in the second person singular "Do you believe this?" is clearly directed to the present time (cf. present tense!). Martha confirms, "Yes, Lord, I have (always) believed" (πεπίστευκα) that you are the Christ, the Son of God, the one coming into the world" (11:27). With this sentence, Martha uses marked Christological titles in the same way that they play a role in Johannine theology. Many exegetes see in 11:27 an expression of true Johannine faith in the same way that John describes it in his summary at the end of the gospel (see 20:30–31). In this regard, Martha confesses her faith not only once. She commits herself to her faith three times: (1) Jesus will receive everything that he asks for from God. (2) The dead will rise again on the last day. (3) Jesus is the Christ, the Son of God, he who comes into the world.

We therefore need not be surprised that Martha is heralded as the great confessor of faith in the interpretive tradition of John 11.[35] Much has been written on this that need not be repeated in detail. Martha believes, speaks about her faith, and knows the correct terms and concepts of the tradition. Nevertheless, it remains surprising that this confession, this climax, appears so early in the narrative. Was the point of this to precede seeing with believing? Is she portrayed as someone who believes although she does not see? Someone who believes even in the face of or rather in spite of death? But then why do we need all the rest of the text? Must the narrative, after this unsurpassable act of confession, not unavoidably flatten out and end in

---

[35] For example, Rudolf Schnackenburg, *The Gospel According to St John* (London: Sheed and Word; 1971), 2.332–33; Klaus Wengst, *Das Johannesevangelium* (TKNT 4.2; Stuttgart: Kohlhammer, 2004), 28; Sandra M. Schneiders, "Death in the Community of Eternal Life: History, Theology and Spirituality in John 11," *Int* 41 (1987): 44–56, esp. 53; Colleen M. Conway, *Men and Women in the Fourth Gospel. Gender and Johannine Characterization* (SBLDS 167; Atlanta: Society of Biblical Literature, 1999), 141–43; Labahn, *Lebensspender*, 420–22; Udo Schnelle, *Das Evangelium nach Johannes* (ThKNT 4; 2d ed.; Leipzig 2004), 190; Schenke, *Johannes,*226; see more references in Moloney, "Can Everyone be Wrong," 515 n. 36.

irrelevance? It is no wonder that earlier interpreters in literary criticism wanted to cut out large parts as superfluous.

As correct as many observations on Martha's faith may be, several details as well as the further narrative progression raise doubt as to whether Martha is a thoroughly positive role model for faith. Drawing on Francis Moloney,[36] we list the following problems:

a) The incompatibility of Jesus' question of faith ("Do you believe this?") with Martha's answer stands out. The response does not really answer the question.[37]

b) The tense of the verb is striking. "I have believed" is the perfect tense (πεπίστευκα), as if to say that Martha has believed for a long time; she would not have needed Jesus to say, "I Am the resurrection and the life." With this, however, the answer is placed in the series of other confessions, each of which are introduced with οἶδα, "I know (already)" (11:22, 24). The two preceding confessions were, however, criticized by Jesus.

c) The confession in v. 27 stereotypically reflects not so much Jewish messianic expectation as especially Johannine christological confessions.[38]

d) V. 28: Martha now speaks of Jesus again as διδάσκαλος (= Rabbi, see 11:8) and uses none of the titles used previously. Does this not demonstrate that she has not yet understood the importance of these predicates?

e) V. 39–40: Martha's behavior at the tomb: she intervenes in Jesus' act of resurrection.

In the face of these problems and especially in view of the further progress of the narrative, we can no longer maintain a purely positive portrayal of Martha's faith. Even if Martha's famous confession in 11:27 concluded the conversation and prompted no reaction from Jesus, Jesus' rhetorical questions at the tomb make it clear that Martha has obviously not yet understood everything. Accordingly, we must read the reaction of Jesus as a clarification or even a rebuke toward Martha: Jesus said to her, "Did I not

---

[36] See Moloney, "Can Everyone be Wrong, 513–15.

[37] That has already been noted in the scholarly discussion, see Francis J. Moloney, *Signs and Shadows. Reading John 5–12* (Minneapolis: Fortress, 1996), 162; Raymond E. Brown, *The Gospel according to John*, (2 vols; AB 29–29a; New York: Doubleday, 1966–1970), 1.434–35. Most, however, consider it to be a genuine and developed statement of faith.

[38] I would like to state Moloney more precisely here: The putting together of the three predicates does not reflect "Jewish messianic expectation" (Moloney, "Can Everone be Wrong," 513), because the Messiah was not characterized as the "Son of God." The "coming into the world" is not typical of messianic expectation either, but it is Johannine language.

say to you, if you believe, you will see the glory of God?" (11:40) Why does she not want the stone to be removed? Does she want to stop the action in order not to be thrown back to the level of materiality, as she has now understood that it is spiritual-theological comprehension that is important? But is this all that is important? It is Jesus himself who wants to reach the dead man; she puts herself in the way of his challenge. In this there are two aspects to Jesus' actions. He is dealing with the concrete present time. Faith must stand the test and prove itself in the here and now of the dead Lazarus. And Jesus himself wants to reach the dead man; he is not stopped by banalities, by the finitude of human existence that could hardly be expressed more graphically than in the stench of decomposition. That is exactly what Martha would like to reject. Her confession – as correct as it may literally be – remains incomplete as long as she cannot admit the necessity of death. The glorification of which Jesus speaks (v. 4) cannot be attained before or on the other side of death, but only through death. Only in this way does the talk of the glorification of Jesus in John 11 remain connected to the other discussions of glorification in the gospel. Especially the subsequent chapter 12 speaks explicitly about the fact that the raising on the cross is regarded as the hour of glorification (12:28–36). New life arises out of death (12:24).[39] Thus the implementation of Martha's confession of faith remains deficient.

5.2. Mary – Model of the Trusting Believer?

Mary's meeting with Jesus is described in a completely different way (11:28–37). We miss here a discursive explanation of the basic principles of death and resurrection. We do not learn why Mary at first remains inside the house. We can rule out disinterest, as is demonstrated by her actions in 11:29 and 31. It is reported twice that Mary "rises quickly" (ταχέως ἀνέστη) to meet Jesus. When she meets Jesus, she greets him with the same statement as her sister, although the following clause is missing. Instead of a confession of trust, we read of an act of trust. She falls at Jesus' feet, possibly representing a foreshadowing of the anointing and drying of the feet, of which was anticipated in the introduction and will be narrated later (see 11:2 and 12:2–3). Falling down is, however, above all a gesture of adoration, which, according to the Jewish understanding, may only be addressed to God. In this way, Mary expresses her trust and her faith in Jesus. Mary weeps; she is emotionally distraught in the face of death. However, the encouragement of the Jews who have come to her can clearly not comfort her. They are portrayed at a distance from her, they follow at a distance, and they misunderstand her actions. Mary comes to Jesus in her

---

[39] See my comments in Ruben Zimmermann, "Das Leben aus dem Tod (vom sterbenden Weizenkorn) – Joh 12,24," in *Kompendium der Gleichnisse Jesu*, 804–16.

inconsolable sadness at the death of her brother. And Jesus reacts adequately. In the same way that he answered the confessing Martha with theological words, here his reaction is on the level of feelings and actions. Also the valuation that is expressed with this is in accordance with Jesus' response to the respective method of handling death sensitively but, simultaneously, he criticizes the sisters. Accordingly he reacts "angrily" to Mary's emotional state. The actual meaning of the verb ἐμβριμάομαι can be understood only in this way. A semantic reinterpretation, as if Jesus is only "moved," is to be rejected, based on the other uses of the verb.[40] It is left up to the reader to decide what exactly Jesus' anger refers to. Is it the form of Mary's adoration, which she expresses by falling at his feet and which seems to be just as wrongly placed here as the literal confessions of Martha? Or is it actually her emotional reaction? As Jesus then himself weeps in front of the tomb, emotionality is not principally rejected, but the different verb (δακρύω instead of κλαίω) expresses the fact that one must clearly differentiate between emotional disturbance and debilitating sadness. Crying is acceptable, but purposeless wailing and lamenting is not. Similar to Martha's case, Mary's countenance and faith are not criticized in principle but ultimately they are portrayed as deficient.

5.3 Preliminary Summary: Mary and Martha as Figures of Contrast

Martha and Mary are both introduced as Jesus' "beloved" (11:5). At the same time they are the sisters of the dead man. They both go to meet Jesus outside Bethany. They both greet Jesus with a sentence, identical in its very words (11:21, 32). But here the parallels end. The contrasts between the sisters are emphasized on this very background of parallel frameworks. Martha acts immediately, Mary remains at first in the house. Martha is an individual confessor of faith, Mary is surrounded by other people. Martha enters into a theological dialogue with Jesus, Mary meets Jesus with gestures. Martha clings to terms, Mary to emotions. In all of these actions we can see aspects and forms of faith.

Ultimately, the contrast between the women comes to its climax in the sense of smell. Martha fears, in the face of death, the stench of decomposition: "He reeks already" – this is the way Martha tries to warn Jesus of death (11:39: κύριε, ἤδη ὄζει, τεταρταῖος γάρ ἐστιν – "Lord, he reeks already for it has been four days since he died." In contrast, Mary anoints Jesus' feet so that "the house is filled with the fragrance of the oil" (12:3: ἡ δὲ οἰκία ἐπληρώθη ἐκ τῆς ὀσμῆς τοῦ μύρου). This smell is also placed in relation to death, which is made clear by Jesus' response to Judas: "Leave

---

[40] See Moloney, "Can Everyone be Wrong," 518: "We must allow the verb ἐμβριμάομαι to have its correct meaning. Both the lexical meaning, and the few New Testament uses of the verb (Mark 1:43; 14:5; Matt 9:30), carry an idea of hostility."

her! Let her keep it for the day of my burial!" (12:7) Anyone who has up to now assumed a one-sidedly positive evaluation of Martha must now certainly smell it. The reader's sense of smell is directed in two extremes in the face of Jesus death. While Martha fears the stench of decomposition, the pleasant fragrance of ointment wafts around Mary.

For Martha, death has retained its cruelty, its finality, its stench. Mary, on the other hand, acts correctly according to John 12:2–3 when she prepares Jesus for his burial. But is she a model for faith because of this? Has she truly understood that there can be no glorification without the death of Jesus?[41] How can she now fall down before Jesus, when he has not yet gone through death? Yet if, on the other hand, not only Martha but also Mary remains incomplete in her faith, there arises in the reader a certain perplexity. "Can Everyone be Wrong?"[42]

5.4. Lazarus – Model of True, Living Faith?

It is characteristic that one of the main characters of the narrative remains almost completely unmentioned in the numerous commentaries – Lazarus himself.[43] Certainly the passage owes to him its name as "The resurrection of Lazarus." Nevertheless, he is subsequently degraded in the discussions to a mere add on. In addition to Jesus, the actors are the disciples, Martha, Mary, and the Jews. But where does Lazarus fit? Where and how does he play a role in the story? Lazarus is introduced in 11:1 with the other characters and the opening verses leave no doubt, through the explicit framing, that Lazarus is the main character:

John 11:1–2 Ἦν δέ τις ἀσθενῶν, Λάζαρος ἀπὸ Βηθανίας ... ἧς ὁ ἀδελφὸς Λάζαρος ἠσθένει.
Now a certain man was sick, Lazarus of Bethany... [their] brother Lazarus was sick

The sisters' message places the sick man into a close relationship with Jesus: "Therefore the sisters sent to him, saying, 'Lord, behold, he whom you love is sick.'" (11:3). Jesus loves Lazarus. The motif of love is then confirmed at the end of the exposition when Jesus' love for all three siblings from Bethany is emphasized, although the name of Mary is not mentioned (11:5: Now Jesus loved Martha, and her sister, and Lazarus.).

---

[41] See also Moloney, "Can Everyone be Wrong," 525: "Mary is the first to accept that the illness and death of Lazarus will be the means by which the Son of God will be glorified (11:4). Jesus' supportive explanation of Mary's gesture in v. 7 indicates that, at last, one of the characters in the story has 'got it right.'"

[42] This is the title of the essay by Francis J. Moloney, "Can Everyone be Wrong," 505.

[43] Although, for example, Ludger Schenke discusses all the people and groups of people of the chapter within the framework of his narrative analysis, Lazarus is missing, see Schenke, *Johannes*, 214–17.

Jesus describes Lazarus's sickness as a "sickness not ending in death but for the glory of God." The reader is even more surprised when, in the subsequent dialogue with the disciples (11:11–15), the death of Lazarus is indeed mentioned. Here Jesus expressly calls Lazarus his "friend" (11:11: "Our friend Lazarus [Λάζαρος ὁ φίλος] sleeps, but I go that I may wake him up."). He knows of his death even before anyone can inform him of it (11:13–14: Λάζαρος ἀπέθανεν, "Lazarus is dead"). But Jesus is not saddened by the death of his friend. Paradoxically, he is even happy about it (11:15). Thus the reader learns several things about Lazarus that would seem to be contradictory: Jesus loves him and calls him "friend," but he is not in a hurry to help him in time of need. Lazarus is weak and ill, but his illness should not lead to death. Nevertheless his death is reported. The relationship between Jesus and Lazarus is consequently characterized by a unique tension.

A direct meeting does not occur until 11:38–44. Jesus comes to Lazarus's tomb. He orders that the stone should be rolled away, the stone that seals the tomb, that marks the finality of death. It is possibly also a reminiscence of the first use in this chapter of the term in the verb "to stone," with which Jesus' risk of death was alluded to (11:8).

Then comes Jesus' cry in a loud voice (11:43: "He cried out with a loud voice"). The cry and especially the loud voice (φωνὴ μεγάλη) of Jesus can be understood as a whole, as a key motif of the gospel. Jesus calls to people to follow him, as the parable of John 10:1–5 in the figurative domain of the shepherd impressively expresses.[44] The scene in front of Lazarus's tomb makes reference, beyond this, explicitly to a saying of Jesus in John 5: "Amen, Amen, I say to you, an hour is coming and now is, when the dead shall hear the voice of the Son of God; and those who hear shall live" (5:25; cf. 5:28). The hour of the call for resurrection has arrived. The resurrection takes place in the presence of Jesus in the here and now. The present tense discussion of resurrection (11:25) must consequently be made visible in present time action. Accordingly, Jesus calls Lazarus to come out, and he hears the voice and lives! How significant this cry of Jesus is, can be seen in a last cross-reference to John 11 in 12:17. The short summary of the Lazarus narrative is expressed precisely with the parallelism of "to call" and "to raise" (12:17 ὅτε τὸν Λάζαρον ἐφώνησεν ἐκ τοῦ μνημείου καὶ ἤγειρεν αὐτὸν ἐκ νεκρῶν.). Lazarus is, after all, the one to whom life is being given. No relativizing or deprecatory questions are posed by Jesus here. Lazarus "simply" receives life through Jesus without any words or actions on his side and thus he becomes the prototype of the

---

[44] On John 10:1–5 see Beate Kowalski, "Ruf in die Nachfolge (Vom Hirt und den Schafen) – Joh 10,1–5," in *Kompendium der Gleichnisse Jesu*, 768–80.

person of faith who, in the Johannine sense, correctly believes in the resurrection and thus in Jesus as the giver of life.

5.5 Conclusions: The Faith Development of Martha, Mary, and Lazarus

If, in the three siblings, we see different prototypes of faith, there is a clear progression from Martha to Mary and finally to Lazarus.

Martha believes in the traditional way. She has already believed, she is a courageous confessor, she is not afraid to use weighty theological terminology. However, she remains fearful and hesitant in the application of her faith in concrete situations, in the implementation of the words in the present. She runs the risk of prematurely rejecting the reality and even the necessity of death with set theological phrases. She demonstrates a cognitive, verbal limitation of faith.

Mary, by contrast, is led in her faith by emotions and gestures. She mourns, weeps, wails, and falls down. Jesus indulges her and accepts her confessions of love and faith, as in the anointing of his feet. However, at the same time, he becomes angry at the paralysis this causes. Mary remains at Jesus' feet; she does not learn to stand on her own feet. She demonstrates the risk of an emotional limitation of faith that is in danger of losing itself in emotion and admiration.

However, development from Martha to Mary is visible. While Jesus' brief, negative response to Martha at the tomb demonstrates that her understanding is still incomplete, the re-adoption of Mary in the anointing narrative shows that she has better understood Jesus' perspective on death. Mary does not speak of the "anointed one" (ὁ χριστός) like Martha (11:27), but she truly anoints him. Characteristically, the word for "to raise" (ἀνίστημι) is used not only in the dialogue with Martha (11:22–25) but also with Mary. She herself "arose" and "went out" (11:31: ἀνέστη καὶ ἐξῆλθεν) just as her brother does later. In doing this, she does not, as the Jews mistakenly assume, go to the tomb, but rather she comes to Jesus (11:32). If we assume that, in the artistic narrative, every detail is of importance, we can recognize subtle allusions to the understanding of faith in the precise description of the coming and calling. Martha speaks of "the one who comes" (11:27: ἐρχόμενος), but she cannot wait for Jesus to come to her. In anticipatory activism, she goes to meet Jesus without even hearing a call. Mary hears the "secret" call passed on to her by her sister (11:28) but she also hurries and goes to meet him (11:29: καὶ ἤρχετο πρὸς αὐτόν). Lazarus, in contrast, lets Jesus come to him (11:38; cf. 11:6, 15). He alone hears Jesus' loud call directly. And this alone seems sufficient. For Lazarus is described as briefly as possible. Lazarus distinguishes himself, not through theological terminology like Martha or through emotional devotion like Mary, but through simple action, through the life itself that is born out of death. Martha remains a busy servant and Mary stays at Jesus' feet,[45] but in the end it is Lazarus who reclines with Jesus at the table and shares supper with him (12:2). We gain the impression that he is fulfilling here the prophecy made in 6:54 and 58: He who eats the bread of and with Jesus "is raised up and will live forever."[46] With regard to faith, Martha's eagerness in confession and Mary's proclamation of trust are, in the end, surpassed by Lazarus's missionary impact. By hearing the voice of Jesus, and by receiving life through Jesus, Lazarus becomes the one who ends up bringing others to believe in Jesus (12:11: "because on account of him many of the Jews went away and believed in Jesus.").

6. Epilogue: The Resurrection of Lazarus, of Jesus, and of the Faithful Reader

The resurrection narrative activates a process of understanding. Using the characters as models, readers of John 11 should discover their own position in dealing with death and in their faith in Jesus as the giver of life. Having said this, we can imagine the first audience of the gospel in a situation that impedes this understanding in two ways. On the one hand, they are lamenting the absence of Jesus after his death. On the other hand, there seem to have been deaths in the Johannine community, perhaps of simple community members who have died due to an illness or maybe as a consequence of persecution. However, it may also be the leader of the community or the favorite disciple himself, who, as we can conclude from 21:23, has died, contrary to the expectations of many community members. How should one deal with such a situation? How should one maintain one's faith in (eternal) life in the face of the reality of death?

The Lazarus story invites readers to find analogies between this story and their own situations. The different possibilities that are exhibited through the three siblings from Bethany are ideal-typical models that do not occur in this pure form in reality. They offer the reader possibilities for identification and, each in their own form, they become mirrors in which people can (re-)recognize their own chances and limitations of faith in the face of death. Thus, it is possible for the three siblings to personify in an ideal-typical way aspects that normally only occur in humans as a mixture. They can also mark different phases of the process of coming to terms with

---

[45] John may be drawing here on the Lukan narrative of the hospitality shown to Jesus by the sisters in Bethany (Luke 10:38–42), see the thesis of Thyen, *Erzählung*; idem, *Johannesevangelium*, 510–11.

[46] For an interpretation of "life" in John 6 as a present gift in faith see also Stare, *Durch ihn leben*, 302–10.

death, phases that do not necessarily relate to each other in a linear progression. It is also conceivable that the characters do not refer only to individual models, but are meant to be understood as prototypes for a group of Jesus-followers. This concept has been explored by Philip F. Esler and Ronald A. Piper within the theoretical framework of social identity theory.[47] It is not necessary to commit to a one-sided definition, for in a group model, individual group members also discover their identity by drawing on and demarcating from the prototypical representatives.[48]

Instead, it is the theology offered in John 11 that is decisive for crisis management. Nevertheless, does not the resurrection narrative of Lazarus come across as sheer mockery, as an unbelievable story, if the community truly is being rocked by the deaths of individual members?

In John 11, death is in no way being evened out or negated. On the contrary, the drama and the uncompromising acceptance of the reality of death are described explicitly in many places. The reality of death is brought to the attention of our eyes – or rather our noses, through our sensory perception of the stench of decomposition. Death is not only recognized, it is also, at least on the narrative level, affirmed. Lazarus's illness need not have led to death. It is the declared will of Jesus, his, at first, incomprehensible hesitation (11:6) that has deadly consequences. If Jesus had been there, Lazarus would not have died. This is the unanimous testimony of the two sisters (11:21, 32).

However, Jesus was not there. He deliberately stayed where he was, so that death became inevitable. We can understand this part of the narrative in two ways. First, christologically – even the death of Jesus is inevitable, in order to demonstrate his glorification. Second, sociologically – in my opinion, Esler and Piper assume correctly that "the explanation for the delay lies in John's insistence on the reality of death . . . Death by natural causes and persecution are certainly on the agenda of the evangelist, and even the very closest followers of Jesus are not exempt."[49]

Thus, death becomes a prerequisite, even a necessity, without which the resurrection of Lazarus and thus the glorification of Jesus would not have been possible. In the parallel between the death of Lazarus and that of Jesus it becomes clear that the death of Jesus in its inevitability, in its necessity, should also be explained here.

---

[47] Philip F. Esler and Ronald Piper, *Lazarus, Mary and Martha. Social-Scientific Approaches to the Gospel of John* (Minneapolis: Fortress, 2006), 108–11.

[48] See Esler and Piper, *Lazarus, Mary, and Martha*, 37: "Prototypes and exemplars provide invaluable models for self-categorizations by group members whenever social identity is salient."

[49] Esler and Piper, *Lazarus, Mary, and Martha*, 111.

While Jesus is present during his ministry on earth, there was healing and life among the people. However, the Gospel of John – as has often been described – was written from the perspective of the absent Jesus, the Jesus who has been taken away. This is also the case in John 11. How should the people understand Jesus' message, now that he is no longer on earth in human form? John 11 answers this unambiguously. It is not the bodily presence of Jesus that is decisive. Even during his life, people did not understand him, as we see here with Martha and Mary. The people around Jesus also did not believe, as we are told in the Gospel of John: "But although he had done so many signs before them, they did not believe in him" (12:37).

More definitive than bodily existence is the enduring closeness to the risen Christ, to the faith in Jesus who identifies himself with life and resurrection (11:25) and thus frees Lazarus from death. Anyone who sees in Lazarus only a foretaste of the future resurrection of the dead also misjudges, like Martha, the primacy of the practice and the presence of the resurrection in John 11. According to John 11, resurrection does not take place later, but in the here and now. Paradoxically, it is illness and weakness and ultimately even death that become, for Lazarus, the eye of the needle of true faith. In relation to Jesus, it is his death on the cross, his entrance into the depths of human finitude that ultimately leads to glorification and true life. Lazarus's fate becomes, in the course of the gospel, a model for Jesus' own passion and resurrection. Turning this around, in the Johannine perspective, the cross and Jesus' death, and, according to 11:45–54 even the representative function of this death, have become the prerequisite for the resurrection of Lazarus and ultimately of all the faithful. Limiting the gift of new life to the eschatological resurrection of all faithful would in no way do justice to the concrete present reality of the resurrection as it is demonstrated in the story.

The allusion to Jesus' own death may represent only a "cold comfort" for some mourners in the community of the first audience of John as well as in our present-day community. We long so strongly for very visible signs and concrete proof of a resurrection like that of the historical Lazarus. Instead, all we have is stories about it, and the facts melt away before we can grasp them. However, it is exactly the text-bound narrative hermeneutics of the Lazarus passage that allow us, still today, to enter into the story and be given new life. Anyone who searches in the Lazarus passage for historical facts about the resurrection remains caught in the crypt of the unrestorable past. Anyone who separates the resurrection of Lazarus as "revivification" from the future "resurrection"[50] fears the possibly of the

---

[50] See on this linguistic differentiation Esler and Piper, *Lazarus, Mary, and Martha*, 1 n. 1.

unpleasant smell of the radicality of the gospel. Those, however, who, in the act of reading, let themselves be drawn into the challenges and encouragement of the present reality of Jesus in writing and faith can, regardless of when death may enter into their lives, experience the counterfactual reality of life.[51] A life that will exist not before or on the other side of death, but in spite of death and through death. No tomb can be so tightly sealed that the voice of Jesus can not enter it and call us out to a new life that cannot be destroyed by any form of death (see 11:26).

---

[51] On this hermeneutical understanding of the "reality of resurrection" with respect to the semiotic of C. S. Peirce see Stefan Alkier, "Die Realität der Auferstehung," in *Theologie zwischen Pragmatismus und Existenzdenken. Festschrift für Hermann Deuser zum 60. Geburtstag* (ed. G. Linde et al.; Marburger Theologische Studien 90, Marburg 2006), 339–59; idem, *Die Realität der Auferweckung* (NET 12; Tübingen: Francke, 2008).

Chapter 5

Jesus' Resurrection in the Farewell Discourses

Jean Zumstein

1. Introduction

The central question of the Farewell Discourses (John 13:31–16:33) can be formulated as follows: How is the Absentee present? How can the one who has returned to the Father establish a relationship with the disciples, who have remained in the world? This questioning leads to an intensive reflection on the interpretation of Jesus' death and the positive, productive nature of his departure. But simultaneously – and this aspect is often neglected – not only is the departure of Jesus subject to interpretation but also his Easter coming, in other words, his resurrection. If this perspective is correct, how should we deal with Jesus' resurrection in the two Farewell Discourses?

I suggest that we proceed in three steps: The first is of a hermeneutical nature. On one hand, we have to identify the hermeneutical perspective that dominates the Farewell Discourses and especially their retrospective or post-Easter point of view (1.1). On the other hand, particular attention has to be given to the question of narrative time and specifically to the Easter prolepses (1.2). Both the point of view as well as the matter of narrative time indicate that the Easter topic shapes the two discourses in their entirety. The second step lies in the exegesis of two passages, despite controversy about their interpretation. One passage (John 14:18–26) expounds in an original way the implied author's interpretation of the traditional faith in Jesus' resurrection (2). The other passage (John 16:16–22) attempts to link Easter faith to the life experience of the Johannine believers (3). The third and final step brings together the results of the analysis, which was developed on several levels, and outlines the Johannine conception of Jesus' resurrection (4).

1.1 The Hermeneutical Horizon of the Farewell Discourses

We begin with a hermeneutical observation. The Fourth Gospel looks back at the story of Jesus from a post-Easter perspective.[1] At first glance this may seem to be an insignificant remark, but attentive reading reveals that the implied author has clearly articulated his point of view. In the first part of the gospel there are proleptic statements about how the disciples will remember what Jesus did (2:22; 12:16). There are also prolepses that anticipate things that will occur outside of the scope of the narrative.[2] These are ways in which the difference between the time before and the time after the resurrection is consciously articulated. Moreover, the gospel is framed by a paratext, consisting of the prologue (1:1–18) and the conclusion of the gospel (20:30–31). This reveals how the story of the incarnate Christ is understood as a whole, which is the way the completed story will function for the reader.

The Farewell Discourses share the same perspective. In the narrative sequence these discourses precede the arrest, trial and, execution. Yet the speaker is simultaneously Jesus on the day before his death and the risen Lord. These aspects of his identity form an indissoluble unity. This fusing of horizons[3] is particularly evident in the way the implied author uses verbal forms. Although the passion has not begun yet, he uses the aorist and perfect tenses when speaking about the revelation and even about the cross. Nevertheless, he can also utilize the future and present tenses when describing the post-Easter period. Such modes of expression point to a stereoscopic point of view.[4]

> The examples supporting this thesis are numerous. In 13:31–32 the glorification is described simultaneously as having already happened (ἐδοξάσθη) and as about to happen (δοξάσει). In 14:9 the revelation, i.e., seeing the Father in the Son, is expressed in the perfect tense (ὁ ἑωρακὼς ἐμὲ ἑώρακεν τὸν πατέρα). In 14:12 and 28 the return of the Son to the Father is described as a present event (ὅτι ἐγὼ πρὸς τὸν πατέρα πορεύομαι). In 14:17 the Spirit represents a present reality (γινώσκετε, μένει). In 14:18 the Easter coming of Christ is expressed in the present tense (ἔρχομαι),[5] and

---

[1] Jean Zumstein, "Mémoire et relecture pascale," in *Miettes exégétiques* (MoBi 25; Genève: Labor et Fides, 1991), 299–316.

[2] R. Alan Culpepper, *Anatomy of the Fourth Gospel. A Study in Literary Design* (Philadelphia: Fortress, 1983), 67; see the external historic prolepses, which are not yet fulfilled (10:16; 11:52; 12:32).

[3] Hans-Georg Gadamer, *Vérité et méthode. Les grandes lignes d'une herméneutique philosophique* (L'ordre philosophique; Paris: Seuil, 1976), 328–29.

[4] Culpepper, *Anatomy of the Fourth Gospel*, 33.

[5] For the meaning of the present tense in connection with verbs of movement for a future statement see Friedrich Blass, Albert Debrunner, and Friedrich Rehkopf, *Grammatik des neu-testamentlichen Griechisch* (Göttingen: Vandenhoeck & Ruprecht, 1976), § 323.3.

by a future tense in 14:23 (ἐλευσόμεθα). In 14:19 the seeing by the disciples and the non-seeing by the world is described as something present, as is the life that is connected to the Easter coming of Christ (ὁ κόσμος με οὐκέτι θεωρεῖ, ὑμεῖς δὲ θεωρεῖτέ με ὅτι ἐγὼ ζῶ καὶ ὑμεῖς ζήσετε). In 14:25 the Johannine Christ looks at his work of revelation from a retrospective point of view, although the passion has not begun yet (ταῦτα λελάληκα ὑμῖν παρ' ὑμῖν μένων).

In 14:28 the revelation belongs to the past (ἠκούσατε ὅτι ἐγὼ εἶπον ὑμῖν), as it does in 14:29, where the pre-Easter period is said to be completed (καὶ νῦν εἴρηκα). The whole passage about the vine refers to the post-Easter relationship of the disciple with his Lord. Moreover in 15:9 and 12 the love of Christ for his own is described as an event fulfilled in the past, even though the cross has not yet occurred in the order of the story. John 15:15 places the revelation in the past (πάντα ἃ ἤκουσα παρὰ τοῦ πατρός μου ἐγνώρισα ὑμῖν; see also 15:11: ταῦτα λελάληκα ὑμῖν). The same is true of the election of the disciples in 15:16 (οὐχ ὑμεῖς με ἐξελέξασθε, ἀλλ' ἐγὼ ἐξελεξάμην ὑμᾶς καὶ ἔθηκα ὑμᾶς; see also 15:19). The epoch described in 15:18–16:4a is undoubtedly a post-Easter period (see, for example, 15:18, where a distinction is made between the time of Jesus and the time of the disciples; 15:20, where the persecution of Jesus is placed in the past [εἰ ἐμὲ ἐδίωξαν]). The same perspective appears in 15:22, where the work of revelation is reflected in retrospect (εἰ μὴ ἦλθον and καὶ ἐλάλησα αὐτοῖς; the same phenomenon in 16:6), whereas the hour of separation marks the present (16:6). Even the Farewell Discourses belong to the past (16:6): The well-known saying in 16:16 structures the time before and after the resurrection (μικρὸν καὶ οὐκέτι θεωρεῖτέ με, καὶ πάλιν μικρὸν καὶ ὄψεσθέ με). Here the time of sorrow after separation (16:22) is described in the present and the time of the pre-Easter revelation is expressed by the past tense (16:25: λελάληκα ὑμῖν and 16:27: ὑμεῖς ἐμὲ πεφιλήκατε καὶ πεπιστεύκατε ὅτι ἐγὼ παρὰ [τοῦ] θεοῦ ἐξῆλθον; 16:28: ἐξῆλθον παρὰ τοῦ πατρὸς καὶ ἐλήλυθα εἰς τὸν κόσμον· πάλιν ἀφίημι τὸν κόσμον καὶ πορεύομαι πρὸς τὸν πατέρα – although the passion has not begun yet!). The perspective of 16:32 (ἰδοὺ ἔρχεται ὥρα καὶ ἐλήλυθεν) is again stereoscopic. Finally 16:33 describes the present time as a time of sorrow for the disciples (post-resurrection period!), whereas the hour of victory over the world, which happens at the cross (νενίκηκα τὸν κόσμον), already belongs to the past.

1.2 The Easter Prolepses of the Farewell Discourses

The topic of Jesus' resurrection appears in a completely different way. The narrative analysis has drawn attention to the significance of narrative time. The first two Farewell Discourses are characterized by several Easter prolepses; i.e., internal prolepses that are fulfilled in chapter 20.[6] In other words: In the Farewell Discourses the Johannine Christ announces his Easter coming and expresses its meaning. Then, what the Farewell Discourses announce on the day before the crucifixion actually comes to pass in chapter 20, in the stories of the empty tomb and the resurrection appearances. Let us note a few examples.

---

[6] Jean Zumstein, *Kreative Erinnerung: Relecture und Auslegung im Johannesevangelium* (2d ed.; AThANT 84; Zürich: Theologischer Verlag, 2004), 284–85.

The most significant question asked in both Farewell Discourses concerns to the departure of the Son. His absence causes tears and mourning for the disciples (16:20). The episode of the empty tomb and the absence of the body form the narrative image of this absence. Mary Magdalene's tears at the entrance to the tomb are the expression of the pain felt by the disciples. Non-seeing is followed by seeing, the departure is followed by a coming: The movement of the first Farewell Discourse also shows how the departure of the revealer is the prerequisite for his return, as is explicitly announced in 14:18. This new coming of the revealer occurs in the form of seeing at Easter (14:19), and this Easter seeing causes the movement from grief to joy (16:20–22). It is this movement from grief to joy, which is caused by seeing the risen Christ, that Mary Magdalene and the group of disciples experience. The connection between the Easter coming of the risen Christ and the gift of the Spirit is made by Christ himself in the first Farewell Discourse, when he assosciates his Easter coming with the coming of the Spirit (14:19–24.25–26). Now this prolepse is fulfilled in the appearance of the risen Christ to his disciples, which reaches its climax in the giving of the Spirit (20:22). The sending of the disciples, which follows the Father's sending of Jesus, is announced in 17:18 and then realized in 20:21. The promise of Jesus' return to the Father, which establishes a new relationship between the disciples and Jesus (15:14–16), is realized in 20:17 in the encounter of the risen Christ with Mary Magdalene.[7]

The conclusion is obvious: The Johannine Easter story is the narrative counterpart to 14:18–26 and its recapitulation in 16:16–22. Whereas the discourse of Christ taking leave of his disciples characterizes the time of Easter and its theological characteristics, chapter 20 shows how this promise has been realized. Therefore chapter 20 must be read in the light of the Farewell Discourses (see 14:18–26 and its recapitulation in 16:16–22).

1.3 Two Controversial Passages

Finally, we turn to two passages: one in the first (14:18–26) and the other in the second Farewell Discourse (16:16–22). Their interpretation is disputed, but they seem to point directly to the theme of Jesus' resurrection and to give an interpretation of it. Before we go into details, three preliminary remarks ought to be made:

First, despite the debate concerning the structure of the first Farewell Discourse,[8] the inclusio found in 14:1–3 and 14:27b–28 seems clearly to

---

[7] The analysis could be pursued in order to show how the announced post-Easter period, which was presented in 14:12 as qualitatively superior and in 14:22–24 as inaccessible for the world, is now realized in chapter 20: The disciples are taking part in a new situation from which the world is excluded.

[8] See Andreas Dettwiler, *Die Gegenwart des Erhöhten. Eine exegetische Studie zu den johanneischen Abschiedsreden (Joh 13:31–16:33) unter besonderer Berücksichtigung ihres Relecture-Charakters* (FRLANT 169; Göttingen: Vandenhoeck & Ruprecht, 1995), 112–21; Christian Dietzfelbinger, *Der Abschied des Kommenden. Eine Auslegung der johanneischen Abschiedsreden* (WUNT 95; Tübingen: Mohr Siebeck,

indicate that the departure and the coming again of Christ represent the main axis of the speech.⁹ Thus, particular attention must be paid to the summary that is given as a conclusion (14:28a): ἠκούσατε ὅτι ἐγὼ εἶπον ὑμῖν· ὑπάγω καὶ ἔρχομαι πρὸς ὑμᾶς. Second one of the most important semantic lines results from the verbs that show movement.¹⁰ The double movement described by the verbs ὑπάγειν/πορεύεσθαι and ἔρχεσθαι is especially rich in meaning: It determines the tone of the whole discourse (13:33, 36; 14:2, 3, 4, 5, 6, 12, 18, 23, 28) and recounts the way of the Johannine Christ. Third, the thesis that the first Farewell Discourse not only reflects on the significance of Christ's death before the beginning of the passion story, but also on the significance of his resurrection, seems quite plausible. This would mean that the Christian kerygma itself would stand in the center of the Johannine Christ's discourse.¹¹

To this first perspective we want to add another: The second text we must consider (16:16–22) is related to the first. Whatever theory one advocates concerning the origin of the Farewell Discourses, the order of the reading compels the reader to connect the motif of the μικρόν, which structures 16:16–22 (see vv. 16, 17, 19) with 14:19. One has to take particular notice of the fact that the dialogue between Jesus and his disciples in chapter 16 is devoted to the detailed explanation of this motif. The implication of this observation – provided the argumentative coherence in the Farewell Discourses is not entirely denied – is that if the μικρόν in the first Farewell Discourse treats the Easter Topic, it will hardly be different in chapter 16. But does the motif of the ἔρχεσθαι really point to the Jesus' resurrection? We now want to devote ourselves to this question.

1997), 15, 70–71; Jörg Frey, *Die johanneische Eschatologie III* (WUNT 117; Tübingen: Mohr Siebeck, 2000), 119–22; Hans-Ulrich Weidemann, *Der Tod Jesu im Johannesevangelium* (BZNW 122; Berlin and New York: de Gruyter 2004), 79–85.

⁹ See the key words that mentioned at the beginning of the discourse and again at the end: ταράσσειν, πιστεύειν/ὑπάγειν, πορεύεσθαι, ἔρχεσθαι. In the same way C. K. Barrett, *The Gospel according to St. John* (2d ed.; Cambridge: Cambridge University Press, 1978), 455.

¹⁰ See the survey in Dettwiler, *Die Gegenwart des Erhöhten*, 114.

¹¹ See Michael Theobald, "Der johanneische Osterglaube und die Grenzen seiner narrativen Mitteilung (Joh 20)," in *Von Jesus zu Christus. Christologische Studien* (ed. Rudolf Hoppe; BZNW 93; Berlin and New York: de Gruyter, 1998), 93–123, esp. 93–94.

2. "The Coming of Christ" in the First Farewell Discourse

2.1 Easter or the Parousia?

In recent exegetical discussion, it is debated whether the coming of Christ in 14:18 refers to the Easter event[12] or the Parousia.[13] This question is legitimate, since certain expressions in the passage are ambiguous[14] (see,

---

[12] For support for the hypothesis of the Easter coming of Christ see Julius Wellhausen, *Das Evangelium Johannis* (Berlin: Reimer, 1908), 67; Wilhelm Heitmüller, *Das Johannes-evangelium* (SNT 4; Göttingen, 1918), 9–184, here 151; Alfred Loisy, *Le quatrième Évangile* (2d ed.; Paris: Picard, 1921), 411; Marie-Joseph Lagrange, *Évangile selon Saint Jean* (Paris: Gabalda, 1927), 385; Rudolf Bultmann, *Das Evangelium des Johannes* (19th ed.; KEK 2; Göttingen: Vandenhoeck und Ruprecht, 1968; orig. 1941), 478–79 (with the following emphasis: "Das Besondere dieser Verheißung bei Joh und an dieser Stelle ist aber dieses, dass die Ostererfahrung als Erfüllung der Parusieerwartung verstanden wird, wie es schon 16:20–22 der Fall war"; C. H. Dodd, *L'interprétation du quatrième Évangile* (LD 82; Paris: Cerf, 1975), 511 (giving up the traditional eschatology and stressing the presence of the living Lord for his own after his death); Barrett, *The Gospel according to St. John*, 455, 464 (who empha-sises the giving up of the apocalyptic register to describe the coming of Christ in its different forms); Raymond E. Brown, *The Gospel according to John II* (AB 29A; New York: Double-day, 1970), 646 (it is not only about Easter appearances of a limited duration, but about the permanent presence of Christ after Easter, which is connected with the presence of the Spirit); Rudolf Schnackenburg, *Das Johannesevangelium III* (HThK 4/3; Freiburg: Herder, 1975), 88–90; Barnabas Lindars, *The Gospel of John* (NCB; London: Oliphants, 1972), 480–81; Josef Blank, *Das Evangelium nach Johannes* (2d ed. Geistliche Schriflesung.NT 4/2; Düsseldorf: Patmos, 1986), 111–12; George R. Beasley-Murray, *John* (WBC 36; Waco: Word, 1987), 258–59; Jürgen Becker, *Das Evangelium nach Johannes II* (3d ed.; ÖTK 4/2; Gütersloh: Gerd Mohn – Echter, 1991), 557–58; Xavier Léon-Dufour, *Lecture de l'Évangile selon Jean III* (Parole de Dieu; Paris: Seuil, 1993), 123; Dettwiler, *Die Gegenwart des Erhöhten*, 191–95; Dietzfelbinger, *Der Abschied des Kommenden*, 53–57; Ulrich Wilckens, *Das Evangelium nach Johannes* (NTD 4; Göttingen: Vandenhoeck & Ruprecht, 1998), 229; Klaus Scholtissek, *In ihm sein und bleiben. Die Sprache der Immanenz in den johanneischen Schriften* (HBS 21; Freiburg: Herder, 2000), 260; D. Moody Smith, *John* (ANTC; Nashville: Abingdon, 1999), 275; Klaus Wengst, *Das Johannesevangelium II* (TKNT 4/2; Stuttgart: Kohlhammer, 2001), 127–28 (Easter interpretation emphasizing the post-resurrection presence of Christ); Theobald, "Der johanneische Osterglaube," 96; Esther Straub, *Kritische Theologie ohne ein Wort vom Kreuz. Zum Verhältnis von Joh 1–12 und 13–20* (FRLANT 203; Göttingen: Vandenhoeck & Ruprecht, 2003), 199; Weidemann, *Der Tod Jesu im Johannesevangelium*, 176–77.

[13] See Theodor Zahn, *Das Evangelium des Johannes* (5th–6th ed.; KNT 4; Leipzig: Deichert, 1921), 568; Udo Schnelle, "Die Abschiedsreden im Johannesevangelium," ZNW 80 (1989): 64–79, 68–69; idem, *Das Evangelium nach Johannes* (3d ed.; THKNT 4; Leipzig: Evangelische Verlagsanstalt, 2004), 256.

[14] See Barrett, *The Gospel according to St. John*, 464; Wengst, *Das Johannesevangelium II*; 128; Frey, *Die johanneische Eschatologie III*, 164–78, defends a position that

for example, ἔρχεσθαι[15] or the expression ἐν ἐκείνῃ τῇ ἡμέρᾳ). In addition, the assertions of the text can change their sense depending on whether they are interpreted as referring to the internal narrative logic of the text or to the post-Easter situation of the reader.[16] Moreover, one can not exclude the possibility that the implied author plays with a certain ambiguity to increase the potential meaning of the text.

Even if one has to beware of passing categorical judgments, a careful study of the text most strongly supports the Easter hypothesis. Let us now have a look at the arguments.

a) The literary context of the first Farewell Discourse clearly shows that the problem of separation that is mentioned in 14:18 refers to the absence caused by Christ's death (13:33, 36; 14:5, 12) and not to the time separating Easter from the Parousia.

b) The μικρόν in 14:19 can only refer to the cross and therefore to Jesus' ascension to the Father. In this way the non-seeing by the world,[17] in contrast to the seeing by the disciples,[18] becomes clear. On the other hand, in early Christianity, the Parousia hope assumes that Jesus will be seen by the world for judgement as well as by believers for salvation (5:28–29). The seeing of the disciples is an Easter seeing (θεωρεῖν see 20:6, 12, 14). This interpretation is confirmed by the causal clause that completes 14:20

---

unites both possibilities: 14:18 is a traditional logion referring to the Parousia, but its contextualisation made an assertion out of it, referring to the present experience of the post-resurrection community and describing the spiritual presence of Christ with his own.

[15] John is the only one to use the verb ἔρχεσθαι in the stories of the Easter appearances (see 20:19, 24).

[16] This aspect was especially emphasized by Schnelle, *Das Evangelium nach Johannes*, 256, and Frey, *Die johanneische Eschatologie III*, 164, who put a special accent on the context of the external communication, i.e., the community of readers (= the Johannine communities).

[17] The fact that in our passage the "world" is excluded from the life created by the Easter turn, is a consequent expression of the Johannine dualism. But the fact itself that such an idea is already presupposed shows that it concerns the post-Easter period and not the Parousia. The dualism indeed results from the coming of the revealer and from the confrontation of the world with the revelation.

[18] The verb θεωρεῖν was used in 14:17, where it designates the non-seeing of the world. The antithesis between the world's inability to see the Spirit and the disciples' ability to recognize it is again discussed in 14:19, where the non-seeing of the world is the opposite of the seeing of the disciples. This parallelism clearly indicates that the focus of attention lies on the post-Easter period and not on the date of the Parousia (see Christina Hoegen-Rohls, *Der nachösterliche Johannes. Die Abschiedsreden als hermeneutischer Schlüssel zum vierten Evangelium* [WUNT II/84; Tübingen: Mohr Siebeck, 1996], 108–9). On the parallelism between 15–17 and 18–21 see Brown, *The Gospel according to John II*, 644–45; Dettwiler, *Die Gegenwart des Erhöhten*, 180, 191.

and uses the related term of life (ζῆν): The fact that Christ is represented as living, results from the Easter event and not from the Parousia.[19]

c) The argument that the expression ἐν ἐκείνῃ τῇ ἡμέρᾳ (14:20) describes the Parousia (16:23, 26; see Matt 7:22; Luke 10:12) is questionable, too, because in the Fourth Gospel the *terminus technicus* describing the last day is ἐν τῇ ἐσχάτῃ ἡμέρᾳ (John 6:39, 40, 44, 54; 11:24; 12:48).

d) The extension of the reciprocal immanence formula to the disciples (14:20) is a prolepse, which finds its fulfilment in the meeting between the risen Christ and Mary Magdalene (see 20:17, where for the first time in the Johannine story, Jesus' Father becomes the Father of the disciples).

e) John 14:21a clearly shows that the period of time under consideration is not the time initiated by the Parousia but the post-Easter period – the period during which the disciple is called to live the commandements of Christ and to keep them (ὁ ἔχων τὰς ἐντολάς μου καὶ τηρῶν αὐτάς). In addition, 14:21b shows that the time experienced by the disciples equals the time of revelation, when God's love is communicated through Christ.

f) The event of revelation that is announced in 14:21 (ἐμφανίζειν) does not describe the appearance of Christ at the Parousia because this appearance is inaccessible to the world, as is shown by Judas's objection in 14:22. The fact that the world does not perceive the resurrection appearance of Christ is a classic objection raised in non-Christian polemic, which expresses doubts about the reality of Jesus' resurrection.[20]

g) John 14:23 describes the historic existence of the disciples: The common presence of Christ and God in the life of the disciple[21] is again linked with the love of Christ and with the keeping of his word. This interpretation is confirmed by 14:24, which expresses the opposite possibility of unbelief. This refers exclusively to the time of faith and thus to the post-Easter period.

h) If the implied author argues in a coherent way, then the second saying about the Paraclete (14:25–26) unquestionably indicates that the period of time in 14:18–24 refers to the historic existence of the post-resurrection disciple.

The conclusion seems clear: In 14:18–26 the focus is on Jesus' resurrection and the Easter experience, the beneficiary of which is the

---

[19] See Luke 24:5.23; Mark 16:11; Acts 1:3; Rev 1:18.

[20] See the material collected by Dietzfelbinger, *Der Abschied des Kommenden*, 60–61.

[21] John 14:23 uses ἔρχομαι in the future. This verb can already be found in 14:18. In 14:23 it clearly relates to the post-Easter existence of the disciples. Is it possible to assume that this event is not connected to 14:18?!

disciple. If this is true, then what is the interpretation of the Easter event represented in this passage?

2.2 The Johannine Interpretation of the Jesus' Resurrection

2.2.1 The Semantic Fields in 14:18–24

As the metaphor of the orphan suggests (14:18), the problem caused by the departure of Jesus is the one of a broken relationship.[22] The argument developed in 14:18–26 aims to describe how this broken relationship can be restored. Thanks to the Easter theme, the implied author is able to show that the Absentee is present and that the Crucified is living. This restoration of the relationship between the disciple and his master is expressed by referring to different semantic fields:

– John 14:18 uses spatial vocabulary (the terminology is again taken up in 14:23): The departure is followed by the coming.

– In 14:19 the spatial vocabulary is replaced by the language of seeing (θεωρέω).[23] The coming of 14:18 is fulfilled in a seeing that bears witness to the life of the departed Christ.

– In 14:20 this seeing turns into a knowing (γινώσκω), the content of which is the reciprocal immanence of Father and Son and its extension to the disciples. This extended reciprocal immanence formula is again taken up in the motif of the mutual coming of Father and Son (14:23).

– The restored relationship, represented by the observance of the commandments, is realized in a relationship of love (14:21; ἀγαπάω), which reaches its climax in a revelation accessible only to the disciples.

– In 14:22–24 we do not find new concepts, but a restatement of 14:18–21.[24]

This sequence of different semantic fields should not be perceived as an addition of different independent motifs. On the contrary, our hypothesis suggests that this sequence constitutes an argumentative process that aims at showing what the implied author understood as the Easter event. This argumentative process requires now our attention.

---

[22] On the crisis and the end of the pre-Easter relationship of the disciple with his Lord, see 13:36–38.

[23] The two occurences of the verb θεωρέω are in the present tense. They are followed by a twofold occurrence of the verb ζάω; one stands in the present and the other in the future. The seeing on the part of the disciples and that of the living Lord are presented as events that are bound to happen in a near future, which will create life for the disciples. In the gospel of John the life granted to the disciple is not an event linked to the Parousia, but a dimension of existence in faith. The conclusion is obvious: Easter is the topic of 14:19.

[24] See Hermann Strathmann, *Das Evangelium nach Johannes* (NTD 4; Göttingen: Vandenhoeck & Ruprecht, 1951), 203; Scholtissek, *In ihm sein und bleiben*, 266.

2.2.2 The Argumentation

The first conceptual change occurs in the transition from 14:18b to 14:19. The imminent and certain coming of Christ to his own, who were separated from their Lord by his death/exaltation, takes shape in the seeing granted to the disciples – and not to the world – and this results from the fact that the Crucified is living. The soteriological correlate of this christological thesis is that this event of seeing implies a promise of life for the disciples. This notion of the Easter event is common in early Christianity.[25]

The second conceptual jump occurs in the movement from 14:19 to 14:20. The experience of seeing, which is the privilege of the earthly circle of Jesus' disciples (see the intratextual communication's context of the Farewell Discourses), is elucidated by an act of knowing.[26] In this way a category is introduced that allows a broader access to the Easter experience. As the "seeing" turns into a "knowing," the relationship with the living Christ is not only reserved for the circle of disciples gathered for the Last Supper, but it becomes an option accessible to every believer. The formulation of the content of this knowledge makes up the Johannine Easter message: It deals with the reciprocal immanence formula, but – and this is the new element – this formula is extended to the disciples (see 2:23).

The movement from 14:21 to 14:22 is characterized by the introduction of the motifs "to keep the commandments" and "to love the risen Christ." This is the way the necessary condition for the disciple's participation in the Easter experience is formulated. Three remarks are appropriate here:

a) First of all, what 14:20 was suggesting, is confirmed: The widening of the Easter experience is completed. The condition expressed in 14:21a not only refers to the disciples present at the Last Supper, but can be practiced by every believer (ὁ ἐκεῖνος). b) Moreover, access to the Easter experience is conditioned by the disciple's love for Jesus, a love consisting of the reception and practice of the revealer's words. The demand to be fulfilled is not primarily of an ethical nature, but originates in the unconditioned acceptance of Christ and his message. c) Finally, this concrete love for Christ has a double consequence: On the one hand it opens access to God, and on the other hand the believer is given Christ's love, which consists of his appearance. The reader will realize that here two threads of argumentation are combined with each other. One thread considers the indissoluble unity of the relationship between the Father and the Son, which has already been announced in the theme of reciprocal immanence;

---

[25] See, e.g., 1 Cor 15:20–28; Rom 4:23–24.

[26] The reference to non-seeing by the world as well as the seeing by the disciples is in the present tense. The announcement of the act of knowing is in the future tense.

the other thread concerns the manifestation (14:21–22) anticipated in the seeing (14:19).

As already mentioned, 14:23–24 respond to the objection of Judas and are a restatement of 14:18–21.

The objection by Judas takes up the motif of the "manifestation (ἐμφανίζω[27]) of Christ," which is understood in the light of the Easter event and not the Parousia. The argument is a classic motif of the ancient polemic against the resurrection. The non-visibility of Christ's resurrection makes the world doubt its credibility. This objection is refuted in 14:24, which again takes up the argument of 14:21: Only those in a loving relationship with Christ, i.e., those who keep his word, receive the divine love. At the same time, the reader may notice an interesting difference between 14:21 and 14:23, in the formulation of the end of the argument. Whereas the last part of 14:21 says that Christ's love for his own will be realized in his imminent appearance, the end of 14:23 mentions the mutual coming of the Father and the Son to the disciple in order to make their home with him. These two assertions are not contradictory. On the contrary, by taking up two different points of view, they express the same Easter experience. Two elements need to be pointed out: a) The gain resulting from the Easter coming of Christ consists in the restoration of a relationship characterized by closeness; b) The meaning of the Son's coming – his appearance – is strictly theological: It should not be separated from the coming of the Father. This indissoluble relationship between the Son and the Father is emphasized in 14:24 and is the negative correlate of 14:23. This verse indeed, by its use of the terminology of sending, claims that the rejection of the revelation (i.e., the words of Christ) corresponds to a rejection of the Father (i.e., a rejection of God).

2.2.3 The Johannine Easter Gospel

In our opinion, the implied author defends a conception of Christ's resurrection that was common throughout early Christianity. The crisis for the disciples that is caused by the death of Jesus – or, in Johannine language, by the departure of Christ – is overcome by his Easter coming; that is, by the resurrection appearances to his own (θεωρεῖν). These appearances of the risen Christ reveal him as the living one. The revelation of the living Christ is a factor in the life of the disciples insofar as it restores the relationship that is interrupted at the cross. In the Fourth Gospel the relationship to Christ and the gift of life are interdependent.

The specifically theological shaping of the passage by the implied author is expressed by the argument of 14:20–21, which is reassumed and

---

[27] Detailed analysis of this expression by Dettwiler, *Die Gegenwart des Erhöhten*, 196.

reformulated in 14:23–24. Two aspects of this interpretation's work especially need to be pointed out.

On the one hand, the relevance of the resurrection appearances appears in a new light. Admittedly, the context of the intratextual communication is taken into consideration, since those addressed by the appearances are the companions of Jesus, who shared a last supper with him. But the transition from the topic of seeing to the topic of knowing, followed by the transition from knowing to "keeping the commandments" and "love," widens the group of potential recipients of resurrection appearances. The encounter with the living Christ is no longer a privilege reserved to a limited circle, but an opportunity offered to any believer in the post-Easter era.[28] From a Johannine perspective, one cannot make a sharp distinction between the appearances of the resurrected Christ and the post-Easter period, since the implied author shows that they are in continuity with each other.

On the other hand, the implied author does make a transition from seeing to knowing (14:20) with respect to the reception of the revelation (14:21). Therefore, it is important to consider the content that is associated with the Easter coming of Christ. In our opinion, the major Johannine statement points to the reciprocal immanence formula that is extended to the disciples. What is gained through Easter consists of a new relationship to God. Whereas the first part of the gospel demonstrated that the reciprocal immanence of the Father and the Son is the center of the revelation, the Easter event allows the disciple to participate in this fundamental relationship. Nevertheless, the disciple has no direct access to God, as Scholtissek correctly noted.[29] The believer is in a close relationship with God insofar as he "loves" Christ. This theocentric conception of the Easter event is corroborated by 14:21, where the Father's love towards the disciple and the manifestation of the Son in the disciple go hand in hand, as well as in 14:23 with the well known motif of the Father and the Son coming to the disciple to make their home with him. One must point out that the encounter of the resurrected Christ with Mary Magdalene – with the well-known statement in 20:17 – confirms this interpretation.

2.2.4 The Second Saying about the Paraclete

The status of the second saying about the Paraclete has often caused problems. For some it is an assertion with no perceptible connection to the

---

[28] This point of view was strongly pointed out by Dietzfelbinger, *Der Abschied des Kommenden*, 76–78. This view is also shared by Becker, *Das Evangelium nach Johannes II*, 558; Dettwiler, *Die Gegenwart des Erhöhten*, 199.

[29] See Scholtissek, *In ihm sein und bleiben*, 260–64.

preceding verses; for others the living Christ and the Paraclete represent one and the same reality (see the famous statement of Heitmüller: "Im Geist kommt Jesus zu den Seinen").[30] A well-grounded interpretation of 14:25–26 is based on the following two arguments, which seem decisive:

On the one hand, these verses must be understood within the argumentative context of the first Farewell Discourse. The fact that the passage about "Christ's coming" is framed by two sayings about the Paraclete is not a coincidence but the deliberate intention of the implied author. This is supported by the often-noted structural parallel between 14:15–17 and 18–21. Also note that 14:25–26 differentiates clearly between the pre- and post-Easter period, and brings up the problem of the interpretation of Christ's words by dealing again with a main aspect of 14:21 (ἐντολή) and 14:23–24 (λόγος).

On the other hand – as J. Frey[31] rightly points out – the risen Christ should not simply be equated with the Paraclete. The implied author always portrays them as two different persons.[32] The wording of 14:26 (ὁ δὲ παράκλητος, τὸ πνεῦμα τὸ ἅγιον, ὃ πέμψει ὁ πατὴρ ἐν τῷ ὀνόματί μου), by reverting to the terminology of sending, clearly shows the perspective taken by the implied author. The incarnate Son represents the Father among human beings and represents him entirely, despite being different from him, and the Paraclete is likewise sent from the Father in order to represent the Son among the disciples during the post-resurrection period.

John 14:26 indicates how one must imagine this representative role of the incarnate Son (see 14:25, a clear reference to the earthly work of Christ) and the risen Christ (ἐν τῷ ὀνόματί μου). The mission of the Paraclete is a double one, but – and this fact is remarkable – it constantly refers to the word of Christ. The first task consists in the teaching of everything (διδάξει πάντα). The content of this comprehensive teaching is clearly defined (epexegetical καί); it consists of the anamnesis of the words of the earthly Jesus. The Paraclete is the architect of memory – he brings to mind the incarnated Christ's revelation among the disciples, as well as for the interpreter – and he interprets the revelation that occurred in the past in terms significant for the present. This remembrance is therefore productive; it results in a creative teaching.

---

[30] Heitmüller, *Das Johannesevangelium*, 151. The same perspective is shared by Bultmann, *Das Evangelium des Johannes*, 477 ("Eben im Kommen des Geistes kommt er [= Jesus] selbst") and also by Becker, *Das Evangelium nach Johannes II*, 558 ("Der lebendige Christus wird als Geist erfahren").

[31] Frey, *Die johanneische Eschatologie III*, 175–76.

[32] On the Paraclete as a distinct person see Takashi Onuki, *Gemeinde und Welt im Johannesevangelium* (WMANT 56; Neukirchen: Neukirchener Verlag, 1984), 72–76, followed by Dettwiler, *Die Gegenwart des Erhöhten*, 204.

3. The Coming of Christ in the Second Farewell Discourse (16:16–22)

3.1 Easter or the Parousia?

The interpretation of 16:16–22 is also disputed. For some, the first μικρόν refers to the death of Jesus and the second to Easter, whereas for others the first μικρόν is an allusion to the return to the Father and to his absence during the post-Easter period and the second μικρόν designates the Parousia. In recent research, both the Easter thesis[33] and the Parousia thesis[34] are vigorously defended.[35]

Even if the wording allows different interpretations – which is often the case in the Fourth Gospel – there are good reasons to prefer the "Easter reading":

---

[33] The Easter thesis is defended by Loisy, *Le quatrième Évangile*, 434–435; Heitmüller, *Das Johannesevangelium*, 160; Zahn, *Das Evangelium des Johannes*, 598; Lagrange, *Évangile selon Saint Jean*, 425; Walter Bauer, *Das Johannes-Evangelium* (HNT 6; Tübingen: Mohr Siebeck, 1933), 199; Bultmann, *Das Evangelium des Johannes*, 445–48; Dodd, *L'interprétation du quatrième Évangile*, 523 (as a reinterpretation of the traditional view of the Parousia); Brown (*The Gospel according to John II*, 729–30), rules out the Parousia thesis, does not only think of the appearances in a restricted sense, but of Christ's presence through the Spirit during the post-resurrection period; Schnackenburg (*Das Johannes-evangelium III*, 175–76) makes a distinction between the primary sense of the text, which refers in a restricted sense to the death and resurrection of Christ, and the extended sense that this resurrection gains for the reader; Lindars, *The Gospel of John*, 506–7; Blank, *Das Evangelium nach Johannes 4/2*, 202; Becker, *Das Evangelium nach Johannes II*, 600; Onuki, *Gemeinde und Welt*; Léon-Dufour, *Lecture de l'Évangile selon Jean III*, 252–53; Dettwiler, *Die Gegenwart des Erhöhten*, 239–42; Dietzfelbinger, *Der Abschied des Kommenden*, 231–32, 245–46; Culpepper, *Anatomy of the Fourth Gospel*, 218; Wilckens, *Das Evangelium nach Johannes*, 254; Konrad Haldimann, *Rekonstruktion und Entfaltung. Exegetische Unter-suchungen zu Joh 15 und 16* (BZNW 104; Berlin and New York: de Gruyter, 2000), 337, 362–64; Wengst, *Das Johannesevangelium II*, 162–63.

[34] Augustine (*In Jo.* 101.6 [PL 35]) stands at the origin of a tradition that interprets this passage as an announcement of the Parousia; Bengel (cited by Dietzfelbinger, *Der Abschied des Kommenden*, 232); Wellhausen, *Das Evangelium Johannis*, 73; Schnelle, *Die Abschieds-reden im Johannesevangelium*, 75–76; Idem, *Das Evangelium nach Johannes*, 275; Johannes Neugebauer, *Die eschatologischen Aussagen in den johanneischen Abschiedsreden. Eine Untersuchung zu Johannes 13–17* (BWANT 140; Stuttgart/Berlin/Köln: Kohlhammer, 1995), 136, 157; Frey, *Die johanneische Eschatologie III*, 205–21.

[35] Barrett, *The Gospel according to St. John*, 491 does not make a decision; in his opinion the terminology is deliberately ambiguous and refers to death/resurrection as well as to the ascension/Parousia.

a) It makes sense to begin by placing the passage within its context. John 16:4b marks a caesura in the second Farewell Discourse. After the long presentation about the hate of the world (15:18–16:4a), the second Farewell Discourse comes back to the issue of separation and farewell (16:4b–6). Both the verses prior to and subsequent to our passage present ways to overcome the crisis arising from the imminent event of the cross. The preceding context consists of two sayings about the Paraclete (16:7–11, 12–15): The first elucidates the mission of the Spirit with respect to the world during the post-Easter period, and the second explains its prospective role. These two sayings enable the disciples of future generations to be fully aware of their identity when facing the threatening world and the future. The later context (16:23–30) outlines the themes of prayer and the understanding of the believers' life after Easter. The major issue is therefore the post-resurrection existence of the disciple, and it is very likely that 16:16–22 is to be placed within this perspective. The point under consideration is the departure of the Son and the ensuing time, not the time before the Parousia.

b) Even the advocates of the Parousia thesis have to admit that on the level of the narrative logic (see the context of Jesus' last supper with his own), the first μικρόν can only point to the period of time separating the Johannine Christ from the cross, and the second to the period of time between the Son's death and his resurrection. The idea that one can shift the meaning of the first μικρόν to the ascension of Jesus and his exaltation during the Easter time, and construe the second as the short period of time that separates the believers from the date of the Parousia, is based on arguments relating to the pragmatic of the communication. It requires that the two occurrences of μικρόν no longer be interpreted within the context of the narrated story but in accordance with the experience of the readers, which is Christ's absence and the expectation of the Parousia.[36]

Numerous arguments work against this interpretation. First of all, the expression μικρόν is a well-known and frequent expression in the Fourth Gospel (7:33; 12:35; 13:33; 14:9), unmistakably describing the complex of cross/exaltation. The causal clause at the end of 16:17a (ὅτι ὑπάγω πρὸς τὸν πατέρα) clearly confirms this interpretation.[37] Second, the first μικρόν

---

[36] See Schnelle, *Das Evangelium nach Johannes*, 275; Frey, *Die johanneische Eschatologie III*, 207–9, who points out (209): "Der Abschnitt 16:16ff. stellt daher eine spezifisch johanneische Form der Auseinandersetzung mit dem Problem der 'Parusieverzögerung' dar."

[37] The verb ὑπάγω describes the departure of the one sent in the Gospel of John, but it is always a departure that is caused by the death upon the cross. The departure/exaltation should therefore not be separated from the cross and Easter. See Gerhard Delling, "ὑπάγω" (*ThWNT* VIII, 508–9); H. Probst, "ὑπάγω" (*EWNT* III, 942). See, e.g., 7:33–35; 8:21–22; 13:3, 33, 36.

poses a problem if the reference point for interpretation consists of the community of readers: The departure of Christ is not imminent, but has already occurred (one cannot attribute a future meaning to the second μικρόν and simultaneously deny it to the first!). Third, the price is high if one wants to argue for the Parousia thesis in light of the second μικρόν: The post-Easter period is semantically equated with the time separating the cross from Easter. The whole argument of the Farewell Discourses, which aims at demonstrating the superiority of the post-Easter period as compared to the pre-Easter period, stands in contrast to such a perspective.[38] It is tantamount to a falsification of the first Farewell Discourse.[39] Fourth, the fact that the implied author presents this saying as a riddle for the disciples is completely coherent with the interpretative line we suggest: The explanation required from Christ shows that the saying in 16:16 has lost its significance for the disciples. Consequently, the point does not consist in shifting the sense of the word, but in defining again its relevance for the post-Easter existence of the disciple.

c) The terminology of "seeing" (ὁρᾶν und θεωρεῖν) is found in 16:16–19 and it also appears in the Easter story of the gospel (ὁρᾶν: 20:18, 20, 25, 29[40]; θεωρεῖν: 20:6, 12, 14), but is not used in the passages that undoubtedly evoke the Parousia (14:3; 21:23; 1 John 2:28).

d) On the level of the terminology, the motif of joy is used outside of our passage to describe the historic existence of the disciple (χάρειν:

---

[38] Schnelle, (*Das Evangelium nach Johannes*, 275) writes for example: "Sie (= die joh Gemeinde) kommt von Ostern her, und es ist zu fragen, ob der erneute Verweis auf die zurückliegenden Ostererscheinungen ausreicht, um die gegenwärtige Situation der Bedrängnis zu bewältigen. Offensichtlich konnten in der joh. Gemeinde bedrängende Glaubenszweifel entstehen, obwohl die Osterbotschaft verkündigt wurde. Kann der Hinweis auf Ostern ein Problem lösen, dessen Entstehung er nicht verhinderte?" In the same sense Frey, *Die johanneische Eschatologie III*, 221: "Trotz der gewährten Gebetserhöhung und der christologisch-soteriologischen Offenbarung ist die Gegenwart der nachösterlichen Leser-gemeinde keineswegs vollendete Zeit."

[39] One of the issues in the first Farewell Discourse consists in showing that the departure of the one sent, i.e., his death upon the cross, is not a loss but a gain. Therefore, the post-resurrection period is not presented as a time of loss but rather as the time of "greater works" (14:12), as the time marked by the coming of the Paraclete (14:16–17.25–26). The second Farewell Discourse subscribes to this perspective (see 16:7: συμφέρει ὑμῖν ἵνα ἐγὼ ἀπέλθω). The victory over the world is no longer to come, but has already occurred at the cross (16,33: ἐγὼ νενίκηκα τὸν κόσμον). According to the Johannine view of the revelation, the decisive event lies in the departure of the revealer with its numerous effects and not in the Parousia.

[40] The verb ὁρᾶν denotes the Parousia in 1 John 3:2; Mark 13:26; 14:62.

14:28; χάρα: 15:11; 17:13; 16:24) and particularly the Easter experience (20:20, where the terminology of joy and seeing are combined!).[41]

e) Eventually the motif of the λύπη is clearly defined in our context. Given the problem expressed in 16:6, it undoubtedly describes the situation that results from the departure of Christ, i.e., from his death.

f) Those who support the thesis that 16:16–22 makes an indirect announcement of the Parousia often link the parable of the woman in labor to texts of an eschatological or apocalyptic character. Isaiah 26:17[42] and 66:7–9 (see also 37:3; 1QH III, 9–18) are often quoted. Two remarks are appropriate here: On the one hand, from a methodological point of view the purported intertextuality is not beyond doubt. The passage does not include a quotation or a reference, but is at best an allusion. And assuming that it is an allusion, one has to note that in the case of Isaiah 26 we cannot even find a single common syntagma, but only a connection between scattered lexemes derived from this source. In this case it would be better to speak of hypertextuality,[43] thus indicating a loose connection between the

---

[41] Becker, (*Das Evangelium nach Johannes II*, 599–600), and Dettwiler, (*Die Gegenwart des Erhöhten*, 241), have pointed out that in this passage we are not only confronted with isolated expressions referring to Easter, but with a constellation of concepts that are found in the christophanies: "seeing" (16:16–19, 22; 20:6, 12, 14); "in that day" (16:23, 26; 20:19); "peace" (16:33; 20:19, 21, 26); "joy" of the disciples (16:10, 22, 24; 20:20); "weeping" (16:20; 20:11, 13, 15). The allusion to Easter therefore becomes more likely.

[42] The parable of the woman in labor was often interpreted with reference to the OT, where the metaphor of the pain of the woman in labor and the birth of the child is often found. Two texts are permanently linked to our passage: Isa 26:17, in which the expectation of divine salvation is described, and 66:14, in which the restoration of Jerusalem is announced. In both texts the metaphor of birth and its preceding pains refer to the experience of God's people, who experience their eschatological salvation like a movement from sadness into joy. The surplus of meaning created by the connection between Isaiah and John 16:21 would consist of helping one detect in the metaphor of the woman in labor the sense of the eschatological divine salvation realized at the cross. Based on further developments of the same metaphor in the Jewish apocalyptic, various authors see in the motif of the birth pains (*1 En.* 62:4; *4 Ezra* 4:42; Mark 13:8, 15–19; Rev 12:1–6) an allusion to the time of grief that immediately precedes the end. In this case the surplus of meaning would consist in reading the passage of sadness into joy against the background of the Parousia expectation. Nevertheless, we have to be aware fact that on the one hand the metaphor can very well be understood by itself, and on the other hand, even supposing an intertextual link, we have to do neither with a citation nor with a reference, but with an allusion, the identification of which depends on the competence of the reader; and its sense also has to be worked out by the reader.

[43] See Gérard Genette, *Palimpseste. La littérature au second degré* (Collection Poétique; Paris: Seuil, 1982), 11–12. In the case of hypertextuality, the connection between the hypo-text (source of the text) and the hypertext is much looser and can include several levels. Unlike the quotation, the hypertext plays freely with the text to which it refers. In our case this means that John is able to take up the metaphorical language that

text's source and its receiver. On the other hand, the parable describes a fundamental experience of human existence that is to be found in all cultures and traditions. Therefore, the text is completely understandable without appealing to an intertextual reference.[44] The signal the parable gives to the reader is not part of an intertextual game, but is the remarkable choice of certain expressions that describe the process of labor and birth (λύπην ἔχειν; θλῖψις; ἦλθεν ἡ ὥρα αὐτῆς!). This shift in terminology is intended: It encourages the reader to understand the parable as an illustration of the believer's existence – and not as a coded announcement of the Parousia.

g) An intertextual connection is often assumed in the application made in 16:22, in this case referring to Isa 66:14 (common syntagma: καὶ χαρήσεται ὑμῶν ἡ καρδία). If the intertextual connection seems to be more evident here, it has to be balanced by the following observations: a) The whole argument has to be understood as a continuation of the riddle and the parable; the application takes up the contrast of "sadness – joy," which structures the parable, and relates it to the believer's existence. b) Joy is a classic johannine category of post-Easter existence; it is not specifically related to the Parousia (see 15:11 where complete joy is linked with revelation; likewise 17:13). c) Provided that the connotations relating to the book of Isaiah are well-founded, evidence must still be provided to show that the hope for salvation can only refer to the Parousia and not to the incarnation and especially to the death/exaltation of the Son (see 16:33).[45]

h) For the use of the expression ἐν ἐκείνῃ τῇ ἡμέρα we refer to point 2.1.

3.2 The Tension Inherent in Post-Easter Existence

Provided that our hypothesis is legitimate and the significance of the Easter event for the disciples is discussed in the 16:16–22, the question arises about the connection between our text and the passage that mentions the Easter coming of Christ in the first Farewell Discourse. In our opinion, a relecture of 14:18–26[46] is performed in 16:16–22. One does not have to

---

is characteristic of the Old Testament, which describes the pains of the woman in labor without adopting the sense that it has in Isaiah 26 and 66.

[44] In this sense see Schnackenburg, *Das Johannesevangelium III*, 177–178. See also Becker, *Das Evangelium nach Johannes II*, 601, who points out the general nature of this traditional topos.

[45] Barrett, *The Gospel according to St. John*, 493, and Gail R. O'Day, *The Gospel of John* (NIB 9; Nashville: Abingdon, 1995), 780, for example, discern in the surplus of meaning that results from the intertextual linking of John 16:21 with Isaiah, the expression of the eschatological salvation that is realized at the cross.

[46] Dettwiler, *Die Gegenwart des Erhöhten*, 266–92 provided an exhaustive analysis of the relecture of 13:31–14:31 in 16:4b–33. For the problem of the relecture, see Zumstein, *Kreative Erinnerung*, 15–30 and idem, "Ein gewachsenes Evangelium. Der Relecture-

share the same opinion to be nevertheless confronted with the hermeneutical question arising from the presence of these two passages in the discourse. Regardless of how one explains the origin of the text, the first Farewell Discourse (13:31–14:31) is – in its final version – dominated by christological problems (How does the departing Christ remain present for his own? What is the future of the revelation?). The emphasis in the second Farewell Discourse (15:1–16:33) lies on ecclesiological issues (To what kind of existence is the community of disciples called, in an hostile world, in which Christ is henceforth absent?). The sequence of these two passages shows that the problem of Easter in the first Farewell Discourse is discussed on a christological level, and that it is taken up again in the second discourse on a soteriological and ecclesiological level. This sequence structures the text in its canonical form and has to be taken seriously.

3.2.1 The Riddle and the Misunderstanding (16: 16–19)

Jesus' saying about his absence and his new appearance (16:16) is deliberately mysterious. Why does the implied author use such mysterious wording to introduce the dialogue between Jesus and his own? As shown previously, it does not deal with an amphibology, i.e., with a statement, which – on the level of the narrative logic – points to the sequence of cross-resurrection and simultaneously – on the level of context of communication – to the sequence of ascension-Parousia. The enigmatic character of 16:16a aims at emphasizing the incomprehension of the disciples, which is highly accentuated in 16:17–19.

The way in which the incomprehension is described deserves our special attention. The inability of the disciples to understand their master's teaching is described in detail. First, the statement of Jesus is discussed not once but twice (16:17, 18), thus illustrating the depth of their incomprehension. Furthermore, this cognitive failure takes place in the absence of Jesus (post-resurrection transparency?). Finally, the points causing difficulties are mentioned. In 16:17 the difficulty consists in relating the teaching on the two occurrences of μικρόν with the announcement of Christ's departure to the Father: How can one who has gone away to the Father be seen anew? In 16:18 it is the term μικρόν that presents a problem.[47]

The reader will not fail to notice that it deals with exactly those questions that were discussed in the first Farewell Discourse. This means

---

Prozess bei Johannes," in *Johannesevangelium – Mitte oder Rand des Kanons? Neue Standortbestim-mungen* (ed. Thomas Söding; QD 203; Freiburg: Herder, 2003), 9–37.

[47] The imperfect ἔλεγον, which follows the aorist εἶπαν in 16:17, shows that the incomprehension of the disciples is not temporary but persistent.

that the way in which the departure of Jesus and his Easter coming were presented has lost its persuasive power. In order to remedy this difficulty, our passage does not simply elaborate an answer that would compensate for the insufficiency of Easter by a further promise – the one of the Parousia.[48] On the contrary: For the implied author the complex of the cross/resurrection has not lost any of its relevance. It keeps its fundamental value. The incomprehension of the disciples requires a detailed explanation, but – and this is the shift of perspective caused by the second Farewell Discourse – it is no longer Christ's fate that demands an explanation but the destiny of the disciples living in the turbulence of the post-Easter era. What relevance does the Easter message expressed in 14:18–24 retain in view of the world's hatred for the disciples (15:18–16:4a)? The argument developed in these verses by the implied author has to show that the experience attributed to the first disciples with regard to the two occurrences of μικρόν has a paradigmatic value. As correctly shown by Dettwiler, the two uses of μικρόν refer to two forms of relationship to Jesus and thus define a fundamental structure of Christian existence: "Christliche Existenz ist eine im Übergang begriffene Existenz: eine Existenz in der Trauer, die durch die jeweilige Erfahrung der unmittelbaren Gegenwart Jesu . . . die Überwindung ihrer negativen Befindlichkeit erfährt."[49] The johannine conception of Easter (14:18–24) as well as the explanation of the two occurrences of μικρόν by the notions of sadness and joy (16:20–24) confirms this interpretation.

The comment of Christ in 16:19 shows that the disciples' incomprehension is a literary device that paves the way for a detailed explanation. By wondering about the meaning of 16:16, the disciples allow the johannine Christ to present a detailed interpretation of his statement. Qualified by his omniscience (16:19: ἔγνω), which enables him to discern human thoughts (2:25), Jesus takes the initiative in clarifying by anticipating the question of the disciples. He begins his speech by stating again the riddle that was previously presented to the disciples, which is now the object of their search (ζητεῖν).

3.2.2 The Thesis (16: 20)

The first part of Jesus' answer is introduced by the solemn formula ἀμὴν ἀμὴν λέγω ὑμῖν and has to be read as a thesis. It establishes a connection

---

[48] That is the way taken by Schnelle, *Das Evangelium nach Johannes*, 205–6, and Frey, *Die johanneische Eschatologie III*, 218, who tries to develop a dialectical interpretation, taking the soteriological statements in the present and with respect to the future (see 218–22).

[49] See Dettwiler, *Die Gegenwart des Erhöhten*, 243; in the same sense Dietzfelbinger, *Der Abschied des Kommenden*, 232–33, 244–46.

between the fate of Christ and the situation of the disciples. The center of the argument is no longer the fate of Jesus in itself (16:16) but its relevance for the existence of the disciples. The clarification is developed by means of the antithetic pair "sadness – joy"; more precisely, the existence of the disciple is presented as a movement from sadness (λύπη) to joy (χαρά). The argument is built on two contrasts: First, the sadness felt in view of Christ's death[50] contrasts (δέ) with the joy of the world (κόσμος). The world, here a symbol for unbelief, thinks that it has gotten rid of the revealer by crucifying him – which is the cause for its joy. So there is a double reason for the sadness of the disciples: The irreversible absence of Jesus and their exposure to a threatening world. Nevertheless, this sadness is not an inevitable fate, as shown by a second contrast, which structures the disciples' movement from sadness[51] into joy. The sadness about Christ's death and absence is transformed by the Easter certitude: The Crucified is living. Sadness arises out of joy.

The reader has to take particular notice of the shift when comparing this with the first Farewell Discourse. Because of the tension between the two occurrences of μικρόν, the post-Easter situation of the disciples is taken seriously. What the first companions of Jesus experienced regarding his farewell is not over-and-done. On the contrary, it is paradigmatic for the situation of every believer during the post-Easter period.

3.2.3 The Parable (16:21)

The transformation of sadness into joy is illustrated by the parable of the woman in labor (16:21). This picture describes a universal experience that is accessible to everyone. With the moment of birth approaching, the woman in labor will experience pain. But as soon the child is born, the joy caused by the presence of this newborn makes her forget the pain she suffered. However, this does not mean a return to the former state. The experience of the woman in childbirth has gained a completely different dimension: She has given life to a new human being. The decisive point of this picture consists of the fact that the woman in labor must go through the pain in order to arrive at the joy of birth. One is not possible without the other.

---

[50] The verbs used (κλαίειν, θρηνεῖν) express grief. The verb "weep" (κλαίειν) is found only in connection with the experience of death (11:31, 33) – particularly in combination with the death of Christ (20:11, 13, 15), whereas "wail" (θρηνεῖν) reminds one of the funeral song ritual. It therefore does not mean a general sorrow, but a grief caused by the loss of a beloved person.

[51] The noun λύπη (sadness, grief) and the verb λυπεῖσθαι (to be sad) do not describe an undefined sadness but the sadness resulting from the separation from Christ (see 16:6).

The wording chosen for the explanation of this picture is surprising: Usually words like "she has pain/sorrow" (λύπην ἔχει) or she remembers her "anguish" (θλῖψις) are not used in connection with a woman in labor; one would more commonly speak about her birth-pangs (ὠδίν). Yet, this shift in the terminology is deliberate: It is a signal inviting one to read the parable of the woman in labor as an illustration of believing existence. The focus is not on the remote future of this believing existence, the Parousia, but on the movement inherent in this existence. The post-Easter as well as the pre-Easter disciple has to cope with the grief caused by the absence of Jesus in order to experience the joy of his new coming. It is not merely a linear sequence, which would indicate the complete elimination of the sadness, but a movement structuring the existence of the disciple again and again. The joy originates in the sadness, so that the sadness also forms a constitutive part of the disciple's life.[52]

3.2.4 The Application (16:22)

John 16:22 describes the application of the parable. It deals with the existence of the disciples. The transformation of sadness into joy is christologically founded. The "now" (νῦν) of the sadness contrasts with future joy (χαρήσεται: future!) and corresponds to the narrative logic.[53] In 16:22b, which describes the future joy of the disciples, there are two new pieces of information. Instead of the expected "you will see me," there is the surprising "I will see you" (πάλιν δὲ ὄψομαι ὑμᾶς). So the disciples are no longer the subject of the seeing, but Christ himself is the subject. In other words, the "new seeing" is not an action of the disciples but an action initiated only by Christ; it consists of his Easter appearance (see 14:21–24), which is a reason for joy (see 20:20, see also 17:13). The indestructible nature of this joy lies in its gift's dimension. Because of its divine origin, the world has no influence on it.

---

[52] See Bultmann, *Das Evangelium des Johannes*, 446: "Vielmehr hat die χαρά in der λύπη ihren Ursprung."

[53] Same distribution of the tenses of the verbs in 16:16, 17, 19: θεωρεῖτε – ὄψεσθε (distinction between an imminent future [the time before the death upon the cross] and a remote future [the time immediately preceding Easter]).

4. Conclusion

The results of this brief study can be summarized as follows:

a) The Fourth Gospel is of great interest because it deals with the topic of Jesus' resurrection on a discoursive (chaps. 14–16) as well as on a narrative level (ch. 20). Each of the two Farewell Discourses makes room for discussing this topic (14:18–26; 16:16–22). If in the Farewell discourses the Easter event is first treated from a discursive point of view, the link between the chs. 14 –16 and the narrative of chap. 20 is explicitly established by the Easter prolepses. We are therefore confronted with a clearly structured treatment in two steps. Moreover, just as the first Farewell Discourse interprets the death of Christ before it has occurred, the same applies for the Easter event. Therefore, the Farewell Discourses represent a hermeneutical "portal" allowing one to decode the significance of the end of Christ's life in its entire meaning.

b) The passage in the first Farewell Discourse that is dedicated to the "coming of Christ" shows an implied author who is the witness of the Easter kerygma as well as its interpreter. If 14:18–19 articulates the traditional Easter faith in johannine language, the following verses provide a typically johannine interpretation of Jesus' resurrection. Three aspects deserve to be pointed out in particular. First, the implied author sets out to extend the significance of the resurrection appearances; i.e., he wants to point out their relevance for the whole post-Easter period. Second, the johannine *proprium* in the interpretation of the resurrection appearances consists in the established connection between these appearances and the reciprocal immanence formula that is extended to the disciples. Easter is understood in a theocentric sense: The ascent of the Son to the Father, manifested in the appearances, gives believers access to a new relationship with God. This is the Easter gain. Third, the implied author has reflected – in connection with the Easter event – the problem of the future of the christological revelation that is henceforth completed. For this reason he has linked the Easter faith to the coming of the Paraclete, who will be in charge of reminding the disciples of the Son and interpreting his significance during the post-resurrection period.

c) The aim of the second Farewell Discourse in 16:16–22 is to relate the Easter faith developed in the first Farewell Discourse to the experience of the reality to which the disciples are exposed: their "sadness" (λύπη). The disciples' situation of distress is caused by the separation from their Lord as well as by the hostility of the world that surrounds them. The implied author reformulates the relevance of the Easter faith for the believers, not by orientating them to the hope for the Parousia, but by inviting them to recognize in the movement between the cross and Easter, with its inherent tension, the key that enables them to found their existence and to understand it.

Chapter 6

Cross and Resurrection in the Gospel of John

Udo Schnelle

> We know that the process of history has another context than the incidental causality of the interests and passions of those through whom it takes place, and that it has another goal than the personal aims of those acting in it[1]
>
> Johann Gustav Droysen

1. The Hermeneutical Perspective

What applies to history as a whole also applies to every good narrative: It is not exhausted in the mere sequence of events or in the portrayal of the actors; rather, it raises what has occurred to a new level of meaning. This is especially true for John, since in writing his gospel under the guidance of the Paraclete he undertakes a completely new way of presenting the story of Jesus Christ.[2] To be sure, the link back to Jesus of Nazareth is as important to the Fourth Evangelist as the reformulation of the message of

---

[1] Johann Gustav Droysen, *Historik*, (ed. V. P. Leyh; Stuttgart and Bad Cannstatt: Wissenschaftliche Buchgesellschaft, 1977; repr. of 1857/1882), 392.

[2] I date the gospel of John between A.D.100–110; for my reasons see Udo Schnelle, *Einleitung in das Neue Testament* (5th ed.; Göttingen: Vandenhoeck & Ruprecht, 2005), 518–21; ET: *The History and Theology of the New Testament Writings* (trans. M. Eugene Boring; London: SCM, 1998), 475–77. The terminus a quo for the dating derives from John 11:48 which assumes the destruction of Jerusalem in A.D. 70; contra Klaus Berger, *Im Anfang war Johannes. Datierung und Theologie des vierten Evangeliums* (Stuttgart: Quell, 1997), 84–90, who in the context of his early dating (shortly before A.D. 66) denies that there is any reference to the destruction of the temple in 11:48. Additionally, the fact that the Fourth Gospel appears rather later in early Christian literature of the second century argues for a late dating; cf. Titus Nagel, *Die Rezeption des Johannesevangeliums im 2. Jahrhundert. Studien zur vorirenäischen Auslegung des vierten Evangeliums in christlicher und christlich-gnostischer Literatur* (Arbeiten zur Bibel und ihrer Geschichte 2; Leipzig: Evangelische Verlagsanstalt, 2000).

Jesus Christ for his own time. For John there is no Christianity apart from the historical Jesus, whose historical-geographical grounding is of utmost importance to him (e.g., John 1:28, 44; 2:1, 13; 3:22; 4:4–5; 5:2; 6:1; 7:1; 11:1; 12:1, 12; 18:1, 13, 24, 28; 19:17, 38–39, 41–42).[3] Yet it is also true that apart from a presentation of the Christ-event that is fresh in its language and concepts, John cannot stabilize the identity of his community, which is threatened by unbelief; understanding will lag behind its possibilities, and proclamation will bear no "fruit" (cf. 15:1–8).[4] Through the writing of his gospel, John opens new access to the story by way of a creative and ongoing appropriation of the revelation of Jesus Christ. According to the evangelist's self-understanding this is not an arbitrary process. Rather, it is through the Paraclete that Jesus interprets himself in the post-Easter remembrance that is found in John's gospel (cf. 2:17, 22; 12:16; 13:7; 20:9).[5]

The presence of the Paraclete (cf. 14:26) makes possible a more profound grasp of the incarnation, public ministry, suffering, exaltation, and glorification of Jesus Christ (cf. 14:15–17, 26; 15:26; 16:7–11, 13–15).[6] John deliberately conceives of what is comes later as having priority. This is not a deficiency, for the fact that remembrance comes later[7] does not mean that insight is lost, because the significance of an event is disclosed only in retrospect. What is past only exists when it is appropriated in the

---

[3] On this topic cf. Martin Hengel, "Das Johannesevangelium als Quelle des antiken Judentums," in *Judaica, Hellenistica et Christiana* (ed. Martin Hengel; WUNT 109; Tübingen: Mohr Siebeck, 1999), 293–334.

[4] On the situation of the Johannine community and its perils, cf. Udo. Schnelle, *Das Evangelium nach Johannes* (3d ed.; THKNT 4; Leipzig: Evangelische Verlagsanstalt, 2004), 8–11.

[5] Cf. Franz Mussner, *Die johanneische Sehweise und die Frage nach dem historischen Jesus* (QD 28; Freiburg, Herder, 1965), 45–51; Udo Schnelle, "Perspektiven der Johannesexegese," *SNTU* 15 (1990): 59–72, 61–64; Paul Ricoeur, *Gedächtnis – Vergessen – Geschichte*, in *Historische Sinnbildung* (ed. K. E. Müller and Jorn Rüsen; Reinbek, 1997), 433–54, esp. 436: "Im Gedächtnis . . . liegt die ursprüngliche Verbindung des Bewußtseins zur Vergangenheit."

[6] On the linguistic aspects of παράκλητος see Joannes Behm, "παράκλητος," *TDNT* 5 (1967), 800–3. The relevant attempts at derivation from the standpoint of the history of religions (Gnosticism, Forerunner-Fulfiller-idea; Advocate-idea, Qumran, Farewell Discourse Genre) are collected in Rudolf Schnackenburg, *Das Johannesevangelium* (4th ed.; HTKNT 4/3; Freiburg: Herder, 1982), 163–69; Gary M. Burge, *The Anointed Community* (Grand Rapids: Eerdmans, 1987), 10–30. On the history-of-religions background of the Paraclete concept cf. U. B. Müller, "Die Parakletvorstellung im Johannesevangelium," *ZTK* 71 (1975): 31–77; parallels are cited in: *Neuer Wettstein I/2* (ed. Udo Schnelle, Michael Labahn, and Manfred Lang; Berlin: de Gruyter, 2001), 689–93.

[7] Eckart Reinmuth, "Neutestamentliche Historik: Probleme und Perspektiven," *Forum Theologische Literaturzeitung* 8 (2003): 47–55, uses the concept "subsequence" (*Nachträglichkeit*).

present, and is continually grasped and made accessible in the context of contemporary identity. Only in this kind of continuous process is there any insight into the relevant past, and only in this way can the significance of the past be communicated and made accessible. A perspective "after the fact" provides the space needed for new achievements in thought and transformation, for the development of the metaphors that bear the content of an event and facilitate understanding. It disentangles things that have just occurred in order to provide the open space needed for objectification and for new interpretations to arise.

By means of post-Easter remembrance, John develops his independent conception and creative solution to the historical-theoretical problem of interpreting "after the fact," as well as the problem that all understanding is "subsequent." Because a narrative point of view that is shaped by a post-Easter retrospective binds the time of Jesus directly to the present time of the community through the guidance of the Paraclete, several levels of understanding typically flow together in Johannine texts. These do not exclude but supplement each other. Post-Easter remembrance makes possible the type of narrative technique that oscillates between the pre- and post-Easter period in ways that are so characteristic of John, allowing the reader to see in the public ministry of the earthly Jesus the activity of the exalted Christ and vice versa.[8]

2. The Potential Inherent in the Gospel Genre

John connects his hermeneutical perspective in a unique way to the narrative and theological potential of a new literary genre: the gospel.[9] Early Christianity faced the task of maintaining continuity with its origins and, at the same time, dealing with current problems. It is impossible to derive the meaning of an event simply from the fact that it happened. Rather, an interpretive narration of the event is needed to draw out the potential meaning inherent in the event, and through such a narration to make it

---

[8] For John 3 and 6, this was emphatically demonstrated by Thomas Popp, *Grammatik des Geistes. Literarische Kunst und theologische Konzeption in Johannes 3 und 6* (Arbeiten zur Bibel und ihrer Geschichte 3; Leipzig: Evangelische Verlagsanstalt, 2001).

[9] On gospel as literary genre, cf. recently Richard A. Burridge, *What are the Gospels? A Comparison With Graeco-Roman Biography* (2d ed.; Grand Rapids: Eerdmans, 2004); Dirk Frickenschmidt, *Evangelium als Biographie. Die vier Evangelien im Rahmen antiker Erzählkunst* (Texte und Arbeiten zum neutestamentlichen Zeitalter 22; Tübingen: Francke, 1997); Detlev Dormeyer, *Das Markusevangelium als Idealbiographie von Jesus Christus, dem Nazarener* (SBB 43; Stuttgart: Katholisches Bibelwerk, 1999); Dirk Wördemann, *Das Charakterbild des bios nach Plutarch und das Christusbild im Evangelium nach Markus* (Paderborn: Schöningh, 2002).

intelligible and relevant. Successful narratives are historical-narrative creations of meaning. They create, unfold, and make plausible frames of meaning and thus translate contingent events into lasting configurations of meaning.[10] From their own theological vantage points and with their own literary capabilities, the evangelists faced the task of shaping the traditions accessible to them, together with their own texts and compilations, into a new narrative, and in that way to form a new reality. This reality had to do three things: first, to transmit and formulate knowledge; second, to secure identity; and third, to communicate norms and to provide orientation. In this process the factors that shape meaning – the guiding principles – are especially significant, for they determine the course of the narrative. The guiding principles determine which kind of orientation particular stories and the entire gospel should provide. They are a central element of the new gospel genre, which intends to preserve the traditions, to continue forming them, and through efforts at interpretation to communicate their meaning from the past to the present.

The gospels generally agree on the basic data of their story of Jesus Christ, yet at the same time they structure the material in different ways and emphasize those aspects that are significant for forming the identity of their own community.[11] If it is true that the formation of meaning is always a constructive interpretation of the contemporary world, we need to ask what is the pattern of the matrix which John used to achieve this, that is, about the factors that order and give orientation to the gospel's thought.

These reflections have the following implications for our central question: Do the cross and resurrection belong to the principles that guide John's narrative and theological presentation of the story of Jesus Christ? Does the gospel contain merely figurative references to the cross as the place of Jesus' death and to the resurrection of Jesus Christ from the dead as a demonstration of God's life-giving power; or do the cross and resurrection belong to the narrative and substantive factors that shape meaning, to the guiding principles that determine the course of the narrative? Again:

---

[10] On aspects of early Christian formation of theology from the perspective of the science of history, cf. Udo Schnelle, *Paulus. Leben und Denken* (Berlin: de Gruyter, 2003), 2–25; ET: *Apostle Paul: His Life and Theology* (trans. M. Eugene Boring; Grand Rapids: Baker Academic, 2005), 26–46.

[11] I regard as unlikely the thesis of Richard Bauckham, "John for Readers of Mark," in *The Gospels for all Christians* (ed. Richard Bauckham; Grand Rapids: Baker Academic, 1998), 147–71, esp. 171: "that the Fourth Gospel was written, not for a Johannine community isolated from the rest of the early Christian movement, but for a general circulation among the churches in which Mark's gospel was already being widely read." What chiefly militates against this is the narrative and theological profile peculiar to each gospel, which is comes to the fore from the respective texts themselves, and not from a (hypothetical) knowledge of the other gospels.

Does not the gospel *genre* demand a special presentation of cross and resurrection? Is it possible that key elements of the story of Jesus Christ are transmitted merely by the force of tradition, without at the same time developing their narrative and theological significance? Finally: Since the hermeneutical starting point of post-Easter remembrance always presupposes the cross and resurrection at the outset, the question cannot be whether but only how the cross and resurrection are integrated into John's story of Jesus Christ.

3. Terminological Considerations

In Johannine exegesis it is disputed whether one can say that the Fourth Evangelist has a theology of the cross.[12] Therefore, we need to clarify the extent to which we can refer to a theology of the cross in John and whether it is a constituent element in Johannine thought.[13] The problem that lies behind this debate is whether the Johannine references to the death of Jesus are neutralized by being incorporated into an overarching scheme of

---

[12] On this topic, cf. U. B. Müller, "Die Bedeutung des Kreuzestodes Jesu im Johannesevangelium," *KD* 21 (1975): 49–71; Udo Schnelle, *Antidoketische Christologie im Johannesevangelium* (FRLANT 144; Göttingen: Vandenhoeck & Ruprecht, 1987), 182–94; ET: *Antidocetic Christology in the Fourth Gospel* (trans. Linda M. Maloney; Philadelphia: Fortress, 1992), 164–75; Herbert Kohler, *Kreuz und Menschwerdung im Johannesevangelium. Ein exegetisch-hermeneutischer Versuch zur johanneischen Kreuzestheologie* (ATANT 72; Zürich: Theologischer Verlag, 1987); Thomas Knöppler, *Die theologia crucis des Johannesevangeliums. Das Verständnis des Todes Jesu im Rahmen der johanneischen Inkarnations- und Erhöhungschristologie* (WMANT 69; Neukirchen: Neukirchener Verlag, 1994); U. B. Müller, "Zur Eigentümlichkeit des Johannesevangeliums. Das Problem des Todes Jesu," *ZNW* 88 (1997): 24–55; Johanna Rahner, *"Er aber sprach vom Tempel seines Leibes." Jesus von Nazareth als Ort der Offenbarung Gottes im vierten Evangelim* (BBB 117; Bodenheim: Philo, 1998); Jörg Frey, "Die *theologia crucifixi* des Johannesevangeliums," in *Kreuzestheologie im Neuen Testament* (ed. Andreas Dettwiler and Jean Zumstein; WUNT 151; Tübingen: Mohr Siebeck, 2002), 169–238; Esther Straub, "Der Irdische als der Auferstandene. Kritische Theologie bei Johannes ohne ein Wort vom Kreuz," in *Kreuzestheologie im Neuen Testament* (ed. Andreas Dettwiler and Jean Zumstein; WUNT 151; Tübingen: Mohr Siebeck, 2002), 239–64; Esther Straub, *Kritische Theologie ohne ein Wort vom Kreuz. Zum Verhältnis von Joh 1–12 und 13–20* (FRLANT 203; Göttingen: Vandenhoeck & Ruprecht, 2003); Jürgen Becker, *Johanneisches Christentum* (Tübingen: Mohr Siebeck, 2004); Udo Schnelle, "Markinische und johanneische Kreuzestheologie," in *The Death of Jesus in the Fourth Gospel* (ed. Gilbert Van Belle; BETL 200; Leuven: University Press - Peeters, 2007), 233–58.

[13] Rahner, *"Er aber sprach vom Tempel seines Leibes,"* 3–117, and Frey, "Die *theologia crucifixi* des Johannesevangeliums," 169–91, offer a sketch of recent research on the topic.

interpretation (e.g., dualism; Christ as the one who is sent; the path of Jesus' self-revelation that comes from the Father and returns to the Father), and thus made into a merely figurative event;[14] or whether John conceived of the cross theologically and Christologically, and whether it had fundamental and abiding significance for him.[15] Further: What is a theology of the cross? In the current debate there are various attempts to define and distinguish it.[16] One should speak of a theology of the cross only when

---

[14] So Rudolf Bultmann, *Theology of the New Testament* (trans. K. Grobel; 2 vols.; New York: Scribner's, 1951–55) 2:52, asserts: "In John, Jesus' death has no preeminent importance for salvation." According to Ernst Käsemann, *The Testament of Jesus according to John 17* (trans. Gerhard Krodel; Philadelphia: Fortress, 1968), 52, John lacks the great "paradox, that the power of the resurrection can be experienced only in the shadow of the cross, and that the reality of the resurrection now implies a position under the cross." U. B. Müller, "Die Bedeutung des Kreuzestodes Jesu," 69, emphatically states: "Die Theologie des Johannesevangeliums entfällt als ein Zeugnis für die urchristliche theologia crucis." See also Esther Straub, *Kritische Theologie ohne ein Wort vom Kreuz*, 214: "Das Kreuz Jesu ist im Joh nicht der Ort, an dem die christologische Identität Jesu allererst in ihren wahren, paradoxen Dimensionen offenbar wird, sondern der Ort, an dem das Eschaton in die Geschichte eingeht"; and Straub, *Der Irdische als der Auferstandene*, 264: "denn die Kreuzigung bedeutet nicht Jesu Tod, sondern Jesus kehrt am Ende seines irdischen Daseins zu seinem Vater zurück."

[15] Thus, e.g., Klaus Wengst, *Bedrängte Gemeinde und verherrlichter Christus* (4th ed.; München: Kaiser, 1992), 199–219; Schnelle, *Antidocetic Christology*, 170–73; Kohler, *Kreuz und Menschwerdung*; Martin Hengel, "Die Schriftauslegung des 4,. Evangeliums auf dem Hintergrund der urchristlichen Exegese," in *"Gesetz" als Thema biblischer Theologie* (Jahrbuch für Biblische Theologie 4; Neukirchen-Vluyn: Neukirchener Verlag, 1989): 249–88; Pierre Bühler, "Ist Johannes ein Kreuzestheologe?" in *Johannes-Studien* (ed. Martin Rose, Zürich: Theologischer Verlag, 1991), 191–207; Knöppler, *Die theologia crucis*; Ulrich Wilckens, "Christus traditus, se ipsum tradens. Zum johanneischen Verständnis des Kreuzestodes Jesu," in Wilckens, *Der Sohn Gottes und seine Gemeinde*. Studien zur Theologie der Johanneischen Schriften (FRLANT 200; Göttingen: Vandenhoeck & Ruprecht, 2003), 29–55; Frey, "Die *theologia crucifixi* des Johannesevangeliums"; Thomas Söding, "Kreuzerhöhung. Zur Deutung des Todes Jesu nach Johannes," *ZTK* 103 (2006): 2–25.

[16] Cf. chiefly Konrad Haldimann, "Kreuz – Wort vom Kreuz – Kreuzestheologie. Zu einer Begriffsdifferenzierung in der Paulusinterpretation," in *Kreuzestheologie im Neuen Testament* (ed. Andreas Dettwiler and Jean Zumstein; WUNT 151; Tübingen: Mohr Siebeck, 2002), 1–25, 3, who suggests "zwischen der Kreuzestheologie als einer bestimmten Form von Theologie und dem Bezug auf das Kreuz (als Konstitutivum christlicher Theologie) zu unterscheiden"; Straub, *Kritische Theologie ohne ein Wort vom Kreuz*, 211: "Die Frage, ob der joh. Entwurf kreuzestheologisch zu nennen ist oder nicht, interessiert nicht als Frage nach der formalen Klassifizierung der joh. Theologie, sondern als Frage nach der Sache, die diese Theologie vertritt und die es in einen Dialog mit der eigenen, kreuzestheologisch geprägten Glaubensidentität zu setzen gilt"; Jens Schröter, "Sühne, Stellvertretung und Opfer," in *Deutungen des Todes Jesu im Neuen Testament* (ed. Jörg Frey and Jens Schröter; WUNT 181; Tübingen: Mohr Siebeck, 2005), 51–71.

four conditions are met: 1) A form of the word σταυρ- must be present; 2) the cross must not be mentioned merely as the location of Jesus' death; 3) rather, the cross must function as the foundation and center of a theological system, giving it its narrative and substantive shape; 4) and finally, an explicit theological reflection on the correlation between the cross and resurrection must be evident.

John also regards the *resurrection* of Jesus Christ from the dead as a protological and exemplary event by which God's life-creating activity begins, bringing about a new reality of salvation that abides and can already be experienced in a comprehensive way in the present. But how does John explicate the theme of resurrection in a narrative and a conceptual-theological manner? Is the resurrection as *the* sign of glory detached from the cross, so that it only functions as a vestige of tradition?[17] Is the Fourth Gospel dominated by a Christology of glory that focuses on Jesus' abiding divinity, so that the incarnation and cross are included merely as stages along the way, though they are no longer developed theologically or carry any weight? Does John ultimately know Jesus Christ as nothing but the Risen One, so that it is correct to say: "With Christ the world of the resurrection has broken in on the earth"?[18] Above all we need to ask: Does John set the reality of the resurrection in relation to the cross in a way that is reflected in the gospel's narrative and theology, or is the evangelist's theological perspective limited to presenting Jesus' exaltation as a confirmation of his glory, while the cross is essentially ignored?[19]

The question of the cross and resurrection in the Gospel of John is no peripheral theme, but one that leads to the center of Johannine theology and is naturally connected to an assessment of the Fourth Gospel as a whole.

4. Cross and Resurrection as Guiding the Composition

In the narrative of John's gospel the revelatory path of the Logos among humankind is explicated and considered in its significance for salvation. This explication occurs as a continually intensifying dispute between faith and unbelief with regard to the message of the cross *and* resurrection! This opposition shapes the narrative structure through which the event is at once

---

[17] Thus Käsemann, *The Testament of Jesus*, 29: "His death occurs on the cross, as the tradition demands. But this cross is no longer the pillory of the one associated with criminals."

[18] Käsemann, *The Testament of Jesus*, 40.

[19] Thus again Becker, *Johanneisches Christentum*, 150, according to whom the death of Jesus is to be understood merely as "Gehorsamstat des Gesandten."

moved forward and differentiated.[20] This is already evident in the *Prologue*, for in 1:5 ("the light shines in the darkness, and the darkness did not overcome it") and 1:11 ("he came to what was his own, and his own people did not accept him"), Jesus' fate is presented as rejection and reception (1:12). There is no explicit reference to the cross and resurrection, but to what else should the rejection of Jesus refer, if not to the cross? One might object that it relates to death in general as the condition of his return.[21] But in the Gospel of John such a "death in general" does not exist. Rather, it is always the unique and concrete death of Jesus of Nazareth on the cross that leads to the resurrection and makes life possible for all believers. What gives the members of the community their certainty in speaking of the times of the light's exceeding brilliance (φαίνει in the present tense in 1:5!) and in understanding themselves as children of God (1:12), if not Jesus' resurrection from the dead as proof of God's power to give life (cf. 1:4)? The prologue, as beginning of the story, is not the place to present the ending in a comprehensive narrative form. Yet subtle allusions from the beginning onward suffice to indicate dimensions of cross and resurrection. Then as now, the hearers or readers of the Fourth Gospel know what is meant, even though it is not verbally expressed.

In the narrative opening of the gospel[22] Jesus appears twice as the *Lamb of God* (ἀμνὸς θεοῦ). To him applies the revelatory word of the Baptist, which, as the first positive description of his status, has programmatic significance: "Look, here is the Lamb of God who takes away the sin of the world" (1:29). The repetition in 1:36 (the Baptist says: "Look, here is the Lamb of God") underscores the importance of what is said about Jesus.[23]

---

[20] Cf. R. Alan Culpepper, *Anatomy of the Fourth Gospel. A Study in Literary Design* (Philadelphia: Fortress, 1983), 97.

[21] Thus Becker, *Johanneisches Christentum*, 151: "Die christologischen Ausführungen sind vielmehr am Weg des Gesandten ausgerichtet, seine Rückkehr nach oben zum Vater ist grundlegend. Dementsprechend ist der Tod Jesu nur impliziter anfänglicher Teil dieser Rückkehr."

[22] On the narratological analysis of the Johannine theology of the cross see especially Jean Zumstein, "Die johanneische Interpretation des Todes Jesu," in Zumstein, *Kreative Erinnerung. Relecture und Auslegung im Johannesevangelium* (2d ed.; ATANT 84; Zürich: Theologischer Verlag, 2004), 219–39; Craig R. Koester, "The Death of Jesus and the Human Condition," in *Life in Abundance: Studies of John's Gospel in Tribute to Raymond E. Brown* (ed. John R. Donahue; Collegeville: Liturgical Press, 2005), 141–57.

[23] Whoever wants to minimize the significance of the cross in John must interpret vs. 29b as secondary without being able to give sufficient reasons (so Becker, *Johanneisches Christentum*), 152; Müller, "Zur Eigentümlichkeit des Johannesevangeliums," 51–52., or deny any reference to Jesus' death *on the cross*; thus Jens Schröter, "Sterben für die Freunde. Überlegungen zur Deutung des Todes Jesu im Johannesevangelium," in *Religionsgeschichte des Neuen Testaments* (ed. A. v. Dobbeler, K. Erlemann, and R. Heiligenthal; Tübingen: Francke, 2000), 263–87, and especially 286–87.; Dietrich Ru-

Precisely at the place where the Johannine Jesus first comes into view, he appears as the Crucified, for the narrative resumes the metaphor of "carrying" in" in 19:17 and makes the connections clear: Jesus himself carries his cross to the place of execution.[24] However it is impossible for Jesus to bear the "sin of the world" as the Crucified One but only as the Crucified *and Risen* One. The hearers or readers know that the way of the preexistent and incarnate Logos leads to the cross and resurrection.[25]

The narrative thread of 1:29–36 is taken up and reinforced in the *Cana Narrative* with 2:1a ("on the third day") and 2:4c ("My hour has not yet come"). For the recipients of the gospel the "third" day can only be the day of resurrection.[26] The ὥρα of Jesus is the "hour" of the passion of the preexistent Son of God (cf. sec. 5 below). The understanding of this event along the lines of a theology of the cross (which has to be assumed from the beginning) is underscored by the presence of Mary. Only at the miracle of the wine and in the scene under the cross (19:25–27) does the mother of Jesus appear, each time addressed as γύναι. The identification of the "hour" as glorification (δοξασθῆναι) in 12:23, 27–28 and 17:1 allows us to recognize another dimension of 2:1–11. The revelation of Jesus' δόξα (2:11) now includes miracles, passion, and resurrection. Here as there his glory is revealed. The first sign (σημεῖον) already points to the fundamental change of the times that is brought about in the cross and resurrection.

Therefore, it is no accident that in the *Epilogue* in 20:30, John uses the word σημεῖον again, which he had used for the last time in 12:37 at the end of Jesus' public ministry. The σημεῖον-concept is particularly suited to evoke the faith-creating, revelatory quality of Jesus' ministry that had been

---

sam, "Das 'Lamm Gottes'" (John 1:29, 36) und die Deutung des Todes Jesu im Johannesevangelium," *BZ* 49 (2005): 60–80.

[24] The verbs αἴρω in 1:29 and βαστάζω in 19:17 possibly represent different tradition-historical connections, but their basic meaning is *de facto* identical; cf. Franz Passow, *Handwörterbuch der griechischen Sprache* I/1 (5th ed.; Leipzig: Wissenschaftliche Buchgesellschaft, 1841), which lists "aufheben, aufnehmen, bes. um zu tragen" as basic meanings for αἴρω (p. 62) and "heben, emporheben, aufheben" for βαστάζω (p. 496). The fact that different verbs are used cannot be used as an argument against the compositional connections that were demonstrated above; to the contrary: using the metaphor of the lamb and αἴρω, John alludes to the traditions of Passover and the Suffering Servant. In 19:17 he then specifies where and in which way the saving event happened.

[25] On the interpretation of John 1:29 cf. also Wilckens, "*Christus traditus, se ipsum tradens*," 33–37; Rainer Metzner, *Das Verständnis der Sünde im Johannesevangelium* (WUNT 122; Tübingen: Mohr Siebeck, 2000), 115–58; Frey, "Die *theologia crucifixi* des Johannesevangeliums," 197–207.

[26] According to Euripides, *Alcestis* 1146, the return from the realm of the dead occurs on the third day (and not later).

described earlier in the gospel.[27] Further, the σημεῖον-concept is appropriately suited to qualify the preceding appearance narratives, for they too have revelatory character and are marked by elements that establish faith in a visual and perceptible way.[28] Because the *doxa* of Jesus is supposed to call forth faith, and because the miracles as well as the reports of his appearance display this *doxa* in a forceful and unmistakable way, John takes up the σημεῖον-concept in the Epilogue of his work, making it the hermeneutical key to the Fourth Gospel.[29] What is more, the striking mention of the disciples becomes intelligible in this context. John reaches back to his interpretation of the Cana miracle in 2:11 and at the same time sets up a contrast to 12:37, which refers to the unbelief of the ὄχλος despite Jesus' many miracles. At the same time, the phrase ἐνώπιον τῶν μαθητῶν may have been occasioned by Jesus' previous appearances to his disciples (20:19–23:24–29). This also sheds light on the purpose of presenting the gospel this way. The disciples were the ones before whom Jesus did many other signs. This means that the Gospel of John is not a missionary tract for Jews or Gentiles, but has *its Sitz im Leben* within the Johannine community's tradition and school. It is a "disciples' gospel."[30]

The position of the *temple cleansing* is one of the most significant differences between the Synoptic gospels and the Gospel of John.[31] While ac-

---

[27] Whoever regards John 20:30–31 as merely the end of a pre-Johannine semeia-source must explain why, at precisely this point in his description, the evangelist takes up the σημεῖον-concept again, which otherwise relates chiefly to concrete miracle stories. This problem is for the most part overlooked. Thus Jürgen Becker, *Das Evangelium nach Johannes II* (3d ed.; ÖTK 4/2; Gütersloh – Würzburg: Gütersloher Verlagshaus Mohn – Echter, 1991), 756, who thinks that in 20:30–31 the evangelist is not at all concerned with the concept of signs, which he is supposed to have merely appropriated from the semeia-source ("E hat diesen Abschluß der SQ übernommen. Er achtete nicht darauf, ob 20,30f auch sein Evangelium angemessen wiedergab"). Is it possible that John shaped the very conclusion of his work without reflection?

[28] Cf. Thomas Söding, *Die Schrift als Medium des Glaubens*, in *Schrift und Tradition* (ed. Knut Backhaus and Franz Georg Untergassmair; Paderborn: Schöningh, 1976), 341–71, esp. 361.

[29] Cf. Gilbert Van Belle, "The Meaning of σημεῖον in John 20:30–31," *ETL* 74 (1998): 300–25, 324; differently, Hans Christian Kammler, "Die Zeichen des Auferstandenen," in *Johannesstudien. Untersuchungen zur Theologie des vierten Evangeliums* (ed. Otfried Hofius and Hans-Christian Kammler; WUNT II/88; Tübingen: Mohr Siebeck, 1996), 191–211, esp 201, who wants to refer σημεῖον "ausschließlich auf die Selbstverweise des Auferstandenen von seinen Jüngern."

[30] Thus the thesis of Joseph Thomas Pamplaniyil, *Crossing the Abysses. An Exegetical Study of John 20:19–20 in the Light of the Johannine Notion of Discipleship* (Biblical Tools and Studies; Leuven: Peeters, 2008).

[31] On the topic cf. Udo Schnelle, "Die Tempelreinigung und die Christologie des Johannesevangeliums," *NTS* 42 (1996): 359–73; Rahner, *"Er aber sprach vom Tempel seines Leibes,"* 176–340.

cording to the Synoptics, the temple cleansing occurs in the context of the entry into Jerusalem, John places it deliberately as a prolepsis at the beginning of Jesus' public activity (2:14–22).[32] Historically, the cleansing of the temple no doubt belongs at the end of Jesus' ministry, for it was a decisive factor causing his arrest, and it is likely that John knew of this original setting. By anticipating the temple cleansing, the Fourth Evangelist follows a theological chronology: Since historically the temple cleansing led to Jesus' death on the cross, and since the cross is one of the factors that determine the dramatic shape of the Fourth Gospel's content and composition from the outset, the temple cleansing *must* stand at the beginning of Jesus' public activity. In 2:17, 22 John uses the hermeneutical concept of "remembrance" to demonstrate explicitly that for him the temple cleansing involves the theology of the cross and resurrection.. Jesus' resurrection from the dead (2:22) is the horizon for understanding the meaning of the temple cleansing. *In the same way, the post-Easter community can only relate the metaphors of the destruction and the rebuilding of the temple in three days (2:19, 21) to the cross and resurrection.* Moreover, the Evangelist identifies the cross and resurrection as a σημεῖον (vs. 18–19.) and thus creates links between 2:11 and 20:30–31. By introducing his hermeneutical concept of post-Easter remembrance right at the temple cleansing, John gives his hearers or readers a clear signal: The temple cleansing is not a random episode from Jesus' life, for even here at this early point it involves the understanding of Jesus' entire mission. *This means that the temple cleansing declares the principle of John's theology of the cross and resurrection!*

By pointed allusions (3:14–16; 10:15, 17–18; 11:51–52; 12:27–32)[33] the theme of the cross and resurrection is made present over and over again in the narrative course of the gospel. The emphasis on the reality of Jesus' death as the condition for the possibility of the Eucharist in 6:51c–58, and the numerous references in 2:23; 5:1; 6:4, 71; 7:2, 10; 11:18, 55–57; 12:1, 12 that connote a theology of the passion, all have the same effect.

With the raising of Lazarus (11:1–44), the irreversible decision by the Jewish leaders to put Jesus to death (11:53), the anointing in Bethany (12:1–8, 9–11), and the entry into Jerusalem (12:12–19), John uses large blocks of narrative to direct attention to the cross and resurrection.[34]

---

[32] On the prolepsis cf. Gerard Genette, *Die Erzählung* (2d ed., UTB 8083, Munich: Fink, 1998), 45–54; Culpepper, *Anatomy of the Fourth Gospel*, 61–70.

[33] On the analysis see section 5 below: Key Conceptual Points.

[34] On the key function of John 11 and 12 in the gospel's structure and narrative dramatic action, cf. Michael Labahn, "Bedeutung und Frucht des Todes Jesu im Spiegel des johanneischen Erzählaufbaus," in *The Death of Jesus in the Fourth Gospel* (ed. G. Van Belle; BETL 200; Leuven: Leuven University Press and Peeters, 2007), 431–56.

The *raising of Lazarus* is the climax of Jesus' public ministry as well as the occasion for the final decision by the Jewish leaders to put Jesus to death (11:53).[35] John deliberately set the greatest miracle in the New Testament at this place in the narrative. Following the heightened controversy with the Jews (10:22ff.) and the emphasis on Jesus' miraculous activity in 10:40–42, this extraordinary miracle occurs in Bethany, in the immediate vicinity of Jerusalem. It brings about faith (11:45) but at the same time it also calls forth unbelief (11:47–53). The revelation of Jesus as life-giver, which is visible to all, is contrasted with the Jews' decision to kill Jesus; the most powerful sign is opposed to the greatest act of unbelief. Numerous references (11:4, 8, 16, 25, 40) intensify the sense that the entire narrative is theologically directed toward the passion, a narrative marked by John's subtle irony: The reason why Jesus must die is that he raised someone from the dead! John 11:4 ("But when Jesus heard it, he said: 'This illness does not lead to death; rather it is for God's glory, so that the Son of God may be glorified through it.'") gives an initial interpretation of the impending event. Lazarus' illness does not lead to death, since it is the occasion for the revelation of δοξα in the miracle. For Jesus, this event irreversibly opens the way to the cross, which John interprets as the mutual glorification of the Father and Son. But the hearers or readers of the gospel also know that just as Jesus raised Lazarus from the dead, God will raise Jesus from the dead, so that the story of Lazarus is also a narrative model of Jesus' own fate. The resurrection theme is present as early as vs. 6 (Jesus' curious delay is a variation on Hosea 6:1–2),[36] and beginning in vs. 27 it forms the theological horizon of the event. Jesus' powerful self-designation in vs. 27 is realized in the fate of Lazarus. Through his word alone, Jesus Christ the Son of God is able to give life back to one who was truly dead. This act proves that Jesus is lord over life and death, a true giver of life. At the end of the narrative, John describes the resurrection of Lazarus in a twofold way as a prefiguration of Jesus' resurrection: a) For Lazarus and for Jesus the final resting place is a rock-hewn grave (cf. 11:38; 20:1); b) both are said to have been buried according to Jewish customs (cf. 11:44; 19:40), and both heads were covered with a face cloth (cf. 11:44; 20:7). At the same time, small details indicate the great difference

---

[35] On John 11:1–44, in addition to the commentaries cf. especially Michael Labahn, *Jesus als Lebensspender* (BZNW 98; Berlin: de Gruyter, 1999), 378–465; Eckart Reinmuth, "Lazarus und seine Schwestern – was wollte Johannes erzählen?" *TLZ* 1124 (1999): 127–37; Jörg Frey, *Die johanneische Eschatologie III. Die eschatologische Verkündigung in den johanneischen Texten* (WUNT 117; Tübingen: Mohr Siebeck, 2000), 403–62; Wendy E. Sproston North, *The Lazarus Story within the Johannine Tradition* (JSNTSup 212; Sheffield: Sheffield Academic Press, 2001).

[36] Cf. Hartwig Thyen, *Das Johannesevangelium* (HNT 6; Tübingen: Mohr Siebeck, 2005), 515.

between Lazarus and Jesus: a) Lazarus' cave-tomb is still closed (11:38), whereas the stone is already rolled away from Jesus' tomb (20:1); b) the one, totally wrapped in bandages, must be carefully released from them (11:43–44.), the other undoes the death wrappings himself (cf. 20:6–7), as is evident by the neatly folded head cloth. Finally the threefold ὃν ἔγειρεν ἐκ νεκρῶν ("whom he had raised from the dead") in reference to Lazarus in 12:1, 9, 17, and the ἠγέρθη ἐκ νεκρῶν in reference to Jesus in 2:22, form a clear connection between the raising of Lazarus and of Jesus, since only in these three passages does ἐγείρειν appear in the sense of "to rise" (cf. 21:14).

The portrait of Jesus in the Lazarus episode contains surprising features, for it is precisely as Lord over life and death (11:27) that he is depicted in his true humanity: Jesus loves Lazarus and his sisters (vss. 3, 5, 36); Jesus weeps (vs. 35) and is disturbed (vs. 38). The community of hearers and readers outside the text understands the raising of Lazarus not only as a prefiguring of the fate of Jesus. They may hope that Jesus will act toward believers as he did toward Lazarus. Beyond this, yet another idea that is basic to Johannine theology shapes the Lazarus episode: in this miracle Jesus reveals his divinity, which paradoxically leads him to the cross. As a whole, the Lazarus episode can be read as a development of the "I Am" saying in vs. 27, and thus as a narrative that teaches about the manner in which the cross, death, and resurrection can be understood.[37] On one level Jesus is shown to be lord over life and death toward Lazarus; on a second level his own path toward the cross is made clear; and on a third level the readers or hearers of the gospel, and thus Christians of all times, can understand the fate of Lazarus as their own story. Precisely here (as in the entire Fourth Gospel), cross, death, and resurrection are not opposites but are deliberately related to each other: The Son of God, Jesus of Nazareth, goes the way of actual suffering, in order that by his resurrection he can make resurrection and real life possible for believers.

Within the narrative movement of the Fourth Gospel, the intention to put Jesus to death is one of the elements that drives the action forward and gives the event a dramatic cast. John reinforces this perspective with numerous prolepses (5:18; 7:1, 19–20, 25, 30, 32, 44; 8:20, 27, 40; 10:31–33, 39). In the Lazarus episode, the reality of death is present on several levels: The irreversible death of Lazarus is accented in 11:39 ("Lord, already there is a stench, because he has been dead four days"); the Jews' intention

---

[37] Cf. Frey, *Eschatologie III*, 425: "To the extent that the raising of Lazarus is to be understood as a σημεῖον only from the perspective of the cross and resurrection, it points forward to the deliverance from ἀσθένεια, sin, which *remoto Christo* is a 'sickness unto death,' but on the basis of Jesus' cross and resurrection, for Lazarus, the paradigmatic believer, it has lost its power to bind one to death."

to put him to death appears in 11:8, 16; and Jerusalem as the location of conflicts and Jesus' death appears in 11:18. The negative connotation of Jerusalem in the theological geography of the Fourth Gospel (cf. 2:23–24; 5:16, 18; 7:6, 10; 8:59; 10:31), is accentuated by the irrevocable decision to put Jesus to death in 11:45–47. It fits Johannine irony and dramatic form for Jesus' greatest sign (11:47) to be the occasion for the definitive decision to put him to death.[38] Though the leaders of the Jews apparently imagine that they will benefit by Jesus' death, the entire event actually occurs according to the will of God. Jesus' death does not prevent the coming of the Romans and the destruction of the temple, but it does indeed establish the redemption of all who believe in him.

The *Anointing in Bethany* (12:1–8, 9–11)[39] and the *Entry into Jerusalem*[40] again are prolepses that reinforce the connections between suffering, death, and resurrection in the Lazarus episode as well as in the passion and Easter event.[41] The passion is anticipated by means of Judas' dishonest behavior (12:4–6) and the decision to put Lazarus to death (12:10). The anointing is a scarcely veiled reference to Easter: (1) In 12:7 there is explicit reference to the burial in 19:38–42. (2) In contrast to the stench of Lazarus, the nard signifies the fragrance of life,[42] that is, it symbolizes the reality of the resurrection which is finally underscored by the refrain-like reference to Lazarus' being raised (12:1, 9, 17). *Mary anoints a living person who remains alive so that she can wipe the ointment away again.* (3) The explicit mention of Jesus' departure to the Father in 12:8b anticipates

---

[38] One can scarcely regard John 11:47–57 as the beginning of a pre-Johannine passion narrative (attempts at reconstruction in Matti Myllykoski, *Die letzten Tage Jesu. Markus und Johannes, ihre Traditionen und die historische Frage*, vol. 1 (AASF 256/272; Helsinki: Suomalainen Tiedeakatemia, 1991), 89 n. 90, for as regards content and language, the text has an altogether Johannine character; cf. Eugen Ruckstuhl and Peter Dschulnigg, *Stilkritik und Verfasserfrage im Johannesevangelium* (NTOA 17; Freiburg and Göttingen: Universitätsverlag, 1991), 224.

[39] Cf. Margareta Gruber, "Die Zumutung der Gegenseitigkeit. Zur johanneischen Deutung des Todes Jesu anhand einer pragmatisch-intratextuellen Lektüre der Salbungsgeschichte Joh 12,1–8," in *The Death of Jesus in the Fourth Gospel* (ed. Gilbert Van Belle; BETL 200; Leuven: University Press and Peeters, 2007), 647–60.

[40] On the analysis cf. Thyen, *Das Johannesevangelium*, 553–67. Due to the immediate (12:7) and wider context, the glorification of Jesus in John 12:16 is clearly to be linked to the cross and resurrection.

[41] Within the sequence of texts there are two striking peculiarities over against Mark: (1) The Fourth Evangelist begins the passion week with the anointing in Bethany, which in Mark appears only at the beginning of the actual passion story (Mark 14:3–9); (2) the anointing of Jesus is placed before to the entry into Jerusalem, which in Mark opens 'passion week' (Mark 11:1–10). For further analysis cf. Thyen, *Das Johannesevangelium*, 547–53.

[42] Cf. Gruber, *Die Zumutung der Gegenseitigkeit*, 3.

the farewell discourses and the entire Easter event. (4) Finally, the saying[43] in 12:24 expressly strikes the theme of Jesus' death and resurrection: "Very truly, I tell you, unless a grain of wheat falls into the earth and dies, it remains just a single grain; but if it dies, it bears much fruit." Jesus must die if he is to bear "fruit," which means that only from his death comes fruit and with it life.

To sum up: The sequence of scenes in John 11 and 12 intends to make clear to the gospel's hearers and readers that Jesus' path does not lead to the void of death but that in his very fate life he triumphs, whereas in the end Lazarus must die again. *Precisely where it is difficult to overlook that the references to Jesus' death are are becoming more frequent, the reality of the resurrection is also clearly in view!*

Mary's anointing of Jesus' feet is taken up with Jesus *washing the disciples' feet* (13:1–20), so that by another large block of narrative material John forcefully enhances the perspective on the cross and resurrection.[44] The footwashing occupies a key position in the structure of the Fourth Gospel. As the prologue to the second main section of the narrative and point of entry to the passion story, it takes up the previous references to the passion and directs the readers' attention decisively to Jesus' imminent fate. Moreover, the central theme of the farewell discourses is already present in 13:1–20: the impending departure to the Father (cf. 13:1, 3), which in Jesus' washing of the disciples' feet is given an interpretation for the benefit of the community outside the text. The footwashing as a prefiguring of Jesus' fate is to motivate the community to act during Jesus' absence just as he did: out of love. Consequently, the farewell discourses also appear in the light of God's love that leads to the cross and into the resurrection. The new commandment of love is deliberately placed at the beginning of the discourses (13:34–35), for only love can overcome the pain of separation and guarantee a lasting relationship.

---

[43] Cf. Epictetus, *Disc.* 4.8.36–39.

[44] On the footwashing cf. Georg Richter, *Die Fusswaschung im Johannesevangelium. Geschichte ihrer Deutung* (BU 1; Regensburg: Pustet, 1967); J. Beutler, "Die Heilsbedeutung des Todes Jesu im Johannesevangelium nach Joh. 13:1–20," in *Der Tod Jesu* (ed. Karl Kertlege; QD 74; Freiburg: Herder, 1976), 188–204; Kohler, *Kreuz und Menschwerdung*, 192–229; Christoph Niemand, *Die Fusswaschungserzählung des Johannesevangeliums. Untersuchungen zu ihrer Entstehung und Uberlieferung im Urchristentum* (SA 114; Rome: Pontificio Ateneo S. Anselmo, 1993); Udo Schnelle, "Die johanneische Schule," in *Bilanz und Perspektiven gegenwärtiger Auslegung des Neuen Testaments* (ed. Friedrich Wilhelm Horn; BZNW 74; Berlin: de Gruyter, 1995), 198–217, esp. 210–16; John Christopher Thomas, *Footwashing in John 13 and the Johannine Community* (JSNT SS 61; Sheffield: JSOT, 1991).

Finally, the Johannine *passion and Easter narratives* are arranged around a theology of the cross.[45] Various lines of the narrative intersect here and give their stamp to the entire gospel. It is beyond doubt that Jesus' self-surrender in 18:1–11 contains features of majesty (18:5a, 6), at the same time, however, suffering is still present in the person of Judas (18:5b), in the word concerning the cup (18:11; cf. Mark 14:23, 36; 1 Cor. 10:16, 21; 11:25–27), and in the motif of seeking (ζητεῖν, John 18:4, 7–8.), which is tightly linked to the intention to put him to death (cf. 5:18; 7:1, 4, 11, 19, 25, 30; 8:21, 37, 40; 10:39; 11:8, 56; 19:12). Further, the recollection of Caiaphas' prophecy in 18:14 (cf. 11:50) allows us to see that John does not separate the motif of Jesus' vicarious giving of his life and salvation (18:9; cf. 17:12) from his actual suffering. Moreover, only here (18:5, 7) and in the inscription of the cross does Jesus appear as ὁ Ναζωραῖος (19:19). In the trial before Pilate the nature of Jesus' kingdom is the subject of debate, in which the reference to Jesus as βασιλεύς (cf. 1:49; 12:13, 15; 18:33, 36, 37, 39; 19:3, 12, 14, 15, 19, 21)[46] takes up and interprets the phrase βασιλεία τοῦ θεοῦ in 3:3, 5. The links between the conversation with Nicodemus and the trial before Pilate are obvious: The first dialogue of Jesus with a Jew and the last with a Gentile correspond to one another in that both dialogue partners fail to recognize Jesus' true nature and are stuck on an earthly and superficial level. The *inscription on the cross* (19:19) makes clear to all the world that Jesus' death on the cross as βασιλεύς is the presupposition and condition of possibility for the believers and the baptized to enter the βασιλεία τοῦ θεου. Further, the inscription underscores the fact that Jesus' transcendent kingdom (18:36) can in no way be separated from his concrete death on the cross.

Maltreated, Jesus of Nazareth carries his own cross (19:7; cf. 1:29), and as king of the Jews he sits naked on his throne: the cross. From the cross Jesus establishes his community, in which Mary can be entrusted to the care of the Beloved Disciple. The scene under the cross is the foundational legend of the Johannine community. Mary represents the believers of all times who, like her, have to depend on the Beloved Disciple. *For John the hour of crucifixion thus becomes the hour of the church's birth, since it is at the same time the hour of exaltation!*[47] In the cross Scripture is fulfilled

---

[45] Cf. Manfred Lang, *Johannes und die Synoptiker. Eine redaktionsgeschichtliche Analyse von Joh 18–20 vor dem markinischen und lukanischen Hintergrund* (FRLANT 182; Göttingen: Vandenhoeck & Ruprecht, 1999), 305–42.

[46] Cf. Frey, *Die johanneische Eschatologie III*, 271–76.

[47] On the topic cf. Artemidorus, *Onir.* 2.53: "If one imagines hanging on a cross in a city, then that portends a public office corresponding to the place where the cross is erected."

(19:28),⁴⁸ and on the cross the one who has become flesh says τετέλεσται (19:30: "it is finished"). The thirsting, exhausted Jesus speaks his last word on the cross, where τελεῖν ("to fulfill/complete") in vss. 28, 30 refers back to the prepositional phrase εἰς τέλος in 13:1, which has a temporal ("to the end") and qualitative ("to the point of completion") dimension. The cross is the place at which the love of Jesus for his own achieves its end and its completion. On the cross the way of the Revealer is completed. In 19:34b, 35, the striking reality of Jesus' death is accented with the issuing of "water and blood" from the wound in his side, with patent references to baptism (3:3, 5) and the Eucharist (6:51–58). Together with the narrator, believers look on the one from whose body the blood and water flow, who thus fulfills the promise of 7:38, and after his exaltation will draw his own to himself (12:32).⁴⁹ The realities of death and life are also visible in Jesus' burial (19:38–42). The unusual amount of burial spices makes clear that the crucified Jesus (19:41) is buried as a king, that true life already shines thus through death.

In the *Easter narratives* in 20:1–29, the glory of Jesus is naturally at the center, but not in a way that takes the attention off the cross and the corporeality of the crucified.⁵⁰ In 20:1–10 the Beloved Disciple becomes the first authentic Easter witness. He immediately recognizes and interprets Jesus' fate: Jesus Christ is neither among the dead nor was his corpse stolen; rather he is risen and will go to the Father. With one look the Beloved Dis-

---

⁴⁸ On the Johannine understanding of scripture cf. Bruce G. Schuchard, *Scripture within Scripture. The Interrelationship of Form and Function in the Explicit Old Testament Citations in the Gospel of John* (SBL.DS 133; Atlanta: Scholars Press, 1992); Martinus J. J. Menken, *Old Testament Quotations in the Fourth Gospel* (CBET 15; Kampen: Kok Pharos, 1996); Andreas Obermann, *Die christologische Erfüllung der Schrift im Johannesevangelium. Eine Untersuchung zur johanneischen Hermeneutik anhand der Schriftzitate* (WUNT II/83; Tübingen: Mohr Siebeck, 1996); Wolfgang Kraus, "Johannes und das Alte Testament," *ZNW* 88 (1997): 1–23.

⁴⁹ On the exposition cf. Schnelle, *Das Evangelium nach Johannes*, 316–19.

⁵⁰ On the analysis of John 20:1–10, 11–18, in addition to the commentaries cf. Gert Hartmann, "Die Vorlage der Osterberichte in Joh 20," *ZNW* 55 (1964): 197–220; Robert Mahoney, *Two Disciples at the Tomb. The background and message of John 20,1–10* (TW 6; Bern and Frankfurt: Lang, 1974); Joachim Kügler, *Der Jünger, den Jesus liebte. Literarische, theologische und historische Untersuchungen zu einer Schlüsselgestalt johanneischer Theologie und Geschichte; mit einem Exkurs über die Brotrede in Joh. 6* (SBB 16; Stuttgart: Katholisches Bibelwerk, 1988), 314–49; Lang, *Johannes und die Synoptiker*, 259–79; Frans Neirynck, "John and the Synoptics: The Empty Tomb Stories"; idem, *Evangelica II* (BETL 99; Leuven: University Press and Peeters, 1991), 571–99; Werner Stenger, "Strukturale Lektüre der Ostergeschichten des Johannesevangeliums (Joh 19:31–21:25)," in *Strukturale Beobachtungen zum Neuen Testament* (ed. Stenger; NTTS 12; Leiden: Brill, 1990), 202–42; Dieter Zeller, "Der Ostermorgen im 4. Evangelium (John 20:1–18)," in *Auferstehung Jesu – Auferstehung der Christen* (ed. Lorenz Oberlinner; QD 105; Freiburg: Herder, 1986), 145–61.

ciple grasps the situation and immediately comes to complete faith in Jesus' resurrection (20:8). There is no lack of understanding concerning the situation here, no need for palpable proof to conquer doubt, as is later the case with Thomas. For the Beloved Disciple it is true that faith arises out of seeing.

In 20:11–18 the empty tomb is construed in a different way, since now not the linen wrappings or head cloth, but rather two angels at the head and feet of where Jesus' body had been laying bear witness to the empty tomb.[51] The shining white garments are a symbol of the heavenly world. The presence of the angels signals that an event that transcends natural understanding has taken place here. Jesus appears in shadowy form and denies Mary the possibility of touching him bodily. That way of obtaining certainty is not yet possible, for Jesus exists in an interim bodily state. He is risen from the dead but has not yet ascended to the Father. John deliberately does not use the verb ὑψόω but rather ἀναβαίνω when referring to Jesus' permanent link with the heavenly world (cf. 1:51) or to the return of the Son to the Father (cf. 3:13; 6:62). The narrative of the appearance before Mary Magdalene clarifies Jesus' whereabouts and emphasizes, as did the race to the empty tomb, that the new identity of Jesus Christ is not immediately accessible. Initially, Mary holds onto to the tomb as the place where one might naturally expect Jesus to be, for she wants to undo what appears to be a grave robbery. But then she is led to understand that Jesus has his legitimate and abiding place with the Father.

John does not report the disciples' reaction to the message brought by Mary Magdalene. Instead he narrates another resurrection appearance (20:19–23), so that Mary's "I have seen the Lord" can lead to the disciples' "we have seen the Lord" (20:20). The disciples' understanding of the resurrection event is elaborated by way of intentional structural analogies between 6:19–20 and 20:19–23. In both instances the disciples are in danger, and each time Jesus appears in a miraculous way to save them. Prior to Easter the disciples do not recognize Jesus on the sea, and 20:20 makes clear that for John (as for Mark) Jesus of Nazareth can be fully understood only as the Crucified and Risen One. Jesus shows his hands and his side and thus changes the disciples' fear into joy.

In the Thomas episode (20:24–29) the identity of the preexistent and incarnate one with the crucified and exalted one takes on tangible dimensions. In a miraculous way Thomas is allowed to verify the identity of the risen with the earthly one in space and time, and in this way he comes to faith. By so doing, he confirms that the *cross and resurrection come together in the identity of the corporeality of the crucified and risen one!* Thus John's story of Jesus Christ both ends and is raised to a new level of

---

[51] On the analysis cf. most recently Pamplaniyil, "Crossing the Abysses," 39–50.

understanding: "Blessed are those who have not seen and yet have come to believe" (John 20:29b). In the post-Easter situation following Jesus' departure, John makes clear that the absence of Jesus' body may not be misconstrued as the absence of his person. Rather, the narratives of the empty tomb and the appearances to Mary Magdalene, the "Twelve," and Thomas *par excellence* make clear that after Easter seeing and believing are transformed on the basis of the disciples' witness.

The structure of John 20 is marked by a twofold movement: There is an unmistakable heightening of the presence of the Risen One as crucified in a new, inaccessible corporeality. While Peter and the Beloved Disciple see only the linen cloths in the empty tomb, Jesus appears to Mary Magdalene without her being allowed to touch him. Jesus then shows the disciples the wounds in his hands and side which Thomas may actually touch in order clearly to grasp the identity of the Crucified with the Risen One. The opposite development can be noticed with regard to the certainty of faith. While the Beloved Disciple believes without seeing, Mary Magdalene believes only when directly addressed by Jesus (20:16). Then it is said of the disciples that they "rejoiced" at the appearance of Jesus (20:20b), and Thomas' doubt must be overcome by the corporeality of the Risen One. By means of this opposite development, the Beloved Disciple embodies in an ideal way the principle, which is now also applicable to the community of hearers and readers outside the text: Blessed are those who have not seen and yet have come to believe (20:29b).

5. Key Conceptual Points

Among the distinctive elements in John's narrative technique is the way that concepts are given new theological connotations, so as to present central themes in compressed form and to achieve effects that cause surprise and foreignness. The most important to be noted in connection with cross and resurrection are the "hour" of Jesus, his "exaltation and glorification," as well as the Johannine "understanding of the signs."

With the concept of the *"hour"* (ὥρα) John places Jesus' entire public ministry in the perspective of a theology of the cross and of the resurrection.[52] The evangelist speaks of the hour of Jesus' glorification (12:23, 27–28; 17:1), the hour that attests to his being sent by the Father (13:1; 7:30; 8:20), the hour of his acceptance the passion (12:27), and the hour that is

---

[52] John probably took this motif from Mark 14:41 ("He came a third time and said to them, 'Are you still sleeping and taking your rest? Enough! The hour has come; the Son of Man is betrayed into the hands of sinners'"). On the exposition of the text, cf. Knöppler, *theologia crucis*, 102–15.

to come (4:21, 23; 5:25; 16:2, 4, 25). As early as in 2:4c ("My hour has not yet come"), the meaning can be discerned only from the wider narrative context, for it is not the hour of the miracle-worker[53] but the hour of the passion and the glorification of the preexistent and incarnate Son of God.[54] As in 7:6, 8, 30 and 8:20, οὔπω ("not yet") separates the time before the passion from the passion itself. With this "not yet" John constructs a narrative tension that is dissolved only by the announcement of "the" hour in 12:23 ("Jesus answers them and says, 'The hour has come for the Son of Man to be glorified'").[55] Jesus' "hour" retains its special dignity by the event that occurs in and with it: the glorification of the Son of Man. By glorification John designates exaltation to the divine sphere, which is an act of God, accomplished by cross and resurrection (12:27–33). The motif of the "hour" also leaves its mark on the narrative of the footwashing (13:1). After concluding his public ministry, Jesus knows about his coming hour of suffering, which will lead to glorification (12:23). In all of this, Jesus' death is not absorbed by his glory and made into an unreal event. Rather, here it is already revealed that the death on the cross is his glorification. In his death Jesus meets the Father.

Another distinctive element in Johannine Christology consists in defining Jesus' death as *lifting up* and *glorification*.[56] In 3:13–14 the *anabasis* of the Son of Man is interpreted as being "lifted up": "No one has ascended into heaven except the one who descended from heaven, the Son of Man. And just as Moses lifted up the serpent in the wilderness, so must the Son of Man be lifted up." Here the cross looms up in a fourfold way: (1) The aorist passive ὑψωθῆναι refers to the accomplishment of Jesus' crucifixion with God as the one doing the "lifting up;" (2) the δεῖ takes up Mark 8:31 and assigns the suffering on the cross to the divine will; (3) within

---

[53] Contra Rudolf Bultmann, *Das Evangelium des Johannes* (19th ed.; KEK II; Göttingen: Vandenhoeck & Ruprecht, 1968), 81; ET: *The Gospel of John. A Commentary* (trans. G. R. Beasley-Murray, R. W. N. Hoare and J. K. Riches; Philadelphia: Westminster, 1971), 116–17. If vs. 4c relates to Jesus' miracle-working activity, then he would be performing the miracle immediately after refusing! According to Straub, "Der Irdische als der Auferstandene," 254, vss. 4bc mean "dass sich Jesus von seiner irdischen Herkunft distanziert." Neither vs. 4c nor the customary use of ὥρα in the Fourth Gospel allows even the hint of such an interpretation.

[54] Cf. Schnelle, *Das Evangelium nach Johannes*, 70–71; Jörg Frey, *Die johanneische Eschatologie II. Das johanneische Zeitverstandnis* (WUNT 110; Tübingen: Mohr Siebeck, 1998), 215; Knöppler, *theologia crucis*, 103.

[55] Cf. Frey, *Johanneische Eschatologie II*, 218.

[56] On the topic cf. Wilhelm Thüsing, *Erhöhung und Verherrlichung Jesu im Johannesevangelium* (3d ed.; NTAbh 21/1.2; Münster: Aschendorff, 1979); Jörg Frey, "Wie Mose die Schlange in der Wüste erhöht hat. . . ," in *Schriftauslegung im antiken Judentum und im Urchristentum* (ed. Martin Hengel and Hermut Löhr; WUNT 73; Tübingen: Mohr Siebeck, 1994), 153–205; Knöppler, *theologia crucis*), 154–73.

John's symbolic language, the verb ὑψοῦν ("to lift up"), used here as in 8:28; 12:32, suggests Jesus' crucifixion;[57] (4) the comparison with the brass serpent assumes the physical nature of the cross as does the thought that the sight of the brass serpent/cross has an apotropaic effect. Like the lifting up of the serpent in the wilderness, the lifting up of Jesus has a saving function. Not just Jesus' exaltation to heaven but already his exaltation on the cross is a saving event. In the New Testament the idea of exaltation is usually tightly linked to the resurrection, as in Phil. 2:9; Acts 2:33, and 5:31. John proposes a new definition by *consistently thinking of cross and resurrection together when referring to exaltation*. As the crucified, Jesus is "exalted" in a twofold way: *He hangs on the cross and is at the same time with the Father; sitting at God's right hand is sitting on the cross!*[58] This interpretation is especially supported by John 12:27–33, where exaltation and glorification mutually interpret each other, making clear that for John, Jesus' glorification is his exaltation and vice versa. In mentioning the agony in vs. 27, John accents the reality of the cross, as he does by his comment in vs. 33 ("He said this to indicate the kind of death he was to die"). Semantically, his understanding of the cross, exaltation, and glorification is expressed precisely by the ποίῳ θανάτῳ (ποῖος = "in what state"). *At issue is not the death of Jesus in general, but the manner of his death/the kind of death, that is, the cross!*[59] On and in the cross Jesus achieves the dignity of exaltation and glorification.[60] For John, exaltation

---

[57] Cf. Thüsing, *Erhöhung und Verherrlichung*, 3–12.

[58] On the factual aspects of the crucifixion cf. Heinz-Wolfgang Kuhn, "Der Gekreuzigte von Givʻat ha-Mivtar. Bilanz einer Entdeckung," in *Theologia Crucis – Signum Crucis* (ed. Carl Andresen and Günther Klein; Tübingen: Mohr Siebeck, 1979), 303–34.

[59] Whoever intends to minimize the theological significance of the crucifixion for the sake of a Johannine Christology of glory, must naturally reduce the importance of John 12:23, by either ignoring this passage (thus Becker, *Johanneisches Christentum*, 151), by interpreting it as 'incidental' (thus Müller, "Zur Eigentümlichkeit des Johannesevangeliums," 44) or by simply reversing the meaning of the text (thus Straub, "Der Irdische als der Auferstandene," 260: "Zwar weist Jesus in 3,14 und 12,32f auf die Art und Weise seines Todes voraus, doch liegt der entscheidende Punkt dieser Stellen darin, dass die Kreuzigung (σταυρόω) auf die Erhöhung (ὑψόω) festgelegt wird." What militates against these theses is the course of the narrative in 12:27–32, which by way of the commentary in 12:33 clearly aims at a conscious identification of glorification, exaltation, and cross. The reference to the cross stands at the end and qualifies the exaltation and glorification; cf. also Thyen, *Das Johannesevangelium*, 565–66; Francis Moloney, *The Gospel of John* (SP 4; Collegeville: Liturgical Press, 1998), 355.

[60] Isaiah 52:13 LXX forms the traditions-historical background of the Johannine Christology of exaltation and glorification: There the text says of the Servant of God: ἰδοὺ συνήσει ὁ παῖς μου καὶ δοξασθήσεται σφόδρα. Cf. Knöppler, *Theologia crucis*, 162–63 for more information on this topic.

on the cross and exaltation to the Father coincide (cf. 13:31–32). The cross is the permanent place of salvation.[61]

The perspective of the *High Priestly Prayer* underscores this idea: "Father, the hour has come; glorify your Son so that the Son may glorify you" (17:1; cf. vss. 4. 5. 22. 24). As Son and the One sent by the Father, Jesus Christ goes to the hour of the cross and exaltation in which the *doxa* of the Father is manifested and the power of death is conquered. Precisely because the saving significance of the cross is accented in this way, Jesus' suffering fades before the Easter victory in John. This is the reason the Fourth Evangelist can understand Jesus' being crucified as "exaltation" and "glorification." In this sense the theology of the cross is the presupposition for the Christology of glory. This makes evident a Christological "concentration," which is also characteristic of other aspects of Johannine thought. The event of salvation is not described primarily in its factual or temporal stages, but is seen as a unity while preserving the individual aspects.

6. Cross and Resurrection as Meaning – Creating Threads through John's Gospel

The question of the relationship between the cross and resurrection in John also involves determining the intellectual profile of the Fourth Evangelist. Is the Johannine reference to Jesus' death neutralized and made into an unreal event by its incorporation into an overarching scheme of interpretation (e.g. dualism; Christology of the One sent; Jesus' way of self-revelation from and to the Father)?[62] Is the gospel dominated by a Christology of glory that allows Jesus' suffering and death on the cross to be absorbed and muted? Does the incarnation as well as the cross become an unreal event?[63]

---

[61] *Contra* Becker, *Das Evangelium nach Johannes II*, 470: "Nicht das Kreuz ist also bleibender Realgrund der Erlösung, sondern die Erhöhung, die sich als Abschluß der Sendung ergibt."

[62] *Contra* Becker, *Johanneisches Christentum*, 151, who wants to interpret the concept of the One sent as the only appropriate interpretive model of the Gospel of John: "Die christologischen Ausführungen sind vielmehr am Weg des Gesandten ausgerichtet, seine Rückkehr nach oben zum Vater ist grundlegend. Dementsprechend ist der Tod Jesu nur impliziter anfänglicher Teil dieser Rückkehr."

[63] It is no accident, but only consistent when those who contest that there is a theology of the cross in John's gospel also relativize the incarnation. See Käsemann, *The Testament of Jesus according to John 17* who speaks of the incarnation as "the absolute minimum of the costume designed for the one who dwelt for a little while among men" (p. 10), of "condescension" (p. 12), of Jesus' earthly life "merely as backdrop for the Son

The foregoing analyses have indicated that this is not the case. As far as the gospel of John is concerned it would be wrong to speak of a diminishment of the cross in favor of a pure Christology of glory. Nor would it be correct to assume that in John there are different Christological models that are parallel or even in opposition to each other. In his re-writing of the story of Jesus Christ, John gives the cross a special place as the historical location of the central illustrative element in his narrative. *As far as the narrative dimension is concerned,* the cross breaks through the usual structure of all events from beginning to end and opens up new dimensions in the resurrection. *Thus the cross undergoes a semantic enhancement and a literary-rhetorical compression in which it becomes an abbreviation for a complex event.* John (as Paul and Mark before him) grasped this possibility, and in his model narrative he gave the historical and theological significance of the cross compositional and conceptual expression. *Within John's story of Jesus Christ, the cross is fact and fiction at the same time, because in the resurrection it exceeds its own possibilities* and makes possible a way of narrating in which the known ending is already present in the potential beginning and which gives the entire event its perspective, forward motion, and tension. Through cross references (above and below), John weaves a network of understanding and, to greater extent than the Synoptics, creates theological connections between the cross and resurrection. The miracles, passion, and resurrection appearances are separately and in their totality locations for the epiphany of the glory of the Son of God, without relativizing each other. It is difficult to imagine tighter narrative configurations of the connections between cross, death, resurrection, and real life than in those in 11:1–44 or 20:1–29! *For John, true death and true life coincide on and in the cross, since for him incarnation, crucifixion and resurrection form a unity; genuine dying and real resurrection are the presupposition for genuine life and vice versa.*

---

of God proceeding through the world" (p. 13); cf. also Becker, *Johanneisches Christentum*, 131: "Man sollte das Interpretationsmodell, Inkarnation' als Matrix für die joh. Christologie am besten aufgeben. Denn nur ganz am Rande hat dieses Stichwort beim Evangelisten Verwendung gefunden und dann in einer Bedeutung, die die Inkarnationstheologen seit Irenäus nicht mehr teilen;" Müller, "Zur Eigentümlichkeit des Johannesevangelims," 54: "Zwei prinzipielle Gründe verhindern, dass die Inkarnation und damit auch der Tod Jesu ein theologisches Eigengewicht bekommen. ... Nicht die Menschheit Jesu und damit die Menschwerdung sind zu unterstreichen" and Straub, "Der Irdische als der Auferstandene," 255: "Dieser wurde Fleisch (Joh 1,14a), d.h. er wurde aus dem Fleisch geboren (vgl. 3,6). Er setzt sich der irdischen Herkunft aus, in die verstrickt der Mensch sein Dasein im Tod fristet."

Taken as a whole, Johannine Christology is characterized by a comprehensive program: Preexistence and incarnation, sending and exaltation/ glorification on the cross intersect in the idea of love.[64] The Father's love for the Son before the foundation of the world and the sending of the Son coincide just as much, according to 17:24–25, as the sending of the Son and his path to the cross motivated by love for the world (3:13–14, 16; 10:17; 13:1). It is scarcely accidental that the first instances of κόσμος in the gospel are linked to preexistence-incarnation (1:9–10), cross (1:29), and sending (3:16). Like all the prominent New Testament authors, John took up Christological patterns that were from different tradition-historical backgrounds, and integrated them into an impressive comprehensive model. For him the Preexistent, Incarnate, and Sent One is none other than the Crucified and Exalted One (cf. 20:24–29), for in the cross the movement of the Son toward the Father and the Father toward the Son are become one.[65] Jesus Christ as preexistent and incarnate, as the One sent and glorified on the cross, is the all-embracing, personal answer to the question concerning an existence in love which is determined by God. For John, the incarnation does not mean letting go of the divinity of Jesus. Rather, in the Fourth Gospel Jesus' humanity is a correlate of his divinity. Jesus became human and at the same time remained God, that is, God in the mode of incarnation. He became human without distance and distinction, a human being among human beings. At the same time he is God's Son, also without distance and distinction in relation to God. For John, incarnation and glory are no more opposites than a Christology of the cross and a Christology of glory. John thinks synthetically. With him differing traditions that belong together as far as content is concerned flow into a unity. Moreover, John's dual patterns in no way reduce the significance of the cross, for they are integrated into an overarching argumentative flow. It is the idea of love that makes the cross, in the resurrection, the place of life. Love also accompanies and interprets John's dual patterns. Jesus' path to the cross into the glory of the resurrection stands in continuity with his entire being and activity, in the continuity of love. Jesus defines love as the readiness to let go of his life for his friends. In exemplary fashion he dies in this love and thus makes possible the gathering and salvation of the children of God.

---

[64] On the topic cf. Enno Edzard Popkes, *Die Theologie der Liebe Gottes in den johanneischen Schriften. Zur Semantik der Liebe und zum Motivkreis des Dualismus* (WUNT II/197; Tübingen: Mohr Siebeck, 2005).

[65] Cf. Kohler, *Kreuz und Menschwerdung*), 201–2.

All things taken together, John proves himself to be a master of interpretive integration by bringing together in his gospel very different streams of tradition guided by the knowledge of God's love for humankind in Jesus Christ.

Translated by Roy A. Harrisville,
Craig R. Koester, and Reimund Bieringer

Chapter 7

Touching the Risen Jesus:
Mary Magdalene and Thomas the Twin in John 20

Sandra M. Schneiders

In the last analysis, anything theology says about the resurrection of the body of those who have died in Christ stands or falls in terms of what we say about the bodily resurrection of Jesus himself. And our only access to the resurrection of Jesus, whether bodily, physical, spiritual, or none of these is the New Testament. Although there is a great deal of material in the New Testament about the resurrection, only three passages focus directly on the bodiliness of the risen one. The first is 1 Cor 15 in which Paul argues with members of the Corinthian community who, for philosophical reasons, regarded the material in general and the body in particular as worthless. Paul argues for the possibility, actuality, and significance of bodily resurrection as such, whether of Jesus or of believers.[1] The second is Luke 24:36–43, the narrative of Jesus' appearance to the startled and terrified disciples who think they are seeing a ghost. The risen one invites them to tactilely verify the solidity of his body, that he has "flesh and bones" in order to convince them that he is indeed the Jesus who was crucified and not a ghostly apparition.[2] Both the Pauline and Lukan texts were addressed to predominantly Hellenistic audiences whose dualistic anthropology made bodily resurrection a priori impossible or meaningless or both.

Interesting as these polemics are, and not unrelated to contemporary issues about the possibility of an afterlife, neither text addresses the primary

---

[1] For references on the probable ideological *Sitz-im-Leben* of the Corinthian correspondence, see Jerome Murphy–O'Connor, "The First Letter to the Corinthians," NJBC, 798-815, esp. 812. For a very good, brief treatment of Paul's position in contrast to the Corinthian position, see Peter Lampe, "Paul's Concept of a Spiritual Body," in *Resurrection: Theological and Scientific Assessments* (ed. Ted Peters, Robert John Russell, and Michael Welker; Grand Rapids: Eerdmans, 2002), 103–14.

[2] Hans-Joachim Eckstein, "Bodily Resurrection in Luke," in Peters, Russell, and Welker, *Resurrection*, 115–23, discusses both the polemic in Luke against the anthropological dualism of his predominantly Gentile community and Luke's subtle alternative to that position.

concerns of this essay, namely, the question of what role the bodiliness of the risen Jesus plays, and how it does so, in the relationship between Jesus and his disciples after the resurrection. Does the body of Jesus, which mediated his pre-Easter relationship with his disciples, continue to play that role for his post-Easter disciples, including us?[3] If bodily is synonymous with physical, then we are caught between two equally unacceptable positions. Either, on the one hand, Jesus is simply resuscitated (i.e., physically revived), which leaves him and us still subject to the conditions of space, time, and causality, and vulnerable to death, or, on the other hand, his resurrection is purely spiritual, and we are outside the Christian community's faith in the "resurrection of the body." By way of prolepsis, I am going to propose that Jesus' resurrection is *not* physical but *is* bodily and therefore that his body continues to mediate his relationship with his disciples but in a way that is both continuous and discontinuous with the way it did in his pre-Easter career.

I will argue this on the basis of the third New Testament text that focuses on the body of the risen Jesus, namely, the Johannine resurrection narrative, John 20, and specifically verses 11–18 (the Mary Magdalene episode) and 24–29 (the Thomas the Twin episode). In the first passage the risen Jesus prohibits Mary Magdalene from touching him and in the second he invites, even commands, Thomas the Twin to touch him. Our question is, what does John 20 say about the body of the risen Jesus and its role in his relationship with his disciples?

1. Presuppositions about the Theology of John

Before turning to the texts in question we have to lay a certain amount of biblical groundwork, first about the theology of the Fourth Gospel relative to resurrection and second about the structure and dynamics of the Johannine resurrection narrative as a whole. In the first section we need to look briefly at the eschatology and anthropology of the Fourth Gospel, which together govern John's approach to the resurrection of Jesus. In the second section we will look at the theological progression within the Johannine

---

[3] Following Marcus Borg in *Meeting Jesus Again for the First Time: The Historical Jesus and the Heart of Contemporary Faith* (San Francisco: Harper, 1994), 15–17, I prefer to use the terms "pre-Easter" and "post-Easter" to designate Jesus' life before the resurrection and his life after the resurrection respectively. The traditional term "earthly Jesus" can set up a theologically problematic dichotomy between the "Jesus of history" and the "Christ of faith" and implicitly deny the ongoing presence of the risen Jesus in the historical experience of his contemporary earthly disciples.

resurrection narrative and at the development within it of the dialectic between seeing, hearing, touching (i.e., sense experience), and believing.

1.1 John's Eschatology[4]

As is commonly recognized, the eschatology of the Fourth Gospel differs strikingly from that of the Synoptic Gospels. This difference is often expressed as the contrast between realized (i.e., present) and delayed (i.e., future) judgment. However, these two eschatologies involve much more than a temporal difference. Each is a theological approach to life, death, judgment, and afterlife.

In the Fourth Gospel Jesus' death is not presented, as it is in the Synoptics, as a *kenosis*, the nadir of his earthly life, a human condemnation from which God vindicated him through resurrection. In John, Jesus' death itself is the apotheosis, the victorious culmination of his life. In and by his death Jesus is glorified by God and exalted to God's presence.[5] He is proclaimed as king and reigns gloriously from the cross (John 19:19). Consequently, Bultmann observed in the mid-twentieth century:

> If Jesus' death on the cross is already his exaltation and glorification, *his resurrection* cannot be an event of special significance. No resurrection is needed to destroy the triumph which death might be supposed to have gained in the crucifixion.[6]

Bultmann and others have suggested that John's Gospel really ends with the crucifixion in chapter 19 and the Johannine resurrection narrative is merely a concession to the tradition which was normative by the time this gospel was written at the end of the first century. While this is hardly a satisfactory conclusion, it raises pointedly the question of what role the resurrection narrative does play in John's Gospel. It clearly does not play the vindicatory role it does in the Synoptics but, I would argue, it is crucial to John's theological purposes.

The two strands or types of eschatology we find in the New Testament are the descendents of two types of eschatological reflection that devel-

---

[4] Following convention among Johannine scholars I will use the term "John" to refer to the Fourth Evangelist or to the Gospel itself. This implies no position on the much-debated issues of Johannine authorship and the identity of the evangelist. My position on these questions is available in *Written That You May Believe: Encountering Jesus in the Fourth Gospel* (rev. ed.; New York: Crossroad, 2003), 233–54.

[5] ὑψόω, "exalt" or "lift up," is used several times in John to speak of Jesus' being lifted up on the cross as his exaltation (e.g., 3:14; 8:28; 12:32) and δοξάζω, "glorify," is used to speak of the effect on Jesus of his being lifted up in crucifixion (e.g., 7:39; 12:16; 12:23; 13:31–32), namely, that he is glorified by God and glorifies God by his death.

[6] Rudolf Bultmann, *Theology of the New Testament* (trans. Kendrick Grobel; 2 vols.; New York: Charles Scribner's Sons, 1951–55), 2:56.

oped in the latest Old Testament and the intertestamental writings.[7] The first type, which we might call "resurrection eschatology," was futuristic and apocalyptic. It developed in the context of the Syrian persecutions and the Hasidean-Hasmonean controversies in Palestine in the second to first centuries B.C.E. Faithful Jews, like the mother and seven brothers in 2 Macc 7, were being persecuted and even martyred for their fidelity to Torah, but they were strengthened by the hope that they would be vindicated by God after death. The clearest Old Testament expression of this eschatology is found in Dan 12:1–3, predicting the awakening of "many . . . who sleep in the dust," and 2 Macc 7, both of which are influenced by the Suffering Servant image of Deutero-Isaiah.[8] The martyrs are assured that they will be restored even in their bodies, that Israel will be reconstituted, and that the unjust will be finally punished.

This type of eschatology, characteristic of the Synoptic Gospels, was that of the Pharisees of Jesus' time. Matthew 25:31–46 portrays such a final vindicatory event, a last judgment, conceived as a sudden cosmic cataclysm (see Matt 24:15–44; Mark 13; Luke 17:22–37), when all will be raised to appear before the glorified Christ who will assign them to eternal reward or punishment on the basis of their comportment in this life. The role of bodily, even physical, resurrection in this eschatology is essentially functional. It renders the just and the unjust present for final judgment in which divine justice will be fully manifest. And it assures the participation of the whole person in the final sentence.

John's Gospel, unlike the Synoptics, operates within the other strand of late pre-Christian Jewish eschatology, which I will label "immortality eschatology." This eschatology is realized and sapiential rather than future and apocalyptic. It developed in the Hellenistic context of Diaspora Judaism, probably in the late second to first century B.C.E. Jews who had remained faithful to Torah even though living in a Hellenistic context were being persecuted and even killed, not only by pagans but by their religiously and culturally assimilated fellow-Jews.[9] Once again, there is appeal

---

[7] Although both the category "intertestamental" itself and the dates for the period and its literature are debated, for my purposes it designates the overlapping of Old Testament and New Testament experience and the writings reflective of that experience, extending roughly from 200 B.C.E. to about 100 C.E. My thanks to my Old Testament colleague, John Endres, for help with this issue.

[8] For a detailed comparison of texts showing the influence of Isa 26:20, 26:19, and 66:24 on Dan 12:1–3, see Sandra M. Schneiders, *The Johannine Resurrection Narrative: An Exegetical and Theological Study of John 20 as a Synthesis of Johannine Spirituality*, (2 vols.; Ann Arbor, Mich.: University Microfilms, 1983), 1:35–86.

[9] An excellent and provocatively suggestive treatment of the Wisdom of Solomon, its eschatology in relation to its *Sitz-im-Leben*, and its possible relation to the New Testa-

to a post-death solution to the problem of the intrahistorical victory of the unjust. The clearest (deutero)canonical expression of this eschatology occurs in Wisdom 1–6.

The wisdom Hero in this story, who epitomizes the faithful Jews, is persecuted unto death by the disciples of folly who mock his fidelity to the law, repudiate his claim to be God's son, and are infuriated by his accusation that they are unfaithful to their training and tradition (cf. Wis 2:10–20).[10] The LXX version of the fourth Suffering Servant song (Isa 52:13–53:12) and of the Dan 7 figure of the Son of Man surely influenced the portrait of the martyred hero in Wisdom of Solomon,[11] which was also influenced by Hellenistic notions of immortality. Unlike the future apocalyptic resurrection eschatology of 2 Maccabees, this sapiential eschatology presents the death of the righteous as an exaltation-for-judgment on his enemies and an immediate entrance into an intimate relationship with God in a non-terrestrial, post-death realm. The text tells us that, even though the hero is physically killed, "the souls of the just are in the hand of God . . . They seemed, in the view of the foolish, to be dead . . . but they are in peace . . . God took them to himself" (Wis 3:1–6).

Bodily, much less physical, resurrection such as we see in resurrection eschatology does not figure explicitly in this sapiential understanding of the destiny of the just and unjust because the judgment of the ungodly takes place in their very choice of evil by which they "summon death" (see Wis 1:16) and the just are exalted by and assumed to God in their very destruction by the unjust. However, the exaltation of the just is not simply immortality of the soul in the Greek philosophical sense, that is, the natural indestructibility of a spiritual substance. Their immortality is *life* in the Jewish sense (i.e., a gift from God), who alone possesses it by nature[12] and who freely bestows it on those who are loyal to the covenant. Furthermore, life, even after death, in which the body did not participate in some way

---

ment is Barbara Green's "The Wisdom of Solomon and the Solomon of Wisdom: Tradition's Transpositions and Human Transformation," *Hor* 30 (2003): 41–66.

[10] For the development of the extra-biblical literary genre of "wisdom tale" within which we meet "wisdom heroes" in non-canonical dress who resemble Joseph, Daniel, and Susanna, see G. W. Nickelsburg, *Resurrection, Immortality, and Eternal Life in Intertestamental Judaism* (HTS 26; Cambridge, Mass.: Harvard University Press, 1972), 49–55. The distinctiveness of the biblical wisdom heroes is that their wisdom consists in fidelity to Torah rather than in secular *savoir faire* or philosophically based ethics.

[11] See Schneiders, *The Johannine Resurrection Narrative*, 98–101, for the textual evidence for this position.

[12] This was explained well by Joseph Moignt, "Immortalité de l'âme et/ou résurrection," *LumVie* 21 (1972): 65–78, who takes essentially the same position as Oscar Cullmann in his classic text, "Immortality of the Soul or Resurrection of the Dead: The Witness of the New Testament," The Ingersoll Lecture, 1955, *Harvard Divinity School Bulletin* 21 (1955–1956): 5–36.

would have been inconceivable to the Jewish imagination. So, while it says nothing explicit about bodily resurrection, sapiential eschatology is fundamentally susceptible to it[13] and even in a way requires it.

This sapiential eschatology is easily discerned in the Fourth Gospel and is operative in John's presentation of the death of Jesus as the wisdom hero. His death is his exaltation in and by which his persecutors are judged and he is glorified (cf. John 16:8–11). This leads to two conclusions about the role of the resurrection narrative in John's Gospel.

(1) Because bodily resurrection is compatible with, perhaps even implicit in, even though not explicitly affirmed by sapiential eschatology, bodily resurrection *could easily become explicit* in this eschatology if the right pressures were brought to bear upon it (e.g., by the Easter experience of the first followers of Jesus).

(2) If bodily resurrection *did* become explicit (as I believe it did) within sapiential immortality eschatology it would not have the same meaning it has in apocalyptic, resurrection eschatology. It would not be seen as vindication of the persecuted since this vindication takes place in the very death/exaltation of the Just One. Nor would resurrection appear as a victory over death because death never has any real power over the one who is a child of God. Resurrection would be essentially a manifestation of the meaning for the whole bodyperson of life in God now lived in all its fullness. And, in the case of Jesus, as we will see, it would be a condition of possibility for his post-Easter personal presence to his disciples and his continuing action in the world.

I would suggest that the bodily resurrection of Jesus in John is presented precisely in terms of sapiential eschatology. The Johannine resurrection narrative in John 20 is, therefore, not a concession to the constraints of early Christian tradition. It is a narrative-theological exploration of the Easter experience of the first disciples and the implications of that experience for the spirituality of the Johannine community and later disciples. In other words, the two dimensions of Jesus' paschal mystery, his *glorification* on the cross (i.e., his passage out of this world to his Father) and his *resurrection* (i.e., his promised return to his own), though related, are not strictly identical in John. The glorification is the condition of possibility of the resurrection. Consequently, the appearances in John are not primarily

---

[13] It is important, however, but beyond the scope of this essay, to note that Jewish anthropology was influenced by Hellenistic philosophy in the immediate pre-Christian period. This is evident in the use of terms such as "incorruption" (ἀφθαρσία) in Wis 2:23 and "immortality" (ἀθανασία) in Wis 3:4. On the other hand, the characteristically biblical approach appears in Wisdom of Solomon in the notion that death is not intended by God but entered the world through the envy of the devil (cf. Wis 2:23–24) in contrast to the notion of death as a natural passage into nonexistence that the enemies of the wisdom hero enunciate in Wis 2:1–22.

about Jesus' post-death experience but about his disciples' experience of his return to them.

1.2 John's Anthropology

Closely related to the eschatology of the Fourth Gospel is its anthropology. Much discussion about bodily resurrection is subverted from the start by the fact that modern westerners tend to read the gospel texts through the lens of a basically dualistic and substantialist philosophical anthropology. John's anthropology, although expressed with Greek vocabulary which has clearly influenced his understanding of the person, is thoroughly rooted in the Hebrew language and sensibility.[14] The pertinent Greek terms, ψυχή (usually translated "soul"), ζωή ("life"), θάνατος ("death"), σάρξ ("flesh"), αἷμα ("blood"), πνεῦμα ("spirit"), and σῶμα ("body"), constitute a complex semantic field in which all the terms are interrelated and mutually qualifying. Although in English these terms each denote a *component or state* of the human being, in biblical usage they each denote the *whole person* from some perspective or under some aspect. Ignoring this difference can result in serious misunderstanding, such as the tendency of many moderns to hear cannibalistic overtones in Jesus' invitation to eat his flesh and drink his blood in John 6:52–58. It is crucial to understand what these anthropological terms meant in the context of John's first century Judaism in order to understand how they function in the Fourth Gospel as a whole, but especially in the account of Jesus' glorification and resurrection.

Space constraints prevent examining each of these terms, but two of them are critical to our purposes here: σάρξ in relation to αἷμα, that is, "flesh" and "blood", and σῶμα or "body." For moderns σάρξ and αἷμα denote two separable components of the human being, one solid and one liquid. However, flesh in John's anthropology is not a part of the human, distinct from bones and blood, but the whole person as natural and mortal.[15]

---

[14] A good introduction to Semitic anthropology is Hans Walter Wolff, *Anthropology of the Old Testament* (London: SCM, 1974; repr. Mifflintown, Pa.: Sigler, 1996). As we have seen in respect to his eschatology, the Gospel of John is not devoid of Hellenistic influences coming probably through Old Testament sapiential materials, esp. Wisdom of Solomon. However, this influence is controlled by Hebrew understandings of God, the human, and the end of human life. A thorough study of Johannine anthropology, which is completely beyond the scope of this paper, would proceed by tracing the path from the concrete and stereometric (to use Wolff's term) Hebrew usage through the changes rung on the terms in the Greek of the LXX into the Fourth Gospel. I suspect that the most original development is precisely John's exploitation of the distinction – not possible in Hebrew but possible in Greek – between σάρξ and σῶμα.

[15] "Flesh" is a good translation of σάρξ, which is a more differentiated term than the Hebrew בשר which denotes the human in his/her infirmity or weakness (Wolff, *Anthropology*, 26–31). But the Hebrew term covers the territory of "body" virtually com-

When flesh is combined with blood it denotes the person, mortal by nature, but actually alive. To say that in Jesus the word of God (λόγος τοῦ θεοῦ) became flesh (σάρξ) is to say that the word became fully human (i.e., mortal).[16] In the psalms especially we see "flesh" used to speak of humanity in its weakness and mortality: "God remembered that they were flesh, a passing breath that returns not" (Ps 145:21, see also 56:5; 65:3; 145:21 and elsewhere). In John 6:51 Jesus says that he *is* the living bread come down from heaven, and that the bread that he will *give* for the life of the world "is [his] flesh." Jesus is not talking about a physical part of himself. He is saying that in giving himself totally in death, which is only possible because he is flesh (i.e., mortal), he gives life to the world as bread gives life to one who eats it.

The most important term in this anthropological semantic field in relation to the resurrection of Jesus, and the one which John uses in a subtle way that marries Semitic and Hellenistic understandings of the human, is σῶμα, "body."[17] Because moderns tend to think of the body as a distinct substance in the human composite, the physical component as distinguished from the spiritual, they tend to equate it with flesh, itself misunderstood as the soft, solid component in distinction from blood and bones. In other words, body tends to be understood as a physical substance which is integral to but only a part of the person.[18]

For John, body is the person in symbolic self-presentation. The person may be living or dead[19] but it is the whole self, the bodyself, who is living

---

pology, 26–31). But the Hebrew term covers the territory of "body" virtually completely whereas Greek distinguishes σάρξ from σῶμα, a crucial distinction for John's theology of resurrection.

[16] For a very rich treatment of the meaning of flesh in John, see Dorothy Lee, *Flesh and Glory: Symbol, Gender, and Theology in the Gospel of John* (New York: Crossroad, 2002), 29–64.

[17] Here I disagree with Lee, *Flesh and Glory*, 45–46, who suggests that there is no significant difference between σάρξ and σῶμα. I will argue that there is a critically important difference. Jesus does not rise as "flesh" (σάρξ) but as "body" (σῶμα).

[18] It is interesting that psychosomatic medicine is discovering in various ways how completely the whole human is "body," not in the reductive sense of being nothing but physical matter, but in the sense of being, as a whole, a "bodyperson." This understanding is closer to the biblical understanding than the reductionistic anthropology spawned by the scientific revolution and the enlightenment. Nevertheless, contemporary understandings of the human are still quite dichotomous as is evidenced by the often mechanistic approaches to medical procedures.

[19] The Hellenistic influence on John's thought as well as the exploitation of the possibilities of the Greek language are clear here. בשׂר is not used to speak of a corpse (although נפשׁ occasionally is) but only of living creatures, whereas John does not use σάρξ (which the LXX uses for בשׂר) but σῶμα to speak of the corpses on the cross (19:31) and specifically of the dead body of Jesus (19:38, 40; 20:12) and of his risen body (2:21–22).

or dead. In Semitic thought, once the body of the dead person begins to decay, to fall apart, the person is no longer a person. Whatever trace of the individual may survive in Sheol, it is not a human being because it does not enjoy subjectivity, community, or union with God.[20] The body is quintessentially the person as self-symbolizing (i.e., as numerically distinct, self-consistent and continuous), a subject who can interact with other subjects, and who is present and active in the world.[21] A corpse, in John's vocabulary, is also called a body (John 19:31, 38, 40; 20:12) precisely because it symbolizes the whole person, the bodyself, in its transition from being to nonbeing or from presence to absence. The corpse is the symbolic (i.e., perceptively real) person in the process of becoming absent and when the person is finally and fully absent, when the corpse has decomposed (which, importantly, does not happen in the case of Jesus), it is no longer considered a body. In short, if the pre-Easter Jesus as *flesh*, that is, as mortal human being, was the symbolic presence of God's glory in this world (cf. John 1:14), Jesus as *body* is his own symbolic presence to his contemporaries. Prior to his death the two, flesh and body (i.e., the mortal human person called Jesus), are coterminous as they are in all humans in this life. The issue of "body" as distinct from "flesh" only arises when Jesus dies and the two are no longer coterminous.[22]

---

[20] I have never seen a better definition of Sheol than that of John L. McKenzie who says in "Sheol," *Dictionary of the Bible* (Milwaukee: Bruce, 1965), 800, that Sheol "is less a positive conception of survival than a picturesque denial of all that is meant by life and activity."

[21] I have dealt at length with the concept of symbol, especially as it functions in John's Gospel, in *Written That You May Believe*, 63–77. See also Lee, *Flesh and Glory*, 9–28. A still very important work on symbol in theology and especially on the body as the primary symbol by which a person is present to himself/herself as well as to others is Karl Rahner, "The Theology of the Symbol," in *Theological Investigations. More recent Writings* (23 vols.; trans. Kevin Smyth, Baltimore: Helicon Press, 1961–), 4:221–52, esp. 245–52 on the body. Joseph A. Bracken, in "The Body of Christ – An Intersubjective Interpretation," *Hor* 31 (2004): 7–21, dialogues with Rahner's position from the standpoint of neo-Whiteheadian metaphysics.

It is especially interesting that the term "body" does not seem to play a distinct enough role in Semitic thought to merit a term of its own in distinction from "flesh." The only bodies known to human experience were fleshly ones, either the potential human, the "earth creature" (האדם) of Gen 2:7, or the living person, נפש or בשר.

[22] I find very suggestive the point made by Mary Coloe in "Like Father, Like Son: The Role of Abraham in Tabernacles–John 8:31–59" *Pacifica* 12 (1999): 1–11: "In speaking of Jesus as both Temple and Tabernacle there is no dichotomy as the two are intrinsically related as the flesh (1:14) is related to the body (2:21). The Tabernacle and the Temple serve the same symbolic function even though they recall different historical eras" (p. 4, n. 6). I think that, in fact, flesh and body denote different and subsequent modes (analogous to historical eras) of the presence of Jesus to his disciples. Flesh indi-

The issue of Jesus' real presence in and after his passage through death dominates the last supper in John (chapters 13–17) as well as the resurrection narrative (chapter 20). Where is the Lord? Has he gone where his disciples cannot follow? Are they orphans, deprived of the glory of God that had been present in the flesh of Jesus? Are future believers condemned to a faith based on hearsay about events in which they did not and do not participate? Unless Jesus is bodily risen, unless he is alive in the full integrity of his humanity (i.e., symbolized bodily), he is not present, either as the presence of humanity in God or as God's divinely human presence to us.

The crucial anthropological/theological issue for the topic of resurrection is then the relation of flesh to body (i.e., of the pre-Easter person of Jesus) as mortal human being to the post-Easter person of Jesus as glorified Son of Man. By way of anticipatory summary, I will propose that the relation of flesh to body is precisely what is altered by Jesus' glorification. In his pre-Easter existence as flesh, the body of Jesus (i.e., his personal symbolic presence) was conditioned by his mortality. He was subject to death and to the limitations of space, time, and causality that natural human life entails. In his glorification Jesus goes to the Father as a human bodyself and in his resurrection he returns to his own in the full integrity of his humanity. His body is real, both continuous and discontinuous with his pre-paschal body. To say that the glorified and risen Jesus is a body-person is to affirm that he is numerically distinct, a personal subject who can be intersubjectively present and active,[23] but he is no longer flesh. And he will be present as this same bodyself throughout post-Easter time in the range of symbols through which his personal presence will be manifest.

2. The Structure and Dynamics of the Johannine Resurrection Narrative

Increasingly Johannine scholars recognize that the resurrection narrative of the Fourth Gospel is not a random collection of interchangeable episodes but an organic literary/theological unity and that the clue to its meaning

---

cates his career as a mortal and body his glorified life. But the two terms denote the same person and the same presence of the glory of God among humans in that person.

[23] A fascinating article on the body of Jesus in its displacements, transformations, and resignifications which brings a confirming postmodern light to bear on this topic is Graham Ward, "Bodies: The Displaced Body of Jesus Christ," in *Radical Orthodoxy: A New Theology* (ed. John Milbank, Catherine Pickstock, and Graham Ward; London/New York: Routledge, 1999), 163–81, esp. 168. See also Ward's article, "Transcorporeality: The Ontological Scandal," *BJRL* 80 (1998): 235–52.

lies in its structure.²⁴ There, however, the consensus ends. Scholars have proposed a surprising number of very plausible structures for John 20, including chronological and geographical, numerological and verbal, narrative and dramatic, theological and spiritual ones, many of which are complementary rather than contradictory, even though they lead to different interpretations.²⁵ Obviously, we cannot review them here but I will propose two complementary structures, one theological and one spiritual, without implying agreement or disagreement with other theories. My proposal is in service of the purpose of this particular paper, namely, responding to the question of how the body of the glorified Jesus functions in the relationship between Jesus and his post-Easter disciples.

2.1 The Theological Structure of John 20

In vv. 1–2 the narrative is introduced. Mary Magdalene comes to the tomb in darkness (always negatively symbolic in John), finds the *stone* taken out of the tomb, and reports to Simon Peter and the beloved disciple that "they have taken the *Lord* out of the tomb and we do *not know where* they have laid him" (20:2). The "we," even though Mary was alone at the tomb, marks the problem as not merely personal but communal.²⁶ The program-

---

²⁴ Dorothy A. Lee, "Partnership in Easter Faith: The Role of Mary Magdalene and Thomas in John 20," *JSNT* 58 (1995): 37–49. Although she regards the structure as an important indication of meaning, Lee does not consider the first scene, the beloved disciple and Simon Peter at the tomb, to be truly integral to the meaning of the Johannine resurrection narrative (pp. 38–40). She considers the pericope a minor prolepsis preparing for chapter 21. I disagree with this position although I find her treatment of Mary Magdalene and Thomas as "narrative partners" in Easter faith encircling the central episode of the appearance to the disciples enlightening.

²⁵ Recently, Robert Crotty, in "The Two Magdalene Reports on the Risen Jesus in John 20," *Pacifica* 12 (1999): 156–68, summarized and criticized a number of the major attempts to decipher the structure of John 20: Francis Moloney, *The Gospel of John* (SP 4; Collegeville, Minn.: Liturgical Press, 1998), 516; Dorothy A. Lee, "Partnership in Easter Faith"; Brendan J. Byrne, "The Faith of the Beloved Disciple and the Community in John 20," *JSNT* 23 (1985): 83–97; Ignace de la Potterie, "Genèse de la foi pascale d'après Jn 20," *NTS* 30 (1984): 26–49; Donatien Mollat, "La foi pascale selon le chapître 20 de l'évangile de saint Jean (Essai de théologie biblique)," in *Resurrexit: Actes du symposium internationale sur la résurrection de Jésus* (ed. E. Dhanis; Rome: Libreria Editrice Vaticana, 1974), 316–34; L. Dupont, C. Lash and G. Levesque, "Recherche sur la structure de Jean 20," *Bib* 54 (1973): 482–98; Raymond E. Brown, *The Gospel according to John XIII-XXI* (AB 29A; New York: Doubleday, 1970), 965. This list is by no means exhaustive. Crotty, of course, offers his own structuring of the chapter.

²⁶ Crotty, in "The Two Magdalene Reports," 159, follows many commentators in seeing the "we" as an "aporia," a trace of a source text which originally included other women (as we find in all three synoptic resurrection narratives) who accompanied Mary Magdalene to the tomb. However, unlike many he suggests that John uses the "we" to make Mary Magdalene a representative of the community vs. the "they" who have taken

matic question which drives the first half of the Johannine resurrection narrative, vv. 3–18, is announced: "Where is the Lord?" after his death. It also suggests one possible answer: Jesus is a corpse. He is truly gone.

In the next episode, vv. 3–10, Simon Peter and the beloved disciple run to the tomb. The evangelist carefully structures this story so that Peter enters the tomb first and sees its contents: the grave clothes and the face veil, the σουδάριον, of Jesus lying not with the clothes but carefully wrapped up and definitively put aside (20:7).[27] The beloved disciple enters second and sees what he did not see from the outside when he first peered in. From outside he had seen only the grave clothes (20:5). Inside, he sees also the face veil and we are told that he "saw and believed," an expression which John uses for the appropriate faith response to a sign (e.g., 2:23; 6:30; 11:40).

This sign, the face cloth now laid aside, is both continuous and discontinuous with the signs done by Jesus in his public ministry. One characteristic of signs in both dispensations is that they are symbolic and therefore intrinsically ambiguous. Everyone present saw the healed man who was born blind in chapter 9 and the raised Lazarus in chapter 11. Some saw and believed. Others saw and did not believe. In this episode both Simon Peter and the beloved disciple see the face cloth. The beloved disciple believes; Peter does not.

But this sign is also different from those worked by the pre-Easter Jesus. Jesus himself is not visibly present doing a work. In this episode the disciples are offered as sign an object that must be interpreted as revelatory, probably in terms of the face veil of Moses, which he wore to shield the Israelites from the glory of his face but removed when he dealt "face to face" with God (cf. Exod 34:29–35).[28]

The finale of the scene (v. 9), however, has often defied exegetes: "for as yet they did not understand the scripture, that he must rise from the dead." So, if not the resurrection, what *did* the beloved disciple believe? I would suggest that he believed what Jesus had repeatedly said of his death (e.g., 13:1; 16:28; 17:1; 17:24), namely, that by it he would be glorified. The beloved disciple believed that on the cross, though he truly died, Jesus was exalted into the presence of God. The face cloth of his flesh (i.e., his mortality in which his glory had been veiled during his pre-Easter career)

---

the Lord (p. 164). I prefer this position to the attribution of redactional clumsiness to a writer of John's skill. I also think it carries ecclesiological freight.

[27] Ἐντετυλιγμένον is in the perfect tense, denoting a punctual action whose effects are permanent or enduring in effect.

[28] For the linguistic argument for this Old Testament background for John's use of σουδάριον, see Schneiders, *Written That You May Believe*, 207–8.

is now definitively laid aside. Jesus, the new Moses, has gone up the mountain to seal the new covenant between God and the new Israel.

The reader now has the beginning of the answer to the question, "Where is the Lord?" He is with God. He is glorified. But there is more, something the disciples do not yet understand, namely, that Jesus is not only *glorified* but *risen* from the dead.

In the next episode, vv. 11–18, Mary Magdalene is again at the tomb. This scene is redolent with allusions to the garden of the first creation and especially the place of trysting of the Song of Solomon, the wedding song of the covenant between Yahweh and Israel. In the tomb Mary sees not grave clothes and face veil but two angels sitting, one at the head and one at the feet of the place where the body (σῶμα) of Jesus had lain. This verbal picture, and even the words, recall the golden throne, the "mercy seat," of the ark of the covenant (cf. Exod 37:6–9 and the LXX version Exod 38:5–8) which was guarded by two cherubim, one at either end of "the meeting place of God and humans."[29] Mary Magdalene is weeping in desolation at the absence of Jesus, whom she clearly equates with a corpse that has been taken away. When Jesus, the good shepherd, calls her by name, she turns, she is converted from her despair to recognition of him as indeed the "teacher" she had known in his pre-paschal life. There is infinitely more in this rich scene, but for our present purpose it provides the second dimension of the answer to the question, "Where is the Lord?" He has returned to his own. When Mary comes proclaiming (ἀγγέλουσα) the Easter gospel to those who are now the "brothers and sisters" of Jesus, she says explicitly, "I have seen the *Lord*" (20:18). The beloved disciple saw and believed through a sign, that Jesus was glorified, alive with God. Mary Magdalene has experienced him risen, returned to his own.

With the proclamation of the Easter gospel, that Jesus is both glorified and risen, the narrative enters its second phase, vv. 19–29, which takes place not at the dawn of the new era in the garden of the tomb to the first apostle but in the evening of the first day of that new era, in Jerusalem "where the disciples were gathered" as a community. The question "Where is the Lord?" now gives way to the question which dominates the second half of the Johannine resurrection narrative, "How can the risen Lord be experienced?" This first scene of this second part, vv. 19–23, Jesus' coming to the community, is the centerpiece of the Johannine resurrection narrative. Despite locked doors, Jesus rises up in the midst of the community. Behind the Greek ἔστη εἰς τὸ μέσον (literally, Jesus "stood into the midst" of the community) stands the Aramaic verb for "rise up" which can refer either to standing up physically or rising from the dead. As he had promised in his first public act in the temple of Jerusalem, Jesus, on the

---

[29] Richard J. Clifford, "Exodus," *NJBC*, 56.

third day, raises up the new temple of his body in the midst of the community. In the temple Jesus' opponents had challenged him:

> "What sign can you show us . . . ?" Jesus answered and said to them, "Destroy this temple, and in three days I will raise it up." . . . But he was speaking about the temple of his body [σῶμα]. Therefore, when he was raised from the dead, his disciples remembered that he had said this, and they came to believe the scripture and the word Jesus had spoken. (John 2:18–22)

The scene then unfolds in two actions, both inaugurated by Jesus' "Peace to you," fulfilling his promise to give them, upon his return, a peace the world cannot give (cf. 14:27; 16:33). The character of the first action is signaled by the verb δείκνυμι ("show" or "manifest"), a Johannine term denoting revelation. Jesus shows them his hands and his side (i.e., he reveals to them the meaning for them of his glorification), and they rejoice at this revelation that the Lord himself is indeed in their midst, glorified but still marked with the signs of his paschal mystery. His bodyself is both continuous and discontinuous with the one they had known who had promised that his going away would constitute a new coming to them (14:28).[30]

The second action, following the repeated gift of peace, is a commissioning of this new people as God had commissioned Jesus. He breathes on them and says "Receive the Holy Spirit." The verb "breathe" (ἐμφύσαω) is a hapax legomenon, occurring only here in the whole New Testament. It occurs only twice[31] in the Old Testament: in Gen 2:7 when God, at the first creation, breathes life into the earth-creature and it becomes the first living human being and in Ezek 37:9–10 when the prophet in God's name breathes life into the dry bones to recreate, to raise from the dead, the people Israel. In this Easter scene it occurs for the third time when Jesus breathes the promised Spirit of the new covenant into the community of disciples, creating them as the new Israel.

The structure of this scene is that of the Sinai covenant experience, in which the great theophany on the mount was followed by the giving of the

---

[30] Both verbs in this text are in the present. One would expect "after I have gone away I will come back to you" but instead we have, literally, "I go away and I come to you." It might be paraphrased, "My going away is my coming to you," i.e., my departure from you in the *flesh* is my coming to you in the *Spirit*. In fact, this is why it is expedient or necessary for the disciples that Jesus depart (cf. John 16:7). As flesh he would be unable to establish the kind of mutual interiority with his disciples that he can in the Spirit who will be with them and in them (cf. John 14:16–17).

[31] Actually, the verb appears four times in the LXX, the two instances adduced here, plus Wis 15:11 which recalls the enlivening of Adam and thus is not an independent third instance, and 1 Kgs 17:21, recounting the prophet Elijah's reanimation of the son of the widow of Zarephath. The LXX inaccurately (but perhaps deliberately) translates the Hebrew for "stretched" or "measured" as "breathed," perhaps alluding to the creation narrative.

law which made Israel the people of God. Through the prophet Ezekiel God had promised a new covenant:

> I will make a covenant of peace with them; it shall be an everlasting covenant with them; and I will bless them and multiply them, and will set my sanctuary among them forevermore. My dwelling place shall be with them; and I will be their God, and they shall be my people. Then the nations shall know that I the Lord sanctify Israel, when my sanctuary is among them forevermore. (Ezek 37:26–28; cf. 34:25 and Isa 54:10)

God now appears not in thunder and lightening but in the person of Jesus glorified and risen. And as promised in Ezek 36:27–28: "I will put my spirit within you, and make you follow my statutes," the Holy Spirit, the new law, is poured forth in their hearts. Jesus, as God had promised, here establishes the new covenant with the new Israel, raising up in its midst the new temple of his body. Thus is the church founded, commissioned to continue Jesus' mission of taking away the sin of the world and holding fast all those whom God had given him. It is important to note that the evangelist does not tell us that Jesus, having completed his work, leaves or departs. Jesus has definitively returned to his own. He will come and come again but he never leaves. That he is present and knows what transpires in his community is clear from what follows.

The final scene in the Johannine resurrection narrative, vv. 24–29 concluding with 30–31, the Thomas episode and its conclusion, at first seems out of place.[32] Nothing in the preceding scene suggested that anyone was missing when Jesus appeared on Easter night. Thomas is identified as "the Twin."[33] His double identity is immediately specified: he is both "one of the Twelve" and thus was a companion of the pre-Easter Jesus and participant in the pre-Easter signs, and he was "not with" the gathered disciples on Easter night when Jesus appeared and thus he is one of those who will

---

[32] Although I cannot deal with it here, there is a hypothesis that seems to have some merit to the effect that this episode might have had anti-gnostic purposes. Mary Magdalene and Thomas are important figures in the gnostic literature and they play very significant roles in John's gospel that they do not play in the synoptic resurrection accounts. See April D. DeConick, "'Blessed Are Those Who Have Not Seen' (Jn 20:29): Johannine Dramatization of an Early Christian Discourse," in *Nag Hammadi Library after Fifty Years* (Leiden: Brill, 1997), 381–98, who proposes that the Thomas episode was composed to refute the Thomasine Christians in Syria whose characteristic soteriology appears in the *Gospel of Thomas*. She proposes that the *Gospel of Thomas* may date from 70–80 C.E. and thus might have been available to the fourth evangelist.

[33] M. de Jonge, "Signs and Works in the Fourth Gospel," in *Miscellanea Neotestamentica II* (ed. T. Baarda, A. F. J. Klijn, and W. C. van Unnik; NovTSup 48; Leiden: Brill, 1978), 119. He calls Thomas "a borderline case" because he is the last of those who see signs and the first of those who must believe on the word of witness. I agree that he stands on the border between the Easter experience and later experience of the risen Jesus but I do not think that signs are replaced by the word of witness. Rather, one kind of sign gives way to a new kind of sign.

know the resurrection not through an Easter experience but through the testimony of the church, "We have seen the Lord."

Thomas refuses this new structure of faith, refuses to enter this new dispensation. He insists that he will believe only if he can touch the very wounds of Jesus, only if he can return to the dispensation of pre-Easter faith, only if he can continue to relate to Jesus in the flesh. Note that Thomas is not spontaneously mistaking the glorified Jesus for the pre-paschal Jesus as had Mary Magdalene. He is demanding that Jesus be for him as he had been prior to the glorification. And note further that Thomas does not "doubt" as is so often averred. He refuses: "I will not believe." In John's Gospel believing and refusing to believe are always a matter of free choice, not the natural response to irrefutable evidence or the lack thereof.

Jesus comes again, a week later, on Sunday night, the time of the early church's eucharistic celebrations. Again he "rises up in the midst of them," greets them with peace, but this time, though the doors are shut marking the boundaries of the church community, there is no mention of fear of the authorities. Jesus' initial gift of peace has cast out fear. We are in post-paschal time. But Jesus directly addresses Thomas whose inner thoughts and outer words he knows perfectly. "I know mine and mine know me" (John 10:14).

He invites Thomas not to do what Thomas had demanded – to physically probe the wounds in his hands and side in order to verify his physical resuscitation – but to a different but just as real experience of his true identity. He says, "Bring here your finger and *see my hands*." One does not "see" with one's finger. The imperative, ἴδε, "Behold!" or "See!" as M. de Goedt pointed out many years ago, functions in the Fourth Gospel as part of a revelation formula.[34] The invitation is not to see physically but to grasp what cannot be seen with the eyes of flesh (e.g., that Nathaniel is a true Israelite without guile or that the beloved disciple on Calvary is now the true son of the mother of Jesus). The wounds of Jesus are not a proof of physical reality but the source of a true understanding of the meaning of Jesus' revelatory death.

Then the invitation reaches deeper. Jesus commands Thomas to put his hand into his open side from which had issued the lifegiving blood and water, symbol of the gift of the Spirit in baptism and the eucharist which Jesus had handed over in his death and had focused in the gift to the community a week earlier when Thomas was absent. This is followed immediately by the imperative μη γίνου ἄπιστος ἀλλὰ πιστός. Note that Jesus does not say, "Do not doubt." Ἄπιστος means to refuse to believe, to be unfaithful, to be treacherous. Thomas's immediate response, not an attempt

---

[34] Michel de Goedt, "Un schème de révélation dans le quatrième évangile," *NTS* 8 (1962): 142–50.

to touch Jesus physically but an acknowledgement of what he can grasp only by faith, makes clear his conversion from unfaithful to faithful, his transition from his stubborn absorption with the flesh of Jesus, "Unless I touch physically I will not believe," to his self-gift to the risen one, "My Lord and my God." In other words, Jesus says to Thomas not what the Lukan Jesus says to his disciples who disbelieve their eyes through startled joy: "Feel me and see that I have flesh and bones, that I am not a ghost," but rather "Thomas, grasp in faith what my saving death means and appropriate in faith the fruits of that death, the Spirit poured forth from my open side." He is saying in effect what he said to Simon Peter at the last supper, "Unless you enter by faith into the new dispensation inaugurated by my glorification you can have no part with me."

Jesus welcomes Thomas's conversion unreservedly and confirms his Easter faith by one of the only two macarisms in the Fourth Gospel. Jesus equates the two kinds of believing. Faith based on seeing pre-paschal signs, which was appropriate to the first dispensation, is supplanted by post-paschal faith that will be based on a new kind of sign, like the folded up face veil, the apostolic testimony of Mary Magdalene and the rest of the disciples, the words of scripture, which will now be mediated by the church. "Blessed are those (now including Thomas) not seeing and believing." It is not later disciples who are assimilated to Thomas, but Thomas who is assimilated to the later believers. The pre-paschal era is over, even for those who participated in it.

The evangelist then concludes the Gospel by directly addressing the disciples of the post-Easter dispensation. The pre-Easter Jesus, says the evangelist, did many visible signs, only some of which are written in the Gospel. But the written gospel has exactly the same function in the faith of later disciples that the signs Jesus performed in Palestine had for the apostolic generation.[35] Through believing, these later disciples will have life in Jesus' name just as did his pre-Easter companions. Contrary to what some exegetes, who insert an adversative conjunction between the two parts of v. 29, would suggest, namely, that Jesus derogates Thomas's faith based on seeing and exalts the faith of those who have not seen signs and yet have believed, Jesus does not assign superiority to either the first generation's experience or that of later disciples. As Dorothy Lee has well said, the faith of future believers is dependent on the witness of the apostolic community but in no way limited by that dependence. "Thomas's confession is a narrative bridge between Easter Sunday and the life of the believ-

---

[35] Peter Judge, "A Note on Jn 20,29," in *Festschrift Frans Neirynck* (ed. F. Van Segbroeck et. al.; 3 vols.; Leuven: University Press, 1992), 3:2183–92, cites U. Schnelle and D. A. Carson as scholars who, like himself, take the position that the Thomas incident itself is a sign and the gospel will function in the same way for later believers.

ing community."[36] The point is neither that faith in response to signs is defective nor that sense experience, seeing and hearing and touching, will have no further role in faith. The mode, not the fact, of seeing must change because the mode, not the fact, of Jesus' bodily presence to his disciples has changed.

2.2 The Dialectic of Sense Experience and Believing

We turn now, very briefly, to make explicit the dialectic between sense experience and believing which emerges as the spiritual structure of the Johannine resurrection narrative before drawing conclusions about the body of the risen Jesus from the Mary Magdalene and Thomas incidents specifically.

After the introductory verses in which the question, "Where is the Lord?" is introduced, we have a scene in which Jesus does not appear visibly. The beloved disciple comes to faith in the glorification of Jesus upon encountering a sign, the folded face veil. At the other end of the Johannine resurrection narrative is the evangelist's conclusion assuring later disciples that in scripture, in which Jesus also does not appear visibly, Jesus is really and salvifically encountered. In other words, at the beginning and the end of the resurrection narrative is an encounter with Jesus through signs, through sensible material realities, in which Jesus does not appear in visible form. Both of these scenes recount experiences that are historically realistic, the kinds of experiences believers have in "ordinary time," if you will, as they taste bread and wine, hear words, feel water.

Moving inward we have three scenes that take place in "extraordinary time," that are clearly a theological narrativizing of spiritual experience, real but not physical, rather than the recounting of ordinary human events taking place in ordinary time. In the very middle is the scene of the establishment of the covenant community that will be in the world the ordinary mode of the glorified Jesus' presence and action (i.e., will be his body). Assured of his identity and presence and enlivened by his Spirit the community will forgive sins and hold fast in communion all those whom God will entrust to it as Jesus took away the sin of the world (cf. 1:29) and held fast all those the Father had given him (cf. 6:37; 6:39; 10:27–29 ; 17:12; 18:9).

Flanking this historicized narration of the founding of the church as the fully realized bodily but nonphysical and definitive presence of Jesus in the world are two episodes that occur in an "in-between" time/place, what we might call Easter time, when Jesus is both present and absent. Their purpose is to narratively unfold the intrinsic relationship between Jesus himself, as a distinct bodyperson, and the ecclesial community which is his

---

[36] Lee, "Partnership in Easter Faith," 48.

body in the world. In other words, they are about the relationship of Jesus to Christ, mediated by the category "body," the body of the risen Jesus, which is the principle of the ecclesial body of Christ. The two are identical, though not reductively so; distinct but inseparable. It is time, then, to examine these two scenes in terms of Jesus' seemingly contradictory commands to Mary Magdalene not to touch him and Thomas the Twin to touch him.

3. Conclusions on Touching the Risen Jesus

Both Mary Magdalene and Thomas the Twin undergo conversions that consist in turning away from a mode of experience that is no longer possible and turning toward a new, unfamiliar, but equally real mode of experiencing Jesus. Both, in response to a negative imperative of Jesus (what they must not do: do not touch, do not be faithless) followed by a positive imperative (what they are now called to: find me in the community, recognize me in believing) must pass over from the pre- to the post-Easter dispensation. But the emphasis in each episode is different. The two actors are in different positions in the story, Mary Magdalene bridging the pre-Easter with the Easter time; Thomas the Twin bridging the Easter with the post-Easter time. And their experiences respond to the two presiding questions: (1) *Where* is the Lord encountered? and (2) *How* is the Lord encountered?

Mary Magdalene is the first pre-Easter disciple to encounter the risen Lord. She erroneously thinks that the past dispensation has been reinstated. Things will be as they had always been. Literal misunderstanding in John's Gospel is a literary technique to describe growth in faith. Mary reaches out to touch Jesus, to relate to him as she had in the past, using a form of address suitable to that time, "Rabbouni," but Jesus forestalls her attempt: "Do not touch me."

There is no textual basis for the often expressed opinion that Mary was clinging hysterically to Jesus or trying to hold him back from ascending.[37] The verb is ἅπτω "touch," not κρατέω, "grasp," or "hold on to." (The verb κρατέω is in John's vocabulary and he uses it in its normal sense in the very next scene, in 20:23.) Jesus' response is μή μου ἅπτου. The imperative verb is in the imperfect tense reflecting an ongoing or continuous activity and the negative particle is in the emphatic position. The point is that

---

[37] See Lee, "Partnership in Easter Faith," 42, against this interpretation which, however, Frank J. Matera, in "John 20:1–18," *Int* 43 (1989): 405, and Teresa Okure, "The Significance Today of Jesus' Commission to Mary Magdalene, *International Review of Mission* 81 (1992): 180, both defend.

physical "touching" – which is an apt metonymy for the physically mediated historical experience of two people relating "in the flesh," that is, as mortal human beings – has come to an end. Jesus says: "Go to my *brothers and sisters*." The place where Mary will now encounter Jesus as he really is, glorified and risen, is the community. Mary must pass over from the pre-Easter to the Easter dispensation. Her proclamation to the other disciples makes clear that she has indeed made that transition. She no longer speaks of "Rabbouni." As first apostle of the resurrection she proclaims "I have seen the *Lord*."[38]

In the Thomas episode things are quite different. The Easter experience has taken place. The ecclesial community, constituted by the new covenant mediated by Jesus on Easter night, proclaims to Thomas, "We have seen the Lord." Mary was the first of the Easter community of apostolic witnesses. Thomas is the first of the post-Easter generation who must respond in faith to their witness.

Thomas does not, like Mary, simply misunderstand his experience; he categorically refuses to believe the testimony of the community. He says, in effect, "You may have seen the Lord, but I haven't, and until I do see physically I will not believe." Thomas does not deny their experience. He simply says he will not substitute their experience for his. What he misunderstands is that it is not *their experience* that he must accept in place of his own but their *witness* upon which *his own experience* must be grounded. It is the problem of all believers down through the centuries who must somehow grasp that faith is not accepting something as true on the basis of external authority. It is allowing the testimony of the church to

---

[38] Although discussing this point is beyond the scope of this essay I want to note the growing consensus among biblical scholars and theologians that Mary Magdalene is, by every criterion available in the New Testament, an apostle. Pheme Perkins, in " 'I Have Seen the Lord' (John 20:18): Women Witnesses to the Resurrection," *Int* 46 (1992): 31–41, says that the Johannine Mary Magdalene episode at least establishes a woman as an independent witness to the resurrection. Teresa Okure in "Jesus' Commission to Mary Magdalene," 184–85, correctly makes the point that Mary Magdalene is not simply "the apostle to the apostles," as if her mission ended once theirs began. She is the apostle commissioned to announce the resurrection to the church. However, her role is not limited to announcing the resurrection (like the Emmaus disciples) but she is commissioned, (like Paul), to proclaim the good news, that is, the new status of believers as children of God. Lee in "Partnership in Easter Faith," 46–47, says that she is the first apostle, the first disciple of the risen Lord, and the representative of the community of faith. A major exegetical/theological study of all the New Testament material on Mary Magdalene, and which comes to virtually the same conclusion, is Gerald O'Collins and Daniel Kendall, "Mary Magdalene as Major Witness to Jesus' Resurrection," *TS* 48 (1987): 631–46. The growing consensus about Mary Magdalene's apostolic identity appeals primarily to the Johannine text.

initiate one into personal experience through the Spirit of the living God present in Jesus.

It is important to note that Thomas's attitude would have been just as problematic during the time of the pre-Easter Jesus as it was after Easter. Sense experience plays an important role in faith but not as physical proof of the "facts." One could eat the bread at the Sea of Tiberias and, precisely as Jesus says to the crowds who sought him afterward, *not* see the sign of Jesus as the bread of life (cf. 6:26) but be seeking a reliable guarantee of material food. The Pharisees in chapter 9 saw the blind man healed and the Jews in chapter 11 saw Lazarus called forth from the tomb after four days. So one could probe the wounds of the risen Jesus and not see the sign of his real presence. Similarly, in post-paschal time, Jesus is available, whether in eucharist or Scripture or mystical experience, only to faith.

Jesus, who is already "there" because he knows what Thomas has said, appears in the community from which Thomas had been separated not only physically but spiritually. And Jesus' being there, his real presence, is precisely what the community mediates to Thomas by its testimony. The community is not reporting a past event that Thomas accidentally missed and now has to accept on someone else's word. It is witnessing, pointing to, a present reality available to him in faith as it is to them in faith. Jesus' command to Thomas is: "Be not unbelieving, but believing." The invitation to touch, as we have seen, is not an invitation to physical verification which cannot cause or ground faith but to sacramental experience, to *seeing* what the crucifixion really means, to *appropriating* what the open side really offers.

Sacramental experience is not disembodied. It is an experience of the spiritual precisely in the material. Jesus invites all his post-Easter disciples to an experience that is in continuity with but different from the faith based on the signs performed in the pre-Easter dispensation. The continuity consists in the material mediation, the actual sensible experience of seeing, hearing, tasting, touching. However, the mediating material is no longer perishable bread at the Sea of Tiberias but the eucharistic meal flowing from the open side of the glorified Jesus, no longer physical eyesight restored in the waters of Siloam, but the baptismal opening of the eyes of faith in the water pouring from that same source. Thomas signifies his conversion in his exclamation, "My Lord and my God," which is a response not to flesh probed but to what Thomas could not see physically but only in faith. He, and all later disciples come to faith through an experience of signs, material mediations of spiritual reality. But the signs in the new dispensation are not the visible flesh of the pre-Easter Jesus but the sacramental body of the Lord which is, and is mediated by, the church.

The whole second half of the Johannine resurrection narrative is an unfolding of the new dispensation of signs that will supplant the signs of the pre-Easter dispensation. The fundamental sign, the ur-sacrament, of the really present Jesus is the ecclesial community itself, which is now the body of Christ, the new temple raised up in the world. The community witnesses in the word of proclamation rooted in Scripture, through the celebration of the sacraments, through its ministry of reconciliation, through its community of mutual love that washes feet and lays down life, and through the mutual indwelling of its members in Jesus in contemplative prayer. The response to that witness, from the first disciples and down through the ages, is the recognition of Jesus as Lord and God to which Jesus replies, "Blessed are you . . . because you believe."

The purpose of these two episodes of "touching" is to help the reader make the same transitions that Mary Magdalene and Thomas the Twin had to make, from a romantic fantasy of contemporaneity with the pre-Easter Jesus through the paschal experience of death and new life to faith in the glorified and risen Lord. But in making this transition two extremes must be avoided. One is to see the church not as a mediation of the risen Jesus himself but as an exhaustive substitute for a Jesus who no longer exists. The other is a gnostic attempt to relate to Jesus in a purely spiritual Jesus-and-I spirituality that rejects the sacramental structure of the ecclesial body of the Lord as a merely human organization that plays no necessary or essential role in our encounter with Jesus. Mary Magdalene had to realize that the church is the *body* of Christ (Jesus is not a corpse) and Thomas had to realize that the Church is the body of *Jesus* (not an unsatisfactory substitute for him).

The ecclesial community, doing in the world the works that Jesus did (cf. 14:12), is truly the body of Christ, the corporate person who is the organ of Jesus' salvific action in the world. But this can only be the case if Jesus himself, the principle of that ecclesial body, is actually alive in the full integrity of his personal humanity. This is the significance of maintaining that Jesus is *bodily* risen from the dead (i.e., that what body signifies, namely, numerical identity, personal subjectivity grounding interpersonal presence and effective action in the world) is verified in him after his death on the cross. Jesus is no longer in the flesh (i.e., he is no longer mortal). He is no longer subject to the conditions of time, space, causality. The description of the tomb as empty of his corpse, his being not recognizable to Mary Magdalene, his being able to appear in the midst of his disciples despite locked doors, his knowing what Thomas thought and said in his absence, are narrative devices for insisting on both the real bodiliness and the non-fleshliness of the risen Jesus.

If Jesus is not a real, distinct, personal subject, a real bodyperson, there is no ontological foundation for the Jesus mysticism that has been a constant feature of the church's spirituality, at least from the stoning of Stephan, who saw *Jesus* standing at the right hand of God, and Paul, who learned that it was *Jesus* whom he was persecuting, down to our own day. But if Jesus is merely physically resuscitated, if he is still in the flesh, then he cannot be mediated by a community from which he would be not only distinct but separate.

In summary, John's resurrection narrative is not about Jesus' vindication after his shameful death. It is about where and how his disciples, the first generation symbolized by Mary Magdalene, and all those who were not with them when Jesus came symbolized by Thomas the Twin, will encounter Jesus as *their* Lord and God.

In the Gospel itself believing is presented as a response to seeing the works of Jesus and hearing his revelatory discourse. Johannine scholars continue to argue over whether John's Gospel was written to *delegitimate* faith based on seeing signs in favor of faith based solely on hearing or to present seeing and hearing as *indispensable* mediators of revelation.[39] I believe that the very nature of the incarnation as the symbolization of the wisdom/word of God in sensible form indicates the latter position. The word of God became flesh; we have seen his glory; our hands have handled the word of Life. And he is still with us.

However, precisely because Jesus appeared in the flesh (i.e., as a mortal human being), his human career as flesh had to come to an end. But if, as I believe to be the case, the dynamic of sensible experience mediating faith is a permanent feature of the revelatory economy of salvation, it must somehow continue after the departure of the pre-Easter Jesus through death. Chapter 20 of John's Gospel, enlightened by the last discourses in which Jesus explains his "going away" through death as a new mode of "coming to" his disciples in the Spirit, is an attempt to elucidate how the sense-experience-mediating-faith dynamic is realized in a new mode after the resurrection. The Mary Magdalene and Thomas the Twin episodes explore the personal appropriation by disciples of the new location and the new mode of experience of Jesus, risen bodily and now acting through his ecclesial body. The category of body, no longer equated with flesh, body that is material in the sense of being a principle of individuation but not in the sense of being a principle of physicality, is used by the evangelist to

---

[39] For a good overview of this dispute ranging from those who regard John's Gospel as a critique and/or rejection of faith based on signs through those who see signs as playing a critical role in faith only during the career of the pre-Easter Jesus to those seeing signs as permanently important in faith even though the kind of sign is different after the resurrection, see Judge, "A Note on Jn 20,29." My position belongs in the last category.

assure the reader that it is Jesus himself who is not only glorified in God's presence but who has returned to us and that we will see him and hear him and touch him, experience his real presence in our lives and in our world, through our participation in the life of the ecclesial community. But we are also assured that we are, and are challenged to be, individually and communally, his real presence, his body in the world. Jesus says that "in that day," namely, our own post-Easter day, "you will know that I am in the father and you in me and I in you" (John 14:20) and that "the works that I do you also will do, and greater than these will you do" (John 14:12).

Chapter 8

Resurrection, Recognition, Reassuring: The Function of Jesus' Resurrection in the Fourth Gospel

Jesper Tang Nielsen

One of the groundbreaking methodological insights from the pioneering work of narrative criticism has been to conceive of a text as an autonomous meaning-producing construct. Neither the intentions of the author nor the effects on the reader determine its significance or exhaust its meaning. To prevent these fallacies – the intentional and the affective – real readers and authors have been rigorously but rightfully separated from implied readers and authors. Nowadays it is commonplace in New Testament studies to place them on separate levels of communication.[1]

Although narrative methodology has made important points and is still a sound starting point for exegetical analysis, the time has come to ask if some aspects of the texts are overlooked by a strict narrative approach. A neglected aspect of interpretation is that the narrative has been constructed to provoke an emotional and cognitive response from its readers. Narrative studies have focused on the reading process of the Fourth Gospel, but it has primarily been to detect an implied reading strategy and thereby show the readers' contribution to the meaning production.[2] This approach tends to overlook the fact that the text involves an implied reading strategy in order to influence its real readers. Even if a text constitutes an internal narrative universe that produces an autonomous meaning independent of ex-

---

[1] The main figure introducing narrative methods in Johannine studies is R. Alan Culpepper, *Anatomy of the Fourth Gospel. A Study in Literary Design* (Philadelphia: Fortress, 1983). An influential work from the field of literary criticism is Seymour Chatman, *Story and Discourse. Narrative Structure in Fiction and Film* (Ithaca and London: Cornell University Press, 1978).

[2] E.g., Jeffrey L. Staley, *The Print's First Kiss: A Rhetorical Investigation of the Implied Reader in the Fourth Gospel* (Atlanta: Scholars Press 1988), and the contributions in R. Detweiler, ed., *Reader Response Approaches to Biblical and Secular Texts* (*Semeia* 31; Chico, Calif.: Scholars Press, 1983).

ternal historical factors, it is constructed to affect the reader either by transforming or confirming a presupposed worldview.[3]

According to this perspective, the resurrection of Jesus in the Fourth Gospel has a function within the Johannine narrative and in relation to the reader. Even though the evangelist honored the demands of tradition by including Jesus' passion and resurrection in his gospel, he did not do so unwillingly.[4] On the contrary, he incorporated it meaningfully into the narrative structures and gave it a function in the overall purpose of the gospel.[5] By being firmly integrated in the narrative, the resurrection obtains a unique Johannine significance that is the basis for the intended effect on the readers.

To analyze both aspects, the well-known narrative text model will be combined with insights from Aristotle's Poetics.[6] Aristotle provides a spe-

---

[3] The social function of the gospel is dominant within exegetical traditions that are informed by social sciences, but these approaches primarily focus on the implicit and possibly unconscious functions of the text and not on the explicit and deliberate intent. See, e.g., Wayne A. Meeks, "The Man from Heaven in Johannine Secterianism," *JBL* 91 (1972): 44–72; David Rensberger, *Johannine Faith and Liberating Community* (Philadelphia: Westminster, 1988); Norman R. Peterson, *The Gospel of John and the Sociology of the Light. Language and Characterization in the Fourth Gospel* (Valley Forge, Pa.: Trinity Press International, 1993). In a completely different way, some feminist, postcolonial and queer readings focus on the actual readers. See, e.g., the articles in Katharine D. Sakenfeld and Sharon H. Ringe, eds., *Reading the Bible as Women: Perspectives from Africa, Asia and Latin America* (*Semeia* 78; Atlanta: Scholars Press, 1997); Musa W. Dube and Jeffrey L. Staley, eds., *John and Postcolonialism* (London: Sheffield Academic Press, 2002); Dale B. Martin, *Sex and the Single Saviour. Gender and Sexuality in Biblical Interpretation* (Louisville: Westminster John Knox, 2006).

[4] Contra Ernst Käsemann, *Jesu letzter Wille nach Johannes 17* (4th ed.; Tübingen: J.C.B. Mohr, 1980), 23.

[5] In the following I understand chaps. 1–20 to constitute the Fourth Gospel. Chapter 21 will not be taken into consideration. The problems about its relation to chapters 1–20 are well known and will not be repeated here. Cf. Christian Dietzfelbinger, *Das Evangelium nach Johannes I* (Zürcher Bibelkommentare 4.1–2; Zürich: Theologischer Verlag, 2001), 350. The findings of my own exegesis will, however, confirm the understanding that the first twenty chapters of the Fourth Gospel constitute a narrative unity to which chap. 21 must be considered an appendix. For a different opinion see, e.g., Hartwig Thyen, *Das Johannesevangelium* (HNT 6; Tübingen: Mohr Siebeck, 2005), 772–74; R. Alan Culpepper, "Designs for the Church Imagery of John 21:1–14," in *Imagery in the Gospel of John. Terms Forms, Themes, and Theology of Johannine Figurative Language* (ed. Jörg Frey, Jan G. van der Watt and Ruben Zimmermann; WUNT 200; Tübingen: Mohr Siebeck, 2006), 369–402.

[6] Aristotle's Poetics has been influential on narrative interpretations of the Fourth Gospel. See, e.g., F. R. M. Hitchcock, "Is the Fourth Gospel a Drama?" in *The Gospel of John as Literature* (ed. Mark W. G. Stibbe; NTTS 17; Leiden: E.J. Brill, 1993), 15–24; repr. from *Theology* 7 (1923); Culpepper, *Anatomy of the Fourth Gospel*, 79–98; idem, *The Gospel and Letters of John* (IBT; Nashville: Abingdon, 1998), 72–86; Pierre Bühler,

cific focus on the emotional relationship between the tragedy and the spectator, which enlightens the relationship and interaction between different levels of communication and illuminates these aspects of the Fourth Gospel.[7]

1. Narrative Theory and Communicative Levels

Some of the fundamental insights of narrative theory stem from investigations into the process of communication, which have been carried out within different fields of research. Semiotic studies in particular have pointed out that communication involves several levels.[8] The relationship between sender and recipient constitutes one level; another consists of the message that is communicated between them. It is appropriate to call the former one the level of communication since it involves the persons who actually communicate. This distinction makes it possible to separate the investigation of the historical situation of communication from the analysis of the message itself. When the message takes the form of a narrative, another pair of levels can be distinguished inside the text. It can be depicted in a model where the sender-recipient relationship has been transformed into an intra-textual structure, as an implied author and an implied reader between whom the narrative is communicated.[9]

In the textual model two intra-textual levels can be separated. An act of communication is established when the implied author communicates the narrative to the implied reader. The implied author gives voice to the entire text and is represented on the textual surface when he gives information

---

"Ist Johannes ein Kreuzestheologe? Exegetisch-systematischer Bemerkungen zu einer noch offenen Debatte," in *Johannes-Studien. Interdisziplinäre Zugänge zum Johannes-Evangelium* (ed. M. Rose; Neuchatel: Secrétariat de l'Université, 1990), 191–207; Mark W.G. Stibbe, *John as Storyteller. Narrative Criticism and the Fourth Gospel* (SNTSMS 73; Cambridge: Cambridge University Press, 1992); Kasper B. Larsen, *Recognizing the Stranger. Recognition Scenes in the Gospel of John* (PhD diss., University of Aarhus, 2006 [Biblical Interpretation Series 93; Leiden: Brill, 2008]). But his ideas of tragic emotions have not yet been taken into account.

[7] Historically, this focus may be due to the philosophical debate about the function and benefit of art that Aristotle was involved in. Cf. Stephen Halliwell, *Aristotle's Poetics* (Chapel Hill, N.C.: University of North Carolina Press, 1986), 1–41; Richard Janko, "From Catharsis to the Aristotelian Mean," in *Essays on Aristotle's* Poetics (ed. Amélie O. Rorty; Princeton: Princeton University Press, 1992), 341–58.

[8] Cf. e.g., Umberto Eco, *A Theory of Semiotics* (Bloomington: Indiana University Press, 1976).

[9] The model exists in different versions. Cf. Umberto Eco, *The Role of the Reader. Explorations in the Semiotics of Texts* (Bloomington: Indiana University Press, 1979), 5; Chatman, *Story and Discourse*, 267; Culpepper, *Anatomy of the Fourth Gospel*, 6.

about the narrated figures or comments on the narrated events. The implied reader, on the other hand, is seldom explicit in the text. The implied reader is rather a reading strategy or a conceptualization of the competence and the reactions that are foreseen by the implied author.[10] This level can be named the discoursive level.[11]

The next level is constituted by the narrative that the implied author tells the implied reader. It can be labeled the narrative level on which the plot takes place. It is important to separate this level from the discourse because the narrative level does not include the information or commentary that is given on the level of the discourse. Furthermore, the narrative level is distinguished by its temporal perspective: A progression of time and a course of action are necessary to construct a proper narrative. Something happens on the narrative level!

---

[10] U. Eco, who calls the implicit reader a 'Model Reader,' thinks that a text produces its own reader by establishing a reading strategy that a concrete reader must follow to realize the *intentio operis*, Umberto Eco, *Interpretation and Overinterpretation* (Cambridge: Cambridge University Press, 1992), 64.

[11] In a Johannine context it is relevant to emphasize that the point of view of the implied author is beyond the narrative. He embraces the entire story and is consequently able to make proleptic statements and construe the plot with an overall structure and meaning. Cf. Algirdas-Julien Greimas & Joseph Courtès, "Énunciation," *Sémiotique. Dictionnaire raisonné de la théorie du langage* (Paris: Hachette Supérieur, 1979), 125–28. A.-J. Greimas and J. Courtès distinguish an enunciator from a narrator. The former is the "voice" of the entire text including the narrator's comments. In contrast to the narrator, the point of view of the enunciator is necessarily beyond the narrative. Due to this distinction the possibility arises that the narrator may be untrustworthy but still integrated meaningfully into the overall purpose of the text. For the interpretation of the Fourth Gospel it is convenient not to separate these two levels, but let them be comprised in the concept of the implied author. This means that the point of view of the Johannine implied author and narrator coincides with the point of view of an enunciator. Consequently, it does not separate the Fourth Gospel from other narratives that the point of view in the Johannine authorial comments (e.g., 2:21.22; 7:39; 12:16) belongs to a time after Easter ("nachösterlich"). For a different interpretation see, e.g., Christina Hoegen-Rohls, *Der nachösterliche Johannes. Die Abschiedsreden als hermeneutischer Schlüssel zum vierten Evangelium* (WUNT II/84; Tübingen: J.C.B. Mohr, 1996), 32–50; Jörg Frey, *Die johanneische Eschatologie II: Das johanneische Zeitverständnis* (WUNT 110; Tübingen: Mohr Siebeck, 1998), 221–23.

2. Aristotle's Theory of Tragedy and Tragic Emotions

Although Aristotle's *Poetics* focuses on ancient Greek tragedies, his analyses have universal narratological importance.[12] According to Aristotle himself, the general relevance of his poetical investigations stems from the fact that epic differs from tragedy only because it has an unchanging meter and a narrative mode. Hence, knowledge of tragedy includes knowledge of epic (*Poet.* 1449b 17–18).

In his treatise Aristotle does not explicitly distinguish different levels of communication, but his famous definition of tragedy implies at least two levels:

> Tragedy, then, is mimesis of an action which is elevated, complete, and of magnitude; in language embellished by distinct forms in its sections; employing the mode of enactment, not narrative; and through pity and fear (ἔλεος καὶ φόβος) accomplishing the catharsis (κάθαρσις) of such emotions (*Poet.* 1449b 24–28).[13]

One level consists of the dramatic enactment of an action of a certain character (elevated, complete, and of magnitude). In the model of communication, this is the narrative level insofar as the tragic representation corresponds to the narrated story. Another level is the emotional response (pity and fear) evoked by the mimesis and the result of these tragic effects (*katharsis*). This level concerns the participants in the communication and not the narrated figures. It corresponds to the discursive level. Aristotle does not distinguish real spectators or readers from implied ones, but he insists on a controllable relationship between the mimesis of the narrative and the effects on the spectator. This leads him to operate with a typified recipient of the narrative level, while readers and spectators do not always react according to conventions.[14] The Aristotelian conception of the spectator correlates with the implied reader of narrative theories.

---

[12] Although the differences between Aristotle's ancient understanding of art and modern conceptions of literature should be noted, cf. Elizabeth Belfiore, "Narratological Plots and Aristotle's Mythos," *Arethusa* 33 (2000): 37–70.

[13] Unless otherwise noted all texts and translations are from LCL.

[14] In his *Rhetoric* Aristotle mentions that not all persons react in a conventional way to a speech. Some people are ruined from suffering too much, others think themselves too fortunate to suffer, and neither is able to feel pity (*Rhet.* 1385b 19–24). Likewise, some people are too self-confident to fear (*Rhet.* 1383b 1–5). The acknowledgement that not all actual listeners, and by implication spectators and readers, will react according to conventions, corresponds to separating real and uncontrollable recipients from the idea of a predictable and conventionally reacting recipient.

The Discoursive Level in Aristotle's Poetics

Aristotle's definition of tragedy has produced a wasteland of unsettled questions. Every element is highly disputed, but the discussion of *katharsis* probably surpasses all. It has been described as "a grotesque monument of sterility."[15] The problems arise from the fact that Aristotle never defines *katharsis* accurately. Although he, in his *Politics*, promises a thorough presentation of the concept in his work on aesthetics (*Pol.* 1341b 40), the term only appears in the quoted definition, and Aristotle never clarifies the intended result of the tragedy. S. Halliwell has proposed the appealing interpretation that *katharsis* means habituation of emotions.[16] Spectators, readers, or listeners experience artistically provoked emotions when they enjoy a work of art. Through this aesthetic experience they are habituated to such emotions and learn to manage them in real life.[17] Consequently, the intended *katharsis* of pity and fear denotes an aesthetic education that furthers the ability to remain in self-control and to keep such emotions in accordance with reason. In this way art has a positive function; it serves the classic virtues of antiquity.

Halliwell bases his interpretations on three arguments. First of all, the aesthetic theory of Aristotle is an answer to Plato's denunciation of mimetic art in the tenth book of the *Republic*. Therefore, the understanding of *katharsis* must be integrated into a rejection of the Platonic theory as part of the Aristotelian defense of poetic emotions. In the end, *katharsis* is the legitimate purpose of arousing emotions. Second, the concept of *katharsis* was used in medical, religious, and philosophical contexts prior to Aristotle. It had already acquired an extended meaning and could be used in a metaphorical – though not necessarily non-physical – manner to denote purgation through various means, such as religious rituals, philosophical training, or music. Third, this metaphorical cathartic function is the topic of Aristotle's treatment of music (*Pol.* 1341b–42b). In the relevant passage he explores the cathartic effects of different kinds of music on different kinds of people. Aristotle divides melodies into ethical, practical, and passionate harmonies, which have different purposes and must be used in dif-

---

[15] J. Morley according to Halliwell, *Aristotle's Poetics*, 184. Halliwell presents a history of interpretations, Halliwell, *Aristotle's Poetics*, 350–56.

[16] Halliwell, *Aristotle's Poetics*, 184–96. To the discussion, cf. Jonathan Lear, "Katharsis," *Phronesis* 33 (1988): 297–326; repr. in *Essays on Aristotle's* Poetics (ed. Amélie O. Rorty; Princeton: Princeton University Press, 1992), 315–40; Janko, "From Catharsis to the Aristotelian Mean;" Stephen Halliwell, "Pleasure, Understanding, and Emotion in Aristotle's *Poetics*," in *Essays on Aristotle's* Poetics (ed. Amélie O. Rorty; Princeton: Princeton University Press, 1992), 241–60.

[17] The "emotions become better attuned to the perception of reality, and, consequently, as Aristotle believed, better disposed towards virtue." Halliwell, *Aristotle's Poetics*, 197.

ferent manners (*Pol.* 1341b 34). In education the ethical must be employed. For listening, the two others are preferred because they produce the kind of emotions that are purged through the musical experience:

> ... for any experience that occurs violently in some souls is found in all, though with different degrees of intensity – for example pity and fear (ἔλεος καὶ φόβος), and also religious excitement; for some persons are very liable to this form of emotion, and under the influence of sacred music we see these people, when they use tunes that violently arouse the soul, being thrown into a state as if they had received medicinal treatment and taken a purge (κάθαρσις); the same experience then must come also to the compassionate and the timid and the other emotional people generally in such degree as befalls each individual of these classes, and all must undergo purgation (κάθαρσις) and a pleasant feeling of relief; and similarly also the purgative melodies (τὰ μέλη τὰ καθαρτικά) afford harmless delight to people (*Pol.* 1342a 4–16).

Taking his starting point in the extreme case of hypersensitive people, who literally fall into religious frenzy when exposed to passionate melodies, Aristotle draws conclusions about the general effect of music. After the passionate experience, these people are left with a kind of relief as if they have found healing or *katharsis*. Not all persons are susceptible to such intense religious feelings, but they are disposed to pity and fear, which music evokes in them. Just like the hyper-sensitive person, the compassionate and timid achieve a kind of *katharsis* when they experience these emotions. The point is that *katharsis* is the result of musical experience because music arouses emotions and lets the listener find relief when the emotional influence ends. So, Aristotle concludes, *katharsis* is a result of the affective response to music, which may be different from person to person, but nevertheless is a possibility for everyone.

The moral value of music comes from the habituation of the emotions that aligns them with moral qualities. Through the artistic production of emotions the listener learns to control his emotions and keep them in accordance with reason, so that he is able to direct them toward the right objects.

By means of the plot-structure, tragedy serves the same objective as music. When the spectators witness events that in real life provoke pity and fear, they have an emotional and cognitive experience that results in ethical education: "... tragic *katharsis* in some way conduces an ethical alignment between the emotions and the reason: because tragedy arouses pity and fear by appropriate means it does not, as Plato alleged, 'water' or feed the emotions, but tends to harmonize them with our perceptions and judgments of the world."[18]

Tragic emotions are pity and fear. In the *Poetics* Aristotle defines them as responses to the tragic structure of the play. They are, however, not

---

[18] Halliwell, *Aristotle's Poetics*, 201.

radically different from sympathetic reactions to real events. The only difference is that the tragic emotions are provoked by a mimesis of a course of actions. Pity and fear arise when the tragic figures experience something that reminds the audience of their own human vulnerability.[19] For that reason both tragic emotions demand a sympathetic relationship to their objects: Pity is oriented towards the tragic characters that must in some way be like the spectators. Fear is directed towards the tragic misery itself, which must be something the spectators fear for themselves.

This interpretation of pity and fear originates in Aristotle's explication of the emotional response of an audience in his treatise on rhetoric.[20] He defines pity:

> Let pity then be a kind of pain excited by the sight of evil, deadly or painful, which befalls one who does not deserve it; an evil which one might expect to come upon himself or one of his friends, and when it seems near. For it is evident that one who is likely to feel pity must be such as to think that he, or one of his friends, is liable to suffer some evil, and such an evil as has been stated in the definition, or one similar, or nearly similar (*Rhet.* 1385b 13–19).

Apart from the fact that the misery must be undeserved, there must be a sympathetic relationship between the subject and the object of pity. Only when the subject can imagine himself in the role of the innocent victim, does he pity the object. Men pity persons suffering something they fear for themselves.

A comparable structure defines fear:

> Let fear be defined as a painful or troubled feeling caused by the impression of an imminent evil that causes destruction or pain (*Rhet.* 1382a 21–22).

Whereas pity concerns someone else, fear concerns oneself or someone closely related. A sympathetic relationship is indispensable for this emotion, since fear is always directed towards the future and the subject only fears what he imagines could happen to himself. Men fear for themselves what they pity in others.

Both pity and fear have a cognitive status. They are not just spontaneous feelings but emotional consequences of the perception of the sufferer's status and situation.[21] At the same time, they depend on an

---

[19] Nussbaum, "Tragedy and Self-Sufficiency: Plato and Aristotle on Fear and Pity," *Oxford Studies in Ancient Philosophy* 10 (1992): 107–59, esp. 118–23.

[20] Cf. e.g., Halliwell, *Aristotle's Poetics*, 168–184; Martha C. Nussbaum, *The fragility of goodness. Luck and ethics in Greek tragedy and philosophy* (Cambridge: Cambridge University Press, 1986), 383–86; idem, "Tragedy and Self-Sufficiency," 133–37; Alexander Nehamas, "Pity and Fear in the *Rhetoric* and the *Poetics*," in *Essays on Aristotle's* Poetics (ed. Amélie O. Rorty; Princeton: Princeton University Press, 1992), 291–314

[21] Cf. Halliwell, *Aristotle's Poetics*, 182.

understanding of one's own identity that establishes a relationship of sympathy to the sufferer.

At this point it can be concluded that the Aristotelian understanding of the effect of a tragedy can be expressed in the model of communication. To adapt Aristotle's approach, we can say that the implied author tries to produce a certain emotional reaction from the implied recipient. This response leads to *katharsis*. Following the interpretation of *katharsis* it may furthermore be stated that the tragedy lets the audience be habituated to the tragic emotions so that they can control them in real life afterwards. Just as the theoretical model of communication demonstrates, the means of producing this effect is the message that is communicated. In the case of Aristotle, the tragedy as a structured and performed play is the medium for the tragic effect, i.e., the narrative level causes the tragic emotions.

The Narrative Level in Aristotle's Poetics

Because *katharsis* through pity and fear is the objective of tragedy, Aristotle focuses his systematic treatment on the best way to produce these effects. Three factors are important in the representation of the tragic object: the plot (μῦθος), moral character (ἦθη), and thought (διάνοια). The *mythos* is synonymous with the "structure of events" (*Poet*. 1450a 4) and is determined to be the most important factor of the tragedy:

> The most important of these things is the structure of events, because tragedy is mimesis not of persons but of action and life (*Poet*. 1450a 15–17).

A tragedy can exist without character but not without a course of action; as a matter of fact, the tragedy portrays the character for the sake of the action, not the other way around (*Poet*. 1450a 21–22). Accordingly, the *mythos* is the foundation (ἀρχή) and soul (ψυχή) of tragedy (*Poet*. 1450a 38–39). It is defined:

> We have stipulated that tragedy is mimesis of an action that is complete, whole, and of magnitude . . . A whole is that which has a beginning, middle, and end (*Poet*. 1450b 23–27).

Although this definition of a whole *mythos* may seem self-evident, it is fundamental to the understanding of narratives that the three phases follow each other logically, either from necessity or from probability.[22] The beginning does not presuppose anything but leads into the middle, which is dependent on the preceding beginning. As a consequence of the middle, the end follows, but after the end nothing more happens (*Poet*. 1450b 24–

---

[22] To Aristotle's notion of a logical development in tragedy see Dorothea Frede, "Necessity, Chance, and 'What Happens for the Most Part' in Aristotle's *Poetics*," in *Essays on Aristotle's* Poetics (ed. Amélie O. Rorty; Princeton: Princeton University Press, 1992), 197–219.

30). From this it follows that the acting persons do not constitute the unity of the *mythos*; it is the action itself that is the unifying factor when it develops from happiness to unhappiness or from unhappiness to happiness.

Although pity and fear may be provoked by other elements of the tragedy, e.g., the enactment of a horrible accident, it is better to arouse the emotions through the course of events:

> In addition, tragedy's most potent means of emotional effect (ψυχαγωγός) are components of plot (μῦθος), namely reversals (περιπέτειαι) and recognitions (ἀναγνωρίσεις) (*Poet.* 1450a 33–35).

The best way to provoke pity and fear is not through a continuous decline or progression in the persons involved. On the contrary, the change must happen as a *peripeteia*, i.e., an unexpected reversal from one situation to its oppo-site (*Poet.* 1452a 1–6, 22–23). These two courses of development form the basis of a distinction between simple and complex *mythoi* (*Poet.* 1452a 12–18). The complex *mythoi* involving *peripeteia* are the better, according to Aristotle. But some of the best *mythoi* involve a cognitive reversal called *anagnōrisis*:

> Recognition (ἀναγνώρισις), as the very name indicates, is a change from ignorance to knowledge, leading to friendship or enmity, and involving matters which bear on prosperity or adversity (*Poet.* 1452a 29–32).

The two factors, reversal and recognition, along with pitiful events (πάθος) (*Poet.* 1452b 10) are the means for evoking the tragic emotions. The best tragedies involve all three elements in a complex structure of events.

The cause of the *peripeteia* is also relevant for the tragic effect. The act that brings the tragic figure into misery can be done in different ways: It may be committed with or without knowledge of its character, and it may or may not be carried out. On that basis Aristotle deduces a schematic presentation of four different tragic *mythoi* (*Poet.* 1453b 27–1454a 15): (1) The tragic act is planned with knowledge of its character but is not carried out. This is actually the story of a change of mind and is not tragic at all. (2) The tragic act is committed with knowledge of its character, as in the case of Euripides' *Medea*. Aristotle does not find it appealing since it hardly evokes fear and pity. (3) The tragic act is committed without knowledge of its character. This is the case in Sophocles' *King Oedipus*. (4) The tragic act that is about to be committed without knowledge of its character but is prevented before it is accomplished. This is the structure of Euripides' *Iphigeneia in Tauris*.

To Aristotle the two procedures last mentioned are the better because they involve not only a *peripeteia* in the reversal from happiness to unhappiness but also an *anagnōrisis* in the recognition of the tragic act.

Recognition happens when the protagonist realizes the cause of his misfortune, whether it is accomplished or not.

But the quality of a tragedy is also dependent on the cause of the transition from ignorance to knowledge. Aristotle evaluates the possible causes in a complex taxonomy (*Poet.* 1454b 19–1455a 21): *Anagnōrisis* may be caused (1) by tokens or signs (ἡ διὰ τῶν σημείων), which may be congenital or acquired, e.g., birthmarks or scars; (2) by elements of the play that do not follow logically from the plot (αἱ πεποιημέναι ὑπὸ τοῦ ποιητοῦ); (3) by memory, when a sight reminds a person of something (ἡ διὰ μνήμης); (4) by logical reflection (ἡ ἐκ συλλογισμοῦ), which sometimes is combined with (5) a false reasoning on the part of the spectators (ἐκ παραλογισμοῦ τοῦ θεάτρου); (6) by a probable consequence of the process of events (ἡ ἐξ αὐτῶν τῶν πραγμάτων), i.e., the recognition follows naturally from the *mythos*. Aristotle prefers the last possibility over the others. It leads to the conclusion that the best *mythoi* involve both a *peripeteia* and an *anagnōrisis* that arises from the structure of the *mythos*.

This taxonomy of *mythoi* is interconnected with Aristotle's assessment of types of characters involved in the tragedy (*Poet.* 1452b 34–1453a 17). To provoke a tragic emotional response the protagonists cannot be evil characters. Neither the fortune nor the misfortune of evil persons provokes pity and fear. But they cannot be good characters, either. Their fortune is not tragic and their misfortune is just repugnant. This leaves the third possibility, that the persons portrayed are in the middle of the moral spectrum, neither good nor evil but comparable to ordinary people, "someone like us," and obvious objects of sympathy:

> Such a person is someone not preeminent in virtue and justice, and one who falls into adversity not evil and depravity, but through some kind of error (ἁμαρτία) . . . (*Poet.* 1453a 7–10).

The concept of *hamartia* takes up a central role in Aristotle's summary of the best-structured tragedies:

> The well-made plot (μῦθος) then, ought to be single rather than double, as some maintain, with a change not to prosperity from adversity, but on the contrary from prosperity to adversity, caused not by depravity but by a great error of a character (ἁμαρτία μεγάλη) either like that stated, or better rather than worse (*Poet.* 1453a 12–16).

It is fundamental to the arousal of tragic emotions that the persons are not to blame for their misery. Consequently, *hamartia* is located in between the situations where one is guilty of one's own misfortune and those where an innocent person is struck by misfortune. *Hamartia* is a conceptualization of human frailty and guarantees the sympathetic emotions of the spectators. The person that commits a *hamartia* is neither innocent, nor can he be blamed for the tragic action. He is indeed a tragic hero, because he causes his own reversal from happiness to unhappiness by an act that he has committed in ignorance of its nature.

The concept of *hamartia* within Aristotelian thinking in general and in his *Poetics* in particular is another vigorously debated area.[23] The main texts for interpreting the central passage of the *Poetics* are texts from the *Nicomachean Ethics* and the *Rhetoric*. A passage of the *Nicomachean Ethics* discusses just and unjust acts and agents, and makes the following distinction:

> When the injury happens contrary to reasonable expectation, it is (1) a misadventure (ἀτύχημα). When, though not contrary to reasonable expectation, it is done without evil intent, it is (2) a culpable error (ἁμάρτημα); for an error is culpable when the cause of one's ignorance lies in oneself, but only a misadventure when the cause lies outside oneself. When an injury is done knowingly but not deliberately, it is (3) an act of injustice or wrong (ἀδίκημα) . . . (*Eth. nic.* 1135b 16–20).

A culpable error (ἁμαρτήματα) is defined as an act done in unnecessary ignorance. The doer did not know the character of his act; therefore he did not commit a wrong (ἀδίκημα). However, it was not impossible for him to anticipate the possible consequences of the act; therefore it was not a misadventure (ἀτύχημα). E.g., Oedipus committed a culpable error (ἁμάρτημα) because he did not know that the man he killed was his father, but he should have known that the man was somebody's father; therefore it was not contrary to reason that it was his own father.

This corresponds to the treatment of excusable acts in the analysis of forensic speech in the *Rhetoric*. Aristotle defines the three unjust acts as equitable (*Rhet.* 1374a–1374b):

> Misadventures (ἀτυχήματα) are all such things as are unexpected and not vicious; culpable errors (ἁμαρτήματα) are not unexpected, but are not vicious; acts of injustice or wrongs (ἀδικήματα) are such as might be expected and vicious, for acts committed through desire arise from vice (*Rhet.* 1374b 6–10).[24]

Aristotle's point is that these unjust acts should not be treated as voluntarily committed wrongful acts. For different reasons and to a different degree they are forgivable, because they live up to the following definition of equity:

> For that which is equitable seems to be just, and equity is justice that goes beyond the written law (*Rhet.* 1374a 26–28).

---

[23] To the history of interpretations see Jan M. Bremer, *Hamartia. Tragic Error in the Poetics of Aristotle and in Greek Tragedy* (Amsterdam: Adolf M. Hakkert, 1969).

[24] The translation is adjusted to the translation of *Eth. nic.*

Since the acts mentioned are unjust according to the actual deed committed but equitable according to the motive or cause of action, they should not be punished in the same way as common violations of the law.

It can be concluded that the reason for the tragic development lies in an act that was not intended to be vicious but turned out to be illegitimate and punishable. Although *hamartia* cannot be reduced to a cognitive concept, lack of knowledge is an inherent aspect of the tragic act. Nobody knowingly commits a *hamartia*. But there may be various reasons why a person would commit it.[25] It includes acts done in ignorance, as it is primarily in the case of Oedipus,[26] but it also involves culpable acts done without knowledge of the long-term consequences, as in Medea's case.[27] Perhaps *hamartia* can be summarized as an act committed because of ignorance of one's own true identity, insofar as knowing oneself includes knowing the right way to act.[28]

That the cognitive element is important in the concept of *hamartia* will be evident from an analysis of some of the ancient tragedies that Aristotle mentions.[29] In the paradigmatic play *King Oedipus* by Sophocles, the scene of recognition is the king's realization of his own identity. This is provoked by the structure of events and is proven by the mark that he carries on his body. In *Iphigeneia in Tauris* by Euripides, the recognition is the uncovering of the identity of Orestes, which prevents his sister from killing him. In this case the *anagnōrisis* precedes the *hamartia* and averts the intended tragic deed. Other plays do not include *anagnōrisis* but have *hamartia* (e.g., Euripides' *Medea*), whereas other genres may have scenes of recognition but no tragic act (e.g., the bath scene of Homer's *Odyssey*).

---

[25] Thomas C.W. Stinton, "*Hamartia* in Aristotle and Greek Tragedy," *CQ* N.S. 25 (1975): 221–54, esp. 254; repr. in *Collected Papers on Greek Tragedy* (Oxford: Clarendon, 1990).

[26] Gerald F. Else, *Poetics: The Argument*, (Cambridge: Harvard University Press, 1957), 383.

[27] Nancy Sherman, "*Hamartia* and Virtue, in *Essays on Aristotle's* Poetics," in *Essays on Aristotle's* Poetics (ed. Amélie O. Rorty; Princeton: Princeton University Press, 1992), 177–96, esp. 189–92.

[28] Amélie O. Rorty, "The Psychology of Aristotelian Tragedy," in *Essays on Aristotle's* Poetics (ed. Amélie O. Rorty; Princeton: Princeton University Press, 1992), 1–22, esp. 11.

[29] Cf. Halliwell, *Aristotle's Poetics*, 224–26; Stephen A. White, "Aristotle's Favorite Tragedies," in *Essays on Aristotle's Poetics* (ed. Amélie O. Rorty; Princeton: Princeton University Press, 1992), 221–40; Elizabeth Belfiore, "Aristotle and Iphigenia," in *Essays on Aristotle's* Poetics (ed. Amélie O. Rorty; Princeton: Princeton University Press, 1992), 359–77.

It may be concluded that *hamartia* indicates a cognitive flaw, and *anagnōrisis* reveals the *hamartia*.[30]

It is possible to summarize the reading of Aristotle's poetic by presenting his ideal of a tragic structure. First, the acting characters must be able to evoke sympathy. They cannot be better or worse than the spectator but rather should be "ourselves writ large."[31] Second, the *mythos* must be complex, involving both *peripeteia* and *anagnōrisis*. Third, the tragic event is caused by a *hamartia*. And finally, in the best *mythoi*, this *hamartia* is disclosed through *anagnōrisis*, which marks a reversal from ignorance to knowledge and subse-quently may produce a reversal from unhappiness to happiness.

Conclusion: Interaction of Communicative Levels to Evoke Tragic Emotions

When the separation of a discoursive and narrative level is introduced in the interpretation of Aristotle's *Poetics*, it is obvious that he consciously and thoroughly determines the best way to control the interaction between the two levels. His analysis of the different *mythoi* should enable the playwrights to influence the discoursive level by their construction of the narrative. They should be able to control the emotions of the spectators and lead them towards *katharsis*.

Aristotle rehabilitates the drama and the emotions within the philosophical tradition when he points out that the arousal of emotions has a moral end. When a tragedy is structured to evoke pity and fear, the spectators experience these emotions and in the cathartic process come to terms with them. It happens because they encounter their own fear in their pity and fear for the tragic figures, and through a process of habituation learn to align it with reason. Consequently, it is essential that the spectators recognize their own fear in the misfortune of the enacted tragedy, but it is also important that the reason for the tragic *peripeteia* is disclosed in *anagnōrisis*. Only when the *hamartia* is revealed, can the fear be rationalized.

In conclusion, Aristotle wants the tragedies to present a world that is consistent and just, but not always transparent. For that reason the figures that risk falling into misfortune are seemingly innocent. But in the end their *hamartia* is revealed and the worldview of the spectators is confirmed.[32] Accordingly, they will learn to control their fear with reason.

---

[30] The relation between *hamartia* and *anagnōrisis* is emphasized strongly by Else, *Poetics: The Argument*, 385.

[31] Rorty, "The Psychology of Aristotelian Tragedy," 12.

[32] For that reason the repugnant *mythoi* of evil men's progress or just men's downfall should not be presented on stage (cf. *Poet.* 1452b 33–36).

This is the result that the implied author wants his message to achieve for the implied reader, and it is this response that the real author hopes for from his real reader.

3. The Fourth Gospel: Christological and Cognitive Structures

The Fourth Gospel is not an Aristotelian tragedy. Although studies occasionally and sometimes successfully claim an influence from Greek drama, it can hardly be persuasively argued that the gospel is constructed as a tragedy.[33] First of all, the protagonist does not fit Aristotle's requirements. Jesus is not "ourselves writ large" and he does not experience a tragic and unexpected *peripeteia* or *anagnōrisis*, and he explicitly cannot be proven guilty of any *hamartia* (John 8:46). On the contrary, he has infallible knowledge of the course of events and acts with a sovereignty that comes from his union with the Father (e.g., 13:1.3; 18:4; 19:28).[34] Jesus is not a tragic hero. Given that the dominant structure of the Johannine narrative is the process of the divine Logos being sent to the world by God, incarnated in the flesh of Jesus, revealing the Father and returning to the heavenly divine unity, the *mythos* of the gospel cannot be called tragic.[35] However, a substructure of the gospel has salient tragic features and this structure is the decisive factor of the resurrection scenes in chap. 20.[36]

The reason for dividing the gospel into several structures is the fact that the dominant structure of Jesus' descent and ascent involves another

---

[33] A number of scholars have compared parts or details of the gospel to Greek tragedy, e.g., Hitchcock, "Is the Fourth Gospel a Drama?"; Stibbe, *John as Storyteller*; idem, *John's Gospel* (London and New York: Routledge, 1994); George L. Parsenios, *Departure and Consolation. The Johannine Discourses in Light of Greco-Roman Literature* (Leiden: Brill, 2005); Larsen, *Recognizing the Stranger*. J.-A. Brant claims that the author of the Fourth Gospel was directly dependent on many conventions and established methods from Greek tragedy, Jo-Ann A. Brant, *Dialogue and Drama. Elements of Greek Tragedy in the Fourth Gospel* (Peabody, Mass.: Hendrickson, 2004).

[34] Cf. Culpepper, *Anatomy of the Fourth Gospel*, 108–9.

[35] Regardless of the fact that the descending and ascending figure can be interpreted in the most diverse and notoriously contradictory ways, e.g., Rudolf Bultmann, *Das Evangelium des Johannes* (KEK II; Göttingen: Vandenhoeck & Ruprecht, 1941) and Käsemann, *Jesu letzter Wille*, there is not much doubt that it is the main structure of the gospel, cf. A. Reinhartz, *The Word in the World. The Cosmological Tale in the Fourth Gospel* (SBLMS 45; Atlanta: Scholars Press, 1992).

[36] Some exegetes define the passion as *peripeteia* insofar it is a contradiction of the expectations to Jesus, e.g., Culpepper, *Anatomy of the Fourth Gospel*, 88; Bühler, "Ist Johannes ein Kreuzestheologie," 202. This stresses the expediency of separating the level of Jesus, whose expectations are certainly not negated, from the level of the human recipients.

structure. It revolves around the humans that are in contact with Jesus and concerns their understanding of him. Although this structure reflects the main structure, it constitutes a separate substructure. Contrary to the main Christological structure, the cognitive substructure can be compared to the Aristotelian tragic *mythos* and it is primarily within this structure that the resurrection scenes are meaningful.[37]

According to the communicative theoretical distinctions, both the main structure and the proposed substructure belong to the narrative level and will be analyzed under that heading. But the Fourth Gospel evidently has a discoursive level as well. In a presentation of this level, the role of the resurrection stories in the substructure will be set in relation to the implied reader and author.

The Narrative Level of the Fourth Gospel

The narrative level consists of the story about Jesus, the Son of God, who descended from heaven, performed signs and proclaimed his identity on earth, was crucified, died and resurrected, and returned to his heavenly Father. Although this structure is not tragic, the general Aristotelian definition of a whole *mythos* illuminates the Johannine plot. All three phases of the whole *mythos* are represented in the Fourth Gospel as Christological epochs.

The Main Structure: Beginning, Middle, and End

In the beginning – understood both as a narrative phase and as an epoch of the theologically interpreted history – the divine logos is in heaven with God (1:1). Before this period nothing must be presupposed; in fact nothing can be presupposed, because nothing existed prior to this epoch (17:5). Until the incarnation the logos belongs to the heavenly realm as an unambiguous divine being in proximity with God, having divine glory (17:5), and indeed being God himself (1:1–3). Though the logos is not generally

---

[37] Cf. Reinhartz, *The Word in the World*, 27f. When R. Bultmann claims that the resurrection of Jesus does not carry any independent theological value in the Fourth Gospel, he focuses exclusively on the Christological structure and does not consider the effect of the resurrection on the human figures in the gospel, Rudolf Bultmann, *Theologie des Neuen Testaments* (9th ed.; Tübingen: J. C. B. Mohr, 1984), 408. In his structural analysis of the Johannine plot M. Stibbe finds a Christological structure to be fundamental, but he is not able to define a relation to the substructure, Stibbe, *John's Gospel*, 38–53. For that reason he does not include the human responses in his analysis. R. A. Culpepper takes the substructure to be fundamental in the construction of the Fourth Gospel, when he defines the plot as being "propelled by conflict between belief and unbelief as responses to Jesus." Culpepper, *Anatomy of the Fourth Gospel*, 97. He overlooks the fact that the responses must refer to something. Therefore, the Christological transformations constitute the main structure on which the cognitive reactions are dependent.

accessible to humans in this period, there is no doubt about his identity, because his *appearance* corresponds to his *being*. In heaven he *appears* and *is* divine.[38]

The transition from the beginning phase to the middle phase takes place in the incarnation. The incarnation results from the sending of the logos, who has to accomplish a mission. Different terms describe his task (ἔργον [4:34; 5:36; 9:3, 4; 10:25, 32, 37, 38; 14:10, 11; 17:4], ῥήματα [3:34; 14:10; 17:8], λόγος [14:24; 17:14; cf. 12:49–50], διδαχή [7:16, 17; cf. 8:28], ἐντολή [10:18; 12:49; 15:10; cf. 14:31], θέλημα [4:34; 5:30; 6:38]). Every concept expresses a different aspect of Jesus' duty: it is inherent to his mission that he has to preach words and do works, including giving his life (cf. the concept of τελεῖν/τελειοῦν [4:34; 5:36; 17:4; 19:30] and ἐντολή/ἐντέλλεσθαι [10:17–18; 12:49–50; 15:10]). However, it is evident that he tries to evoke faith in himself as the Son of God during his earthly ministry (10:37–38; 14:9–11).[39] His mission to save the world cannot be successfully accomplished if he does not lead people to believe in him (3:16; 5:24 etc.). Nevertheless, his earthly period ends in the crucifixion, where he fulfils the Father's demand but apparently fails to convince anybody of his divine being.[40]

There are several confession-like statements (1:49; 3:2; 4:19, 29, 42; 6:14, 68–69; 9:38; 11:27; 12:13) in the Johannine presentation of the earthly ministry of Jesus. But in different ways they are all disqualified. Jesus or the narrator states that the confession has an inadequate founda-

---

[38] A systematic treatment of the relation between *appearing* and *being* is found in Greimas and Courtès, "Véridictoires (modalités)," *Semiotique*, 419; cf. J. Dušek, "Saying 'True' according to A.J. Gremas," in *Philosophical Hermeneutics and Biblical Exegesis* (ed. Petr Pokorný and Jan Roskovec; WUNT 153, Tübingen: Mohr Siebeck, 2002), 94–100. The English speaking part of the semiotic tradition from Greimas normally uses *seeming* for the French *paraître*. *Appearing*, however, seems to be a less confusing translation of the concept that denotes the manifest, explicit side of an object or a person that may and may not correspond to the immanent, implicit side: the *being*. A conflict between *appearance* and *being* occurs when an object or a person *appears* as something he *is* not. In this case he is in the semiotic status of *lie* according to Greimas. On the other hand, if an object or a person *is* something he does not *appear* to be, he is in the status of *secrecy*. Only when *appearance* and *being* corresponds, the object or the person is in the status of *truth*. This is the semiotic status of the divine *logos* in heaven, of course.

[39] A dominant exegetical tradition in the 20th century understood Jesus' preaching as kerygmatic proclamation, Bultmann, *Theologie des Neuen Testaments*, 418–19. But in fact he tries to convince people of his identity. This has been proven beyond reasonable doubt through the investigations of recognition scenes as type genres in the Fourth Gospel, Culpepper, "The Plot of John's Story of Jesus," *Int.* 49 (1995): 347–58; idem, *The Gospel and Letters of John*, 72–86; Brant, *Dialogue and Drama*, 50–57; Larsen, *Recognizing the Stranger*.

[40] Cf. Culpepper, *The Gospel and Letters of John*, 77–86.

tion and is premature. This is the case when Jesus refers Nathanael to future revelations (1:50–51), tells Nicodemus that he must be born from above to see the divine kingdom (3:3), withdraws from the people who want to make him king (6:15), and informs Peter that one of the disciples is the devil though Peter has just included him in his confession (6:70). When he is received as king in Jerusalem, the narrator discloses that this could not be understood before his resurrection (12:16). On some occasions the confessing characters themselves contradict their confession. Martha hears that Jesus is "the resurrection and life" and confesses that he is "Christ, the Son of God," but shortly after that she refuses to open Lazarus's grave and has apparently not understood who Jesus is (11:39–40). Only the confession of the Samaritans (4:42) is not contradicted, but their role in the gospel is restricted to chapter 4. In the farewell discourses the same pattern appears. Philip reveals that he has not understood Jesus (14:9), and by the end of the discourses the disciples claim to have realized where Jesus is from (16:30), but in the following verses Jesus predicts that they will be scattered and he will be left alone (16:31–32). In his earthly existence Jesus cannot be fully recognized: "No declaration of Jesus' identity prior to his being lifted up, his death and resurrection, could be a full *anagnōrisis*."[41] For that reason the recognition scenes in the corpus of the gospel are indeed a bent genre.[42] At best they consist of partial recognitions with very little persistence. Note the description of the disciples as a timid, insecure group hiding behind locked doors (20:19). The point is that Jesus before his resurrection is not particularly successful. His true identity remains unrecognized, and complete belief has not yet arisen.

The reason for the ambiguous answers to Jesus' proclamation during his earthly life lies in the complicated relationship between his appearance and his being. Because of the incarnation he *appears* to be only human in the middle phase of the narrative, but he also *is* divine. There is no direct access to his divinity. He is incognito, and consequently he cannot immediately convince the humans of his divine status.[43] However, fulfilling his task by being slain on the cross (19:30) leads into the final phase of the

---

[41] Culpepper, *The Gospel and Letters of John*, 83.

[42] H. Attridge has proposed that John appropriates established literary forms and genres, but bends them because they are not adequate to express John's message, Harold W. Attridge, "Genre Bending in the Fourth Gospel," *JBL* 121 (2002): 3–21.

[43] This does not mean that R. Bultmann's interpretation of 1:14 is preferred over E. Käsemann's. For Bultmann 1:14a is the central part of the incarnation verse, whereas Käsemann stresses 1:14b, Bultmann, *Das Evangelium des Johannes*, 38–42; Käsemann, *Jesu letzter Wille*, 28. The point is that the divine Jesus (cf. Käsemann) cannot be immediately recognized as divine because of his human flesh (cf. Bultmann). Conversely, the revelation of his divinity (cf. Bultmann) presupposes his ability to communicate with humans (cf. Käsemann).

narrative. According to the logic of events, the willing death of Jesus results in his resurrection and ascension to heaven (10:17–18; 13:1; 17:5; 20:17). The glorification of Jesus is his re-entering the heavenly realm and resuming his position by God, which follows his death on the cross (12:23; 13:31–32; 17:5).[44] In this way the narrative moves with necessity and probability to the final phase.

In the end, the logos has resumed his unambiguously divine status, and this is the way he appears to his disciples in the resurrection narratives (20:19–23, 26–29). At this point he again both *appears* and *is* divine. The middle phase leads naturally into this phase by establishing the necessary precondition for the re-entry into the original and immediately recognizable divine status, which God gives him after he has fulfilled his task on earth, including his voluntary crucifixion. The death on the cross is the culmination of the middle phase because it causes the glorification that establishes the transition to the final phase. For that reason the death of Jesus in the Fourth Gospel may be called the *peripeteia* of the narrative, because it produces the reversal of Jesus' appearance from human to divine which corresponds to a transformation from an ambiguous to unambiguous divine status. In the end of the gospel Jesus is placed in the same position as the logos in the beginning. His identity has not changed; he has only temporarily been incarnated and appeared in human form. Apparently, nothing has happened!

If one of the requirements of a complete narrative is that something changes during the story, it may be questioned if the Fourth Gospel is a genuine narrative.[45] The affirmative answer to that question lies in the substructure.

The Substructure: Beginning and Middle

The three narrative and Christological phases are not just characterized by the transformation of Jesus' appearance; they have correlates in the human response to him. It is almost a matter of course that the main Christological structure has a corollary in a human cognitive substructure, because Jesus' mission so obviously is directed towards the human world and expects a response from the persons he addresses. Already in the Prologue two groups of people are radically separated on the basis of their reaction to the

---

[44] On the concept of glory/glorification see below.

[45] T. Onuki rightly demands that every interpretation of the Fourth Gospel should be able to account for the fact that the Johannine Christology is expressed in a gospel, Takashi Onuki, *Gemeinde und Welt im Johannesevangelium. Ein Beitrag zur Frage nach der theologischen und pragmatischen Funktion des johanneischen "Dualismus"* (WMANT 56; Neukirchen-Vluyn: Neukirchener Verlag, 1984), 193, 201. According to the proposed Aristotelian definitions this question can be reformulated as the problem of the narrative development in the gospel. What changes in the course of the narrative?

incarnated logos: those who did not accept him and those who did (1:11–12). The first group corresponds to the world that did not know him (1:9) and the second group consists of those who believe in his name and were given the right to be God's children (1:12). These two groups are constructed in the following narrative when the Christological transformations provoke cognitive transformations.

The gospel narrative begins with the logos being in a divine state in heaven, and the corollary is the general human ignorance of him and of God (5:37; 6:46). God is unknown until he is revealed by his Son, who is sent for exactly that purpose (1:18). The world is under the wrath of God (3:36). Metaphorically, the state of the world is presented as darkness (1:5; 8:12; 11:10; 12:35, 46; cf. 3:2; 13:30), death, and judgment (3:36; 5:24–25; 12:48). Therefore, the persons who believe in Jesus come to light (3:19–21; 8:12; 9:5; 12:35f, 46) and receive eternal life (3:15–16, 36; 5:24; 6:40, 47; 10:10, 28; 11:25–26; 20:31). Furthermore, the humans' lack of knowledge of God corresponds to an ignorance of their own being, as it can be seen when Jesus comes to his own (οἱ ἴδιοι) who reject him. They neither know his identity nor their own.[46] The gospel never explains why the world, which is the creation of God and continuously the object of his love (1:3; 3:16), was separated from him and fell under his wrath. The negative state of affairs is the unquestioned starting point of the narrative.[47] The situation changes with the incarnation of the divine logos.

When Jesus appears on earth as a human being in the middle phase of the gospel, he makes the otherwise inaccessible God known in his own person and through his words and deeds (e.g., 14:8–11). Ignorance is no longer an inescapable condition of human life. But the ambiguous status of Jesus, being human and divine, complicates the understanding of his relationship to God. It is not immediately apparent that he represents God; therefore humans must accept his status in faith. Accepting (πιστεύειν) that Jesus reveals God leads directly into the divine unity of Father and Son, hence it involves salvation and eternal life (3:15–16, 36; 5:24; 6:40, 47; etc.). Conversely, rejecting Jesus equals an affiliation with the negatively determined world and hence eternal death (3:19, 36; 12:48). Unbelief means remaining in the ignorance that characterized the first

---

[46] This point is implied in 1:11 and is presented in a parable in 10:3f. The logos came to its own (τὰ ἴδια), but his own (οἱ ἴδιοι) did not receive him (1:11). Likewise, the shepherd calls his own sheep (τὰ ἴδια πρόβατα), and his own (τὰ ἴδια) hear his voice (10:3–4). However, to recognize the shepherd's voice includes knowing to be of his sheep.

[47] It is not the case that this situation comes into being when the Son of God establishes a crisis (κρίσις), Bultmann, *Theologie des Neuen Testaments*, 373. Before the incarnation the world is not in a neutral status but it is already negatively determined, Onuki, *Gemeinde und Welt*, 42, 50.

phase of the gospel. But exactly the possibility of knowing God through his Son changes the character of ignorance. It is no longer just a given status but a consequence of the negative response to Jesus. Ignorance of God corresponds to ignorance of the identity of his Son (14:9). It is *hamartia* (16:8–9)!

Hamartia in the Fourth Gospel

Johannine scholarship is fairly consistent in its overall understanding of *hamartia*.[48] Chapter 9 is an appropriate starting point for the analysis of this Johannine concept because different groups of people use the term. The Jews apply it according to traditional conceptions, linking it to a blasphemous attitude toward God or the law (9:24, 34). Sin is an intentional or unintentional act that destroys or infects the relationship to God (cf. Leviticus 4–5). Consequently, it would be self-contradictory if God listened to sinners (John 9:31). On one occasion the disciples ask Jesus about the sin of the blind born man (9:2). Their question presupposes a concept of sin that corresponds to the one the Jews advocate.[49] They believe someone – presumably the man himself or his parents – must have committed a sinful act, and that the man's blindness is punishment for the sin. Characteristically, Jesus does not accept either the disciples' or the Jews' concept of sin. He explicitly dismisses the reasoning of his disciples (9:3), and in the subsequent miracle story he rejects the Jewish concept of sin and replaces it by an understanding of sin that is based on a person's perception of him:

> And Jesus said, "I came into the world for judgment so that those who do not see may see, and those who do see may become blind." Some of the Pharisees near him heard

---

[48] The general definition sin = unbelief is uncontroversial. The controversy concerns the more precise understanding of this reaction to Jesus. M. Hasitschka claims that sin is the world's broken relation to God, which results in the rejection of Jesus, Martin Hasitschka, *Befreiung von Sünde nach dem Johannesevangelium. Eine bibeltheologische Untersuchung* (Innsbrucker theologische Studien 27; Innsbruck and Vienna: Tyrolia-Verlag, 1989), 167. R. Metzner defines sin Christologically. He takes it to be the attitude of the world towards God's revelation in Jesus, Rainer Metzner, *Das Verständnis der Sünde im Johannesevangelium* (WUNT 122; Mohr Siebeck, 2000), 354. J. Zumstein thinks that sin characterizes the world seen in light of the revelation. The world is exposed as a godless space, but this characteristic of the world influences human cognition: Sin is the inability to recognize Jesus' identity, Jean Zumstein, *Kreative Erinnerung. Relecture und Auslegung im Johannesevangelium* (2d ed.; AThANT 84; Zürich: Theologischer Verlag, 2004), 98, 100. All three exegetes agree that sin culmi-nates and is exposed at the cross, but at the same time it is defeated, Hasitchka, *Befreiung von Sünde*: 163f; Metzner, *Verständnis der Sünde*, 354; Zumstein, *Kreative Erinnerung*, 99.

[49] Whether this is a historically correct presentation of the Jewish understanding of sin and its consequences, is a matter of dispute, cf. Klaus Wengst, *Das Johannesevangelium. 1. Teilband: Kapitel 1–10* (Theologischer Kommentar NT 4.1; Stuttgart: Verlag Kohlhammer, 2000), 352–53.

this and said to him, "Surely, we are not blind, are we?" Jesus said to them, "If you were blind you would not have sin (ἁμαρτία). But now you say, 'We see,' your sin (ἁμαρτία) remains" (9:39–41).

In a radically transforming interpretation, Jesus changes the basis of understanding sight and blindness. According to him, blindness is not primarily a matter of physical eyesight but equals ignorance of his true identity; hence the man born blind comes to see in two ways. First and foremost seeing means accepting Jesus as the Son of God. But this metaphorical interpretation of the concepts is related to a concrete understanding of seeing. The Jews claim to be seeing, i.e., they trust their access to Jesus' identity through their physical sight, and for that reason their *hamartia* remains. Had they not based their relationship to Jesus on appearance, i.e., if they had been blind, they would not have sin. *Hamartia* in this passage is to trust the physical senses in the judgment of Jesus' identity. Hence blindness is a necessary condition for accepting Jesus, because the blind do not base their understanding of Jesus on appearance. In conclusion, the blind become seeing in the true sense of the word when they do not perceive Jesus' appearance but see his true identity. In contrast, the seeing become blind when they trust their physical sight of Jesus and never see his true identity. *Hamartia* is defined according to this interpretation of sight and blindness. It is an error to let the physical sight be the basis of the understanding of Jesus, thus remaining in ignorance of his identity and not accepting his revelation of God.[50]

As it is already hinted at in 9:39, this concept of *hamartia* is a consequence of Jesus actually appearing to people:

> If I had not come and spoken to them, they would not have sin (ἁμαρτία); but now they have no excuse for their sin (ἁμαρτία). If I had not done among them the works that no one else did, they would not have sin (ἁμαρτία). But now they have seen and hated both me and my Father (15:22–24).

Without the incarnation that makes the unseen God visible in an ambiguous manner, there would not be *hamartia*. The possibility of knowing God through his Son is the precondition for defining the erroneous understanding as *hamartia*. For that reason the Johannine concept of *hamartia* can be strictly Christologically defined as the error of letting Jesus' appearance be decisive of one's relationship to him.

This interpretation is confirmed by the definition of *hamartia* in the farewell discourses (16:8–9). When the Paraclete is said to convince the world of *hamartia*, the concept is explicitly defined as not believing in

---

[50] Note the parallel to Sophocles' *King Oedipus*. Oedipus has eyesight while his *hamartia* is unrecognized. When he realizes the truth, he becomes blind, cf. Larsen, *Recognizing the Stranger*.

Jesus. Conversely, Jesus cannot be convicted of any *hamartia*, because he has access to the truth from the Father (8:46–47). Similarly, Jesus leaves a world whose situation is defined as sin because it did not believe in him, as opposed to the community that is not of the world (15:19; 17:14, 16). Accordingly, his followers forgive sin when they let people come into the community (20:23).

Hamartia can be defined as ignorance of Jesus' true identity, or more precisely, as an understanding of his identity on the basis of his appearance while neglecting his true being. It leads, according to the theological logic of the Fourth Gospel, directly into misfortune. It lets the unbelieving humans remain in the negatively determined world from which Jesus will set the believers free (8:34–36; cf. 5:14):

> I have told you that you will die in your sins (ἁμαρτίαι); unless you believe that I am, you will die in your sins (ἁμαρτίαι) (8:24; cf. 8:21).

It has now been demonstrated that according to John the *hamartia* came into the world by one man, namely Jesus, the Son of God. In the rejection of him *hamartia* emerges as an erroneous perception of his ambiguous identity.[51] *Hamartia* is to understand him according to his human appearance and refuse to accept the proclamation about his divine being. Connected to this *hamartia* is the humans' ignorance of their own identity. They do not understand themselves as Jesus' *idioi*, which again causes their hostile and violent reaction toward him. But the gospel states programmatically that Jesus as the Lamb of God will take away the *hamartia* of the world or the worldly *hamartia* (1:29).[52] The expression "Lamb of God" refers to the crucifixion scene where Jesus is depicted as a Passover lamb (19:14, 29, 36),[53] which indicates that the removal of the Johannine *hamartia* takes place in the final phase of the gospel.

The Substructure: End

According to the main Christological structure, Jesus is unambiguous in the end. He has unambiguously resumed the divine status that he had from

---

[51] This understanding of sin differs from other interpretations by connecting the inability to recognize Jesus' identity to his Christological constitution which is a result of the incarnation.

[52] The alternative translation has been suggested by Dieter Rusam, "Das 'Lamm Gottes' (Joh 1,29.36) und die Deutung des Todes Jesu im Johannesevangelium," *BZ* 49 (2005): 60–74. It accentuates the interpretation that "the sin of the world" (ἡ ἁμαρτία τοῦ κόσμου) means "the sin that the world has" or "the worldly sin," namely unbelief.

[53] For the problems concerning the Lamb of God, cf. Jesper T. Nielsen, "The Lamb of God: The Cognitive Structure of a Johannine Metaphor," in *Imagery in the Gospel of John. Terms, Forms, Themes, and Theology of Johannine Figurative Language* (ed. Jörg Frey, Jan G. van der Watt, and Ruben Zimmermann; WUNT 200; Tübingen: Mohr Siebeck, 2006), 217–56.

eternity. He *appears* and *is* divine. For that reason there is no doubt whether it is the Son of God that meets the disciples in the resurrection scenes.[54] What is doubtful is whether the divine being in front of the disciples is identical with to the earthly Jesus who was crucified. As proof Jesus shows his stigmata (20:20).[55] When the identity of the resurrected one is established the uncertainty of the identity of the earthly Jesus is removed, and hence unbelief is proven wrong. The resurrection provokes recognition, i.e., an *anagnōrisis* which eliminates the *hamartia*.[56] After the crucifixion and resurrection, unbelief is not an option on the same level as belief. Unbelief has been exposed as *hamartia*. Consequently, the disciples are given authority over the *hamartia* when they are sent out to continue the mission of Jesus (20:23). Now that the *hamartia* of the world has been "taken away" (1:29), i.e., exposed and defeated, Jesus' disciples forgive or retain sin when they carry his revelation forward.[57]

To emphasize this interpretation, as it were, the resurrection scene is repeated for the sake of Thomas. He refuses to believe because he has not seen the resurrected Jesus or verified his identity by means of the stigmata (20:25). This is granted him in the final resurrection scene, and he

---

[54] Significantly, the mysterious scene of Mary meeting the resurrected Jesus (20:14–18) is placed between his death as a human and his appearance as divine. Consequently, Mary cannot see him as divine but mistakenly thinks he is the gardener (20:15). Even when she recognizes his voice, she addresses him 'rabbi' (20:16) revealing an inadequate understanding of his identity (cf. 3:2). According to Mary's reaction Jesus appears at this point still ambiguously and cannot immediately be recognized as divine. He explains why himself: "I have not yet ascended to the Father" (20:17). When she later uses the term *kyrios* about Jesus (20:18), it is probably not a confession of his true identity (cf. 4:11). Although, she does not point to Mary's inability to recognize Jesus, M. D'Angelo has persuasively argued that "the state of Jesus is different when he encounters Mary from when he meets the disciples and Thomas and invites Thomas' touch." Mary R. D'Angelo, "A Critical Note: John 20:19 and Apocalypse of Moses 31," *JTS* 41 (1990): 535; cf. Harold W. Attridge, "'Don't Be Touching Me': Recent Feminist Scholarship on Mary Magdalene," in *A Feminist Companion to John*. Volume 2 (ed. Amy-Jill Levine; Cleveland: Pilgrim Press, 2003), 140–66.

[55] Jörg Frey, "Die '*theologia crucifixi*' des Johannesevangeliums," in *Kreuzestheologie im Neuen Testament* (ed. Andreas Dettwiler and Jean Zumstein; WUNT 151; Tübingen: Mohr Siebeck, 2002), 235.

[56] With reference to 8:28–29 Zumstein claims that the cross is the place for the decisive recognition, Zumstein, *Kreative Erinnerung*, 99. But according to 8:28 the 'uplifting' – and not the cross per se – leads to realizing Jesus' *ego eimi*. This is significant because the concept of uplifting comprise both crucifixion and resurrection. Both are needed to provoke the final recognition. On the cross Jesus reveals himself as the Father's faithful representative, as Zumstein notes, but he also acquires the marks or signs that are necessary to prove his identity when the Father has glorified him in recognition of his completed task.

[57] Cf. Hasitschka, *Befreiung von Sünde*, 421; Metzner, *Verständnis der Sünde*, 272.

responds by making the culminating confession of the gospel (20:27–28). Thomas declares Jesus to be Lord and God, and thereby expresses his identity in relation to both hu-mans and God.[58]

The resurrection scenes correspond to the recognition scene in the Greek drama. Just as Ulysses' identity is revealed by way of his birthmarks, and Oedipus is convinced of his own identity when his scars match the story he is told, and Iphigeneia is recognized as the sister of Orestes because of her letter, so Jesus in the Fourth Gospel is recognized because of his stigmata.

According to the Aristotelian taxonomy, the evangelist is a quite competent playwright insofar as his construction of the resurrection scenes honors several of the demands in Aristotle's *Poetics*. The recognition is based on bodily signs when Jesus' stigmata evoke the recognition, but the wounds and the recognition itself follows naturally from the course of events, as Aristotle recommends. For the interpretation of the Fourth Gospel this observation shows the intimate relationship of the two independent events: crucifixion and resurrection. The crucifixion is the *peripeteia* of the narrative, which marks the culmination of the middle phase and results in the glorification that initiates the final phase. In the final phase the stigmata of the resurrected one evoke the *anagnōrisis* which could not have happened without the crucifixion. In the narrative of the Fourth Gospel the *peripeteia* produces the *anagnōrisis* which is the disclosure of the *hamartia*.

At the conclusion of this section the tragic character of the human substructure can be formulated. *Hamartia* is a possibility in the middle phase of the gospel because Jesus is in an ambiguous status. To understand his identity on the basis of his appearance and physical sight is *hamartia* because this approach erroneously rejects his divinity. Because of this *hamartia* humans fall into a misfortune that consists of remaining in a situation of ignorance of God and oneself, i.e., being under the wrath of God. In the resurrection scenes the *hamartia* is exposed as a false understanding of Jesus when he reveals his divine identity and provokes recognition, which establishes the necessary change from ignorance to knowledge or from unbelief to belief (cf. 8:28; 13:19; 14:20, 29; 16:23).[59] In order to protect humans from death, his death produces the needed conditions for the *anagnōrisis* that removes *hamartia*.

---

[58] Cf. Jan G. van der Watt, "The Cross/Resurrection-Events in the Gospel of John with Special Emphasis on the Confession of Thomas (20:28)," *Neot.* 37 (2003): 127–45.

[59] In the gospel this transformation is also described as a change from grief to joy (16,6–7, 20, 22; cf. 20:19): Grief when Jesus is absent, but joy when he as resurrected initiates a new presence. I am grateful to Professor Harold Attridge for important comments in this regard.

One of the characteristics of the Fourth Gospel is that its dominant structures are expressed in terms of glory/glorification. This conception cannot be presented in detail here.[60] The purpose is just to show that the tragic feature of the Johannine structures is evident in the use of glory/glorification terminology also.

The use of the term δόξα for the divine glory goes back to the LXX translation of the noun כבוד. Generally, it also translates the verbal forms of כבד with δοξάζειν. Through this translation the Greek word achieves new meaning potential.[61] Prior to the LXX it denoted "expectation," "opinion," or "repute,"[62] but due to the LXX it takes on another meaning in the Jewish-Christian tradition. It designates the divine way of appearing (e.g., Exod 24:16; 40:34–35; Mark 8:38; Rev 15:8) and expresses acknowledgement of status (e.g., Isa 42:12; 48:11; Matt 6:2; Luc 14:10). God is glorious and must be given glory by his adherents, i.e., they acknowledge his superiority by recognizing him as God (e.g., Exod 14:4.17–18; Acts 12:23; Rev 1:6). The other way around, the believers may be given divine glory because of their relationship to God (e.g., Isa 43:4; Rom 5:2; 1 Cor 15:40–43). Glory/glorification has a semantic potential that includes both material and relational connotations. The material part denotes the divine being and appearance, and the relational part concerns social recognition.

In the Fourth Gospel, language of glory/glorification describes every phase of the narrative. The noun designates the divine being and appearance that the logos had in its pre-existent state (John 1:14; 17:5, 22, 24; cf. 12:41), and it denotes the divine being that Jesus reveals in his

---

[60] The classic monograph on the subject is Wilhelm Thüsing, *Die Erhöhung und Verherrlichung Jesu im Johannesevangelium* (NTA 21; Münster: Aschendorffsche Verlagsbuchhandlung, 1960); see also G. B. Caird, "The Glory of God in the Fourth Gospel: An Exercise in Biblical Semantics," *NTS* 15 (1969): 265–77; Margaret Pamment, "The meaning of *doxa* in the Fourth Gospel," *ZNW* 74 (1983): 12–16; Yu Ibuki, "Die Doxa des Gesandten. – Studie zur johanneischen Christologie," *AJBI* 14 (1988): 38–81; Joong Suk Suh, *The Glory in the Gospel of John. Restoration of Forfeited Prestige* (Oxford, Ohio: M. P. Publications, 1995). See now also Nicole Chibici-Revneau, *Die Herrlichkeit des Verherrlichten* (WUNT II/231; Tübingen: Mohr Siebeck, 2007).

[61] To the history of language and the relation between the Hebrew *kbd* and the Greek *doxa*, see August Freiherr von Gall, *Die Herrlichkeit Gottes. Eine biblisch-theologische Untersuchung ausgedehnt über das Alte Testament, die Targume, Apokryphen, Apokalypsen und das Neue Testament* (Giessen: J. Ricker'sche Verlagsbuchhandlung, 1900); Johannes Schneider, *Doxa. Eine bedeutungsgeschichtliche Studie* (Gütersloh: C. Bertelsmann, 1932); Helmuth Kittel, *Die Herrlichkeit Gottes. Studien zu Geschichte und Wesen eines Neutestamentlichen Begriffs* (BZNW 16; Giessen: A. Töpelmann, 1934); Carey C. Newman, *Paul's Glory-Christology. Tradition and Rhetoric* (NTS 69; Leiden: Brill, 1992).

[62] "δόξα," *LSJ*, 444.

signs (2:11; 11:4, 40), but it is also used for his state after he has accomplished his task on earth. At that point he will be glorified with the glory he had in his pre-incarnation status (17:5, 24). His course involves three phases: pre-incarnation with unambiguous glory, incarnation with ambiguous glory, and post-incarnation with unambiguous glory. His incarnation transforms him from state one to two and his glorification from two to three.[63] This is equivalent to the main Christological structure of the gospel.

The language of glory/glorification describes the substructure as well. Jesus glorifies his Father by fulfilling his task (17:4), which according to the interpretation above involves winning a persistent recognition of his own identity as the Son of God and of God as his Father. But this recognition does not follow until the resurrection; therefore Jesus must be glorified in order to glorify his Father (17:1), although he has glorified his Father by accomplishing his earthly work (17:4). This is another way of saying that Jesus' work on earth needs the final sanction of his glorification to be fulfilled and produce the glorification of the Father (13:31–32). Jesus must appear in his unambiguous divine glory to win the requested recognition.

Finally, glorifying the Father and Son (14:13; 15:8; 17:10) is the human recipients' acceptance of Jesus' proclamation and recognition of his relationship to God. It consequently includes in the divine unity of glory (17:22), which involves an eschatological expectation of seeing Jesus' heavenly glory (17:24).[64]

In conclusion, the Johannine language of glory/glorification describes all the important phases in the Johannine narrative. Its objective has not been completed and its end not reached, before the appearance of the unambiguously glorified Son of God in the resurrection.

But the resurrected and glorified Jesus is not generally present. After the appearance to the disciples he disappears and cannot be seen. For that reason the Johannine Jesus places the recognition of the resurrection witnesses in relation to a belief that is not grounded in a vision (20:29). The group that believes without seeing is, of course, the recipients of the gospel. Unlike Thomas and the other disciples in the narrative, they have not seen the resurrected one; hence their belief does not stem from meeting Jesus in his unambiguously divine nature. That is the reason the Johannine

---

[63] "In Rahmen des Gesamtentwurfs wird damit die Passion zur letztgültigen Bestätigung der Zugehörigkeit Jesu zum Vater, und in solcher Zugehörigkeit besteht seine Doxa von Anfang an." Christian Dietzfelbinger, *Abschied des Kommenden. Eine Auslegung der johanneischen Abschiedsreden* (WUNT 95; Tübingen: J. C. B. Mohr, 1997), 289.

[64] Cf. Thüsing, *Erhöhung und Verherrlichung*, 217.

Jesus praises their belief and call them "blessed." They accomplish what the disciples did not: believing without seeing.

The Discoursive Level of the Fourth Gospel

The remarks about 20:29 anticipated the discoursive level by identifying the believers that had not seen the resurrected one with the readers of the gospel. This is the main quality of those whom the narrative is meant to affect. Or to put it in Aristotelian terms, the plot of the gospel is constructed to provoke an emotional response from an audience that has not had direct contact with the earthly or resurrected Jesus.

In order to react emotionally there must be "someone like us," who functions as an object of sympathy. The readers must in some way be able to see their own situation reflected in the narrative figures, otherwise a sympathetic relationship cannot exist. But to discover who is "someone like us," the situation of the intended and implied group of readers must be defined.

According to the gospel, the most important feature of the implied readers is that they are situated after the departure of Jesus.[65] He is visibly absent in their presence. The Johannine community has no direct access to Jesus. Nevertheless, the community is described as being in an intimate relationship to him and his Father, which most characteristically is expressed in the reciprocal immanence formula (17:11, 21–23).[66] At the same time it seems that the Johannine community understood itself to be in a severe conflict with the world in general (7:7; 15:18–19; 17:14) and the Jewish community in particular.[67] According to the picture drawn in the

---

[65] There are several more or less hypothetical reconstructions of the social history of the Johannine community, but they tend to neglect this basic fact of the community's cognitive constitution, e.g., J. Louis Martyn, *History and Theology in the Fourth Gospel* (New York: Harper & Row, 1968); Raymond E. Brown, *The Community of the Beloved Disciple. The Life, Loves, and Hates of an Individual Church in New Testament Times* (New York: Paulist Press, 1979); Klaus Wengst, *Bedrängte Gemeinde und verherrlichter Christ. Ein Versuch über das Johannesevangelium* (3d ed.; München: Chr. Kaiser, 1992).

[66] Klaus Scholtissek, *In ihm sein und bleiben. Die Sprache der Immanenz in den johanneischen Schriften* (HBS 21; Freiburg: Herder, 2000).

[67] This is stressed by the investigations into the social history of the community. But see the discussion about the historical relation between the Johannine community and its Jewish contemporaries, e.g., Jörg Frey, "Das Bild 'der Juden' im Johannesevangelium und die Geschichte der johanneischen Gemeinde," in *Israel und seine Heilstraditionen im Johannesevangelium* (ed. Michael Labahn, Klaus Scholtissek, and Angelika Strotmann; Paderborn: Ferdnand Schöningh, 2004), 33–53; Adele Reinhartz, "The Johannine Community and its Jewish Neighbors: A Reappraisal," in *"What is John?" Volume II: Literary and Social Readings of the Fourth Gospel* (ed. Fernando F. Segovia; SBLSS 7; Atlanta.: Scholars Press, 1998), 111–38; and the contributions in *Anti-Judaism and the*

Fourth Gospel, the Johannine believers are expelled from the synagogues and exposed to life threatening hostility from the Jews (9:22; 12:42; 16:2). The reason is that they understand Jesus in a way that is different from their hostile contemporaries. The believing community is constituted by recognition of Jesus' divinity despite his apparent absence (17:6–8, 20–23). Thus, the most important description of the community is Jesus' final blessing:

> You believe because you have seen me; blessed are those who have not seen and yet believe (20:29).

In this way, the situation of the community is characterized by incongruity between belief and sight. Their belief is apparently contradicted because they cannot see. For that reason the Johannine community is potentially threatened by the arguments of opponents who see Jesus' absence as the logical result of his death and consequently a negation of his divinity.

Structurally, this situation matches the narrative level of the gospel, where the relationship between the human appearance of Jesus and his divine being causes the conflict of interpretations. The readers of the gospel are comparable to the humans who act on the narrative level because both groups have to come to term with a fundamental incongruity between the experience of Jesus and the belief in him. The situations differ since the incongruity at the narrative level is constituted by the difference between Jesus' appearance and his being; at the discoursive level the community's belief in the presence of Jesus is contradicted by his apparent absence. Nevertheless, the common structures make a sympathetic relationship between the levels possible. The reader is supposed to feel pity and fear towards the humans at the narrative level because their situation is characterized by an incongruity parallel to his own.

The tragic emotions arise when the narrative protagonists experience what the readers fear for themselves. The readers of the Fourth Gospel are meant to fear the loss of their belief in the identity of Jesus; hence they should feel pity and fear towards the narrative figures that tend to judge Jesus according to appearance and physical sight. It is exactly the mistake the readers could but should not make; and consequently, it is called *hamartia*.[68] But when the *anagnōrisis* of the resurrection scene reveals the *hamartia*, it is an affirmation of the readers' belief.

Fourth Gospel (ed. Reimund Bieringer, Didier Pollefeyt and Frederique Vandecasteele-Vanneuville; Assen: Royal Van Gorcum, 2001).

[68] Cf. "Der johanneische Christus spricht die nachösterliche Zeit an – eine Zeit, in der Sünde sich durch die Abwesenheit des erhöhten Christus und dessen Unerreichbarkeit definiert." Zumstein, *Kreative Erinnerung*, 98.

At the end, the readers have had their own problematic situation played out in the narrative conflict over understanding the Johannine Jesus; and they have in the resurrection seen a confirmation of their basic belief system. This may be called a cathartic process, since the fundamental challenge to the belief of the readers is presented as the *hamartia* of the narrative figures and it is finally defeated by the *anagnōrisis*. The tragic emotions were evoked by the reactions to Jesus' ambiguity in the gospel narrative, but are reassured by his unambiguous appearance as the resurrected one. Through this process the readers' belief system has been challenged but was proven right. In this way the gospel teaches its readers to align the potential doubts with reason, i.e., to let the conflict between appearance and being be corrected by the *anagnōrisis* of the narrative resurrection scenes.

However, it is important to notice that the readers do not experience the same *anagnōrisis* as the resurrection witnesses. They have not seen the resurrected and are still in the problematic situation of a belief that is apparently contradicted by the absence of Jesus. This situation has not been surmounted by the resurrection, because the resurrected one is seemingly absent in the Johannine community. But in the absence of the resurrected Jesus, the gospel itself serves to affirm the belief of the readers. What Thomas experiences in the narrative of his encounter with the resurrected Jesus, namely the realization of Jesus' true identity and consequently the removal of *hamartia*, the Johannine reader experiences through the reading of the gospel. In this way the gospel itself has the function of the resurrected Jesus, and the readers take part in the change from grief over Jesus' absence to joy over his presence in the gospel.

This is the often overlooked relationship of 20:29 and 20:30–31. The purpose of the gospel is that the readers should remain in the belief that Jesus is Christ, the Son of God. Its relationship to the readers corresponds to relationship of the resurrected Jesus to Thomas. He believes because he has seen; the readers cannot see but must read.[69]

---

[69] Cf. Thomas Söding, "Die Schrift als Medium des Glaubens. Zur hermeneutischen Bedeutung von Joh 20,30f," in *Schrift und Tradition* (ed. Knut Backhaus, Franz G. Untergaßmair; Paderborn: Ferdinand Schöningh, 1996), 343–71.

Conclusion: Interaction of Communicative Levels to Reassure the Readers

The Aristotelian reading of the basic structures in the Fourth Gospel has demonstrated an intimate relationship between the main Christological structure and the substructure concerning the human response on the one hand, and the narrative and discoursive level on the other.

Jesus' transformation through the three narrative phases corresponds to three different stages of knowledge of God. In the final phase, the initial ignorance of God is replaced by acceptance of Jesus as God's interpreter. His revelation, however, was not accepted until he was seen by the disciples with complete congruence between his being and appearance. In the resurrection he *was* and *appeared* divine, hence provoking recognition. This was not possible in the middle phase when Jesus was divine but appeared to be merely human. The apparent contradiction between who he claimed to be and what he seemed to be made him incomprehensible to those who based their evaluation on physical sight. The gospel exposes this way of comprehending him as intrinsically wrong; it is *hamartia*.

Exactly at this point the relationship between the levels of communication emerges. According to the portrayal of the readers, they experience a structurally equivalent contradiction when they believe Jesus, whom they have not seen and cannot see. For that reason the author wants his readers to feel pity and fear when the narrative persons base their opinion on physical appearance; and he wants them to be reassured when the resurrection proves this judgment wrong, i.e., establishes *anagnōrisis* and removes *hamartia*.

The text affirms the readers' basic belief system and fundamental worldview. The conflict between the physical absence of Jesus and faith in him is worked out in the emotional response to the events at the narrative level. In the end the readers' understanding of Jesus is substantiated by his resurrection, their doubts are brought into accordance with the reason of the Fourth Gospel, and their faith without – or rather despite – physical sight is validated. Just as the resurrection verifies Jesus' proclamation, it confirms the readers' acceptance of it. Thus the gospel is written that they may remain in their faith.

4. Final Remarks

Aristotle's relevance for Johannine studies depends first and foremost on his original insights into the nature of narratives. His explorations have general and universal value because they expose intrinsic narrative structures and elements. They are helpful even if the author of the Fourth Gospel had no acquaintance with Aristotle's work. Even the concept *hamartia*, which in the

Fourth Gospel seems closely related to the Aristotelian concept, does not necessarily testify to a direct relationship. Nevertheless, it is worth noting that Aristotle in his definition draws on legal traditions, which may have been commonly known.[70] John may have been influenced by juridical currents rather than dramaturgical.[71]

Finally, many aspects and problems of the Fourth Gospel have not been treated above. We have focused on the role of the resurrection within the Johannine communication. It has been demonstrated how it functions on the narrative level and the discoursive level, but the communicative level has been left out. It is one thing to ask how the resurrection and the gospel text are meant to influence its readers; it is another thing to ask whether it achieves this ambition with real readers. Does the gospel manage to take the place of the resurrected Jesus and confirm the readers' belief system in the conflict between faith and physical sight? Apparently, it does not! The text includes a new conflict between being and appearance. It claims to be fact, but it appears to be fiction; it declares that it is truth, but it could be lie; it purports to be reality, but it is a text. For that reason the success of the gospel depends on its ability to convince its readers that it is more than it appears to be, just as the earthly Jesus had to. But if the truth of Jesus' claim was proven right by his resurrection, according to the Fourth Gospel, the proof of the truth of the Fourth Gospel remains an eschatological expectation.

---

[70] Eckart Schütrumpf, "Traditional Elements in the Concept of *hamartia* in Aristotle's *Poetics*," *HSCP* 92 (1989): 137–56.

[71] It is noteworthy that even though most commentators acknowledge the innovative understanding of the concept *hamartia* in the Fourth Gospel as compared to Jewish and early Christian traditions, they place John's interpretation firmly within a Jewish-Christian tradition, e.g., Zumstein, *Kreative Erinnerung*, 83–103. R. Metzner refers several times to the genre *Rechtsstreit* and its importance for the Johannine concept of sin, which he defines as forensic, Metzner *Verständnis der Sünde*, 194–201. But he does not relate the concept *hamartia* to legal traditions or practices. Likewise, the interpretations that focus on the legal aspects of the gospel do not mention the concept of *hamartia*, e.g., A. E. Harvey, *Jesus on Trial. A Study in the Fourth Gospel* (London: SPCK, 1976); Andrew T. Lincoln, *Truth on Trial. The Lawsuit Motif in the Fourth Gospel* (Peabody, Mass.: Hendrickson, 2000).

Chapter 9

"I am ascending to my Father and your Father, to my God and your God" (John 20:17): Resurrection and Ascension in the Gospel of John

Reimund Bieringer

John 20:17 is mainly known in the Western world for the words of the risen Jesus to Mary Magdalene: μή μου ἅπτου. These words became even more famous in the Latin translation, *Noli me tangere*, which gave the name to a longstanding tradition of representing the post-resurrection encounter of Jesus and Mary in the visual arts. However, the most prevalent theme in 20:17 is not μή μου ἅπτου, but Jesus' ascension to the Father. In this study we shall investigate the Johannine theme of the ascension, which is an important theme in the gospel in its resurrection context. We shall first investigate the syntax of 20:17, entering into discussion with a variety of proposals. In a second step we shall discuss some of the major tradition-critical and redaction-critical approaches. Finally we shall present our own composition-critical study of the text, which reads 20:17 as a Johannine redaction of Matt 28:9–10.

1. Syntactic Analysis of John 20:17

At first sight the syntactic structure of John 20:17 is rather straightforward. The verse consists of six coordinated clauses that are linked with the conjunctions γάρ, δέ and καί. However, the logical progression of thought within the six clauses is far from unambiguous, since we do not know how the evangelist would have used punctuation with regard to these six clauses. Various attempts have been made to interpret the Greek sentence structure. Before we discuss them, we present John 20:17 in sense lines to facilitate communication about the various parts of the verse. At this point we do not introduce punctuation, except the colon introducing direct speech (at the end of 20:17a and 17e):

20:17a λέγει αὐτῇ Ἰησοῦς·
20:17b μή μου ἅπτου
20:17c οὔπω γὰρ ἀναβέβηκα πρὸς τὸν πατέρα
20:17d πορεύου δὲ πρὸς τοὺς ἀδελφούς μου
20:17e καὶ εἰπὲ αὐτοῖς·
20:17f ἀναβαίνω πρὸς τὸν πατέρα μου καὶ πατέρα ὑμῶν καὶ θεόν μου καὶ θεὸν ὑμῶν

In the exegetical discussion several syntactic interpretations of 20:17 are defended (see the appendix). The focus is here on the meaning of γάρ in 20:17c: οὔπω γὰρ ἀναβέβηκα πρὸς τὸν πατέρα. The vast majority of interpreters understand γάρ as a "marker of cause or reason,"[1] introducing a clause that motivates the prohibition expressed in 20:17b.[2] This means that "I have not yet ascended to the Father" in 20:17c is understood as the reason why Jesus says: μή μου ἅπτου in the immediately preceding clause. The causal connection between 20:17b and 17c has important implications for the interpretation of μή μου ἅπτου.

If this prohibition means "do not touch me," then the motivation given in 20:17c is surprising and raises many questions. Does this suggest implicitly that after having ascended to the Father Jesus may well be touched? Should not the fact that Jesus has not yet ascended to the Father imply that he can still be touched?[3] Does the prohibition perhaps have more to do with something in Mary Magdalene than in Jesus? But if the latter is the case, what is the meaning of the motivating clause in 20:17c? If in 20:27 Thomas is invited to touch, does this demonstrate that Jesus has in the meantime actually ascended and is now in a state in which he can be touched?

If, however, μή μου ἅπτου means "do not hold on to me" or "do not cling to me," then the motivation given in 20:17c makes more sense. In this case the prohibition μή μου ἅπτου is understood as signaling a radical discontinuation of a this-worldly relationship with Jesus. The text would be suggesting that Jesus' mode of existence as the risen one is only provisional and transitional. The prohibition thus contains a critique of attaching

---

[1] BDAG, 189.

[2] See the current modern versions and commentaries.

[3] Cf. D. A. Carson. *The Gospel According to John* (Leicester: Inter-Varsity and Grand Rapids: Eerdmans, 1991), 643: "If Jesus *has* ascended between v. 17 and v. 27, the implication is that the disciples are permitted to touch Jesus after the ascension but not before – exactly the reverse of what might have been expected." Similar is Sandra M. Schneiders, *Written That You May Believe. Encountering Jesus in the Fourth Gospel* (New York: Crossroad, 1999), 198: "If Jesus is not yet ascended, that is, if he is still present in the earthly sphere, it would seem that Mary, like the pre-ascension disciples in Luke 24:29, could be invited to touch him and verify his bodily reality."

too much value to the resurrection appearance and deflects the attention to the ascension.[4] A rather nuanced version of this position was defended by Michael Theobald.[5] According to him, οὔπω γὰρ ἀναβέβηκα πρὸς τὸν πατέρα 20:17c is needed in the context to explain why Mary Magdalene should not hold on to Jesus. He paraphrases 20:17 as follows: "Do not hold on to me, for (as the one who is standing before you now, namely as *the one who is raised from the tomb*) I have not yet ascended to the Father; (my mode of existence as *risen one* is not yet my actual mode of existence with the Father, but it is only provisional."[6] For Theobald, in 20:11–18 the Fourth Evangelist addresses a more fundamental issue than a prohibition to touch and more than a prohibition of holding him fast in this earthly reality.[7] Instead, the question is whether the risen Christ whom Mary sees in bodily form represents the true Easter reality or is only a sign of it.[8] According to Theobald, the evangelist would consider the resurrection appearances only to be the sign of his true Easter reality.

Some scholars, however, are convinced that "I have not yet ascended to the Father" cannot be the reason for the prohibition in 20:17b and have looked for alternative syntactic options. Maximilian Zerwick agrees that γάρ introduces a reason that follows, but suggests that it does not follow immediately, but rather in 20:17d, making the words that follow γάρ parenthetical. He suggests the following translation: "Do not keep hold of me, for (I am not yet ascended to My Father) go rather to My brethren and tell them . . ."[9] The motivation for the prohibition would thus be found in the

---

[4] In this article we use the noun "ascension" to refer to the reality that in 20:17 is described with the Greek verb ἀναβαίνω. This choice of vocabulary is not intended to suggest that what John calls ἀναβαίνω is the same as what we see in Luke 24:50–51 and Acts 1:2.9–11. For a discussion of the difference between the two see Pierre Benoit, "L'Ascension," *RB* 56 (1949): 161–203. For Luke "ascension" means the terminus of the appearances, for John the glorification of Jesus in the Father's presence.

[5] Michael Theobald, "Der johanneische Osterglaube und die Grenzen seiner narrativen Vermittlung (Joh 20)," in *Von Jesus zum Christus. Christologische Studien. Festgabe für Paul Hoffmann zum 65. Geburtstag* (ed. Rudolf Hoppe and Ulrich Busse; BZNW 93; Berlin and New York: de Gruyter, 1998), 93–123.

[6] Theobald, "Der johanneische Osterglaube," 111–12: "Halte mich nicht fest, denn (als derjenige, der ich jetzt vor dir stehe, nämlich als *der aus dem Grab Erweckte*) bin ich noch nicht zum Vater gegangen; (meine Existenzweise als *Auferweckter* ist noch nicht meine eigentliche beim Vater, sie ist vorläufig)."

[7] The more physical idea of "Do not hold me back," i.e., do not prevent me from ascending, is still defended by Frank J. Matera, "John 20:1–18," *Int* 43 (1989): 402–6, esp. 405; and Teresa Okure, "The Significance Today of Jesus' Commission to Mary Magdalene," *International Review of Mission* 81 (1992): 177–88, esp. 180.

[8] Theobald, "Der johanneische Osterglaube," 111 n. 71: "ob der *Erweckte*, wie Maria ihn leibhaft vor sich sieht, schon Jesu *wahre* österliche Wirklichkeit repräsentiert."

[9] Maximilian Zerwick, *Biblical Greek. Illustrated by Examples* (ed. Joseph Smith; Scripta Pontificii Instituti Biblici 114; Rome: Biblical Institute, 1963), 160 (§476).

task Jesus gives to Mary Magdalene to go to his brothers. Zerwick paraphrases: "let go of me because you must go . . ." According to Zerwick, 20:17bc is an instance of the classical μὲν γάρ . . . δέ construction, which he describes as follows: "sometimes the real reason is expressed in the second place only, preceded by something not alleged as a reason but merely conceded parenthetically as well known."[10] In this interpretation the fact that Jesus has not yet ascended has nothing to do with the prohibition in 20:17b. It is only mentioned in passing as a well-known concession ("although, as everyone knows . . ."). Zerwick is convinced that John 20:17c is one of the many cases where μέν is not explicitly expressed but assumed.[11]

The major difficulty with this syntactic interpretation is that the content of "I have not yet ascended to the Father" in 20:17c and "Go to my brothers" in 17d is too different to be correlated in a μέν . . . δέ construction.[12] For the resulting meaning could then be paraphrased as follows: "[Although] I have not yet ascended to the Father, [I give you the task that already now you] go to my brothers and tell them: I am ascending to my Father and your Father, to my God and your God." This would suggest that normally one would expect that Mary Magdalene could only go and tell Jesus' brothers that he is ascending *after* he has ascended, because the fact that he has not yet ascended is given as a concession. However, to assume that the disciples may only be told that he is ascending after he ascended does not make sense, and to suggest that 20:17cd implies making an exception to this sequence is equally nonsensical. If one followed Zerwick's basic assumption that the reason of μή μου ἅπτου is found in πορεύου δὲ πρὸς τοὺς ἀδελφούς μου, without accepting his hypothetical assumption of a μέν γάρ . . . δέ correlation, one might simply consider οὔπω γὰρ ἀναβέβηκα πρὸς τὸν πατέρα to be one of the typically Johannine parentheses that interrupts the line of thought.[13] This brings the prohibition in 20:17b and the commands in 20:17d and 17e closer together, but

---

[10] Zerwick, *Biblical Greek*, 159 (§474).

[11] Zerwick, *Biblical Greek*, 159 (§475): "The μέν however is often omitted." This aspect is overlooked by Carson (*The Gospel According to John*, 642) when he formulates his decisive argument against Zerwick: "It would help Zerwick's case if it had been introduced by a concessive word like 'although' . . . but this is not the case."

[12] In the examples Zerwick gives (Matt 22:14; 24:6 and Acts 13:36–7) the two sides of the correlation are much more parallel.

[13] This is the suggestion of Gilbert Van Belle, *Les parenthèses dans l'évangile de Jean: Aperçu historique et classification. Texte grec de Jean* (Leuven: Leuven University Press and Peeters, 1985), 323. Alfred Loisy, *Le quatrième Évangile. Les Épîtres dites de Jean* (2d ed.; Paris: Picard, 1921), 505 considers 20:17c to be "une interpolation rédactionnelle."

the question remains as to what the function of the parenthesis in 20:17c is and how the conjunction γάρ is to be understood.

The positions we discussed so far assume that γάρ is a marker of cause or reason and that it motivates the preceding clause, namely the prohibition in 20:17b. Michael McGehee, however, suggests understanding the γάρ as an anticipatory γάρ. This means that there is a full stop after μη μου ἅπτου and that in 20:17c a new, unconnected thought begins. The γάρ clause in 20:17c does not motivate 20:17b but the following clauses in 20:17d and 17e. He therefore paraphrases 20:17 as follows: "Don't cling to me. Since I have not yet ascended (*anabebēka*) to the Father, go to my brothers and tell them I am ascending (*anabainō*) to my Father and your Father . . ." Here the prohibition is isolated from its succeeding context. The focus is on the reason why Mary Magdalene is commissioned to tell the disciples that he is in the process of ascending.[14] This interpretation can hardly escape trivializing the text, for it seems tautological to say that the reason Mary Magdalene is sent to the brothers to tell them that Jesus is in the process of ascending to the Father is that he has not yet ascended to the Father. Moreover, others have pointed out that in the New Testament "there is no certain example"[15] of anticipatory γάρ. Moreover it would be surprising if the prohibition in 20:17b was not motivated at all in the text.

M.-J. Lagrange also sees a correlation between γάρ and δέ, but according to him γάρ does not have a motivational meaning. He rather understands the conjunction as concessive ("it is true that") and sees the motivation for the prohibition in 20:17b elsewhere, as we shall see. Moreover, he suggests that δέ in 20:17d does not apply to this clause, but rather to ἀναβαίνω πρὸς τὸν πατέρα μου . . . in 20:17f.[16] This means that 20:17d and 17e are seen as parenthetical.[17] The effect is that now "I am ascending to my Father and your Father, my God and your God" in 20:17f becomes the actual motivation for the μή μου ἅπτου prohibition in 20:17b. Jesus

---

[14] Michael McGehee, "A Less Theological Reading of John 20:17," *JBL* 105 (1986): 299–302. This position received support from Stanley E. Porter, *Verbal Aspect in the Greek of the New Testament, with Reference to Tense and Mood* (Studies in Biblical Greek 1; New York: Lang, 1989), 356; and Xavier Léon-Dufour, *Lecture de l'évangile selon Jean* (Parole de Dieu 34/4; Paris : Seuil, 1996), 223.

[15] Carson, *The Gospel According to John*, 642.

[16] M.-J. Lagrange, *Evangile selon Saint Jean* (6th ed.; Paris: Gabalda, 1936), 512 paraphrases: "n'insiste pas pour me toucher, car, si, je ne suis pas encore monté vers mon Père, cependant je ne tarderai pas beaucoup à y remonter . . . ce que tu diras à mes frères, afin qu'ils soient préparés mieux que tu ne l'as été à comprendre de quelle nature est ma présence." Similarly, C. K. Barrett, *The Gospel According to St John* (London: SPCK, 1956), 470.

[17] Lagrange, *Evangile selon Saint Jean*, 512 : "Le message donné à Magdeleine n'est qu'une parenthèse."

would then be saying to Mary Magdalene: "It is understandable and possible that you are touching me in this post-resurrection and pre-ascension state to show the continuity with my earthly existence and to prove the reality of the resurrection.[18] But stop touching me now because now the ascension begins and this implies that there will now be a new spiritual mode of contact in which physical aspects are no longer appropriate." Lagrange's interpretation is based on the assumption that μή μου ἅπτου refers to an action that is already going on and is not in itself considered to be wrong during a resurrection appearance, but that needs to stop because something new is happening, namely the ascension. The strength of this interpretation is that it brings 20:17 into the fold of 20:27 and the other resurrection appearance narratives where touch is not prohibited. However, it is purchased at too high a price, namely a clear disrespect for the text of 20:17d and 17e. To declare πορεύου δὲ πρὸς τοὺς ἀδελφούς μου καὶ εἰπὲ αὐτοῖς to be a negligible parenthesis, and to do so as if the conjunction δέ in 20:17d was not there but in 20:17f, does violence to the text.

All the positions we have discussed so far have in common that they understand οὔπω γὰρ ἀναβέβηκα πρὸς τὸν πατέρα in 20:17c as a declarative sentence. Sandra Schneiders suggested reading the clause as a question. The adverb οὔπω would then indicate that the question suggests the answer "yes." The correct translation of 20:17c would then be: "For I have already ascended to the Father, haven't I?"[19] Schneiders is right in saying, "The grammar and syntax of the sentence allow its translation as a question, . . ."[20] This is, however, not just a grammatical question. It is theologically motivated, for on the same page Schneiders states: "It is virtually impossible, theologically, to understand Jesus in this scene as being somewhere in between (whether ontologically, spatially, or temporally) his resurrection and his ascension. The Jesus Mary encounters in the garden is clearly the glorified Jesus." Understanding οὔπω γὰρ ἀναβέβηκα πρὸς τὸν

---

[18] It is obvious that in such an interpretation the Johannine scenes of Mary Magdalene and Thomas are perfectly parallel.

[19] Schneiders (*Written That You May Believe*, 198) says that she understands 20:17c "as a rhetorical question expecting a negative reply, that is, 'Am I as yet (or still) not ascended?' The proper answer to the question is, 'No, you are indeed ascended, that is, glorified.'" Even though this seems to be saying the opposite of what we are saying, Schneiders is saying the same, namely that Jesus is saying in 20:17c that he is already ascended.

[20] Schneiders is an application of the position of Albert Vanhoye, "Interrogation johannique et exégèse de Cana (Jn 2,4), " *Bib* 55 (1974): 157–67 to 20:17c. Vanhoye argued that οὔπω ἥκει ἡ ὥρα μου in John 2:4 means: "my hour has come, hasn't it? See also Raymond F. Collins, "Cana (Jn 2:1–12). The First of His Signs or the Key to His Signs?" in *These Things Have Been Written. Studies in the Fourth Gospel* (LTPM 2; Leuven: Peeters and Grand Rapids: Eerdmans, 1990), 158–82.

πατέρα as a question suggesting the answer "yes," Schneiders is able to make this clause say the exact opposite of what it would mean as a declarative sentence. According to Schneiders, "Jesus' ascension to the Father, that is, his glorification, is precisely the reason Mary will now encounter him in the community of the church rather than in his physical or earthly body, which may appear to be resuscitated but is not."[21] Thus for Schneiders, the γάρ clause in 20:17c clearly gives the reason for the prohibition in 20:17b, but by understanding 20:17c as a question suggesting the answer "yes," Schneiders' theological position comes close to that of Lagrange who, in a problematic syntactic construction, sees the motivation for the prohibition of 20:17b in the announcement "I am ascending . . ." in 20:17f. For both positions, the prohibition signals a transition to something utterly new, where the old ways no longer work.[22]

Schneiders' position of reading 20:17c as a question has mostly met with skepticism. The major difficulty is whether οὔπω γὰρ ἀναβέβηκα πρὸς τὸν πατέρα is correctly understood as a question expecting the answer "yes."[23] In four of the twenty-six occurrences in the NT οὔπω is, at least if we follow the common interpretation, used in questions, some of them even questions which suggest the answer "yes," i.e., exactly the meaning that Schneiders postulates for John 20:17c. All four of them are found in the Synoptic gospels. In Mark 4:40 Jesus asks the disciples who woke him during the storm on the sea: "Do you still have no faith?" In the context of the multiplication of loaves Jesus asks the disciples: "Do you still not understand/perceive?" (Mark 8:17: οὔπω νοεῖτε οὐδὲ συνίετε; par. Matt 16:9: οὔπω νοεῖτε . . .; as well as in Mark 8:21: οὔπω συνίετε; par. Matt 16:11: πῶς οὐ νοεῖτε . . .;). It is not clear here whether Jesus asks an open question or a rhetorical question suggesting that they will answer: "Yes, we have understood, and that they will behave accordingly." In none of these instances is οὔπω used with γάρ. However, γάρ is often used in questions.[24] In Gen 15:16 LXX, 2 Macc 7:35, and John 3:24, the

---

[21] Schneiders, *Written That You May Believe*, 198.

[22] See Sandra M. Schneiders, "Touching the Risen Jesus: Mary Magdalene and Thomas the Twin in John," in this volume, p. 171: "The point is that physical 'touching' – which is an apt metonymy for the physically mediated historical experience of two people relating "in the flesh," that is, as mortal human beings – has come to an end."

[23] See the criticism of Harold W. Attridge, "'Don't be touching me': Recent Feminist Scholarship on Mary Magdalene," in *A Feminist Companion to John* (ed. Amy-Jill Levine; Feminist Companion to the New Testament and Early Christian Writings 5/2; London and New York: Sheffield Academic Press, 2003), 140–66, 151: "Unfortunately the construal of οὔπω as an interrogative is artificial. The adverb quite normally means 'not yet,' . . . another expression, such as οὐ (or perhaps better οὐχί) νῦν, would have been necessary to convey the meaning that Schneiders seeks."

[24] See BDAG, 189.

instances where οὔπω γάρ is used in Biblical Greek besides John 20:17, the expression is clearly not used in questions. Taking these observations into account, it can hardly be denied that it is grammatically possible that John 20:17c expresses a question, maybe even a question expecting the answer "yes." However, it is difficult to maintain this interpretation in the immediate context. For if Jesus in 20:17c is suggesting the answer: "Yes, I have ascended to the Father," how can he commission Mary Magdalene to tell the disciples: "I am ascending . . ."?

We need to draw attention to the precise meaning of οὔπω in John 20:17c. If the negation οὐ is used, the meaning is rather undetermined, leaving open whether it ever happened before or whether it is expected ever to happen in the future. The negation with οὐ excludes the idea hat an action is in the process of happening, especially when it is used with the present indicative. If the negation οὐκέτι is used, it suggests that something happened before, but did not happen again; or was going on until a certain moment, but then stopped happening. The negation οὔπω, however, is used for actions that never happened before but are expected to happen, or have already begun but are not yet completed. The question as to whether an action that is negated by οὔπω has already started or not depends on the *Aktionsart* implied in the semantics of the verb and in the tense in which it is used. In Gen 15:16 LXX ἀναπληρόω occurs in the perfect, and in John 7:8 the *verbum simplex* πληρόω is found in the same tense. Both times the verb is negated with οὔπω. The interplay between the semantics of the verb and the tense means that the negated action has already started, but is not yet completed. With verbs that carry a more semelfactive *Aktionsart* than a durative one, the perfect tense used with οὔπω adds to the idea that the action has not started. In Gen 18:12 LXX Sarah says within herself concerning the prediction that she will have a son: "This thing has not yet happened to me up to now." In 2 Macc 7:35, in the context of the martyrdom of the seven brothers, the youngest says to King Antiochus: "You have not yet escaped the judgment of the almighty, all-seeing God." Here the perfect implies: "You have not even begun to escape." In John 20:17c the semantics of the verb ἀναβαίνω imply an action that takes time. The durative *Aktionsart* together with the perfect tense suggests that Jesus is saying in this verse: "I have not yet completed the process of ascending to the Father." This would be in keeping with the use of the present tense ἀναβαίνω in 20:17f, which could be paraphrased: "I am in the process of ascending."[25] In this interpretation 20:17c does not

---

[25] Porter (*Verbal Aspect*, 356) describes the verbal aspect of the perfect as "the process as a state of affairs not yet attained" and the verbal aspect of the present tense as "the process as in progress." See also Léon-Dufour, *Lecture de l'évangile selon Jean*, 223: "le présent ne peut être entendu comme un futur, fût-it immanent, au sens de 'je vais mon-

contradict the Johannine interpretation of the cross as exaltation and glorification.

The question remains, however, as to whether and in which way οὔπω γὰρ ἀναβέβηκα πρὸς τὸν πατέρα can be seen as a motivation of the prohibition μή μου ἅπτου. The grammatical attempts to separate these two clauses from each other are not convincing. Therefore, no interpretation of 20:17 can escape facing the difficulty as to how 20:17c can be a reason for the prohibition in 20:17b.

We conclude this first section by noting that οὔπω γὰρ ἀναβέβηκα πρὸς τὸν πατέρα (John 20:17c) was subjected to the complete arsenal of grammatical and style-critical techniques, which are all designed to undo or transform its connection with the preceding prohibition μή μου ἅπτου. It was seen as a parenthesis (Van Belle), the first part of a μὲν γάρ . . . δέ construction (Zerwick), a concessive clause (Lagrange), and an anticipated motivational clause (McGehee). All of these techniques had the effect that the link between 20:17b and 17c was undone. The technique of understanding 20:17c as a question expecting the answer "yes" (Schneiders) does not undo the link between 20:17b and 17c but makes 20:17c say the opposite of what it otherwise says. However, none of these attempts to come up with a smoother text is convincing. With that in mind we now turn to a literary-critical analysis of our text.

2. Tradition-Critical and Redaction-Critical Approaches to John 20:17

In John 20:1–18 scholars have identified strong parallels with the synoptic Easter narratives (Matt 28:9–10; Mark 16:7, 9–11; Luke 24:12). At the same time John 20:1–18 also contains elements that are unique. There is a discussion as to whether they have their origin in earlier traditions or in Johannine redaction. This complex situation is at the root of the great variety of literary-critical theories that have been developed to explain the composition of John 20:1–18 and that form the context for the question of the origin of the various parts of 20:17.

Gert Hartmann reconstructed a rather extensive traditional story at the basis of 20:1–18.[26] According to him, John's redactional activity was lim-

---

ter'. Il convient donc de l'interpréter immédiatement de l'exaltation dans la sphère céleste, qui est en acte dès la mort de Jésus." See also Hartwig Thyen, *Das Johannesevangelium*, (HNT 60; Tübingen: Mohr Siebeck, 2005), 763: "Wie die Fortsetzung zeigt, ist Jesus bereits unterwegs zu seinem Vater."

[26] Gert Hartmann, "Die Vorlage der Osterberichte in Joh 20," *ZNW* 55 (1964): 197–220, see esp. 219–20 for his reconstruction of the "Vorlage."

ited to the addition of the Beloved Disciple in 20:3–10 and to the introduction of the vision of angels in 20:11b–13. In the other verses he also ascribes to the evangelist a number of elements that caused perceived inconsistencies. Even though Hartmann reconstructed an extensive *Vorlage* for John 20:1–18, he considers v. 17 to be by the evangelist himself.[27] He sees very clearly that there is a contradiction between the first nineteen chapters of John's gospel, where death and resurrection are understood as one event, and 20:17, where after crucifixion and resurrection the ascension is said not to have happened yet. On the other hand, he comes to the conclusion that for the most characteristic aspects of 20:17, the prohibition of touch and the reference to the ascension, no parallels can be found in the tradition.[28] Therefore, he concludes that 20:17 is the work of the evangelist and that the tension between the exaltation that already happened on the cross according to the gospel up to 19:30 and the ascension that has not yet happened according to 20:17 needs to be accepted as Johannine.

Rudolf Bultmann also postulates one basic story as the *Vorlage* of the evangelist, but his is much shorter than the one of Hartmann. Important for our concerns in this article is that Bultmann ascribes Jesus' appearance to Mary Magdalene in 20:14–18 to the evangelist's free creation.[29] This also includes 20:17 and the idea of the ascension. For Bultmann there is no problem in seeing the "not yet" of the ascension as Johannine, since "οὔπω refers to Mary rather than to Jesus; she cannot yet enter into fellowship with him until she has recognized him as the Lord who is with the Father, and so removed from earthly conditions."[30] This makes it possible for Bultmann to read 20:17 as presuming that Jesus had already ascended before he appeared to Mary Magdalene.

Barnabas Lindars and Michael Theobald see John's style and theology in 20:14–18, but also assume that the evangelist used the same tradition

---

[27] Hartmann, "Die Vorlage," 207: "V. 17 ist demnach von Johannes formuliert." See, however, Georg Richter, "Der Vater und Gott Jesu und seiner Brüder in Joh 20,17. Ein Beitrag zur Christologie im Johannesevangelium," in *Studien zum Johannesevangelium* (ed. Josef Hainz; BU 13; Regensburg: Pustet, 1977), 266–80, esp. 268–70. He is one of the few authors who does not consider 20:17 to be from the hand of the Fourth Evangelist.

[28] Hartmann thinks that John 20:17c would fit well in the Farewell Discourses as a promise. However, 20:17c differs from the traditional material which John used in the Farewell Discourses and elsewhere in so far as ἀναβαίνω is not combined with the Son of Man title as is the case in the tradition (see 3:13–14; 6:62; 8:28 and 12:32).

[29] Rudolf Bultmann, *The Gospel of John: A Commentary* (trans. by George R. Beasley-Murray et al.; Philadelphia: Westminster, 1971), 682: "Vv. 14–18 reflect entirely the view of the Evangelist."

[30] Bultmann, *The Gospel of John*, 682.

that is at the root of the Synoptics and Matthew in particular.[31] Theobald is also convinced that 20:17 is thoroughly Johannine.[32] He also points out the tension between the understanding of ascension in 3:14 and 6:62 in the perspective of the cross and the understanding of ascension in 20:17, where it is seen as entering into the heavenly world after the resurrection. Theobald points out that in a number of late books in the New Testament, resurrection and entering into the heavenly world are linguistically differentiated (Eph 1:20; 1 Pet 1:21; 3:21–22) and he suggests that tradition-critically this is where John 20:17c comes from.[33] According to Theobald, John intends the prohibition in 20:17b (do not hold on to me, do not pin me down to an appearance) and the ascension (20:17c and 17f) to be a critique of paying too much attention to appearances. The evangelist wants to show that the Easter reality of the exalted Christ transcends the appearances in many ways. Thus, demonstrating that we may not cling to the resurrection appearances but have to read them as signs which point beyond themselves to the Easter reality of the exalted Christ, 20:17 is the hermeneutical key to John 20.

Pierre Benoit postulates two basic stories that the evangelist combined by making direct use of the synoptic tradition (20:11b–14a).[34] One of the two traditions supposedly was a non-Synoptic story (20:1–10), while the other was Synoptic-like (20:11a.14b–18). For the latter he assumes that both John and Matthew depend on the same story in the tradition, which both adapt in their own ways to their contextual theological needs.[35] Benoit does not make any attempt in this study to explain the tradition history of 20:17.

---

[31] Barnabas Lindars, "The Composition of John 20," *NTS* 7 (1961): 142–47; Michael Theobald, "Der johanneische Osterglaube und die Grenzen seiner narrativen Vermittlung (Joh 20)," in *Von Jesus zum Christus. Christologische Studien. Festgabe für Paul Hoffmann zum 65. Geburtstag* (ed. Rudolf Hoppe and Ulrich Busse; BZNW 93; Berlin and New York: de Gruyter, 1998), 93–123, esp. 102–3.

[32] Theobald, "Der johanneische Osterglaube," 103: "Die Rede vom 'Aufstieg Jesu zu seinem Vater verrät also die redaktionelle Hand des Evangelisten, der V. 17, so wie er dasteht, auf der Basis seines überlieferten Gerüsts selbst formuliert hat."

[33] Theobald, "Der johanneische Osterglaube" 107: "In 20,17 wird er, *traditionskritisch* betrachtet, in der eben dokumentierten Sprachkonvention neutestamentlicher Spätschriften stehen, die Jesu Auferweckung aus den Toten und seinen Eingang in die himmlische Welt als zwei voneinander zu differenzierende Aspekte bzw. Etappen des einen österlichen Erhöhungsgeschehens begreift."

[34] Pierre Benoit, "Marie-Madeleine et les Disciples au Tombeau selon Joh 20,1–18," in *Judentum, Urchristentum, Kirche. Festschrift für Joachim Jeremias* (ed. Walther Eltester; BZNW 26; Berlin: Töpelmann, 1960), 141–52.

[35] Benoit. "Marie-Madeleine," 145: "Ne depend-il pas ici du récit sous-jacent à Joh 20 14–18, qu'il aura résumé et adapté."

Raymond E. Brown assumes that at the origin of John 20:1–18 there were three basic stories from different traditions, a visit to the tomb by women, a visit to the tomb by male disciples, and an appearance of Jesus to Mary Magdalene. He finds it difficult to answer the question as to whether these three stories were combined on the pre-Johannine level or whether the evangelist joined them together. Brown admits that the evangelist adapted his *Vorlagen* "as a vehicle for his own theology."[36] He is convinced that in 20:17 John is not dependent on the Lukan ascension tradition, but rather develops his own understanding of ascension as a process of exaltation and glorification which began on the cross.[37] Brown also warns against attempts to establish a chronological sequence of resurrection and ascension. According to Brown 20:17 is an

> effort to fit the resurrection into the process of Jesus' passing from this world to the Father. If John reinterprets the crucifixion so that it becomes part of Jesus' glorification, he dramatizes the resurrection so that it is obviously part of the ascension.[38]

Erika Mohri is also convinced that at the root of John 20:1–18 there are three traditions. The earliest is an Easter morning narrative of women at the tomb to which a narrative of a Christophany is added, and the two stories are thoroughly interwoven[39]. The last addition is the race to the tomb (20:3–10) for which the evangelist made use of oral tradition. According to Mohri, even 20:17 comes from tradition, because it is unique among all the Johannine statements about Jesus departure or ascension to the Father in so far as in 20:17 ascension is not identified with crucifixion and in so far as 20:17 postulates a phase of appearances between resurrection and ascension. Nevertheless, the understanding of ascension in 20:17 fits well with other aspects of the gospel of John like Jesus' descending into the world. Similarly nowhere else does John use the expression "your Father," but the basic idea of 20:17f ("my Father and your Father") can be compared to 14:20, 24; 15:15; and 17:21, 23. According to Mohri, in 20:17 John preserves an ancient tradition because it is close to John's thinking.[40]

According to Frans Neirynck, John depended directly on the Synoptics. For John 20:1–10 the evangelist's inspiration was Luke 24:12 and for John

---

[36] Raymond E. Brown, *The Gospel according to John* (2 vols. AB 29–29A; Garden City, N.Y.: Doubleday, 1966, 1970), 2.996–1004, esp. 998.

[37] Brown, *The Gospel according to John,* 2.1013.

[38] Brown, *The Gospel according to John,* 2.1013–14.

[39] Erika Mohri, *Maria Magdalena. Frauenbilder in Evangelientexten des 1. bis 3. Jahrhunderts* (MTSt 63; Marburg: Elwert, 2000), 131 and 137–38.

[40] Mohri, *Maria Magdalena,* 140: "Joh 20,17 fügt sich in diesen Hintergrund des JohEv und hebt sich gleichzeitig davon ab. Dies ist verständlich, wenn in V. 17 ältere Tradition gesehen wird, die aufgrund ihrer Nähe zu joh. Vorstellungen bewahrt wurde."

20:11–18 it was Matt 28:9–10[41]. On the basis of these texts John is seen as having composed his texts with much redactional freedom and creativity. Neirynck also explains 20:17 on the basis of synoptic parallels and Johannine redaction. He considers the opposition in "do not touch me any more" and "go to my brothers and tell them . . ." to be the slightly explicated Matthean structure. There is also in Matt 28:10 the striking reference to "my brothers," which is unique in John. Neirynck is also convinced that there is no essential difference between ἅπτομαι in John and κρατέω in Matthew. He finds support for this in the fact that in Matt 8:15 the verb κρατέω of the Markan parallel is replaced by ἅπτομαι. Moreover in Luke 7:39 the verb ἅπτομαι is used for more or less the same action of touching Jesus' feet as in Matt 28:9.[42] Onto this basic Matthean structure John grafted his own theology of the ascension in 20:17c, which Neirynck thinks might have its origin in John 7, where we find Jesus in a dispute with his brothers about going up (ἀναβαίνω) to Jerusalem for the feast. According to Neirynck, μή μου ἅπτου has two opposites: Mary Magdalene's commission to go to the brothers and Jesus' going to the Father. μή μου ἅπτου, therefore, is seen to have the connotation "do not make me lose time, for I need to go to the Father," and at the same time it implies "do not lose any time, for you need to go to my brothers."[43]

Our overview of the tradition-critical and redaction-critical approaches to John 20:17 has brought to the surface the same problems as the syntactic analysis. The main issue is how the prohibition in 20:17b and the γάρ clause in 20:17c fit together. The question is whether 20:17b and 20:17c and 17f are contradictory to or in harmony with the rest of the gospel of John. This mainly raises the question of how death, resurrection, and ascension relate to one another in John, what the prohibition in 20:17b actually forbids, and why it is forbidden. In our third and final subsection we shall enter more deeply into these questions.

---

[41] Frans Neirynck, "John and the Synoptics: The Empty Tomb Stories," in *Evangelica II 1982–1991: Collected Essays* (ed. Frans Van Segbroeck; BETL 99; Leuven: Leuven University Press and Peeters, 1991), 571–600.

[42] Frans Neirynck, *Evangelica. Gospel Studies – Etudes d'évangile. Collected Essays* (BETL 60; Leuven: University Press and Peeters, 1982), 292–93; (= "Les femmes au tombeau. Etude de la rédaction matthéenne (Matt. xxviii. 1–10," originally *NTS* 15 [1968-69] 168–90, esp. 187–88): "La tradition sousjacente à Jean xx. 17 sera donc fort semblable à Matt. xxviii. 9–10 et rien ne s'oppose à ce qu'il s'agisse d'une tradition qui remonte à Matthieu lui-même."

[43] For this interpretation Neirynck finds the support of Heinrich Julius Holtzmann, *Evangelium des Johannes* (ed. W. Bauer; 3d ed.; HKNT 4/1; Tübingen: Mohr Siebeck, 1908), 303.

3. A Composition-Critical Approach to John 20:17

In our own composition-critical approach, we shall work with the hypothesis of John's direct dependence on the Synoptics, but with special emphasis on John's own redactional contribution. We begin with a comparison of John 20:16–17 with Matt 28:9–10:[44]

John 20:14–17	Matt 28:9–10
14–15	9 καὶ ἰδοὺ Ἰησοῦς ὑπήντησεν αὐταῖς
16 λέγει αὐτῇ Ἰησοῦς·	λέγων·
Μαριάμ.	χαίρετε
στραφεῖσα ἐκείνη	αἱ δὲ προσελθοῦσαι
λέγει αὐτῷ Ἑβραϊστί·	
ραββουνι	
ὃ λέγεται διδάσκαλε	
	ἐκράτησαν αὐτοῦ τοὺς πόδας
	καὶ προσεκύνησαν αὐτῷ.
17a λέγει αὐτῇ Ἰησοῦς·	
17b μή μου ἅπτου	
	10 τότε λέγει αὐταῖς ὁ Ἰησοῦς·
	μὴ φοβεῖσθε·
17c οὔπω γὰρ ἀναβέβηκα	
πρὸς τὸν πατέρα	
17d πορεύου δὲ	ὑπάγετε
πρὸς τοὺς ἀδελφούς μου	
17e καὶ εἰπὲ αὐτοῖς·	ἀπαγγείλατε
	τοῖς ἀδελφοῖς μου
	ἵνα ἀπέλθωσιν
17f ἀναβαίνω	εἰς τὴν Γαλιλαίαν,
πρὸς τὸν πατέρα μου	
καὶ πατέρα ὑμῶν	
καὶ θεόν μου	
καὶ θεὸν ὑμῶν	
	κἀκεῖ με ὄψονται.

The basic structure in John 20:14–17 and Matt 28:9–10 is similar: meeting – exchange of words – approach – something about touching – negative command – positive command to move away and bring a message to Jesus' brothers – content of the message about moving to a different place. But within this structure, practically every element is different. The only part that is literally the same is "my brothers," but even this differs in so far as Matthew mentions the brothers as the recipients of the message whereas John mentions them as the people to whom Mary Magdalene is to go and give a message. In Matt 28:9 Jesus meets Mary Magdalene and the other

---

[44] Cf. Jürgen Becker, *Das Evangelium nach Johannes* (ÖTK 4; Gütersloh: Gütersloher Verlagshaus and – Würzburg: Mohn and Echter, 1981), 617: "Ohne einen Blick auf Mt 28,9 wird nun das Folgende (V 17) kaum verständlich."

Mary and says to them: "Greetings." In John 20:14–16a this scene is much more developed by the presence of the non-recognition and Mary Magdalene's preoccupation about Jesus' body having been carried away. In Matt 28:9 the two women seize the feet of Jesus and worship him. There is no prohibition of touching, but only the negative command not to be afraid. In John 20:16–17 nothing is said about an attempted touching, but there is an unexpected prohibition that uses ἅπτομαι instead of κρατέω and is about the whole person (μου) instead of just the feet. John has nothing about the worshiping of Jesus. The closest he gets to that is Mary addressing Jesus as ραββουνι, but much depends on the way one understands this address. The Johannine reference to the ascension in 20:17c has no corresponding element in Matt 28:9–10. The command to move away is parallel, but the vocabulary is different (ὑπάγω and πορεύομαι). The part about bringing a message to Jesus' brothers also differs in vocabulary. In Matt 28:10 what they are to tell the brothers is a command in indirect speech (ἀπαγγέλλω), in John 20:17f it is a piece of information reporting a direct speech of Jesus (λέγω). The message the risen Jesus sends to his brothers is very different in both gospels, but it is about movement. In Matt 28:10 the brothers are to go to Galilee, in John 20:17f Jesus is going to the Father.

A number of differences between the Matthean and the Johannine version can easily be recognized as Johannine characteristics: the reduction of a group of people to just one person,[45] the misunderstanding (thinking that Jesus was the gardener), the dialogue (in Matt 28:9–10 the women are not saying anything), the reference to Jesus as rabbi, the use of "Hebrew" words and their translation in a parenthesis, the reference to God as Father, the idea of Jesus' ascending to the Father. What is unique in John is the use of the verb ἅπτομαι, the reference to the disciples as Jesus' brothers, the combination of ἀναβαίνω with the prepositional phrase πρὸς τὸν πατέρα, and finally the expression πρὸς τὸν πατέρα μου καὶ πατέρα ὑμῶν καὶ θεόν μου καὶ θεὸν ὑμῶν. What is unique in John in this expression is referring to God as "your Father" and for Jesus to refer to God as "my God."

Our analysis has brought to the fore that the most important redactional activity of the Fourth Evangelist in John 20:14–17 is the introduction of Jesus' ascension to the Father. While the precise wording of 20:17c and

---

[45] In John 20:2 Mary Magdalene, after having gone to the tomb alone and having witnessed the stone removed from the tomb, says to Simon Peter and the disciple whom Jesus love: "They took the Lord out of the tomb and *we* do not know (οὐκ οἴδαμεν) where they laid him." The fact that she speaks here in the first person plural is sometimes seen as a leftover of the fact that in the synoptic tradition more than one woman went to the tomb and thus an indication that John knew about the tradition of more than one woman at the tomb.

17f is not found anywhere else in the gospel, the idea is very prevalent. The reason why John used ἀναβαίνω here, and not πορεύομαι or ὑπάγω as he did earlier in the gospel, is probably twofold. As we have tried to show earlier, in 20:17c John is speaking about a process of ascension that is not yet completed. For this he needed a verb that semantically could express a durative *Aktionsart*. The use of ὑπάγω would have been incorrect here since, even though he has not yet completed his ascension, i.e., he has not yet arrived, he did depart at the moment of his death. We suggest that John did not use πορεύομαι because he was interested in a specific connotation of the verb ἀναβαίνω that πορεύομαι does not have, a connotation that makes a connection with the temple.

We encounter the expression ἀναβαίνω εἰς Ἱεροσόλυμα[46] in each of the four gospels.[47] Five of the six synoptic occurrences are found in the third passion prediction in Mark 10:32-33; par. Matt 20:17-18; par. Luke 18:31 (εἰς Ἱερουσαλήμ). Luke uses ἀναβαίνω εἰς Ἱεροσόλυμα in 19:28[48] where Mark 11:1 and Matt 21:1 use the verb ἐγγίζω. John uses ἀναβαίνω εἰς Ἱεροσόλυμα in 2:13 and 5:1 with Jesus as subject and in 11:55 with "many" as subject. In addition the Fourth Evangelist also uses ἀναβαίνω εἰς τὸ ἱερόν in 7:14 and ἀναβαίνω εἰς τὴν ἑορτήν in 7:8 (bis) and 10 (cf. 12:20). In the Bible ἀναβαίνω as a translation of עלה is a technical term of cultic language referring to going to Jerusalem for worship (cf. John 12:20: τινες ἐκ τῶν ἀναβαινόντων ἵνα προσκυνήσωσιν ἐν τῇ ἑορτῇ and Acts 24:11 ἀνέβην προσκυνήσων εἰς Ἱερουσαλήμ).

In addition to the frequent use of cultic terminology for going up to Jerusalem, John also uses ἀναβαίνω with regard to the divine sphere in the expressions ἀναβαίνω εἰς τὸν οὐρανόν (3:13)[49] and ἀναβαίνω ὅπου ἦν τὸ πρότερον (6:62). The fact that John uses ἀναβαίνω πρὸς τὸν πατέρα in 20:17 is not unprepared for in John, since in the second part of the gospel he frequently uses πρὸς τὸν πατέρα in more or less synonymous expressions with the verbs ὑπάγω (16:10.17), πορεύομαι (14:12.28; 16:28), and even μεταβαίνω (13:1). Moreover, ὑπάγω is used with πρὸς τὸν θεόν in 13:3.[50] It is true that with ἀναβαίνω πρὸς τὸν πατέρα in 20:17 John uses a combination he has not used before. However, this does not force us to postulate a source or tradition that John might have used.[51] We agree with Neirynck that John may have worded 20:17 consciously as a counter-

---

[46] In the some cases Ἱερουσαλήμ is used.
[47] The other occurrences are in Acts 11:2; 21:12, 15; 24:11; 25:11 and Gal 2:1.
[48] See also ἀναβαίνω εἰς τὸ ἱερόν in Luke 18:10.
[49] Cf. also John 1:51 where with heaven open the angels are ascending and descending upon the Son of Man.
[50] Cf. ὑπάγω πρὸς τὸν πέμψαντά με in 7:33. See also the frequent uses of ὑπάγω with ὅπου throughout the gospel.
[51] Pace Mohri, *Maria Magdalena*, 139-40.

point to John 7:1–18, where the brothers of Jesus pressure him to go up to the feast and where Jesus states: ἐγὼ οὐκ ἀναβαίνω εἰς τὴν ἑορτὴν ταύτην and where he stays back in Galilee (7:8–9) only to go up himself in hiding a little later (καὶ αὐτὸς ἀνέβη).

On this background we suggest that προσεκύνησαν in Matt 28:9 and τοῖς ἀδελφοῖς μου as well as εἰς τὴν Γαλιλαίαν in 28:10 reminded John of the scene with the brothers of Jesus in 7:1–18. Along with Matthew, in 20:17 John now uses ἀδελφοί in the new meaning of disciples. For this, however, he is not only dependent on Matthew. It is also a consequence of theologically transcending the concept of going up the temple/feast into the sense of going up to the Father. After using the expression πρὸς τὸν πατέρα in 20:17c without a possessive pronoun[52] and πρὸς τοὺς ἀδελφούς μου in 20:17d, the evangelist has already prepared πρὸς τὸν πατέρα μου καὶ πατέρα ὑμῶν in 20:17f where the last doubts are removed as to the exact meaning of ἀδελφοί.[53] John 7:1–18 is centered on the issue of Jesus' ἀναβαίνειν from Galilee to Jerusalem, 20:17 is about Jesus' ἀναβαίνειν from Jerusalem to the Father.

For the evangelist this is probably also connected with the issue of true worship in 4:19–24, where the verb προσκυνέω is used with high frequency. With his own ἀναβαίνειν to his Father and his God, the Johannine Jesus opens the possibility of worshiping the Father neither on Mount Gerizim nor in Jerusalem, but ἐν πνεύματι καὶ ἀληθείᾳ.[54] It seems that what the evangelist found in Matt 28:9–10 was the occasion for him to reinterpret the scene with the help of his earlier writing in chapters 4 and 7. John reconfigures the Matthean appearance narrative by resolutely refocusing it on God and the relationship of the disciples with God. He does so with the help of the ἀναβαίνω motif, recentering worship from Jerusalem to God.

John's redactional change from ἐκράτησαν αὐτοῦ τοὺς πόδας καὶ προσεκύνησαν αὐτῷ in Matt 28:9 to μή μου ἅπτου is also part of this same reinterpretation.[55] In the gospel of Matthew the verb προσκυνέω is prevalent in the descriptions of how people approach Jesus. From the be-

---

[52] The presence of μου in 𝔓[66] A and a variety of ancient witnesses is usually seen as a secondary harmonization with πρὸς τὸν πατέρα μου in 20:17f.

[53] See also John 19:25–27 where he lays the foundation of the new family relations after his death.

[54] See Benny Thettayil, *In Spirit and Truth. An Exegetical Study of John 4:19–26 and a Theological Investigation of the Replacement Theme in the Fourth Gospel* (Contributions to Biblical Exegesis and Theology 46; Leuven: Peeters, 2007).

[55] See Becker, *Das Evangelium nach Johannes*, 618; and Gerhard Schneider, "Auf Gott Bezogenes 'mein Vater' und 'euer Vater' in den Jesus-Worten der Evangelien. Zugleich ein Beitrag zum Problem Johannes und die Synoptiker," in *The Four Gospels 1992. Festschrift Frans Neirynck* (ed. F. Van Segbroeck et al.; BETL 100/3; Leuven: Leuven University Press and Peeters, 1992), 1751–81, esp. 1779.

ginning of the gospel when the magi come to pay homage to the new-born King of the Jews (2:2, 8, 11) to the end in the resurrection appearance (28:9, 17), this verb plays a prominent role in interpreting who Jesus is. This is quite explicit in center of the gospel when after the stilling of the storm Matthew says: "And those in the boat worshiped him, saying, 'Truly you are the Son of God'" (Matt 14:33). The verb προσκυνέω is also used regularly of people who come up to Jesus to ask him for something (8:2; 9:18; 15:25; and 20:20[56]). "Behind this customary posture of petition there is probably a reference on the part of the authors of the gospels to Jesus' divinity,[57] for the spontaneous reaction to an encounter with a deity is throwing oneself down."[58] In Mark προσκυνέω is only used concerning the Gerasene demoniac in 5:6 as a recognition that Jesus is the Son of the Most High and in the scene of the soldiers mocking Jesus before the crucifixion in 15:19. After using προσκυνέω in the temptation story (4:7–8), Luke reserves the use of this verb for the very end of the gospel at the moment of Jesus' being carried up into heaven: "And they worshiped him,[59] and returned to Jerusalem with great joy; and they were continually in the temple blessing God" (24:52–53).

In Matt 28:9 ἐκράτησαν αὐτοῦ τοὺς πόδας is best read in light of the following statement about worship (καὶ προσεκύνησαν αὐτῷ). When Jesus allows them to seize his feet, the focus is not on Jesus allowing himself to be touched but on allowing them to worship him. Since προσκυνέω means worshiping by bowing down to the ground, it is directly associated with the feet. When Jesus appears to the eleven in Galilee, they worship him as soon as they see him (28:17). Luke moved this act of worship away from the appearances to the moment after Jesus was carried up into heaven (24:52). Next to the discussion about the true worship of the Father in 4:19–24, the only uses of προσκυνέω in John are found in 9:38 where the man born blind after coming to faith worships Jesus and in 12:20 with regard to temple worship. Thus 9:38 is the only use of προσκυνέω with Jesus as recipient. This verse and the first part of v. 39 is missing in $\mathfrak{P}^{75}$ ℵ* W and some early versions. The fact that the act of worshiping Jesus is found only here in John is a reason for Raymond E. Brown to suggest that "[p]erhaps we have here an addition stemming from the association of

---

[56] See See also 4 Βασ 4:37 (cf. v. 27): καί ἔπεσεν ἐπί τούς πόδας αὐτου καί προσεκύνησεν ἐπί τήν γῆν.

[57] The link with Jesus' divinity is reinforced by the fact that during the temptation Jesus tells the devil, who wants Jesus to worship him: "Worship the Lord your God, and serve only him" (4:10).

[58] Silvia Schroer and Thomas Staubli, *Body Symbolism in the Bible* (trans. Linda M. Maloney; Collegeville: Liturgical Press, 2001), 195.

[59] A part of the textual tradition (D it sy^s) lacks even this reference to worship.

John ix with the baptismal liturgy and catechesis."[60] Rudolf Schnackenburg opposes Brown's view and considers the element of worship necessary in the context. According to him προσκυνέω expresses more than paying respect to a person and less than formal adoration of Jesus. It is rather an expression that Jesus is the true temple, the true place of worshiping the Father.[61]

Given this background it is not surprising that the Johannine redaction of Matt 28:9 avoids any reference to worshiping Jesus. This is part of re-centering the scene on the Father. We shall try to demonstrate that μή μου ἅπτου fits well within this intention. This is the only place in John where ἅπτομαι occurs. Neirynck tried to explain ἅπτομαι here by suggesting it to be a variation of κρατέω in Matt 28:9. He claims that there is no essential difference between the two verbs in these verses. He finds support for this position in the observation that in Matt 8:15 Mark's κρατήσας (1:31) is replaced by ἥψατο. This is, however, not completely correct. In Mark 1:31 Jesus seized the hand of Peter's mother-in-law and lifted her up (ἤγειρεν). In Matt 8:15 the idea of lifting up is not present. The seizing of the hand to lift her up has become a simple touching of the hand. Matthew's change of the verb is precisely proof that he perceived a difference between κρατέω and ἅπτομαι. Neirynck also refers to Luke 7:39 where the whole action concerning Jesus' feet described in v. 38 ("she began to wet his feet with her tears, and wiped them with the hair of her head, and kissed his feet, and anointed them with the ointment") is referred to by the Pharisee as ἅπτεται αὐτοῦ. After our analysis of ἐκράτησαν αὐτοῦ τοὺς πόδας in Matt 28:9 as an expression of worship,[62] this parallel seems less convincing. Luke 7:39 rather seems to be evidence that ἅπτομαι is an umbrella term that can refer to different ways of touching. It is also possible that in 7:39 it has sexual overtones. Another reason why Neirynck's proposal of a redactional explanation of μή μου ἅπτου was not convincing is that he did not give an explanation as to why κρατέω in Matt 28:9 is permitted whereas ἅπτομαι in John 20:17 is prohibited.

On the basis of this critique and in line with what we have said so far we shall make a fresh attempt to find a redactional explanation of μή μου ἅπτου. First, we note that in John the element that corresponds to Matthew's αἱ δὲ προσελθοῦσαι is στραφεῖσα ἐκείνη. Many have remarked that this second turning of Mary Magdalene is strange since, taken literally, it would mean that she turns away from him. For this reason it is

---

[60] Brown, *The Gospel according to John*, 1.375.

[61] Rudolf Schnackenburg, *Das Johannesevangelium* (vol. 2; HTK 4/2; Freiburg et al.: Herder, 1971), 323.

[62] We acknowledge that the precise meaning of the expression ἐκράτησαν αὐτοῦ τοὺς πόδας remains cryptic because of the scarcity of parallels (but cf. 4 Βασ 4:27, 37).

likely that it expresses an inner turning from her non-recognition of Jesus to recognizing him. The use of προσέρχομαι in Matt 28:9 is not surprising, taking into consideration that 59% of all NT occurrences of this verb are in Matthew. It is also to be expected that John did not take over this verb, since in the Fourth Gospel there is only one instance of this verb (in 12:21). We suggest that John's choice for ἅπτομαι in 20:17 is occasioned at least as much by προσελθοῦσαι in Matthew's text as by ἐκράτησαν.[63]

Second, we need to have a close look at the semantic domain of ἅπτομαι. LSJ gives the following meanings for this verb in extra-biblical Greek: to fasten oneself, to grasp, to engage in, to undertake, to fasten upon, to attack, to lay hands on, to touch, to affect, to grasp with the senses, to have intercourse with, to come up to, to reach, to attain, to make use of, to be in contact (of bodies and surfaces). In the LXX ἅπτομαι means to touch in the vast majority of occurrences. This is confirmed by the fact that in those cases it translates the Hebrew verb נגע. ἅπτομαι can be used of touch that sanctifies and touch that makes unclean. נגע can also mean to reach or to draw near, and in a few instances where ἅπτομαι translates נגע it has this meaning. These are Judg 20:41 ("evil had come upon[64] them"); Job 20:6 ("reach the clouds"); Jer 4:18 ("reach to thy heart"); 48:32 (31:32 LXX: "they reached the cities of Jazer"), and Micah 1:9 ("reached the gate of my people"). There are also a couple of instances where the Hebrew verb קרב (to come near, to approach) is translated by ἅπτομαι, namely Gen 20:4 ("Abimelech had not approached her"); Num 3:10 ("the stranger that comes near shall die"), 3:38 ("the stranger that comes near[65] shall die"); 17:28 (13) ("come near the tabernacle – τῆς σκηνῆς"), and Ezek 42:14 ("whenever they come in contact with people"). The majority of occurrences of קרב are translated with ἐγγίζω and προσέρχομαι respectively.

It is important to note that there is only one case where the Hebrew verb for to take hold of, to seize, to grasp (אחז) is translated with ἅπτομαι, namely in Ezek 41:6. The meaning here is, however, not "to take hold of" but the touching of surfaces. Normally אחז is rendered by λαμβάνω, ἐπιλαμβάνω, and κατέχω. The Hebrew verb for to cleave, to cling (דבק, usually rendered as κολλάομαι) is translated twice as ἅπτομαι, in Job 31:7 and in 2 Chron 3:12. In none of these cases, however, does ἅπτομαι mean to cleave. In Job 31:7 the text of the LXX differs from the MT. The LXX

---

[63] We note that προσέρχομαι immediately precedes the use of ἅπτομαι in the narrative of the woman with a hemorrhage in Matt 9:20 par Luke 8:44 and in the narrative of the raising of the son of the widow of Nain in Luke 7:14.

[64] In addition to ἧπται there is also the variant reading συνήντησεν.

[65] Note the variant reading προσπορευόμενος for ἁπτόμενος. προσπορευόμενος is used in Num 1:51 and 18:7 in almost identical expressions.

speaks of touching gifts with one's hands, whereas the MT has it over a spot that clings to one's hands. In 2 Chron 3:12 דבק is used in a parallel construction with נגע to express the idea of the contact of surfaces (wall and wing respectively) and both verbs are rendered with ἅπτομαι. On the basis of these observations we conclude that in the LXX there is no evidence that ἅπτομαι means to seize or to cling. The prevalent meaning is to touch (both positive and negative). But there is also a significant number of instances where ἅπτομαι means to draw near, to reach.

The 37 NT occurrences of ἅπτομαι are mainly found in the Synoptic gospels and express touching by or of Jesus. The majority of instances speaks about the healing touch of Jesus. He touches the hand, the tongue or the eyes of a sick person. He touches children and blesses them (Mark 10:13; par. Luke 18:15). There is also a woman who touches the hem of his clothes and is healed (Mark 5:24–34 par.) and the woman who anoints Jesus' feet. In addition ἅπτομαι is used for sexual intercourse (1 Cor 7:1), for harmful contact (1 John 5:18), and for contact with unclean things (2 Cor 6:17).[66]

In John 20:17 the negated present imperative of the verb ἅπτομαι is used. It has become commonplace among commentators to interpret this form as a command not to continue with an action that has already begun. This is the reason why recent commentators and modern versions (in Western languages) translate μή μου ἅπτου as "Do not hold (on to) me" or "Do not cling to me."[67] This interpretation is based on the durative *Aktionsart* of the present tense. It is the interpretation of the negated present imperative in the handbooks and grammars of the Greek language.[68] However, as we shall see, it is only partly correct. In the Gospel of John, there

---

[66] Other verbs that belong to the semantic domain of touching are rather infrequent in the NT. Among them κρατέω is the most frequent. There are some occurrences of ψηλαφάω (Luke 24:39; Acts 17:27; Heb 12:18; and 1 John 1:1), κολλάω (Matt 19:5 and some references in Luke/Acts), and ἐπιλαμβάνομαι (Matt 14:31; Mark 8:23; most occurrences are in Luke/Acts). None of these can be found in John except a single occurrence of κρατέω, namely in 20:23. On the discussion whether the verb here means "to retain" or "to hold fast" see Sandra M. Schneiders, "The Raising of the New Temple: John 20.19–23 and Johannine Ecclesiology," *NTS* 52 (2006): 337–55; and Jan Lambrecht, "A Note on John 20,23b," *ETL* 83 (2007): 165–68.

[67] For Theobald, "Der johanneische Osterglaube," 110 n. 65, Thyen (*Das Johannesevangelium*, 763, and Jean Zumstein, *L'évangile selon Saint Jean (13–21)* (Commentaire du Nouvau Testament 4b; Genève: Labor et Fides, 2007), 279, this is a foregone conclusion. There are, however, some exceptions to this near consensus. For instance, Frank Schleritt, *Der vorjohanneische Passionsbericht. Eine historisch-kritische und theologische Untersuchung zu Joh 2,13–22; 11,47–14,31 und 18,1–20,29* (BZNW 154; Berlin and New York: de Gruyter, 2007), 491–92.

[68] See, e.g., BDF §335: "the present imperative is durative or iterative, the aorist imperative punctiliar."

are 58 occurrences of the present imperative and 74 of the aorist imperative. Sixteen of the 58 instances of the present imperative have a negation, but none of the 74 instances of the aorist imperative does.[69]

Among the 16 occurrences of the present imperative, there is only one that clearly forbids an action that has already begun, namely John 2:16: "Stop making my Father's house a marketplace!" (NRSV). In 10:37 it is impossible that the negated present imperative μὴ πιστεύετε μοι refers to an ongoing action that is to discontinue ("If I am not doing the works of my Father, then do not believe me," NRSV). In 5:14 the present imperative ἁμάρτανε is negated with μηκέτι in place of μή, which suggests that the author did not trust the negated present imperative to be understood as a command to stop an ongoing action. This observation is confirmed by the original German edition of the grammar of Blass-Debrunner-Rehkopf §335, which states that in a number of cases the difference between the present and aorist imperatives has disappeared and it is left to the personal preference of the authors to decide whether they use the harsher command of the aorist or the milder command of the present tense.[70] These observations caution against blindly assuming that the negated present imperative μή μου ἅπτου in John 20:17 means "Stop touching me," i.e., "do not hold me" or "do not cling to me." Neither the semantics of the verb nor the *Aktionsart* of the verb form necessitate this. The fact that in the immediately preceding context nothing suggests that Mary Magdalene actually touches Jesus. We only hear that she turns and says "Rabbouni."[71]

Interpreting μή μου ἅπτου in 20:17 as John's redactional reworking of Matthew's αἱ δὲ προσελθοῦσαι ἐκράτησαν αὐτοῦ τοὺς πόδας καὶ προσεκύνησαν αὐτῷ and keeping in mind that there are virtually no other instances of verbs of the semantic domain of touching in John, it is necessary to look for the precise connotations of the meaning "to touch" when translating μή μου ἅπτου. This is also suggested by the strong emphasis on ἀναβαίνω in John's redactional reworking of the scene as we have seen above, and by an analysis of the verbs of movement in John 20:1–18.[72]

---

[69] This observation is confirmed by Herbert Weir Smyth, *Greek Grammar* (rev. Gordon M. Messing; Cambridge, Mass.: Harvard University Press, 1956; repr. 1984; orig. 1920), 409: "The aorist imperative is rare in prohibitions."

[70] In the English translation of BDF this sentence is conspicuously absent. See, however, Smyth, *Greek Grammar*, 410: "In many cases, however, μή with the present imperative does not refer to the interruption of an action already begun, but to an action still in the more or less distant future against which the speaker urges resistance."

[71] This was perceived by the scribe in ℵ* who added καὶ προσέδραμεν ἅψασθαι αὐτοῦ. But even then, this only expresses the intention of touching, not that the touching has already started.

[72] See Reimund Bieringer, "'They have taken away my Lord': Text-Immanent Repetitions and Variations in John 20:1–18," in *Repetitions and Variations in the Fourth Gos-*

Any touching includes a movement toward a thing or a person. As we saw above, there are a number of instances in the LXX where the focus of the use of ἅπτομαι seems to be more on the movement toward than the actual touching. Such a nuance would also be present if we understood the *Aktionsart* of the present imperative as conative. Not attempting to touch would amount to not coming near, not approaching someone. As we already saw, there are three instances in the Book of Numbers where ἅπτομαι is used in a cultic context: 3:10, 28; 17:28 (13).

The book of Numbers speaks frequently about coming near the tabernacle, holy things, the holy of holies giving precise rules as to who can come near under which circumstances. In 3:10, 28 we read καὶ ὁ ἀλλογενὴς ὁ ἁπτόμενος ἀποθανεῖται. In 18:7 an almost identical construction is used except that ὁ προσπορευόμενος takes the place of ὁ ἁπτόμενος. In 1:51 we read almost exactly the same, only that the verb in the future indicative is replaced by an aorist imperative (ὁ ἀλλογενὴς ὁ προσπορευόμενος ἀποθανέτω). Similar wordings are also found in 17:28 (πᾶς ὁ ἁπτόμενος τῆς σκηνῆς κυρίου ἀποθνῄσκει), in 18:3 (καὶ πρὸς τὸ θυσιαστήριον οὐ προσελεύσονται καὶ οὐκ ἀποθανοῦνται καὶ οὗτοι καὶ ὑμεῖς), and in 18:4 (καὶ ὁ ἀλλογενὴς οὐ προσελεύσεται πρὸς σέ).[73] In all these verses the verbs ἅπτομαι, προσπορεύομαι, and προσέρχομαι translate the Hebrew verb קרב (to come near, to approach). They are used in more or less identical contexts. In 3:38 part of the textual tradition reads ὁ προσπορευόμενος in place of ὁ ἁπτόμενος. It is not possible to find any reason why ἅπτομαι is used in 3:10, 28 and 17:28 and προσπορεύομαι/προσέρχομαι in the others. Since in these verses the object of ἅπτομαι is the tabernacle (σκηνή), it seems unlikely that the act of literally touching is meant. However, there are also many instances in the book of Numbers where ἅπτομαι refers to the touching of holy or unclean objects.

---

pel: Style, Text, Interpretation (ed. G. Van Belle, M. Labahn, and P. Maritz; BETL; Leuven: Leuven University Press and Peeters, 2008): "The spell that hangs over the movement of this pericope (20:11–18) is only broken after it has reached its climax in Jesus prohibiting even the small movement that Mary seems to intend in coming close to him (μή μου ἅπτου in 20:17). The dynamism of the movement is regained when Jesus announces his moving up to the Father (ἀναβαίνω in 20:17) and sends Mary back to his brothers (πορεύου δὲ πρὸς τοὺς ἀδελφούς μου in 20:17) and the evangelist tells us that Mary does what she was commanded (ἔρχεται Μαριὰμ ἡ Μαγδαληνή in 20:18)." We might add: 'and Jesus is about to ascend to the Father.'

[73] Cf. Num 17:5: μνημόσυνον τοῖς υἱοῖς Ισραηλ ὅπως ἂν μὴ προσέλθῃ μηθεὶς ἀλλογενής.

On this background we return to John 20:17. We recall our assumption that in 20:17 the Fourth Evangelist is rewriting Matt 28:9–10. He mainly does so by refocusing the scene on God and by introducing the cultic concept of ἀναβαίνειν (עלה). If we assume that John's redactional activity in 20:17 is coherent, μή μου ἅπτου needs to be understood in the same perspective. As we have seen, in Numbers ἅπτομαι is used in a way that fits within the Johannine context. μή μου ἅπτου then means: "Do not come near to me the way one approaches the tabernacle." This would imply that, in an attempt to correct Matt 28:9–10, the Fourth Evangelist says that even the risen Christ is not someone to be worshiped. The γάρ clause that follows in 20:17c is then saying that by ascending to God, Jesus will prepare the access to the Father, the one to be worshiped (together with the Son and the Holy Spirit). This is even more forcefully said in 20:17f when John states that through Jesus' ascension his Father will become the Father of the disciples and his God will become the God of the disciples. Jesus' ascension or pilgrimage to the Father will prepare the way for the ascension or pilgrimage of the disciples.[74] In the prohibition the word order μή μου ἅπτου is significant, since the personal pronoun μου is emphasized by being placed before the verb. The risen Christ is thus saying to Mary Magdalene in 20:17: "It is not me as the risen Christ whom you have to approach and worship, but I will open the access to God. When I have made the pilgrimage to the Father and have prepared a place in my Father's house for you, you will be able to make this pilgrimage also and in my Father's house we shall all together experience the new communion" (cf. 14:1–2). Both μή μου ἅπτου and the expression "my Father and your Father, my God and your God" thus serve to shift the focus away from the risen Christ to God.[75]

---

[74] Cf. Lagrange, *Evangile selon Saint Jean*, 512: "La formule: 'mon Père et votre Père, mon Dieu et votre Dieu', insinue que les disciples aussi iront un jour au Père et qu'ils arriveront à lui par le Christ, comme Jésus le leur a dit après la cène (xiv, 1–2,6) ; c'est pourquoi il les appelle maintenant ses frères, enchérissant sur le discours, où il les a nommés ses 'amis.'" See also Zumstein, *L'évangile selon Saint Jean*, 280 : "la résurrection comprise comme élévation suscite un saut qualitatif, une nouvelle forme de communion avec Dieu. C'est en cela que consiste, selon Jn, l'évangile de Pâques."

[75] Cf. Rudolf Schnackenburg, *Das Johannesevangelium* (vol. 3; HTK 4/3; Freiburg et al.: Herder, 1975), 377: "Jetzt ist die Stunde des Aufstiegs Jesu zum Vater, und das bedeutet für seine 'Brüder', daß er auch ihnen einen Platz beim Vater bereitet, daß er ihnen jene Gemeinschaft mit Gott vermittelt, die er ihnen als Frucht seines Weggangs vorhergesagt hatte (vgl. 14,21.23.28). Das dürfte der Hauptgrund sein, warum der Evangelist jene zwei interpretierenden Worte vom 'Aufstieg' Jesu (V 17a.c) seiner Quelle hinzugefügt hat. Damit wird das Ostergeschehen in die theologische Linie des Evangeliums einbezogen und finden andererseits die Ankündigungen der Abschiedsrede ihre österliche Bestätigung und Verwirklichung."

4. Conclusion

The enormous variety of interpretations of John 20:17, of which we could only represent a selection in this study, is evidence for the well-known fact that this verse is one of the most difficult and certainly among the most disputed in the New Testament. The fact that so many different syntactic and literary-critical interpretations of the verse have been developed is due above all to the fact that the theological content of this verse presents many puzzles to the exegete and the biblical theologian. The main theological question is how in John resurrection and ascension are related to one another. This relationship is often discussed in terms of "chronological" sequence. Some say that resurrection and ascension are the same for John and that it all happened in Jesus' exaltation on the cross. Such an interpretation assumes that 20:17c means: "I have already ascended to the Father, haven't I?" (Sandra Schneiders). Others interpret the present ἀναβαίνω in 20:17f to be strictly present and place the ascension between the appearance to Mary Magdalene and the appearance to the disciples without and with Thomas (e.g., Hartwig Thyen). A third group of scholars understands the present ἀναβαίνω as having a future meaning and suggests that the ascension happened after the resurrection to the disciples with Thomas (e.g., Gert Hartmann).

However, such a "chronological" framework seems not to do justice to John's literary-theological style. We interpreted the perfect ἀναβέβηκα as indicating an action that is still in progress (cf. also the present ἀναβαίνω, "I am ascending"). In 20:11–18 the Fourth Evangelist interprets Jesus' resurrection and its implications in terms of his own theology which was developed throughout the gospel and with special intensity in the Farewell Discourse. John 20:17 is a theological, not a chronological interpretation. In 20:17 John gives the resurrection a theocentric perspective. The going up to Jerusalem to the temple in pilgrimage is the model for Jesus going up to the Father through his crucifixion and resurrection. In doing so Jesus opens up the access to God for the believers and God becomes their Father and their God. The hour has now definitely come "when the true worshipers will worship the Father in Spirit and truth" (4:23). It is the day when Jesus raises the temple again after it had been destroyed (2:19). This is the temple of his body, the community of his brothers and sisters with whom he is united in a new communion through his death and resurrection, the community to which Mary Magdalene is sent. But this temple is also the house of Jesus' Father in which there are many dwelling places (14:2a). "If it were not so, would I have told you that I go to prepare a place for you? And if I go and prepare a place for you, I will come again and will take you to myself, so that where I am, there you may be also" (14:2b–3). In

20:17 the Johannine Jesus deflects the attention away from himself in two directions, to the Father and to the "brothers." Mary Magdalene cannot yet expect Jesus to take her along with him on the heavenly pilgrimage. She will first have to join the earthly temple of the believing community and instill in them the vision of a house with many dwellings in God's presence.

Appendix

The motivational clause is highlighted in boldface.
// indicates a caesura
Parenthetical clauses are indented and in round brackets ( ).
Square brackets [ ] indicate additions to the text which are postulated.

Majority Position
20:17a λέγει αὐτῇ Ἰησοῦς·
20:17b μή μου ἅπτου,
20:17c οὔπω γὰρ ἀναβέβηκα πρὸς τὸν πατέρα.//

20:17d πορεύου δὲ πρὸς τοὺς ἀδελφούς μου
20:17e καὶ εἰπὲ αὐτοῖς·
20:17f ἀναβαίνω πρὸς τὸν πατέρα μου καὶ πατέρα ὑμῶν καὶ θεόν μου καὶ θεὸν ὑμῶν.

Theobald
20:17a λέγει αὐτῇ Ἰησοῦς·
20:17b μή (not) μου ἅπτου,
20:17c οὔπω γὰρ ἀναβέβηκα πρὸς τὸν πατέρα.
20:17d πορεύου δὲ (rather) πρὸς τοὺς ἀδελφούς μου
20:17e καὶ εἰπὲ αὐτοῖς·
20:17f ἀναβαίνω πρὸς τὸν πατέρα μου καὶ πατέρα ὑμῶν καὶ θεόν μου καὶ θεὸν ὑμῶν.

Zerwick
20:17a λέγει αὐτῇ Ἰησοῦς·
20:17b μή μου ἅπτου,
    (20:17c οὔπω γὰρ [μέν] ἀναβέβηκα πρὸς τὸν πατέρα)
20:17d πορεύου δὲ πρὸς τοὺς ἀδελφούς μου
20:17e καὶ εἰπὲ αὐτοῖς·
20:17f ἀναβαίνω πρὸς τὸν πατέρα μου καὶ πατέρα ὑμῶν καὶ θεόν μου καὶ θεὸν ὑμῶν.

Van Belle
20:17a λέγει αὐτῇ Ἰησοῦς·
20:17b μή μου ἅπτου
    (20:17c οὔπω γὰρ ἀναβέβηκα πρὸς τὸν πατέρα)
20:17d πορεύου δὲ πρὸς τοὺς ἀδελφούς μου
20:17e καὶ εἰπὲ αὐτοῖς·
20:17f ἀναβαίνω πρὸς τὸν πατέρα μου καὶ πατέρα ὑμῶν καὶ θεόν μου καὶ θεὸν ὑμῶν.

McGehee
20:17a λέγει αὐτῇ Ἰησοῦς·
20:17b μή μου ἅπτου.//

20:17c οὔπω γὰρ ἀναβέβηκα πρὸς τὸν πατέρα
20:17d πορεύου δὲ πρὸς τοὺς ἀδελφούς μου
20:17e καὶ εἰπὲ αὐτοῖς·
20:17f ἀναβαίνω πρὸς τὸν πατέρα μου καὶ πατέρα ὑμῶν καὶ θεόν μου καὶ θεὸν ὑμῶν.

Lagrange
20:17a λέγει αὐτῇ Ἰησοῦς·
20:17b μή μου ἅπτου,
20:17c οὔπω γὰρ ἀναβέβηκα πρὸς τὸν πατέρα
    (20:17d πορεύου δὲ πρὸς τοὺς ἀδελφούς μου
    20:17e καὶ εἰπὲ αὐτοῖς·)
20:17f ἀναβαίνω πρὸς τὸν πατέρα μου καὶ πατέρα ὑμῶν καὶ θεόν μου καὶ θεὸν ὑμῶν.

Schneiders
20:17a λέγει αὐτῇ Ἰησοῦς·
20:17b μή μου ἅπτου.
20:17c οὔπω γὰρ ἀναβέβηκα πρὸς τὸν πατέρα;
20:17d πορεύου δὲ πρὸς τοὺς ἀδελφούς μου
20:17e καὶ εἰπὲ αὐτοῖς·
20:17f ἀναβαίνω πρὸς τὸν πατέρα μου καὶ πατέρα ὑμῶν καὶ θεόν μου καὶ θεὸν ὑμῶν.

Chapter 10

Resurrection and the Forgiveness of Sins.
John 20:23 against Its Traditional Background

Johannes Beutler, S.J.

The Johannine narrative of the appearance of the Risen Christ to his disciples on the day of Easter ends rather unexpectedly with Jesus giving his disciples the authority to forgive or retain sins. "Forgiving" sins occurs only here in the Gospel of John and "retaining" sins is a hapaxlegomenon in the New Testament. Commissioning the disciples to forgive sins occurs only here in the Easter narratives and is unique in the whole New Testament. According to Mark 2:1–12 par. forgiving sins is an action that only God and the Son of Man can perform. So it is not surprising that John 20:23 has generated considerable interest in recent exegetical literature.[1] Instead of discussing the secondary literature at length, we will focus on the Johannine text and refer to recent studies on a case by case basis.

---

[1] Among recent literature about the verse in this context see Johannes Beutler, *Habt keine Angst. Die erste johanneische Abschiedsrede (Joh 14)* (SBS 116; Stuttgart: Katholisches Bibelwerk 1984), 90–104; G. Korting, "Binden und Lösen. Zu Verstockungs- und Befreiungstheologie in Mt 16,19; 18,18.21–35 und Joh 15,1–17; 20,23," *SNTU* 14 (1989): 39–91; Thomas R. Hatina, "John 20,22 in Its Eschatological Context," *Bib* 74 (1993): 196–219; Gérard Claudel, "Jean 20,23 et ses parallèles matthéens," *RevSR* 69 (1995): 71–86 ; A. F. Mohamed and T. Sorg, "Friede sei mit euch! (Joh 20,19–23)," *TBei* 26 (1995): 113–17; E. Haag, "Aus Angst zur Freude, aus Resignation zu Perspektiven, aus Müdigkeit zu Vollmacht (Joh 20,19–23)," *TBei* 27 (1996): 57–60; Steven E. Hansen, "Forgiving and Retaining Sin: A Study of the Text and Context of John 20:23," *HBT* 19 (1997): 24–32; Johannes Beutler, "Friede nicht von dieser Welt? Zum Friedensbegriff des Johannesevangeliums," in *Studien zu den johanneischen Schriften* (SBAB 25; Stuttgart: Katholisches Bibelwerk, 1998), 163–73; idem, "Peace not of this world?" *ThD* 39 (1992): 131–35; William S. Kurz, "Test case: 'Whose sins you shall forgive' in John 20: Applying Scripture with the Catechism," in *The Future of Catholic Biblical Scholarship. A Constructive Conversation* (ed. Luke Timothy Johnson and William S. Kurz; Grand Rapids: Eerdmans, 2002), 237–48; Hans-Ulrich Weidemann, "Nochmals Joh 20,23. Weitere philologische und exegetische Bemerkungen zu einer problematischen Bibelübersetzung," *MTZ* 52 (2001) 121–27; Sandra M. Schneiders, "The Raising of the New Temple: John 20:19–23 and Johannine Ecclesiology," *NTS* 52 (2006): 337–55.

We will proceed in several steps: First, we will interpret John 20:23 in its context in John as a whole, in chapter 20, and more specifically in 20:19–23. Second, we will analyze the text from the perspective of the New Testament tradition that it reflects. Finally, we will consider the Old Testament and Jewish traditions behind the text. In our first section we will see that the authority to forgive or retain sins is given to the disciples as a result of the resurrection of Christ, of his new presence among his disciples, and of his mission for these disciples into the world. In the second section we will show that the resurrection account of Luke 24:36–49 has probably influenced the resurrection narrative of John. Direct influence of the commissioning of Peter or the disciples in Matt 16:19 and 18:18 is less likely. In our third section we will consider the influence of the eschatological promises of the later prophets on John 20:23. The connection of the Johannine text with the announcement of the new covenant will be studied and evaluated.

1. John 20:23 in Its Johannine Context

The "Easter chapter" John 20 is structured in two parts. At the beginning there are three scenes that focus on the empty tomb. They occur early on Easter morning (vv. 1–18): the visit of Mary Magdalene to the tomb (vv. 1–2), the arrival of Peter and the Beloved Disciple at the tomb (vv. 3–10), and the encounter of Mary Magdalene and the Risen Lord in front of the tomb (vv. 11–18). In this part of John 20, we see Jesus as he is about to ascend to the Father (note his words to Mary Magdalene in v. 17: "Do not hold on to me, because I have not yet ascended to the Father"). In the second part of the chapter we see Jesus coming to his disciples. The first scene takes place on Easter evening (vv. 19–23). Two more scenes follow days later: an appearance to the disciples with Thomas, who had not been present on Easter (vv. 24–25), and an encounter of Jesus with the whole group of the disciples (vv. 26–29) before the first conclusion of the gospel (vv. 30–31). If we include this section, John 20 is structured in seven parts, with the scene of the appearance of Jesus to the disciples on Easter evening at the center. If the author of the chapter intended this sevenfold structure, the scene in John 20:19–23 receives particular emphasis.[2]

John 20:19–23 is structured in two parts, which are parallel to some extent: vv. 19–20 and vv. 21–23. The first part of the passage reports the

---

[2] For the structure of the chapter see among other contributions the unpublished dissertation of Sandra M. Schneiders, *The Johannine Resurrection Narrative* (Rome: Pontifical Gregorian University, 1975), extract published in 1976, and Schneiders, "The Raising of the New Temple."

coming of Jesus to his disciples and his being recognized by them, while the second part reports the commissioning of the disciples. A comparison shows the following structure:

> Jesus comes to his disciples and meets them with a greeting of peace: v. 19
> A gesture of Jesus: he shows the disciples his hands and his side: v. 20ab
> A reaction of the disciples: they are filled with joy: v. 20cd
>
> Jesus renews his greeting of peace and prepares for the commissioning of the disciples: v. 21
> A gesture of Jesus: he breathes upon the disciples: v. 22ab
> An interpretation of the gesture and a word of commissioning to the disciples: vv. 22cd–23.

Let us briefly consider the two parts. John 20:19–23 forms a separate unit, which is set off from the preceding context by indications of time, place, and participating persons. In v. 19, every word merits attention. Jesus comes "in the evening of the first day of the week." The event takes place on the day of Easter. In the future, the "first day of the week" will be the day when the Christian community gathers for worship. This interpretation is confirmed by the place: Jesus appears "where the disciples were gathered." It seems reasonable to interpret this place of Christ's appearance in a deeper sense. The verb with which the appearance of Jesus is described merits particular attention: Jesus "comes." This verb occurs only here in the resurrection narratives of the gospels and the other NT texts that relate to this event. With Sandra S. Schneiders we can consider this choice of expression as intentional.[3]

Generally, the New Testament speaks about the "coming" of Jesus or the Son of Man with reference to Jesus' return at the end of time. The most important text is found in Mark 13:26, in the eschatological discourse of Jesus: "Then they will see the Son of Man coming in clouds with great power and glory" (cf. Matt 24:30; Luke 21:27). The verse quotes part of Dan 7:13. The context is clearly eschatological-apocalyptic. Apparently, John has intentionally moved the expected coming of the Son of Man into the present time of his community. This was anticipated in John 14, a chapter that is divided into two parts as is John 20: First, the departure of Jesus and the ongoing connection with him by faith (14:1–14). Second, the new coming of Jesus in the arrival of the Spirit, the coming of Jesus alone, and together with the Father (14:15–24). John explicitly uses the verb "to come" for the new encounter with Jesus (14:18), and the text continues with the announcement of a future "coming" of Jesus and the Father (14:23). This "coming" will take place in a moment of history, that is, in the "hour" of Jesus and from this hour onward. The promise of an eschato-

---

[3] Schneiders, *The Johannine Resurrection Narrative*.

logical coming of God to his people and his future dwelling among them (cf. Ezek 37:26) will be fulfilled.[4] One may question whether the future "coming" of Christ according to John 14:18 refers more to the Parousia or to the coming of Jesus to his own on Easter. Nevertheless, these alternatives seem to be misleading, since Easter is the "hour" of Jesus and the fulfillment of Johannine eschatology.

Jesus' greeting of peace in vv. 19 and 21 takes up his promise of peace from the Farewell Discourses (14:27; 16:33) and transforms it into his paschal gift. The joy of the disciples was also announced in the Farewell Discourses ("you would rejoice" in 14:28 and their joy is likened to that of a woman in labor looking forward to the hour of giving birth in 16:20–22). Here again we see an eschatological use of the subject of joy, which will be dealt with below (section 3). In John 20:20, the joy promised by Jesus to the disciples has become reality.

In the second part of the scene in 20:19–23, Jesus' repeated greeting of peace is followed by the words: "As the Father has sent me, so I send you" (20:21). This statement prepares for the gift of the Spirit and the commissioning of the disciples to forgive or retain sins in the following verses. Jesus compares the sending of the disciples to his own being sent from the Father. Such Johannine comparisons mean more than a correspondence. In fact, the sending of the disciples is rooted in Jesus being sent by the Father (as in 17:18). Given the central role of the "mission" of Jesus by the Father in the Gospel of John (he is the "Sent One," 3:34; 5:38; 8:42; 10:36; 17:3), the mission of the disciples is deeply rooted in Jesus' mission. If they are given authority to forgive or retain sins, their authority continues Jesus' mission into the world.

The gesture by which Jesus manifests his identity is paralleled by the one through which he initiates the mission of his disciples (v. 22). He breathes on them and says: "Receive Holy Spirit." In the command, "Receive Holy Spirit," the definite article is lacking, so that we do well not to translate it, "Receive the Holy Spirit." The eschatological gift of the Spirit as a life-giving principle has been anticipated since chapter 1, as has been shown by T. R. Hatina[5] among others:

1:33: the baptism in the Spirit (with parallels in Rabbinic literature)
3:34: God (rather than Jesus) as the one who gives the Spirit in abundance
4:7–14, 23–24: the Spirit given in eschatological time, allowing the authentic cult
7:37–39: the Spirit that flows from Jesus as the living rock in eschatological time
14:1–16:33: the promise of the Spirit-Paraclete (14:16–17, 26; 15:26; 16:7–14).

---

[4] For more details see Beutler, *Habt keine Angst*, chapter 3.
[5] Hatina, "John 20,22."

To understand v. 23 it is important to notice that Jesus, according to v. 19, appears to the "disciples." It is on them that Jesus breathes and it is to them that he gives his commission. The proposal of W. Kurz[6] (together with the Catechism of the Catholic Church) and of J. Swetnam[7] to narrow down the group of the disciples to the apostles or the ministers of the church is not backed by the wording of John 20:23. The strongest argument in favor of a limited group of disciples would be that Thomas is said to be "one of the Twelve" in v. 24. This group, however, is not mentioned in vv. 19–23 and in vv. 24–29. The authors who favor the idea that the commissioning is given to a limited group of recipients generally interpret v. 23 in a sacramental sense. As we shall see below, an alternative interpretation is more likely.

The problems with the interpretation of v. 23 start with the translation of the verse. The remission of sins is to be distinguished from "forgiving sins," since this ability belongs exclusively to God or his agent (Mark 2:1–12). The translation of the verb κρατέω is more difficult. On the basis of a comparison with Matt 18:19 some translators render κρατέω as "to refuse forgiveness" (e.g., the German Einheitsübersetzung: "verweigert"). This proposal has been contested for good reasons, since it overlooks the fact that passages in Matthew and John use different verbs.[8] Some authors have tried to avoid interpreting κρατέω as a negative action on the part of the disciples with regard to the sins of the persons to whom they are sent. Thus, W. E. Seitz interprets the κρατέω of sins as "overcoming" them and sees in John 20:23 a synthetic rather than an antithetic parallelism.[9] This view has been rejected by H.-U. Weidemann on the basis of grammar: "retaining" in 20:23 is used in the present tense, over against the "forgiving" in the aorist. Thus, an ongoing activity is envisaged.[10] A proposal similar to the one by W. E. Seitz has been made by S. M. Schneiders.[11] She suggests that ἄν τινων κρατῆτε should be understood in the sense of the community "holding fast" its members. However, it is unlikely that the meaning of τινων shifts from that of a possessive pronoun (i.e., retaining the sins "of any") to that of a pronoun functioning as the object of the verb (i.e., holding "any" persons fast). The words of v. 23 are better translated with the New Revised Standard Version (and the Luther Bible): "if you retain the sins of any, they are retained."

---

[6] Kurz, "Test case."

[7] James Swetnam, "Bestowal of the Spirit in the Fourth Gospel," *Bib* 74 (1993): 556–76, esp. 572.

[8] Cf. Weidemann, "Nochmals Joh 20,23."

[9] Wendelin Eugen Seitz, "Philologische Bemerkungen zu einer problematischen Bibelübesetzung: Joh 20,22.23," *MTZ* 51 (2000): 55–61.

[10] Weidemann, "Nochmals Joh 20,23."

[11] See Schneiders, "The Raising of the New Temple."

According to its form, the saying of Jesus in 20:23 follows an antithetical parallelism. Two conditional clauses, introduced by the typical Johannine ἄν, are placed opposite each other. The positive statement is mentioned first. If the disciples forgive the sins of any, they are forgiven them. The authority of the disciples is rooted in Jesus, the "Lamb of God who takes away the sin of the world" (1:29).[12] The text says nothing about an institution by which the disciples are to give this forgiveness of sins. The early Church Fathers thought of baptism and later ecclesiastical tradition focused on the sacrament of penance. Today authors interpret the commission of Jesus – with good reason – in the sense of Christian proclamation, which confronts people with the Christian message, which they must accept or refuse. This interpretation is defended among other authors by R. Metzner.[13] The double mission of the disciples to transmit forgiveness of sins and to confront the unbelief of a part of the audience corresponds to the twofold mission of Jesus, namely, proclaiming the saving message and bringing judgment against the unbelieving world (cf. 9:39–41; 12:31; 15:22–24; 16:8–11).

As is generally noted, John ordinarily uses the word ἁμαρτία in the singular. The plural is found in 8:24 "you will die in your sins," but the parallel verse 21 uses the singular. This means that the sins of the audience of Jesus ultimately consist in "sin" as such, that is, the refusal to accept Jesus as God's agent. In the remaining texts, only the "Jews" speak of sins in the plural, as, for instance in 9:34, where they reproach the man born blind after his healing by Jesus: "You were born entirely in sins, and are you trying to teach us?" The use of the plural in 20:23 can be explained by the assumption that John is using a formula that is also attested in 1 John 1:9 and 2:12.

According to the studies of M. Hasitschka,[14] the texts of the Gospel of John that deal with "sin" are found in four major textual units. At the beginning there is the testimony of the Baptist, who points to Jesus with the words: "Here is the Lamb of God who takes away/bears the sin of the world!"(John 1:29). If we see in this verse a reference to the Paschal

---

[12] A full discussion of this debated verse is beyond the scope of this article. The present writer understands John 1:29 in the light of the Suffering Servant. For the importance of this subject for the Gospel of John see Johannes Beutler, "Greeks Come to See Jesus (John 12,20f.)," *Bib* 71 (1990): 333–47.

[13] Rainer Metzner, *Das Verständnis der Sünde im Johannesevangelium* (WUNT 122; Tübingen: Mohr Siebeck, 2000), chapter 8.

[14] Martin Hasitschka, "Befreiung von Sünde nach dem Johannesevangelium," in: *Sünde und Erlösung im Neuen Testament* (ed. Hubert Frankemölle; QD 161; Freiburg: Herder 1996), 92–107; idem, *Befreiung von Sünde nach dem Johannesevangelium. Eine bibeltheologische Untersuchung* (Innsbrucker theologische Studien 27; Innsbruck-Wien: Tyrolia 1989).

Lamb, it forms an inclusion with the Passion Narrative (cf. 18:28; 19:14, the hour when judgment is pronounced against Jesus is the time when the Paschal lambs are slaughtered). A further dimension of the image of the lamb is found in connection with the fourth Servant Song (Isa 53:7). Here we also find the concept of "bearing" the infirmities of many (53:4) as well as their guilt (53:11–12). Hasitschka thinks also of the theophany on Mount Sinai in Exod 34:7, where God manifests himself as the one who "forgives iniquity and transgression and sin."[15]

Another context where the Gospel of John deals with "sin" is the feast of Tabernacles. We have already referred to John 8:21 and 24, where sin appears as a realm of power and influence from which Jesus liberates. The whole section in 8:21–30 revolves around the subject of sin, and this theme is deepened in 8:31–59 (cf. 8:34, 46) and continues to be a major element in chapter 9. There a development can be seen from the question about the sin of the man born blind (9:2–3) to the sin of Jesus' Jewish opponents who claim to see but are blind and thus remain in their sin (9:41). In the Farewell Discourses, Jesus looks back to the experience of having been rejected. If he had not revealed himself in word and deed, those who had rejected him would be without guilt. Yet, they are now inexcusable (15:2, 24). The Paraclete will convince the "world" of its sin of rejecting Jesus (16:8–9).

John 20:23 should be interpreted against the background of these texts. In contrast to the Synoptic saying about "binding" and "losing," the Johannine statement in 20:23 has the positive statement precede the negative one: "If you forgive the sins of any, they are forgiven them; if you retain the sins of any, they are retained." The perfect tense ἀφέωνται is not attested in all ancient manuscripts; there are variant readings. But it is confirmed by the parallel expression κεκράτηνται, which is attested unanimously. From a Johannine perspective, all individual sins are rooted in and culminate in the one sin of rejecting Jesus and his message of salvation. Thus, the authority to forgive sins may not always achieve its goal. In some cases, the lack of readiness to accept the message may have to be pointed out, and this means "retaining sins." If we interpret Jesus' saying in 20:23 in this sense, it fits the Johannine perspective on sin and forgiveness.

---

[15] Cf. Hasitschka, *Befreiung von Sünde*, 95.

2. New Testament Traditions

The relationship of John to the Synoptic Gospels is still a matter of debate. A recent volume edited by Francisco Lozada, Jr. and Tom Thatcher notes that the tendency has been to see John as independent from the Synoptic Gospels.[16] The problem is made more complex by the fact that John's relationship to the Synoptics is unlike the relationship of the Synoptics to each other. The way John relates to the Synoptics is different from the way that Matthew and Luke relate to Mark, for example. I have been convinced by the Louvain School of Frans Neirynck, which maintains that the Synoptic Gospels have directly influenced the Gospel of John. There may have been an increase of this influence during the time when John was being redacted, as I have recently proposed with regard to John 6.[17] Apparently, John makes rather free and independent use of the Synoptic materials and sources, and makes them serve his literary and theological purposes. This procedure can also be observed in 20:19–23.

The strongest literary connections can be observed between John 20:19–23 and the Lukan account of the appearance of Jesus among all disciples on Easter evening in Luke 24:36–49. The correspondences start with the setting of the scene. Apparently, John has adopted it from Luke. At the beginning of 20:19, John takes over from Luke 24:1 the indication of the first day of the week (all following scenes take place in Luke on the same day) and adds that the disciples were together in fear of the Jews.

ἔστη εἰς τὸ μέσον καὶ λέγει αὐτοῖς in John 20:19 corresponds to ἔστη ἐν μέσῳ αὐτῶν καὶ λέγει αὐτοῖς in Luke 24:36. A characteristic element in John is the addition of the "coming" of Jesus, by which the Fourth Evangelist interprets the appearance of Jesus as his eschatological coming.[18] Jesus' greeting of peace has the same wording in both gospels: εἰρήνη ὑμῖν. In Luke the motif of unbelieving surprise follows, and Jesus responds by showing his hands and his feet. John omits the motif of doubt and replaces the showing of Jesus' hands and feet by the showing of his hands and his side. By directing our attention to Jesus' side, the evangelist recalls John 19:34–37, where blood and water flow from the side of Christ as symbols of salvation.

---

[16] Francisco Lozada, Jr. and Tom Thatcher, eds., *New Currents through John: A Global Perspective* (SBLRBS 54; Atlanta: Society of Biblical Literature, 2006).

[17] Cf. Johannes Beutler, "Joh 6 als christliche 'relecture' des Pascharahmens im Johannesevangelium," in *Damit sie das Leben haben. (Joh 10,10). Festschrift für Walter Kirchschläger zum 60. Geburtstag* (ed. Ruth Scoralick; Zürich: Theologischer Verlag, 2007), 43–58.

[18] See above section 1.

Another important point of convergence between the versions of Luke and John is the common occurrence of words related to "peace, joy, and Holy Spirit," which will be dealt with later.[19] We have already mentioned the concept of "peace." According to Luke 24:41, the disciples cannot comprehend their encounter with the Risen One because of their joy and surprise, and according to John 20:20 the disciples simply rejoice when they see the Lord. After the second greeting of peace, John adds a saying about the mission of the disciples and the gesture of breathing on them with the invitation: "Receive Holy Spirit" (20:22). In Luke, the scene concludes with the command not to leave the Holy City until what Jesus has promised is given to the disciples: the power from above (Luke 24:49). The gift of the Spirit will be bestowed upon the disciples after fifty days, on the day of Pentecost. Thus, the differences between the two gospels can be largely explained by the different theological positions of the evangelists.

One of the common elements in both gospel texts is the forgiveness of sins, which is our subject. In Luke, the topic is connected with the mission of the disciples to preach the gospel. Jesus had to suffer, and in his name repentance for the forgiveness of sins has to be preached to all nations (Luke 24:47). The plural used by Luke for "sins" returns in John, where it deviates from John's common usage, but could be traditional, since the expression "forgiving sins/forgiveness of sins" seems to correspond to a formula (cf. Mark 1:4).

The double expression "forgiving" and "retaining" sins is not explained by the Lukan tradition but seems to have a different source. Authors often compare this to the "binding" and "losing" of Matt 16:19 and 18:18. It is impossible to refer the discussion about this parallel and its relevance for John in detail. It seems to be justified that we follow the judgment of H. Thyen, presented in his monograph *Studien zur Sündenvergebung im Neuen Testament und seinen alttestamentlichen und frühjüdischen Voraussetzungen*.[20] According to Thyen, it is impossible to derive the Johannine saying of Jesus from the two Synoptic ones.[21] Both variants seem to go back to a common Hellenistic Jewish tradition. The two versions in Matthew could go back to controversies in Antioch about the competence of Peter or the group of the apostles to interpret Jesus' understanding of the Torah authentically.[22] The authority to forgive sins is reserved for the Jo-

---

[19] See below section 3.

[20] Hartwig Thyen, *Studien zur Sündenvergebung im Neuen Testament und seinen alttestamentlichen und frühjüdischen Voraussetzungen* (FRLANT 96; Göttingen: Vandenhoeck & Ruprecht, 1970).

[21] Cf. Thyen, *Studien zur Sündenvergebung im Neuen Testament*, 247.

[22] Cf. Thyen, *Studien zur Sündenvergebung im Neuen Testament*, 218–43.

hannine saying of Jesus. Both versions may go back to traditions that attributed the words of commission to the Risen Christ.

Correspondences between the sayings of Jesus in Matthew and the saying in John 20:23 are recognized also by G. Claudel.[23] The author nevertheless insists on the Johannine character of the saying in its present form. To the reasons for this hypothesis belongs the double conditional ἄν at the beginning of the two antitheses. This use is attested in the New Testament only in John 13:20 and 16:23.[24] As mentioned earlier, the "forgiveness of sins" is found twice in 1 John (1:9; 2:12) and thus in the literary tradition of the Gospel of John. The perfect that is used for the two verbs "being forgiven" and "being retained" (ἀφέωνται/ κεκράτηνται) is in keeping with the Johannine perspective, according to which salvation in Christ has come definitively, and thus it is in keeping with Johannine eschatology. According to Claudel the origin of the saying may be found in the circles of John the Baptist (cf. Mark 1:4). This observation paves the way for our third section in which we shall deal with the Old Testament and Jewish background of John 20:23.

3. Old Testament and Jewish Traditions

The verb used in John 20:22 (ἐμφυσάω) recalls two important episodes of the history of salvation. God "breathes on" Adam and bestows upon him the breath of life (Gen 2:7 LXX), and the prophet Ezekiel is exhorted to call the Spirit to breathe on the dry bones as a symbol for Israel being restored to life after its destruction (Ezek 37:9 LXX). The prophetic text stands in between creation and the new creation in Christ. The verb ἐμφυσάω is infrequent in the Septuagint. It also occurs in Wis 15:11 where it echoes Gen 2:7, and in 1 Kings 17:21 where Elijah breathes new life on the son of the widow of Zarephath, in whom no breath was left (v. 17). The only other occurrences are Ezek 21:36 where the verb is used for the outpouring of divine wrath, and Tob 6:9 where it is used for breathing on the eyes of the blinded Tobit after his treatment with the gall of a fish.[25]

As has been shown above,[26] the semantic field of "peace," "joy," and "Spirit" (in Luke as "promise" and "power from above") is found in Luke 24:36–49 and John 20:19–23. The Johannine Easter narrative recalls the

---

[23] Cf. Claudel, "Jean 20,23 et ses parallèles matthéens."

[24] In John 5:19 and 12:32 ἄν is found in part of the textual transmission, but is admittedly less well attested than ἐάν.

[25] Claudel ("Jean 20,23 et ses parallèles matthéens," 80), in addition to Tob 6:9 S, also refers to 11:12 S, where the "breathing" heals the blind eyes.

[26] See above section 2.

twofold announcement of these subjects in the Farewell Discourses. The semantic field is found for the first time in John 14:15–24 in a section that could be called "the eschatological gifts of Jesus." Jesus will go to the Father and come back (14:1–3 is the announcement and 14:14–14, 15–24 the realization). He will not come with empty hands. He promises the Spirit (14:26) and leaves behind his peace (14:27). If the disciples loved him, they would be glad that he goes to the Father (14:28). The same themes recur in 16:4–33. Jesus departs with the announcement of his peace (16:33). He promises joy to his disciples at the moment of his "hour" by using the image of a woman rejoicing about her newborn child (16:20–22), and he promises his Spirit (16:7–14). In addition, Jesus speaks about "justice" which will be done in connection with his departure – a subject found only here (16:8, 10) in John.

There are good reasons for seeing behind this semantic field an old tradition. In a monograph on John 14 I have pointed to Rom 14:17 as a key to this tradition.[27] This is a section where Paul is debating the question of dietary laws and their validity for the new Christian congregation. In the end, dietary laws have no relevance for him, "for the kingdom of God is not food and drink but righteousness (or better: justice) and peace and joy in the Holy Spirit." This text is of great importance from the point of view of the history of tradition. Paul almost never refers to the Synoptic Jesus tradition about the "kingdom of God." Instead, he normally uses his key concept, "justice of God." Here in Rom 14:17 he gives a definition of the Kingdom of God that remains unique not only in his writings, but in the whole of the Bible. There are good reasons to think that the semantic field mentioned above (whether mediated by Luke 24:36–49 or not) has influenced the two sections of Jesus' Farewell Discourses in John and the Easter narrative in John 20:19–23. What Jesus bestows on his disciples on Easter are the eschatological gifts of peace, joy, and Holy Spirit.

The elements of the semantic field mentioned above go back to the biblical tradition of Israel, especially to texts found in the exilic and post-exilic prophets. The most relevant texts are found in the latest strata of the book of Isaiah. According to Isa 61:1–2, the spirit of God will rest upon the Messiah. He will bring the good news to the poor (this text is used in Luke 4:18–19). In Isa 61:1–11 the message of salvation is proclaimed to the post-exilic community. The one anointed with God's Spirit will bring not only law and justice (vv. 3, 8, 10) but also joy (vv. 1, 3, 7, 10). Relationships with neighboring nations will be characterized by peace; they will be astonished about the salvation granted to Israel and will serve the People of God (vv. 5–7). The time of slavery and the humiliation of Israel will come to an end (vv. 1–4).

---

[27] Cf. Beutler, *Habt keine Angst*, 90–104.

A similar text is found in Isa 11:1–10. This section announces a future messianic ruler who is to be filled with the spirit of the Lord. He will judge in righteousness (vv. 3–5) and establish an order of peace which extends into nature and which is described in paradisiacal colors (vv. 6–8). Without the mention of a messianic ruler, peace and justice are the fruit of the eschatological outpouring of God's Spirit as promised in Isa 32:15–20. This text also belongs to the later strata of the book of Isaiah. Again, paradisiacal motives occur: plants and animals participate in the eschatological order established by the Spirit. The community hears the words: "Be blessed" (אשריכם, v. 20). It can rejoice about the new order of salvation.

Such texts go back to a twofold tradition. On the one hand, they are inspired by the eschatological hope of Israel, according to which God was expected to send the Spirit to his people in the last days in order to revive it (cf. Ezek 36:26–27; 37:1–14; Joel 3). On the other hand, an archaic motif of the Ancient Near East is adopted. The hymns sung on the occasion of the ascendance of Pharaohs and the rulers of Mesopotamia to the throne praise the new order of peace and justice brought about by the new ruler. The result of the new order of justice and peace will be the joy of the people.[28]

It is not possible to explain the motif of the forgiveness of sins in John 20:23 in the light of these texts. Some traces of this motif in the Old Testament have been hinted at previously.[29] Thus, the Servant of God was presented as someone who carried the sin of the people (Isa 53:11–12). A connection with a cultic liberation of the people from guilt cannot be recognized in John 20:23. This is rather the case in the Epistle to the Hebrews, which ascribes to Jesus what the rites of atonement could not achieve in Israel: permanent forgiveness of sins (cf. Heb 9:22; 10:18).

Hebrews 10:18 may, however, help us to discover the traditional background of John 20:23. Here, the forgiveness of sins is presented in connection with the announcement of the new covenant in the book of Jeremiah. In Heb 10:11–18 the author contrasts many sacrifices that proved unable to achieve atonement with the unique sacrifice of Jesus: "For by a single offering he has perfected for all time those who are sanctified. And the Holy Spirit also testifies to us, for after saying, 'This is the covenant that I will make with them after those days, says the Lord: I will put my laws in their hearts, and I will write them on their minds,' he also adds, 'I will remember their sins and their lawless deeds no more.' Where there is forgiveness of these, there is no longer any offering for sin" (Heb 10:14–18). The text successively takes up Jer 31:31 and 31:34 according to the LXX text (where the quotations are in Jer 38:31, 34).

---

[28] Cf. Beutler, *Habt keine Angst*, 103–4.
[29] See above section 1.

For the interpretation of John 20:23 it is important to note that in Heb 10:14–18 the forgiveness of sins is explicitly connected with the announcement of the new covenant of Jer 31:31–34. This, in turn, leads to the tradition of the Last Supper. What is probably the earliest version of the saying over the cup reads, according to Luke (22:20) and Paul (1 Cor 11:25): "This cup that is poured out for you is the new covenant in my blood." It is likely that the more recent version is found in Mark 14:24. It identifies not the cup, but its content, with a reference to the Sinai covenant (Exod 24:8): "This is my blood of the covenant, which is poured out for many." This leads to the text in Matt 26:27–28: "Drink from it, all of you; for this is my blood of the covenant, which is poured out for many for the forgiveness of sins." At this stage, the traditions of the Sinai covenant and of the new covenant according to Jer 31:31–34 have merged.

In John 20:23, there is no direct reference to the new covenant. Thus, the question remains as to whether this theological motif can be assumed to be present in the Johannine text. A comparative look at John 14 can help to answer the question in the affirmative. In John 14:15–24, the Jesus of the First Farewell Discourse speaks about his "coming" to his own through the Spirit-Paraclete (vv. 16–17), personally (v. 18) and together with the Father (v. 23). There are good reasons to see in Jesus' announcement that he would come together with his Father and make his dwelling among his own an allusion to Ezek 37:26–28, where God promises his future dwelling among his people. Together with Ezek 36:26–28, this text stands in the tradition of the new covenant according to Jer 31:31–34. This way, the connection between the motifs of the gift of the Spirit and of the forgiveness of sins in John 20:22–23 can also be explained. In fact, the gift of the Spirit in John 20:22 recalls Ezek 36:26. This topic was introduced in John 14:16, where John uses the verb of "to give," which points back to Ezek 36:26. A connection between these texts can hardly be denied.

For the relationship between John 20:22–23 and the promise of the Spirit according to Ezekiel 36, it is important to note that in Ezekiel 36 the forgiveness of sins is announced. In Ezek 36:25 we read: "I will sprinkle clean water upon you, and you shall be clean from all your uncleannesses, and from all your idols I will cleanse you." The wording is influenced by the vocabulary and theology of Ezekiel, which are strongly cultic and priestly. The same idea is taken up in Ezek 36:29: "I will save you from all your uncleannesses." Accordingly, the themes of John 20:22–23 are basically prepared for in the announcements of a new or renewed covenant of God with Israel according to Jeremiah 31 and Ezekiel 36–37.

In the Judaism of the time of the New Testament, the idea of an eschatological forgiveness of sins brought about through by the Spirit was not widespread. As has been shown by H. Thyen, rabbinic Judaism knows liberation from sin, but it is through penance and the endurance of punishment.[30] Here also it is God who pardons. Thus there remains a tension between human effort and divine grace.[31]

In this respect the community of Qumran is closer to the New Testament. The self-understanding of this community is eschatological-apocalyptic. "The transfer from darkness to light and from death to life is achieved by the forgiveness of sins, which is announced to those who enter the community" (cf. 1QH VI, 13).[32] For the community of Qumran as well, the forgiveness of sins is achieved by new creation in a new covenant.[33] Apparently Isa 66:22-23 has influenced this idea. Note also *Jub* 5:12: "And he made for all his works a new and righteous nature so that they might not sin in all their nature forever and so that they might all be righteous . . ."[34]

Recent study has shown that the new covenant of Jer 31:31-34 does not play a prominent role in the Qumran writings. Although there is some reference to a new covenant in the Dead Sea Scrolls, these texts do not seem to develop the ideas found in Jeremiah to any great extent.[35] This leads to the conclusion that the New Testament writers adopted their identification of the new covenant with the order of salvation brought about by Jesus rather directly from the Old Testament, in particular the Septuagint, and not from contemporary Judaism in general or the theology of the scrolls in particular. The "Bible" of the first Christians was the sacred Scriptures of Israel as read in the liturgy.

The coming of John the Baptist with his call for repentance and his announcement of the coming eschatological judgment and salvation in connection with his baptism is of fundamental importance for the New Testament. Mark and Luke report the beginning of the activity of the Baptist with almost the same words: "John the baptizer appeared in the wilderness, proclaiming a baptism of repentance for the forgiveness of sins" (βάπτισμα μετανοίας εἰς ἄφεσιν ἁμαρτιῶν, Mark 1:4; cf. Luke 3:3). John's baptism is distinguished from the ritual baths of the community of Qumran in a twofold way: it is administered and it is received only once. This follows from its eschatological character, which is also manifest in the preaching of the Baptist. It exhorts people to escape the coming judgment of wrath by repentance and baptism.

---

[30] Thyen, *Studien zur Sündenvergebung*, 64-68.
[31] Thyen, *Studien zur Sündenvergebung*, 76.
[32] Thyen, *Studien zur Sündenvergebung*, 84.
[33] Thyen, *Studien zur Sündenvergebung*, 87-8.
[34] Thyen, *Studien zur Sündenvergebung*, 88.
[35] Cf. Susanne Lehne, *The New Covenant in Hebrews* (JSNTSup 44; Sheffield: Academic Press, 1990).

At this early stage the texts concerning the Baptist do not show any direct connection with the announcement of Jesus as the Coming One and of the Spirit. This is only the case in Mark 1:7–8 par. In the Acts of the Apostles, Luke tells about a group of disciples, met by Paul, which had only received the baptism of John. Allegedly, they had never heard about a Holy Spirit (Acts 19:1–7). We may see here the confirmation of an early tradition about the Baptist, in which people did not yet know about a witness of John the Baptist to Jesus or of the announcement of a baptism in the Spirit to be administered by Jesus.

Both elements are found in Mark 1:7–8 par. and especially in John's Gospel. As the Synoptics before him, John knows the quotation from Isa 40:3 (see John 1:23) and understands it in a Christological sense: John the Baptist invites people to prepare the way for the coming Lord. He baptizes with water, but among his listeners stands the One of whom he is not worthy to untie the thong of his sandal. He will baptize not with water, as John does, but with the Holy Spirit (1:26–27, 30–33). According to the Fourth Evangelist, John the Baptist saw the Spirit descending upon Jesus and remaining upon him. The actual baptism of Jesus by John is omitted. Only the element of the Spirit, which came upon Jesus in the form of a dove, is important for the evangelist, and this element is reinforced by the statement that the Spirit remains upon Jesus.

In accordance with the Johannine perspective, John the Baptist appears right from the beginning as a witness to Jesus (1:7–8, 15, 19), and thus, the response of the Baptist to the delegation sent to him from Jerusalem ends with the words: "And I myself have seen and have testified that this is the Son of God" (1:34).[36] In an extended process, the call of the Baptist for repentance and his baptism for the forgiveness of sins have been transformed into the announcement of the baptism of the Spirit by the Messiah and Son of God and into a testimony for Jesus.

However, even the report of the Fourth Evangelist conserves the original element of the call for a baptism of repentance. It is contained in the words of the Baptist: "Here is the Lamb of God who takes away the sin of the world!" (1:29, cf. v. 36). This way, we have reached our starting point. From a synchronic point of view, the reference to Jesus, the Lamb who takes away the sin of the world, frames the whole of the Gospel of John. From the diachronic point of view, this reference points back to the oldest preaching of the Baptist precisely in the element of the forgiveness of sins. It will retain its influence until John 20:23.

---

[36] Cf. Johannes Beutler, *Martyria. Traditionsgeschichtliche Untersuchungen zum Zeugnisthema bei Johannes* (FTS 10; Frankfurt: Knecht, 1972), 237–52.

Chapter 11

Realized Eschatology in the Experience of the Johannine Community

R. Alan Culpepper

The understanding of resurrection and eternal life in the Gospel of John is distinctive, and often labeled "realized eschatology." Much that is anticipated, hoped for, and expected in the future in ancient Jewish writings and other books of the New Testament is understood to be already present in a real sense in the Gospel of John. There is still the hope for the future realization of that which is not yet present, but John is distinctive in its proclamation that eternal life is already a present reality for those who believe in Jesus.

Jörg Frey has submitted the Gospel of John to a comprehensive review of its eschatology in light of the history of research, the gospel's distinctive use of language, its narrative design, and its historical context. Frey found that the gospel exhibits a stylistic unity that allows neither the reconstruction of earlier source documents, nor the exclusion of passages that contain a future-oriented eschatology.[1] While both future and present (or realized) eschatology are visible in John, the accent falls on realized eschatology. The Johannine community is called to the conviction "that its present is the time of the Spirit, in which the 'greater works' (John 14:12) will be realized through the disciples and their preaching, in which salvation and 'eternal life' are granted, and in which the eschatological destiny of men is decided in the encounter with the Word of Christ."[2]

David E. Aune's exploration of *The Cultic Setting of Realized Eschatology in Early Christianity* in 1972 was an attempt "to demonstrate that the crux of the problem created by the emphatic Johannine emphasis on realized eschatology is the necessity of understanding the meaning which that eschatology had for the community, the function which it had within their

---

[1] Jörg Frey, *Die johanneische Eschatologie I* (WUNT 96; Tübingen: Mohr Siebeck, 1997), 445.

[2] Jörg Frey, *Die johanneische Eschatologie II* (WUNT 110; Tübingen: Mohr Siebeck, 1997), 298; idem, *Die johanneische Eschatologie III* (WUNT 117; Tübingen: Mohr Siebeck, 2000), 464–76.

religious thought, and the mode or modes of conceptualization which enabled the Johannine community to experience aspects of eschatological salvation in the present."[3] His exploration of this question led him to the conclusion that the gospel's realized eschatology finds "a most appropriate setting with the cultic worship and life of the Johannine community."[4]

This essay returns to this perennial crux of Johannine scholarship, looking at the intersection of text and context and asking, "What did it mean to the early Johannine Christians to live in a community in which the hope of the resurrection was already being fulfilled?" In theological language, what effect did the realized eschatology of the early Johannine Christians have on their ecclesiology? The question does not presuppose a direction of influence, for one could just as easily argue that the gospel's eschatology was shaped by the life of the Johannine community, as Aune does when he concludes with that "the Johannine Jesus was primarily the product of the retrojected beliefs, values and aspirations of the community."[5] Although we cannot distinguish the ways in which theology shaped the community from ways the community projected its theology in the narrative of the gospel, the currents of influence must have flowed in both directions over time.

The first step is to hear from John what is distinctive about Johannine eschatology, what has already been fulfilled and what remains to be fulfilled. Then, we can sketch more clearly how their theology of the present and the future defined the lives of the Johannine believers.

1. Realized and Future Eschatology in John

The Gospel of John often uses various Greek terms synonymously and interchangeably.[6] The distinctions John maintains in the language of resurrection are therefore all the more important. The term "resurrection" (ἀνάστασις) occurs only four times in the gospel and never in the epistles. In all four references the resurrection lies in the eschatological future:

> for the hour is coming when all who are in their graves will hear his voice and will come out – those who have done good to the resurrection of life, and those who have done evil, to the resurrection of condemnation. (5:28–29)

---

[3] David E. Aune, *The Cultic Setting of Realized Eschatology in Early Christianity* (NovTSup 28; Leiden: Brill, 1972), 133.

[4] Aune, *Cultic Setting*, 223.

[5] Aune, *Cultic Setting*, 222.

[6] Raymond E. Brown, "Appendix I: Johannine Vocabulary," in *The Gospel according to John* (2 vols.; AB 29–29A; Garden City, N.Y.: Doubleday, 1966, 1970), 2.497–518.

Then, at Lazarus's tomb Martha replies to Jesus, "I know that he will rise again (ἀναστάσει) in the *resurrection* on the last day" (11:24), and Jesus answers, "I am the *resurrection* and the life" (11:25). The verb ἀνίστημι occurs four times transitively ("to raise up"), each time in reference to raising believers "in the last day" (6:39, 40, 44, 54), and four times intransitively ("to rise again") for the resurrection of Lazarus (11:23–24, 31) and the resurrection of Jesus (20:9). The verb is not used for the Father raising the Son. The verb ἐγείρω, to "raise" or "rise," is used in various ways, including raising the temple (metaphorically) in three days (2:19–20), the resurrection of Jesus (2:22; 21:14), the Father raising the dead (5:21), and the resurrection of Lazarus (11:29; 12:1, 9, 17). John also maintains a distinction between eternal life and resurrection that is most apparent in the separation of the present from the future in John 6:40 and 6:54.

> This is indeed the will of my Father, that all who see the Son and believe in him may have eternal life; and I will raise them up on the last day. (6:40) Those who eat my flesh and drink my blood have eternal life, and I will raise them up on the last day. (6:54)

Believers who "see the Son" and participate in the community's sacred meal have eternal life (now), and Jesus will raise them up on the last day. Whereas elsewhere eternal life is typically linked to resurrection from the dead, as the life of the resurrected person, John distinguishes eternal life from resurrection, claiming that it is the present experience of those who believe. In this way, John moves beyond the common early Christian understanding that the righteous dead are taken to the place of blessedness before the resurrection (Luke 16:22–24, 23:43; Phil 1:23; Rev 6:9–10).[7] For the faithful, the experience of blessedness, the life of eternity, is not withheld until death – it is a present reality. Eternal life is the present experience of those in the Johannine community.

Readers of the Gospel of John encounter early the claim that in the *Logos* was life (1:4), that the *Logos* came to "his own" (1:11), and that they had "seen his glory" (1:14). The significance of these Christological claims is adumbrated in the chapters that follow. Jesus claims that the Son of Man must be lifted up, "that whoever believes in him may have eternal life" (3:15). The time when the believer will possess this eternal life is not specified, but the parallel with Moses' action in lifting up the serpent in the wilderness (Num 21:9) implies that the attainment of eternal life will be immediate. The much loved and often quoted John 3:16 can be understood as a promise of life that is either present or future: ". . . so that everyone

---

[7] D. R. A. Hare, Introduction to "The Lives of the Prophets," in *Old Testament Pseud-epigrapha* (ed. James H. Charlesworth; 2 vols.; Garden City, N.Y.: Doubleday, 1985), 2.383. Hereafter abbreviated *OTP*.

who believes in him may not perish but may have eternal life" (cf. 3:36). Those who do not believe in him are already condemned (3:18), and the judgment, presumably the judgment of all persons and nations that is a standard feature of early Jewish and Christian eschatology, has already occurred in the revelation of the light, God's Son, in the world (3:19). The "living water" that Jesus gives "will become a spring of water gushing up to eternal life" (4:14, 36).

John's understanding of eternal life is further clarified in the next chapter. In response to the charges of Sabbath violation and blasphemy, Jesus contends that "just as the Father raises the dead and gives them life, so also the Son gives life to whomever he wishes" (5:21). Here, the giving of life (eternal life) is separated from resurrection of the dead: "Anyone who hears my word and believes him who sent me has eternal life, and does not come under judgment, but has passed [μεταβέβηκεν, literally "crossed over"] from death to life" (5:24; cf. 13:1; 1 John 3:14). The verb here is perfect, indicating a completed action with continuing effects. Foreshadowing the resurrection of Lazarus, Jesus claims that the hour is coming when the dead (i.e., the physically dead)[8] will hear the voice of the Son of God and live (5:25), when "all who are in their graves will hear his voice and will come out – those who have done good, to the resurrection of life, and those who have done evil, to the resurrection of condemnation" (5:28–29; cf. Dan 12:2). The expected resurrection of the dead still lies in the future, however.

Just as Jesus gives living water, he is himself "the bread of life" (6:35). The will of the Father is that "all who see the Son and believe in him may have eternal life; and I will raise them up on the last day" (6:40).[9] This hope of the resurrection of the dead is reiterated in 6:39, 44, along with the affirmation that "whoever believes has eternal life" (6:47). Jesus is the bread of life (6:48) and the light of life (8:12). Similarly, "whoever eats of this bread will live forever" (6:51), because one "may eat of it and not die" (6:50). John 6:54 draws together the present realization and the future expectation: "Those who eat my flesh and drink my blood *have* eternal life, and I *will* raise them up on the last day." In other words, those who believe in him have eternal life (already) and (therefore) will be raised from the dead in the future. This life comes from the Father through Jesus to those who believe in him (6:57). Jesus has the words of eternal life (6:63, 68).

Later, Jesus affirms that he has come in order that his sheep may have eternal life (10:10): "My sheep hear my voice. I know them, and they follow me. I give them eternal life, and they will never perish" (10:28).

---

[8] Aune, *Cultic Setting*, 117–19. See also sec. 2.5 below.
[9] The phrase "the last day" also appears in the *Life of Adam and Eve* (Apocalypse) 41:3 (*OTP* 2.293).

Therefore, when Jesus declares to Martha that he is the resurrection and the life, correcting her future eschatology, "I know that he will rise again in the resurrection on the last day" (11:24), Jesus is not only leading Martha a step beyond the teachings of the Pharisees regarding the resurrection but making resurrection a metaphor or sign for the possession of eternal life. Consistent with the future references to resurrection in John 6, Jesus does not eliminate the future hope but emphasizes the present reality of eternal life for those who believe in him. When Jesus raises Lazarus, calling the dead out of the tomb, he acts out in an individual case the fulfillment of his promise to all whom he loves and who love him (11:3), who are his friends (11:11; 15:13) and his own (13:1). They have eternal life now, and he will raise them from the dead in the future.

Adapting a saying found in the Synoptics (Matt 16:25; Mark 8:35; Luke 17:33), Jesus asserts in John 12:25 that one who loves his life will lose it, while one who hates his life in this world will safeguard it into eternal life. The Father's commandment is eternal life (12:50). Following this intensive reinterpretation of eternal life and resurrection in the first half of the Gospel, John makes surprisingly few references to the subject in the latter half of the gospel. Jesus tells the disciples that he is going to prepare a place for them and that he will come again for them (14:3), but by the end of the chapter a present reality has been defined: Jesus has made his abiding place in those who love him (14:23). The hope for the future is already being fulfilled in the present, and their present experience serves as a sign of the eventual fulfillment of the future hope. In John 14:6, Jesus declares that he is "the way, the truth, and the life," that is, the process, the goal, and the result.[10]

Then, in Jesus' prayer in John 17, Jesus petitions the Father to glorify the Son so that the Son may glorify him, "since you have given him authority over all people, to give eternal life to all whom you have given him" (17:2). In what appears to be an aside or an insertion, Jesus explains, "And this is eternal life, that they may know you, the only true God, and Jesus Christ whom you have sent" (17:3). Eternal life, therefore, is the present experience of the believer who lives in the knowledge and fellowship of God through the revelation of Jesus.

The only other reference to eternal life in John appears in the statement of the gospel's purpose at the end of John 20: that the readers may believe that Jesus is the Christ, the Son of God, "and that through believing you may have life in his name" (20:31). Some interpreters take this verse as an indication that the gospel was written to lead unbelievers to believe, while others contend that the purpose is rather to encourage believers to go on

---

[10] See William E. Hull, *John* (Broadman Bible Commentary 9; Nashville: Broadman, 1970), 334.

believing and to see more clearly what their faith means.[11] In either case, the final appeal is that believing leads to eternal life.

2. Elements of Jewish and Early Christian Eschatology

Jewish thought generally posited two ages, "this age" (העולם הזה) and "the age to come" (העולם הבא).[12] This age is characterized by sin, struggle, and persecution. The age to come will be a time of blessing, peace, and presence with God. In some instances, the age to come was expected to be inaugurated by the coming of the Messiah. Although one can hardly speak of Jewish eschatological expectations as though they were monolithic, Jewish expectations generally embraced the following elements: (1) the coming of the Messiah, (2) the vindication of the faithful, (3) the restoration Israel, (4) the gathering of the saints and (following Deutero-Isaiah) the elect from every nation, (5) the raising of the dead, (6) the final judgment, (7) the punishment of the wicked, and (8) the granting of eternal life to the righteous.

For Mark, Paul, and other early Christians, belief that Jesus was the long-expected Messiah modified their understanding of the ages. The church lived in the overlap of the two ages. The messianic era had come, but this age had not been brought to an end. The restoration of Israel had been reshaped into the promise of the Kingdom of God. The gathering of the elect from all nations was occurring in the Gentile mission. In isolated instances the dead were raised (Mark 5:41–43; 9:26–27; Luke 7:1–10, 11–15; Acts 9:36–42; 20:7–12; Heb 11:35). Important aspects of Jewish and early Christian eschatology remained unrealized, however, especially the resurrection of the dead, the last judgment, and the punishment of the wicked and the blessing of the righteous (cf. Dan 12:1–2). Paul and his fol-

---

[11] D. A. Carson, "The Purpose of the Fourth Gospel: John 20:30–31 Reconsidered," *JBL* 108 (1987): 639–51. Carson notes that the determination of the purpose of the gospel does not depend on the resolution of the textual issue regarding the tense of the verb to believe and argues that the gospel had an evangelistic purpose. He further proposes that the syntax of the verse supports the translation "that you may believe that the Christ, the Son of God, is Jesus." In this judgment he has been followed by Howard M. Jackson, "Ancient Self-Referential Conventions and Their Implications for the Authorship and Integrity of the Gospel of John," *JTS* 50 (1999): 18–20, but Jackson concludes that the intended readers are Christians, that the purpose statement is anti-docetic: "the Gospel of John and I John were both directed at the same audience and both similarly intended to maintain the christological loyalty of this audience against the threat of the same docetist dissenters" (p. 20).

[12] See Pseudo-Philo, *L.A.B.* 3:10; 16:3; 19:7, 13; 32:17; 62:9; *2 Bar.* 74:2; *2 En.* 65:7–10.

lowers resisted those who maintained that the resurrection was already past (2 Tim 2:18, and possibly 1 Cor 15:12).[13] John's thought is distinctive in importing to this overlap between the two ages more of the hope traditionally lodged in the age to come than was the case with other lines of early Christian theology.

Following the survey of eschatological references in John above, we can assess the gospel's handling of the eight elements of Jewish and early Christian eschatology.

2.1. The Coming of the Messiah

Like the synoptic evangelists, John attributed messianic titles to Jesus (1:41; 4:25–26; 6:14; 11:27; 20:31). John also speaks of the coming of Jesus as the risen Lord in the future (14:3, 18, 23; 21:22–23–see below), but more often the gospel makes an issue of where Jesus was going (7:34, 36; 8:21–22; 13:33; 16:5; 17:11, 13). John also speaks of the coming of the Paraclete in the narrative future and the functions of the Paraclete, which include abiding with the disciples (14:17), teaching and reminding them (14:26), testifying on Jesus' behalf (15:26), "proving the world wrong" (16:8), and guiding the disciples in all truth (16:13), but significantly Jesus does not include raising the dead among the functions of the Paraclete.

2.2. The Vindication of the Faithful

Jewish apocalyptic literature often looked forward to a violent vindication of the faithful. *Second Baruch* 72:6 promises, "All those, now, who have ruled over you or have known you, will be delivered up to the sword" (*OTP* 1.645). In the Gospel of John Jesus speaks often of the vindication of the faithful, but it is almost always a promise of what will occur in this world rather than what will occur after death, and it is not a vindication of Israelites before the nations (contrast *Pss. Sol.* 17). Jesus will lose no one who is given to him (6:37, 39), except the one who betrayed him (17:12; 18:9). The Good Shepherd lays down his life for the sheep, and no one will snatch them out of his hand (10:18, 27–30). Jesus' followers will be hated and persecuted, but the Paraclete will testify on their behalf (15:18–27).

---

[13] Denial of a future resurrection on the basis of a spiritual interpretation of the resurrection continued in isolated instances. Justin reports that a Samaritan magician named Menander "even convinced those who followed him that they would never die" (*Apol.* 1.26.4), and Irenaeus adds that Menander taught that his disciples "obtain the resurrection by being baptized into him, and can die no more, but never grow old and are immortal" (*Haer.* 1.23.5). See Martin Dibelius and Hans Conzelmann, *The Pastoral Epistles* (trans. P. Buttolph and A. Yarbro; ed. H. Koester; Hermeneia; Philadelphia: Fortress, 1972), 112; and William D. Mounce, *Pastoral Epistles* (WBC 46; Nashville: Thomas Nelson, 2000), 539–40.

Then, Jesus prays for the protection of his own from "the evil one" (17:11–15). There is also a future dimension to Jesus' assurance of the vindication of the faithful: Jesus will raise them on the last day (6:39, 40, 44, 54).

2.3. The Restoration of Israel

One of the marks of Jewish apocalyptic literature is that the dispersed of Israel will be gathered and vindicated. The *Testament of Benjamin* affirms, "all Israel will be gathered to the Lord" (10:11; *OTP* 1.828). *Second Baruch* 78:7 recalls that the Lord has promised "that he will not forever forget or forsake our offspring, but [will] with much mercy assemble all those again who were dispersed" (*OTP* 1.648).

The theme of the restoration of Israel appears early in John, setting the context for the rest of the gospel.[14] John the Baptist announces that he came baptizing with water so that the one who was coming after him "might be revealed to Israel" (1:31). Then, when Philip calls Nathanael to Jesus, Jesus identifies him as "an Israelite in whom there is no deceit" (1:47), which echoes the description of Jacob in Gen 27:35 (before he became Israel, Gen 32:28). Jesus explains that he saw Nathanael while he was sitting under the fig tree. The first thing one notices when one reviews the references to fig trees in the Old Testament and Apocrypha is that sitting under one's fig tree was the identifying element of the memory of peace and security in Israel in the time of Solomon:

1 Kings 4:25 from	During Solomon's lifetime Judah and Israel lived in safety, Dan even to Beer-sheba, all of them under their vines and fig trees.
1 Macc 14:11–12	He established peace in the land, and Israel rejoiced with great joy. All the people sat under their own vines and fig trees, and there was none to make them afraid.

Sitting under one's fig tree could therefore characterize the prophetic vision of the restoration of peace and security to Israel in the future: "they shall beat their swords into plowshares, and their spears into pruning hooks; nation shall not lift up sword against nation, neither shall they learn war any more; but they shall all sit under their own vines and under their own fig trees" (Mic 4:3–4). The restoration of Israel would also be the time for the builder of a new temple to arise, one called "the branch" (cf. Ps 132:17; Isa 4:2; 11:1; Jer 23:5; 33:15). Zechariah declares that "On that day, says the Lord of hosts, you shall invite each other to come under your vine and fig tree" (Zech 3:8–10). The original reference was apparently to Zerubbabel, but this passage later came to be understood messianically, so

---

[14] This theme is the subject of a fine dissertation by John A. Dennis, *Jesus' Death and the Gathering of True Israel* (WUNT 217; Tübingen: Mohr Siebeck, 2006).

that Jesus' activity could be understood as a reconstitution of the temple, the household of God, in a metaphorical sense.[15] Nathanael, the Israelite in whom there is no guile, can therefore confess that Jesus is the Son of God, the King of Israel (John 1:49; cf. 12:13), and Nicodemus, a leader of the Jews (3:1), can refer to Jesus as "a teacher of Israel" (3:10). By gathering those who believed in him, Jesus was fulfilling the hope of the restoration of Israel and the building of a new temple, a central feature of the restoration of Israel.

2.4. The Gathering of the Saints and the Elect from Every Nation

The restoration of Israel would be the signal for the nations to come to Jerusalem. Isaiah declared, "Thus says the Lord God, who gathers the outcasts of Israel, I will gather others to them besides those already gathered" (Isa 56:8), and "my house shall be called a house of prayer for all nations" (Isa 56:7). Then, near the end of the book, the prophet records the words, "I am coming to gather all the nations and tongues; and they shall come and shall see my glory" (Isa 66:18). Micah shares this vision and looks forward to the day when "Peoples shall stream to the temple, saying, "Come, let us go up to the mountain of the Lord, to the house of the God of Jacob; that he may teach us his ways" (Mic 4:1–2). The *Psalms of Solomon* look forward to the fulfillment of this promise: "And he will purge Jerusalem (and make it) holy as it was even from the beginning, (for) nations to come from the ends of the earth to see his glory, to bring as gifts her children who had been driven out, and to see the glory of the Lord with which God has glorified her" (17:30–31; *OTP* 2.667).[16]

John announces that the Word became flesh, "and we have beheld his glory" (1:14). Those who believe in him are given authority as "children of God" (1:12), and part of Jesus' work as the Revealer is to gather the children of God who have been scattered:

> I have other sheep that do not belong to this fold. I must bring them also, and they will listen to my voice. So there will be one flock, one shepherd (10:16)
>
> [Caiaphas] prophesied that Jesus was about to die for the nation, and not for the nation only, but to gather into one the dispersed children of God. (11:52)
>
> And I, when I am lifted up from the earth, will draw all people to myself. (12:32; cf. 21:11)

---

[15] On the interpretation of Zechariah 3:8–10, see Craig R. Koester, "Messianic Exegesis and the Call of Nathanael (John 1.45–51)," *JSNT* 39 (1990): 23–34; Mary L. Coloe, *God Dwells with Us. Temple Symbolism in the Fourth Gospel* (Collegeville: Liturgical Press, 2001); idem, *Dwelling in the Household of God. Johannine Ecclesiology and Spirituality* (Collegeville: Liturgical Press, 2007), 49–50.

[16] Regarding Jewish expectations about Gentiles, see further Dennis, *Jesus' Death and the Gathering of True Israel*, 303–6.

In a careful recent study of the theme of the restoration of Israel in John, John A. Dennis contends that the concept of "the children of God" is thoroughly restorational and that the Fourth Gospel "is centered squarely on *Jewish* concerns," so he quotes approvingly Barrett's comment that in a Jewish document John 11:52b would mean, "the gathering together of the dispersed Israelites to their own land in the messianic age."[17] Nevertheless, as Dennis notes, Barrett went on to say "It is however unlikely that John was thinking of the gathering of dispersed Christians at the last day, but rather the gathering of men into the church, the *one* body of Christ (cf. 17.21 . . .)."[18] Dennis interprets the conflict with the synagogue as an intra-Jewish debate and therefore reads the gathering of the children of God primarily as a gathering of believing Jews. The gathering of believers from the nations is secondary. He argues that John 11:52b should be translated, ". . . Jesus had to die for the nation and not for the nation only but in order that he might *also* gather into one the children of God who are dispersed."[19] Taking a different view, I have interpreted the conflict with the synagogue as the separation of Johannine believers from the synagogue and the time when the Johannine community was established as a distinctly Christian community that was defining itself over against its Jewish origins.[20] John 1:12 redefines the "children of God" as those who believe in Jesus' name. As a self-designation for the Johannine community, it includes both Jewish and Gentile believers. Accordingly, John 11:52 looks not only to the mission to Israel (ὁ ἔθνος) but to Gentiles also.

Related references underscore the importance of the community's witness to Gentiles: the reception of Jesus by the Samaritans and their confession that he was "the Savior of the world" (4:42), the ironic misunderstanding that Jesus was going to the Dispersion "and teach Greeks" (7:35), the Greeks' request to see Jesus (12:20–21), the inscription of the *titlus* on the cross in three languages (19:20), and perhaps the symbolism of the 153 large fish (21:11). In these various ways the gospel of John recognizes the eschatological role of Jesus as the Messiah who would gather the children of God from all nations. While that gathering was not complete, it began in the ministry of Jesus, was represented at the crucifixion, and – as imaged in the great catch of fish (21:1–14) – continued in the work of the disciples following the resurrection. What the prophet Isaiah looked forward to in

---

[17] Ibid., 293, quoting C. K. Barrett, *The Gospel according to St. John* (2d ed.; Philadelphia: Westminster, 1978), 407.

[18] Barrett, *The Gospel according to St. John*, 407.

[19] Dennis, *Jesus' Death and the Gathering of True Israel*, 258.

[20] See R. Alan Culpepper, "Anti-Judaism in the Fourth Gospel as a Problem for Christian Interpreters," in *Anti-Judaism and the Fourth Gospel: Papers of the Leuven Colloquium, 2000* (ed. R. Bieringer, D. Pollefeyt, and F. Vandecasteele-Vanneuille; Assen: Van Gorcum, 2001), 68–91.

the future had already begun in the ministry of the Revealer and was being accomplished in the mission of the church. It was no longer a future expectation but a reality already in process.

2.5. The Resurrection of the Dead

Daniel looked forward to the time when the angel Michael would arise, and "many of those who sleep in the dust of the earth shall awake, some to everlasting life, and some to shame and everlasting contempt" (Dan 12:2). Paul corrected the Corinthians, insisting that "at the last trumpet . . . . the dead will be raised imperishable" (1 Cor 15:52). *Second Baruch* extends the description of the blessing of the faithful in the resurrection:

> And it will happen after these things when the time of the appearance of the Anointed One has been fulfilled and he returns with glory, that then all who sleep in hope of him will rise. And it will happen at that time that those treasuries will be opened in which the number of the souls of the righteous were kept, and they will go out and the multitudes of the souls will appear together, in one assemblage, of one mind. And the first ones will enjoy themselves and the last ones will not be sad. For they know that the time has come of which it is said that it is the end of times. But the souls of the wicked will the more waste away when they shall see all these things. For they know that their torment has come and that their perditions have arrived. (*2 Bar.* 30:1–5; *OTP* 1.631).

The *Testament of Job* contains the following vivid description, though the italicized phrase may well be a Christian interpolation: "*And you shall be raised up in the resurrection.* For you will be like a sparring athlete, both enduring pains and winning the crown. Then will you know that the Lord is just, true, and strong, giving strength to his elect ones" (*T. Job* 4:9–11; *OTP* 1.841).

The Gospel of John reflects a realistic realized eschatology in that it recognizes the reality of physical death while maintaining that believers already participate in the eternal life of the resurrection. John uses the noun θάνατος eight times. Those who believe have eternal life; they have passed from death to life (5:24). Those who keep Jesus' word will never see/taste death (8:51, 52). Lazarus's illness would not lead to death (11:4), but Jesus spoke of Lazarus's death as sleep (11:13). The other three occurrences are proleptic references to the manner of the deaths of Jesus (12:33; 18:32) and Peter (21:19). Νεκρός, an adjective ("dead") that can be used substantively, occurs eight times in John, always in the plural (referring to death literally as "the dead" (pl.) and often with the verb "to raise" (ἐγείρω: 2:22; 5:21 [cf. 5:25]; 12:1, 9, 17; 21:14). The exception is 20:9, where it occurs with ἀνίστημι ("to rise"). θάνατος is the more abstract term and can mean either physical or spiritual death.

Because John speaks of various kinds of death, one must be careful about discerning the different nuances of the verb "to die" (ἀποθνήσκω) in

John. Jaime Clark-Soles finds that "death appears to have a double meaning in [the Fourth Gospel], signifying both physical death, which no one escapes, and Holy-Spiritual death, which only believers escape,"[21] but other nuances can be distinguished also:

(a) *Physical death.* Abraham and the prophets died (8:52–53), and the apostle Peter (21:19) and the Beloved Disciple (21:23) would die. The official's son was at the point of death (4:47, 49), and Lazarus died (11:14, 16, 21, 32). Even Jesus died (11:51; 12:33; 18:14, 32; 19:30). These references to physical death say nothing about the condemnation or hope of those who die.

(b) *Death without the hope of eternal life.* Such death appears to be the end of life both physical and spiritual. The people of Israel who ate manna in the wilderness died [sense (a)], but one who eats the true bread from heaven will not die [sense (b)] (6:49, 50, 58). Those who do not believe will "die in their sins" (8:24). On the other hand, those who keep Jesus' word will never die (8:51, 52). In this sense, Lazarus's illness would not lead to death (11:4).

(c) *Death of self seeking and false love.* Jesus speaks of death as a metaphor for self-denial. Like a grain of wheat that falls into the ground and dies, those who die to self and the pursuits of this world out of the love of God and of others will live and bear much fruit (12:24–25).

(d) *Physical death as merely a transition for those who already enjoy eternal life.* For those who believe in Jesus, dying physically is going to sleep and waking (11:11–14). Therefore, Jesus could assure Martha that her brother would rise again (11:23). Beyond the hope of resurrection in the future, however, is the reality that "Those who believe in me, even though they die [physical death – sense (a)], will live, and everyone who lives and believes in me will never die [death without the hope of eternal life – sense (b)]" (11:25–26).

The dead will be raised on "the last day" (6:39, 40, 44, 54; 11:24). On this point the Gospel of John agrees, at least to a degree, with the hope of the resurrection affirmed by the Pharisees and the Essenes (*On Resurrection* [4Q521] and *Pseudo-Ezekiel* [4Q385]).[22] John's affirmation of the resurrection of the dead on the last day seems to be limited to those who have been given to Jesus by the father (6:39), who believe in Jesus (6:40), are drawn by the father (6:44), and eat his flesh and drink his blood (6:54). The resurrection on the last day is therefore affirmed for those who already have eternal life in Jesus.

John 5:29, which refers to resurrection of both those who have done good and those who have done evil (cf. 3:20), clearly alludes to Daniel

---

[21] See the excellent discussion of Johannine eschatology by Jaime Clark-Soles, "'I Will Raise [Whom?] Up on the Last Day': Anthropology as a Feature of Johannine Eschatology," in *New Currents through John: A Global Perspective* (ed. Francisco Lozada, Jr. and Tom Thatcher; Atlanta: Society of Biblical Literature, 2006), 29–53, esp. 42.

[22] James H. Charlesworth, "Resurrection: The Dead Sea Scrolls and the New Testament," in *Resurrection: The Origin and Future of a Biblical Doctrine* (ed. James H. Charlesworth; New York: T. & T. Clark, 2006), esp. 145–53.

12:2. Jörg Frey argues that the evangelist adopts a traditional formulation in John 5:29 not to make Johannine eschatology more orthodox but to persuade the Christian reader of the gospel of the reality of judgment and life in Jesus the Christ now.[23] John neither denies nor develops the declaration, validated by Scripture and tradition, that the wicked will experience "the resurrection of condemnation." On the other hand, the distinctively Johannine affirmation is that the judgment occurs in the present through one's belief or refusal to believe in Jesus, and that those who believe already have eternal life. That eternal life continues after death through the believer's future resurrection from the dead.

2.6. The Last Judgment

The expectation of the last judgment at the end of time is a standard feature of Jewish and early Christian eschatology – "when the Son of Man comes in his glory" (Matt 25:31–46). *First Enoch* warns that the sins of the sinner are being written down every day (104:7), but exhorts the righteous to be steadfast because they will be vindicated in the eternal judgment. Nevertheless, an element of John's eschatology is already present in *1 Enoch*: the righteous will not be called to judgment: "You shall not have to hide on the day of the great judgment, and you shall not be found as the sinners; but the eternal judgment shall be (far) away from you for all the generations of the world" (104:5; *OTP* 1.85). *Second Enoch* 65:11 offers the same assurance: the righteous "will escape the Lord's great judgment, for their faces will shine forth like the sun" (*OTP* 1.193; cf. *2 Enoch*, Appendix, *OTP* 1.221).

For John the final judgment is already taking place in how persons respond to Jesus' words and the light that has come in him. Those who do not believe in him "perish" (3:16), that is, they do not have eternal life. Those who do not believe are condemned already (3:18): "This is the judgment, that the light has come into the world, and people loved darkness rather than light because their deeds were evil" (3:19). In the soliloquy at the end of Jesus' public ministry, Jesus declares: "I do not judge anyone who hears my words and does not keep them, for I came not to judge the world, but to save the world. The one who rejects me and does not receive my word has a judge; on the last day the word that I have spoken will serve as judge" (12:47–48). It is a subtle point. Jesus did not come to judge, but life comes only through receiving Jesus and his word, i.e. his revelation of the Father.

2.7. The Punishment of the Wicked

According to the *Psalms of Solomon*, the wicked will not be raised:

---

[23] Frey, *Die johanneische Eschatologie III*, 386, 390–91.

The destruction of the sinner is forever, and he will not be remembered when (God) looks after the righteous. This is the share of sinners forever, but those who fear the Lord shall rise up to eternal life, and their life shall be in the Lord's light, and it shall never end. (*Pss. Sol.* 3:10–11; *OTP* 2.655; cf. *Pss. Sol.* 14:9).

First Enoch warns that at the judgment sinners "shall be driven from the face of the earth . . . and where [is] the resting place of those who denied the name of the Lord of the Spirits? It would have been better for them not to have been born" (*1 En.* 38:2; *OTP* 1.30).

John says remarkably little about the fate of those who do not believe and have life, in Jesus.[24] The logic of the affirmation that those who believe have passed from death to life is that those who do not believe remain in spiritual death, do not have eternal life, and therefore will not be resurrected. For John, the fate of the wicked is that they will "perish" (ἀπόληται, 3:16; 10:28; 17:12; cf. Bar 3:3). John does not describe Hades, hell, or a place of torment. Perishing is simply eternal death, separation from the presence of God and denial of the gift of eternal life. One who does not believe has already been judged (3:18; 5:24). Jesus' words in John 5, somewhat surprisingly, follow the traditional pattern of the resurrection of all the dead, the good to "the resurrection of life," and the evil "to the resurrection of condemnation" (5:29), as in Dan 12:2. John 3:36 declares that "whoever believes in the Son has eternal life; whoever disobeys the Son will not see life but must endure God's wrath" (NRSV), literally, "God's wrath remains [or abides] on him." Those who do not believe die in their sin (8:21). God's wrath abiding on the disobedient is the counterpart to the Father and the Son making their dwelling place with those who keep Jesus' word (14:23). John never speaks of gehenna, or an unquenchable fire, but says only that those who do not abide in him are "cast out" (ἐβλήθη ἔξω) like branches that are "gathered, thrown into the fire, and burned" (15:6).[25] In light of the other references to the fate of the wicked, the image of fire here is probably a metaphor for destruction rather than a reference to eternal torment.

2.8. The Granting of Eternal Life to the Righteous

The heavenly reward of the righteous is a favorite theme of the apocalyptic writings. Our interest here is limited, however, to parallels to John's view of eternal life as the present possession of the faithful. The Prayer of Jacob allows the righteous one to say, "As an ear[th]ly angel, as//[hav]ing become immortal, as having receiv[ed] the gift which (is) from [yo]u, [a]men, amen" (*Prayer of Jacob* 19; *OTP* 2.723). Mary L. Coloe finds in the Wisdom of Solomon "a type of realized eschatology in which the end-

---

[24] Frey, *Die johanneische Eschatologie III*, 306.
[25] Clark-Soles, "'I Will Raise [Whom?] Up on the Last Day,'" 45–46.

time realities impinge on life in this world."[26] Death for the righteous is not a disaster. They only "seemed to have died," but their souls are in the hand of God (Wis 3:1–2). The righteous martyrs are those who have been perfected in a short time and then quickly taken up: "Being perfected in a short time, they fulfilled long years" (4:13), and "the righteous who have died will condemn the ungodly who are living, and youth that is quickly perfected [or "ended"] will condemn the prolonged old age of the unrighteous" (4:16); because "the righteous live forever" (5:15). Wisdom "passes into holy souls" in every generation "and makes them friends of God" (7:27; cf. John 15:13–15; 3 John 15). James H. Charlesworth notes that "The Qumran community considered itself to be an antechamber of heaven and that the elect (the Essenes) formed with the angels one lot," [27] citing 1QH VI, 13: "For you have brought [your truth and your] glory to all the men of your council and in the lot, together with the angels of the face, without there being an [sic] mediator between the intelligent and your holy ones" (cf. 1QH III, 21–22; IV, 24–25).[28]

The term "heaven" occurs eighteen times in John, but John speaks of heaven distinctively, not as the place to which believers will go after they die, but as the place above from which Jesus has come down. Clark-Soles observes that "'heaven' language in [the Fourth Gospel] designates the realm of God the Father; that is, it serves as a metonym for God."[29] Jesus comes "from above," from God. In John, consequently, "heaven" often occurs in conjunction with the verb καταβαίνω, to come down or descend (1:32, 51; 3:13; 6:33, 38, 41, 42, 50, 51, 58).

John 14:2–3 is the key passage that speaks of the future of believers: "In my Father's house there are many dwelling places (μοναί). If it were not so, would I have told you that I go to prepare a place for you? And if I go and prepare a place for you, I will come again and will take you to myself, so that where I am, there you will be also." The context is Jesus' departure from the disciples and their concern about not seeing him again, not their anxiety about their own deaths. In this context Jesus assured them that he would continue to be present with them. Later in the chapter, Jesus explains, answering Judas (not Iscariot), "Those who love me will keep my word, and my Father will love them, and we will come to them and make our home (μονή) with them" (14:23). The latter verse clearly refers not to heaven but to the present communion of believers with Jesus through the Spirit. This recasting of the promise in John 14:2–3 shifts the believer's

---

[26] Coloe, *Dwelling in the Household of God*, 72.
[27] *OTP* 2.718 n. 11.
[28] Florentino García Martínez, *The Dead Sea Scrolls Translated* (Leiden: Brill, 1994), 340.
[29] Clark-Soles, "'I Will Raise [Whom?] Up on the Last Day,'" 48.

hope from the eternal future to present, from traditional future eschatology to John's realized eschatology, without denying the future coming of Jesus.

David Aune agrees that John is here referring to the future Parousia: "The passage refers, with sufficient clarity, to a final eschatological return of Jesus for his followers in order that they may ascend to the heavenly realm with him where they will eternally contemplate his protological glory (cf. 12:26; 17:24). This apocalyptic return of Jesus is referred to in Johannine literature only here, John 21:22f., I John 2:28; and 3:2."[30] James McCaffrey also finds a reference to the heavenly temple,[31] and Francis Moloney rejects the exclusively present interpretation of John 14:23.

> The departed Jesus comes to those who love and believe as they experience the presence of the absent one (vv. 18–21), and they can also look forward to a final coming, when Jesus and the Father will set up their dwelling with them (v. 23). I am rejecting the widespread interpretation of v. 23 as 'in terms of the mystical abiding of God with the believer.'[32]

Moloney adds that the present interpretation removes the need for the "other Paraclete," but one may equally understand that the abiding of the Father and the Son referred to in 14:23 occurs through the work of the Paraclete, which is explained in John 14:26.

Jürgen Becker argued that John affirms the traditional expectation of the future Parousia in 14:2–3 but then introduces the distinctively Johannine view that the community already enjoys the presence of God's glory because the Father and Son have come to make their dwelling place in the one who believes (14:23).[33] Mary Coloe takes the argument a step further, maintaining that "the Temple [in 14:2] is now reinterpreted in a radically new way as the household of God, where the Divine Presence dwells within the community of believers."[34]

Some readers may well recognize that John's concern is more the present experience of the community than the return of Jesus in the future, and recall that John has already interpreted the language of the temple in terms of Jesus himself (2:21), but for many readers John starts with a traditional reference to the Parousia and moves the reader to understand that

---

[30] Aune, *Cultic Setting*, 129. So also Frey, *Die Johanneische Eschatologie III*, 145–53.

[31] James McCaffrey, *The House with Many Rooms: The Temple Theme of Jn 14, 2–3* (AnBib 114; Rome: Biblical Institute Press, 1988), 256.

[32] Francis J. Moloney, "The Gospel of John: A Story of Two Paracletes," in *The Gospel of John: Text and Context* (Biblical Interpretation Series 72; Leiden: Brill, 2005), 253. Moloney's footnote refers to Barrett, *Gospel according to St. John*, 466.

[33] This is the interpretation of Jürgen Becker, "Die Abschiedsreden Jesu im Johannesevangelium," *ZNW* 61 (1970): 215–46. See Frey's critique of Becker in *Die Johanneische Eschatologie III*, 173–75.

[34] Coloe, *Dwelling in the Household of God*, 112.

hope for the future is already being fulfilled in the present experience of the community. Once again, while the distinctively Johannine emphasis is on the present experience of the community, the expectation of the Parousia is not denied.[35]

There is no eschatological discourse such as Mark 13 in the Gospel of John, but Jesus does speak explicitly of his coming again in the future in John 21:22–23. The reference to his coming again in John 14:18 is ambiguous, but the explanation that follows in verse 23 and the summary reference in 14:28 make it clear that in this context at least Jesus is speaking of his return to the disciples after his death, in the experience of the Johannine community – not of the Parousia in the future: "I have told you this before it occurs, so that when it does occur, you may believe" (14:29). Without denying the hope of abiding with God, therefore, John recasts it in terms of present fulfillment through Jesus' death and resurrection.

3. Realized Eschatology in the Johannine Community

We are now in a better position to explore the implications of the experience of eternal life for the Johannine community. In what ways did its realized eschatology change the life of the community? The gospel and letters of John suggest that the community's realized eschatology shaped the experience of the community in the following five areas:

3.1. Living in the Community of the Resurrection Offered an Experience of Oneness with God.

This unity with God was experienced through abiding in Jesus, the presence of the Paraclete, and participation in the community's resurrection meal. The essence of the resurrection life for John was the transformation of life that came through the knowledge and fellowship of God through Jesus Christ (17:3). Living in daily communion with God through the revelation in Jesus, Jesus' revelatory words and deeds, the study of Scripture, the continuing presence of the Holy Spirit, regular worship and observance of the community's sacred meal, obedience of Jesus' love command, and fellowship with fellow believers gave their lives a distinctive quality: ζωὴ αἰώνιων (the life of eternity).

One implication of the realization of the eschatological hope of union with God was John's distinctive mysticism, at the center of which is oneness with God.[36] Jesus' followers abide in him by eating his flesh and

---

[35] Frey, *Die Johanneische Eschatologie III*, 177–78.
[36] Cf. Mark L. Appold, *The Oneness Motif in the Fourth Gospel. Motif Analysis and Exegetical Probe into the Theology of John* (WUNT II/1; Tübingen: Mohr, 1976).

drinking his blood (6:56). As children of God, believers are accorded the status of a son rather than a servant and therefore abide in God's household forever (8:35).[37] The Father abides in Jesus, the Son (14:10). Similarly, the Spirit of Truth abides in the disciples (14:17), and Jesus abides in them and they in him (15:4). Jesus and the Father will make their "abiding place" in the disciples (14:23). The disciples abide in Jesus' love by keeping Jesus' commandments, just as Jesus abided in the Father's love by keeping his commandments (15:10). Jesus' relationship to the Father, moreover, is the model and indeed the basis for the disciples' abiding in God (17:21). This indwelling, or unity, has a missiological purpose (17:18, 21, 23) to which we will return below. The believer's unity with God therefore has a Christological foundation (Jesus as the model and basis for the believer's unity with God), an ethical norm (keeping Jesus' words and commandments), and a missiological goal (that the world may believe).

Closely related to this mysticism is Jesus' promise of the coming of the Paraclete. The Paraclete will abide in the disciples (14:17), so even though the world will not see Jesus, his followers will see him (14:19). The Paraclete will instruct believers and remind them of what Jesus said (14:26) and testify on his behalf (15:26). The Paraclete, therefore, will serve juridical, apologetic, and missiological functions within the community of believers (16:7–11). When Jesus appeared to the disciples following his resurrection, he "breathed" the Holy Spirit on them (20:22).

Participation in the community's sacred meal was a vital element in sustaining the life of the resurrection. This assertion may appear to be odd or even unfounded since John does not report the giving of the bread and the cup or the words of institution of the Lord's Supper. The discourse on the bread of life in John 6 contains Christological and wisdom themes (Prov 9:5; Sir 24:19),[38] and Bultmann's thesis that the eucharistic emphasis in John 6:51c–58 was a later addition by an "ecclesiastical redactor"[39] is now generally rejected.[40] Maarten J. J. Menken concludes that John 6:51c–58 is

---

[37] Mary Coloe has recently significantly advanced David Aune's insight that οἰκία ("household") reflects the self-designation of the Johannine community": Aune, *Cultic Setting*, 130; Coloe, *Dwelling in the Household of God*, 111.

[38] See, for example, Marianne Meye Thompson, "Thinking about God: Wisdom and Theology in John 6," in *John 6* (ed. R. Alan Culpepper; Biblical Interpretation Series, 22; Leiden: Brill, 1997), 221–46, esp. 225–30.

[39] Rudolf Bultmann, *The Gospel of John: A Commentary* (trans. G. R. Beasley-Murray et al.; Philadelphia: Westminster, 1971), 218–19, 234–37; D. Moody Smith, *The Composition and Order of the Fourth Gospel: Bultmann's Literary Theory* (New Haven: Yale University Press, 1965), 134–37, 145.

[40] See the range of views noted by Maarten J. J. Menken, "John 6:51c–58: Eucharist or Christology," in *Critical Readings of John 6* (ed. R. Alan Culpepper; Biblical Interpretation Series, 22; Leiden: Brill, 1997), 183–204, esp. 184–85.

an integral part of the Christological discourse in John 6, and that it need not be considered anti-docetic but emphasizes the salvific significance of Jesus' death.[41] Nevertheless, he acknowledges "there is no reason to doubt that the Johannine Christians celebrated the Eucharist; the fact that John makes use of the words of institution in John 6:51c testifies to this practice."[42]

The emphasis on life in these verses is noteworthy. Whereas the Pauline tradition associated the eucharistic meal with Jesus' death (1 Cor 11:23–26), the Johannine tradition did not. One who does not eat the flesh of the Son of Man and drink his blood does not have life (6:53), whereas those who do participate in the sacred meal have both eternal life and the promise of future resurrection (6:54). The sacramental eating and drinking are the means by which believers abide in Jesus (6:56), so "whoever eats me will live because of me" (6:57), and "the one who eats this bread will live forever" (6:58). Throughout this section, the emphasis is on life.

In the last chapter, when the risen Lord appears to the disciples on the shore of the Sea of Galilee, the disciples share a meal of bread and fish with the risen Lord. The meal scene in John 21 is connected with the feeding of the 5,000 and the discourse on the bread of life both linguistically and thematically. Both John 6:11 and 21:13 describe Jesus' action of taking bread and fish and giving them to his disciples.

6:11a	Then Jesus took the loaves (ἔλαβεν οὖν τοὺς ἄρτους)
6:11b	and when he had given thanks,
	he distributed (διέδωκεν) them to those who were seated;
6:11c	so also the fish (τῶν ὀψαρίων).
21:13a	Jesus came and took the bread (λαμβάνει τὸν ἄρτον)
21:13b	and gave (δίδωσιν) it to them
21:13c	and did the same with the fish (τὸ ὀψάριον).

Fish was often consumed at funerary meals in antiquity, and in early Christian iconography the fish is closely associated with Christ, the Eucharist, death, resurrection, and new life.[43] Similarly, in John the sacred meal occurs after the resurrection rather than before Jesus' death. Mathias Rissi suggested that the latter was a celebration of the resurrection.[44] John Perry

---

[41] Menken, "John 6:51c–58," 201. For a summary of other perspectives on John 6:51–59 in the same volume see p. 253.

[42] Menken, "John 6:51c–58," 202.

[43] Lawrence H. Kant, *The Interpretation of Religious Symbols in the Graeco-Roman World. A Case Study of Early Christian Fish Symbolism* (3 vols.; Ph.D. Dissertation; Yale University, 1993), 602.

[44] Mathias Rissi, "'Voll grosser Fische, hundertdreiundfünfzig': Joh. 21, 1–14," *TZ* 35 (1979): 73–89, esp. 85. So also Lars Hartman, "An Attempt at a Text-Centered Exegesis of John 21," *ST* 38 (1984): 29–45, esp. 40: "It is probable that, as the episode of the

pressed the argument further, contending that "originally the eucharistic memorial of the Johannine Community was of an earliest Jewish Christian type that celebrated the Resurrection of Jesus and his anticipated return in glory without memorializing his passion and death."[45] Taking together the emphasis on life in the discourse on bread in John 6, the connections between the meal scene in John 21 and the discourse in John 6, the post-resurrection placement of the sacred meal in John, and the symbolism of the bread and fish, it appears that when the community gathered for its sacred meal, it celebrated the resurrection life it experienced through the death and resurrection of Jesus.

3.2. The Ideals of Life in the Community of the Resurrection, because It Is Life in the Spirit, Were Expressed in the Love Command, κοινωνία, Peace, and Joy

The internal life of the community was marked by the ideal of adherence to the ethic of Jesus' teaching. Jesus commanded his followers to love one another as he loved them (13:34; 15:12). Fellow believers were therefore φίλοι, beloved friends (3 John 15), and the community was known for its love (13:35; 1 John 3:17; 4:19–21). Lazarus, whom Jesus raised from the dead, was such a friend (11:11). When persecution threatened, this love required that one be ready to lay down his or her life for "the friends" (15:13–15). The ceremony of footwashing, which Jesus had commanded his disciples to observe, reenacted not only their love and service to one another but Jesus' preparation for his death, loving "his own" to the end by laying aside his garment (and his life – 10:17–18), washing their feet, and taking up his garment (and his life) again.[46] Mary Coloe has recently

---

catch of fish has a symbolic meaning, so has the meal. Then the interpretations of the meal in Jn 6 present themselves: . . . . Passages like these suggest that the meal on the shore symbolizes the gift of eternal life." John Dominic Crossan, *The Historical Jesus* (San Francisco: HarperSanFrancisco, 1991), 398–99 and 402, concludes that "the bread and fish Eucharist was originally a postresurrectional confession of Jesus' continued presence at the ritualized meals of the believing community" (402). Also proposing that the Eucharist in John was a celebration of Jesus' resurrection and life, see Ernst Lohmeyer, "Vom urchristlichen Abendmahl," *TRu*, NF 9 (1937): 312; and Gail R. O'Day, "The Love of God Incarnate: The Life of Jesus in the Gospel of John," in *Life Abundant: Studies of John's Gospel in Tribute to Raymond E. Brown* (ed. John R. Donahue; Collegeville, MN: Liturgical Press, 2005), 158–67, esp. 166.

[45] J. M. Perry, "The Evolution of the Johannine Eucharist," *NTS* 39 (1993): 22–35, esp. 22. See further R. Alan Culpepper, "Designs for the Church in the Imagery of John 21:1–14," in *Imagery in the Gospel of John: Terms, Forms, Themes and Theology of Figurative Language* (ed. Jörg Frey, Jan G. van der Watt, and Ruben Zimmermann; WUNT 200; Tübingen: Mohr Siebeck, 2006), 369–402.

[46] See R. Alan Culpepper, "The Johannine *hypodeigma*: A Reading of John 13," *Semeia* 53 (1991): 133–52.

shown how the footwashing ceremony was an appropriate preparation for those entering the Johannine community – the household of God.⁴⁷

This community ethic/experience receives the insider label κοινωνία in the Johannine epistles but not in the gospel. The epistles appear to represent a later stage in the community's history, and it may be that in the interim the community had begun to refer to its distinctive ethos by using this term. Their κοινωνία was with each other, with "the Father and with his Son, Jesus Christ," and with any who received their witness to what they had seen and heard (1 John 1:3, 6, 7).

Peace and joy were further tokens of the community's distinctive love and κοινωνία. Jesus' peace did not mean the absence of threat, hostility, or danger (cf. 14:27; 16:33); it was rather the sense of completeness and security in God's fellowship. Even behind doors locked in fear of the threat of persecution, the community could know peace in the worship and fellowship of their Lord (20:19, 21, 26), so they greeted one another with expressions of peace (2 John 3; 3 John 15). Similarly, John the baptizer likened his experience to the joy of the "friend" of Jesus, the bridegroom (3:29). Behind these sayings one can detect the formula that the joy of Jesus' followers should be "fulfilled" (πεπληρωμένη) or some other form of the verb: 3:29; 15:11; 16:24; 17:13; 1 John 1:4; 2 John 12). Only if they have Jesus' joy will their joy be complete, an experience of life in the age to come. Such joy, which Jesus likened to the joy of the mother of a newborn baby, causes the hostility of the world to pale in significance (16:20–24). The elder writes that he has no greater joy than to hear that his children are walking in the truth (3 John 4).

This strong, internal ethos, however, was matched by, and perhaps in part produced by, an equally strong awareness of separation from the rest of society which did not share in their experience of the resurrection life.

3.3 The Reality of Sin Became Problematic for the Community of the Resurrection

Because the community already shared in the life of the resurrection, its members could not continue in sin, as though the ruler of this world continued to have power over them. John describes the root or essence of sin, which is unbelief (16:8), rather than the conduct that results from sin. First John reflects the theological quandary that the ideal of perfection created

---

⁴⁷ Coloe, *Dwelling in the Household of God*, 123–44; idem, "Welcome into the Household of God: The Footwashing in John 13," *CBQ* 66 (2004): 400–15; idem, "Sources in the Shadows: John 13 and the Johannine Community," in *New Currents through John: A Global Perspective* (ed. Francisco Lozada, Jr. and Tom Thatcher; Atlanta: Society of Biblical Literature, 2006), 69–82.

for the community.[48] On the one hand it could not deny the reality of sin (1 John 1:8, 10). On the other hand, the Johannine believers could not continue to sin (1 John 3:3–10). They were to live as Jesus lived (1 John 1:7; 2:6), righteously (1 John 2:29). Specifically, they were to keep his commandments, which were especially to believe in him and to love one another (1 John 3:23), which means at least that one should care for a brother or sister in need (1 John 3:17). Commentators have wrestled to resolve this quandary, while recognizing that it is a logical inconsistency born of Johannine realized eschatology. Had John not placed such emphasis on the new status of those who had already been born from above and shared in the life of the age to come, the attendant affirmation of deliverance from the power of sin would not have been such an acute problem.

3.4. Institutional Authority Was Difficult to Establish because All Believers are Children of God, and All Possess the Paraclete

The gospel adopts the language of kinship to characterize those who believe. They are children of God (1:12; 11:52). This new kinship has the effect of leveling all other differences. Whether one is a Galilean or a Judean, a Jew, Samaritan, or Gentile, male or female, poor or a person of status, Jesus called to each one as a shepherd calls his sheep. Nicodemus, a Pharisee of rank, must be born of the Spirit just like others. Privilege based on one's birth counts for nothing. Likewise the Samaritan woman is offered living water. Neither marginality based on birth nor her life experience excluded her. Jesus loved his own completely (13:1), and promised the Spirit to all without exception or distinction.[49]

First John is instructive again in regard to the kind of difficulties this elevated and undistinguished status created for the community. They had no need for teachers because all of them had received the Lord's anointing (1 John 2:27). Jesus was therefore their example, and members of the community were to keep his commandments.

The gospel also illustrates the community's struggle over succession.[50] Jesus promised not a successor but the Paraclete, the Spirit of Truth, who would guide them in all truth and remind them of what Jesus had taught them. Other communities had recognized Peter as the leader of the early church, but the Fourth Gospel maintains the primacy of the Beloved Disciple without denying that Peter had a special role as a shepherd who had

---

[48] John Bogart, *Orthodox and Heretical Perfectionism* (SBLDS 33; Missoula, Mont.: Scholars Press, 1977).

[49] See R. Alan Culpepper, "Inclusivism and Exclusivism in the Fourth Gospel," in *Word, Theology and Community in John* (ed. John Painter, R. Alan Culpepper and Fernando F. Segovia; St. Louis: Chalice Press, 2002), 85–108, esp. 90–95.

[50] D. Bruce Woll, *Johannine Christianity in Conflict* (SBLDS 60; Chico, Calif.: Scholars Press, 1981).

been commissioned by Jesus and who would lay down his life as a "Good Shepherd," following Jesus' example. The Beloved Disciple's leadership, like that of every other believer, would have been measured by faithfulness to the teachings of Jesus and the functions of the Paraclete.

This egalitarian nature of the community was also related to its realized eschatology. Because it already partook of the life of the age to come, it could not be a community in which some had greater authority than others.

3.5. Living in the Community of the Resurrection Produced Enmity with the World. The Other Side of Enmity with the World was a Strong Mandate of Mission to the World

The Johannine community's relationship to the world was highly paradoxical. On the one hand, the gospel maintains an ethical dualism in which one belongs to the light or the darkness, truth or falsehood, God or Satan. Those who do not belong to the community of believers are labeled "the world," and just as Jesus' followers live in Jesus, so the world stands under the power of "the ruler of this world" (12:31; 14:30; 16:11). The world hates Jesus' followers, just as it hated Jesus (15:18–19; 17:14). Jesus' followers are therefore not to love the things of the world (1 John 2:15; John 12:25). Jesus has overcome the world (16:33).

Both the world and the community love their own (7:7; 13:34–35; 15:19), but members of the Johannine community are to love the world as well. God loves the world (3:16–17), and Jesus is the savior of the world (4:42; 12:47) who gives his own flesh as the bread that gives life to the world (6:33, 51). Just as the Father sent the Son into the world, so Jesus sends his disciples to bear a redemptive witness (17:18; 20:21). Jesus promised that when he was lifted up he would draw all people to himself (12:32), and in the last chapter the community's mission is portrayed symbolically as gathering a great catch of fish (21:10–11).[51] The community, therefore, maintains its ethical separation from the world, while continuing to seek to be a redemptive, revelatory presence in it.

4. Conclusion

The realized eschatology of the Gospel of John originated from the experience of the believing community that produced a distinguishing sense of oneness with God, a strong community ethos, and an equally strong sense of alienation from the world. This heightened experience of oneness with God, participation in the resurrection of Jesus, and the continuing presence of the Spirit led the community to distinguish eternal life from the hope of

---

[51] See Culpepper, "Designs for the Church in the Imagery of John 21:1–14," 369–402.

resurrection on the last day. Through the life of the community, the Johannine believers experienced life that was marked by the quality of eternity, and this became a unifying theme of their gospel and its theology. So powerful was the experience of "eternal life" that it altered the Johannine community's theological vocabulary, mysticism, ethics, sacramental thought, separation from the world, ideal of sinless perfection, internal organization, and mission. Therefore, while the Gospel of John testifies to the revelation in Jesus of Nazareth, it also bears witness to the way in which that revelation transformed the lives of those who sought to be faithful to it in one early Christian community.

Chapter 12

Eschatology as Liturgy:
Jesus' Resurrection and Johannine Eschatology

Hans-Ulrich Weidemann

The Gospel of John, like the other gospels, does not end with the death of Jesus but goes on to describe the discovery of the empty tomb and the appearances of the risen Jesus. However, the Fourth Evangelist does not simply narrate the Easter story after the passion account. In John's gospel, the events of the passion and resurrection are anticipated by Jesus himself in the Farewell Discourses "before they occur."[1] The aim of this is to enable the reader or hearer to understand the following narratives of the passion and resurrection "correctly," i.e., in the Johannine sense. Discourse and story belong together in the development of Johannine theology: the words of Jesus and the events related by the evangelist mutually condition each other.

In contrast to other parts of the Fourth Gospel in which Jesus' discourse or dialogue *follows upon* the narrative text (as in John 5 and 6), the reflection about the coming events *precedes* their narration in the second major section of the book. In John 14:29, Jesus emphasizes that he is speaking of the coming events *before* (πρίν) they occur. In this way the Farewell Discourses are anchored in the *pre-Easter* situation. Jesus speaks to his disciples before his death and thus as an earthly being. So, from a strictly literary point of view, the revelation of Jesus' death and return and of the destiny of the post-Easter community is set in a pre-Easter context. Paradoxically, Jesus speaks to his disciples before the occurrence of the events that are required to understand what he is saying (cf. 2:22; 7:39; 12:16; 14:26).

Of course, for the *reader* of the Fourth Gospel the Easter account is not the surprising ending of a fictional story. The implied reader of the gospel is no hypothetical "first-time reader" who does not know the "happy end" of the Jesus story and is surprised by the fact that the victim of the crucifixion overcomes death and is glorified by his heavenly Father. Instead, every Christian knows that Jesus is resurrected – and even non-Christians

---

[1] Cf. John 14:29, also 13:19 and 16:1, 4, which speak of the future of the disciples.

certainly know that Christians believe this.² Thus, when the Johannine Jesus tells his disciples that he will explain to them the meaning of the events before they occur, the evangelist presupposes a reader who is already familiar with the events to come.

In order to focus upon the interrelationship between the Easter account and the Farewell Discourses, we will first consider the Easter account to see the special emphases that the evangelist has imprinted on it. Moreover, a careful analysis of John 20 and the comparison to its Synoptic counterparts shows that the Fourth Evangelist builds upon older traditions that were known in the Johannine community. Regarding the Easter account, we are well-positioned to appreciate the Johannine shaping of the text.

1. The Easter Assembly of the Disciples (John 20)

The Johannine Easter chapter (John 20) follows immediately after the passion narrative (John 18–19) and is linked to this narrative by the account of the burial (19:38–42).³ The "Epilogue" (20:30–31) suggests that this chapter originally constituted the concluding chapter of the Fourth Gospel and that it was only later augmented by the supplementary chapter 21.⁴ It would appear that only in the course of this expansion of the gospel was the Beloved Disciple (who plays an important role in John 21 and there appears as a witness to the resurrection) inserted alongside Peter into the scene of the visit to the tomb (20:2–10).⁵

The Fourth Evangelist clearly put his own stamp on the Easter narratives, but this does not mean that in John 20 he was entirely independent of older traditions. The comparison between the Johannine and synoptic Easter stories reveals a particular affinity to the *Lukan* Easter account, an affinity also shown by comparison with the passion narratives. Since there

---

² Richard Bauckham, "The Audience of the Fourth Gospel," in *Jesus in Johannine Tradition* (ed. Robert T. Fortna and Tom Thatcher; Louisville: Westminster John Knox, 2001), 101–11, 109, rightly emphasizes that the "knowledge the readers have to bring to the text" is not some esoteric secret lore, but rather "the fact that Jesus is going to be crucified and then rise from the dead. Even non-Christian readers interested enough to read F[ourth]G[ospel] would surely know that Christians believed this about Jesus."

³ Among other points, through the theme of the grave (John 19:41–42; 20:1, 3–8, 11–15) and the theme of the garden (κῆπος) (19:41; 20:15).

⁴ Cf. Raymond E. Brown, *The Gospel According to John II* (AB 29A; New York: Doubleday, 1970), 1057.

⁵ See for details Michael Theobald, "Der Jünger, den Jesus liebte. Beobachtungen zum narrativen Konzept der johanneischen Redaktion," in *Geschichte–Tradition–Reflexion III. Frühes Christentum* (ed. H. Lichtenberger; Tübingen: Mohr Siebeck, 1997), 219–55.

is no proof of John's literary dependence on the Gospel of Luke, and since even an acquaintance with Luke's Gospel on the part of the Fourth Gospel is most unlikely, the best explanation of this affinity is to assume that both Easter accounts derive from a common tradition, i.e., a pre-Johannine/ Lukan passion and Easter narrative that the Third Evangelist used alongside the Gospel of Mark and one that was closely related to the ancient passion and Easter account which (alone) was current in the Johannine community.[6] Thus with a brief look at the Lukan material it is possible to trace out, in terms of tradition criticism, the most important accents given by the Fourth Evangelist.

At the center of the Johannine Easter account stands the appearance of the risen Jesus before his assembled disciples on the evening of the first day of the week (20:19–23). The most striking peculiarity of the Johannine account is the fact that Jesus appeared to his disciples *behind locked doors* (20:19). Particularly striking is the divergence from Matthew: there the closing Easter appearance with the mission command takes place in the open, on a mountain in Galilee (Matt 28:16). Since Jesus does not enter a house, the greeting "Peace be with you" is absent here.[7] In Luke, however, the central appearance of Jesus to the eleven apostles and the other disciples, among them the Emmaus disciples (Luke 24:33), takes place in a room in Jerusalem, though this place is not further identified.

Thus the Easter appearance within a room in Jerusalem is a specific element of the Lukan/Johannine Easter tradition. From this tradition, both evangelists took over in almost identical wording the introductory observation that Jesus came and "stood among them and said to them 'Peace be

---

[6] The most plausible model is that offered by Hans Klein, *Lukasstudien* (FRLANT 209, Göttingen: Vandenhoeck & Ruprecht, 2005), 66–84, see also Hans Klein, *Das Lukasevangelium* (KEK I/3, Göttingen: Vandenhoeck & Ruprecht, 2006), 46. Alongside Mark, Luke made use of an already written special tradition, which is closely related to the passion and Easter tradition of the Gospel of John. The decisive argument for the postulation of an older passion and Easter tradition shared by Luke and John is that where they go beyond the Markan text, the Lukan and Johannine accounts strikingly coincide, whereas for Lukan theology the additions to the Markan materials typically find no parallel in John. Examples in the passion account are the Herod scene (Luke 23:5–16), the mourning for Jerusalem (23:28–31), and the two criminals crucified with Jesus (23:28–31). Likewise in the Easter story, the parallels are not to be found where Luke puts his own emphasis (so in the Emmaus and ascension accounts), but rather where he follows his tradition (so in Luke 24:36–43; cf. John 20:19–23). This common tradition must have been available to Luke and John already in written form. This is evidenced by the numerous minor verbal parallels.

[7] Matt 28:9 has only the salutation χαίρετε ("be glad"). By contrast, the greeting "peace be with you" upon entering a house is alluded to in Matt 10:12 / Luke 10:5, where Jesus gives instructions to the apostles sent on mission.

with you!'"[8] The Fourth Evangelist, however, develops this tradition in a way that is characteristic for him, emphasizing here, as in the second appearance, that *the doors were locked* (John 20:19, 26) and adding in the second case (20:26) that the disciples were *inside* (ἔσω). In addition, he gives a motive for closing the doors: "for fear of the Jews" (20:19).[9] The point here is in no way to stress the marvelous ability of the Risen One to pass through solid matter. Instead, the point is that the Sunday evening assemblies of the Johannine community *always* take place behind locked doors. This detail is thus an indication of their own self-understanding.

Although the evangelist gives much weight to the fact that the Easter appearances take place inside, behind locked doors, he does not tell us *where* this locked room is to be found. Indirectly, we can conclude that as before, the disciples are still in Jerusalem: the scene with Mary Magdalene takes place at the grave in the garden near the place of crucifixion (19:41–42), and in contrast to Matt 28:16 we hear nothing of a displacement of the disciples.[10] Again the comparison with Luke shows that the ancient tradition which the Fourth Evangelist uses localized the Easter appearances in *Jerusalem*, though he does not specifically mention this detail, which is so important to Luke (cf. Luke 24:33, 49, 52–53).

In contrast, it is the *time* indication that is important for the Fourth Evangelist: we hear that the disciples gathered together on *the evening of the first day of the week* (John 20:19), a detail that was probably rooted in the pre-Johannine tradition,[11] but which was emphasized by the Fourth

---

[8] Compare Luke 24:36 (αὐτὸς ἔστη ἐν μέσῳ αὐτῶν καὶ λέγει αὐτοῖς·εἰρήνη ὑμῖν) – a text containing no specifically Lukan expressions – with John 20:19 (ἦλθεν ὁ Ἰησοῦς καὶ ἔστη εἰς τὸ μέσον καὶ λέγει αὐτοῖς· εἰρήνη ὑμῖν) and John 20:26 (ἔρχεται ὁ Ἰησοῦς τῶν θυρῶν κεκλεισμένων καὶ ἔστη εἰς τὸ μέσον καὶ λέγει αὐτοῖς εἰρήνη ὑμῖν). On this comparison see Klein, *Lukasstudien*, 66–70.

[9] On this point, see John 7:13; 9:22; 19:38. In the following appearance a week later, the doors are again locked, but the motive of fear of the Jews is not explicitly mentioned.

[10] Consistently, the Easter appearance in Matt 28:16–20 is clearly localized in Galilee (cf. 26:32; 28:7, 10 and Mark 14:28; 16:7), but it is by no means indicated that it took place on Easter Sunday; in fact, no date at all is mentioned.

[11] With Luke it is clear that all the events described in chapter 24 take place on the first day of the week (Luke 24:1). The Emmaus disciples go "on this day" (24:13) to Emmaus and return to Jerusalem directly after the evening (24:29) appearance of Jesus, where they meet the other disciples. Although we are not told directly when the disciples gather, one can surmise, on the basis of 24:29 ("the day is now nearly over") and the mention of broiled fish (24:42), that it was at the time of the usual evening meal (see also Mark 16:14). Following his words to them, Jesus then leads the disciples out to Bethany, where he is taken up into heaven (Luke 24:50–51). In contrast to the localization of the Easter appearances in *Jerusalem*, the time factor is of little importance to Luke here. This is shown by the tension with Acts 1, where multiple appearances during forty days are mentioned.

Evangelist. That the first day of the week (and not the Passover feast) is important for the evangelist is shown by the repetition of the disciples coming together eight days later (20:26). These meetings on the first day of the week, when the Easter appearances of Jesus to his disciples take place, are evidently taken for granted by the narrator.

Striking in these accounts is *the open-ended character* of the scene. With the gift of the Spirit and the power to forgive or retain sins, the first scene ends (20:22–23).[12] The same holds true for the second appearance before the disciples "on the eighth day." The appearance ends with the macarism in 20:29. The epilogue of the book follows. In both cases, there is no farewell scene and no indication of how Jesus withdrew from the scene.[13]

If one asks, *why* the disciples came together on the evening "on that day, the first day of the week," the answer will be found in the foregoing scene with Mary Magdalene (20:1–18). This scene in 20:1–2 and 20:11–12 evidently goes back to the older tradition,[14] although the Fourth Evangelist concentrates his focus on Mary Magdalene. The grounds for this become clear when one takes into consideration the parallels between 20:11–18 and the account of the calling of the disciples in John 1.[15] Mary Magdalene is called by the Risen One himself into post-Easter discipleship. In analogy

---

[12] By contrast, Luke 24:50 adds: ἐξήγαγεν δὲ αὐτοὺς ἔξω ἕως πρὸς Βηθανίαν. Most of the "building blocks" found in John 20:19–23 were taken over from the older tradition: Thus one finds also in the Lukan Easter account the theme of Easter joy (Luke 24:41), the power to forgive sins (24:47), the sending forth (24:28) and the gift of the Spirit (24:49). It would appear, however, that especially towards the end of the scene, John is closer to the original tradition (Klein, *Lukasstudien*, 68).

[13] Here too Luke differs, describing a blessing of the disciples in 24:50. A look at Matthew is instructive. Here too there is no scene of bidding farewell. Rather, the Risen One proclaims his presence "with you" until the end of the age (Matt 28:20; cf. 1:23): "That Jesus does not ascend is a fitting sign of his eternal presence: the risen Lord remains with his people" (W. D. Davies and Dale C. Allison, *The Gospel According to St Matthew III* [ICC; Edinburgh: T&T Clark, 1997], 687).

[14] A glance at Luke shows that a visit to the grave by women, among them Mary Magdalene (Luke 24:10), was a part of the earlier tradition. The plural form in John 20:2 (οὐκ οἴδαμεν) suggests that the Fourth Evangelist likewise was familiar with a tradition of a grave visit by several women, though he focuses exclusively on Mary Magdalene. To the earlier tradition belong the appearance of the angel at the grave and the "announcement" made to the disciples (compare Luke 24:9: ἀπήγγειλαν, with John 20:18: ἀγγέλλουσα) and also Peter's dash to the grave and the seeing of Jesus' ὀθόνια.

[15] Note the following parallels: the address (John 1:38: Ραββί / 20:16: Ραββουνι), which is immediately translated (1:38 / 20:16: διδάσκαλε); the "standing" of the Baptist with his disciples and the "standing" of Mary (1:35 / 20:11: εἰστήκει), the act of "seeing" Jesus (1:36: ἐμβλέψας τῷ Ἰησοῦ / 20:14: θεωρεῖ τὸν Ἰησοῦν), the question put by Jesus (1:38: τί ζητεῖτε; / 20:15: τίνα ζητεῖς;). Compare also the motive of "turning around" (1:38: στραφεὶς δὲ ὁ Ἰησοῦς / 20:16: στραφεῖσα).

to John 1, it is she who tells the others.[16] That the circle of disciples comes together again on the evening of Easter Sunday and that it meets behind locked doors thus follows the logic of the Johannine "call" accounts. Mary Magdalene becomes the "apostle to the apostles." On the basis of her message (ἑώρακα τὸν κύριον), the disciples convene on the evening of Easter day.

The third appearance of Jesus (20:26–29) is, from a literary point of view, constructed analogically, except that here the group and the individual exchange roles. In a clear analogy to Mary Magdalene, it is now "the other disciples" who tell Thomas: "We have seen the Lord (ἑωράκαμεν τὸν κύριον)." Thomas indeed poses conditions for his belief, but he takes part in the following Sunday assembly (20:26: καὶ Θωμᾶς μετ' αὐτῶν)! Thus we find twice the same structural scheme in the text: the Easter message (20:18, 25) brings about the assembly of the disciples on the first day of the week behind locked doors – in the second case, it causes the participation of Thomas in the assembly (20:19, 26).[17] In the midst of these assemblies constituted by the Easter message, the Risen One appears and speaks the greeting of peace (20:19, 26).

Even the Thomas story, which is peculiar to the Fourth Gospel, has at least two roots in the older tradition: the touching of the Risen One's body[18] and the motif of unbelief.[19] Thomas is indeed a member of the

---

[16] Compare John 20:18 with 1:35–37 (the Baptist points out Jesus to two of his disciples and they follow him) and with 1:40–42 (Andrew finds Simon his brother and leads him to Jesus) and also 1:45–51 (Philip and Nathanael).

[17] Similarly Luke 24:33–34: on returning to Jerusalem the two Emmaus disciples find the eleven and those with them already assembled on the basis of the Easter appearance to *Peter* (24:34)!

[18] In Luke 24:39, the Risen One tells his disciples to look at his hands and feet (ἴδετε τὰς χεῖράς μου καὶ τοὺς πόδας μου) and to touch him (ψηλαφήσατε), to demonstrate that he is not a spirit (πνεῦμα, cf. 24:37). In Luke 24:40, he then shows them his hands (ἔδειξεν αὐτοῖς τὰς χεῖρας) and his feet. As Klein, *Lukasstudien*, 69–70, rightly emphasizes, Luke shows no particular interest in this element of the tradition before him; his own concern comes to expression in 24:44–49 (fulfillment of Scripture, message of forgiveness of sins, promise of the Spirit). The Fourth Evangelist puts the showing of the hands in the Easter evening scene (20:20: ἔδειξεν τὰς χεῖρας) and replaces the reference to his feet by a reference to his (pierced) side (ἡ πλευρά, cf. 19:34): The command to look at him and touch him, however, he puts off until the Thomas scene (20:27, cf. 20:25). So also Klein, *Lukasstudien*, 68: The command to the disciples to look at and to touch his hands is divided and inserted into two distinct stories following upon each other.

[19] The motive of the disciples' *unbelief* in the face of the Easter message (compare Luke 24:11: ἠπίστουν αὐταῖς, with John 20:25: οὐ μὴ πιστεύσω, and 20:27: καὶ μὴ γίνου ἄπιστος ἀλλὰ πιστός) probably belongs to the old pre-Lukan and pre-Johannine Easter tradition (Matt 28:17 speaks only of the doubts of some disciples – and that, as a

Twelve, as the evangelist in emphasizes in 20:24, thus reflecting the conviction, widespread in early Christianity, that the Risen One appeared to the Twelve.[20] However he is not present at the first appearance on Easter evening. At this assembly it is the disciples (οἱ μαθηταί)[21] who are present according to 20:19–20, which seems to open up the circle of those who attended the Sunday meeting behind locked doors.

2. Signs for "Those Who Have Not Seen"

The second Easter appearance to the disciples ends with the blessing for "those who have not seen and yet have come to believe" (20:29). In contrast to the Gospel of Matthew, the Gospel of John does not end with the sending of the disciples. This is clearly indicated in John 20:21, but it is not as developed in the narrative.

The macarism in 20:29 is directed to subsequent generations, who do not belong to the circle of Easter witnesses. Here the central concern of the evangelist comes to expression. It is important to understand this verse entirely in the context of John 20, where it becomes clear that the worshiping assembly of the disciples on the first day of the week continues: the evangelist has described the *first two instances* of an ongoing chain of further assemblies.

What πιστεύειν means becomes clear from the preceding verses. With the words "be not unbelieving but believing (πιστός)," Jesus awakens faith in Thomas (20:27). Thomas expresses his faith with the acclamation "My Lord and my God" (20:28), to which Jesus replies, "You do believe now, because you have seen me (ὅτι ἑώρακάς με πεπίστευκας)" (20:29). Faith thus means belief in Jesus as "Lord and God"; blessed are those who have this faith without having received an Easter appearance. In this faith they find life (20:31).

However, it is not said directly how this "believing (πιστεύειν) without seeing" will come to pass. The evangelist probably refers here to the proclamation of the word and the witness of the first disciples as well as to the written witness of the gospel itself, which is hinted at in the concluding

---

response to the *appearance* of Jesus. In the secondary conclusion of Mark, this motive is expanded in dependence upon Luke and John, see Mark 16:11, 13, 14).

[20] See 1 Cor 15:5 and also Acts 1:2–3 ("the apostles"), further Luke 24:33–36; Acts 1:21–22; Matt 28:16 (the eleven disciples, cf. Mark 16:14).

[21] In contrast to Matthew: Matt 28:8–10 (Mary Magdalene and the other Mary) and 28:16–20 (the eleven disciples). Also in contrast to Luke: Luke 24:33–34 (the eleven and the others with them plus the Emmaus disciples) and to Acts 1:2f–3 (the apostles); cf. 1:13.

words of the evangelist, which follow immediately in the epilogue to the Easter chapter. Here the Easter appearances are described as "signs in the presence of his disciples" (σημεῖα ἐνώπιον τῶν μαθητῶν),[22] and they are thus put on the same plane as the pre-Easter wonders performed by Jesus. The only difference with respect to the pre-Easter wonders is that according to 20:30, the disciples are the *exclusive* witnesses of the Easter appearances.[23] In particular, the evangelist says that the Easter stories have been "written down in this book" as exemplary signs (20:31).

For the evangelist, Jesus reveals his divine glory in his "signs."[24] The same holds true for the Easter appearances, as the corresponding reaction of Thomas shows (20:28). These Easter *semeia* are not limited to the mere visible appearances of Jesus, but include also the gift of the Spirit and the overcoming of Thomas's incredulity. At the center of the Johannine Easter chapter is the giving of the Spirit to the disciples on Easter. Playing on the text of Gen 2:7, John 20:22 describes this act as one of "breathing upon" (ἐνεφύσησεν). This means that Jesus here performs a new divine act of creation,[25] which is entirely within the context of sending the disciples "as the Father has sent me" and is connected with the of the power *to forgive or retain sins* (20:23). With good reason, F. Porsch emphasizes the "correspondence between the sending of Jesus by the Father and the sending of the disciples by Jesus": "this means that the sending of the disciples has an analogical structure."[26] The gift of the Spirit is thoroughly *imbedded in this process*. By analogy to the sending of the Son by the Father, the sending of *the disciples* by the Risen One is linked with the *gift of the Spirit* (cf. 1:29–34). Because *Jesus* sends the disciples and gives them the Spirit, he relates to the disciples as the Father relates to the earthly Jesus. As the Son received the Spirit from the Father (cf. 1:31–34; 6:27), so the believers receive the Spirit from Jesus (cf. 3:34). This means that in 20:21–23 the divinity of Jesus is implicitly expressed, so that Thomas' later response "My

---

[22] It is important here to keep the whole text in mind. Factually, the Easter appearances are *semeia* like the wonders worked by the earthly Jesus (cf. 2:11). However, the latter were worked ἔμπροσθεν αὐτῶν (12:37), referring to the Jewish ὄχλος. In contrast, the Easter *semeia* occur exclusively ἐνώπιον τῶν μαθητῶν.

[23] The disciples are also present at the pre-Easter wonders (cf. 2:1, 11; 6:5–10, 12–13, 16–21; 9:2–5; 11:7–16), but they are by no means the exclusive witnesses of these wonders (cf. 2:9; 7:4 and 12:37).

[24] 2:11: καὶ ἐφανέρωσεν τὴν δόξαν αὐτοῦ. The same connection occurs in 12:37–41. The lack of belief on the part of the people despite *semeia* is here demonstrated with two quotations from the prophet Isaiah, who in the temple saw the *his* glory and spoke *of him*, namely of Jesus.

[25] Cf. Gen 2:7 LXX, also Ezek 37:9 and Wis 15:11.

[26] Felix Porsch, *Pneuma und Wort. Ein exegetischer Beitrag zur Pneumatologie des Johannesevangeliums* (FTS 16; Frankfurt: Knecht, 1974), 366.

Lord and my God"[27] is the fitting Johannine reaction to this situation. Reading the Johannine Easter accounts as *semeia*, they indicate what in fact takes place in the assembly of the community.

Since *semeia* in the Fourth Gospel, can only be performed by Jesus,[28] they belong – in the perspective of reader of the gospel (who is implied in 20:29 and directly mentioned in 20:30) – to *the past*. With John 20:29, the way to πιστεύειν through *seeing* the Risen One – i.e., the way of Thomas – is indirectly declared to be ended. For the community of readers, the *semeia* of Jesus are only accessible as they are written down in the book of the gospel, making them simultaneously *readable and audible* signs. This, however, in the eyes of the Fourth Evangelist is no disadvantage. Just the opposite. Already in his first appearance to Mary Magdalene, Jesus said that he appears as *one who is ascending* (ἀναβαίνω) and thus as one who has "not yet (οὔπω) ascended to the Father" (20:17). That means that the Risen One, whom Mary sees bodily, does *not yet* represent the full Easter reality of Jesus.[29] This begins only when he has ascended (ἀναβέβηκα).[30] It is to this full reality that the signs of the Risen One refer as they are written down in the book of the gospel.

The Sunday assemblies of the disciples go on, but the visible appearances of Jesus, in which he is identified by his wounds (20:20, 27), come to an end. The place of the Easter appearances before the Easter witnesses is now taken by the *semeia*-stories "written in this book," concretely – and this is fundamental for the understanding of John 20:29–31 – in the book of the gospel as it is read in the worshipping assembly of the community.

---

[27] Cf. Ps 34:23 LXX, but also Zech 13:9 LXX (κύριος ὁ θεός μου).

[28] See John 10:41. This is not the case for Luke: see Acts 2:43; 4:16, 22, 30; 5:12 ("signs" of the Jerusalem apostles); 6:8 (Steven); 8:6, 13 (Philip); 14:3; 15:12 (Paul and Barnabas). Also Paul in 2 Cor 12:12 speaks of signs of the apostles.

[29] Michael Theobald, "Der johanneische Osterglaube und die Grenzen seiner narrativen Vermittlung (John 20)," in *Von Jesus zum Christus. Christologische Studien* (ed. R. Hoppe and U. Busse; BZNW 93; Berlin and New York: Walter de Gruyter 1998), 93–123, esp. 109–13.

[30] In the background here is the differentiation – especially by Luke! but also in other early Christian texts – between Jesus' resurrection and his entry into the heavenly world (ascension). The Fourth Evangelist uses this differentiation like the Third Evangelist, but to express his own specific concern. Although the ascension story in Luke 24:50–53 is strongly marked in its verbal formulation by Luke, it would appear that he knew an older ascension story which he quite freely made use of to form his own narrative (Klein, *Das Lukasevangelium*, 741). Perhaps this tradition was a part of the pre-Lukan or pre-Johannine Easter account, which would then have ended with the story of Jesus being taken up (on the evening of Easter?). Klein, *Lukasstudien*, 80, is of a different opinion. This could account for the discrepancies between the two "ascension narratives" in Luke 24 and Acts 1 and would help explain how this motif was taken up and (strongly) transformed in the Gospel of John.

This explains why the "listeners," who are already indicated in the macarism of 20:29, are directly addressed in 20:31.

> Thus in the post-Easter community, the gospel book (20:30) takes the place of the visible Risen One (in his "intermediate" status, 20:17). To understand this process, a look at the later liturgical dramatization of the meeting with the risen Jesus in the presentation of the gospel (book) can be of help. In the ancient church, "the Gospels are part of the Orthodox liturgical tradition not only in their reading, but precisely as a *book*." This "is because, for the Church, the gospel book is a verbal icon of Christ's manifestation to and presence among us. Above all, it is an icon of his resurrection. The entrance with the gospels is therefore . . . the image of the appearance of the risen Lord."[31]

After analyzing the Johannine Easter account, we now turn to the Farewell Discourses. We have to limit ourselves to the question of how the evangelist (and probably also later authors from the community) "sets the stage" for the Easter and post-Easter liturgical assemblies of the community. If his version of the Easter account makes transparent allusions to the dominical assemblies of the Johannine community, we should consider whether the Farewell Discourses contain analogous references to the readers' contemporary experience. The question is whether Jesus' predictions, promises, and prophecies only relate to the (literary) disciples and their situation or whether they refer to later generations of believers. But first a brief look at the Farewell Discourses from a literary and editorial point of view is necessary.

3. Easter Account and the Farewell Discourses

That the Farewell Discourses and the Johannine passion and Easter narratives are closely related is no new discovery.[32] On the level of the final text, the Farewell Discourses stand on the threshold of the passion. Jesus addressed these discourses to the disciples, but only after Judas – and with

---

[31] Alexander Schmemann, *The Eucharist. Sacrament of the Kingdom* (Crestwood, N.Y.: St. Vladimir's Seminary Press, 1988), 71. He goes on to point out that in the liturgy the reading and proclamation of the word is preceded by its *appearance*. The solemn entrance with the gospels is "a joyous meeting with Christ, and this meeting is accomplished by means of the bringing out to us of this book of books, the book that is always transformed into power, life and sanctification."

[32] On this point, see among others Christian Dietzfelbinger, *Johanneischer Osterglaube* (ThSt 138; Zürich: Theologischer Verlag, 1992); Theobald, "Osterglaube"; Hans-Ulrich Weidemann, *Der Tod Jesu im Johannesevangelium. Die erste Abschiedsrede als Schlüsseltext für den Passions- und Osterbericht* (BZNW 122; Berlin-New York: Walter de Gruyter, 2004); Jean Zumstein, "Die Deutung der Ostererfahrung in den Abschiedsreden des Johannesevangeliums," *ZThK* 104 (2007): 117–41.

him Satan, who had gone into him (13:27) – had been sent away (13:30).³³ Before Judas returns with a whole Roman cohort and with servants of the high priests and Pharisees (18:3) – and with him the "Ruler of this World" (14:31) – Jesus uses the time with "his own" (John 13:1) to speak to them about what will happen, before it takes place (14:29).

It is noteworthy, that the Farewell Discourses show structural analogies to the Easter chapter (John 20). Again, it is not stated, *where* Jesus met with his disciples; indirectly, one can deduce that it is in Jerusalem (cf. 18:1), but it is not said so explicitly.³⁴ Jesus meets with his disciples in the evening, at the time of the principal meal (13:2, 4; δεῖπνον). Clearly, they are *inside* a building – for Judas, after taking the morsel *goes out* (ἐξῆλθεν). Outside, however, it is night (13:30).

> In his study "Worship in the Fourth Gospel," J.H. Neyrey – linking up with Mary Douglas and Bruce J. Malina – calls attention to the point that the Gospel of John abandons the notion of "fixed sacred space" (i.e., temple) for a notion of "fluid sacred space," namely the space occupied by *the group*.³⁵ In their relationship to Jesus, the group of the disciples constitutes a fluid sacred space replacing the fixed sacred space.³⁶ One can expand Neyrey's observation by attending to the structural similarity between John 13–17 and John 20. In these texts, it is the group around Jesus that stands in the foreground; concrete references to the place of their meeting remain in the background, though it is stated that the group is together in an interior room as contrasted to the "outside," where it is dark and dangerous.³⁷

A further structural analogy between the Farewell Discourses and John 20 lies in the fact that the presence of the reader is not only indicated by the reference to promises for the future; the presence of the figures mentioned in the narration is clearly devalued in comparison to the future presence of the community of readers. Thus it is not the Easter witnesses who are called blessed, but rather those who do not see and nevertheless believe (20:29).

In the Farewell Discourses it is conspicuous that, despite all the material and literary differences, two themes traverse the whole passage: the logion about prayer in the name of Jesus being heard (14:13–14; 15:7–8, 16;

---

³³ That Satan had entered Judas is a motif found in both Luke and John but not in Mark (see Luke 22:3 and John 13:27). Evidently this motif was found in the pre-Lukan/ pre-Johannine passion tradition.

³⁴ In contrast, Luke 22:10–13 par.

³⁵ Jerome H. Neyrey, "Worship in the Fourth Gospel. A Cultural Interpretation of John 14–17," *BTB* 36 (2006): 107–17.155–63, 158–59, 161–62.

³⁶ In contrast, Luke says that at least the Jerusalem Community continued to take part in the worship services in the temple (Acts 2:46; 3:1 and elsewhere; see also 21:26, 27–28).

³⁷ An analogy can be found in the description of the nightly Eucharistic worship service on the first day of the week in Troas (Acts 20:7–21) and the Christian Passover behind closed doors in Acts 12.

16:23–24, 26–27) and the five logia about the Paraclete (14:16–17, 26; 15:26; 16:7–11, 13–15). It is precisely these texts, decidedly pointing to the post-Easter time, that hold the Farewell Discourses together.[38]

There is general agreement that neither the Farewell Discourses (13:31–17:21) nor the passion and Easter accounts (John 18–21) are of one piece, though different explanations for this are to be found in the discussion. The principal argument for the disparity is based on the passage that seems to end the First Farewell Discourse (14:30–31) and on the text that concludes the Easter account in John 20, which has the character of an epilogue and a conclusion to the whole book. In both cases there are extensive texts that follow, and they betray a certain tension with respect to the preceding texts.[39] Thus, roughly speaking, the texts of John 15–17 in the context of the Farwell Discourses and the text of John 21 in the context of the Easter narratives can be viewed as updating continuations of the foregoing texts.[40] This suggests a prolonged growth process for the Fourth Gospel within the Johannine community.

> In recent years, the genesis of the Farewell Discourses has been the subject of much discussion. The model of "relecture" (= re-reading), applied by A. Dettwiler systematically to the whole corpus of the Farewell Discourses, has proven quite fruitful.[41] Dettwiler was able to demonstrate that the passage about the grapevine in 15:1–17 is a re-reading of the foot-washing scene in 13:1–17 and 13:34–35 and that the Farewell Discourse in 16:4b–33 is a re-reading of the First Farewell Discourse in 13:31–14:31.
>
> K. Haldimann takes up this result but emphasizes more than Dettwiler the coherence of the final text, taking account of the diachronic insights. In the context of a "redaction-historical" model, Haldimann attempts to demonstrate, on the one hand, the coherence of the final text and, on the other hand, to expand the prevailing notion

---

[38] This is demonstrated in the case of the saying about prayer being heard not only by the use of the future tense – John 14:13–14 (ποιήσω), 15:7 (γενήσεται ὑμῖν), 16:23 (δώσει ὑμῖν), 16:24 (λήμψεσθε), 16:26 (αἰτήσεσθε) – but also by the fact that, according to 14:14, the one to whom prayer of petition is addressed is Jesus himself (αἰτήσετέ με), something which naturally can refer only to the exalted and glorified Jesus. Moreover, in 16:23, 26, the prayer of petition is dated as occurring on "that day" (ἐν ἐκείνῃ τῇ ἡμέρᾳ, cf. 14:20; 20:19).

[39] Thus in John 14:30 Jesus says that he will "not much more" speak with his disciples (οὐκέτι πολλὰ λαλήσω μεθ' ὑμῖν), and in 14:31 he gives the signal to depart (ἐγείρεσθε, ἄγωμεν ἐντεῦθεν). Then the chapters 15–17 (almost three times as much discourse) follow without a break or transition. Significant in John 21 is the abrupt change of place (Galilee!) and the change in terminology (φανεροῦν instead of σημεῖα).

[40] See also Theobald, "Osterglaube," 93.

[41] Andreas Dettwiler, *Die Gegenwart des Erhöhten. Eine exegetische Studie zu den johanneischen Abschiedsreden (Joh 13,31–16,33) unter besonderer Berücksichtigung ihres Relecture-Charakters* (FRLANT 169; Göttingen: Vandenhoeck & Ruprecht, 1995).

of coherence to include diachronic insights.[42] Haldimann argues that in the last stage of redaction, "the earlier text was deliberately transformed into a coherent whole," thus contesting the view that the Farewell Discourses are the product of an anonymous process of growth. It is a property of the coherence of the final text that the linear character of the text development in chapters 13–16 is deliberately intended. For Haldimann, John 15–16 – in contrast to 13:31–14:31 – is not the product of an essentially homogeneous conception but rather the result of a prolonged redactional process.

Taking up and extending this line of interpretation, we may proceed as follows. First, according to 14:29, the First Farewell Discourse is to be interpreted as a key text for understanding the Johannine Easter account. In a second and third step, the significance of John 15–16 is then to be considered. In doing so one must take into account that, on the one hand (with Dettwiler, Haldimann and others), these texts *presuppose* John 13–14, constituting in part a *re-reading* of that passage; on the other hand (going beyond Dettwiler), one must also take into account that John 15–17 presupposes not only the First Farewell Discourse but also the passion and Easter accounts by the evangelist. The re-reading of the First Farewell Discourse likewise *presupposes John 20!* That 14:31 and 20:30–31 have been left standing shows, moreover, that the various redactors deliberately intended not to eliminate the connections indicated by these texts.

4. The First Farewell Discourse (John 13:31–14:31) as the Key to the Easter Account

With the First Farewell Discourse, the ground is laid for the narratively developed exposition of the Easter events in John 20. On the one hand, the pre-Easter circle of disciples is fitted out, before the passion and Easter events, with the information needed to understand these events when they take place later. On the other hand, it is made clear that for the pre-Easter circle of disciples, in contrast to the post-Easter community, the decisive presuppositions for such understanding were not yet available (cf. 7:39).

The basic problem of the First Farewell Discourse is formulated in 13:33: it is the departure (ὑπάγειν) of Jesus,[43] which implies the separation of Jesus from his disciples. This appears to put the disciples on the

---

[42] For what follows, see Konrad Haldimann, *Rekonstruktion und Entfaltung. Exegetische Untersuchungen zu Joh 15 und 16* (BZNW 2000; Berlin and New York: Walter de Gruyter, 2000), 39–42.

[43] Probably an older saying with sapiential background; see Michael Theobald, *Herrenworte im Johannesevangelium* (HBS 34; Freiburg: Herder, 2002), 424–55; Jürgen Becker, *Johanneisches Christentum. Seine Geschichte und Theologie im Überblick* (Tübingen: Mohr Siebeck, 2004), 101, 107–8.

same plane as the "Jews."[44] The basic similarity between the disciples and the Jews[45] is grounded in the fact that both groups will soon seek after him but that they will not able to get to where he is going. To put it more exactly, the separation that Jesus will shortly put between himself and both the "Jews" and "his own" disciples cannot be overcome by either the one or the other party by their own devices ("Where I am going, *you* cannot come"). In contrast to the Jews, however, a perspective beyond the separation is opened up for the disciples, as is shown by "the temporal qualification of the coming separation"[46] indicated by the phrase "so *now* I say to you" (καὶ ὑμῖν λέγω ἄρτι).

With his question, Κύριε, ποῦ ὑπάγεις; (13:36), Peter makes clear that he has not understood Jesus' statement. The answer that Jesus gives to Peter's query sharpens the problem, shifting the conversation to the theme of "following" (ἀκολουθεῖν) Jesus, unto death. By introducing the foretelling of Peter's betrayal (13:38) – a theme belonging to his older passion tradition[47] – the evangelist emphasizes the impossibility of "following" Jesus before Easter.

It is crucial to realize that Peter (like the other disciples, cf. 14:5, 8, 22) does not know what the readers already know. Thus from the very beginning of the Farewell Discourse, the readers (or hearers) of the text are reminded that their situation is *fundamentally different* from that of the figures in the story: "The situation of the community is not simply a repetition of that of the disciples."[48] This fundamental *difference* between the fictional narrative situation of the disciples on the evening before Jesus' death and the real situation of the readers is intended to oppose an all too quick identification of the two audiences. The readers are "in a better posi-

---

[44] Compare 13:33 with 7:33–34 and 8:21.

[45] Fernando F. Segovia, *The Farewell of the Word. The Johannine Call to Abide* (Minneapolis: Fortress, 1991), 74, n. 33.

[46] Segovia, *Farewell*, 78.

[47] Compare Luke 22:33–34 and Mark 14:29–30 par. Again the Lukan and the Johannine versions of the betrayal prediction are more closely related. In Luke as in John (against Mark), Peter addresses Jesus as κύριε and offers to lay down his life *before* his betrayal is predicted. In Mark, by way of contrast, Peter speaks of dying with Jesus only *after* the prediction. See Klein, *Lukasstudien*, 74; he overlooks, however, that also in Mark Peter expresses his readiness to die with Jesus (Mark 14:31).

[48] This is rightly emphasized by Klaus Berger, *Exegese des Neuen Testaments. Neue Wege vom Text zur Auslegung* (3d ed.; Heidelberg and Wiesbaden: Quelle & Meyer, 1991), 99, albeit in a different context. According to Berger, the misunderstandings of the Fourth Gospel serve as an *introduction to the Christian image-language*. The 'outsiders' in John's Gospel and the only 'insider,' Jesus himself, are in this position only from a literary point of view. The reader, however, should note the misunderstanding in the Gospel and should be protected against confusion (*ibid*, 230). In the same direction point the remarks of Bauckham, "Audience" 108–9.

tion than any of the characters in the story,"⁴⁹ and are in possession of the very knowledge that Peter and the other disciples lack in the literary situation.

As I pointed out before, the readers already know the "end of the story," so the aim of the Farewell Discourse is no to keep them in suspense about the outcome of the narrative, but rather to provide them with the specific Johannine interpretation of the Easter events. So the point of the discourse is not to impart *new* information, but rather to combine the passion and Easter traditions with other traditions; e.g., eschatological or ecclesiological proverbs. The effect of this literary technique is that "Easter" and "Parousia" traditions creatively influence each other.

With John 13:31–38, the evangelist has formulated the fundamental problem of the First Farewell Discourse and linked it to the context of the passion. In 14:1, a new section of the Farewell Discourse begins, one set off formally and content-wise. In contrast to 13:31–38, Jesus now speaks also about his "return" (πάλιν ἔρχομαι). Saying this and adding that he will come to take the believers to himself (καὶ παραλήμψομαι ὑμᾶς πρὸς ἐμαυτόν), he gives an initial answer to the problem marked off so sharply in 13:33–38.

With John 14:2–3, which is probably a traditional saying, the Johannine Jesus alludes to the *Parousia*. Notably, the return of Jesus is not fixed temporally or connected with other end-time events (e.g., the "sounding of the trumpets"); the saying thus remains open, which is a prerequisite for its being taken up by the Fourth Evangelist in the course of the Farewell Discourse. This openness, however, by no means prevents the reader, who it may be assumed is acquainted with the saying,⁵⁰ from relating it to the Parousia and the rapture of the believers.⁵¹ In this case, Jesus appears to foretell an event that even from the point of view of the reader is *located in the future*. That this is the case is suggested not only by the parallels (despite all differences) between this saying and other New Testament and early Christian conceptions of the Parousia, but also by the evident presence of such conceptions in the Johannine community.⁵²

---

⁴⁹ Bauckham, "Audience," 109.

⁵⁰ That is why Jesus says: "Would I have told you that I am going off to prepare a place for you? (εἰ δὲ μή, εἶπον ἂν ὑμῖν ὅτι πορεύομαι ἑτοιμάσαι τόπον ὑμῖν)." (14:2) Although there is no reference for this saying within the gospel itself, the formulation indicates that the audience is familiar with it.

⁵¹ Cf. for (πάλιν) ἔρχομαι: Mark 8:38 par. Matt 16:27 (Dan 7:13–14); Luke 9:26; Mark 13:26–27 and 1Thess 4:16; for παραλήμψομαι 1Thess 4:17 and Luke 17:34–35 (= Q); for ἑτοιμάζειν (τόπον) Rev 12:6; Matt 20:23; 25:34, 41; Heb 11:16. See Theobald, *Herrenworte*, 506–521.

⁵² Cf. John 21:22–23; 1 John 2:28; 3:2.

In the following verses the evangelist leads his hearers into the present time of the post-Easter community, i.e., into *their own present*. This is the intention of the sayings in 14:12–14, which from the point of view of the disciples in the story are formulated as a prediction of the future. They are expressed as amen-sayings, thus emphasizing their importance. The concrete connection to the passion narrative recedes at first into the background. The repetition of πορεύομαι at the beginning (14:2; cf. 13:3) and at the end (14:12) of the first part of the sayings about Jesus' departure represents an inclusion. In this connection 14:12 is particularly significant, for the statement ἐγὼ πρὸς τὸν πατέρα πορεύομαι *gives the grounds* (ὅτι) for the promise that those who believe in Jesus will perform even greater works (ἔργα) than Jesus himself performed. Thus the promise that the post-Easter period will be *a time of intensified salvation* rests on Jesus' departure. Immediately following this is the double promise that petitions in the name of Jesus will be heard (14:13–14), which gives precision to the promise of greater works by representing these as being *asked of* and *worked by* the exalted Jesus.[53] The post-Easter period is thus distinctly presented as a time of Jesus' working, in particular in the worshiping liturgical scene, for it is *there* that prayers of petition in the name of Jesus are offered by the assembled community.[54]

In the second major portion of the First Farewell Discourse (14:15–27), the evangelist comes to speak of the real theme, which he puts in the context of the preceding texts, namely *Easter as the return of Jesus*, that is to say, *Jesus' return as the Easter experience*. To understand the First Farewell Discourse also in reference to the following passion and Easter account, it is fundamental to see that the tradition cited in 14:2–3 receives *a twofold Johannine re-interpretation*, indicated by the keywords ἔρχομαι and μονή. In the first place, the promise πάλιν ἔρχομαι (14:3) finds fulfillment for the evangelist on *the day of Easter*. In this way, the reader of the Farewell Discourse learns that the "Parousia" spoken of in 14:2–3 has already occurred, namely on Easter. After the death of Jesus, the disciples are by no means orphans, for they will see him after a short time (14:19: θεωρεῖτέ με). As in Rev 2:5 and 2:16, the coming of Jesus does not refer to the Parousia. The fact that the cosmos *does not* see Jesus proves that here the Parousia is not intended (cf. 14:22, in contrast to Mark 13:26). The promise of life (καὶ ὑμεῖς ζήσετε) follows upon the Easter vision of the living Jesus. However, the evangelist reformulates the experience of *seeing*, which is a privilege of the Easter witnesses, into an act of *knowing* (John 14:20: γνώσεσθε) and thus opens up broader access to the Easter ex-

---

[53] However the final clause, ἵνα δοξασθῇ ὁ πατὴρ ἐν τῷ υἱῷ, makes clear that Father and Son act together and in unity (see 14:1, 10–11 and 14:23).

[54] See Theobald, *Herrenworte*, 167.

perience.⁵⁵ "Easter" thus becomes the knowledge of the mutual immanence of Jesus and the believers: the visible perception of the Risen One is no longer essential. This knowledge is dated to "that day" (ἐν ἐκείνῃ τῇ ἡμέρᾳ), which does not mean some day to come but, as the wording of 20:19 indicates, the day of Easter.⁵⁶ The expansion of the reciprocal immanence statement in 14:20 is a prolepsis of 20:17, where for the first time in the Johannine narrative, the God and Father of Jesus is said to be the God and Father of the disciples.⁵⁷ Then, by way of conclusion in 20:30–31, the *writing down* (γέγραπται) of the Easter *semeia* in the book of the gospel, which makes the Easter appearances accessible to all believers who "do not see," is connected with the promise of life (cf. 20:31: ἵνα πιστεύοντες ζῆν ἔχετε with 14:19).

In contrast to the figures in the story, for whom both the Parousia and Easter are still in the future, the reader or hearer in the Johannine community *looks back* upon the Parousia which was fulfilled at Easter. Nevertheless, the reinterpretation of 14:2–3 by 14:18–20 does not yet reach its climax and endpoint. With the repetition of μονή creating a keyword link between 14:2–3 and 14:23, the evangelist shows that the events spoken of in 14:2–3, which clearly reflects the end-time Parousia of Christ, are also realized in the life of the individual believer. Thus the evangelist pursues here what may be called the "Vergrundsätzlichung von Ostern" (= foundation-making of Easter), i.e., the postulation of Easter as the basis of Christian belief.⁵⁸ The expressions ἔρχομαι πρὸς ὑμᾶς (14:18, cf. 20:19, 26) and ὑμεῖς δὲ θεωρεῖτέ με (14:19, cf. 20:19–20, 26–27) are thus made into models for the expressions ἐμφανίσω αὐτῷ ἐμαυτόν (14:21) and πρὸς αὐτὸν ἐλευσόμεθα καὶ μονὴν παρ' αὐτῷ ποιησόμεθα (14:23), which are said of *each and every individual believer*, whereby 14:23 clearly is given greater emphasis by the additional mention of *the coming of the Father* to the believer (a statement missing in the context of 14:18–20).

Easter thus finds a kind of counterpart in the individual biography of the believer. This counterpart is by no means inferior to the Easter experience but rather surpasses it. Not only has the decisive event *already taken place*,⁵⁹ it *now takes place* in the presence of the reader and hearer of the

---

⁵⁵ Zumstein, "Deutung," 125–26.

⁵⁶ 20:19: οὔσης οὖν ὀψίας τῇ ἡμέρᾳ ἐκείνῃ τῇ μιᾷ σαββάτων, cf. Brown, *Gospel according to John II*, 1019: "It would not be at all unlikely that John would regard as the eschatological day this Sunday on which, through the gift of the spirit, Jesus makes possible his permanent presence among his followers."

⁵⁷ Zumstein, "Deutung, 123, cf. 128.

⁵⁸ Cf. Dettwiler, *Gegenwart*, 195–202. Similarly Zumstein, "Deutung," 126: "Entschränkung der Ostererfahrung."

⁵⁹ In the "classical" formulation of Rudolf Bultmann, "The Eschatology of the Gospel of John" (orig. 1928), in *Faith and Understanding I* (trans. L. P. Smith; ed. R. W. Funk;

gospel, even though the physical "seeing" of the Risen One is absent and thus no longer mentioned in 14:21–24 (cf. 20:29!). The Easter event which, for the disciples in the story is still a future event, is in fact both past and present for the hearers of the gospel. By the transformation of the traditional logion concerning the many dwellings in the Father's house (14:2–3) into a saying about the indwelling of the Father and the Son in the individual believer (14:23), it becomes clear that for the evangelist the Parousia *has already taken place at Easter* and that – at the same time because of that! – the Easter events are the "archetypes" of Jesus coming to the individual believer. Thus in these verses is contained the whole program for the literary formulation of the Easter stories and their narrative and terminological presentation as *semeia* in a liturgical context.[60]

Strikingly, this reinterpretation of 14:2–3 in 14:18–24 is "framed" by the two Paraclete-logia (14:16–17, 26). Structurally, these sayings are fully imbedded in their individual contexts, but it is striking that the evangelist comes to speak of the Paraclete at the *beginning* and at the *end* of this passage. Thus, making Easter foundational and making the Parousia present, so that the post-Easter period can be identified as the real time of salvation, are done on the basis of Johannine Christology and pneumatology, whereby the first represents the *factual basis* and the second the *horizon*.

The Johannine Jesus speaks of the gift of the Spirit-Paraclete and of "Pentecost" (14:16–17), *before* he comes to speak of Easter (14:18–20). Analogously, the water flows from the side of the crucified Jesus (19:34) before he comes to the disciples at Easter (20:19).[61] In the Paraclete-logion the circle of the literary hearers (ὑμεῖς) is already transcended, as is made clear by the final clause ἵνα μεθ' ὑμῶν εἰς τὸν αἰῶνα ᾖ (14:16c). The ὑμεῖς spoken of at the level of the story are the first of a long series of re-

---

New York and Evanston: Harper & Row, 1969), 165–83, 175: "Therefore it is not true that the *Parousia* expected by others as an event to occur in time is denied by John or transformed into an event in the soul, an experience. John rather opens the reader's eyes to see that the *Parousia has already occurred*! The naïve division into a first and a second coming which we find elsewhere has been discarded."

[60] David E. Aune, *The Cultic Setting of Realized Eschatology in Early Christianity* (NovTSup 28; Leiden: Brill 1972), 126–27, 129 concludes, that the "coming" of Jesus in the relevant passages from John 14 refers primarily to the recurring cultic "coming" of Jesus in form of a pneumatic or prophetic *visio Christi* within the setting of worship "in the Spirit" as celebrated by the Johannine community. Unfortunately, he does not take chapter 20 into account in his study.

[61] Cf. John 19:34 with 4:10–14 and 7:37–39. In John 4 and 7, the "(living) water" is clearly a metaphor for the Holy Spirit. Taking these texts together with the first Paraclete saying (14:16), it becomes clear that the scene with the lance (19:34) represents the fulfillment of the promise made to the Samaritan woman (4:10, 14) and again on the last day of the Feast of Tabernacles (7:37–39).

cipients of the Spirit reaching up to the present of the reader; however, they are "only" the first of such recipients.

In John 14:28, the Johannine Jesus looks back at the whole discourse, summarizes the content under a single point (ὑπάγω καὶ ἔρχομαι πρὸς ὑμᾶς), and gives the instruction to relate the content of the discourse to the coming events, in order that the discourse may achieve its goal (ἵνα ὅταν γένηται πιστεύσητε, 14:29).

The mention of the coming of the Ruler of the World (14:30–31) fits in well at this point. The reader is thus prepared to properly locate the coming of Judas, which will soon be reported (18:1–3). With Judas comes the Ruler of the World (13:27), whose appearance introduces the end-time events. *This means that not only the Parousia but also the coming of the Ruler of the World (and the victory over him) already lie behind the Johannine community* (cf. 12:31–32; 14:30–31; 16:11, 33; 18:5–6).

6. Inside and Outside: the Second Farewell Discourse (John 15:1 – 16:4a)

There follows the Second Farewell Discourse (15:1–16:4a),[62] which has in focus the post-Easter reality of the Church.[63] The Vine-Discourse (15:1–8) together with its immediately following supplement (15:9–11) functions as the base text. Here *the relationship between the disciples and Jesus* is elaborated "anachronistically" under the supposition of Jesus' elevation[64] – and thus in the light of the Easter chapter, John 20. Jesus' first charge, μείνατε ἐν ἐμοί (15:4) presupposes the knowledge promised "for that day," namely for Easter (14:20, cf. 20:19), that "you are in me and I am in you" (14:20). This presupposes the fulfillment of the promise of the μοναί for the believers (14:2–3), that is, respectively the making of a μονή with the believer (14:23).[65]

In John 15:12–17, there follows the command of mutual love within the community, a text which is framed by the clause ἵνα ἀγαπᾶτε ἀλλήλους

---

[62] Regarding the delineation and structure of this discourse, see Theobald, *Herrenworte*, 415–16.

[63] Theobald, *Herrenworte*, 416: Perhaps the redactors were acquainted with the traditional location of the eucharist theme within the Last Supper of Jesus.

[64] On this point, see D. François Tolmie, *Jesus' Farewell to the Disciples. John 13:1 – 17:26 in Narratological Perspective* (BIS 12; Leiden.: Brill, 1995), 154–55. It is noteworthy that most of the verbs having Jesus as their subject are in the aorist or perfect tenses. Thus Ulrich Wilckens, *Das Evangelium nach Johannes* (NTD 4; Göttingen: Vandenhoeck & Ruprecht, 1998), 236, rightly observes: "the pre-Easter viewpoint of farewell and promise is transformed into the post-Easter viewpoint of enduring union with Jesus."

[65] See Haldimann, *Rekonstruktion*, 405.

(15:12, 17). Beginning in 15:18, Jesus announces to the disciples the *future* of the community (which is the *present* for the reader).⁶⁶ The central theme is now the hatred of the world for the community.⁶⁷ The strict division between the true vine and the κόσμος, which is presupposed here is in fact already indirectly indicated in 15:6, where it is stated that those who do not remain in Jesus will be "thrown *outside*" (ἐβλήθη ἔξω). In 15:18–16:4a, the "outside" is defined as the realm of the hostile cosmos, which "hates" and "persecutes" first Jesus, and then his disciples.

The Vine-Discourse as a whole thus links up with the situation described in 20:19–23 (20:26–29), concretely with *the worshiping and liturgical* situation of the post-Easter community of the disciples in which the Easter appearances were located, namely "inside" (20:26: ἔσω) behind locked doors (20:19, 26), where the Sunday assembly of the community takes place.

The fact that the Second Farewell Discourse presupposes the situation of chapter 20 is shown in a variety of ways: (1) In order to thematize the relationship between Jesus, the Father, and the disciples, the author introduces Jesus' discourse with a traditional text (15:1–2, 5–6).⁶⁸ which presumably had its place in the *eucharistic* liturgy of the Johannine community.⁶⁹ Significant in this connection is the immanence-promise in 15:5–6, which links the Vine Discourse with the eucharistic supplement to the Bread Discourse (6:51–58).⁷⁰

---

⁶⁶ Note the future tense in 15:20, 21, 26; 16:2, 3. Programmatic for 15:18–16:4a are the texts 15:20 and 16:1, 4a, whereby particularly in 15:20 and 16:4 the keyword "remember" appears: when the events later occur, the disciples should "remember" that Jesus had foretold them.

⁶⁷ Seven times the word μισεῖν appears in 15:18, 19, 23, 24, 25.

⁶⁸ See Theobald, *Herrenworte*, 404–9. The tradition is evident in 15:1–2, 5–6. Striking is the tension between 15:2 (the Father purges [καθαίρει] the vine) and 15:3 (the disciples are already purged [καθαροί ἐστε] through Jesus' word). This is best explained by understanding verse 3 as a commentary to the older verse 2 (see also 13:10). And by contrast to the old verses 15:1–2, verse 4 makes a *comparison* (καθώς . . . οὕτως . . .).

⁶⁹ Thus one encounters the "vine" (ἄμπελος) in the chalice thanksgiving in the *Didache* (*Did.* 9:1–2), but also in Jewish meal prayers, whose date however is uncertain. In John 15:1–2, as in John 6:35, the eucharistic term (ἄρτος, ἄμπελος) is put in a christological context through ἐγώ εἰμι, something typically Johannine. Further arguments in Wilckens, *Johannes*, 242–43, and in Theobald, *Herrenworte*, 410–15. A "tree of life" likewise appears in a eucharistic context in Rev 22:6–21, a text full of liturgical allusions; see also Rev 22:2, 14 and Rev 22:16 ("I am . . . the root").

⁷⁰ Expressions of immanence are not typical of the imagery of the vine and thus in the context of John 15 they catch the eye. Above all it is striking that *only* in John 6:56 and in John 15:5–6 is a reciprocal immanence between Jesus and his disciples expressed through the verb μένειν. This connection between the thought of a mutual immanence of Jesus and his disciples expressed with μένειν would appear to belong to an older Johannine eucharistic tradition. See Michael Theobald, "Eucharistie in John 6. Vom pneumat-

(2) In both of the passages of the discourse that are directed "inwards" (15:1–11, 12–17), the Johannine Jesus explicitly refers to *the promise that prayer will be heard* (15:7, 16).[71] With this reference to the assembly of the community and its liturgical prayer,[72] the Vine Discourse links up with the post-Easter worship situation of the community, as this is suggested in John 20.

(3) The first major section of the discourse closes with Jesus' remark: "I have said these things to you so that my joy (ἡ χαρὰ ἡ ἐμή) may be in you, and that your joy (ἡ χαρὰ ὑμῶν) may be complete (πληρωθῇ)" (15:11). This remark presupposes the Easter joy of the disciples, as it is awakened by the self-identification of the Risen One in 20:20.[73] The striking formulation ἡ χαρὰ ὑμῶν πληρωθῇ shows that the author of chapter 15 views the joy at seeing the Risen One as only *the beginning*, a beginning that is brought to perfection only after Easter.[74]

(4) In direct connection with the notion of the "completion of Easter joy," the author develops in 15:12–17 his conception of *intensification of discipleship*. In doing so, he emphasizes the motif of *friendship*.[75] Friendship with Jesus is realized in keeping his commandments (15:14) and receiving his instructions (15:15).[76] This represents a correction to 13:12–

---

ologischen zum inkarnationstheologischen Verstehensmodell," in *Johannesevangelium – Mitte oder Rand des Kanons? Neue Standortbestimmungen* (ed. Thomas Söding; QD 203; Freiburg.: Herder, 2003), 178–257, 222–23.

[71] In 15:7, the promise of prayer being heard is put under the condition (ἐάν) of "remaining" in the immanence; it thus has a eucharistic foundation (see above, note 70). In 15:16, this promise is linked with the theme of fruit-bearing, which otherwise goes unmentioned in 15:12–17 and thus refers back to the "eucharistic" first part of the Vine Discourse.

[72] Theobald, *Herrenworte*, 415.

[73] John 20:20: ἐχάρησαν οὖν οἱ μαθηταὶ ἰδόντες τὸν κύριον. Compare Luke 24:52 (μετὰ χαρᾶς), and also the perplexing formulation in Luke 24:41: ἔτι δὲ ἀπιστούντων αὐτῶν ἀπὸ τῆς χαρᾶς. Klein, *Lukasevangelium*, 737, surmises that Luke here has expanded his tradition with "in their joy" (as an excuse for the disciples? See Acts 13:14). However, he also suggests, on the basis of John 20:20, that the joy of the disciples might originally have been mentioned in Luke's source. But see also Matt 28:8 (the Easter joy of the women).

[74] πληροῦν with the accusative (τὴν χαράν) means in John 15:11 (compare 16:24; 17:13) as in Phil 2:2 "bringing something as yet incomplete to completion," see Walter Bauer, *Griechisch-deutsches Wörterbuch zu den Schriften des Neuen Testaments und der frühchristlichen Literatur* (ed. K. and B. Aland; 6th ed.; Berlin and New York: Walter de Gruyter, 1988), 1349. The same holds for λύπη, compare 16:6 (ἡ λύπη πεπλήρωκεν ὑμῶν τὴν καρδίαν)!

[75] Also in Luke 12:4, Jesus speaks of his disciples as his friends; see also Acts 27:3 and 3 John 15 ("friend" as a self-designation for Christians).

[76] See also Theobald, "Jünger," 244: "To be a disciple would thus appear to be merely the *first stage* of initiation into the following of Jesus; the *second* stage would then be

16,[77] which however presupposes 20:17,[78] where, talking to Mary Magdalene, Jesus for the first time in the gospel (!) speaks of the disciples as his *brothers* (ἀδελφοί μου).[79] It is only through his elevation and glorification that the disciples are put into a new relationship to Jesus and to God. In contrast to the Hellenistic ethic of friendship, however, the relationship of friendship to Jesus is by no means one of equality.[80] Prayer is the expression of friendship with Jesus.[81]

(5) Again in the context of John 20, John 15:18–16:4a presents a fundamental reflection about the relationship of the community to the "outside." The fact that the disciples on Easter evening keep the doors shut "for fear of the Jews" (20:19; cf. 20:26) is further developed by the author of John 15 by indicating that the threat to the community described in 15:18–16:4a is concretely the work of "the Jews." It is clear that the expression "world" refers to "the Jews" who are hostile to the Johannine community. This is already suggested where Jesus says that the cosmos first hated him (15:18: ἐμὲ πρῶτον μεμίσηκεν).[82] Shortly thereafter it is made more concrete, where Jesus speaks of "persecution" (15:20: ἐμὲ ἐδίωξαν), a clear reference to John 5:16, where Jesus' persecution by "the Jews" is re-

---

represented by the intimacy of friendship founded on receipt of Jesus' knowledge through instruction. One might ask whether a special self-awareness of the Johannine community comes to expression here, putting them on a higher plane than the Christians of the greater church?" The expression of this imparting of knowledge to the Johannine Christians would then be the Gospel of John itself, which was read in the liturgy and in which is written "everything that I have heard from my Father" (15:15).

[77] In the course of the second interpretation of the footwashing, Jesus speaks of himself as κύριος (13:14, compare verse 13: εἰμί) and indirectly of his disciples as δοῦλοι. In John 15:15, this way of speaking is abrogated (οὐκέτι λέγω ὑμᾶς δούλους). See Tolmie, *Farewell*, 155.

[78] Perhaps the perfect εἴρηκα and the aorist ἐγνώρισα in 15:15 refer to this event.

[79] Compare John 21:23. "Brothers" appears as a self-designation of the Johannine community members in 1 John 2:9–11; 3:10, 12–17; 4:20–21, 5:16; 3 John 3:5, 10. "Friends" appears in 3 John 15. According to the Gospel of John, both "brotherhood" and "friendship" receive their foundation only in Jesus' death.

[80] The friendship with Jesus is founded in his act of love (15:13) and his election (15:16). Moreover, though he calls the disciples φίλοι μου (compare 11:11, where Lazarus is called ὁ φίλος ἡμῶν), he does not speak of himself as friend of the disciples.

[81] As in John 15:15–16, the theme of friendship with God is connected with prayer as in Epictetus, *Disc.* 2.17.29: καὶ εἰς τὸν οὐρανὸν ἀναβλέπειν ὡς φίλον τοῦ θεοῦ. The phrase "looking up to heaven" suggests prayer. For a more thorough discussion, see Erik Peterson, "Der Gottesfreund. Beiträge zur Geschichte eines religiösen Terminus," *ZKG* 42 (1923): 161–202, 170.

[82] Perhaps the statement "I have chosen you out of the world" (John 15:19) is meant to indicate the Jewish origin of the disciples.

ported.⁸³ It becomes fully clear in 15:22–24, where Jesus refers to his preaching and his deeds performed "among *them*" and then speaks of the fulfillment of "the word that is written in *their law*" (ἐν τῷ νόμῳ αὐτῶν!) (15:25, cf. 7:19; 8:17: 10:34).⁸⁴ In 16:1–4a, the text is then concretized with reference to the disciples (ὑμεῖς): Jesus foretells their exclusion from the synagogues and their martyrdom, which is seen as performing "worship (λατρεία) to God."⁸⁵

The equation of "world" and "Jews" is expressed in 18:20 and is presupposed in 15:1–16:4a. Jesus' public speaking "to the world" takes place concretely in his teaching in the synagogue and in the temple, "where all the Jews (!) come together."⁸⁶

(6) In this connection – in contrast to John 14 – the theme of sin is introduced (15:22–24). This theme is likewise present in the Johannine Easter account as the power to forgive or retain sins (20:23) and would appear to belong to the pre-Johannine Easter account.⁸⁷ The author of John 15 here makes clear that sin in the strict sense of the term only becomes possible through the rejection of Jesus.⁸⁸ For this thesis, he offers two witnesses (compare Deut 19:15 and John 8:13, 18), namely Jesus' speaking to "them" (ἐλάλησα αὐτοῖς) and the works (τὰ ἔργα) that he performed "among them."

(7) As with the promise of prayer being heard, the author of John 15 also takes up the Paraclete theme of John 14. It is noteworthy, however, that in 15:26 (ὃν ἐγὼ πέμψω ὑμῖν) and again in 16:7 (πέμψω αὐτὸν πρὸς

---

⁸³ The διώκειν of the Jews is accentuated in 5:18 into a desire for their death; compare 7:1, 19, 25, 30; 8:37, 40; 11:53; 18:14.

⁸⁴ See Christian Dietzfelbinger, *Der Abschied des Kommenden. Eine Auslegung der johanneischen Abschiedsreden* (WUNT 95; Tübingen: Mohr Siebeck, 1997), 163: "With the mention of *nomos*, it finally becomes clear, where the threat to the community comes from, namely from the synagogue, for which the *nomos*, the Torah, marks the center."

⁸⁵ It is also clear from the formulation in 16:2 that the attacks come from the side of the Jews (λατρείαν προφέρειν τῷ θεῷ).

⁸⁶ See the structural analysis and interpretation in Weidemann, *Tod*, 289–91.

⁸⁷ See John 20:23 together with Luke 24:47. Whereas the announcement in Luke that in the name of Jesus "repentance for the forgiveness of sins will be proclaimed to all nations" betrays strong Lukan influence, John 20:23 would appear to have preserved an older, two-part commission formula (see Klein, *Lukasstudien*, 67–68). For this interpretation speak not only the tradition-historical connection with Matt 18:18 (16:19) but also the fact that John 20:23 speaks of "sins" in the plural. In contrast to Matt 18:18 (with its inner-ecclesial orientation), John 20:23 (with its mission orientation) represents an older version of an originally independent logion, which reached the Fourth Evangelist in the context of his pre-Johannine Easter tradition (convincingly argued in Theobald, *Herrenworte*, 193).

⁸⁸ See Haldimann, *Rekonstruktion*, 251.

ὑμᾶς) it is *Jesus* who sends the Paraclete.[89] This evidently presupposes the Easter scene in 20:21–22, in which Jesus sends forth the disciples and breathes into them the Spirit. Analogously to the sending of Jesus by the Father, the sending of the disciples through Jesus is connected with the gift of the Spirit (cf. 1:29–34). This Easter sending of the disciples is accentuated in 15:26 as the witness to Christ produced by the Paraclete, which becomes audible in the witness of the disciples (15:27). For in contrast to the two Paraclete sayings in the First Farewell discourse, the Paraclete saying in 15:26 does not thematize the working of the Spirit "within,"[90] but rather speaks in the context of 15:18–16:4a (where the relationship of the community to the surrounding "world" is thematized) about the μαρτυρεῖν of the Spirit-Paraclete (15:26) and of the community (15:27). The context makes clear that what is at stake is the witness to Christ given by the Spirit-Paraclete in the situation of hatred, persecution, expulsion from the synagogue, and condemnation to death.

7. The Transition from Grief to Joy. Easter as a Symbol for Christian Existence in the Third Farewell Discourse (16:4b–33)

With John 16:4b, the theme and the context of the Farewell Discourses is again shifted.[91] In contrast to the Vine Discourse, it is again the situation of leave-taking that is evoked (16:5: νῦν δὲ ὑπάγω), thus clearly connecting to the First Farewell Discourse. Unlike that text, however, the author here accentuates the despondent reaction of the *disciples* to the coming separation.[92] Thus the focus has been shifted from that of the First Farewell Discourse, where this motif is also encountered (14:1, 27), but it recedes into the background in contrast to the development of christological and eschatological themes.

The Third Farewell Discourse begins with a brief introduction, announcing the basic motif (16:4b–7). A double Paraclete saying (16:8–11,

---

[89] This differs from the Paraclete-saying in the First Farewell Discourse. According to John 14:16, 26, it is the Father who "gives" or "sends" the Spirit-Paraclete, although at the bidding of Jesus (14:16) or in the name of Jesus (14:26).

[90] In John 14:16–17, it is said, that the Paraclete will "be with you forever," will "abide with you" and will "be in you." In 14:26 it is said that the Spirit-Paraclete "will teach you (!) everything, and remind you (!) of all that I have said to you (!)."

[91] On the structure and delineation of the Third Farewell Discourse (John 16:4b–33), see Dettwiler, *Gegenwart*, 213–16.

[92] This is also shown by the contradiction between 13:36; 14:5, where the disciples ask Jesus where he is going, and 16:5, where they are reduced to silence.

13–15) follows. Jesus' departure is the presupposition for the coming of the Paraclete and thus his death is an "advantage" for the disciples. Again *Jesus* sends the Paraclete. The first saying (16:8–11) thematizes the relationship of the Paraclete to the κόσμος, the second (16:13–15) deals with the activity of the Paraclete *ad intra*, concretely, with reference to the ὑμεῖς. In contrast to 14:26, however, the activity of the Paraclete is not related to the past (the works of the earthly Jesus), but rather to the *future*.

The first task is to "prove the world wrong (ἐλέγξει τὸν κόσμον; cf. 3:20; 8:46) about sin and righteousness and judgment." R. Bultmann called attention to the absence of the article in front of these three terms linked by περί and has rightly concluded that "what is at stake is not three *instances* but three *notions* of sin, righteousness and judgment," in short, "what do ἁμαρτία, δικαιοσύνη, and κρίσις *mean*?"[93] Sin is then clearly defined as lack of faith in Jesus (16:9). Jesus' righteousness is shown forth in his death, which is not the expression of a separation from God but rather the contrary: "that I am going to the Father."[94] Furthermore, his righteousness manifests itself in that "you will see me no longer." Inasmuch as the believers no longer see Jesus because he has gone to the Father, they show themselves to be "blessed" in the sense of 20:29! The concluding "definition" of judgment (16:11) now makes fully clear what was adumbrated in the beginning of the Paraclete saying, namely, that the judgment has already taken place; "the ruler of this world has been condemned."[95] The task of the Paraclete thus consists in "uncovering" this eschatological victory, which has already taken place. Note, however, that this must be understood in the Johannine sense: the ruler of the world has by no means been annihilated, but through Jesus' death on the cross he has definitively been separated from the community (cf. 12:31–32; 13:27, 30; 14:30; 18:5–6; and also 1 Corinthians 5).[96]

With the fifth and last Paraclete saying, the open-ended character of revelation is thematized.[97] R. Bieringer, in the context of an extensive dis-

---

[93] Rudolf Bultmann, *Das Evangelium des Johannes* (21st ed.; KEK II; Göttingen: Vandenhoeck & Ruprecht, 1986), 433–34.

[94] Jesus as δίκαιος appears also in 1 John 1:9; 2:1, 29; 3:7. This motif is likewise found in the Lukan death scene: the fact that Jesus at the ninth hour (cf. Acts 3:1) gives up his spirit to the Father, fully trusting in God and with Ps 31:6 on his lips, demonstrates for the god-fearing centurion that he was just (δίκαιος ἦν) (Luke 23:46–47, cf. Acts 3:14; 7:52; 22:14).

[95] Note the perfect tense κέκριται in John 16:11 and the similar ἐγὼ νενίκηκα τὸν κόσμον in 16:33. This means that the devil will not finally be condemned only at the end of time, as for example in Rev 22:10, 14 (see also 1 Cor 15:26).

[96] For details, see Weidemann, *Tod*, 423–50 ("Der Teufel und das Blut des Lammes").

[97] Dettwiler, *Gegenwart*, 234, rightly speaks here of a "Leerstelle" (= blank).

cussion of the variant readings in 16:13, has shown that the history of the texts demonstrates a tendency "of mitigating the revelatory role of the Spirit and avoiding a competition with the revelatory activity of Jesus."[98] However, the connection between 16:12 and 16:16 indicates that "the earthly Jesus has many more things to tell the disciples which they cannot yet bear. What Jesus cannot complete, will be done by the Paraclete in close union with Jesus."[99] It is debated, whether under τὰ ἐρχόμενα the events of the passion and Easter (cf. 16:16, 22, 28) or "the whole future of the post-Easter church"[100] is intended. In the second case, τὰ ἐρχόμενα would refer to the λύπη and the θλίψις of the community, as these are concretized in 16:1–4. However, the text that follows and above all the complex relationships between chapters 14, 16, and 20 demonstrate that such an alternative is falsely postulated: Instead, Easter is so described in 16:16–33 as to become the symbol for the experience of the community and its further history.

For all of the Paraclete sayings one can assume a liturgical Sitz im Leben. In the early Christian worship service, three things occur: (1) the "remembrance" of Jesus' words, (2) the "conviction" of the world (the revelation of unbelief in Jesus as constituting sin, the proclamation of Jesus' return to the Father, and the ultimate victory over the ruler of the world), and (3) the proclamation of the "things to come." That the Paraclete will also announce future events, hints at the phenomenon of early Christian prophecy, which was evidently still active in the worship services of the Johannine community.[101] Specific for the Johannine form of spirit-worked

---

[98] Reimund Bieringer, "The Spirit's Guidance into all the Truth. The Text-Critical problems of John 16,13," in *New Testament Textual Criticism and Exegesis* (ed. A. Denaux; BETL 161; Leuven: Leuven University Press, 2002), 183–207, 206. Bieringer makes a convincing case for the reading in Codex B (ὁδηγήσει εἰς τὴν ἀλήθειαν πᾶσαν - ἀκούσει).

[99] Bieringer, "Guidance," 205, cf. 201: "If one interprets 16:13b in the light of 16:12 and correlates πᾶσα with πολλά, it is hard to see how one could avoid the conclusion that the Spirit will reveal things that Jesus did not reveal."

[100] Wilckens, *Johannes*, 252; Dietzfelbinger, *Abschied*, 193–94.

[101] See Acts 11:27–28 (the prophet Agabus foretold a famine διὰ τοῦ πνεύματος); Acts 21:11 (through Agabus the Holy Spirit predicts – τάδε λέγει τὸ πνεῦμα τὸ ἅγιον – Paul's capture). On the early Christian prophets see also Acts 13:1–3; 15:32, and Did 11–13. On Sunday (!) the Seer of Patmos is seized by the spirit, though not in a liturgical situation: see Rev 1:10 (ἐγενόμην ἐν πνεύματι ἐν τῇ κυριακῇ ἡμέρᾳ), also Rev 19:10 (ἡ γὰρ μαρτυρία Ἰησοῦ ἐστιν τὸ πνεῦμα τῆς προφητείας, likewise Rev 13:1–2 and 11:27–30). For Paul, prophecy counts as a charism (1 Cor 12:10.28) and is exercised in the *worship service* (1 Cor 14:4–39). The connection between prophecy, foretelling the future, and the Holy Spirit is documented also in Justin Martyr, *Apol* 1.31.1, who writes about the Old Testament prophets: "There were, then, among the Jews certain men who were prophets of God, through whom the prophetic Spirit published beforehand things

prophecy, however, is the radical connection with Christology, even in the foretelling of the future (16:13–15).

The Paraclete sayings are followed immediately by a groundbreaking statement by Jesus: "A little while (μικρόν), and you will no longer see me, and again a little while (καὶ πάλιν μικρόν), and you will see me" (16:16). This statement gives rise to a circuitous discussion among the disciples, dealing in essence with the μικρόν (16:17–19: τί ἐστιν τοῦτο τὸ μικρόν;). Jesus' reply – accentuated as a solemn amen-saying – begins by calling attention to the Easter experience as described in chapter 20: There one finds the theme of weeping (κλαίειν), namely, the weeping of Mary Magdalene (20:11, 13, 15; cf. 16:20), and also the theme of the doors locked out of fear (φόβος) (20:19). At the sight of the Risen One, identified by his wounds, the disciples rejoice (χαίρειν) (20:19–20, cf. 16:22). However, precisely the comparison between chapter 16 and chapter 20 shows that the mourning and the joy spoken of in chapter 16 has been extended and generalized[102] in a way that *goes far beyond* John 20. Furthermore, the mourning of the disciples is contrasted with the joy of the cosmos.

All this makes possible an *identification* of the reader with the literary situation of the disciples.[103] In contrast to the First Farewell Discourse, the readers should recognize their own situation of persecution and fear in Jesus' clear predictions. The Third Farewell Discourse, like the Second, evokes a parallel between the present and the imminent future of the *disciples*, who are filled with sadness, and the situation of the Johannine *community*. It is possible that the Johannine community increasingly identified itself with the abandoned disciples, contrasting the original intention of chapter 14, doubting the presence of the risen Lord in their midst. The Third Farewell Discourse focuses on demonstrating that the Easter experience and the encounter with the risen Lord occur in *this* very situation. Moreover, the situation of sadness and despair, even persecution, is an element of the basic human condition in which the Easter resurrection is repeatedly experienced. The disciples' situation "in the world" (16:33) is in no way simply ended by the appearances of Christ, since Easter bears the promise of encountering the victorious resurrected Lord.

Thus Chr. Dietzfelbinger has with good reason called attention to the fact that the statement ὑμεῖς οὖν νῦν μὲν λύπην ἔχετε in 16:22 de-

---

that were to come to pass, ere ever they happened (προεκήρυξε τὰ γενήσεσθαι μέλλοντα πρὶν ἃ γενέσθαι)."

[102] John 16:20 speaks not only of the disciples' "weeping" (!) but also of their "mourning" (!) and their "pain" (!). Furthermore, the nouns λύπη and χαρά appear repeatedly. According to 16:6. the λύπη of the disciples is "completed" (πεπλήρωκεν).

[103] Dettwiler, *Gegenwart*, 251.

scribes not only the literary situation of the disciples at the threshold of the Passion but also the oppressive situation of the community in the present. The same holds for the promised transition from mourning into joy: "What the disciples on Easter experienced for the first time and in a fundamental way – the text does not do without past experiences – is repeated in the post-Easter existence of the disciples whenever the abandoned and sorrowing community recalls the presence of Jesus."[104]

Thus it becomes clear that the Easter stories narrated in John 20 – with their transition from weeping to gladdening encounter with Jesus, from fear to joy in the light of 16:16–24 –become stories about the very *basic structure of Christian existence itself*. The existence of the believers is fundamentally characterized by the transition from mourning and distress to Easter joy. The metaphor of the woman in labor (16:21–22) reinforces the idea that without the experience of sorrow and pain there can be no experience of joy.[105]

The importance of the amen-saying that immediately follows (16:23b–24) is often underestimated. Referring back to John 14:13–14 and 15:7–8, 16, it locates precisely the place where this transition takes place, namely in Christian worship, concretely in liturgical prayer "in my name." This, however, is possible only in the post-Easter period, for "until now" (ἕως ἄρτι), the disciples have of course asked nothing "in my name" (16:24a). But for the time of the reader, the command holds good: "Ask and you will receive, so that your joy may be complete" (16:24b). As in 15:11, the text here speaks of the πληροῦν of the Easter χαρά. The initial joy of the Easter witnesses at the sight of the Risen One will be "completed" in the post-Easter experience of their prayers being heard, that is to say, in the liturgy of the Church.

The concluding passage 16:25–33 marks the transition to the passion. Jesus' introductory statement that he has till now spoken ἐν παροιμίαις but in the future will speak παρρησία about the Father (15:25) is surprising, since the preceding remarks were by no means "enigmatic." But the reaction of the disciples in 16:29–30 (ἴδε νῦν ἐν παρρησίᾳ λαλεῖς. . . νῦν οἴδαμεν. . . ἐν τοῦτο πιστεύομεν. . .) shows that the "problem" is on the side of the disciples, whose ability to understand (in contrast to that of the reader!) must first be created by the coming events. Once again the disciples serve as contrast figures to the readers, whereby their deficiency – in contrast to 13:31–14:31 – does not consist in lack of knowledge. In

---

[104] Dietzfelbinger, *Abschied*, 232. Similarly Dettwiler, *Gegenwart*, 242: "The Easter experience of the first disciples is in this sense removed from its historical setting and transposed to the level of the theologically fundamental truths: it is presented as a paradigmatic experience."

[105] On this point, see Dietzfelbinger, *Abschied*, 231.

fact, their "profession of belief" in 16:30, which takes up Jesus' own statement in 16:28, is fully "orthodox" in the Johannine sense. Nevertheless, Jesus' reply makes clear that their *behavior* at the passion will belie this confession.

It is striking that in 16:32 the tradition of the flight of the disciples has been worked into the text, as it is described in the Gospel of Mark (Mark 14:50 par. Matt 26:36), but not in Luke or in the rest of John. In the Johannine passion account, the disciples are dismissed by Jesus (John 18:8); there is no mention of a flight. However, John 16:32 shows that this tradition was familiar to the Johannine community. It is possible that Luke and the Fourth Evangelist independently of each other eliminated this detail for internal reasons.[106] The prediction that the disciples will be scattered, "each one to his own (εἰς τὰ ἴδια)" evidently refers to their return to *Galilee* and to their former *professions*, a detail unknown to the Third and Fourth Evangelist, but which is taken up in John 21.[107]

In 16:26, the text again speaks of the prayer of petition in the name of Jesus, i.e., the liturgical prayer of those assembled in the name of Jesus. This prayer is now connected to a time specification "on that day" (ἐν ἐκείνῃ τῇ ἡμέρᾳ), which we have already seen in 16:23 (cf. 14:20): "On that day you will ask in my name. . ." Here at the latest, it becomes clear that "that day" refers not to the Parousia, but rather to the post-Easter assembly of the community, the first of which took place "on the evening of *that day*" (20:19). At the same time, a possible misunderstanding is eliminated, namely, the opinion that Jesus might function as a mediator or advocate and thus as an interlocutor between the disciples and God.[108] In

---

[106] The Gospel of Luke likewise fails to report a flight of the disciples. For this reason, they should be included under "all (!) his acquaintances," who observe the crucifixion "at a distance" (Luke 23:49). Thus Luke suppresses the notice in Mark 14:50 : "All of them deserted him and fled." On the basis of John 16:32, one might conclude that the pre-Lukan/ pre-Johannine passion account contained a similar remark, which was dropped by the Fourth Evangelist in John 18, but was then taken up again by the redactor in chapter 16.

[107] According to John 21:1, Jesus appeared to the disciples, among them Peter and the two sons of Zebedee, at the Sea of Tiberias in Galilee. Peter goes fishing; the others accompany him (21:3). That Peter and the sons of Zebedee (and Andrew as well) were *fishermen*, we learn from Mark 1:16 par.; cf. also Luke 5:1–11. Both Mark and Matthew report Easter appearances in Galilee (see Mark 16:7, in contrast to Luke). Matthew (28:16), however, locates the appearance on (!) the mountain (τὸ ὄρος) of the Sermon on the Mount (Matt 5:1; 8:1), which however lies in the vicinity of the Sea of Galilee (Matt 15:29; cf. John 6:1–3, 15).

[108] John 16:26: καὶ οὐ λέγω ὑμῖν ὅτι ἐγὼ ἐρωτήσω τὸν πατέρα περὶ ὑμῖν. John 17 represents such a "prayer of petition," but it is spoken in the pre-Easter situation. However 1 John 2:1–2 appears to indicate that the earlier notion of Jesus as an advocate was familiar to the Johannine community.

16:27 (αὐτὸς γάρ ὁ πατὴρ φιλεῖ ὑμᾶς), the author thus modifies the statement in 14:23 (καὶ ὁ πατήρ μου ἀγαπήσει αὐτόν). This manner of taking up the disciples into Jesus' own "immediate presence to God" naturally presupposes 20:17.[109]

The discourse ends with the resumption of the peace motif. Once again John 20 stands in the background: ἐν ἐμοί the disciples will have peace (thrice repeated in 20:19, 21, 26), ἐν κόσμῳ, by way of contrast, they will have distress[110] (see 20:19), yet the world has already been overcome, the ruler of the world condemned (see 16:8–11). This resounds when the disciples are promised "peace," namely in the "room" of their liturgical assembly. In chapter 16, the (traditional) Easter peace salutation of the Risen One becomes a proclamation of the victory over the cosmos!

8. Conclusions

(1) The study of the genesis and literary organization of the Johannine Easter texts reveals an astonishingly creative process of interpretation and actualization of the original Easter faith and its earliest narrative formulation within the Johannine community. Strikingly, this process of growth and re-reading manifests itself particularly in the Farewell Discourses. Even those parts that evidently presuppose the elevation of Jesus are located in the pre-Easter situation. In this way, the concern of the Fourth Evangelist has been preserved. The coming events – *both* the passion and Easter events (which belong to the past for the reader) *and* the post-Easter reality of the community (which constitutes the present for the reader) – are foretold and interpreted by the earthly Jesus. Thus the Farewell Discourses take place before a non-comprehending (and thus "staged") circle of disciples, which is fundamentally different from the circle of the gospel's readers.

In this way, the authors of John 15 and 16 do not merely link up with the so-called First Farewell Discourse. Their "relecture" of John 13–14

---

[109] In John 20:17, the risen Jesus widens his relationship to God to include also his "brothers," without however overriding the enduring distinction: "I am ascending to *my* Father and *your* Father, to *my* God and *your* God." On this point Theobald, "Osterglaube," 112, observes: "Jesus takes up those who believe in him into his own relationship to God and Father and thus can henceforth call them his *brothers* (verse 17). In this way, the full Easter reality of the Exalted One enormously transcends the appearances of the Risen One." In the words of the Second and Third Farewell Discourses, the Easter joy of the Easter witnesses is "fulfilled" in the post-Easter worship services (John 15:11; 16:24).

[110] θλίψις; cf. Rev 1:9; 2:9–10; Acts 14:22, etc.

takes place against the background of the Easter account in John 20, which is formulated as a paradigm for the post-Easter community.

(2) The Fourth Evangelist set the Easter appearances of Jesus in the Sunday assembly of the disciples. He described the coming of the Risen One to his disciples as an eschatological event, merged with the end-time Parousia of Christ. Thus "that day," which Jesus announced, is no longer a still forthcoming "last day" in the sense of a "futurist" eschatology,[111] but rather it is the Easter day itself (20:19), which is however *the first* of an ongoing series of "first days" of the week (20:26).

The oft remarked and frequently described "presentist" eschatology of the Fourth Gospel should thus be defined more exactly as a *liturgical eschatology* or as a *liturgically realized eschatology*. It is rooted in liturgical experiences. In their attempt to overcome the crisis situation of the community, the texts refer back to the worship services of the Johannine community as the place where Easter joy can be experienced time and again anew.

Already the Fourth Evangelist had strongly accentuated his older Easter tradition in this direction, in order to open up the Easter accounts for the Christians of his own generation, who "do not see and yet believe" (20:29). From the Easter evening on, the encounter with Christ takes place in the context of the liturgical assembly. This is shown also by the Thomas story (20:26), which marks the threshold between the first two Sunday assemblies, where Jesus appears in visible (and tangible) form, and the following Sunday assemblies, where he is indeed present but no longer visibly and tangibly.

It is striking, how the Fourth Evangelist explicitly links up the end of the visible Easter appearances, the beginning of the Sunday repetition of worship services, and the committing of the gospel to written form (20:29–31). The worship service in which the gospel is read takes the place of the Easter appearances, which were only accessible to a limited circle of Easter witnesses. In fact, these appearances are transformed into "written" (and thus readable) signs. The identity of the Risen One and the possibility of his presence are thus connected with the repetition of the assembly of the disciples. Leo the Great describes this connection quite appropriately in Johannine terms: "What was visible on our Redeemer has gone over into the holy rites (mysteries). In order that our faith might become more distinguished and more firm, the doctrine has taken the place of the Easter appearances."[112]

---

[111] As in Matt 7:22; Luke 10:22; 2 Tim 1:12, 18. See Haldimann, *Rekonstruktion*, 368–69.

[112] Leo the Great, *Sermo LXXIV* (second sermon on the Ascension): "Quod itaque Redemptoris nostri conspicuum fuit in sacramenta transivit; et ut fides excellentior esset

But this process occurs under the sign of the gift of the *pneuma* (20:22), which already in the First Farewell Discourse took on the function of an interpreter of Jesus' words (14:26). Through the Spirit, the voice of Jesus is heard in the event of the liturgy and thus the Jesus, who has returned to the Father, becomes again present (as the Easter *semeia* indicate).

(3) Often the Farewell Discourses allude to the visible Easter appearances in the circle of the Easter witnesses as reported in chapter 20.[113] Nevertheless, the real background of the Farewell Discourses is constituted by the frequent allusions to the promise of prayer being heard together with the Paraclete sayings. Both of these series of sayings have a liturgical Sitz im Leben.

But when one compares the Paraclete saying with the brief remarks in John 20:22, one discovers a strong lack of balance between the promise of the Holy Spirit in the Farewell Discourses – extremely complex and spanning the whole situation of the community *ad intra* and *ad extra* – and the fulfillment on Easter. Thus, according to 20:19–23, the recipients of the Spirit are solely the disciples assembled on Easter evening; that is to say, only a *restricted circle* of Easter witnesses – 20:24–25 speaks indeed of the Twelve. The gift of the Spirit, however, does not stand alone in 20:21–23; neither does it mark the highpoint of the scene. Instead it is a consequence of the sending forth of the disciples, "as the Father has sent me" (20:21) and it explains the power to forgive or retain sins (20:23). Noting this, the church fathers like Eusebius of Caesarea, explained that on that Easter evening the Easter witnesses received only "a certain portion of the power of the Spirit."[114]

Correct in this interpretation is the observation that the Farewell Discourses give rise to a remaining promise, which is not entirely fulfilled in John 20. Evidently, the intended effect of this way of presenting the material is to enable the Farewell Discourses to address the present time of the reader and thus not to be limited to the Easter and Pentecost stories which belong to the past. On the contrary, the Easter joy of the original witnesses will be "completed" in the praying and fruit-bringing community (15:11; 16:24). The eschatology of the Fourth Gospel is thus "presentist" in the sense that it can be actualized liturgically in the present time of the community.

---

ac firmior, visioni doctrina successit" (ed. R. Dolle; 74, 2 [= SC 74, 1961], 140]). With R. Dolle, one should translate *sacramenta* better as "les rites sacrés" (*op. cit.* 141). To understand Leo's text it is important to note that he has cited John 20:29 in the immediately preceding passage (74, 1). Thus, referring to the ascension story in Acts 1:9, Leo comments on *this* verse with the sentence cited.

[113] So in John 14:18–20 and in 16:16–24.
[114] Eusebius, *Suppl. Quaest.* (PG 22, 1016) , calling attention to the absent article in πνεῦμα: μερικήν τινα τοῦ Πνεύματος ἐνέργειαν δίδωσιν αὐτοῖς.

(4) The Johannine Easter texts probably hint at the historical situation of the Johannine community, at least in its *self-perception*. The situation of the worship service behind locked doors, which is evoked by John 20, differs significantly from that of the Pauline community in Corinth, where nothing is said of fear or persecution and where Paul reckons with "unbelievers," i.e., non-Christians, who take part in the worship services of the Corinthian ecclesia (see 1 Cor 14:23). When the Corinthians "come together as ecclesia" (see 1 Cor 11:18), the doors are not locked.[115] By contrast, the Johannine scenario – as also Acts 12 – reflects a situation of opposition that will soon escalate to persecution.[116]

Already the Fourth Evangelist presupposes the exclusion of the Johannine community from the synagogue because of its high christology (cf. John 9:22, 34–35; 12:42). In the course of the Farewell Discourses, one notices how the feeling of being threatened grows and becomes more concrete. Perhaps, the Farewell-Discourses reflect an increasingly threatening situation of the Johannine community. At the same time, they also show what an important function, in the Johannine system, that the threat-scenario has for the stabilization of the community *ad intra*.

It is striking how the authors of the Second and Third Farewell Discourses (John 15–16) link up with the scene in 20:19–23 and elaborate on it both with respect to the liturgical assembly of the disciples and with respect to the threatened situation of the community. This fact demonstrates that according to John 20 the Johannine Christians' attitude probably endured over several generations and that this community now as before "defined" itself primarily in terms of its liturgy. At the same time, the liturgical experiences of these early Christians evidently remained lively and strong throughout this whole period, so that the appeal to the hearing of prayers and the recourse to the Paraclete could remain plausible despite the increasingly threatening situation of the community, indeed, even when the original answers contained in the First Farewell Discourse had lost their

---

[115] Bruce W. Winter, *After Paul Left Corinth. The Influence of Secular Ethics and Social Change* (Grand Rapids and Cambridge: Eerdmans, 2001), 135, points out that the vestibules of Roman houses were open to the street. The House was specifically designed to be open to *politeia*. As such, an outsider could come in. We know that this was precisely what they did, and were meant to do, in the Christian gathering.

[116] An instructive analogy is offered by Acts 12, which reports the persecution of the community by King Herod, in the course of which James the Son of Zebedee is put to death and Peter is arrested (12:1–4). In this situation of persecution, the doors to the vestibule of the house are likewise kept locked. Behind the locked doors, the community has assembled for prayer (12:5, 12) and for the celebration of the Passover (12:3–4, 6). Thus Peter, after his miraculous deliverance from prison, has to knock on the door (12:13, 16) in order to be admitted.

convincing power.[117] In this way the stories of the Easter appearances and the transformation of mourning into joy, which is described in them, could become paradigmatic for the life of the faithful.

The fact that the Farewell Discourses and especially the Paraclete-sayings contained in them could prove so "productive" in a literary sense shows that the liturgy in the Johannine sense was essentially a pneuma-related reality[118] and that the liturgical experiences could enter into a fruitful exchange with the pneumatological reflection. In the end, this means that "in this perspective, revelation is an ongoing reality"[119] and that the ἀναγγέλειν of the Paraclete (16:12–15) – like his διδάσκειν and ὑπομιμνῄσκειν (14:26), his μαρτυρεῖν (15:26) and the ἐλέγχειν τὸν κόσμον (16:8) – is realized in the context of the liturgy. The Fourth Gospel is itself a documentary of this action of the Paraclete: it originated out of and for the sake of the worship services.

---

[117] Cf. Zumstein, "Deutung," 136–37.

[118] On this point see John 4:23–24, worship of the Father "in spirit and truth" (cf. "Spirit of truth" in 14:17; 15:26; 16:13).

[119] Bieringer, "The Spirit's Guidance," 205.

Chapter 13

The Significance of the Resurrection Appearance in John 21

Martin Hasitschka

Several times in the Gospel of John, the author conveys announcements and indications concerning future events[1] as well as memories of past incidents or encounters.[2] Through anticipating future events and referring back to the past, he creates mental links and establishes relationships between certain parts of his work. Such special connections are also recognizable between John 21 and the rest of the gospel. The following article analyzes how John 21 is connected to individual parts and statements in John 1–20, and it seeks to show how chapter 21 can be read as an integral part of the gospel.[3] The resurrection appearance in John 21 is structured in two parts: John 21:1–14 (the miraculous catch and the meal at the shore) and 21:15–23 (the dialogue between Jesus and Peter). In both parts the same two disciples play a special role: Peter and the disciple "whom Jesus loved."

---

[1] Explicit references by the author are given, e.g., in John 2:22 (the announcement that after Jesus' resurrection the disciples will "remember" his words), 7:39 (the prospective statement about the Spirit which will be given after the glorification of Jesus), 11:2 (the indication as to what Mary, the sister of Lazarus, will do), 12:16 (the announcement that after the glorification of Jesus the disciples will "remember" the words of the Scripture).

[2] We find references to the past, e.g., in 18:14 (remembering the "advice" of Caiaphas), 19:39 (remembering the encounter between Nicodemus and Jesus), 21:20 (remembering a scene at the last supper).

[3] For this question see also Martin Hasitschka, "'Danach offenbarte sich Jesus den Jüngern noch einmal' (Joh 21,1). Erfüllung von Verheißungen des irdischen Jesus und nachösterliche Antwort auf offene Fragen in Joh 21," in: *Verantwortete Exegese. Hermeneutische Zugänge – exegetische Studien – systematische Reflexionen – ökumenische Perspektiven – praktische Konkretionen. Franz Georg Untergaßmair zum 65. Geburtstag* (ed. Gerhard Hotze and Egon Spiegel; Berlin: LIT, 2006), 231–43.

1. Relationship between John 21:1–14 and John 1–20

1.1 The Inclusio in John 21:1 and 21:14

John 21:2–13 is framed by 21:1 and 14. At the same time 21:14 is, in a striking way, an interruption of the story that continues in 21:15. This shows that the two framing verses are of special importance. The geographical indication "Sea of Tiberias" in 21:1 reminds the reader of the "Sea of Galilee, which is the Sea of Tiberias" in 6:1. This geographical indication already establishes a connection to the story of the feeding of the five thousand (6:2–15).[4]

John 21:1 starts with the expression "after this" (μετὰ ταῦτα), which follows the summary by the author in 20:30–31[5] and guides the reader back to the narrative level. In a similar way, the report about the burial in 19:38 is introduced by "after this" (μετὰ ταῦτα) following 19:35–37, where a summary at the end of the passion events is given.[6] The verb φανερόω, translated as "reveal," also means "to show" or "to make known."[7] In 21:1 as in 7:4 φανερόω is used with the reflexive pronoun. The passive form of the verb in 21:14 has a reflexive meaning. With his first "sign" at the beginning of his earthly activity, Jesus reveals his glory (2:11). In connection with the last sign of Easter he reveals "himself," namely as the Risen One. John 21:1 also says that Jesus reveals himself "again" (πάλιν). This statement throws light on the previous Easter stories in John 20. They too are guided by the thought that the Easter appearances are basically a self-revelation of Jesus. "Seeing" the Risen One (20:18, 20, 25) is connected with his initiative (he "revealed himself").[8] The narrative

---

[4] In the entire NT the place-name Tiberias is found only in John 6:1, 23 and 21:1.

[5] The comment in 20:30–31, together with that in 21:24–25, can be seen as kind of literary frame around 21:1–23. According to Hartwig Thyen, (*Das Johannesevangelium* [HNT 6; Tübingen: Mohr Siebeck, 2005], 774) John 20:30–31 and 21:24–25 constitute "an artistic inclusion for John 21."

[6] The words "after this" (μετὰ ταῦτα) also mark a break in the course of the story in 3:22; 5:1; 5:14; 6:1; and 7:1. Similarly the expression "after this" (μετὰ τοῦτο) in 11:7, 11; 19:28 helps to structure the story.

[7] The verb φανερόω also refers to Jesus in other passages: John 1:31 (the activity of John has the aim that Jesus "might be revealed to Israel"); 2:11 (Jesus "manifests" his glory); 7:4 (the brothers of Jesus tell him: "show yourself to the world"); 17:6 (Jesus "manifests" the name of the Father); 1 John 1:2 ("the life was made manifest"); 2:28 and 3:2 (Jesus "appears" at his Parousia); 3:5, 8 (Jesus "appeared" in order to remove sin and to destroy the works of the devil).

[8] This connection is already suggested in John 14:18–24. On the one hand, Jesus promises his own that they (soon) will "see" (θεωρέω, 14:19) him (cf. also 16:16–18); on the other hand Jesus promises that he (out of his own initiative) will "manifest himself" (ἐμφανίζω, 14:21, 22). The verb ἐμφανίζω (used in a reflexive mode) has a similar sense as φανερόω, as appears from a comparison between 7:4 and 14:22.

reference to the following (οὕτως, "in this way") especially emphasizes the manner of Jesus' self-revelation.

John 21:14 stresses: "This was now the third time that Jesus was revealed to the disciples after he was raised from the dead." The expression "raised from the dead" is the same as in 2:22. This suggests a literary connection. After Easter Jesus' disciples "remember" the prediction of his resurrection in 2:19 and are strengthened in their faith. The numerical indication "the third time" suggests "that there is full certainty as to the fact of the resurrection."[9] The counting of Easter appearances, which are also to be understood as "signs,"[10] can be compared with the enumeration of "signs" during the Galilean activity of Jesus (2:11; 4:54). John 21:14 does not say that Jesus' third appearance is his last one. "Much more, this initiates the long story of his coming to his own people, which extends until the end of time."[11]

The third appearance of the Risen One to a group of disciples happens at a temporal and spatial distance from the appearances in Jerusalem, which were described in John 20. It takes place in the Galilean homeland of these disciples[12] and in their everyday life. By that the Gospel of John shows that the Risen One does not abandon his own, wherever and in whatever situation they may be. Again, Jesus takes the initiative as in his appearances in John 20. He does not only disclose his identity but comes to help his own in a difficult situation.[13] This self-revelation of Jesus is also connected with a mission (21:15–19), as in the other appearance narratives (20:17; 20:21–23).

1.2 The Group of the Seven Disciples in John 21:2

John 21:2 mentions the reunion[14] of a group of seven disciples. Three of them are called by name: First, Simon Peter is mentioned.[15] The last time he was mentioned was in 20:2–10. Through the figure of Thomas, another

---

[9] G. Delling, "τρεῖς, τρίς, τρίτος," *TDNT* 8 (1972): 215–25, esp. 222.

[10] See Gilbert Van Belle, "The Meaning of σημεῖα in Jn 20:30–31," *ETL* 74 (1998): 300–25.

[11] Thyen, *Das Johannesevangelium*, 786.

[12] The Gospel of John says explicitly that Simon Peter (cf. 1:44) and Nathanael (21:2) come from Galilee.

[13] The difficult situation of the disciples in John 20:19–29 is shown by the fact that they, "for fear of the Jews," are behind locked doors (20:19, 26). In John 21:2–13 the difficult situation is that the disciples worked the whole night without result.

[14] The adverbial expression "they were together (ὁμοῦ)" forms a contrast and counter image to Jesus' announcement in John 16:32: "you will be scattered (σκορπίζω)."

[15] Beginning in John 1:42, the Gospel of John mostly uses the double name Simon Peter (= rock). Only a few passages use the name Peter alone (e.g., John 18:16).

link with the previous Easter appearance (20:24–29) is established.[16] Moreover, as "one of the twelve" (20:24), he was presumably present already at the events in John 6. Nathanael is mentioned in 1:45–51 and 21:2, but nowhere else in the NT. Only in 21:2 do we learn that he comes from "Cana in Galilee."[17] He therefore is likely to know about the two "signs" that Jesus performed in Cana (2:1–11; 4:46–54). Looking at Nathanael, the readers of John's gospel ask themselves: Is this, after 2:1–11 and 4:46–54, the climax of the fulfillment of the promise in 1:50–51? Given this earlier promise, the scene in 21:2–13 can be interpreted as follows: Nathanael sees "greater things" and "heaven opened" insofar as Jesus reveals himself as the Risen One.

By bringing Thomas and Nathanael together, the evangelist invites us to think about these two disciples, who in the Gospel of John, express the first and the last great confessions of faith in Jesus.[18] Simon Peter, as spokesperson for the Twelve, also bears witness to Jesus in the context of a previous episode (6:68–69). At the same time, the three disciples mentioned by name can be regarded as witnesses for the two earlier meal miracles (wedding at Cana, feeding of the five thousand).

In addition there are "the sons of Zebedee." One may assume that these are the two sons of Zebedee – James and John – who are known from the Synoptic authors. In the Gospel of John they are mentioned at this point for the first and only time. Two additional disciples remain completely anonymous ("two others"). Among the pairs of disciples mentioned last, there is also that "disciple whom Jesus loved" (21:7).[19] The number seven (like the number twelve) can be understood as symbolic number.[20] It is a symbol for the totality of all believers.

---

[16] The epithet "the Twin" is also found in 11:16 and 20:24 and nowhere else in the NT.

[17] This place name is found in the NT only in John 2:1, 11; 4:46; and 21:2.

[18] Common motives and subjects in the presentation of the two figures are: To both, others bear witness of Jesus (John 1:45–46; 20:25). Both express doubts that are overcome in the encounter with Jesus. Nathanael as well as Thomas expresses a double testimony (1:49; 20:28). Jesus' answer refers to more than the concrete situation and relates to many (1:50–51; 20:29). The wine miracle at Cana follows the testimony of Nathanael and Jesus' promise to him; the miraculous catch at the Sea of Tiberias follows the testimony of Thomas and the related beatitude.

[19] Is he, as the nameless companion of Andrew, already present in John 1:35–40? Recently Thyen (*Das Johannesevangelium*, 782, 795), answers in the affirmative. This disciple is therefore a witness of the life of Jesus from the beginning (cf. John 21:24).

[20] In Revelation 2–3 the number "seven" is symbol for the whole church.

1.3 The Miraculous Catch of Fish and the Meal at the Shore in John 21:3–13

1.3.1 Reference to the Miraculous Feeding of the Crowd in John 6:1–15

Simon Peter has a leading role in this group of disciples, who gather after Easter (as he did in the circle of the Twelve in 6:66–71). Spontaneously the others follow his plan: "I am going fishing" (21:3). It is their everyday professional activity. That the disciples work hard in vain throughout the whole night and catch nothing can be seen as an illustration of 15:5 ("apart from me you can do nothing"). Even with regard to language, 21:4 shows a link to John 20. The temporal reference ("Just as day was breaking") reminds us of the early morning discovery of the open tomb in 20:1. The verb "stand" (ἵστημι, also: "to step before somebody, to go up to somebody, to step over to somebody") is also used for Jesus' appearances to his disciples in 20:19 and 26 (Jesus "stood among them"). The words, "yet the disciples did not know (οἶδα) that it was Jesus" (21:4), points to an (intended?) similarity with 20:14: Mary "did not know that it was Jesus."[21] The statement in 21:4, that the disciples "did not know," is the opposite of the declaration in 21:12: "They knew (οἶδα) it was the Lord."

The conversation between Jesus and the group of disciples in 21:5–6a starts with the intimate address, "Children" (παιδία – cf. 1 John 2:14, 18). It sounds similar to John 13:33 ("Little children" – τεκνία).[22] It can be compared with the personal address in 20:16 ("Mary!"). In the term "child" there is also the idea of needing help and protection. The expression προσφάγιον in this context means "fish." The literary means of repeating the verb ("cast!" – "they cast" [both times βάλλω])[23] expresses briefly that the disciples trust this stranger and rely on his word.

In John 21:6 the miraculous catch is described in a brief, rather than a detailed way. It can be understood as a "sign" that is performed by the risen Lord. John 21:3–13 can be compared with two "signs" that Jesus performed, namely the sign at the wedding at Cana (2:1–11) and the sign of the feeding of the five thousand (6:1–15). All three stories speak at first of a shortage.[24] Then, in various ways, the gospel tells of Jesus giving a gift

---

[21] Cf. also Luke 24:16 (the disciples of Emmaus): "But their eyes were kept from recognizing him."

[22] Παιδίον and τεκνίον are basically synonymous terms for a small child (cf. 1 John 2:14, 18 with 2:1, 12, 28; 3:7, 18; 4:4; 5:21).

[23] Also in John 2:7–8 ("fill! " – "they filled"; "take it!" – "they took it") and in John 6:12–13 ("gather up!" – "they gathered up"), by the literary means of repeating the verb, it is emphasized that people agree to a word of Jesus and do exactly what he says.

[24] At the wedding at Cana there is a shortage of wine (John 2:3). In view of the big crowd at the sea, Jesus asks: "How are we to buy bread, so that these people may eat?" (6:5). Looking at the five loaves and the two fish that are brought by a child, Andrew

in abundance.²⁵ All three "signs" happen in Galilee. They concern gifts for earthly life (wine, bread, fish), which are given by Jesus in abundance in a situation of shortage; all of them have the nature of a sign. And all three stories are put in the context of a communal meal, where Jesus is present (wedding meal, meal of the five thousand,²⁶ early meal at the shore). John 21:2–13 suggests that such a communion with Jesus continues after Easter.

According to John 21:7, it is the disciple "whom Jesus loved" that recognizes Jesus first.²⁷ He tells only Peter: "It is the Lord (κύριος)!" The reaction of Peter shows that he wants to reach Jesus as quickly as possible (and as the first). The putting on of "clothes" is a sign of honor towards his Lord. John 21:8 then directs attention to the other disciples. First, their activity is described. With their boat they "drag" (σύρω) the net with the fish (ἰχθύς) to the shore. Then the gospel notes what they perceive (21:9).²⁸ They see (βλέπω) a charcoal fire (ἀνθρακιά),²⁹ fish (ὀψάριον)³⁰ lying on it, and bread.³¹ The singular expression (without the article) of fish and bread can be interpreted in two ways: (a) a single fish and loaf of bread or (b) a collective expression for a number of fish and loaves of bread. Interpretation (b) is better.

---

asks: "but what are they among so many?" (6:9). After the futile catch by night the Risen One asks his disciples from the shore: "'Children, have you any fish?' They answered him, 'No.'" (21:5).

²⁵ At the wedding at Cana, Jesus gives wine in abundance (six jars each holding approximately one hundred liters). The five thousand at the sea are given bread and fish by Jesus in abundance (the leftovers fill twelve baskets). The disciples at the shore receive fish in abundance from the Risen One (153 large fish). There are various attempts of interpretation concerning the number 153. Corrado Marucci, "Il significato del numero 153 in Gv 21,11," *RivB* 52 (2004): 403–40 thoroughly examines all models of interpretation since the ancient world. According to him none of the symbolic interpretations is convincing. In my opinion the number can also be understood as the sober and exact statement of an eye witness. At the same time one might note that the number 153 consists of 12 times 12 (= 144) plus 3 times 3 (= 9). The number 3 and multiples of it also play a role in John 2:1–11 (6 jars) and 6:1–15 (12 baskets).

²⁶ It is a regular meal where people "sit down" (ἀναπίπτω in John 6:10 as in 13:12).

²⁷ In John 20:8 he is he first one who takes up the Easter faith.

²⁸ John 21:9 is introduced with the words ὡς οὖν. As in other passages (4:1, 40; 11:6; 18:6; 20:11), they signal that now something new or surprising or unexpected is to come.

²⁹ The Gospel of John uses this expression only in John 18:18 (charcoal fire in the courtyard of the high priest) and here. Should the charcoal fire remind Peter at his denial?

³⁰ Apart from προσφάγιον (John 21:5) and ἰχθύς (21:6, 8, 11), this is the third term for fish in 21:1–14. This expression (diminutive of ὄψον = "the cooked") means side dish, everything that is eaten together with bread (particularly meat and fish). In the NT it is found only in 6:9, 11; and 21:9, 10, 13.

³¹ Please note that what the disciples see or perceive is not Jesus but his gifts.

In John 21:10 Jesus asks the disciples: "Bring some of the fish (ὀψάριον) that you have just caught!" This demand stands in a strange tension with the statement of 21:9 that fish (ὀψάριον) are already on the charcoal fire. In 21:9 ὀψάριον is a gift of the Lord; in 21:10 the term is connected also with the participation of the disciples. The disciples take part in realizing the meal by contributing something of what they have caught themselves, albeit with the assistance of the Lord. The large quantity of fish can be seen as a symbol: the disciples are chosen and enabled to participate, so that for many people (meal) communion with the Lord is made possible. John 21:8–10 interrupts the report about Peter. He seems to reach the shore even later than the others (21:11). It is surprising that he alone "hauls" (ἕλκω) the net ashore.[32]

The symbolic nature of the catch is often related to the mission to the Gentiles.[33] The "untearable" net and the amount of fish are interpreted as images for the church in her unity and entirety, and as images for her gathering of many peoples. Peter, who drags the "one" net, is seen as the head of the mission and the "tool" by whom the Lord draws the people to him. In my opinion, however, the idea of mission and gathering is more fully conveyed in the following image of the shepherd (21:15–17).

John 21:12 presents Jesus' last words within 21:2–13, namely his invitation to the meal. "Have breakfast" (ἀριστάω)[34] means rest and refreshment after laborious work, and above all communion with the Lord. A strange tension is shown in 21:12. On the one hand, the disciples do not "dare ask" (ἐξετάζω) who he is,[35] but on the other hand, they "know" (οἶδα) that "it is the Lord." By this it is shown that now the whole group of disciples has attained the certainty at first reached only by the disciple "whom Jesus loved" (21:7).

By his action in John 21:13, Jesus answers the question that the disciples did not dare to ask, which reminds us of the feeding of the five thou-

---

[32] The literary construction of John 21:7–11 shows a chiastic structure if we focus on the acting persons: (A) Peter leaves the boat. – (B) The other disciples haul the net. – (B¹) The other disciples leave the boat and go "ashore." – (A¹) Peter drags the net "ashore." If we focus on the action, the structure is parallel (A – B – A¹ – B¹).

[33] The miraculous catch is connected to the mission to the Gentiles also by Ulrich Busse, "Die 'Hellenen.' Joh 12,20ff. und der sogenannte 'Anhang' Joh 21," in *The Four Gospels 1992. Festschrift Frans Neirynck* (ed. Frans Van Segbroeck; BETL 100/3; Leuven: Leuven University and Peeters Press, 1992), 2083–2100. For him, John 21 is "von Anfang an ein genuiner Bestandteil des Gesamtwerkes" (p. 2100). The last "sign" in the Gospel serves "der narrativen Umsetzung und 'internen' Bestätigung für die universale Heilsvorhersage Joh 12,32" (p. 2098). Busse bases his reasoning particularly on the verb "haul" (ἕλκω) which is used in 12:32 and 21:11.

[34] This verb means not only "have breakfast" but also "eat a meal" in a wide and general sense (cf. Luke 11:37).

[35] Concerning the question "Who are you?" cf. John 1:19 and 8:25.

sand in 6:1–15. By his action, the Risen One manifests his identity with the earthly Jesus.[36] When observing the way the Risen One takes and gives bread and fish they realize: He is no one else than Jesus of Nazareth. A linguistic comparison between John 6:11 and 21:13 makes that clear:

> John 6:11: "Jesus then took (λαμβάνω) the loaves (ἄρτος), and when he had given thanks, he distributed (διαδίδωμι) them to those who were seated; so (ὁμοίως) also the fish (ὀψάριον), as much as they wanted."
>
> John 21:13: "Jesus came and took (λαμβάνω) the bread (ἄρτος) and gave (δίδωμι) it to them, and so (ὁμοίως) with the fish (ὀψάριον)."

In both passages the words "take" (λαμβάνω), "bread" (ἄρτος), "fish" (ὀψάριον, a term used only in these two passages and their contexts), and "so" (ὁμοίως – apart from these two passages only in 5:19) are used. The verbs "distribute" (διαδίδωμι) and "give" (δίδωμι) are cognates. The expression "the bread," used with the definite article in 21:13, is the same as in 6:23. In John 6:23 the scene of the feeding of the five thousand is described as the place "where they ate the bread after the Lord had given thanks (εὐχαριστέω, as in 6:11)." Furthermore, the reports in 6:11 and 21:13 have in common that Jesus passes bread and fish to everyone personally, but it seems that he does not eat.[37] The non-verbal and symbolic event in 21:13 delivers, so to speak, the "proof" that the mysterious person at the shore actually is the Lord, who is identical with the earthly Jesus.[38]

1.3.2 The Giving of the Bread and the Promises in John 6:27 and 6:51

The rite of bread in John 21:13 also recalls two predictions from conversations in the synagogue at Capernaum (6:25–59).[39] In these conversations the predominant idea is that Jesus in his person embodies the "bread from

---

[36] Mary learns about this identity when the Risen One calls her by name (20:16). The disciples on Easter eve and later Thomas recognize this identity by looking at the wounds (20:20, 27).

[37] As reason for that we can suppose that the bread (in the sense of the conversations in 6:25–59) in a special way points to himself.

[38] The self-revelation of the Risen One in the context of a meal in John 21:9–13 is comparable to the recognition of the Risen One during the breaking of the bread in Luke 24:30–31 (Emmaus; cf. Luke 24:35).

[39] The conversation in John 6:25–59 can be divided into six sections. In the first four sections (6:25–27, 28–29, 30–33, 34–40), the interlocutors turn to Jesus with a question; Jesus takes notice and uses it as starting point for his preaching. In the last two sections of the conversation (6:41–51, 52–59), "the Jews" do not turn to Jesus directly but talk about him; they "murmur" (6:41) and "dispute" among themselves (6:52). But also here Jesus responds to their problem and tries to lead them to an understanding of his message. A thorough examination of John 6, especially for the sections 6:25–59 and 6:60–71, is presented by Mira Stare, *Durch ihn leben. Die Lebensthematik in Joh 6* (NTAbh 49; Münster: Aschendorff, 2004).

heaven," which the Father "gives" (6:32, δίδωμι in present tense) and by which those who believe in Jesus already have life (6:35, 47–48, 51). But there are two passages where Jesus talks about a future gift of bread. The first section of the conversation (6:25–27) culminates in the promise of "the food (βρῶσις) that endures to eternal life, which the Son of man will give to you" (δίδωμι in the future tense, 6:27).[40] This food, symbol for the "gift of salvation per se," will be mediated by Jesus "the glorified Lord, the 'Son of man' ascended again to heaven."[41]

On the one hand, in the fifth section of the conversation (6:41–51), where Jesus defends his claim against the "murmuring" Jews, he uses the present tense to confirm the statement that is already contained in the fourth section (6:34–40): "I am the bread of life" (6:48, 51; cf. 6:35). On the other hand, he interprets this bread as future gift: "the bread that I shall give (δίδωμι in the future tense) for the life of the world is my flesh" (6:51).

In the sixth section of the conversation (6:52–59) there is again, as in the first section, talk of the Son of man (6:53). He gives "food" (βρῶσις) and "drink" (πόσις) (6:55), and this is connected to his flesh and blood (indicating the sacrifice of his life). The conversations in 6:25–59 are to some extent framed by the promise that the Son of man – namely because of sacrificing his life – will give the bread and food that will mediate lasting salvation and eternal life. The statements in the present tense (Jesus' "I am" sayings; the promise that the believer [6:40, 47] or the one who eats and drinks [6:54] "has" eternal life) are complemented by this announcement in the future tense. The gift of bread in the full sense is still to come. The meaning of the conversation is elucidated only after the event of the sacrifice of life and the raising of Jesus. The disciples come to understanding in connection with their experience which is reported in 21:2–13. It is perhaps not accidental that the verb δίδωμι, which is in the future tense in 6:27, 51, is used in present tense in 21:13.

1.3.3 The Meal at the Shore and the Promise in John 6:62

The meal and the communion with the Risen One at the shore recall a further prediction. The conversations in the synagogue of Capernaum (6:25–59) cause negative reactions. The Jews "murmur" (γογγύζω – 6:41) and

---

[40] Some manuscripts have the present tense as a variant reading. But the future tense is clearly to be preferred. See Bruce M. Metzger, *A Textual Commentary on the Greek New Testament* (2d ed.; Stuttgart: German Bible Society, 1994), 182. John 6:27 can be compared with 4:14: "The water that I shall give him (δίδωμι in the future tense) will become in him a spring of water welling up to eternal life." Together with 7:37–39 this promise can be related to the post-Easter gift of the Spirit.

[41] Rudolf Schnackenburg, *Das Johannesevangelium*, vol. 2 (HTKNT IV/2; Freiburg: Herder 1985), 49; ET: *The Gospel according to St John* (New York: Seabury, 1980), 37.

"dispute" among themselves (6:52). John 6:25–59 is followed by a conversation of Jesus with the disciples. It has two parts (6:60–65 and 6:66–71) and begins as follows: "Many of his disciples, when they heard it, said, 'This is a hard (σκληρός) saying (λόγος); who can listen to it?'" (6:60) In his answer Jesus talks first about himself (6:61–63); then he makes a statement about the disciples (6:64–65). John 6:61–63 reads as follows: "But Jesus, knowing in himself that his disciples murmured (γογγύζω) at it, said to them, Do you take offense (σκανδαλίζω) at this? Then what if you were to see the Son of man ascending where he was before? It is the spirit that gives life, the flesh is of no avail; the words that I have spoken to you are spirit and life."

"Many" (!) of Jesus' disciples, who have experienced the "sign" of the feeding of the five thousand as well as the conversations in the synagogue,[42] "murmur" (as the Jews in 6:41) and "take offense." The demonstrative pronoun "this" (τοῦτο) refers (as the expression "this saying" in 6:60) to the whole conversation of Jesus with the people and the Jews in 6:25–59. Jesus contrasts the question "Do you take offense at this?"[43] with what can be interpreted as an implied promise in 6:62.[44] The incomplete sentence (aposiopesis) could be completed accordingly: "If you were to see the Son of man ascending where he was before – then you will come to faith and see." So, "this saying" loses its toughness and is no longer intolerable. Then the statement of 6:63 can also be understood.

There are two more linguistic reasons for an interpretation of the ἐάν-sentence (6:62) as an implied promise. The first one: the evangelist John often forms sentences with ἐάν; however, in the context of a question only in 3:12 (in connection with the interrogative adverb πῶς) and in 7:51 (in connection with μή). Would he not also use an interrogative adverb in 6:62 if this ἐάν-sentence were meant as a question? The second reason: Several ἐάν-sentences are placed in the context of a promise: John 8:31, 36 (ἐάν οὖν as in 6:62); 8:51–52; 11:40; 12:32 (in connection with the term Son of man as in 6:62).[45] Also, John 8:28 can be considered as part of this

---

[42] Because of John 6:65 (linked back to 6:37, 39; cf. also 6:44), it is clear that the disciples were present during the conversations in 6:25–59.

[43] The question mark is not necessary. One can read the sentence also as a statement: "You take offense at this."

[44] Most Bible translations interpret John 6:62 as a question. But the aposiopesis of 6:62 does not necessarily have to be interpreted as question. Wilhelm Thüsing (*Die Erhöhung und Verherrlichung Jesu im Johannesevangelium* [2d ed.; NTAbh 21; Münster: Aschendorff, 1970], 262) paraphrases John 6:62 with good reasons as follows: "Wenn ihr das Aufsteigen des Menschensohnes 'schaut,' dann werdet ihr in dieser Glaubensschau meine Rede vom Lebensbrot verstehen."

[45] "Ascend" (John 6:62) and "to be lifted up" (12:32) have an inner connection (cf. 3:13–14).

group (the conjunction ὅταν, which is used here, has a similar meaning as ἐάν, as is evident from a comparison between 8:28 and 12:32). These promises always have a positive connotation. Assuming that 6:62 is a promise,[46] we can say: A full understanding of "this saying (λόγος)" (i.e., the conversations in 6:25–59) is in any case only possible after Jesus' "ascent" (ἀναβαίνω)[47] and after his resurrection and exaltation.

Jesus' message is "hard" for many disciples. They distance themselves and leave him (6:66). The "Twelve" (6:67) are, so to say, the remaining few who stay.[48] But can it be Jesus' intention that his activity (signs, conversations) causes complete and lasting rejection (unbelief), where only the behavior of the Twelve forms an exception? In the light of promises like 8:28 and 12:32, we can say that the present negative reaction of the disciples can be transformed into positive approval and faith by the event of Jesus' death and resurrection.

Only in 3:13, 6:62, and 20:17 does the verb ἀναβαίνω have the meaning of ascension into the heavenly realm. There is a special relationship between 6:62 and 20:17. The promise of the earthly Jesus in 6:62 gets new relevance from the words of the risen Jesus to Mary Magdalene in 20:17: "Do not hold me, for I have not yet ascended (ἀναβαίνω) to the Father; but go to my brethren and say to them, I am ascending (ἀναβαίνω) to my Father and your Father, to my God and your God." Jesus' resurrection is completed in the ascent, in the return to his position with God, which he had as the preexistent Christ (cf. 6:62; 17:5, 24). The words "not yet" imply that when Jesus is fully with God, a new way of communion with him will be possible. The Easter message of Mary Magdalene reminds Jesus' disciples (i.e., "his brethren") of the promise in 6:62. The Easter message is like a "key" for the right understanding of Jesus' words in 6:25–59, which are "hard" for the disciples before Easter (6:60).

The general and fundamental statement in John 6:63 ("It is the spirit that gives life, the flesh is of no avail; the words that I have spoken to you are spirit and life") is connected with the promise in 6:62. The verb "to give life" (ζῳοποιέω) can be found a second time in 5:21.[49] In 6:63 the ac-

---

[46] Thyen, (*Das Johannesevangelium*, 374–76), also regards the aposiopesis of John 6:62 as promise. According to his opinion this passage points to the Synoptic tradition of Jesus' "ascension."

[47] In John 6:25–59 the verb "to descend" (καταβαίνω in 6:33, 38, 41, 42, 50, 51, 58 always has the meaning 'to descend from heaven') is used seven times. In 6:62 the verb "to ascend" (ἀναβαίνω, namely to the place of pre-existence, i.e., heaven) is used for the first time in this context.

[48] The term "the Twelve," which is familiar from the Synoptics, occurs in the Gospel of John only in 6:67, 70, 71; 20:24.

[49] John 5:21: "For as the Father raises the dead (ἐγείρω) and gives them life (ζῳοποιέω), so also the Son gives life (ζῳοποιέω) to whom he will."

tivity of the Spirit (πνεῦμα) on Jesus and through him as the exalted Christ is described.⁵⁰ The term "flesh" (σάρξ) must therefore be referring to Jesus. The flesh (i.e., Jesus in his earthly, transitory existence) alone, taken for itself, is of no avail at all (the double negation οὐκ . . . οὐδέν implies a strong negation), i.e., it is incapable of mediating everlasting life.⁵¹ Made alive by the activity of the πνεῦμα, Jesus himself passes on life-creating πνεῦμα.

Jesus' statement that the flesh and blood of the Son of man, who descended (which is true right up to his death), are food and drink (6:52–58) is something that is only intelligible in light of the ascended Christ. "Only when the Son of man is exalted and glorified his true identity be recognized (cf. 8:28). Only then will the Son of man give the food of eternal life (v. 27c) and offer people his flesh and blood, which they must eat to have eternal life (v. 53)."⁵² The resurrected and exalted Christ is identical with the earthly Jesus, and because of that his earthly life (his preaching, his activity and behavior, as well as his willingness to sacrifice his life) has lasting importance. For a life in faith it is like food and is important and precious like bread. John 6:63 stresses also that the life-giving Spirit and life itself become a (beginning) reality when a person accepts Jesus' words (ῥήματα – plural).

1.4 Summary

The Risen One shows again that he is identical with the earthly Jesus. The group of disciples at the Sea of Tiberias recognizes this by the special meal ritual (21:13). It is the same as at the time of the feeding of the five thousand (6:11). The miraculous catch of fish is a "sign" similar to the miracle of Cana (2:1–11) and the multiplication of the loaves (6:1–15). It symbolizes that Jesus came so that we might have life in abundance (cf. 10:10). The (overabundant) gifts (wine, bread, fish) are always connected with a communal meal (for many) and especially with companionship with the giver. The pre-Easter communion meal with Jesus is continued after

---

⁵⁰ The Spirit as life-giving power is mentioned already during the conversation with Nicodemus in John 3:5–8. One may think of the Spirit mediated by Jesus (cf. John 3:34). Also in John 3:5–8 Spirit and flesh are set against each other. But this contrast refers to the believer, except in John 6:63.

⁵¹ For this "christological" interpretation of flesh cf. Schnackenburg, *Das Johannesevangelium*, 105–6; ET: *The Gospel according to St John*, 71–72. An "anthropological" interpretation was argued recently by Ulrich Wilckens, *Das Evangelium nach Johannes* (NTD 4; Göttingen: Vandenhoeck & Ruprecht, 1998), 109 and Udo Schnelle, *Das Evangelium nach Johannes* (THKNT 4; Leipzig: Evangelische Verlagsanstalt, 1998), 139.

⁵² Schnackenburg, *Das Johannesevangelium*, 104; ET: *The Gospel according to St John*, 71.

Easter. A new understanding of the conversations in 6:25–59, particularly the announcements in 6:27 and 6:51, also result from 21:1–14. An indication that the conversations can be understood in the right way only after Easter is also contained in 6:62. The relationship between John 21:1–14 and John 6 is reciprocal. The memory of the earthly Jesus (bread rite) helps the disciples in the story – as well as readers of the text – recognize the identity of the Risen One. And vice versa: The encounter with the Risen One sheds new light on words and deeds of the earthly Jesus.

2. Conversation between the Risen One and Peter in John 21:15–22

The most extensive conversation between the Risen One and a single person is within the Easter narrative in 21:15–22. Jesus' words in this conversation are at the same time his last words in the Gospel of John. The conversation is structured in two sections: John 21:15–19 and 21:20–23. It deals with the two disciples who in 21:2–13 and previously in 20:2–10 played an important role and were shown in their relationship to one another. We look for the thematic links with John 1–20.

2.1 Peter is Reminded of his Denial (John 18:15–18, 25–27)

The address, "Simon, son of John" is found only in John 21:15–17 and 1:42. It also reminds us of that first encounter with Jesus and of the giving of the symbolic name Cephas (i.e., rock). The following conversation shows that Simon can only be the "rock" as one who loves the Lord. The preeminence of Simon is connected with "greater" love. The expression "more than these" (21:15) is elliptical and has to be understood as follows: "more than they love me."[53] One may hear in this an allusion to 13:37: Peter's readiness even to give his life for Jesus.

After Jesus' third question, Simon "is grieved" (λυπέω) (21:17), and this can be interpreted as follows: The "charcoal fire" (21:9; cf. 18:18) and the question asked three times remind us of the scene of denial (18:15–18.25–27). According to the Synoptics, Peter expresses his sadness immediately after his denial and the cockcrow (cf. "weep" in Matt 26:75; Mark 14:72; Luke 22:62). However, in the Gospel of John this takes place only in chapter 21. Peter tells Jesus: "you know (οἶδα) everything" (John 21:17). This can also refer to his failure at the denial. But at the same time this does not prevent Peter from stressing a third time: "you know that I

---

[53] The following paraphrase would not be correct: "more than you love these (other disciples)."

love you." Without John 21, the story of the denial would lack a very important element, namely the account of Peter's attitude after his denial, which the Synoptics emphasize by pointing out how Peter "remembers" Jesus' prediction (Matt 26:75; Mark 14:72; Luke 22:61–62).

2.2 Relationship to the Good Shepherd Discourse (John 10:1–18)

Jesus' thrice repeated commission to Peter to "feed my lambs," "tend my sheep" and "feed my sheep" (John 21:15–17) stands in clear relation to the symbolic discourse about the "good shepherd" (10:1–18). It is about Jesus' own lambs and sheep. Characteristics of the "good" shepherd are: he leads the flock to pasture (= to life); he "knows" his own (10:14); he is ready to protect them when the "wolf" comes (10:12), and for them he "lays down his life" (τὴν ψυχὴν τίθημι; 10:11, 15, 17; cf. 15:13). Everything that characterizes Jesus, the good shepherd, is now transferred to Peter. Peter is destined to embody Jesus' role as shepherd. Through him, what Jesus said in 10:16 about his own future role as shepherd is realized: "And I have other sheep, that are not of this fold; I must bring them also, and they will heed my voice. So there shall be one flock, one shepherd." Peter is the "tool" through which Jesus, the Risen One, leads those other sheep. In line with Caiaphas' "prophecy," influenced by the metaphorical speech about the shepherd, he will "gather into one the children of God who are scattered abroad" (11:52).

2.3 Updating the Subject of Following Jesus (John 13:36–38)

Jesus' last word to Peter in John 21:15–19 is the imperative: "Follow me (ἀκολούθει μοι)!" In the same way, the following section 21:20–22 closes with the words: "Follow me!" These are also the last words that Jesus speaks in John's gospel. The call to follow Jesus reminds us of 13:36–38: the dialogue between Peter und Jesus in the farewell discourse, prompted by Jesus' announcement to his disciples: "Little children, yet a little while I am with you. You will seek me; and as I said to the Jews so now I say to you, Where I am going you cannot come" (13:33).

The dialogue in John 13:36–38 begins at Peter's initiative and takes place in two steps:

> "Simon Peter said to him (i.e., Jesus), 'Lord, where are you going?' Jesus answered, 'Where I am going you cannot follow me (ἀκολουθέω) now; but you shall follow afterwards.' Peter said to him, 'Lord why can I not follow you now? I will lay down my life (τὴν ψυχὴν τίθημι) for you.' Jesus answered, 'Will you lay down your life for me? Very truly, I tell you, before the cock crows, you will have denied me three times.'"

In a first step (13:36) Jesus speaks of a following that "now" (νῦν) is not possible. The adverb "afterwards" (ὕστερον) can be understood as a reference to 21:19. For Peter, his real following as a disciple in the right and full sense begins only after the experience of Easter and the connected chastening.[54] It will lead him to suffering (cf. 12:26 with the background of 12:24–25). In a second step (13:37–38), Peter expresses his readiness to lay down his life for Jesus. The expression "lay down the life" (τὴν ψυχὴν τίθημι) is the same as in 10:11, 15, 17 and 15:13. It is typical for John's gospel. Jesus' answer can be read as a question ("You will lay down your life for me?") as well as a statement and announcement ("You will lay down your life for me."). In this case, there is no doubt that Peter is ready to give his life and Jesus acknowledges this in a statement that anticipates the future. However, this readiness cannot be realized "now" (ἄρτι –13:37), but only after Peter's denial which is announced by Jesus in one of his Amen sayings.

Similarly, with an Amen saying, Jesus announces to Peter in 21:18 that his readiness to give his life is actually expected. Jesus' announcement in 21:18 is connected with the mission mentioned before (service as shepherd) and indicates that Peter, as the "good" shepherd (10:11, 15, 17), gives his life for those who are entrusted to him. Through a particular selection of words, the author of the comment in 21:19 hints at the thought of a parallel between Peter and his Lord. Like the passion and death of Jesus (cf. 12:28; 13:31; 17:1), Peter's suffering and dying also lead to the situation that God will be "glorified" (δοξάζω).

In John 21:15–19 various lines of John's gospel come together: Peter's denial, the image of the shepherd and the subject of following Jesus, together with the readiness to give even his own life for him. Without 21:15–19 the announcements to Peter in 13:36 ("you shall follow afterwards") and 13:38 ("you will lay down your life for me") would in a strange way remain vague and open.

2.4 Jesus "Coming" for the Parousia (John 14:2–3)

John 21:20 interrupts the conversation between Peter and John: "Peter turned (ἐπιστρέφω) and saw the disciple whom Jesus loved following (ἀκολουθέω – participle, present tense). This disciple had reclined next to him at the supper and had said, "Lord, who is it [that is going to betray you]?" This passage reminds us of 1:38 (Jesus turns [στρέφω] and sees the two disciples of John "following [ἀκολουθέω, participle, present tense])." As in 1:38 the verb "to follow" is used in 21:20 in an absolute sense. Unlike Peter, this disciple was (perhaps already since 1:38) and is continu-

---

[54] Peter can actually follow Jesus only "afterwards," i.e., after Easter. Only now he can understand what Jesus did at the washing of the feet. In John 13:7 Jesus promises Peter: "What I am doing you do not know now, but afterwards (μετὰ ταῦτα) you will understand."

ally a follower. In the narrative context this disciple appears in 21:20 for the last time. A link with 13:25 is explicitly made; this is a reminder of the first passage in which this disciple was mentioned (13:23–26).

With the expression "When Peter saw him" in 21:21 the interrupted conversation (cf. 21:20) between Jesus and Peter is continued and completed. Peter's question "Lord, what about this man?" is answered by Jesus (21:22), and at the same time these are his last words: "If it is my will that he remain until I come, what is that to you? Follow me!" The verb "to remain" (μένω, cf. 1:38–39; 15:1–8) means here: "stay here / stay alive." The phrase "until I come (ἔρχομαι)" can be interpreted in the context of expecting the Parousia.[55] The imminent Parousia not only plays a significant role in the letters of Paul and in the Synoptics, but also in the Johannine literature, albeit only in a few passages: John 14:3 and 16:13;[56] 1 John 2:28 and 3:2.[57]

John 14:3 introduces the subject of Jesus coming again to his own, which plays an important role in the Farewell Discourses: "And when I go and prepare a place for you, I will come (ἔρχομαι) again and will take you to myself, that where I am you may be also." The perfection of salvation (full communion with him) is the aim of the coming of Jesus. We can find similar promises in John 12:26 and 17:24 (cf. 1 Thess 4:16–17). But the coming of Jesus not only takes place at the Parousia, but happens already in the present time. After John 14:3 Jesus also announces that he is coming soon (ἔρχομαι) to his own (14:18, 28), that he and his Father are coming (ἔρχομαι), and he speaks of being with the one who loves him ("make our home with him," 14:23), as well as of the coming (ἔρχομαι) of the Counselor (15:26; 16:7, 8, 13). These announcements, which are different from the promise in 14:3, refer to the mysterious presence of the Risen One with his own after a short period of separation (16:16–18), as experienced by the disciples in John 21 in a special way. John 21:22 ("until I come") and

---

[55] Jörg Frey (*Die johanneische Eschatologie III* [WUNT 117; Tübingen: Mohr Siebeck, 2000], 19) interprets the phrase "bis ich komme" in connection with John 14:3 as an expression of "Erwartung der Parusie Christi."

[56] John 16:13 promises that the Paraclete will proclaim "the things that are to come" (τὰ ἐρχόμενα). This expression can be interpreted with regard to the immortal life which the Risen One already reached, and the "glory" in which he already is (cf. 17:5, 24). If one sees "the things that are to come" as longed-for salvation, then this cannot be separated from the person of Jesus – as is also shown by the context (16:13–15). Frey (*Die johanneische Eschatologie III*, 195–204) examines thoroughly the meaning of "the things that are to come." He recommends the assumption, to see "in den vom Geist verkündigten ἐρχόμενα zuerst den Bezug auf den ἐρχόμενος, auf Jesus selbst, in seinem erwarteten Wieder-Kommen bzw. dem erhoffen Wieder-Sehen mit ihm (16,16ff)" (p. 203).

[57] 1 John 2:28 and 3:2 are an expression of the conviction that Jesus "appears" again (φανερόω as in John 21:1, 14) at his "Parousia" (παρουσία).

14:3 ("I will come again") speak of the coming of Jesus at his Parousia. Jesus, who after Easter comes to his disciples in a hidden way, will then emerge from his concealment and reveal himself. Then the disciples will see him as he really is (cf. 1 John 3:2).

2.5 Summary

True following of Jesus only begins after the event of Easter, and it occurs in a new manner (this distinguishes John 21:19, 22 from Luke 5:11).[58] Following Jesus presupposes the faith of Easter; it means "to walk behind someone" who is present in a mysterious way. Peter, as well as the disciple whom Jesus loved, follow the risen Jesus. But their ways are different. Peter follows Jesus in the role of the shepherd, who – at the risk of his life – stands up for those whom the Risen One has entrusted to him ("my" lambs and sheep). The other disciple follows Jesus in the role of the reliable witness (John 21:24; cf. 19:35). He is spared a violent death. The continuation of Jesus' mission (cf. 20:21) is accentuated concerning Peter through the image of the shepherd, and concerning that disciple through the idea of bearing witness.

3. Main Results

The numbering of the appearances (21:14: "This was now the third time that Jesus was revealed to the disciples.") can be understood as referring to the possibility that – in principle – an encounter with the Risen One can still take place for the readers. The seven disciples (the number 7 stands for completeness) in John 21 infer the deeper meaning of the "sign" of the feeding of the five thousand and the words and announcements in John 6 through the encounter with the Risen One; this was not yet possible before the event of Easter. In the light of the faith of Easter they grasp in which sense Jesus is bread and food for eternal life (6:27, 51). The encounter with the Risen One is the starting point for a new following of Jesus. Peter begins a way of following Jesus that was not possible before. For that disci-

---

[58] Although we cannot see a direct literary dependence, Luke 5:1–11 and John 21:1–19 show the same subjects and motives, starting from the motive of futile work during the night to the subject of following Jesus. See further Frans Neirynck, *Jean et les Synoptiques: Examen critique de l'exégèse de M.-E. Boismard* (BETL 49; Leuven: Leuven University Press and Peeters, 1979), 140–160. The motive of the meal, however, can be found only in the Gospel of John. We may assume that the Gospel of John knows of a tradition, which we find also in Luke 5:1–11, but it is put (deliberately) in the time after Easter. This is true especially for the subject of following Jesus, motivated by his words and deeds. According to Luke 5:11, we follow the earthly Jesus, according to John 21:19 we follow the risen Lord.

ple "whom Jesus loved" following Jesus is marked by hope for his final coming.

Index of References

Old Testament

Genesis
1	145	3:28	231
1:30	45	3:38	228, 231
2:7	28, 42, 45, 90, 161, 166, 246, 286	14:11	62
		14:27	62
		17:5	231
		17:28	228, 231
3	30	18:3	231
3:8	44	18:4	231
15:16	215, 216	18:7	228, 231
18:12	216	21:9	256
20:4	228		
27:35	260	*Deuteronomy*	
32:28	260	4:4	90
49:10	56	18:15–18	61
		19:15	301

Exodus
12:14–20	60	*Judges*	
14:4	202	20:41	228
14:17–18	202		
16:4	61	*1 Kings*	
24:8	249	4:25	261
24:16	33, 202	17:17–24	75
25:8	33	17:17	246
29:46	33	17:21	166, 246
34:7	243		
34:29–35	164	*2 Kings*	
37:6–9	165	4:18–37	75
38:5–8	165	5	42
40:34–35	202		
40:35	33	*4 Bασ*	
		4:27	226, 227
Leviticus		4:37	226
4–5	197		
		2 Chronicles	
Numbers		3:12	229
1:51	228, 231	6:17	229
3:10	228, 231		

12:12	287	54:10	167
		54:13	8
Job		56:7	261
20:6	228	56:8	261
31:7	229	61:1–11	247
		61:1–4	247
Psalms		61:1–2	247
16:11	90	61:1	247
21:5	90	61:3	247
31:6	303	61:5–7	247
32:23	287	61:7	247
36:10	90	61:8	247
56:5	160	61:10	247
65:3	160	66	120
78	7	66:7–9	119
88:13	85	66:14	119, 120
132:17	261	66:18	262
145:21	160	66:22–23	250
		66:24	156
Proverbs			
9:5	271	*Jeremiah*	
		4:18	228
Ecclesiastes		23:5	261
24:8	33	23:6	56
24:10	33	31	249
		31:31–34	249, 250
Isaiah		31:31	248
4:2	261	31:32	228
11:1–10	248	31:34	248
11:1	261	33:15	261
11:3–5	248	33:16	56
11:6–8	248	38:31	248
26	119, 120	38:34	248
26:17	119	48:32	228
26:19	156		
26:20	156	*Ezekiel*	
32:15–20	248	21:36	246
32:20	248	34:25	167
37:3	119	36	249
40:3	251	36:25	249
40:6–8	31	36:26–28	249
42:12	202	36:26–27	248
43:4	202	36:26	249
48:11	202	36:27–28	167
52:13–53:12	157	36:29	249
52:13	147	36–37	249
53:4	243	37	28
53:7	243	37:1–14	248
53:11–12	243, 248	37:9	28, 45

37:26–28	167, 249	*Hosea*	
37:26	240	6:1–2	138
37:9–10	166		
37:9	246, 286	*Joel*	
41:6	229	3	248
42:14	228	*Micah*	
		1:9	228
Daniel		4:1–2	262
7	157	4:3–4	261
7:13–14	293		
7:13	239	*Zechariah*	
12:1–3	5, 156	3:8–10	261
12:1–2	259	3:8	56
12:2	256, 263, 265, 267	6:12–13	56
		13:9	287

Apocrypha

Tobit		15:11	28, 45, 166, 246, 286
6:9 S	246		
11:12 S	246	*Sirach*	
		22:11	85
Wisdom		24:19	271
1–6	157		
1:16	157	*Baruch*	
2:1–22	158	3:3	267
2:10–20	157		
2:23–24	158	*1 Maccabees*	
2:23	158	14:11–12	261
3:1–6	157		
3:1–2	267	*2 Maccabees*	
3:4	158	7	156
4:13	268	7:35	215, 216
4:16	268		
5:15	268		
7:27	268		

New Testament

Matthew		5:1	307
1:23	283	6:2	202
2:2	226	7:22	110, 309
2:8	226	8:1	307
2:11	226	8:2	226
4:10	226	8:15	221, 227

9:18	226	28:17	226, 284
9:20	228	28:20	283
10:12	281		
10:32–33	224	*Mark*	
12:13	41	1:4	245, 246, 250
14:27	62	1:7–8	251
14:31	229	1:16	307
14:33	226	1:31	227
15:25	226	2:1–12	237, 241
15:29	307	4:40	215
15:30	14	5:6	226
15:31	41	5:21–43	75
16:9	215	5:24–34	229
16:11	215	5:34	41
16:19	238, 245, 301	5:41–43	259
16:25	257	6:50	62
16:27	293	8:17	215
18:18	238, 245, 301	8:21	215
18:19	241	8:23	229
19:5	229	8:35	257
20:17–18	224	8:38	202, 293
20:20	226	9:26–27	259
20:23	293	10:13	229
21:1	224	11:1–10	140
24:15–44	156	11:1	224
24:30	239	13	156, 270
25:1–46	5	13:8	119
25:31–46	156, 266	13:15–19	119
25:34	293	13:26–27	293
25:41	293	13:26	118, 239, 294
26:27–28	249	14:3–9	140
26:32	282	14:23	142
26:36	307	14:24	249
26:75	325, 326	14:28	282
28:2–4	69	14:29–30	292
28:7	282	14:31	292
28:8–10	285	14:36	142
28:8	299	14:41	145
28:9	221, 222, 223, 225, 226, 227, 228, 281	14:50	307
		14:62	118
		14:72	325, 326
28:9–10	209, 217, 221, 222, 223, 225, 232	15:19	226
		16:5	69
		16:7	217, 282, 307
28:10	221, 222, 223, 225, 282	16:9–11	217
		16:11	110, 285
28:16–20	282, 285	16:13	285
28:16	281, 282, 285, 307	16:14	282, 285

Luke

3:3	250
4:7–8	226
4:18–19	247
5:1–11	307, 329
5:11	329
7:1–10	259
7:11–17	75
7:11–15	259
7:14	228
7:38	227
7:39	221, 227
8:44	228
9:26	293
10:5	281
10:12	110
10:22	309
10:38–42	98
11:37	319
12:4	299
14:10	202
16:22–24	255
17:22–37	156
17:33	257
17:34–35	293
18:10	224
18:15	229
18:31	224
19:28	224
21:27	239
22:3	289
22:10–13	289
22:20	249
22:33–34	292
22:61–62	326
22:62	325
23:5–16	281
23:28–31	281
23:32–33	281
23:43	255
23:46–47	303
23:49	307
24	282, 287
24:1	244, 282
24:4–5	69
24:5	110
24:9	283
24:10	283
24:11	284
24:12	217, 220
24:13	282
24:16	317
24:23	110
24:29	210, 282
24:30–31	320
24:33–36	285
24:33–34	284, 285
24:33	281, 282
24:34	284
24:35	320
24:36	244, 282
24:36–43	153, 281
24:36–49	238, 244, 246, 247
24:37	284
24:39	229, 284
24:40	284
24:41	245, 283, 299
24:42	282
24:44–49	284
24:47	245, 283, 301
24:48	283
24:49	245, 282, 283
24:50	283
24:50–53	287
24:50–51	211, 282
24:52–53	226, 282
24:52	226, 299

John

1–20	178, 313, 314–325, 325
1–12	55–66
1	283
1:1–18	21, 23–25, 38, 39, 104
1:1–13	26, 31
1:1–5	30, 37
1:1–3	25, 25–27, 37, 37–42, 40, 192
1:1–2	25, 26, 27, 32, 38, 39, 40, 43
1:1	38, 45, 47, 192
1:2	26
1:3	21, 26, 31, 32, 33, 37, 38, 39, 40, 41, 42, 196
1:4–5	21, 25, 27–29, 29
1:4	24, 27, 28, 43,

Reference	Pages
1:5	134, 255
	21, 29, 30, 134, 196
1:6–18	30, 37
1:6–13	25, 29–31
1:6–8	29, 30, 36
1:7–8	251
1:7	24
1:9–13	29, 30
1:9–10	21, 29, 150
1:9	21, 24, 27, 30, 196
1:10–13	30, 33
1:10–12	29
1:10–11	30
1:10	24, 32, 33, 37
1:11	134, 196, 255
1:11–12	196
1:12–13	30, 51
1:12	47, 62, 134, 196, 262, 263, 275
1:12c	38
1:14–18	25, 26, 27, 31, 31–46, 43
1:14	21, 24, 25, 26, 31, 32, 33, 34, 35, 36, 37, 38, 39, 43, 47, 161, 194, 203, 256, 262
1:14a	194
1:14b	194
1:14c	35
1:15–18	24
1:15	23, 36, 251
1:16–18	24, 36
1:16	37
1:17	37
1:18–19	22
1:18	25, 26, 34, 37, 37–42, 38, 39, 40, 43, 196
1:19–4:54	22
1:19–34	36
1:19	251, 319
1:23	251
1:25	283
1:26–27	251
1:27	23, 36
1:28	128, 283
1:29–36	135
1:29–34	286, 302
1:29	134, 135, 142, 150, 170, 199, 200, 242, 251
1:30–33	251
1:30	23, 36
1:31–34	286
1:31	260, 314
1:32	268
1:33	240
1:34	251
1:35–51	55
1:35–40	316
1:35–37	55, 284
1:36	134, 135, 251, 283
1:38–39	328
1:38	55, 327
1:39–41	56
1:39	56
1:40	203
1:40–42	284
1:41–42	56
1:41	259
1:42	315, 325
1:44	128, 315
1:45–51	284, 316
1:45–46	316
1:45	56
1:46	56
1:47–49	56
1:47	260
1:49	142, 193, 261, 316
1:50	56
1:50–51	74, 194, 316
1:51	56, 144, 224, 268
2:1–11	2, 135, 316, 317, 318, 324
2:1	128, 286, 316
2:1a	135
2:3	52, 317
2:4b–c	146
2:4c	135, 146
2:7–8	317
2:9	286
2:11	52, 53, 57, 74, 135, 136, 137, 203, 286, 314,

Index of References

2:13	315, 316	3:19–21	21, 29, 29, 196
2:14–22	128, 224	3:19	5, 27, 196, 256, 266
2:16	137		
2:17	230	3:20	265, 303
2:18–22	68, 128, 137	3:22	128, 314
2:18–19	43, 166	3:24	215
2:18	137	3:27–36	24
2:19–22	18, 52, 53	3:29	274
2:19–20	52	3:31–36	24
2:19	255	3:34–35	39
2:20–21	35, 137, 233, 315	3:34	193, 240, 286, 324
2:21–22	13		
2:21	160	3:35	40, 41, 42
2:22	35, 67, 137, 161, 180, 269	3:36	6, 196, 256, 267
	35, 43, 50, 68, 104, 128, 137, 139, 180, 255, 264, 279, 313, 315	4	22, 194, 225, 296
		4:1	318
		4:4–5	128
		4:7–14	240
		4:10–14	296
		4:10	2, 51, 89, 296
2:23–25	53	4:14	256, 296, 321
2:23–24	140	4:19–24	225, 226
2:25	122	4:19	193
2:23	112, 137, 164	4:21	146
3	128	4:23–24	240, 312
3:1	261	4:23	146, 233
3:2	21, 29, 193, 196, 200	4:25–26	259
		4:26	62
3:3	142, 143, 194	4:29	193
3:5–8	51, 324	4:34	39, 193
3:5	142, 143	4:36	256
3:10–21	24	4:40	318
3:10	261	4:42	193, 194, 263, 277
3:12	322		
3:13–14	146, 150, 218, 322	4:46–5:16	60
		4:46–54	316
3:13	51, 144, 224, 268, 323	4:46	316
		4:47	57, 84, 264
3:14–16	137	4:48	18, 57
3:14	2, 155, 219	4:49	84, 264
3:15–16	196	4:50–53	74
3:15	256	4:50	57
3:16–18	51	4:50a	57
3:16–17	32, 36, 46, 277	4:50b	57
3:16	26, 32, 34, 38, 40, 42, 150, 193, 196, 256, 266, 267	4:51–53	58
		4:53	68
		4:54	315
		5–12	22
3:17	32, 33	5–6	6, 12
3:18	34, 256, 266, 267	5	5–7, 9, 11, 22,

	28, 41, 42, 59, 267, 279	5:28	255, 256 1, 7, 60, 96
5:1–16	58	5:29	6, 265, 267
5:1	137, 224, 314	5:30	39, 193
5:2	128	5:36	193
5:3	41, 324	5:37	196
5:4	58	5:38	240
5:5	41	5:39	37
5:6	41	5:43	62
5:7	58	5:45–47	37
5:8	59, 60	5:51c–58	271–272
5:9–10	22	6	7–10, 16, 22, 78, 98, 128, 272, 273, 279, 316, 325, 329
5:9	41		
5:9a	59		
5:9b	59		
5:10	59	6:1–21	60
5:11–13	59	6:1–15	60, 317, 317–320, 318, 320, 324
5:11	41		
5:13	41		
5:14	41, 60, 199, 230, 314	6:1–3	307
		6:1	128, 314, 314
5:15	41	6:2–15	314
5:15–16	60	6:4	137
5:16–18	22	6:5	317
5:16	54, 140	6:5–10	286
5:17–47	60	6:9	318
5:17	26, 40, 41, 43	6:10	318
5:18	5, 41, 139, 140, 142, 301	6:11	55, 272, 318, 320, 324
5:19–47	5	6:11a	272
5:19–21	43	6:11b	272
5:19–20	39, 40, 41, 42, 43	6:11c	272
5:19	246, 320	6:12–13	286, 317
5:20	40	6:12	60
5:21–29	28	6:14–15	54
5:21	5, 6, 7, 28, 43, 60, 255, 256, 264, 323	6:14	60, 193, 259
		6:15	61, 62, 194, 307
		6:16–21	62, 286
5:22	5	6:17	29
5:24–25	28, 196	6:19–20	144
5:24	1, 5, 6, 49, 60, 193, 196, 256, 264, 267	6:19	62
		6:19c	62
		6:20	62
5:25	6, 89, 96, 146, 256, 264	6:21	62
		6:22–59	60
		6:23	314, 320
5:26	6, 28, 43, 49	6:25–59	320, 321, 322, 323, 325
5:27	6		
5:28–29	2, 3, 6, 11, 28, 49, 60, 78, 109,	6:25–27	320, 321
		6:25	89

Index of References

6:26	18, 173	6:52–59	320, 321
6:27	286, 320–321, 321, 325, 329	6:52–58	8, 9, 159, 324
		6:52	62, 320, 322
6:27c	324	6:53	272, 321
6:28–29	320	6:54	8, 87, 98, 255, 257, 260, 265, 272, 321
6:30–33	320		
6:30	53, 164		
6:31–32	37	6:55	321
6:31	7	6:56–58	8, 9
6:32–35	60	6:56–57	12
6:32	321	6:56	9, 110, 271, 272, 298
6:33	268, 277, 323		
6:34–40	320, 321	6:57–58	89
6:35	55, 62, 89, 256, 298, 321	6:57	9, 272
		6:58	9, 84, 90, 98, 265, 268, 272, 323
6:37	170, 260, 322		
6:38	193, 268, 323		
6:39	110, 170, 255, 256, 260, 265, 322	6:60–71	320
		6:60–65	322
		6:60	322, 323
6:39–40	49, 60, 65	6:61–63	322
6:39	8, 72, 87	6:62	144, 218, 219, 224, 321–324, 322, 323, 325
6:40	8, 87, 110, 196, 255, 256, 260, 265, 321		
		6:63	257, 322, 323, 324
6:41–51	320, 321		
6:41	62, 268, 320, 322, 323	6:64–65	322
		6:65	322
6:42	268, 323	6:66–71	317, 322
6:43	62	6:66	62, 323
6:44	8, 87, 110, 255, 256, 260, 265, 322	6:67	323
		6:68–69	193, 316
		6:68	63, 257
6:45	8	6:70	194, 323
6:46	196	6:71	137, 323
6:47–48	8, 321	7	221, 225, 296
6:47	8, 196, 256, 321	7:1–18	225
6:48	62, 89, 256, 321	7:1	128, 139, 142, 301, 314
6:49	84, 265		
6:50	84, 90, 257, 265, 268, 323	7:2	137
		7:4	142, 286, 314
6:51–59	272	7:6	140, 146
6:51–58	2, 143, 298	7:7	204, 277
6:51	8, 35, 89, 160, 257, 268, 277, 320–321, 321, 323, 325, 329	7:8–9	225
		7:8	146, 216, 224
		7:10	137, 140, 224
		7:11	142
6:51c–58	137	7:13	282
6:51a	89	7:14	224
6:51c	272	7:16	193

7:17	193	8:42	240
7:19–20	139	8:46–47	199
7:19	142, 301	8:46	191, 243, 303
7:23	41	8:51–52	322
7:25	139, 142, 301	8:51	264, 265
7:30	139, 142, 145, 146, 301	8:52–53	264
		8:52	84, 264, 265
7:32	139	8:53	84
7:33–35	117	8:59	140
7:33–34	292	9	22, 41, 42, 63, 173, 197, 243
7:33	78, 117		
7:34	259	9:1–5	59
7:35	78, 263	9:2–5	286
7:36	259	9:2–3	243
7:37–39	2, 51, 240, 296, 321	9:2	197
		9:3	193, 197
7:38	143	9:4–5	21, 29, 55
7:39	155, 180, 279, 291, 313	9:4	41, 193
		9:5	196
7:44	139	9:6	42
7:51	322	9:7	42, 63, 74
8:3	29	9:9	63
8:4	29	9:11	63
8:12	21, 29, 55, 89, 196, 256	9:12	63
		9:13–14	22
8:13	301	9:13–34	42
8:17	301	9:14	41
8:18	301	9:16	22, 37, 54, 63
8:20	139, 145, 146	9:17	63
8:21–30	243	9:22	22, 205, 282, 311
8:21–22	78, 117, 259	9:24–34	37
8:21	84, 142, 199, 242, 243, 267, 292	9:24	197, 199
		9:28	63
		9:31	197
8:24	84, 242, 243, 265	9:33	63
8:25	319	9:34–35	311
8:27	139	9:34	22, 63, 197, 242
8:28–29	200	9:35	63
8:28	39, 147, 155, 193, 200, 201, 218, 322, 323, 324	9:36	63
		9:37–38	63
		9:37	74
		9:38	193, 226, 227
8:31–59	35, 243	9:39–41	42, 198, 242
8:31	146, 322	9:39	21, 29, 198, 227
8:34–36	199	9:41	243
8:34	243	10	80
8:35	271	10:1–18	326
8:36	322	10:1–5	96
8:37	142, 301	10:3–4	70, 196
8:40	139, 142, 301	10:7	89

10:9–10	89		85, 86, 93, 95, 138, 203, 264, 265
10:9	89		
10:10	196, 257, 324		
10:11	28, 36, 43, 85, 89, 90, 326, 327	11:5	12, 82, 94, 96, 139
10:12	326	11:6–16	81, 82
10:14	89, 168, 326	11:6	82, 97, 99, 138, 318
10:15	36, 43, 85, 137, 326, 327	11:7–16	286
10:16	70, 104, 262, 326	11:7	77, 78, 95, 314
10:17–18	43, 47, 85, 137, 193, 195, 274	11:8	77, 78, 82, 92, 96, 138, 140, 142
10:17	36, 67, 150, 326, 327	11:9–10	78, 82, 85
		11:10–11	83
10:18	193, 260	11:10	196
10:22–24	138	11:11–15	96
10:25	193	11:11–14	265
10:27	70	11:11–13	83
10:27–30	260	11:11	12, 78, 86, 96, 257, 274, 300, 314
10:27–29	170		
10:28	196, 257, 267		
10:30	26	11:12–16	82
10:31–33	139	11:13–14	96
10:31	140	11:13	82, 84, 264
10:32	193	11:14	49, 84, 87, 264
10:34	301	11:15	78, 82, 84, 87, 96, 97
10:36	240		
10:37–38	193	11:16	71, 77, 78, 81, 83, 84, 85, 138, 140, 264, 316
10:37	193, 230		
10:38	193		
10:39	139, 142	11:17–37	82
10:40–11:1	64	11:17–27	81, 81, 82, 90
10:40–42	80, 138	11:17–22	81
10:41	287	11:17	49
11:1–12:11	82	11:18	78, 137
11	2, 10–12, 11, 75–101, 80, 137, 141, 164	11:19	82
		11:21	10, 64, 84, 87, 90, 94, 99, 264
11:1–54	80	11:22–25	97
11:1–53	80	11:22	64, 92
11:1–44	48, 64, 80, 81, 137, 138, 149	11:23–27	81
		11:23–24	64, 83, 255
11:1–16	81	11:23	87, 265
11:1–5	82	11:24–26	11
11:1–2	95	11:24	1, 66, 75, 78, 88, 92, 110, 255, 257, 265
11:1	80, 95, 128		
11:2	23, 80, 82, 93, 313		
		11:25–26	28, 49, 52, 55, 64, 65, 76, 78, 83, 87, 88, 90,
11:3	12, 95, 139, 257		
11:4	52, 78, 82, 84,		

	196, 265	11:48	81, 84, 127
11:25	1, 10, 28, 43, 49, 84, 89, 96, 100, 138, 255	11:49–52	86
		11:50	84, 86, 142
		11:51–52	83, 86, 137
11:26	10, 84, 89, 101	11:51	84, 264
11:27	64, 74, 84, 91, 92, 97, 138, 139, 193, 259	11:52	104, 262, 263, 275, 326
		11:52b	262
11:28–37	81, 82, 93	11:53	85, 137, 138, 301
11:28–32	81	11:54–57	81
11:28	92, 97	11:55–57	137
11:29	93, 97, 255	11:55	224
11:30	82	11:56	142
11:31–32	83	12	137, 141
11:31	82, 86, 93, 97, 123, 255	12:1–11	80, 81, 82
		12:1–8	13, 81, 137, 140
11:32	10, 84, 94, 97, 99, 264	12:1–2	81
		12:1	128, 137, 139, 140, 255, 264
11:33–45	81		
11:33–44	81	12:2–3	93, 95
11:33	83, 86, 123	12:2	11, 90, 98
11:35–37	82	12:3	23, 94
11:35	87, 139	12:4–8	83
11:36	12, 139	12:4–6	81, 140
11:37	84	12:6	13
11:38–44	81, 82, 96	12:7–10	78
11:38	97, 138, 139	12:7	13, 95, 140
11:39–40	92, 194	12:8b	140
11:39	64, 85, 94	12:9–11	13, 137, 140
11:40	65, 74, 78, 82, 84, 93, 138, 164, 322	12:9	81, 139, 140, 255, 264
		12:10	85, 140
11:41–42	90	12:11	80, 81, 84, 98
11:41b–42	82	12:12–19	137
11:42	84	12:12–18	65, 66
11:43–44	65, 90, 139	12:12	128, 137
11:43	87, 96	12:13	142, 193, 261
11:44	55, 68, 78, 80, 86, 138	12:15–16	68
		12:15	142
11:45–57	77, 81, 82	12:16	43, 50, 104, 128, 140, 155, 180, 194, 279, 313
11:45–54	100		
11:45–53	65, 81		
11:45–47	80, 140	12:17	96, 139, 140, 255, 264
11:45	53, 80, 84, 86, 138		
		12:20–21	263
11:46–53	81	12:20	11, 224, 226
11:46–50	65	12:21	228
11:47–57	140	12:23–27	85
11:47–53	85, 138	12:23	135, 145, 146, 147, 155, 195
11:47	54, 140		

Index of References   341

12:24–25	265, 327	13:4	289
12:24	84, 93, 141	13:7	128, 327
12:25	257, 276	13:10	298
12:26	269, 327, 328	13:12–16	36, 299–300
12:27–33	146, 147	13:12	318
12:27–32	137	13:13	300
12:27–28	44, 135, 145	13:14	300
12:27	145, 147	13:15	12, 42
12:28–36	78, 93	13:19	201, 279
12:28	327	13:20	246
12:29	29	13:23–26	328
12:31–32	297, 303	13:23–25	68
12:31	218, 276	13:23	39
12:32–34	66	13:25	39, 328
12:32–33	87	13:27	13, 289, 297, 303
12:32	2, 104, 143, 147, 155, 242, 246, 277, 319, 322, 323	13:30	21, 29, 85, 196, 289, 303
		13:31–17:21	290
		13:31–16:33	103–126
12:33	84, 147, 264	13:31–14:31	120, 121, 290, 291, 291–297, 306
12:34	29		
12:35–36	21, 29, 196		
12:35	29, 117, 196	13:31–38	293
12:37–41	286	13:31–32	104, 148, 155, 195, 203
12:37	53, 100, 135, 136, 286		
		13:31	12, 16, 327
12:41	203	13:33–38	293
12:42	205, 311	13:33	107, 109, 117, 259, 291, 292, 317, 326
12:44	49		
12:46	21, 29, 196		
12:47–48	266	13:34–35	36, 42, 46, 141, 277, 290
12:47	277		
12:48	110, 196	13:34	273
12:49–50	193	13:35	274
12:49	193	13:36–38	111, 326, 326–327
12:50	49, 257		
13–21	27	13:36	107, 109, 117, 292, 302, 326, 327
13–17	22, 162, 289		
13–16	291		
13–14	291, 308	13:37–38	327
13:1–20	141	13:37	325, 327
13:1–17	290	13:38	292, 327
13:1	36, 42, 85, 141, 143, 145, 146, 150, 164, 191, 195, 224, 256, 257, 276, 289	14–17	13–15
		14–16	240, 125
		14	13–14, 16, 239, 247, 249, 301, 304, 305
13:2	289	14:1–14	239
13:3	117, 141, 191, 225, 294	14:1–3	106, 247
		14:1–2	232

14:1	294, 302	14:18–21	111, 113, 115, 269
14:2–3	72, 268, 269, 293, 294, 295, 296, 297, 327–329	14:18–20	295, 296, 310
		14:18–19	70, 125
		14:18	14, 104, 106, 107, 108, 109, 110, 111, 239, 249, 259, 270, 295, 328
14:2	14, 107, 269, 293, 294		
14:2a	233		
14:2b–3	234		
14:3	14, 104, 107, 118, 257, 259, 294, 328, 329	14:18b	112
		14:19–24	106
		14:19	14, 89, 105, 106, 107, 109, 111, 112, 113, 271, 294, 295, 314
14:4–14	247		
14:4	107		
14:5	107, 109, 292, 302		
		14:20–21	113
14:6	28, 43, 89, 107, 232, 257	14:20	109, 110, 111, 112, 114, 176, 201, 220, 290, 294, 295, 297, 307
14:7	71		
14:8–11	196		
14:8	292		
14:9–11	193	14:21–24	124, 296
14:9	104, 117, 194, 197	14:21–22	113
		14:21	110, 112, 113, 114, 115, 232, 271, 295, 314
14:10–11	294		
14:10	193, 271		
14:11	193	14:21a	110, 112
14:12–14	294	14:21b	110
14:12	106, 107, 109, 118, 174, 224, 253, 294	14:22–24	106, 111
		14:22	110, 112, 292, 294, 314
14:13–14	289, 290, 294, 306	14:23–24	113, 114, 115
		14:23	72, 105, 107, 110, 111, 113, 114, 232, 239, 249, 257, 259, 267, 268, 269, 270, 294, 295, 296, 297, 308
14:13	203		
14:14	290		
14:15–27	294		
14:15–24	239, 247, 249		
14:15–17	115, 128		
14:16–17	45, 70, 118, 166, 240, 249, 290, 296, 302		
		14:24	110, 113, 193, 220
14:16	249, 296, 302	14:25–26	106, 110, 115, 118
14:16c	296		
14:17	14, 72, 104, 109, 259, 271, 312	14:25	105, 115
		14:26–27	45
14:18–26	103, 106, 108–115, 110, 120, 125	14:26	51, 70, 115, 128, 240, 247, 259, 269, 271, 279, 290, 296, 302, 303, 310, 312
14:18–24	110, 111, 122, 296, 314		

14:27	44, 70, 166, 240, 247, 274, 302	15:15–16	300
14:27b–28	106	15:15	105, 220, 299, 300
14:28	72, 104, 105, 107, 119, 166, 224, 232, 240, 247, 270, 297, 328	15:16	105, 289, 299, 300, 306
		15:18–27	260
		15:18–19	204, 276
		15:18–16:4a	105, 117, 122, 298, 300, 302
14:28a	106		
14:29	105, 201, 270, 279, 289, 291, 297	15:18	105, 298, 300
		15:19	105, 199, 277, 300
14:30–31	290, 297	15:20	105, 298, 300
14:30	276, 290, 303	15:21	298
14:31	39, 78, 193, 289, 290, 291	15:22–24	198, 242, 301
		15:22	105
15–17	290, 291	15:24	243
15–16	121, 291, 311	15:25	301, 306
15:1–16:4a	297, 297–302, 301	15:26–27	14, 45, 51, 73
		15:26	70, 128, 240, 259, 271, 290, 298, 301, 302, 312, 328
15	14, 298, 299, 300, 301, 308		
15:1–17	290		
15:1–11	299	15:27	302
15:1–8	128, 297, 328	16	107, 304, 305, 307, 308
15:1–7	12		
15:1–2	298	16:1–4	304
15:2	243, 298	16:1–4a	301
15:3	298	16:1	279, 298
15:4	73, 271, 297, 298	16:2	146, 205, 298, 301
15:5–7	14		
15:5–6	298	16:3	298
15:5	317	16:4–33	247
15:6	14, 267, 298	16:4	146, 279, 298
15:7–8	289, 306	16:4a	298
15:7	290, 299	16:4b–33	120, 290, 302, 302–308
15:8	203		
15:9–11	297	16:4b–7	302
15:9	73, 105	16:4b–6	117
15:10	14, 193, 271	16:4b	117, 302
15:11	16, 105, 119, 120, 274, 299, 306, 308, 310	16:5	72, 259, 302
		16:6–7	201
		16:6	105, 119, 123, 299, 305
15:12–17	297, 299		
15:12	105, 273, 298	16:7–15	45
15:13–15	268, 274	16:7–14	240, 247
15:13	12, 16, 85, 257, 300, 326, 327	16:7–11	117, 128, 271, 290
15:14–16	106	16:7	15, 70, 118, 166, 301, 328
15:14	299		

16:8–11	158, 242, 302, 303, 308	16:23b–24	306
16:8–10	14	16:24	119, 274, 290, 299, 308, 310
16:8–9	197, 198, 243	16:24a	306
16:8	247, 259, 275, 312, 328	16:24b	306
		16:25–33	306
16:9	303	16:25	105, 146
16:10	119, 224, 247	16:26–27	290
16:11	276, 297, 303	16:26	110, 119, 290, 307
16:12–15	117		
16:12	304	16:27	105, 308
16:13–15	51, 128, 290, 303, 305, 328	16:28	67, 72, 105, 164, 224, 304, 307
16:13	260, 304, 312, 328	16:29–30	306
		16:30	194, 307
16:13b	304	16:31–32	194
16:16–33	304	16:32	105, 307, 315
16:16–24	306, 310	16:33	70, 105, 118, 119, 120, 166, 240, 247, 274, 276, 297, 303, 305
16:16–22	103, 106, 107, 116–124, 117, 119, 120, 125		
16:16–19	118, 119, 121–122	17	44, 257, 307
16:16–18	314, 328	17:1	85, 135, 145, 148, 164, 203, 327
16:16	105, 107, 118, 121, 122, 123, 124, 304, 305	17:2	47, 258
16:16a	121	17:3	240, 258, 270
16:17–19	121, 305	17:4	148, 193, 203
16:17	47, 107, 121, 124, 224	17:5	38, 39, 148, 192, 195, 203, 323, 328
16:17a	117		
16:18	121	17:6–8	205
16:19	107, 122, 124	17:6	314
16:20–24	122, 275	17:8	193
16:20–22	106, 240, 247	17:10	203
16:20	106, 119, 122–123, 201, 305	17:11–15	260
		17:11	51, 72, 204, 259
16:21–22	87, 306, 306	17:12	142, 170, 260, 267
16:21–15	312		
16:21	119, 120, 123, 123–124	17:13	119, 120, 124, 259, 274, 299
16:22	105, 119, 120, 124, 201, 304, 305	17:14	193, 199, 204, 276
		17:16	199
16:22b	124	17:18–26	46
16:23–30	117	17:18	44, 106, 240, 271, 277
16:23–24	290		
16:23	110, 119, 201, 246, 290, 307	17:20–23	205
		17:21–23	204

17:21	46, 220, 262, 271	19:15	87, 142
17:22	148, 203, 203	19:17	84, 128, 135
17:23	46, 220, 271	19:19	142, 155
17:24–25	150	19:20	263
17:24	39, 40, 42, 49, 55, 64, 72, 148, 164, 203, 269, 328	19:21	142
		19:25–27	135, 225
		19:26–27	68
		19:28	143, 191, 314
17:25	323	19:29	199
18–21	290	19:30	2, 143, 193, 194, 218, 265
18–19	22, 280		
18	307	19:31	35, 160, 161
18:1–11	142	19:32	66
18:1–3	297	19:34–37	244
18:1	128, 289	19:34	284, 296
18:3	289	19:34b	143
18:4	142, 191	19:35–37	314
18:5–6	297, 303	19:35	143, 329
18:5	142	19:36	199
18:5a	142	19:38–42	66, 140, 143, 280
18:5b	142	19:38–39	128
18:6	142, 318	19:38	35, 160, 161, 282, 314
18:7–8	142		
18:7	142	19:39	313
18:8	43, 307	19:40	35, 78, 138, 160, 161
18:9	142, 170, 260		
18:11	142	19:41–42	128, 280, 282
18:13	128	19:41	143, 280
18:14	84, 142, 265, 301, 313	20–21	15–16, 21
		20	2, 15, 18, 22, 43, 66–72, 105, 106, 125 145, 153–176, 154, 162, 175, 191, 219, 238, 239, 258, 280, 280–285, 285, 289, 290, 291, 297, 298, 299, 300, 304, 305, 306, 308, 309, 310, 311, 314, 315, 317
18:15–18	325, 325–326		
18:15–16	68		
18:16	315		
18:18	318, 325		
18:20	301		
18:24	128		
18:25–27	325, 325–326		
18:28	128, 243		
18:32	84, 264, 265		
18:33	142		
18:36	61, 142		
18:37	142		
18:39	142	20:1–29	143, 149
18:40	87	20:1–18	217, 218, 220, 231, 238, 283
19	15, 155		
19:3	142	20:1–10	143, 219, 220
19:7	142	20:1–2	163, 238, 283
19:8	87	20:1	21, 43, 67, 138, 129, 280, 317
19:12	87, 142		
19:14	142, 199, 243	20:2–10	280, 315, 325

20:2	67, 163, 223, 283		224, 225, 227,
20:3–18	164		228, 229, 230,
20:3–10	67, 164, 218, 220, 238		231, 232, 233, 234, 238, 287,
20:3–8	280		288, 295, 300,
20:5–12	47		308, 315, 323
20:5–8	44	20:17a	209, 210, 222,
20:5	67, 164		232, 235, 236
20:6–7	139	20:17b	210, 211, 212,
20:6	67, 109, 118, 119		213, 215, 217,
20:7	78, 138, 164		219, 221, 222,
20:8	17, 67, 144, 318		235, 236
20:9–10	68	20:17bc	212
20:9	128, 255, 264	20:17c	210, 211, 212,
20:11–18	143, 144, 154, 165, 211, 221, 231, 233, 238, 283		213, 214, 215, 216, 217, 218, 219, 221, 222, 223, 224, 225, 232, 233, 235,
20:11–15	280		236
20:11–12	283		
20:11	119, 123, 283, 305, 318	20:17cd 20:17d	212 210, 211, 212,
20:11a	219		213, 214, 222,
20:11b–14a	219		225, 235, 236
20:11b–13	218	20:17e	209, 210, 212,
20:12	35, 69, 109, 118, 119, 160, 161		213, 214, 222, 235, 236
20:13	69, 119, 123, 305	20:17f	210, 213, 214,
20:14–18	200, 218, 219		215, 216, 219,
20:14–17	222, 224		220, 221, 222,
20:14–16a	223		223, 224, 225,
20:14–15	222		232, 233, 235,
20:14	109, 118, 119, 283, 317	20:18	236 118, 165, 172,
20:14b–18	219		200, 231, 283,
20:15	4, 69, 119, 123, 200, 280, 283, 305	20:19–29 20:19–23	314 44, 165, 315 136, 144, 165,
20:16–17	223		195, 238, 239,
20:16	17, 69, 145, 200, 222, 283, 317, 320		240, 241, 244, 246, 247, 281, 283, 298, 310, 311
20:17–18	69		
20:17	38, 43, 47, 106, 110, 114, 195, 200, 209, 209–236, 210, 211, 213, 214, 216, 217, 218, 219, 220, 221, 222,	20:19–20 20:19	238, 285, 295, 305 4, 45, 47, 70, 109, 119, 194, 201, 239, 240, 241, 244, 274, 281, 282, 284,

		290, 295, 296, 297, 298, 300, 305, 307, 308, 309, 315, 317	20:27–28 20:27		201 210, 214, 284, 287, 320
20:20		118, 119, 124, 144, 200, 240, 245, 287, 299, 314, 320	20:28 20:29–31 20:29		71, 285, 286, 316 50, 51, 287, 309 18, 34, 53, 70, 72, 118, 167, 169, 203, 204,
20:20ab		239			205, 206, 283,
20:20b		145			285, 287, 288,
20:20cd		239			289, 296, 303,
20:21–23		238, 286, 310, 315	20:29b		310, 316 145
20:21–22		302	20:30–31		18, 53, 91, 104,
20:21		44, 70, 106, 119, 239, 240, 274, 277, 285, 308, 310, 329	20:30		136, 137, 167, 206, 238, 280, 291, 295, 314 135, 286, 287,
20:22–23		249, 283			288
20:22		4, 17, 45, 46, 70, 106, 240, 245, 246, 249, 271, 286, 310	20:31 21		48, 65, 73, 196, 258, 259, 285, 286, 288, 295 2, 15, 18, 22, 23,
20:22ab		239			163, 178, 272,
20:22cd–23		239			280, 290, 307,
20:23		171, 199, 200, 229, 237, 237– 252, 238, 241, 242, 243, 246, 248, 249, 251, 286, 301, 310	21:1–25 21:1–23 21:1–19		313, 313–330, 314, 319, 325, 326, 328, 329 22 314 329
20:24–29		136, 144, 150, 154, 167, 241, 316	21:1–14 21:1		263, 313, 314– 325, 318, 325 307, 313, 314,
20:24–25		238, 310			314–315, 328
20:24		109, 241, 285, 316, 323	21:2–14 21:2–13		316 314, 315, 318,
20:25		53, 71, 118, 201, 284, 314, 316	21:2		319, 321, 325 315, 315–317,
20:25a		70			316
20:25b		70	21:3–13		317, 317–324
20:26–29		195, 238, 284, 298	21:3 21:4		307, 317 317, 317
20:26–28		53	21:5–6a		317
20:26–27		295	21:5		318
20:26		47, 119, 274, 282, 283, 284, 295, 298, 300, 308, 309, 315, 317	21:6 21:7–11 21:7 21:8–10 21:8		317, 318 319 68, 316, 318, 319 319 318

21:9–13	320	2:46	289
21:9	318, 319, 325	3:1	289, 303
21:10–11	277	3:14	303
21:10	318, 319	4:10	41
21:11	262, 263, 318, 319	4:16	287
		4:22	287
21:12	18, 317, 319	4:30	287
21:13	272, 318, 319, 320, 321, 324	5:12	287
		5:31	147
21:13a	272	6:8	287
21:13b	272	7:52	303
21:13c	272	8:6	287
21:14	139, 255, 264, 314, 314–315, 315, 328, 329	8:13	287
		9:36–42	75, 259
		11:2	224
21:15–23	313	11:27–28	304
21:15–22	325, 325–329	12	289, 311, 311
21:15–19	315, 325, 326, 327	12:1–4	311
		12:3–4	311
21:15–17	319, 325, 326	12:5	311
21:15	314, 325	12:6	311
21:17	325, 325	12:12	311
21:18	327	12:13	311
21:19	264, 327, 329	12:16	311
21:20–23	325	12:23	202
21:20–22	326	13:1–3	304
21:20	313, 327, 328	13:14	299
21:21	328	14:3	287
21:22–23	259, 269, 270, 293	14:22	308
		15:12	287
21:22	328, 329	15:32	304
21:23	49, 84, 98, 118, 264, 300	17:27	229
		19:1–7	251
21:24–25	23, 314	20:7–21	289
21:24	316, 329	20:7–12	75, 259
		21:11	304
		21:12	224
Acts		21:15	224
1	282, 287	21:26	289
1:2–3	285	21:27–28	289
1:2f–3	285	22:14	303
1:2	211	24:11	224
1:3	110	25:11	224
1:9–11	211	27:3	299
1:9	310		
1:13	285	*Romans*	
1:21–22	285	4:23–24	112
2:33	147	5:2	202
2:43	287	14:17	247

1 Corinthians			Titus	
5	303		2:8	41
7:1	229			
10:16	142		Hebrews	
10:21	142		6:8	14
11:18	311		9:22	248
11:23–26	272		10:11–18	248
11:25–27	142		10:14–18	248, 249
11:25	249		10:18	248
12:10	304		11:16	293
12:28	304		11:35	259
14:4–39	304		12:18	229
14:23	311			
15	153		1 Peter	
15:1–8	19		1:21	219
15:5	285		3:21–22	219
15:12	259			
15:20–28	112		1 John	
15:26	303			33
15:40–43	202		1:1	229
15:52	2631		1:2	314
			1:3	274
2 Corinthians			1:4	274
2:14	13		1:6	274
			1:7	274, 275
Galatians			1:8	275
2:1	224		1:9	242, 246, 303
			1:10	275
Ephesians			2:1–2	307
1:20	219		2:1	303, 317
			2:6	275
Philippians			2:9–11	36, 300
1:23	255		2:12	242, 246, 317
2:2	299		2:14	317
2:9	147		2:15	276
			2:18	317
1 Thessalonians			2:27	276
4:16–17	328		2:28	118, 269, 293, 314, 317, 328
4:16	293			
4:17	14, 293		2:29	275, 303
			3:2	118, 269, 293, 314, 328, 329
2 Timothy				
1:12	309		3:3–10	275
1:18	309		3:5	314
2:17–18	6		3:7	303, 317
2:18	259		3:8	314
			3:10	300
			3:12–17	300
			3:14–18	36

3:14	256	*Revelation*	
3:17	274, 275	1:6	202
3:18	317	1:9	308
3:23	275	1:10	304
4:4	317	1:18	110
4:9–12	42	2–3	316
4:9	34	2:5	294
4:16	16, 42	2:9–10	308
4:19–21	274	2:11	89
4:19	42	2:16	294
4:20–21	300	6:9–10	255
5:16	300	11:27–30	304
5:18	229	12:1–6	119
5:21	317	12:6	293
		13:1–2	304
2 John		15:8	202
3	274	19:10	304
12	274	20:6	89
		20:11–15	5
3 John		20:14	14, 89
3	300	21:8	89
4	275	22:2	298
5	300	22:6–21	298
10	300	22:10	303
15	268, 274, 299	22:14	298, 303
		22:16	298

Extra-Canonical Jewish Writings

2 Baruch		*4 Ezra*	
30:1–5	264	4:42	119
72:6	260		
74:2	258	*Jubilees*	
78:7	260	5:12	250
1 Enoch		*Life of Adam and Eve (Apocalypse)*	
42:2	33	41:3	256
62:4	119		
104:5	266	*Odes of Solomon*	
104:7	266	12:12	33
2 Enoch		*Prayer of Jacob*	
38:2	266	19	267
65:7–10	258		
65:11	266	*Psalms of Solomon*	
		3:10–11	266
		14:9	266

17	260	32:17	258
17:30–31	262	62:9	258

Pseudo-*Philo*
Liber antiquitatum biblicarum (L.A.B.)

Testament of Benjamin
10:11   260

3:10	258
16:3	258
19:7	258
19:13	258

Testament of Job
4:9–11   264

Dead Sea Scrolls

1 QH

III, 9–18	119
III, 21–22	268
VI, 13	250
IV, 24–25	268

Pseudo-Ezekiel

4Q385	265
4Q521	265

Extra-Canonical Early Christian Writings

Didache

9:1–2	298
11–13	304

Eusebius
Supplementa quaestionum ad Marinum
PG 22, 1016   310

Ignatius
Ephesians
2:20   9

Irenaeus
Adversus haereses (Haer.)
1.23.5   259

Justin Martyr
Apology

1.26.4	259
1.31.1	304

Classical Writings

Aristotle
Nichomachean Ethics
1135b 16–20   188

Poetics

1449b 17–18	181
1449b 24–28	181
1450a 4	185
1450a 15–17	185
1450a 21–22	185
1450a 33–35	186
1450a 38–39	185
1450b 23–27	185
1450b 24–30	185–186
1452a 1–6	186
1452a 12–18	186
1452a 22–23	186
1452a 29–32	186
1452b 10	186
1452b 33–36	190
1452b 34–1453a 17	187
1453a 7–10	187
1453a 12–16	187
1454b 19–1455a 21	187

1454b 27–1454a 15	186

Politics
1341b 34	183
1341b 40	182
1341b–42b	182
1342a 4–16	183

Rhetoric
1374a–1374b	188
1374a 26–28	188
1374b 6–10	188
1382a 21–22	184
1383b 1–5	181
1385b 13–19	184
1385b 19–24	181

Cicero
Pro Sestio
48 §103	61

Dio Chrysostom
Orations
32.31	61

Epictetus
Discourses
2.17.29	300

Euripides
Alcestis
266	85

Fronto
Correspondance
2.17	61

Homer
Illiad
4.461	85

Juvenal
Satires
10.44–46	61
10.73–80	61

Index of Modern Authors

Aland, Barbara 299
Aland, Kurt 42, 299
Alkier, Stefan 101
Allison, Dale C. 283
Anderson, Paul N. 7, 9
Andresen, Carl 147
Appold, Mark L. 271
Ashton, John 27, 66
Attridge, Harold W. 2, 50, 194, 200, 202, 215
Aune, David E. 58, 253, 254, 256, 269, 271, 296
Avemarie, Friedrich 77

Baarda, Tjitze 18, 167
Backhaus, Knut 50, 136, 206
Ball, David Mark 62
Barrett, C. K. 24, 25, 26, 27, 29, 31, 33, 34, 35, 37, 38, 46, 49, 56, 67 107, 108, 116, 120, 213, 262, 269
Bauckham, Richard 1, 61, 77, 130, 280, 292, 293
Bauer, Walter 116, 221, 299
Beasley-Murray, George R. 108
Becker, Jürgen 53, 108, 115, 116, 119, 120, 131, 133, 134, 136, 147, 148, 149, 222, 226, 269, 291
Behm, Joannes 128
Belfiore, Elisabeth 181, 189
Bengel, Johann Albrecht 116
Bennema, Cornelis 17
Benoit, Pierre 17, 211, 219
Berger, Klaus 85, 127, 292
Bernard, J. H. 23
Beutler, Johannes 141, 237, 240, 242, 244, 247, 248
Bieringer, Reimund 2, 76, 77, 205, 231, 263, 303, 304, 312
Black, C. Clifton 16, 27
Blank, Josef 108, 116

Blass, Friederich 104, 230
Bockmuehl, Markus 1, 76
Bogart, John 275
Bonney, William 71
Borg, Marcus 154
Borgen, Peder 7, 27, 30, 37, 38
Bracken, Joseph A. 161
Brant, J.-A. 191, 193
Bremer, Jan M. 188
Brock, Ann Graham 4
Brouwer, Wayne 14
Brown, Dan 17
Brown, Raymond E. 17, 32, 35, 47, 48, 51, 55, 62, 65, 92, 108, 109, 116, 163, 204, 220, 227, 254, 273, 280, 295
Buch-Hansen, Gitte 16
Bühler, Pierre 132, 178, 191
Bultmann, Rudolf 12, 15, 22, 23, 34, 53, 54, 108, 115, 116, 124, 132, 146, 155, 191, 192, 193, 194, 196, 218, 271, 272, 295, 303
Burge, Gary M. 72, 128
Burkett, Delbert 6, 10, 79
Burridge, Richard A. 129
Busse, Ulrich 211, 219, 287, 319
Byrne, Brendan J. 68, 79, 163

Caird, G. B. 202
Carson, D. A. 169, 210, 212, 213, 258
Casey, Maurice 16
Cavallin, H. C. 77
Cebulj, Christian 88
Charlesworth, James H. 17, 77, 265, 268
Chatman, Seymour 177, 179
Clark-Soles, Jaime 49, 264, 267, 268
Claudel, Gérard 237, 246
Clifford, Richard J. 165
Coakley, Sarah 18

Collins, John J. 1
Collins, Raymond F. 54, 214
Coloe, Mary L. 35, 161, 261, 267, 269, 271, 274
Conway, Colleen M. 65, 91
Conzelmann, Hans 259
Courtès, Joseph 180, 193
Courtney, Edward 61
Crossan, John Dominic 273
Crotty, Robert 163
Cullmann, Oscar 157
Culpepper, R. Alan 7, 9, 16, 23, 27, 38, 50, 62, 104, 116, 134, 137177, 178, 179, 191, 192, 193, 194, 263, 271, 272, 273, 274, 276, 277

D' Costa, Gavin 16, 19
D'Angelo, Mary R. 200
Dahl, Nils A. 7
Davies, W. D. 283
de Jonge, Marinus 18, 167
Debrunner, Albert 104, 230
DeConick, April D. 167
Delling, Gerhard 117, 315
Denaux, Adelbert 304
Dennis, John A. 260, 262, 263
Dettwiler, Andreas 48, 50, 106, 107, 108, 109, 113, 114, 115, 116, 119, 120, 122, 131, 132, 200, 290, 295, 302, 303, 305, 306
Detweiler, Robert 177
Deuser, Hermann 101
Dhanis, E. 163
Dibelius, Martin 258
Dietzfelbinger, Christian 89, 90, 106, 108, 110, 114, 116, 122, 178, 203, 288, 301, 304, 305, 306
Dilthey, Wilhelm 22
Dobbeler, Axel von 85, 134
Dodd, C. H. 23, 30, 31, 34, 35, 38, 108
Dolle, R. 310
Donahue, John R. 19, 32, 35, 47, 134, 273
Dormeyer, Detlev 129
Douglas, Mary 289
Droysen, Johann Gustav 127
Dschulnigg, Peter 140
Dube, Musa W. 178
Dupont, L. 163

Dušek, J. 193

Eckstein, Hans-Joachim 76, 153
Eco, Umberto 179, 180
Else, Gerald F. 189, 190
Eltester, Walther 17, 219
Eriksson, Anders 5
Erlemann, K. 134
Esler, Philip F. 64, 99, 100
Evans, C. F. 2

Fee, Gordon D. 73
Fehribach, Adeline 18
Fortna, Robert T. 7, 280
Frankemölle, Hubert 242, 243
Frede, Dorothea 185
Frey, Jörg 2, 3, 5, 7, 10, 11, 12, 13, 14, 49, 50, 77, 78, 79, 80, 81, 86, 88, 107, 108, 109, 115, 116, 117, 118, 122, 131, 132, 135, 138, 139, 142, 146, 178, 180, 199, 253, 265, 267, 269, 270, 273, 328
Frickenschmidt, Dirk 129
Funk, R. W. 295

Gadamer, Hans-Georg 104
Gall, August Freiherr von 202
García Martínez, Florentino 268
Gaventa, Beverly R. 7
Genette, Gérard 119, 137
Giblin, Charles H. 13
Gnilka, J. 80
Goedt, Michel de 168
Gourges, Michel 51
Grässer, Erich 48
Grassi, Joseph 9
Green, Barbara 157
Greig, J. C. G. 22
Greimas, Algirdas-Julien 180, 193
Gruber, Margareta 140
Gunkel, Hermann 23

Haag, E. 237
Haenchen, Ernst 54
Hahn, Ferdinand 48
Hainz, Josef 218
Haldimann, Konrad 116, 132, 290, 291, 297, 301, 309

Halliwell, Stephen 179, 182, 183, 184, 189
Hansen, Steven E. 237
Hare, D. R. A. 255
Harrington, D. J. 77
Harris, J. Rendel 23, 31
Hartenstein, Judith 86
Hartin, P. J. 11, 79
Hartman, Lars 273
Hartmann, Gert 143, 217, 218, 233
Harvey, A. E. 208
Hasitschka, Martin 197, 200, 242, 313
Hatina, Thomas R. 17, 237, 240
Hays, Richard B. 76
Heil, John P. 2
Heiligenthal, R. 134
Heitmüller, Wilhelm 108, 115, 116
Hempelmann, Heinzpeter 76
Hengel, Martin 128, 132, 146
Hitchcock, F. R. M. 178, 191
Hoegen-Rohls, Christina 109, 180
Hoffmann, Paul 211, 219
Hofius, Otfried 16, 18
Holtzmann, Heinrich Julius 221
Hoppe, Rudolf 107, 211, 219, 287
Horn, Friedrich Wilhelm 141
Hotze, Gerhard 313
Hull, William E. 257

Ibuki, Yu 202

Jackson, Howard M. 258
Janko, Richard 179, 182
Janowski, C. 86
Jeremias, Joachim 219
Johns, Loren L. 18
Johnson, Luke Timothy 237
Judge, Peter 169, 175

Kammler, Hans-Christian 2, 3, 5, 16, 18, 136
Kant, Lawrence H. 273
Käsemann, Ernst 15, 34, 132, 133, 148, 178, 191, 194
Kendall, Daniel 172
Kertlege, Karl 141
Kessler, Hans H. 76
Kinlaw, Pamela 16
Kirchschläger, Walter 244

Kirk, J. R. Daniel 76
Kittel, Helmuth 202
Kitzberger, Ingrid Rosa 11, 17, 79
Klein, Günther 147
Klein, Hans 281, 283, 282, 284, 287, 292, 299, 301
Klijn, A. F. J. 18, 167
Knöppler, Thomas 131, 132, 145, 146, 147
Koester, Craig R. 8, 50, 52, 56, 66, 83, 85, 134, 261
Koester, Helmut 259
Kohler, Herbert 131, 132, 141, 150
Koperski, V. 2
Korting, G. 237
Köstenberger, Andreas J. 18
Kowalski, Beate 96
Kraus, Wolfgang 143
Kremer, Jacob 79
Kügler, Joachim 143
Kuhn, Heinz-Wolfgang 147
Kurz, William S. 237, 241
Kysar, Robert 54

Labahn, Michael 43, 54, 79, 89, 128, 137, 138, 204, 231
Lagrange, Marie-Joseph 108, 116, 213, 214, 217, 232, 235
Lambrecht, Jan 229
Lampe, Peter 153
Lang, Manfred 128, 142, 143
Larsen, Kasper B. 179, 191, 193, 198
Lash, C. 163
Lataire, B. 2
Lear, Jonathan 182
Lee, Dorothy A. 17, 70, 160, 161, 163, 169, 170, 172
Lehne, Susanne 250
Léon-Dufour, Xavier 108, 116, 213, 216
Levesque, G. 163
Levine, Amy-Jill 200, 215
Leyh, V. P. 127
Lichtenberger, Hermann 77, 280
Lierman, John 61
Lincoln, Andrew T. 1, 15, 28, 30, 48, 65, 68, 208
Lindars, Barnabas 108, 116, 218, 219
Linde, G. 101
Lohmeyer, Ernst 273

Löhr, Hermut 146
Loisy, Alfred 108, 116, 212
Longenecker, Richard N. 1, 28, 48, 77
Lozada, Francisco, Jr. 49, 244, 264, 274
Lüdemann, Gerd 76

Mahoney, Robert 143
Malina, Bruce J. 289
Maritz, P. 49, 52, 53, 231
Martin, Dale B. 178
Martyn, J. Louis 51, 55, 61, 62, 72, 204
Marucci, Corrado 318
Matera, Frank J. 171, 211
McCaffrey, James 269
McGehee, Michael 213, 217, 235
McKenzie, John L. 161
Meeks, Wayne A. 16, 178
Menken, Maarten J. J. 2, 9, 143, 272
Merk, Otto 48
Metzger, Bruce M. 58, 321
Metzner, Rainer 59, 135, 197, 208, 242
Milbank, John 162
Miller, Douglas V. 18
Minear, Paul S. 11, 18
Mohamed, A. F. 237
Mohri, Erika 220, 225
Moignt, Joseph 157
Mollat, Donatien 163
Moloney, Francis J. 10, 26, 27, 59, 65, 68, 71, 79, 81, 90, 91, 92, 94, 95, 147, 163, 269
Morley, J. 182
Moule, C. F. D. 48
Mounce, William D. 259
Müller, K. E. 128
Müller, U. B. 128, 131, 132, 134, 147, 149
Muncaster, R. O. 77
Murphy-O'Connor, Jerome 153
Mussner, Fraz 128
Myllykoski, Matti 140

Nagel, Titus 127
Nehamas, Alexander 184
Neirynck, Frans 143, 220, 221, 225, 226, 227, 244, 319, 329
Neugebauer, Johannes 116
Neusner, Jacob 76
Neville, Robert C. 76

Newman, Carey C. 202
Neyrey, Jerome H. 289
Nicholson, Godfrey C. 68
Nickelsburg, George W. E. 1, 77, 157
Nicol, W. 54
Nielsen, Jesper Tang 50, 199
Niemand, Christoph 141
North, Wendy E. Sproston 138
Nussbaum, Martha C. 184

O'Collins, Gerald 172
O'Day, Gail R. 32, 36, 57, 62, 68, 72, 79, 120, 273
Oberlinner, Lorenz 143
Obermann, Andreas 143
Okure, Teresa 17, 171, 172, 211
Olbricht, Thomas H. 5
Onuki, Takashi 115, 116, 195, 196

Painter, John 25, 26, 27, 28, 43, 46, 48, 276
Pamment, Margaret 202
Pamplaniyil, Joseph Thomas 136, 144
Pao, David W. 4
Parsenios, George L. 14, 191
Passow, Franz 135
Peirce, C. S. 101
Perkins, Pheme 172
Perry, John 273
Peters, Ted 76, 153
Peterson, Erik 300
Peterson, Norman R. 178
Petzer, J. H. 11, 79
Phillips, D. Z. 18
Pickstock, Catherine 162
Piper, Ronald A. 64, 99, 100
Pokorný, Petr 193
Pollefeyt, Didier 205, 263
Popkes, Enno Edzard 150
Popp, Thomas 129
Porsch, Felix 286
Porter, Stanley E. 213, 216
Potterie, Ignace de la 68, 163
Probst, H. 117

Rahner, Johanna 131, 136
Rahner, Karl 161
Rehkopf, Friederich 104, 230
Reinhartz, Adele 191, 192, 204

Reinmuth, Eckart 76, 79, 128, 138
Rensberger, David 178
Rese, Martin 76
Revneau-Chibici, Nicole 202
Richter, Georg 3, 79, 141, 218
Ricoeur, Paul 128
Riley, Gregory 3
Ringe, Sharon H. 178
Rissi, Mathias 273
Rorty Amélie O. 179, 182, 184, 185, 189, 190
Rose, Martin 132, 179
Roskovec, Jan 193
Ruckstuhl, Eugen 140
Ruhr, Mario von der 18
Rusam, Dietrich 135, 199
Rüsen, Jorn 128
Russell, Robert John 76, 153

Sakenfeld, Katharine D. 178
Salier, Bill 61, 73
Salier, Willis Hedley 53
Schenke, Ludger 80, 81, 90, 91, 95
Schleritt, Frank 229
Schmemann, Alexander 288
Schmidt, Hans 23
Schnackenburg, Rudolf 48, 62, 64, 65, 68, 91, 108, 116, 119, 128, 227, 232, 321, 324
Schneider, Gerhard 226
Schneider, Johannes 202
Schneiders, Sandra M. 11, 18, 19, 35, 47, 51, 65, 67, 73, 91, 156, 157, 164, 210, 214, 215, 217, 229, 233, 235, 237, 238, 239, 241
Schnelle, Udo 12, 13, 15, 52, 53, 54, 91, 108, 109, 116, 117, 118, 122, 127, 128, 130, 131, 132, 136, 141, 143, 146, 169, 324
Scholtissek, Klaus 12, 14, 43, 108, 111, 114, 204
Schottroff, Luise 53
Schroer, Silvia 226
Schröter, Jens 85, 132, 134
Schuchard, Bruce G. 142
Schulz, Siegried 88
Schütrumpf, Eckart 208
Scoralick, Ruth 244
Segovia, Fernando F. 18, 205, 276, 292

Seitz, Wendelin Eugin 241
Sherman, Nancy 189
Simonis, Walter 77
Smith, Dwight Moody 2, 7, 27, 108, 272
Smith, Joseph 211
Smith, Robert H. 1, 76
Smyth, Herbert Weir 230
Söding, Thomas 50, 121, 132, 136, 206, 299
Sorg, T. 237
Spiegel, Egon 313
Staley, Jeffrey L. 177, 178
Stare, Mira 89, 98, 320
Staubli, Thomas 226
Stenger, Frans 143
Stenger, Werner 143
Stewart, Robert B. 76
Stibbe, Mark W. G. 11, 79, 80, 81, 178, 179, 191, 192
Stinton, Thomas C. W. 189
Strathmann, Hermann 111
Straub, Esther 131, 132, 146, 147, 149
Strotmann, Angelika 43, 204
Suh, Joong Suk 202
Swetnam, James 17, 241

Thatcher, Tom 49, 244, 264, 274, 280
Theissen, Gerd 75
Theobald, Michael 107, 108, 211, 218, 219, 229, 234, 280, 287, 288, 290, 291, 293, 294, 297, 298, 299, 301
Thettayil, Benny 225
Thiede, Carsten P. 76
Thomas, John Christopher 59, 141
Thompson, Marianne Meye 18, 48, 54, 71, 73, 271
Thüsing, Wilhelm 146, 147, 202, 203, 322
Thyen, Hartwig 2, 4, 6, 10, 14, 18, 79, 88, 98, 138, 140, 147, 178, 217, 233, 245, 249, 250, 314, 315, 316, 323
Tolmie, D. François 297, 300
Tuckett, Christopher M. 10, 79

Übelacker, Walter 5
Unnik, W. C. van 18, 167
Untergassmair, Franz G. 50, 136, 206, 313

Van Belle, Gilbert 10, 36, 49, 51, 53, 66, 79, 86, 131, 136, 137, 140, 212, 217, 231, 235, 315
Van Segbroeck, Frans 10, 73, 79, 169, 221, 226, 319
Vandecasteele-Vanneuville, Frederique 205, 263
Vanhoye, Albert 214
Verheyden, J. 79

Wagner, Josef 2, 10, 79
Ward, Graham 162
Warren, David H. 4
Watt, Jan G. van der 2, 49, 52, 53, 89, 178, 199, 201, 273
Weidemann, Hans-Ulrich 70, 107, 108, 237, 241, 288, 301, 303
Welck, Christian 83
Welker, Michael 76, 153
Wellhausen, Julius 108, 116
Wengst, Klaus 57, 65, 68, 70, 91, 108, 116, 132, 197, 204

Wesley, Charles 28
Westcott, Brooke Foss 21, 26, 31, 33
White, Stephen A. 189
Wilckens, Ulrich 108, 116, 132, 135, 297, 298, 304, 324
Wilkens, Wilhelm 53
Williams, Rowan 19
Winter, Bruce W. 311
Wolff, Hans Walter 159
Woll, D. Bruce 276
Wördermann, Dirk 129
Wright, N. T. 1, 2, 3, 4, 6, 15, 19, 76
Wuellner, Wilhelm 11, 79, 80, 81

Zahn, Theodor 108, 116
Zeller, Dieter 77, 143
Zerwick, Maximilian 211, 212, 217, 234
Zimmermann, Ruben 2, 80, 83, 85, 87, 88, 93, 178, 199, 273
Zumstein, Jean 50, 51, 70, 104, 105, 120, 131, 132, 134, 197, 200, 206, 208, 229, 232, 288, 295, 312

Wissenschaftliche Untersuchungen zum Neuen Testament
Alphabetical Index of the First and Second Series

Ådna, Jostein: Jesu Stellung zum Tempel. 2000. *Vol. II/119.*
Ådna, Jostein (Ed.): The Formation of the Early Church. 2005. *Vol. 183.*
– and *Kvalbein, Hans* (Ed.): The Mission of the Early Church to Jews and Gentiles. 2000. *Vol. 127.*
Alexeev, Anatoly A., Christos Karakolis and *Ulrich Luz* (Ed.): Einheit der Kirche im Neuen Testament. Dritte europäische orthodox-westliche Exegetenkonferenz in Sankt Petersburg, 24.–31. August 2005. 2008. *Vol. 218.*
Alkier, Stefan: Wunder und Wirklichkeit in den Briefen des Apostels Paulus. 2001. *Vol. 134.*
Allen, David M.: Deuteronomy and Exhortation in Hebrews. 2008. *Vol. II/238.*
Anderson, Paul N.: The Christology of the Fourth Gospel. 1996. *Vol. II/78.*
Appold, Mark L.: The Oneness Motif in the Fourth Gospel. 1976. *Vol. II/1.*
Arnold, Clinton E.: The Colossian Syncretism. 1995. *Vol. II/77.*
Ascough, Richard S.: Paul's Macedonian Associations. 2003. *Vol. II/161.*
Asiedu-Peprah, Martin: Johannine Sabbath Conflicts As Juridical Controversy. 2001. *Vol. II/132.*
Attridge, Harold W.: see *Zangenberg, Jürgen.*
Aune, David E.: Apocalypticism, Prophecy and Magic in Early Christianity. 2006. *Vol. 199.*
Avemarie, Friedrich: Die Tauferzählungen der Apostelgeschichte. 2002. *Vol. 139.*
Avemarie, Friedrich and *Hermann Lichtenberger* (Ed.): Auferstehung – Ressurection. 2001. *Vol. 135.*
– Bund und Tora. 1996. *Vol. 92.*
Baarlink, Heinrich: Verkündigtes Heil. 2004. *Vol. 168.*
Bachmann, Michael: Sünder oder Übertreter. 1992. *Vol. 59.*
Bachmann, Michael (Ed.): Lutherische und Neue Paulusperspektive. 2005. *Vol. 182.*
Back, Frances: Verwandlung durch Offenbarung bei Paulus. 2002. *Vol. II/153.*
Baker, William R.: Personal Speech-Ethics in the Epistle of James. 1995. *Vol. II/68.*
Bakke, Odd Magne: 'Concord and Peace'. 2001. *Vol. II/143.*

Baldwin, Matthew C.: Whose *Acts of Peter*? 2005. *Vol. II/196.*
Balla, Peter: Challenges to New Testament Theology. 1997. *Vol. II/95.*
– The Child-Parent Relationship in the New Testament and its Environment. 2003. *Vol. 155.*
Bammel, Ernst: Judaica. Vol. I 1986. *Vol. 37.*
– Vol. II 1997. *Vol. 91.*
Barton, Stephen C.: see *Stuckenbruck, Loren T.*
Bash, Anthony: Ambassadors for Christ. 1997. *Vol. II/92.*
Bauernfeind, Otto: Kommentar und Studien zur Apostelgeschichte. 1980. *Vol. 22.*
Baum, Armin Daniel: Pseudepigraphie und literarische Fälschung im frühen Christentum. 2001. *Vol. II/138.*
Bayer, Hans Friedrich: Jesus' Predictions of Vindication and Resurrection. 1986. *Vol. II/20.*
Becker, Eve-Marie: Das Markus-Evangelium im Rahmen antiker Historiographie. 2006. *Vol. 194.*
Becker, Eve-Marie and *Peter Pilhofer* (Ed.): Biographie und Persönlichkeit des Paulus. 2005. *Vol. 187.*
Becker, Michael: Wunder und Wundertäter im frührabbinischen Judentum. 2002. *Vol. II/144.*
Becker, Michael and *Markus Öhler* (Ed.): Apokalyptik als Herausforderung neutestamentlicher Theologie. 2006. *Vol. II/214.*
Bell, Richard H.: Deliver Us from Evil. 2007. *Vol. 216.*
– The Irrevocable Call of God. 2005. *Vol. 184.*
– No One Seeks for God. 1998. *Vol. 106.*
– Provoked to Jealousy. 1994. *Vol. II/63.*
Bennema, Cornelis: The Power of Saving Wisdom. 2002. *Vol. II/148.*
Bergman, Jan: see *Kieffer, René*
Bergmeier, Roland: Das Gesetz im Römerbrief und andere Studien zum Neuen Testament. 2000. *Vol. 121.*
Bernett, Monika: Der Kaiserkult in Judäa unter den Herodiern und Römern. 2007. *Vol. 203.*
Betz, Otto: Jesus, der Messias Israels. 1987. *Vol. 42.*
– Jesus, der Herr der Kirche. 1990. *Vol. 52.*

Beyschlag, Karlmann: Simon Magus und die christliche Gnosis. 1974. *Vol. 16.*
Bieringer, Reimund: see *Koester, Craig.*
Bittner, Wolfgang J.: Jesu Zeichen im Johannesevangelium. 1987. *Vol. II/26.*
Bjerkelund, Carl J.: Tauta Egeneto. 1987. *Vol. 40.*
Blackburn, Barry Lee: Theios Aner and the Markan Miracle Traditions. 1991. *Vol. II/40.*
Blanton IV, Thomas R.: Constructing a New Covenant. 2007. *Vol. II/233.*
Bock, Darrell L.: Blasphemy and Exaltation in Judaism and the Final Examination of Jesus. 1998. *Vol. II/106.*
Bockmuehl, Markus N.A.: Revelation and Mystery in Ancient Judaism and Pauline Christianity. 1990. *Vol. II/36.*
Bøe, Sverre: Gog and Magog. 2001. *Vol. II/135.*
Böhlig, Alexander: Gnosis und Synkretismus. Vol. 1 1989. *Vol. 47* – Vol. 2 1989. *Vol. 48.*
Böhm, Martina: Samarien und die Samaritai bei Lukas. 1999. *Vol. II/111.*
Böttrich, Christfried: Weltweisheit – Menschheitsethik – Urkult. 1992. *Vol. II/50.*
– */ Herzer, Jens* (Ed.): Josephus und das Neue Testament. 2007. *Vol. 209.*
Bolyki, János: Jesu Tischgemeinschaften. 1997. *Vol. II/96.*
Bosman, Philip: Conscience in Philo and Paul. 2003. *Vol. II/166.*
Bovon, François: Studies in Early Christianity. 2003. *Vol. 161.*
Brändl, Martin: Der Agon bei Paulus. 2006. *Vol. II/222.*
Breytenbach, Cilliers: see *Frey, Jörg.*
Brocke, Christoph vom: Thessaloniki – Stadt des Kassander und Gemeinde des Paulus. 2001. *Vol. II/125.*
Brunson, Andrew: Psalm 118 in the Gospel of John. 2003. *Vol. II/158.*
Büchli, Jörg: Der Poimandres – ein paganisiertes Evangelium. 1987. *Vol. II/27.*
Bühner, Jan A.: Der Gesandte und sein Weg im 4. Evangelium. 1977. *Vol. II/2.*
Burchard, Christoph: Untersuchungen zu Joseph und Aseneth. 1965. *Vol. 8.*
– Studien zur Theologie, Sprache und Umwelt des Neuen Testaments. Ed. by D. Sänger. 1998. *Vol. 107.*
Burnett, Richard: Karl Barth's Theological Exegesis. 2001. *Vol. II/145.*
Byron, John: Slavery Metaphors in Early Judaism and Pauline Christianity. 2003. *Vol. II/162.*
Byrskog, Samuel: Story as History – History as Story. 2000. *Vol. 123.*
Cancik, Hubert (Ed.): Markus-Philologie. 1984. *Vol. 33.*

Capes, David B.: Old Testament Yaweh Texts in Paul's Christology. 1992. *Vol. II/47.*
Caragounis, Chrys C.: The Development of Greek and the New Testament. 2004. *Vol. 167.*
– The Son of Man. 1986. *Vol. 38.*
– see *Fridrichsen, Anton.*
Carleton Paget, James: The Epistle of Barnabas. 1994. *Vol. II/64.*
Carson, D.A., O'Brien, Peter T. and *Mark Seifrid* (Ed.): Justification and Variegated Nomism.
Vol. 1: The Complexities of Second Temple Judaism. 2001. *Vol. II/140.*
Vol. 2: The Paradoxes of Paul. 2004. *Vol. II/181.*
Chae, Young Sam: Jesus as the Eschatological Davidic Shepherd. 2006. *Vol. II/216.*
Chester, Andrew: Messiah and Exaltation. 2007. *Vol. 207.*
Chibici-Revneanu, Nicole: Die Herrlichkeit des Verherrlichten. 2007. *Vol. II/231.*
Ciampa, Roy E.: The Presence and Function of Scripture in Galatians 1 and 2. 1998. *Vol. II/102.*
Classen, Carl Joachim: Rhetorical Criticsm of the New Testament. 2000. *Vol. 128.*
Colpe, Carsten: Iranier – Aramäer – Hebräer – Hellenen. 2003. *Vol. 154.*
Crump, David: Jesus the Intercessor. 1992. *Vol. II/49.*
Dahl, Nils Alstrup: Studies in Ephesians. 2000. *Vol. 131.*
Daise, Michael A.: Feasts in John. 2007. *Vol. 229.*
Deines, Roland: Die Gerechtigkeit der Tora im Reich des Messias. 2004. *Vol. 177.*
– Jüdische Steingefäße und pharisäische Frömmigkeit. 1993. *Vol. II/52.*
– Die Pharisäer. 1997. *Vol. 101.*
Deines, Roland and *Karl-Wilhelm Niebuhr* (Ed.): Philo und das Neue Testament. 2004. *Vol. 172.*
Dennis, John A.: Jesus' Death and the Gathering of True Israel. 2006. *Vol. 217.*
Dettwiler, Andreas and *Jean Zumstein* (Ed.): Kreuzestheologie im Neuen Testament. 2002. *Vol. 151.*
Dickson, John P.: Mission-Commitment in Ancient Judaism and in the Pauline Communities. 2003. *Vol. II/159.*
Dietzfelbinger, Christian: Der Abschied des Kommenden. 1997. *Vol. 95.*
Dimitrov, Ivan Z., James D.G. Dunn, Ulrich Luz and *Karl-Wilhelm Niebuhr* (Ed.): Das Alte Testament als christliche Bibel in orthodoxer und westlicher Sicht. 2004. *Vol. 174.*

Dobbeler, Axel von: Glaube als Teilhabe. 1987. *Vol. II/22.*
Dryden, J. de Waal: Theology and Ethics in 1 Peter. 2006. *Vol. II/209.*
Du Toit, David S.: Theios Anthropos. 1997. *Vol. II/91.*
Dübbers, Michael: Christologie und Existenz im Kolosserbrief. 2005. *Vol. II/191.*
Dunn, James D.G.: The New Perspective on Paul. 2005. *Vol. 185.*
Dunn, James D.G. (Ed.): Jews and Christians. 1992. *Vol. 66.*
– Paul and the Mosaic Law. 1996. *Vol. 89.*
– see *Dimitrov, Ivan Z.*
–, *Hans Klein, Ulrich Luz* and *Vasile Mihoc* (Ed.): Auslegung der Bibel in orthodoxer und westlicher Perspektive. 2000. *Vol. 130.*
Ebel, Eva: Die Attraktivität früher christlicher Gemeinden. 2004. *Vol. II/178.*
Ebertz, Michael N.: Das Charisma des Gekreuzigten. 1987. *Vol. 45.*
Eckstein, Hans-Joachim: Der Begriff Syneidesis bei Paulus. 1983. *Vol. II/10.*
– Verheißung und Gesetz. 1996. *Vol. 86.*
Ego, Beate: Im Himmel wie auf Erden. 1989. *Vol. II/34.*
Ego, Beate, Armin Lange and *Peter Pilhofer* (Ed.): Gemeinde ohne Tempel – Community without Temple. 1999. *Vol. 118.*
– and *Helmut Merkel* (Ed.): Religiöses Lernen in der biblischen, frühjüdischen und frühchristlichen Überlieferung. 2005. *Vol. 180.*
Eisen, Ute E.: see *Paulsen, Henning.*
Elledge, C.D.: Life after Death in Early Judaism. 2006. *Vol. II/208.*
Ellis, E. Earle: Prophecy and Hermeneutic in Early Christianity. 1978. *Vol. 18.*
– The Old Testament in Early Christianity. 1991. *Vol. 54.*
Endo, Masanobu: Creation and Christology. 2002. *Vol. 149.*
Ennulat, Andreas: Die 'Minor Agreements'. 1994. *Vol. II/62.*
Ensor, Peter W.: Jesus and His 'Works'. 1996. *Vol. II/85.*
Eskola, Timo: Messiah and the Throne. 2001. *Vol. II/142.*
– Theodicy and Predestination in Pauline Soteriology. 1998. *Vol. II/100.*
Fatehi, Mehrdad: The Spirit's Relation to the Risen Lord in Paul. 2000. *Vol. II/128.*
Feldmeier, Reinhard: Die Krisis des Gottessohnes. 1987. *Vol. II/21.*
– Die Christen als Fremde. 1992. *Vol. 64.*
Feldmeier, Reinhard and *Ulrich Heckel* (Ed.): Die Heiden. 1994. *Vol. 70.*

Fletcher-Louis, Crispin H.T.: Luke-Acts: Angels, Christology and Soteriology. 1997. *Vol. II/94.*
Förster, Niclas: Marcus Magus. 1999. *Vol. 114.*
Forbes, Christopher Brian: Prophecy and Inspired Speech in Early Christianity and its Hellenistic Environment. 1995. *Vol. II/75.*
Fornberg, Tord: see *Fridrichsen, Anton.*
Fossum, Jarl E.: The Name of God and the Angel of the Lord. 1985. *Vol. 36.*
Foster, Paul: Community, Law and Mission in Matthew's Gospel. *Vol. II/177.*
Fotopoulos, John: Food Offered to Idols in Roman Corinth. 2003. *Vol. II/151.*
Frenschkowski, Marco: Offenbarung und Epiphanie. Vol. 1 1995. *Vol. II/79* – Vol. 2 1997. *Vol. II/80.*
Frey, Jörg: Eugen Drewermann und die biblische Exegese. 1995. *Vol. II/71.*
– Die johanneische Eschatologie. Vol. I. 1997. *Vol. 96.* – Vol. II. 1998. *Vol. 110.* – Vol. III. 2000. *Vol. 117.*
Frey, Jörg and *Cilliers Breytenbach* (Ed.): Aufgabe und Durchführung einer Theologie des Neuen Testaments. 2007. *Vol. 205.*
– and *Udo Schnelle* (Ed.): Kontexte des Johannesevangeliums. 2004. *Vol. 175.*
– and *Jens Schröter* (Ed.): Deutungen des Todes Jesu im Neuen Testament. 2005. *Vol. 181.*
–, *Jan G. van der Watt,* and *Ruben Zimmermann* (Ed.): Imagery in the Gospel of John. 2006. *Vol. 200.*
Freyne, Sean: Galilee and Gospel. 2000. *Vol. 125.*
Fridrichsen, Anton: Exegetical Writings. Edited by C.C. Caragounis and T. Fornberg. 1994. *Vol. 76.*
Gäbel, Georg: Die Kulttheologie des Hebräerbriefes. 2006. *Vol. II/212.*
Gäckle, Volker: Die Starken und die Schwachen in Korinth und in Rom. 2005. *Vol. 200.*
Garlington, Don B.: 'The Obedience of Faith'. 1991. *Vol. II/38.*
– Faith, Obedience, and Perseverance. 1994. *Vol. 79.*
Garnet, Paul: Salvation and Atonement in the Qumran Scrolls. 1977. *Vol. II/3.*
Gemünden, Petra von (Ed.): see *Weissenrieder, Annette.*
Gese, Michael: Das Vermächtnis des Apostels. 1997. *Vol. II/99.*
Gheorghita, Radu: The Role of the Septuagint in Hebrews. 2003. *Vol. II/160.*
Gordley, Matthew E.: The Colossian Hymn in Context. 2007. *Vol. II/228.*
Gräbe, Petrus J.: The Power of God in Paul's Letters. 2000. *Vol. II/123.*

Gräßer, Erich: Der Alte Bund im Neuen. 1985. *Vol. 35.*
– Forschungen zur Apostelgeschichte. 2001. *Vol. 137.*
Grappe, Christian (Ed.): Le Repas de Dieu / Das Mahl Gottes.2004. *Vol. 169.*
Green, Joel B.: The Death of Jesus. 1988. *Vol. II/33.*
Gregg, Brian Han: The Historical Jesus and the Final Judgment Sayings in Q. 2005. *Vol. II/207.*
Gregory, Andrew: The Reception of Luke and Acts in the Period before Irenaeus. 2003. *Vol. II/169.*
Grindheim, Sigurd: The Crux of Election. 2005. *Vol. II/202.*
Gundry, Robert H.: The Old is Better. 2005. *Vol. 178.*
Gundry Volf, Judith M.: Paul and Perseverance. 1990. *Vol. II/37.*
Häußer, Detlef: Christusbekenntnis und Jesusüberlieferung bei Paulus. 2006. *Vol. 210.*
Hafemann, Scott J.: Suffering and the Spirit. 1986. *Vol. II/19.*
– Paul, Moses, and the History of Israel. 1995. *Vol. 81.*
Hahn, Ferdinand: Studien zum Neuen Testament.
Vol. I: Grundsatzfragen, Jesusforschung, Evangelien. 2006. *Vol. 191.*
Vol. II: Bekenntnisbildung und Theologie in urchristlicher Zeit. 2006. *Vol. 192.*
Hahn, Johannes (Ed.): Zerstörungen des Jerusalemer Tempels. 2002. *Vol. 147.*
Hamid-Khani, Saeed: Relevation and Concealment of Christ. 2000. *Vol. II/120.*
Hannah, Darrel D.: Michael and Christ. 1999. *Vol. II/109.*
Hardin, Justin K.: Galatians and the Imperial Cult? 2007. *Vol. II /237.*
Harrison; James R.: Paul's Language of Grace in Its Graeco-Roman Context. 2003. *Vol. II/172.*
Hartman, Lars: Text-Centered New Testament Studies. Ed. von D. Hellholm. 1997. *Vol. 102.*
Hartog, Paul: Polycarp and the New Testament. 2001. *Vol. II/134.*
Heckel, Theo K.: Der Innere Mensch. 1993. *Vol. II/53.*
– Vom Evangelium des Markus zum viergestaltigen Evangelium. 1999. *Vol. 120.*
Heckel, Ulrich: Kraft in Schwachheit. 1993. *Vol. II/56.*
– Der Segen im Neuen Testament. 2002. *Vol. 150.*
– see *Feldmeier, Reinhard.*
– see *Hengel, Martin.*

Heiligenthal, Roman: Werke als Zeichen. 1983. *Vol. II/9.*
Heliso, Desta: Pistis and the Righteous One. 2007. *Vol. II/235.*
Hellholm, D.: see *Hartman, Lars.*
Hemer, Colin J.: The Book of Acts in the Setting of Hellenistic History. 1989. *Vol. 49.*
Hengel, Martin: Judentum und Hellenismus. 1969, ³1988. *Vol. 10.*
– Die johanneische Frage. 1993. *Vol. 67.*
– Judaica et Hellenistica. Kleine Schriften I. 1996. *Vol. 90.*
– Judaica, Hellenistica et Christiana. Kleine Schriften II. 1999. *Vol. 109.*
– Paulus und Jakobus. Kleine Schriften III. 2002. *Vol. 141.*
– Studien zur Christologie. Kleine Schriften IV. 2006. *Vol. 201.*
– and *Anna Maria Schwemer:* Paulus zwischen Damaskus und Antiochien. 1998. *Vol. 108.*
– Der messianische Anspruch Jesu und die Anfänge der Christologie. 2001. *Vol. 138.*
Hengel, Martin and *Ulrich Heckel* (Ed.): Paulus und das antike Judentum. 1991. *Vol. 58.*
– and *Hermut Löhr* (Ed.): Schriftauslegung im antiken Judentum und im Urchristentum. 1994. *Vol. 73.*
– and *Anna Maria Schwemer* (Ed.): Königsherrschaft Gottes und himmlischer Kult. 1991. *Vol. 55.*
– Die Septuaginta. 1994. *Vol. 72.*
–, *Siegfried Mittmann* and *Anna Maria Schwemer* (Ed.): La Cité de Dieu / Die Stadt Gottes. 2000. *Vol. 129.*
Hentschel, Anni: Diakonia im Neuen Testament. 2007. *Vol. 226.*
Hernández Jr., Juan: Scribal Habits and Theological Influence in the Apocalypse. 2006. *Vol. II/218.*
Herrenbrück, Fritz: Jesus und die Zöllner. 1990. *Vol. II/41.*
Herzer, Jens: Paulus oder Petrus? 1998. *Vol. 103.*
– see *Böttrich, Christfried.*
Hill, Charles E.: From the Lost Teaching of Polycarp. 2005. *Vol. 186.*
Hoegen-Rohls, Christina: Der nachösterliche Johannes. 1996. *Vol. II/84.*
Hoffmann, Matthias Reinhard: The Destroyer and the Lamb. 2005. *Vol. II/203.*
Hofius, Otfried: Katapausis. 1970. *Vol. 11.*
– Der Vorhang vor dem Thron Gottes. 1972. *Vol. 14.*
– Der Christushymnus Philipper 2,6–11. 1976, ²1991. *Vol. 17.*
– Paulusstudien. 1989, ²1994. *Vol. 51.*

- Neutestamentliche Studien. 2000. *Vol. 132.*
- Paulusstudien II. 2002. *Vol. 143.*
- and *Hans-Christian Kammler:* Johannesstudien. 1996. *Vol. 88.*

Holtz, Traugott: Geschichte und Theologie des Urchristentums. 1991. *Vol. 57.*

Hommel, Hildebrecht: Sebasmata.
Vol. 1 1983. *Vol. 31.*
Vol. 2 1984. *Vol. 32.*

Horbury, William: Herodian Judaism and New Testament Study. 2006. *Vol. 193.*

Horst, Pieter W. van der: Jews and Christians in Their Graeco-Roman Context. 2006. *Vol. 196.*

Hvalvik, Reidar: The Struggle for Scripture and Covenant. 1996. *Vol. II/82.*

Jauhiainen, Marko: The Use of Zechariah in Revelation. 2005. *Vol. II/199.*

Jensen, Morten H.: Herod Antipas in Galilee. 2006. *Vol. II/215.*

Johns, Loren L.: The Lamb Christology of the Apocalypse of John. 2003. *Vol. II/167.*

Jossa, Giorgio: Jews or Christians? 2006. *Vol. 202.*

Joubert, Stephan: Paul as Benefactor. 2000. *Vol. II/124.*

Jungbauer, Harry: „Ehre Vater und Mutter". 2002. *Vol. II/146.*

Kähler, Christoph: Jesu Gleichnisse als Poesie und Therapie. 1995. *Vol. 78.*

Kamlah, Ehrhard: Die Form der katalogischen Paränese im Neuen Testament. 1964. *Vol. 7.*

Kammler, Hans-Christian: Christologie und Eschatologie. 2000. *Vol. 126.*
- Kreuz und Weisheit. 2003. *Vol. 159.*
- see *Hofius, Otfried.*

Karakolis, Christos: see *Alexeev, Anatoly A.*

Kelhoffer, James A.: The Diet of John the Baptist. 2005. *Vol. 176.*
- Miracle and Mission. 1999. *Vol. II/112.*

Kelley, Nicole: Knowledge and Religious Authority in the Pseudo-Clementines. 2006. *Vol. II/213.*

Kieffer, René and *Jan Bergman (Ed.):* La Main de Dieu / Die Hand Gottes. 1997. *Vol. 94.*

Kierspel, Lars: The Jews and the World in the Fourth Gospel. 2006. *Vol. 220.*

Kim, Seyoon: The Origin of Paul's Gospel. 1981, ²1984. *Vol. II/4.*
- Paul and the New Perspective. 2002. *Vol. 140.*
- "The 'Son of Man'" as the Son of God. 1983. *Vol. 30.*

Klauck, Hans-Josef: Religion und Gesellschaft im frühen Christentum. 2003. *Vol. 152.*

Klein, Hans: see *Dunn, James D.G.*

Kleinknecht, Karl Th.: Der leidende Gerechtfertigte. 1984, ²1988. *Vol. II/13.*

Klinghardt, Matthias: Gesetz und Volk Gottes. 1988. *Vol. II/32.*

Kloppenborg, John S.: The Tenants in the Vineyard. 2006. *Vol. 195.*

Koch, Michael: Drachenkampf und Sonnenfrau. 2004. *Vol. II/184.*

Koch, Stefan: Rechtliche Regelung von Konflikten im frühen Christentum. 2004. *Vol. II/174.*

Köhler, Wolf-Dietrich: Rezeption des Matthäusevangeliums in der Zeit vor Irenäus. 1987. *Vol. II/24.*

Köhn, Andreas: Der Neutestamentler Ernst Lohmeyer. 2004. *Vol. II/180.*

Koester, Craig and *Reimund Bieringer* (Ed.): The Resurrection of Jesus in the Gospel of John. 2008. *Vol. 222.*

Konradt, Matthias: Israel, Kirche und die Völker im Matthäusevangelium. 2007. *Vol. 215.*

Kooten, George H. van: Cosmic Christology in Paul and the Pauline School. 2003. *Vol. II/171.*

Korn, Manfred: Die Geschichte Jesu in veränderter Zeit. 1993. *Vol. II/51.*

Koskenniemi, Erkki: Apollonios von Tyana in der neutestamentlichen Exegese. 1994. *Vol. II/61.*
- The Old Testament Miracle-Workers in Early Judaism. 2005. *Vol. II/206.*

Kraus, Thomas J.: Sprache, Stil und historischer Ort des zweiten Petrusbriefes. 2001. *Vol. II/136.*

Kraus, Wolfgang: Das Volk Gottes. 1996. *Vol. 85.*

Kraus, Wolfgang and *Karl-Wilhelm Niebuhr* (Ed.): Frühjudentum und Neues Testament im Horizont Biblischer Theologie. 2003. *Vol. 162.*
- see *Walter, Nikolaus.*

Kreplin, Matthias: Das Selbstverständnis Jesu. 2001. *Vol. II/141.*

Kuhn, Karl G.: Achtzehngebet und Vaterunser und der Reim. 1950. *Vol. 1.*

Kvalbein, Hans: see *Ådna, Jostein.*

Kwon, Yon-Gyong: Eschatology in Galatians. 2004. *Vol. II/183.*

Laansma, Jon: I Will Give You Rest. 1997. *Vol. II/98.*

Labahn, Michael: Offenbarung in Zeichen und Wort. 2000. *Vol. II/117.*

Lambers-Petry, Doris: see *Tomson, Peter J.*

Lange, Armin: see *Ego, Beate.*

Lampe, Peter: Die stadtrömischen Christen in den ersten beiden Jahrhunderten. 1987, ²1989. *Vol. II/18.*

Landmesser, Christof: Wahrheit als Grundbegriff neutestamentlicher Wissenschaft. 1999. Vol. 113.
— Jüngerberufung und Zuwendung zu Gott. 2000. Vol. 133.
Lau, Andrew: Manifest in Flesh. 1996. Vol. II/86.
Lawrence, Louise: An Ethnography of the Gospel of Matthew. 2003. Vol. II/165.
Lee, Aquila H.I.: From Messiah to Preexistent Son. 2005. Vol. II/192.
Lee, Pilchan: The New Jerusalem in the Book of Relevation. 2000. Vol. II/129.
Lichtenberger, Hermann: Das Ich Adams und das Ich der Menschheit. 2004. Vol. 164.
— see *Avemarie, Friedrich.*
Lierman, John: The New Testament Moses. 2004. Vol. II/173.
— (Ed.): Challenging Perspectives on the Gospel of John. 2006. Vol. II/219.
Lieu, Samuel N.C.: Manichaeism in the Later Roman Empire and Medieval China. ²1992. Vol. 63.
Lindgård, Fredrik: Paul's Line of Thought in 2 Corinthians 4:16–5:10. 2004. Vol. II/189.
Loader, William R.G.: Jesus' Attitude Towards the Law. 1997. Vol. II/97.
Löhr, Gebhard: Verherrlichung Gottes durch Philosophie. 1997. Vol. 97.
Löhr, Hermut: Studien zum frühchristlichen und frühjüdischen Gebet. 2003. Vol. 160.
— see *Hengel, Martin.*
Löhr, Winrich Alfried: Basilides und seine Schule. 1995. Vol. 83.
Luomanen, Petri: Entering the Kingdom of Heaven. 1998. Vol. II/101.
Luz, Ulrich: see *Alexeev, Anatoly A.*
—: see *Dunn, James D.G.*
Mackay, Ian D.: John's Raltionship with Mark. 2004. Vol. II/182.
Mackie, Scott D.: Eschatology and Exhortation in the Epistle to the Hebrews. 2006. Vol. II/223.
Maier, Gerhard: Mensch und freier Wille. 1971. Vol. 12.
— Die Johannesoffenbarung und die Kirche. 1981. Vol. 25.
Markschies, Christoph: Valentinus Gnosticus? 1992. Vol. 65.
Marshall, Peter: Enmity in Corinth: Social Conventions in Paul's Relations with the Corinthians. 1987. Vol. II/23.
Martin, Dale B.: see *Zangenberg, Jürgen.*
Mayer, Annemarie: Sprache der Einheit im Epheserbrief und in der Ökumene. 2002. Vol. II/150.
Mayordomo, Moisés: Argumentiert Paulus logisch? 2005. Vol. 188.

McDonough, Sean M.: YHWH at Patmos: Rev. 1:4 in its Hellenistic and Early Jewish Setting. 1999. Vol. II/107.
McDowell, Markus: Prayers of Jewish Women. 2006. Vol. II/211.
McGlynn, Moyna: Divine Judgement and Divine Benevolence in the Book of Wisdom. 2001. Vol. II/139.
Meade, David G.: Pseudonymity and Canon. 1986. Vol. 39.
Meadors, Edward P.: Jesus the Messianic Herald of Salvation. 1995. Vol. II/72.
Meißner, Stefan: Die Heimholung des Ketzers. 1996. Vol. II/87.
Mell, Ulrich: Die „anderen" Winzer. 1994. Vol. 77.
— see *Sänger, Dieter.*
Mengel, Berthold: Studien zum Philipperbrief. 1982. Vol. II/8.
Merkel, Helmut: Die Widersprüche zwischen den Evangelien. 1971. Vol. 13.
— see *Ego, Beate.*
Merklein, Helmut: Studien zu Jesus und Paulus. Vol. 1 1987. Vol. 43. – Vol. 2 1998. Vol. 105.
Metzdorf, Christina: Die Tempelaktion Jesu. 2003. Vol. II/168.
Metzler, Karin: Der griechische Begriff des Verzeihens. 1991. Vol. II/44.
Metzner, Rainer: Die Rezeption des Matthäusevangeliums im 1. Petrusbrief. 1995. Vol. II/74.
— Das Verständnis der Sünde im Johannesevangelium. 2000. Vol. 122.
Mihoc, Vasile: see *Dunn, James D.G..*
Mineshige, Kiyoshi: Besitzverzicht und Almosen bei Lukas. 2003. Vol. II/163.
Mittmann, Siegfried: see *Hengel, Martin.*
Mittmann-Richert, Ulrike: Magnifikat und Benediktus. 1996. Vol. II/90.
Miura, Yuzuru: David in Luke-Acts. 2007. Vol. II/232.
Mournet, Terence C.: Oral Tradition and Literary Dependency. 2005. Vol. II/195.
Mußner, Franz: Jesus von Nazareth im Umfeld Israels und der Urkirche. Ed. von M. Theobald. 1998. Vol. 111.
Mutschler, Bernhard: Das Corpus Johanneum bei Irenäus von Lyon. 2005. Vol. 189.
Niebuhr, Karl-Wilhelm: Gesetz und Paränese. 1987. Vol. II/28.
— Heidenapostel aus Israel. 1992. Vol. 62.
— see *Deines, Roland*
— see *Dimitrov, Ivan Z.*
— see *Kraus, Wolfgang*
Nielsen, Anders E.: "Until it is Fullfilled". 2000. Vol. II/126.
Nissen, Andreas: Gott und der Nächste im antiken Judentum. 1974. Vol. 15.

Noack, Christian: Gottesbewußtsein. 2000.
Vol. II/116.
Noormann, Rolf: Irenäus als Paulusinterpret.
1994. Vol. II/66.
Novakovic, Lidija: Messiah, the Healer of the
Sick. 2003. Vol. II/170.
Obermann, Andreas: Die christologische Erfüllung der Schrift im Johannesevangelium.
1996. Vol. II/83.
Öhler, Markus: Barnabas. 2003. Vol. 156.
– see *Becker, Michael.*
Okure, Teresa: The Johannine Approach to Mission. 1988. Vol. II/31.
Onuki, Takashi: Heil und Erlösung. 2004.
Vol. 165.
Oropeza, B. J.: Paul and Apostasy. 2000.
Vol. II/115.
Ostmeyer, Karl-Heinrich: Kommunikation mit
Gott und Christus. 2006. Vol. 197.
– Taufe und Typos. 2000. Vol. II/118.
Paulsen, Henning: Studien zur Literatur und
Geschichte des frühen Christentums. Ed.
von Ute E. Eisen. 1997. Vol. 99.
Pao, David W.: Acts and the Isaianic New Exodus. 2000. Vol. II/130.
Park, Eung Chun: The Mission Discourse in
Matthew's Interpretation. 1995.
Vol. II/81.
Park, Joseph S.: Conceptions of Afterlife in Jewish Insriptions. 2000. Vol. II/121.
Pate, C. Marvin: The Reverse of the Curse.
2000. Vol. II/114.
Pearce, Sarah J.K.: The Land of the Body. 2007.
Vol. 208.
Peres, Imre: Griechische Grabinschriften und
neutestamentliche Eschatologie. 2003.
Vol. 157.
Philip, Finny: The Origins of Pauline Pneumatology. 2005. Vol. II/194.
Philonenko, Marc (Ed.): Le Trône de Dieu.
1993. Vol. 69.
Pilhofer, Peter: Presbyteron Kreitton. 1990.
Vol. II/39.
– Philippi. Vol. 1 1995. Vol. 87. – Vol. 2 2000.
Vol. 119.
– Die frühen Christen und ihre Welt. 2002.
Vol. 145.
– see *Becker, Eve-Marie.*
– see *Ego, Beate.*
Pitre, Brant: Jesus, the Tribulation, and the End
of the Exile. 2005. Vol. II/204.
Plümacher, Eckhard: Geschichte und Geschichten. 2004. Vol. 170.
Pöhlmann, Wolfgang: Der Verlorene Sohn und
das Haus. 1993. Vol. 68.
Pokorný, Petr and *Josef B. Souček:* Bibelauslegung als Theologie. 1997. Vol. 100.
– and *Jan Roskovec* (Ed.): Philosophical
Hermeneutics and Biblical Exegesis. 2002.
Vol. 153.
Popkes, Enno Edzard: Das Menschenbild des
Thomasevangeliums. 2007. Vol. 206.
– Die Theologie der Liebe Gottes in den
johanneischen Schriften. 2005. Vol. II/197.
Porter, Stanley E.: The Paul of Acts. 1999.
Vol. 115.
Prieur, Alexander: Die Verkündigung der Gottesherrschaft. 1996. Vol. II/89.
Probst, Hermann: Paulus und der Brief. 1991.
Vol. II/45.
Räisänen, Heikki: Paul and the Law. 1983,
²1987. Vol. 29.
Rehkopf, Friedrich: Die lukanische Sonderquelle. 1959. Vol. 5.
Rein, Matthias: Die Heilung des Blindgeborenen (Joh 9). 1995. Vol. II/73.
Reinmuth, Eckart: Pseudo-Philo und Lukas.
1994. Vol. 74.
Reiser, Marius: Bibelkritik und Auslegung der
Heiligen Schrift. 2007. Vol. 217.
– Syntax und Stil des Markusevangeliums.
1984. Vol. II/11.
Rhodes, James N.: The Epistle of Barnabas and
the Deuteronomic Tradition. 2004.
Vol. II/188.
Richards, E. Randolph: The Secretary in the
Letters of Paul. 1991. Vol. II/42.
Riesner, Rainer: Jesus als Lehrer. 1981, ³1988.
Vol. II/7.
– Die Frühzeit des Apostels Paulus. 1994.
Vol. 71.
Rissi, Mathias: Die Theologie des Hebräerbriefs. 1987. Vol. 41.
Roskovec, Jan: see *Pokorný, Petr.*
Röhser, Günter: Metaphorik und Personifikation
der Sünde. 1987. Vol. II/25.
Rose, Christian: Theologie als Erzählung im
Markusevangelium. 2007. Vol. II/236.
– Die Wolke der Zeugen. 1994. Vol. II/60.
Rothschild, Clare K.: Baptist Traditions and Q.
2005. Vol. 190.
– Luke Acts and the Rhetoric of History. 2004.
Vol. II/175.
Rüegger, Hans-Ulrich: Verstehen, was Markus
erzählt. 2002. Vol. II/155.
Rüger, Hans Peter: Die Weisheitsschrift aus der
Kairoer Geniza. 1991. Vol. 53.
Sänger, Dieter: Antikes Judentum und die Mysterien. 1980. Vol. II/5.
– Die Verkündigung des Gekreuzigten und
Israel. 1994. Vol. 75.
– see *Burchard, Christoph*
– and *Ulrich Mell* (Hrsg.): Paulus und Johannes. 2006. Vol. 198.

Salier, Willis Hedley: The Rhetorical Impact of the Semeia in the Gospel of John. 2004. *Vol. II/186.*
Salzmann, Jorg Christian: Lehren und Ermahnen. 1994. *Vol. II/59.*
Sandnes, Karl Olav: Paul – One of the Prophets? 1991. *Vol. II/43.*
Sato, Migaku: Q und Prophetie. 1988. *Vol. II/29.*
Schäfer, Ruth: Paulus bis zum Apostelkonzil. 2004. *Vol. II/179.*
Schaper, Joachim: Eschatology in the Greek Psalter. 1995. *Vol. II/76.*
Schimanowski, Gottfried: Die himmlische Liturgie in der Apokalypse des Johannes. 2002. *Vol. II/154.*
– Weisheit und Messias. 1985. *Vol. II/17.*
Schlichting, Günter: Ein jüdisches Leben Jesu. 1982. *Vol. 24.*
Schließer, Benjamin: Abraham's Faith in Romans 4. 2007. *Vol. II/224.*
Schnabel, Eckhard J.: Law and Wisdom from Ben Sira to Paul. 1985. *Vol. II/16.*
Schnelle, Udo: see *Frey, Jörg.*
Schröter, Jens: Von Jesus zum Neuen Testament. 2007. *Vol. 204.*
– see *Frey, Jörg.*
Schutter, William L.: Hermeneutic and Composition in I Peter. 1989. *Vol. II/30.*
Schwartz, Daniel R.: Studies in the Jewish Background of Christianity. 1992. *Vol. 60.*
Schwemer, Anna Maria: see *Hengel, Martin*
Scott, Ian W.: Implicit Epistemology in the Letters of Paul. 2005. *Vol. II/205.*
Scott, James M.: Adoption as Sons of God. 1992. *Vol. II/48.*
– Paul and the Nations. 1995. *Vol. 84.*
Shum, Shiu-Lun: Paul's Use of Isaiah in Romans. 2002. *Vol. II/156.*
Siegert, Folker: Drei hellenistisch-jüdische Predigten. Teil I 1980. *Vol. 20* – Teil II 1992. *Vol. 61.*
– Nag-Hammadi-Register. 1982. *Vol. 26.*
– Argumentation bei Paulus. 1985. *Vol. 34.*
– Philon von Alexandrien. 1988. *Vol. 46.*
Simon, Marcel: Le christianisme antique et son contexte religieux I/II. 1981. *Vol. 23.*
Smit, Peter-Ben: Fellowship and Food in the Kingdom. 2008. *Vol. II/234.*
Snodgrass, Klyne: The Parable of the Wicked Tenants. 1983. *Vol. 27.*
Söding, Thomas: Das Wort vom Kreuz. 1997. *Vol. 93.*
– see *Thüsing, Wilhelm.*
Sommer, Urs: Die Passionsgeschichte des Markusevangeliums. 1993. *Vol. II/58.*
Sorensen, Eric: Possession and Exorcism in the New Testament and Early Christianity. 2002. *Vol. II/157.*
Souček, Josef B.: see *Pokorný, Petr.*
Southall, David J.: Rediscovering Righteousness in Romans. 2008. *Vol. 240.*
Spangenberg, Volker: Herrlichkeit des Neuen Bundes. 1993. *Vol. II/55.*
Spanje, T.E. van: Inconsistency in Paul? 1999. *Vol. II/110.*
Speyer, Wolfgang: Frühes Christentum im antiken Strahlungsfeld. Vol. I: 1989. *Vol. 50.*
– Vol. II: 1999. *Vol. 116.*
– Vol. III: 2007. *Vol. 213.*
Sprinkle, Preston: Law and Life. 2008. *Vol. II/241.*
Stadelmann, Helge: Ben Sira als Schriftgelehrter. 1980. *Vol. II/6.*
Stenschke, Christoph W.: Luke's Portrait of Gentiles Prior to Their Coming to Faith. *Vol. II/108.*
Sterck-Degueldre, Jean-Pierre: Eine Frau namens Lydia. 2004. *Vol. II/176.*
Stettler, Christian: Der Kolosserhymnus. 2000. *Vol. II/131.*
Stettler, Hanna: Die Christologie der Pastoralbriefe. 1998. *Vol. II/105.*
Stökl Ben Ezra, Daniel: The Impact of Yom Kippur on Early Christianity. 2003. *Vol. 163.*
Strobel, August: Die Stunde der Wahrheit. 1980. *Vol. 21.*
Stroumsa, Guy G.: Barbarian Philosophy. 1999. *Vol. 112.*
Stuckenbruck, Loren T.: Angel Veneration and Christology. 1995. *Vol. II/70.*
– , *Stephen C. Barton* and *Benjamin G. Wold* (Ed.): Memory in the Bible and Antiquity. 2007. *Vol. 212.*
Stuhlmacher, Peter (Ed.): Das Evangelium und die Evangelien. 1983. *Vol. 28.*
– Biblische Theologie und Evangelium. 2002. *Vol. 146.*
Sung, Chong-Hyon: Vergebung der Sünden. 1993. *Vol. II/57.*
Tajra, Harry W.: The Trial of St. Paul. 1989. *Vol. II/35.*
– The Martyrdom of St.Paul. 1994. *Vol. II/67.*
Theißen, Gerd: Studien zur Soziologie des Urchristentums. 1979, ³1989. *Vol. 19.*
Theobald, Michael: Studien zum Römerbrief. 2001. *Vol. 136.*
Theobald, Michael: see *Mußner, Franz.*
Thornton, Claus-Jürgen: Der Zeuge des Zeugen. 1991. *Vol. 56.*
Thüsing, Wilhelm: Studien zur neutestamentlichen Theologie. Ed. von Thomas Söding. 1995. *Vol. 82.*
Thurén, Lauri: Derhethorizing Paul. 2000. *Vol. 124.*
Thyen, Hartwig: Studien zum Corpus Iohanneum. 2007. *Vol. 214.*

Tibbs, Clint: Religious Experience of the Pneuma. 2007. *Vol. II/230.*
Tolmie, D. Francois: Persuading the Galatians. 2005. *Vol. II/190.*
Tomson, Peter J. and *Doris Lambers-Petry* (Ed.): The Image of the Judaeo-Christians in Ancient Jewish and Christian Literature. 2003. *Vol. 158.*
Trebilco, Paul: The Early Christians in Ephesus from Paul to Ignatius. 2004. *Vol. 166.*
Treloar, Geoffrey R.: Lightfoot the Historian. 1998. *Vol. II/103.*
Tsuji, Manabu: Glaube zwischen Vollkommenheit und Verweltlichung. 1997. *Vol. II/93.*
Twelftree, Graham H.: Jesus the Exorcist. 1993. *Vol. II/54.*
Ulrichs, Karl Friedrich: Christusglaube. 2007. *Vol. II/227.*
Urban, Christina: Das Menschenbild nach dem Johannesevangelium. 2001. *Vol. II/137.*
Vegge, Ivar: 2 Corinthians – a Letter about Reconciliation. 2008. *Vol. II/239.*
Visotzky, Burton L.: Fathers of the World. 1995. *Vol. 80.*
Vollenweider, Samuel: Horizonte neutestamentlicher Christologie. 2002. *Vol. 144.*
Vos, Johan S.: Die Kunst der Argumentation bei Paulus. 2002. *Vol. 149.*
Wagener, Ulrike: Die Ordnung des „Hauses Gottes". 1994. *Vol. II/65.*
Wahlen, Clinton: Jesus and the Impurity of Spirits in the Synoptic Gospels. 2004. *Vol. II/185.*
Walker, Donald D.: Paul's Offer of Leniency (2 Cor 10:1). 2002. *Vol. II/152.*
Walter, Nikolaus: Praeparatio Evangelica. Ed. von Wolfgang Kraus und Florian Wilk. 1997. *Vol. 98.*
Wander, Bernd: Gottesfürchtige und Sympathisanten. 1998. *Vol. 104.*
Waters, Guy: The End of Deuteronomy in the Epistles of Paul. 2006. *Vol. 221.*
Watt, Jan G. van der: see *Frey, Jörg*
Watts, Rikki: Isaiah's New Exodus and Mark. 1997. *Vol. II/88.*
Wedderburn, A.J.M.: Baptism and Resurrection. 1987. *Vol. 44.*
Wegner, Uwe: Der Hauptmann von Kafarnaum. 1985. *Vol. II/14.*
Weissenrieder, Annette: Images of Illness in the Gospel of Luke. 2003. Vol. II/164.
–, *Friederike Wendt* and *Petra von Gemünden* (Ed.): Picturing the New Testament. 2005. *Vol. II/193.*
Welck, Christian: Erzählte ‚Zeichen'. 1994. *Vol. II/69.*
Wendt, Friederike (Ed.): see *Weissenrieder, Annette.*
Wiarda, Timothy: Peter in the Gospels. 2000. *Vol. II/127.*
Wifstrand, Albert: Epochs and Styles. 2005. *Vol. 179.*
Wilk, Florian: see *Walter, Nikolaus.*
Williams, Catrin H.: I am He. 2000. *Vol. II/113.*
Wilson, Todd A.: The Curse of the Law and the Crisis in Galatia. 2007. *Vol. II/225.*
Wilson, Walter T.: Love without Pretense. 1991. *Vol. II/46.*
Wischmeyer, Oda: Von Ben Sira zu Paulus. 2004. *Vol. 173.*
Wisdom, Jeffrey: Blessing for the Nations and the Curse of the Law. 2001. *Vol. II/133.*
Wold, Benjamin G.: Women, Men, and Angels. 2005. *Vol. II/2001.*
– see *Stuckenbruck, Loren T.*
Wright, Archie T.: The Origin of Evil Spirits. 2005. *Vol. II/198.*
Wucherpfennig, Ansgar: Heracleon Philologus. 2002. *Vol. 142.*
Yeung, Maureen: Faith in Jesus and Paul. 2002. *Vol. II/147.*
Zangenberg, Jürgen, Harold W. Attridge and *Dale B. Martin* (Ed.): Religion, Ethnicity and Identity in Ancient Galilee. 2007. *Vol. 210.*
Zimmermann, Alfred E.: Die urchristlichen Lehrer. 1984, ²1988. *Vol. II/12.*
Zimmermann, Johannes: Messianische Texte aus Qumran. 1998. *Vol. II/104.*
Zimmermann, Ruben: Christologie der Bilder im Johannesevangelium. 2004. *Vol. 171.*
– Geschlechtermetaphorik und Gottesverhältnis. 2001. *Vol. II/122.*
– see *Frey, Jörg*
Zumstein, Jean: see *Dettwiler, Andreas*
Zwiep, Arie W.: Judas and the Choice of Matthias. 2004. *Vol. II/187.*

For a complete catalogue please write to the publisher
Mohr Siebeck • P.O. Box 2030 • D–72010 Tübingen/Germany
Up-to-date information on the internet at www.mohr.de